Introducing Social Psychology

Introducing
Social Psychology

Colin Fraser and Brendan Burchell

Dale Hay and Gerard Duveen

Polity

First published in 2001 by Polity Press in association with Blackwell Publishers Ltd

Editorial office:
Polity Press
65 Bridge Street
Cambridge CB2 1UR, UK

Marketing and production:
Blackwell Publishers Ltd
108 Cowley Road
Oxford OX4 1JF, UK

Published in the USA by
Blackwell Publishers Inc.
350 Main Street
Malden, MA 02148, USA

ISBN 0–7456–1093–5
ISBN 0–7456–1094–3 (pbk)

A catalogue record for this book is available from the British Library.

Library of Congress Cataloging-in-Publication Data

Introducing social psychology / edited by Colin Fraser and Brendan
Burchell with Dale Hay and Gerard Duveen.
    p. cm.
Includes bibliographical references and index.
  ISBN0–7456–1093–5 (HB : acid-free paper) ISBN 0–7456-1094–3 (PB :
acid-free paper)
  1. Social psychology. I. Fraser, Colin. II. Burchell, Brendan.
  HM1033.I587 2001
  302—dc21   00–012849

Typeset in 10 on 12 pt Times
by Kolam Information Services Pvt Ltd., Pondicherry, India
Printed in Great Britain by TJ International, Padstow, Cornwall

This book is printed on acid-free paper.

Contents

PART IV   Social Issues 289

PART V   The Nature of Social Psychology 381

Detailed Chapter Contents

List of Contributors

Abigail Buckle   St Catherine's College, Cambridge.

Brendan Burchell   Department of Social and Political Sciences, University of Cambridge.

Gerard Duveen   Department of Social and Political Sciences, University of Cambridge.

Colin Fraser   Department of Social and Political Sciences, University of Cambridge.

David Good   Department of Social and Political Sciences, University of Cambridge.

David Halpern   Department of Social and Political Sciences, University of Cambridge.

Dale Hay   School of Psychology, Cardiff University.

Robert A. Hinde   Sub-Department of Animal Behaviour, University of Cambridge.

Patrick Leman   Department of Psychology, Goldsmiths' College, University of London.

Nicola Morant   Department of Psychology, Anglia Polytechnic University, Cambridge.

Fraser Watts   Faculty of Divinity, University of Cambridge.

Preface

There are many textbooks, mainly from North America, aimed at university students studying social psychology for the first time. There is a very small number of English-language textbooks intended for British and European students taking a second or subsequent course in social psychology. We believe that this book uniquely offers a comprehensive introductory-level text in social psychology primarily for university students outside North America, although if some American students do find our book congenial, we shall be delighted.

Of course, there are not two clearly distinct social psychologies, a European or non-American social psychology and a North American one. The best work spans geographical boundaries. In practice, however, there are differences in emphases and in the sources of ideas and findings most likely to be selected for presentation. Although this book offers a great deal of American material, it does try, wherever possible, to balance that with work from Europe, including Britain, and from other parts of the non-American world.

In addition to creating a genuine introductory text, we also hope we are presenting a somewhat broader view of social psychology than our competitors. Readers will find not only the generally accepted core topics of social psychology but also chapters on developmental social psychology, social representations and social issues, including health and illness, employment and unemployment, and social policy.

Our title, *Introducing Social Psychology*, was also the title of a book edited more than twenty years ago by the late Henri Tajfel and one of the current editors, Colin Fraser. This is not a revised edition of that work. The structure of the present book does overlap somewhat with that of the earlier one but the contents have been completely reworked. Like the earlier editors, however, 'we have tried to adopt a social perspective on social psychology'. We have done that by means of the range of topics covered, an awareness of the world outside the social psychology laboratory, a willingness to recognize cultural differences and, where appropriate, contributions from other social sciences, as well as from experimental psychology. We believe our efforts to offer a broad, social view of social psychology have been aided by a number of our contributors coming from the interdisciplinary Department of Social and Political Sciences of the University of Cambridge. Indeed all our contributors are, or have been, teachers and researchers in Cambridge. We do not, however, claim to be offering a peculiarly Cambridge view of social psychology.

We are obliged to our contributors for their cooperation and patience in meeting our requests for additions, deletions and other modifications and to one unknown reviewer whose impressively detailed and constructive critique of an earlier version of the manuscript far exceeded normal expectations. We are very grateful to Kathrin Buhr for her knowledgable and meticulous assistance with editorial matters, including the extensive glossary and references, to Jane Nolan for her assistance in the final stages of the preparation of the manuscript, and to Joy Labern for her skilled and sympathetic support regarding word processing and preparing the manuscript. The staff of Polity have been very helpful in turning manuscript into textbook, and we are especially appreciative of the thoughtful and detailed copy-editing of Fiona Sewell.

Naturally, we hope this book appeals to students and teachers of social psychology and we will welcome, from both, feedback and suggestions for future improvements.

Colin Fraser and Brendan Burchell

Acknowledgements

The authors and publishers wish to thank the following for permission to use copyright material:

Annual Reviews for **Table 1** from J. M. Digman (1990) 'Personality structure: emergence of the five-factor Model', *Annual Review of Psychology*, 41, Table 1, pp. 423. Copyright © 1990 by Annual Reviews;
The British Journal of Psychiatry for **Fig. 17.2** from C. Vaughn and J. Leff (1976) 'The influence of family and social factors in the course of psychiatric patients', *British Journal of Psychiatry*, 129, pp. 125–37;
W. H. Freeman and Company for **Fig. 2.7** from H. H. Kelley, E. Bershceld, A. Christensen, J. H. Harvey, T. L. Huston, G. Lavingar, E. McClintock, L. A. Paplatt and D. R. Peterson (1983) *Close Relationships*. Copyright © 1963 by W. H. Freeman and Company;
HarperCollins Publishers for **Fig. 10.2** from Lawrence Kohlberg (1984) *Essays on Moral Development: The Psychology of Moral Development*, Vol. II. Copyright © 1984 by Lawrence Kohlberg;
Harvard University Press for **Box 3.2** from A. R. Luria (1976) *Cognitive Development: Its Cultural and Social Foundations*, pp. 108–9. Copyright © 1976 by the President and Fellows of Harvard College;
Open University Press for **Fig. 12.2** from I. Ajzen (1988) *Attitudes, Personality and Behavior*, p. 133;
Taylor and Francis Books Ltd for **Fig. 10.1** from J. Piaget (1932) *The Moral Judgement of the Child*, Routledge, p. 118;
D. C. Thomson & Co Ltd for **Fig. 3.3** from 'The Numskulls', *Beano*, 26.8.00, Issue no. 3032;

Every effort has been made to trace the copyright holders but if any have been inadvertently overlooked the publishers will be pleased to make the necessary arrangement at the first opportunity.

1

A Brief Introduction

- Introduction
- A definition of social psychology
- The organization of this book

Introduction

This textbook is intended as an introduction to social psychology for university students and others with little or no prior knowledge of the field. What usually attracts people to social psychology is a desire to understand more about the self, interpersonal relations, aggression, prejudice and the variety of other issues that make up social psychology. This introduction is deliberately brief in order not to stand in the way of you, the reader, getting quickly to chapters 2 to 18, which provide a broader view of social psychology than do most textbooks.

As you discover what social psychologists do or do not know about the issues which interest you, and how they go about finding out, you will almost certainly ask yourself questions about the adequacy of the research methods they use and about the nature of social psychology as a whole. Textbooks usually start with chapters on those issues, offering abstractions and generalizations regarding social psychology about which the reader, as yet, knows little that is concrete or specific. The writers of this book believe that, before trying to grapple with 'the nature of social psychology' and 'methods of research', you should sustain your interest by satisfying your curiosity about the content of social psychology, and so we reserve our general chapters for the very end of the book. That, of course, does not mean you have to wait until you have completed seventeen other chapters before you can read about research methods, the history of the field and alternative conceptions of social psychology, including 'the broader view' which underpins this book. Feel free to read the final chapters when you feel ready to put the substance of what you have read in earlier chapters into a broader context. You may even wish to compare your own emerging impressions of the nature of social psychology against what we claim in chapters 19 and 20.

Meanwhile, there are two aims to this purposefully short introduction. The first is to present our definition of social psychology, which underlies the organization of this book. The second is to outline the book's structure and contents.

A definition of social psychology

Social psychology is the study of the interrelations amongst individuals, their interactions and the societies they live in. The key feature of that definition is that it emphasizes that social psychology is continually concerned with interrelating ideas and phenomena at three different levels of analysis: the personal, the interpersonal and the societal. Social psychologists are fascinated by the internal psychological processes and observable behaviours of the individual person. We are also extemely interested in what happens when two or more people interact together, particularly when they are face to face, and form relationships. In addition, we try to understand how individuals, dyads (i.e. pairs of people) and small groups are influenced by, and sometimes succeed in influencing, the larger-scale social, economic and political processes and institutions of society. We struggle to attempt to integrate what we have learned about those three very rich sets of issues. Those issues and their interrelations are what make social psychology so exciting, and such a potentially ambitious discipline. It is sometimes described as the link between psychology and the biological sciences, on the one hand, and sociology and the social sciences, on the other. Ambitious indeed! It is only honest to admit, perhaps to your relief, that by no means all of those ambitions have as yet been achieved. It is also true that some social psychologists hold more modest conceptions of social psychology, as we shall see in chapter 20. But it is this ambitious and broad view which underlies this textbook, and this view provides the rationale for the way in which the book is organized.

The organization of this book

Social psychology should be continually concerned with relations amongst the individual, interaction and society. Yet, in practice, one of those levels of analysis frequently seems to be focused on at the expense of the other two. I would argue that in good social psychological theory and research that is something of an illusion. The individual or the interpersonal or larger-scale social influences may, at first sight, seem to be the focus, but in fact the primary concern will not be understood unless the other two sets of concerns are adequately accounted for. One of the three levels of analysis may be foregrounded but the other two will be lurking not far behind. Thus, parts I, II and

III of this book are organized according to whether the individual, social interaction and relationships or the social world seems to be the primary focus. Part IV examines a number of major social issues, which span all three levels and to the study of which social psychology fruitfully contributes. Part V considers the general nature of social psychology.

Part I   The Social Individual

The first part attempts to capture the social nature of the individual by considering in turn what we know about the personalities, cognitive bases of social behaviour, feelings and language abilities of individuals. You might expect chapter 2, 'Personality and the Self', to deal exclusively with personal and individualistic concerns, and you will see that efforts to understand personality as traits or in Freudian terms partly confirm those expectations. But a third approach to the study of personality, in terms of how the self emerges and functions, forces us to grasp the idea that a person's sense of self is in large part socially constructed through both interaction with particular others and the influences of society at large, thereby providing a particularly good illustration of what was argued in the previous section. Chapter 3, 'Cognition and Social Behaviour', begins to make clear, as do many subsequent chapters, the importance for social psychology of understanding the cognitive abilities, and limitations, of individuals. The chapter considers not only how the thought, judgement and decision-making of individuals affect their social behaviour but also how culture and society influence their cognitive functioning. Although social psychology continues to be dominated by a concern for cognition, or thinking, it has relatively recently rediscovered the importance of emotion, or feelings. Chapter 4, 'Emotion', examines how the emotions operate in our social life, and in doing so reveals both the interdependence of our thoughts and feelings and striking cultural differences, as well as similarities, in how feelings are expressed. Chapter 5, 'Language and Communication', which analyses how individuals communicate, especially through the use of language, applies this analysis to gender differences in language use. This is the first of many discussions throughout the book of relations between the sexes and possible gender differences. The inclusion of this chapter in part I helps round off an analysis of the individual which is inherently social. It could also, of course, have been the first chapter in part II.

Part II   Social Interaction and Relationships

In part II, the apparent focus is now firmly on interaction and interpersonal relations, rather than on the individual. Chapter 6, 'The Development of Social Relationships', begins, appropriately enough, at the beginning, by examining the infant's early interaction with adults before looking at the increasingly complex relationships engaged in by children as they grow older. Although interpersonal phenomena are central, the importance of internal psychological processes and of differing cultural contexts is also made apparent. Many social psychologists build a barrier between social psychology and developmental psychology which we, on principle, will ignore (and, in chapter 20, will justify ignoring), hence the inclusion of chapters 6 and 10 and various other discussions of relevant developmental matters. Chapter 7, 'Interpersonal Relationships', carries the study of relationships into adulthood. It sets out a broad framework within which we can see what should be taken into account if we are to begin to understand the variations in and richness of interpersonal relations. In chapter 8, 'Interaction in Groups', the examination of social interaction switches from dyads to small groups of people. A consideration of what constitutes a group is followed by the main issue of the chapter, an analysis of how members of a group, whether in a majority or a minority within the group, are influenced by other group members. Chapter 9, 'Altruism and Aggression', examines particularly positive and particularly negative facets of social interaction. The main emphasis in the treatment of these far-reaching issues is on interpersonal manifestations of prosocial and antisocial behaviours.

Part III   Understanding The Social World

Part III contains five chapters on the theme of how we understand the social world and represent it to ourselves and to others. Although the primary focus is now the social world around us, the individual's cognitive and emotional processes as well as interpersonal relations remain very relevant. Chapter 10, 'The Development of Moral Reasoning', for example, looks at how we acquire a system of morality. It does so by examining cognitive processes which, at least in part, underlie, amongst other things, the prosocial and antisocial behaviours of the previous chapter, and by emphasizing the role of interpersonal relations in the development of moral reasoning in the individual, especially in childhood. The most salient part of our social world is other people and chapter 11 is on 'Perceiving and Understanding People'. This chapter includes a major topic in social psychology, attribution making, which deals with how we interpret the behaviour of others as well as our own behaviour. Traditionally, our views of the social world have been studied by social psychologists as 'attitudes', and these are examined in the next two chapters. Chapter 12, 'Attitudes and Actions', includes a discussion of varying conceptions of attitudes but its main theme is the complex, and at times rather unexpected, relations between our views of the world and our behaviours in it. Chapter 13, 'Attitude Organization and Change', asks whether our attitudes and actions are as organized as the 'consistency theories' imply. It also considers how attitudes can be changed. A more recent way of studying people's views of the social world is the focus of Chapter 14, 'Social Representations'. A social representation can be thought of as a shared, sometimes widespread, view of a facet of the world, such as the body or mental illness. This chapter shows why, for social psychology, it is at least as important to understand why many people share similar views of the world as it is to understand differences amongst individuals in their views.

Part IV   Social Issues

This part also focuses on our social world, with its four chapters analysing major social issues. Chapter 15, 'Prejudice and Intergroup Relations', which deals with prejudice and hostility mainly between ethnic groups, is a prime example of the need to consider processes at different levels of analysis. The chapter critically examines four contrasting types of theories put forward by social psychologists and asks what social psychology has to offer with regard to improving intergroup relations. Chapter 16, 'The World of Paid Work', asks what employees might hope to get from paid work and what, in the way of job satisfaction, they do appear to gain from work. It also examines the psychological impact of unemployment and insecure employment, especially on people's mental health, a topic which reappears in Chapter 17, 'Health and Illness'. This chapter presents ideas and research on psychological aspects of both physical and mental health and illness, in keeping with the considerable interest in recent years in a 'health psychology' more broadly based than psychology's traditional and much narrower interest in just mental illness. Prejudice, employment and health, amongst other topics, all raise important issues of social policy to which social psychology is potentially capable of making more major contributions than has often been recognized. That is the theme of the final chapter of part IV, a chapter possibly unique in social psychology textbooks. Chapter 18, 'Social Psychology and Policy', makes clear that social psychology is about not only understanding but also changing the social world and the social individuals who interact in it.

Part V   The Nature of Social Psychology

The final part consists of two chapters which aim to place the specific contents of parts I to IV into a broader, more general context. Chapter 19, 'Research Methods', offers a broad introduction to methods of inquiry in social psychology, with an emphasis on the multiplicity of research methods available to the social psychologist. Finally, Chapter 20 examines 'The Nature of Social Psychology' in two ways. First, it offers a brief and selective history of Social Psychology. Then it looks at alternative conceptions of what social psychology is and contrasts a common narrower view with the broader view of social psychology which underpins this book.

PART I

The Social Individual

2

Personality and the Self

- Introduction
- Traits, types and individual differences
- Freud and the psychoanalytic tradition
- The self
- Conclusions
- Recommended reading

Introduction

For the newcomer to social psychology, the most obvious way to try to understand the social individual is to get to grips with the notion of 'personality', a notion which attempts to capture what is most distinctive about an individual. In this chapter you will be introduced to two contrasting views of personality favoured by different sets of psychologists, a trait approach and a Freudian approach. You may conclude that while both views have interesting things to tell us about the individual, neither approach is particularly social. Thus, a third view of personality, as self, will help you see how personality can be understood as an individual's view of himself or herself that is only possible through interaction with others and with society at large.

While some parts of social psychology describe people and society in unfamiliar ways, or use strange terms and concepts, most of the subject matter of personality is not foreign to us at all. Everyone has ideas about it, and we know it intimately. All human languages are full of words and expressions for it. We readily describe people as having good, bad, odd or strange personalities, and a really damning judgement is to describe someone as having no personality at all. It is no surprise that we apply these descriptions to those we know very well, but we are so involved with the idea of personality that we apply these terms very widely. We quickly form clear, if questionable, judgements as to the personalities of those whom we hardly know at all, for example sports or media celebrities, and it is not unusual to find ourselves describing animals, machines, buildings and many other things as having a personality. In other words, personality is a very real, rich, complex and ever-present part of human life, and, as a topic in psychology, it has matched this richness by attracting a greater range of theories and perspectives than any other part of the discipline. A brief examination of a classic compendium personality text such as C. S. Hall, Lindzey, and Campbell (1998) or Pervin and John (1997) demonstrates this range.

The scope and diversity of these theories can be bewildering for the newcomer, particularly when he or she attempts to compare the different accounts. Definitions can seem vague and contradictory, and can leave the newcomer wondering if the many different theories have anything in common at all. Indeed, Reber in his dictionary of psychology simply observes that personality is 'a term so resistant to definition and so broad in usage that no coherent simple statement about it can be made' (1985, p. 533). Reber may be right, but this does not mean that we should throw up our hands in despair, or that we cannot put some order into the field. We can begin to do this by recognizing that there are three important historical roots for the many theories which have been offered.

First, a large number of theories have been developed by psychologists who have sought to classify and type persons, and to provide a way of distinguishing between these types. Some of this work has been done in a clinical setting, but most of it has been done for non-clinical reasons ranging from personnel selection to computer dating. A key element in this work has been the development of standardized techniques for assessing someone's personality in terms of various traits. Unsurprisingly, these accounts are often known as trait theories, and the term nomothetic is applied to theories with this root. The word derives from the Greek, '*nomos*' meaning law and '-*thetic*' meaning something like 'laying out a positive statement'. This reflects the focus on what, it is hoped, will prove to be the laws of personality.

Second, other theories have been developed by clinical psychologists, psychiatrists and psychotherapists to help them with their work in counselling and treating their clients. These theories often stand as an explanation of and justification for the therapies these clinicians have used. The theories are also, therefore, a way of developing the diagnostic and therapeutic procedures which the clinician uses. A number of theories which have this root are often known as idiographic, a term which again derives from the Greek, in this case from '*idios*' meaning personal or private and '-graph' meaning written. This reflects the focus on the description of individuals.

Third, personality theorists have often developed their ideas in reaction to what else has been going on in social and general psychology. At many different times in the history of psychology, progress in understanding how different features of the mind work has led to the neglect of the whole person as an individual, and a number of theories have been developed as a reaction to this. Necessarily, the reactive ideas are as diverse as the original theories, and the picture is complicated by the fact that some personality theories are reactions against other personality theories. For this reason,

C.S. Hall, Lindzey and Campbell (1998) argue that personality psychology occupies an important dissident role in the development of psychology.

Despite these different roots there is, however, one theme which is common to all the most important theories of personality. This is a focus on those features of a person's actions and behaviour which reliably distinguish him or her from other people, which are consistent across time and space, and which derive from stable internal factors. This theme does not exhaust the concerns of all the theories by any means, but the idea that someone's personality is revealed by consistently different behaviour is fundamental. Broadly speaking the analysis of this has been approached in one of two ways. One has focused directly on the individuals' behaviour to find the consistent elements within it which distinguish us one from another. The other has focused more on the underlying psychological structures and processes which are claimed to generate this behaviour.

There are many traditions in the study of personality which show the influence of these three roots, and follow one or other of the approaches to the question of personal distinctiveness. Two, however, stand out and provide us with excellent examples of how personality might be analysed, what the goals of that analysis might be, and where the study of personality might go in the future. Both have, in their origins, a strong reactive and dissident element even though they have become part of the establishment in their own different ways, and they differ in that one reflects the nomothetic tradition and the other the idiographic. First, there is work on personality traits which was begun by theorists such as Cattell and Eysenck. Second, there is the psychodynamic tradition originating from the work of Freud. A consideration of these will form the first and major part of this chapter before we turn at the end to consider how work on personality relates to work on accounts of self-hood. These are a type of personality theory, but are different in approach when compared to trait and psychodynamic traditions. In a sense they might be seen as theories which individuals hold about themselves, rather than being theories about the individual which psychologists offer in their role as external observers.

Traits, types and individual differences

The beginnings in everyday speech

As we have noted already, natural languages are full of terms for describing people. In an unusual study, G. W. Allport and Odbert, (1936) looked at this vocabulary in American English by combing Webster's *New International Dictionary*. They found almost 18,000 words which could be used to describe elements of someone's personality. A number of these were rare, or of a similar meaning to one another, but even when the duplications, oddities and rarities were removed, the list still contained 4,500 words. A vocabulary of this size and diversity does not come into existence by chance, and there is every reason to believe that it represents meanings and distinctions which have proved useful to people in talking about themselves and others. While the existence of a word for something does not guarantee that it exists – unicorns, and mermaids have yet to be found – the sheer scale of this vocabulary, our daily use of it, and our endless discussions over which terms fit which people suggest strongly that it refers to something which we find to be very real. This simple insight has encouraged many to use the vocabulary and the ideas which it offers as the starting point for their theorizing.

Among the first of these was Gordon Allport himself. He carefully classified the various trait terms according to their meaning, distinguished between traits, habits and attitudes, and specified what might be meant by a personality type (G. W. Allport 1937). He argued that our central personality traits are revealed in characteristic ways of behaving towards other people and reacting to events, which we share with some people, but which distinguish us from others. These traits are neither as impermanent as passing fads and fancies, nor so common that they are present in the way that everyone behaves. Equally, a trait can be distinguished from a habit and an attitude because it is not directed towards a single object, or kind of object (see chapter 12 on 'Attitudes and Actions' for more on this). An individual's personality is, then, a collection of enduring traits which lead to consistent and distinctive behaviour over time. For Allport, and those who have followed him, the aim of personality research has been the description and explanation of these traits.

His strategy for doing this was like the one he employed in his work on attitudes. He offered a broad-ranging story which addressed many aspects of the human psyche which are dismissed or ignored by other trait theorists who followed him. Subsequent accounts, however, have offered assessment techniques which provide ways of measuring traits, classifying individuals, and investigating their behaviour, making it easier to build on and develop these accounts than did the wide-ranging views of Allport. Among the most important of these other theorists are Hans J. Eysenck and Raymond B. Cattell.

Their work has often been compared, and their positions have a number of significant similarities, but there are differences, and the two were at one time seen as transatlantic rivals. The similarities are due to the early training which they received. Although Cattell spent most of his working life in the USA, he was born in England, and spent the first thirty-two years of his life there. By contrast, Eysenck was born in Germany and was forced to flee to England from the Nazis when he was in his early twenties. As a result, both came under the influence of what is sometimes referred to as the London School.

The origins of this school lie in work done in the nineteenth century by Francis Galton, who was responsible for the introduction of various measurement techniques throughout the human sciences. The school laid great store by the numerical analysis of an individual's mental capacities through the use of various mental tests. An important statistical technique, factor analysis, was being developed by Charles Edward Spearman, a British psychometrician (1863–1945), in London in the 1920s and 1930s and was widely used in studies of intelligence. These studies focused on individual differences in intellectual ability, and gave rise to what is sometimes called differential psychology. Both Eysenck and Cattell effectively extended the techniques for measuring individual differences in intelligence to the study of personality differences, and this has resulted in their theories often being referred to as factor analytic theories.

Taxonomy, factor analysis and assessment

Hans Eysenck has been strongly associated with the view that psychology will only make advances and have credibility if it adopts the practices and procedures of the natural sciences. He offers in his work an uncompromising account of how personality research in particular, and psychology in general, should proceed. He argues that the investigation of any phenomenon must begin with the description and classification of examples of it. Doing this will produce a taxonomy, that is, it will place all the examples of the phenomenon into a limited number of categories which allow us to see the important similarities and differences between them. So, for example, if we wish to investigate the insects found in a particular meadow, we should collect as many as we can, and sort them into different categories on the basis of such obvious features as how many legs they have, the size of their different body parts, whether they have wings, and so forth. Once we have done this, the taxonomy can form the basis for further investigation through the development of measuring techniques, the elaboration of theories, and the experimental testing of hypotheses derived from those theories. This may lead to the revision and refinement of the taxonomy and the further elaboration of these theories, and the cycle may be repeated. It is this strategy which Eysenck has pursued in studying personality.

Taxonomy Eysenck's first attempt at developing a taxonomy of personality was conducted at a clinic in London for psychiatrically disturbed soldiers during World War II, and reveals the clinical background found in many personality theories. He analysed the case histories of 700 patients by isolating thirty-nine recurring dimensions of their behaviour, experience and disposition, which their psychiatrists had used to describe them and to distinguish their condition. His working assumption was that the personality characteristics which are to be found to a greater or lesser extent in the population as a whole would receive their greatest expression in the extreme cases provided by the mentally disturbed. The psychiatrists who had treated them would also be expert in spotting and describing these features, and thereby would provide him with access to what was most significant in the patients' behaviour.

His analysis revealed that a number of descriptions often co-occurred in the same cases. For example, the description of a patient as dependent often went with a description of him or her as having a disorganized personality and a history of odd behaviour before becoming ill, but rarely with a description as being obsessional. By the use of factor analysis, Eysenck was able to discover a significant pattern in this covariation which he argued was due to two important dimensions of personality. He termed these extraversion–introversion and neuroticism–stability. The former reflects an individual's tendency to be outgoing, sociable and sensation-seeking vs. inward-looking, shy and sensation-avoiding. The latter reflects a tendency to worry and be anxious, a tendency which in the extreme is characterized by a neurotic breakdown, or a tendency to be calm and relaxed even in very anxiety-provoking situations. Everyone can be located somewhere on these two dimensions, and a person's position on one is claimed to be independent of his or her position on the other. For example, someone who is very neurotic could be very extroverted, very introverted, or somewhere in between.

Eysenck confirmed the existence of these dimensions in subsequent work, and was able to elaborate and refine their description. He also subsequently added a third dimension, psychoticism. Individuals who score highly on this dimension tend to be solitary, uncaring, hostile, lacking in empathy, etc. In some formulations of his position, he has also included intelligence as a fourth dimension.

Cattell's early work began around the same time, but initially followed a different path. Following Allport and Odbert, he took a number of trait words from American

English and some popular terms from psychology. After much weeding out of syno-
nyms, overspecialized words and the like, he derived 171 terms on which he asked a
number of subjects to rate friends and colleagues. As Eysenck found with the terms
which the psychiatrists had chosen to use, Cattell discovered that clusters of items often
went together. He too used factor analysis to identify this clustering, but, in contrast to
Eysenck, he initially discovered no fewer than twelve traits and argued that these
provide the necessary basis for the description of personality. Initially, he developed a
series of labels to describe these traits which have no simple reflection in everyday
language. This was to emphasize the distinctiveness of his claims. An example of these
labels is 'Parmia vs. Threctia', which in ordinary terms means 'Outgoing vs. Shy'.
Subsequently, he described another four traits to bring the total to sixteen.

Cattell's proposal of so many more dimensions than Eysenck's seems to leave us with
a substantial conflict, but this is more apparent than real. To understand why, it is
necessary to appreciate a little of the principles underlying factor analysis, to
understand what it can do for the investigator, and, importantly, to understand what
it does not do.

Factor analysis   The very term 'factor analysis' can send the numerically challenged into
a state of shock, but, although the arcane details of different versions of it are complex,
the essential ideas behind it and what it enables us to do are simple. The simplicity can
be best illustrated through an example. Imagine that a group of fifty students have taken
nine brief tests assessing their skills in trigonometry (T), geometry (G), algebra (A),
calculus (C), logic (L), set theory (S), essay writing (E), poetry (P), and vocabulary (V).
We could correlate their fictitious scores on each test with that on each of the other tests
to reveal the extent to which performance on one is linked to performance on the other.
Correlational statistics range from $+1$ through 0 to -1. A correlation of $+1$ means that
doing very well on one test is precisely tied to a corresponding high performance on
another test. A correlation of -1 means that doing very well on one test is precisely tied
to doing very badly on another. A correlation of zero means there is no relation between
them. Now consider the matrix shown as table 2.1.

Table 2.1 A correlation matrix

Trigonometry	I								
Geometry	+0.8	I							
Algebra	+0.5	+0.5	I						
Calculus	+0.5	+0.5	+0.8	I					
Logic	+0.3	+0.3	+0.8	+0.8	I				
Set theory	+0.3	+0.5	+0.8	+0.8	+0.8	I			
Essay writing	0	−0.2	0	+0.3	+0.3	0	I		
Poetry	−0.4	−0.2	0	−0.2	0	−0.2	+0.8	I	
Vocabulary	0	−0.3	−0.3	−0.3	0	0	+0.8	+0.5	I
	T	G	A	C	L	S	E	P	V

This matrix indicates the correlations between the scores on the different tests. So, students who scored well on trigonometry tended to do well on geometry, as indicated by the correlation of 0.8, but increasingly better performance on trigonometry was associated with a worsening performance on poetry (correlation −0.4). If we look at this table, the pattern of correlations suggests that those doing well on any one mathematical test will do well on any other mathematical test. Similarly, those doing well on any literary test will do well on other literary tests. So, we might infer that these tests show evidence of two independent abilities, mathematical and literary. We would assume from this that each test assessed the use of these general mathematical or literary competencies and some capacities specific to that test.

Spotting these groupings for a table presented in this way is easy, but the groupings are not so clear cut when one is dealing with real data. The correlations do not fall simply into clear categories, and the number may be very large. Cattell's early use of 171 items generated 14,535 inter-item correlations. This is the first point where factor analysis is of use. It enables us to find patterns in large and ambiguous correlation matrices, but this is not all that it does. If, for example, in our demonstration case above, we did want to assume that there was a general mathematical ability, it would be valuable to know how much of an individual's score on any one test was due to that general ability, and how much was due to test-specific matters. This is the second advantage of factor analysis. It enables the investigator to see how much variability in performance is accounted for by any hypothesized factor across all items in a correlation matrix. The importance of these benefits of factor analysis, and the other benefits which follow, should not be underestimated, but it is also important to know what the method does not do.

When applying factor analysis to a large correlation matrix, it is often the case that one can find a number of different factor solutions, as they are known. On some occasions, statistical criteria can be applied to choose between them, but often the choice is made on independent criteria. This is one reason why Eysenck found far fewer factors than Cattell. He took the view that the important dimensions would not be correlated with one another, and so extracted what are referred to as orthogonal or independent factors. Cattell, however, worked to the idea that different traits were correlated to a limited extent, and so extracted what are known as oblique factors. When Cattell applied a further factor analysis looking for orthogonal structures to the correlations between the factors he found, he discovered dimensions which were similar to Eysenck's.

The other important thing which factor analysis does not do is name the factors which are extracted. It is important to remember that it is a statistical technique which deals purely with the numbers to which it is applied. The labelling of the factors depends on the theorist's interpretation of the items which correlate highly. In the make-believe case above, it was a simple matter to choose the labels 'mathematical ability' and 'literary ability', but what would we have done if there had been a subgroup of poetry, vocabulary, algebra and geometry?

Not only has factor analysis been important in developing taxonomies of the personality domain for Eysenck and Cattell, it has also been important in developing the questionnaires they have used to assess individual personalities.

Assessment   Both Eysenck and Cattell have been associated with two important personality questionnaires, the Eysenck Personality Questionnaire (EPQ) for the former, and the Sixteen Personality Factor Inventory (16 PFI) for the latter. The essence of the construction of these questionnaires lies in the analysis of large sets of potential questionnaire items which are believed to be revealing about an individual's personality. The questions typically refer to how one might behave in everyday life, and the assumption is that an individual's traits will lead him or her to answer related items in a consistent way. The analysis proceeds by examining the answers to these questions from many different subjects, and discovering which items produce systematically related answers from similar subjects. Questions which result in answers which are unrelated to the broad pattern of answers in the questionnaire as a whole are rejected.

So, for example, if we find that our subjects who answer 'yes' to questions 1, 4, 14, 23, 24 and 35 in our set of potential questionnaire items also tend to answer 'no' to questions 3, 7, 13, 21, 28 and 39, then we infer that these twelve questions are tapping the same trait, and retain them in our questionnaire. If, by contrast, we find that answers to questions 2, 5, 6, 29, 36 and 47 are unrelated to how our subjects answer any other questions, then these are not retained in the questionnaire. Recognizing the patterns in the answers is in fact an extremely difficult matter, so, in the development of questionnaires, factor analysis has again been very important.

Once a set of items which result in coherent responses has been discovered, the characteristics of people who answer them in different ways can be examined and related to various other descriptions of their behaviour. Through this process the questionnaire is validated, resulting in instruments like the 16 PFI and the EPQ which can be used to assess personality, investigate its basis, and explore its consequences.

The uses of assessment

Eysenck always argued that the development of assessment techniques was just the prelude to developing a mature science of personality. In this spirit, he and many others have used these measurement techniques in researching the bases and consequences of different personality types. He has been in the forefront of those arguing that the most important and fundamental aspects of our personality are biologically based and inherited (Eysenck 1982; 1998), and that these aspects explain a wide variety of social phenomena, including a number which relate to highly charged social and political issues. In particular, he has offered personality-based, and thus heredity-based, explanations of why some people are more likely to be deviant, and embark on a life of crime (Eysenck 1977); who is more likely to smoke and which smokers will develop cancer (Eysenck 1980; 1991); why some people will have a more extravagant and adventurous sex life than some others (Eysenck 1978; Eysenck and Nias 1978); and why some people are more likely to be attracted to the political extremes of left and right (Eysenck 1954; 1999). By his own admission (see Eysenck 1997; D. Cohen 1995) he always enjoyed stimulating debate in these areas, and has argued strongly for the role of personality in explaining matters which are often seen to be the province of sociology, political science and anthropology as well as social psychology.

Personality tests have not only been used in the investigation of various phenomena, but have also been applied to personnel selection in business and industry to select the right person for the right job. Here, however, their validity and reliability has often been questioned (Blinkhorn and Johnson 1990). While many companies and recruitment agencies still use them, many other means of evaluating candidates for jobs are also used.

One problem which has always affected the use of these assessment techniques for both research and selection purposes is the sheer diversity of the traits proposed, and their varying definitions. Eysenck's three traits as compared to Cattell's sixteen are only two of the many options which have been on offer. However, since about 1990, there has been a growing appreciation that there is great overlap and similarity between the different accounts. This idea was first voiced many years ago by D. W. Fiske (1949), and has since led to a focus on what are now known as the 'big five' traits (see Digman 1990; Wiggins 1996). Focusing on the big five has given a new lease of life to the analysis of personality traits in recent years, and we shall return to them below, but the whole issue of the consistency in behaviour which these theories are seeking to explain has been haunted by what has become known as the 'situationist critique'.

Consistency and the situationist critique

The main aim of trait theories has always been to describe and explain those distinctive features of an individual's behaviour which are neither due to other characteristics such as age, gender, ethnic background and intellectual ability, nor due to the variations of the situation in which that behaviour occurs. In 1968, at the same time as Wicker was challenging the idea that attitudes were reliably linked to behaviour and could thus be seen as driving what an individual does (see chapter 12 below), Walter Mischel attacked the corresponding idea that personality characteristics were linked to any reliable consistency in the individual's behaviour (Mischel 1968; 1996). This attack was of some consequence for trait theories, and was taken more seriously within that literature than elsewhere in the study of personality, but Mischel also offered it as a critique of the full range of personality theories.

A vital assumption for these theories is that there is consistency in an individual's behaviour across time, and that this is due to his or her personality traits rather than anything else. In the case of trait theories, for example, extroverts should reliably behave in an extroverted way, introverts in an introverted way, and so on. If they do not, the claim that they are extroverts or introverts has little interest or explanatory power. Mischel's argument was that whatever consistency there is in an individual's behaviour is due to similarity in the circumstances or situations in which he or she is behaving, and that there is nothing for the hypothesized personality traits to explain. He offered a large number of studies to support this point. A classic which is often cited is May and Hartshorne's study of honesty amongst schoolchildren (May and Hartshorne 1928). These researchers claimed to have found that whether or not children exploited an opportunity to cheat in an exam was due not to how honest they were (i.e. a trait) but to the opportunities to cheat and the prospect of being detected (i.e. the situation). All children cheated in their study if the opportunity arose, if other children were cheating, and if there was no chance of being detected.

Mischel's attack gave rise to an important debate within the literature which is of some significance for social psychology as a whole. If an individual's personality really did dictate the most important elements of his or her social behaviour, and if it was formed and stabilized early in life, or even depended mostly on his or her genetic inheritance, then the field of social psychology would be much reduced in that there would be far less for the social psychologist to explain. The net result of that debate may be simply described as an acceptance by both sides that it is the interaction between personality and situation which gives rise to a person's actions, but in getting to that consensus a number of important issues were clarified. Key amongst these is the elaboration of how the ideas of situation and consistency are to be understood.

If we took consistency of behaviour to mean that people always did the same thing no matter what situation they found themselves in, we would be contemplating a ludicrous proposition. No one has ever doubted that circumstances play a role in constraining and determining our actions. Equally, if we restricted ourselves to examining consistency with respect to claims about personality only when exactly the same situation recurred, we would limit ourselves to a very small sample of behaviour indeed. Arguably, no situation is ever repeated in every last detail. These two points force the conclusion that in understanding how a person's behaviour relates to and derives from her or his personality, it is essential that we analyse consistency with respect to types of situation and types of behaviour.

On the former, A. H. Buss (1989) argued that some types of situation demand consistency and say very little about a person's personality, and others permit that personality to be expressed. For example, in the situation where we are at home, the phone rings and no one else is in, it is very likely that we will answer it, but the new situation which follows in the phone call might lead to great variety in our behaviour which seems to be more reflective of our personality. In general, Buss argued that to the extent to which a situation is well structured, formal, public and brief it is likely that an individual's personality will not show through, but when a situation is unstructured, informal, private, well known and likely to last a long time, it is more likely that personality factors will come into play. Interestingly, the former is more likely to occur in the laboratory, and many of the cases which Mischel cited to show that the situation was the key determinant of behaviour were drawn from psychological experiments.

Concerning types of behaviour, Epstein (1979; Epstein and O'Brien 1985) argued for the importance of seeing consistency as a property of behaviour over time where we do not focus on single instances of behaviour, but see it in a broader perspective. He pointed out that we would think it odd to expect a single question on a personality questionnaire to correlate perfectly with an underlying trait, and that inasmuch as we see a trait as indicated by a set of questions, so too we must look at a range of behaviour. (A similar point will be made in chapter 12 about matching attitudes and behaviour for specificity or generality.)

The whole picture receives a further twist in the proposals from D. J. Bem and Funder (1978), who point out that persons do not by chance find themselves in a situation, but make choices as to where they go and what they do and are likely to choose situations which fit their personality, or at least to avoid those they find difficult. Thus, in the cases where this holds it becomes quite difficult to disentangle the relative contributions of situation and personality in the determination of behaviour. For this reason and others see, for instance, chapter 11, where it is argued that our expectations about the personalities of others can make them behave in a particular way. Cronbach (1975) has been somewhat pessimistic as to the prospects of ever disentangling the two.

Prospect

At one stage, it looked as if Mischel's attack and the analysis which followed might relegate trait theories to a quiet backwater where they would be nurtured by only a few devotees. In the late 1970s, even personnel managers and recruiters were beginning to doubt that personality traits could be reliably assessed in a way which suited their specific purposes. This decline has not, however, happened, and in recent years work on traits has developed through a convergence by personality psychologists on the big five personality traits, which were mentioned briefly above, together with recognition that we might have lower expectations as to the role of personality in the determination of behaviour.

The idea that there are five important factors underlying personality has its origins many years ago in work by W. T. Norman (1963). It has been developed since the mid-1980s by a variety of authors, and while there is some disagreement as to the appropriate labels for these five dimensions, and even some suggestion that there might be a sixth (McKenzie 1998; Becker 1999), the labels and brief definitions offered by Digman (1990), and given in table 2.2, are relatively uncontentious (with perhaps the qualification that number V, 'intellect', is also often referred to as 'openness'). The relationship of these factors to many previous theories is quite straightforward in many respects. For example, Eysenck's factors of extroversion and neuroticism relate quite straightforwardly to I and IV respectively.

Table 2.2 Traits of the five-factor model

Trait name	Typical characteristics
I Extroversion	Sociable vs. retiring
	Fun-loving vs. sober
	Affectionate vs. reserved
II Agreeableness	Soft-hearted vs. ruthless
	Trusting vs. suspicious
	Helping vs. uncooperative
III Conscientiousness	Well-organized vs. disorganized
	Careful vs. careless
IV Neuroticism	Calm vs. anxious
	Secure vs. insecure
	Self-satisfied vs. self-pitying
V Intellect	Imaginative vs. practical
	Prefers variety vs. prefers routine
	Independent vs. conformist

The presence of this structure in persons living in a wide variety of cultures and societies has been attested to in a number of studies through the use of the Five-Factor Personality Inventory (FFPI). This inventory has been successfully translated from English into languages as diverse as Chinese, Hebrew, Hungarian, Slovak and Spanish (Hendriks, Hofstee and de Raad 1999), and for the most part successfully used in those societies. There have been some studies which have questioned whether all five factors are reliably found in all societies. Extroversion and neuroticism are fairly robust in this respect, but there have been queries over the other three and most usually the factor of intellect (L. R. Goldberg and Shmelov 1993; Hofstee, et al. 1997; Somer and Goldberg 1999). All of this work has had a very descriptive character, although some writers have tried to provide a rationale for the five factors. L. R. Goldberg (1990) has, for example, tried to link them to major themes in anyone's life, the argument being that personality traits reflect the ways in which different people address those themes.

The combination of the general acceptance of the five-factor model with a more cautious agenda on the part of trait theorists has given a much more stable role to this work in social psychology as a whole. Much of what goes on in this respect is dedicated to the exploration of specific traits in relation to specific domains of activity or outcomes, as we shall see in a number of subsequent chapters. For example, there has been much interesting work which has related personality traits to health, and has led to interesting and potentially valuable suggestions on how personality and situation interact to produce disease or well-being (Suls and Wan 1989). (See also chapter 17 for examples of the link between personality and health.) It has also become part of work on biology and temperament which again has important practical consequences (Pervin 1990; 1999; Zuckerman 1991). But no one really expects an overarching theory of personality traits to provide a unified explanation of human social behaviour as Cattell once hoped it might, and even the five-factor model has its critics (Block 1995). In short the study of personality traits only gets us a small way towards understanding the social individual.

Freud and the psychoanalytic tradition

Trait theories of personality have sought to advance their case by seeking consistencies and regularities in behaviour, and then hypothesizing what must lie beneath these regularities. The tradition which Freud founded took the alternative route of trying to build an account of the psychic structure which lay behind the behaviour we see, and which would by its very nature reveal what the consistencies are. A summary of Freud's key ideas can be found in box 2.1. Unsurprisingly, this grand ambition has never been satisfied, and psychoanalysis has found itself attacked from many sides, including by trait theorists such as Eysenck (Eysenck and Wilson 1973). Failing to achieve a grand ambition does not mean, however, that the whole endeavour has failed, and some still believe that psychoanalysis has much to offer. To understand what it has to offer, and how the ideas have been developed, it is important to get certain basic issues clear. Doing this is not, in itself, a simple matter, and a whole academic industry has grown up around deciding what Freud might have meant, and how he might be read (see Stafford-Clark 1965). It is not possible to consider these debates here, but there is one point from them which is worth bearing in mind. Freud, like all of us, was heavily influenced by the spirit of his time. This is reflected in his work by the metaphors he exploited, and the conventional wisdom and morals which would have affected both the clinical material he saw (i.e. his patients) and his ideas as to what was likely and possible in human life.

It is also important to acknowledge that while Freud's own work has been historically very significant, it has not used the methods and principles which underpin other parts of psychology, and many reject it as unscientific. We will return to these points below, but for now and with these caveats in mind, we will focus on his ideas of development, structure and process in a way which illustrates their distinctiveness and potential.

Box 2.1   Sigmund Freud (1856–1939)

Freud was born in 1856 in the small town of Freiberg, Moravia (now Pribor, Czech Republic). He was the first child of the third wife of a cloth merchant, and although his mother went on to have seven more children, she always favoured Sigmund, referring to him as her 'undisputed darling'. An intellectually precocious child, with strong interests in literature and philosophy, Freud, somewhat reluctantly, decided on a career in medicine, entering the University of Vienna at the age of 17.

After graduating in 1881, he entered the General Hospital in Vienna, specializing in Neurology. Here, he met Josef Breuer who had developed a technique for treating hysteria that encouraged patients to recall, under hypnosis, emotionally painful experiences. Freud's interest in hypnosis was further developed during a period of study in Paris (1885–6) with Charcot. Jean-Martin Charcot (1825–93) was a French physician and neurologist who ran the Sâlpetrière Hospital in Paris. Freud spent some time there studying Charcot's use of hypnosis with psychiatric patients. Subsequent to his

Plate 2.1 Sigmund Freud

stay there, he used hypnosis in his own work for a number of years. It was in Paris that his interests shifted from neurology to psychopathology.

At 30, he married Martha Bernays and together they had six children. Immediately after his marriage, Freud started in private practice, and from his experiences with patients and through analysing his own dreams and discussing childhood memories with his mother, he went on to generate psychoanalysis. His ideas were met with much hostility by many of his contemporaries, but he managed to gather disciples around him, including Alfred Adler and Carl Jung. In 1908 this group called themselves the Vienna Psychoanalytic Society, but tensions grew rapidly amongst the members and by 1913, both Adler and Jung had broken with Freud. Freud was undeterred, however, and went on to publish many influential works, such as *Totem and Taboo* (1913) and *The Ego and the Id* (1923) (Freud 1919; 1927). Following the Nazi occupation of Austria, Freud moved to London, where he died in 1939 of cancer of the jaw.

Freudian psychoanalysis, as a theory of personality, consists of three basic ideas:

1   *Psychosexual development* For Freud, sexuality or libido is the underlying motivating force behind most human behaviour. He used the term 'sexuality' in its broadest sense, however, to denote any kind of body stimulation that produces pleasure. As a child develops, its sexuality is located in different erogenous zones, and Freud names the phases of development after the zone in question. Children develop through oral, anal and phallic stages. Fixation at any one of these stages may influence later adult personality.
2   *Psychodynamics* Adult behaviour is governed by the conflict between three different aspects of personality: (a) the id, which is the drive for satisfaction of biological needs; (b) the ego, which develops out of the id, and is the perceptual aspects of personality and the source of conscious, volitional activity; (c) the superego, the moral, regulatory side of personality, which develops as children assimilate broader societal values. Psychodynamics explores the ways in which people cope with this conflict by employing various defence mechanisms.
3   *The unconscious* Essentially, Freud believed that unconscious processes determine much of human behaviour and adult personality.

While revised versions of psychoanalysis are still used as therapeutic techniques, many academic social psychologists find Freud's ideas extravagant and unscientific. This is principally because his claims appear to be unfalsifiable. That is, almost any aspect of behaviour can be explained using psychoanalytic concepts, which cannot therefore be tested. Another reason why social psychologists are wary of Freudian theory is that they feel it is a determinist account of personality, granting little importance to conscious experience. Finally, in building his theory, Freud looked, to a large extent, to his own childhood. By doing so he extrapolated from his own experiences as a boy growing up in a nineteenth-century, middle-class Jewish family to the human population as a whole.

Despite these difficulties, however, Freud's influence can still be felt in many other fields of study: criminology, sociology, anthropology, history, cultural studies and literary theory all sometimes draw on psychoanalytic concepts, though usually in a form modified by later theorists.

A classical cast

Freud's account is distinctive in personality theory for its psychogenetic perspective. The older sense of this term, and the one which is relevant here, refers not to the study of the genetic basis of human psychology, but to the study of the growth of the psyche in the developing child. It is in this developmental progression that the basic structures and functions which constitute the adult psyche and personality are said to be formed. In the days before there was much concern with sexist terminology, this position was captured by the saying 'the child is father of the man'.

In writing about development and its consequences, Freud made much use of figures and ideas from classical literature. In the process, he made some quite striking claims about sexual knowledge and sexual desire in young children. This can make the account he gives both fascinating and unbelievable in many eyes, and this has led many to reject completely what he said. Such outright rejection may well be a case of throwing the baby out with the bath water, and there are many elements of what he says which, when translated into less dramatic language, or seen as metaphorical, appear to have more than a grain of truth.

Eros and Thanatos The important driving force in life is a complex set of instincts which have a degree of psychic energy associated with them. According to Freud's later work, there are two classes of instinct, Eros and Thanatos.

Eros was the Greek god of love, and these instincts are essentially life-preserving ones. Central to them is the pleasure–pain principle, often referred to as the pleasure principle, which simply reflects the most basic of operating principles for the individual – avoid pain, seek pleasure. Within this complex, Freud placed great emphasis on the sexual instinct and the libido, which is the psychic energy associated with it. His use of the term 'psychic energy' is an example of how contemporary ideas were reflected in his work. Although he wrote as if there were a psychic energy which had the characteristics of physical energy, there is no reason to believe that it, or the different kinds of neurological structures which he thought would be its medium, exist in any shape or form. This is an instance where even if Freud did not intend his readers to understand his terminology metaphorically, we necessarily do so today.

How the notion of sexuality is to be understood in Freud's work is not straightforward. In the developing child, as distinct from the adult, it is to be understood as sensual rather than sexual. For the child, the sexual (or sensual) instinct is differentiated as a function of the number of different bodily needs and erogenous zones (his or her mouth, genitals and anus), and it is only in the adult that these differentiated elements become fused and oriented towards a sexual goal in the more common sense of the term.

Thanatos was the Greek god of death, and this instinct is the converse of Eros. It was proposed by Freud much later in his career, and has a somewhat mystical air in that he saw it as linked to the tendency of all complex organic matter to return to the simpler inorganic states from which it is a deviation. Some have argued that it was witnessing the horrors of World War I that led him to postulate this instinct and the related aggressive drive, which is essentially the death instinct turned away from oneself. As with Eros, there is a specific psychic energy associated with it, but Freud left it unnamed.

All instincts are claimed to have their source in some bodily irritation and excitation, and the associated aim is to restore the body to its prior state of equilibrium or home-ostasis through the release of the energy deriving from that irritation. For this reason, Freud's account has been referred to as a homeostatic theory. An important property of this energy is that while it has a particular origin, and in some sense its most satisfactory expression relates simply to that origin, it can be displaced or sublimated in the service of some other activity. For example, the energy associated with sexual desire could be diverted into various creative arts. It is the redirection of this energy which makes possible, according to Freud, all the important features of human life and civilization. To understand how he thought this happens, it is necessary to understand the basics of his account of psychic structure and its development.

Id, Ego and Superego   At birth, the id is the only element of mentality which the child possesses, and Freud's characterization of it and its operation is highly reminiscent of many other biologically based accounts of behaviour. It is the well-spring of all psychic energy throughout life, and, apart from simple reflex actions, its only process is what Freud termed primary process. This is the id's capacity to form an image of the object which would enable the release of the energy associated with a desire. These images are necessarily unconscious, as conscious life requires the formation of the ego. The id is often thought of as the unconscious, but in Freud's formulation, there were also elements of ego and superego function which were unconscious. Images by themselves cannot satisfy a desire, and to engage with reality, the id needs the actions of the ego.

The ego is formed out of the id, and is essential for the satisfaction of the id's desires. It does this through what is known as secondary process, and its activity is constrained by objective reality. Secondary processes enable the discovery of things in the world which will correspond in some way or another to the images formed by primary process, and thus enable the release of the energy associated with the provoked desire. This means that it is the id's contact with reality, and it is the embodiment of the reality principle.

Another important ego function, especially in the adult, is the operation of defence mechanisms. For the individual, many of the unconscious desires arising from the id are too anxiety-provoking for them to be expressed in their raw form, and thus to appear in consciousness. The most potent defence is repression, where all knowledge of a desire is banished from consciousness, but it is a defence with a cost. The energy associated with the desire does not go away, and continually seeks expression. Other defence mechanisms do not produce a total blocking of expression, but transform the content of the desire, allowing the energy to be released in a related form. For example, if a man had a deep-seated hate of his father, but consciously believed that he loved him, he might well find it impossible to express that hate directly, but would be able to express it towards a similar figure, such as an uncle or his boss. This would be the defence known as displacement. Others include projection, when we attribute our own unacceptable thoughts to someone else (for example, assuming that another person hates you but you do not hate them, when the reverse is the case), reaction-formation, when we embrace the opposite of what we actually feel (for example, being ostentatiously enamoured of someone whom we really hate) and many others.

According to Freud, these defence mechanisms, together with the differences in individual development in childhood, form the basis of the distinctive differences between people in everything that we do. He strongly believed in the principle of psychic determinism, which held that the individual's underlying psychic dynamic made itself present in everything we do. His best-known account of this view can be found in his most popular book, *The Psychopathology of Everyday Life*, where he analysed a large number of everyday slips of the tongue and the like to show how someone's obsessions and neuroses are expressed in the simplest of actions. This style of analysis is captured in the popular description of something as a Freudian slip.

If the ego were simply combined with the id, the resulting individual would be an awful, amoral, self-obsessed person. This outcome is prevented by the presence of the superego, which balances the demands of the id and which also, in part, necessitates the defence mechanisms.

The superego is the final part of the individual's psychic structure to be developed. It is effectively the internal representation of the mores, conventions and constraints of society, and acts as what we often refer to as one's conscience. This representation is developed by the child incorporating into its mentality the specific beliefs of its parents, but why the child should do this leads us to a controversial part of Freud's account, the Oedipus complex. (Chapter 10 considers the development of moral thinking from other theoretical perspectives.)

Oedipus   According to Freud, as the child develops, its sexuality is located in different erogenous zones, and he names the phases of development after the zone in question. The first two phases, the oral and the anal, relate to the child's early experiences of eating and defecation. The sensory receptors of both the mouth and the anus are highly developed at an early stage in life. As a result, the child experiences pleasure in its actions and their consequences, but also reactions from the parents which lead to the development of control of both activities, through weaning and toilet-training. Both Freud and subsequent commentators have made claims about how the resolution of these phases can have consequences for later development, but it is the third phase, the phallic phase and the associated Oedipus complex, which is the basis of the superego's development, and thus is of the greatest structural consequence. The complex is named after King Oedipus in the play by the Greek tragedian Sophocles. Oedipus killed a man, Laius, whom he later discovered was his father, and married Laius' widow Jocasta, who unbeknownst to Oedipus was his mother.

Around the time of the child's fifth year of life, after he or she has passed through the oral and anal phases, the focus of pleasure moves to auto-erotic activity which focuses on the genitals. Initially, this is associated with sexual fantasies about the mother for both sexes, and a rejection of the father, who is seen as a competitor for the mother's love. Like Oedipus, all children have the desire to do away with the father and possess the mother. As their sexual knowledge grows, however, they follow a different pathway.

For the boy, this is marked by castration anxiety. He recognizes that his father is a powerful and dominant rival for his mother's love, and begins to fear that his father will remove the source of his lust and pleasure by castrating him, a fate which he believes has befallen little girls. This fear is so great that it leads to a repression of both the desire for the mother and the fear of the father. The boy then begins, defensively, to identify with the father, and take on his apparent attitudes, beliefs and mores as a standard by which to behave. This identification is the basis of superego development, and is completed by the repression of any awareness of the oedipal phase. The boy then enters the latent phase, which only ends when puberty reawakens sexual interest in the form of the genital sexuality of the adult.

For the girl, things are said to be more complicated. The complications centre on her discovery that in fact she has already been castrated. This she blames on her mother, with whom she then competes for her father's love. She experiences a desire for him as part of a desire for what she has lost, referred to as penis envy. She does not see her mother as a feared competitor, and so she neither totally represses her desire, nor fully identifies with an adult figure in the way that the boy does. Thus superego formation is less clear-cut in the female. She too enters a quiescent period which is reawakened in puberty. At this stage, her earlier penis envy is transformed into a desire for a child to substitute for this loss.

As with earlier phases, there are many ways in which the child's development through the oedipal phase can vary and the tensions associated with it be more or less satisfactorily resolved. The very nature of the parents, and the way they are accepted as models or challenged as competitors, also offers a basis for great variety in the adult personality which is formed as a result.

A classic, but is it relevant?

Freud's own writings (e.g. Freud 1905/1953–74; 1907/1953–74), particularly his case studies, provide a fascinating read. They can also seem fairly fantastic. The brief account given here necessarily risks becoming a caricature, but even in their original form Freud's claims seem extravagant and unsupportable to many, for their possible plausibility depends on accepting the operation of a powerful, dominating unconscious to which the individual has normally no access. That is a notion of which most social psychologists are sceptical. Yet others have been quite won over by Freud's ideas and the tradition which he initiated. These reactions have often polarized into two hostile camps where Freud is either praised or reviled, and it can seem that there is no middle ground. If one focuses on the standards for evidence which are accepted in psychoanalytic work, then many would argue it is simply unscientific because claims cannot be challenged and falsified, and we should not even consider the theory at all. However, to do this would ignore the fact that much of what Freud proposed has been very influential, and elements of his thinking have found their way into other parts of psychology, including social psychology (e.g. Chapter 15 on the authoritarian personality). It is also important to remember that Freud's work is not a single theory, but is composed of many parts, and that the weaknesses of some parts does not necessarily affect them all. Underpinning all of these difficulties is the fact that psychoanalytic theory grapples with the meaning of behaviour in relation to people's wishes and desires, and this gives rise to very difficult interpretative and investigative problems.

Problems of interpretation   The mechanisms of defence which were mentioned above lie at the heart of queries over the status of psychoanalytic claims and the evidence on which they are based. By themselves, each mechanism can seem quite plausible, and we can often think of occasions when we have directly experienced something like their operation. The problems arise when it is recognized that as a set, their net effect is to make any specific behaviour a possible outcome of many different drives or instincts. In making claims about instincts, drives and motives, Freud has much in common with a whole variety of other psychologists who work on both human and animal behaviour. The important difference comes with his claim that the cause of what someone is doing can be so transformed by various defensive manoeuvres that it ends up producing something quite different from what one would expect. Indeed, it might end up producing the complete opposite when something like reaction-formation is operating, or it might result in nothing at all if repression and denial are at work. Unless there is a clear way of linking behaviour with an underlying psychological structure which is said to be its basis, the claim that the existence of that behaviour supports the theory of the underlying structure cannot be entertained.

So very different?   At face value many of Freud's claims are very different from those offered by other theories, and in many respects they are simply wrong. A clear case of this is to be found if we read the account of the oedipal phase as a series of literal claims. The available evidence says that young children usually have little if any knowledge of genital differences, and base their understanding of gender on various superficial features. It would also seem from observational studies that little girls engage in as much auto-erotic activity in the phallic phase as little boys do (see Greenberg and Fisher 1977; 1996). Furthermore, the sense of sexual desire which is being proposed for the child cannot be the same as for the adult.

However, if we view Freud's claims as being about the growth of understanding of relationships in an emotional context, a growing recognition on the child's part of differences between men and women in power, position and status, and a claim about the importance of role modelling, the story becomes quite a familiar one which has a surprising amount in common with that which one would find in other traditions. The difference in Freud's case, however, lies in his attempt to integrate a variety of emotional and cognitive factors into a single account. The breath-taking breadth of his attempt is also its weakness, particularly when allied to outdated metaphors and a sensationalist treatment of infantile sexuality.

The self

Personality theorists of the type represented by Eysenck and Cattell offer accounts of the individual on the basis of the observer's perspective. In this sense, they are in the same position as the lay member of society who attempts to understand the behaviour of other people (see chapter 11). In addition to the observer's position, there is, of course, another angle for the lay person on what people do. This is the individual's own perspective on what he or she is as a person, and what makes himself or herself distinctive. These personal understandings of oneself have been studied extensively, are often referred to as theories of the self, and form a distinctive contribution to work on personality. A significant and seemingly paradoxical thread which runs through these theories is that, despite being concerned with the individual's own reflections on her or his self and behaviour, they have placed great emphasis on the way in which other persons and social groupings are central to our understanding of ourselves. A principle figure in these developments was G. H. Mead, who worked not in psychology but in the Philosophy Department of the University of Chicago in the early part of the twentieth century, and has subsequently exerted considerable influence on social psychologists' thinking about the individual. Box 2.2 gives a brief biography of Mead.

Box 2.2 George Herbert Mead (1863–1931)

George Herbert Mead was born in South Hadley, Massachusetts, in 1863. At the age of 16 he entered Oberlin College, graduating with a BA degree in 1883. Mead went to Leipzig to pursue a PhD in philosophy and physiological psychology in 1888, but his work was interrupted by the offer of a lectureship at the University of Michigan. Mead took the job in 1891 and married Helen Castle in October of the same year. He never completed his PhD.

At Michigan, he met the philosopher John Dewey and the two men became close personal and intellectual friends. When Dewey moved to the University of Chicago, he did so only on condition that Mead was also offered a position. Thus, the University of Chicago became the new centre of American Pragmatism, the philosophical tradition that interprets truth in terms of the practical effects and usefulness of belief systems. Mead spent the rest of his life in Chicago and made substantial contributions to both social psychology and philosophy. Mead was hit hard by the death of Helen in 1929 and, gradually becoming ill himself, died in 1931.

Mead's major contribution to social psychology was his attempt to show how the human self arises in the process of social interaction,

Plate 2.2 G. H. Mead

particularly through linguistic communication ('symbolic interaction'). As humans, we have a unique capacity to create shared meanings, and to bring those meanings to life in a social relationship. Like Freud (see Box 2.1), Mead placed a heavy emphasis on childhood socialization as the source of adult personality. Central to understanding his work are three concepts: the 'I', the 'generalized other' and the 'me'.

The 'I' is the active, creative and impulsive element of the person, which, prior to socialization, is the basis for all of our actions.

The 'generalized other' develops as the child engages with others and begins to understand the necessity of give and take in social exchanges, and the meaning and implications others attribute to his or her actions.

The 'me' is the bedrock of self-consciousness and represents the efforts of the 'I' to experience itself, which it can do only through the lens provided by the 'generalized other'. Mead saw each of these elements as existing in a dynamic relationship to one another.

While Mead himself was not involved in any empirical social psychological research, his ideas inspired much important work, especially within what became known as symbolic interactionism.

George Herbert Mead

Mead's work, which was mostly published after his death in 1931, had at its heart a single key question: how do we know who we are? This can either seem to be somewhat trivial, as we all seem to know who we are without much difficulty, or it can be heard as a profound spiritual or metaphysical question for which we cannot hope to find an answer. Mead viewed it as neither, but instead as made up of two difficult but answerable questions: first about what is it that we experience about ourselves when we gain knowledge of the self, and second about how a child develops the capacity to experience and know herself or himself in this way.

Social experience and self-knowledge   Mead's first observation was that we do not experience ourselves in the same way as we experience other objects or even our own body. Our self is bound up with our experience of other objects, but it is not part of them. However, when the self becomes an object of experience it is at one and the same time the subject and the object of experience, and so the self enters into the experience of the self. This recognition enables us to identify, he argued, 'the essential psychological problem of selfhood or self-consciousness . . . . how can an individual get outside himself (experientially) in such a way as to become an object to himself?' (Mead and Strauss 1964, p. 202). The answer for him lay in 'the importance of what we term "communication" [which] provides a form of behaviour in which the individual may become an object to himself' (Mead and Strauss 1964, p. 203).

He believed the kind of communication humans could engage in through the use of human language was fundamentally different from the communication systems found in other creatures in its ability to create shared meanings, and to bring those meanings to life for those in a social relationship. Through this capacity, it enables us to become self-conscious because it allows us to see and understand ourselves as others do, and to act with foresight. Because of this representational ability, we can change what we wish to do in the light of our understanding of what an action will generate as a reaction, and thereby tailor it to achieve a specific goal. None of this tailoring can be perfect because all of us are anticipating what each other will do, and so the interactional landscape is forever shifting, but this does not matter. Human awareness and self-consciousness are the result irrespective of these imperfections, and thereby also the past and the future are brought into the present moment to provide that extended sense of human self-hood beyond the here and now.

Social development and psychological structure   An important implication of Mead's claims is that self-hood depends upon the child's socialization into a social world, and through this the acquisition of the relevant mental capacities for knowing the self. Central to his account of this are three concepts: the I, the generalized other and the me.

The I is the active creative and impulsive element of the person, and before the child is socialized it is the basis of all his or her actions. In this respect, it is reminiscent of Freud's conceptualization of the id, but unlike the id the I does not require any ego functions at all to relate to the world, nor does Mead endow it with any particular drives or desires. As the child begins to act in the world on the basis of these I impulses, he or she witnesses the reactions of other people to those actions and also acquires a language to describe them. Through this an understanding of the meaning of what he or she has done develops, as does an understanding of the attitudes and values of other people.

This first understanding of the views of others, and the give and take it permits in social exchanges, which Mead referred to as the play stage, is the prelude to the formation of an understanding of what views and attitudes people as a whole in a social group hold, and thereby what meanings different actions have. When the child has achieved this, she or he will engage in interaction in a more reflective fashion because her or his actions are being governed by more than just the actions of the person to whom she or he is relating at that moment. Once the child has achieved this level she or he will be in what Mead referred to as the game stage, and will have developed an understanding of the generalized other. This enables the child to have a broader understanding of the meaning of his or her actions, and to be driven by the simple demands of the present.

Over time, the child will then develop a sense of the me, which is his or her under-standing of the potential and actual actions of the I as filtered through and organized by the acquired beliefs and attitudes of the generalized other. The me is the bedrock of self-consciousness, and represents the efforts of the I to experience itself, which it can only do through the lens provided by the generalized other. None of these elements is static, and they exist in a dynamic relationship to one another as experience changes the ambition and content of each.

After Mead   While Mead never sought deliberately to found a research tradition, his work led to the establishment of symbolic interactionism, which has been important in both social psychology and sociology. And although Mead himself did not engage in empirical work, the symbolic interactionists who followed him have made a strong commitment to understanding persons, their identity and the social order they create through an examination of how the significant symbols in a social group are deployed and understood. Amongst the most important of Mead's followers was Erving Goff-man, who studied in some detail the ways in which people achieved the kinds of self and personhood which Mead only theorized (see Goffman 1959; Goffman, Lemert and Branaman 1997). Much of this work has sought to move beyond a framework for understanding the general properties of the self to understanding the specific content of individuals' beliefs about themselves, and where those beliefs come from. An important contribution to this in social psychology comes from social identity theory.

Social identity and self-categorization

A significant figure in the development of social identity theory was Henri Tajfel (Tajfel 1974; 1981; 1982). His initial concerns lay with the issues of person perception (chapter 11) and, importantly, prejudice and intergroup relations (see chapter 15). If one examines how the latter operate, it becomes clear that a number of factors relating to self-identity derive from ones experience of one's own group, and that in turn depends on the group's relationship to other groups. In essence, what an individual knows about himself or herself depends upon understanding what other members of the social group in which he or she is placed are like. In a manner of speaking, we might be said to be working to the assumption that birds of a feather flock together, and that we understand ourselves by seeing which flock we are in. Understanding the nature of our own social group depends upon seeing it in contrast to other social groups, because we can only understand the characteristics of our own group when we compare it to others.

Through a number of strategies we seek to preserve and even heighten these differences through the way we think about and act towards others. We do our best to increase the differences between the groups, we often favour our own group excessively and are blind to its failings, we compete with the members of other groups, and as a result of all this, there is an important impact on our self-esteem when our group is prospering or failing (see chapter 15 for details of Tajfel's analysis).

Group membership is neither a passive matter nor a static condition, and an important development of social identity theory has come from the work of one of Tajfel's collaborators John Turner (Turner et al. 1987). He and his co-workers have proposed self-categorization theory, which argues that how we categorize ourselves is the important process which produces the phenomena considered within social identity theory. It focuses on the way in which we classify ourselves as members of different groups in different contexts as a function of the representations we hold in memory of groups we know as either an ingroup or an outgroup member. This process, it is argued, is constrained by the general properties of our memory and its schematic organization. This simplification can produce a measure of depersonalization in those contexts where group membership comes to the fore, with the effect that we behave more and more like the stereotype of the group ideal. This can be seen in many ways, including, for example, the changes in the way we speak as predicted by speech accommodation theory (see chapter 5) and the social influence exerted by fellow group members (see chapter 8).

The merely social self?

The two lines of work on the self considered here have placed great emphasis on the role of social processes in generating a sense of self or identity of personality. This can seem to suggest that the individuality of people is being denied in one way or another, but this is not so. In her introduction to her novel *The Golden Notebook*, Doris Lessing observed that one of the many surprising aspects of human life is the similarities we necessarily share while at the same time witnessing our own lives as following our own unique pathway (Lessing 1972). These theories are about some part of those similarities, but they do not deny the wide basis for individuality. At the very least, the unique elements of our own history are enough to ensure our individuality, but without our commonalities through a shared social world, we would not, as Lessing observed, be able to know each other at all.

Conclusions

The study of personality has always had a curious position within social psychology. This is strangely captured by the fact that one of the major journals in the discipline is called the *Journal of Personality and Social Psychology*. This can be read as emphasizing either the importance of personality in the discipline, or how it is not really part of it, but needs to be considered too. The incorporation of personality into the discipline has always seemed to be simplest when social psychology as a whole has taken a very individualistic turn, and has seen societies as simply collections of isolated individuals. Personality theorists as different as Eysenck and Cattell on the one hand, and Freud on the other, have attempted to provide grand theories which are ideally suited to this individualistic view. It is often the case that attempts at grand theory fail in social psychology, but the problems are always worse when there is no real sense of what the theory is about. Personality theory in its grandest sense has always suffered from being about everything and nothing, and neither provides a sensible target.

The prospects for the study of personality can be best understood by considering again the three historical roots mentioned at the start of this chapter. The most promising prospects arise when the peculiarities of the individual pose a puzzle in the clinic, the laboratory or the outside world. In this view, it is likely that personality theory will see greater success in the future in those moments where it is linked to the pursuit of a clear goal. On the one hand this could be in the context of work such as Zuckerman's, which is tying various claims about personality to a well-specified biological account of temperament. On the other, it could be where the goal is tied to some applied need such as therapy or assessment.

The third root which was considered focused on the way in which personality theories had often developed as a reaction to other developments in psychology. As can be seen from the rest of this book, there is less for the personality theorist to rebel against these days, if the concern is that important issues are being neglected. The theories of the self which we considered above are an important part of that wider context, although it must be recognized that the maturity of this field does not mean that these different theories are not in competition. This is most importantly the case when we recognize that personality theories of all types overlap in what they seek to explain, and that they cannot all be correct.

Ultimately we are left with a strange irony. 'Personality' is the kind of thing which many non-psychologists think psychology, and especially social psychology, should be about. Psychology in that sense is about what makes people tick. Yet, when one delves into people's personalities and lives, one finds that all of human life is there, and that what makes people tick is to be found in many places and not just in the study of personality, as the remaining chapters of this book make clear. As the next step in understanding the social individual, we shall examine some of the cognitive bases of an individual's social behaviour.

RECOMMENDED READING

There are many books which offer a collection of overviews of the various different personality theories which have been offered. Any reader wishing to find out more about the breadth and variety of theories within this field would do well to consult one of them. Each will provide further readings on each of the specific positions. The items mentioned above by L. A. Pervin and co-authors, and by C. S. Hall and G. Lindzey and their collaborators, provide excellent examples of the type which have been continuously revised over the years.

Baumeister, R. F. (1999) *The Self in Social Psychology*. Philadelphia and Hove: Psychology Press/Taylor and Francis.
For work on theories of the self, this provides the best contemporary overview of the field.

Gay, P. (ed.) (1995) *The Freud Reader*. London: Vintage.
Many would argue that Freud's own writings provide the best way of understanding his approach. The Penguin Freud Library provides the full range of his writings in a readily accessible form. For the newcomer, this reader provides an interesting selection from his earliest to his last publications together with a helpful commentary.

Hogan, R., Johnson, J. and Briggs, S. (eds) (1997) *Handbook of Personality Psychology*. London: Academic Press.
This is one volume which provides an advanced resource in the field beyond what can be covered in such books of overviews.

Wiggins, J. S. (1996) *The Five-factor Model of Personality: Theoretical Perspectives*. New York: Guilford Press.
Within trait-based approaches, the five-factor model is becoming increasingly important, and this provides a good overview of the history and ideas relevant to it.

Wollheim, R. (1991) *Freud*. London: Fontana Press.
This is one of the simplest and clearest introductions to Freud's work.

3

Cognition and Social Behaviour

Introduction

Our ability to function as ordinary members of society depends upon a wide range of psychological capacities and processes. These underpin our ability to interpret, understand, make judgements about and represent in memory the persons we meet, the societies in which we live and the ways in which we are related to them. Many theories within social psychology address the use of these capacities and processes with respect to specific phenomena; for example, in the study of attitude change, person perception and social judgements. These phenomena are the subject matter of what is referred to as social cognition or cognitive social psychology within the social psychological literature, and they are considered at length in many of the chapters which follow. The aim of this chapter is to set the scene for those later discussions by considering accounts of those basic processes and capacities in a more general way. In doing this, it will draw not only on work in social psychology, but also on mainstream cognitive psychology. Theories of social cognition have been inspired and influenced in many ways by that mainstream, using ideas and results from it, and adapting them, as appropriate, to the different subject matter in which social psychologists are interested, and it has made a significant contribution to the development of cognitive social psychology as a whole. In the first part of this chapter we will consider certain important lessons for our understanding of the cognitive basis of social behaviour which derive from work on perception, memory and judgement.

Focusing on these cognitive abilities independently of the social world in which they have developed and in which people live is not without its problems, however. It can lead to the assumption that these abilities are unaffected by that world, and this is far from true. With this in mind, the chapter will also examine how social and cultural conditions in both the short term and the long term determine and constrain our cognitive abilities. Amongst the important questions to be considered with respect to the short term is that of whether or not living in different societies or cultures changes not only the content of our ideas and beliefs, but also the very way we understand the world, reason and solve problems. There have been numerous studies which explore the psychological abilities of people from different societies and cultures which have offered quite surprising results. The long term in this instance can also be very long. One of the claims we will consider is the view that the evolution of the human intellect was driven by factors associated with the kind of social life our ancestors led in the period since we separated some five million years ago from the ancestral line which we share with our nearest genetic relatives, chimpanzees. The second part of the chapter will be devoted to differing effects of social circumstances on human cognitive abilities.

Throughout both parts of the chapter, four important themes will recur. First, we need to be careful how we idealize human mental capacities. In the age of high-powered computers with perfect memories and faultless logic, it can be tempting to take such machines as the paradigm for human reasoning, but there are many dangers in doing this. Second, many features of our cognitive capacities are designed to deal with the uncertainty and ambiguity we regularly confront in every area of our lives. As we will see shortly, even when we experience the world as well defined and clear cut, as in your experience of looking at this printed text, the basis for that experience does not lie only in the sensory information arriving at your eye from the page; it is also due to your understanding of what ought to be there. Third, our social cognition does not operate independently of the content matter to which it is applied, and in any sphere, human purposes and meanings play a central role in the organization of our cognitive activity. Finally, a repeated concern is the extent to which studies in this area properly reflect the actual cognitive demands of daily life (see chapter 19 on 'Research Methods' for more on this particular point).

Perception

The study of human perception has been an important part of psychology since its modern foundation, and is an area where we have seen many important advances in our understanding of psychological phenomena. By far the greatest proportion of this work has focused on vision and hearing. While many of the results are not of direct relevance to social cognition, the models which have been developed have inspired a number of analyses of perceptual and cognitive processes which have been exploited in the study of social cognition. In particular, they have assisted our thinking on the essential ambiguity which faces us when we try to understand the world around us, and the relationship between what the world presents to our senses and the knowledge we already possess.

Ambiguity

Take a quick look at the pictures in figures 3.1 and 3.2, and make a mental note of what you first thought could be seen in them before reading any further.

The first was developed by the Czech psychologist Joseph Jastrow, and the second comes from a magazine called *Puck* and was published in 1915. Both of them can be seen as two very different things. In figure 3.1, which is often referred to as the 'duck-rabbit', it is fairly easy to see that there are two possible ways of viewing it – either as a duck or as a rabbit. Notice as you see it first as one, and then the other, how your centre of attention shifts. Notice also how the rabbit's nose, which is a significant feature when you see it as a rabbit, becomes an insignificant detail on the back of the duck's head when you see it as a duck.

Figure 3.2 represents much more of a challenge to many people in that having seen one interpretation of it, usually the young woman, they find it hard to see the other. The original title of this picture was 'Wife and Mother-in-Law', and this refers to the two interpretations which it offers – a young woman and an old one. If, with this suggestion alone, you cannot see both, focus on either the tip of the young woman's chin or the tip of the old woman's nose depending on which you can see, for they are created by the same line. If that does not help, then try to see the young woman as looking away from the viewer with her head in the air, and the old woman as looking down to the bottom left-hand corner with her chin in her chest. Again, notice how your attention shifts when you see it as one or the other of the interpretations, and how the significance of different

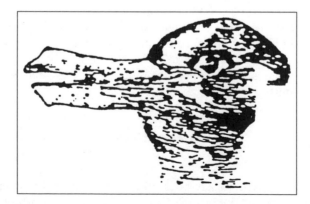

Figure 3.1 Duck or rabbit?

Figure 3.2 Young woman or old woman?

parts varies again. Also, notice two other things. First, it is seemingly impossible to see both at exactly the same time, no matter how rapidly you switch between the two views. Second, if you only saw one interpretation of it in the first instance, and can now see two, notice how it is impossible to recapture that sense which you originally had of not seeing the second interpretation. You might be able to lose it by squinting or blurring your vision in some other way, but you will find it nigh on impossible to retain the state of ignorance in which you were when you could not see it at all.

This kind of ambiguity, and the work we do in resolving it, reveal the challenges we face in performing even the most seemingly clear-cut perceptual task, and the active role we take in perceiving the world around us. This point is emphasized if we bear in mind the structure of the back of the eye, where the image we are seeing has fallen. Unless one knows better, it is tempting to think that the retina is like some kind of photographic plate, and that all the receptors on it have an uninterrupted exposure to the light coming into our eye. The reality is, however, quite different. The various structures which link the receptors on the retina to the optic nerve and to the brain pass across the face of the retina, so that any light reaching the receptors must first pass through the structures which lie in front of them. Furthermore, where the optic nerve leaves the eye, there is a complete lack of receptors, so that there is a literal blind spot in the visual field. Yet when we look at some visual scene, we are aware of none of this. What we experience is a coherent field. If we can take such an active role in visual perception, then it is unsurprising to discover that the idea of an active role for the perceiver has been very readily exploited within studies of social perception, where the information from the world is even less clear cut than in the case of visual perception (see chapter 11).

The coherence of our visual field is due to many features of our visual system. At the lowest level, it includes various properties of the retina, and other physical characteristics of the system which connects the retina to the other parts of the brain. At the highest level, it depends upon the knowledge of the perceiver which seemingly guides the perceptual process, as you will have experienced in seeing figures 3.1 and 3.2. This leads us to the second idea from work in perception.

Top-down and bottom-up

The recognition that our knowledge of what is in the world can drive our perception of it has led to the description of the relevant psychological processes as being top-down or bottom-up. The former is also referred to as knowledge-driven processing and the latter as data-driven processing. The implication of these names is that, on the one hand, the basic sensory input is the raw data with which we begin and which comes in at the bottom of the processing system, and, on the other, knowledge is at the top. In visual perception, both top-down and bottom-up processes can be in operation, and depending upon the circumstances, there will be a different balance between the two.

In interpreting this idea, it is tempting to think that when, for example, we see something, the top-down aspect is associated with some internal agent or eye which is doing the viewing. This tendency is supported by the fact that we can, of course, reflect on the experience of having perceived something, and we can seemingly guide our perception by a conscious effort of will, but this is a dangerous and misleading temptation.

There was once a comic strip called *The Numskulls* in the *Beezer*, a British weekly for children, which exploited this idea. As the reader, you were shown the inner life of the main character as he went about his daily business (see figure 3.3 for an example). His inner life was made up of a collection of other smaller characters, the Numskulls of the title. The main character could see because there was a vision Numskull behind his eye with a telescope, there was a hearing one behind his ear with a hearing trumpet, and so on. His perceptions of and actions in the world were explained as the result of the behaviour of the Numskulls.

If we interpret the idea of knowledge driven in this way, then we do not explain anything because we have simply said that some inner agent, be it a Numskull or something else, has done the job. This leaves us to explain the working of the inner agent, whatever it may be, and if we explained the working of that in a similar way we would embark on an infinite regress, where each explanation required a further explanation of some subcomponent of it (Pylyshyn 1973). To avoid this infinite regress, the knowledge involved in top-down processing must be embedded in the process itself.

Memory and meaning

When it comes to remembering anything, it seems that computers can put us all to shame. If you ask humans to remember a sequence of random numbers, most probably they will be able to remember about seven plus or minus two (G. A. Miller 1968). Mnemonists who can remember many more are of a special type and are very rare (Luria 1969). By contrast, even the simplest pocket computer can remember seemingly endless sequences with absolute perfection. Furthermore, when we deal with something

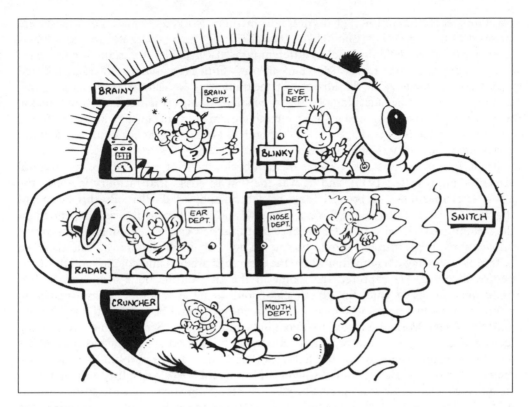

Figure 3.3 Does this go on inside your head?

more meaningful, such as a passage of prose describing a scene or an event, we can remember much more, but we are very likely to make errors again and it takes a real effort to remember the passage word for word, whereas the computer can provide a perfect rendition.

These failings of our memory can be depressing, but there are other areas where our memories outshine the computer's for the strange and simple reason that we can forget. In our daily lives we are exposed to huge amounts of information. If we were to remember it all in the manner in which a computer does, we would face a major problem in finding any particular memory when we need it. We do, of course, have problems remembering the things we want to remember, and we find that we can surprise ourselves with the odd details we do recall, but a distinctive and highly important feature of human memory, especially for the study of social cognition, is that meaning plays a major role in its operation, affecting both what we remember and what we forget.

Effort after meaning

From the beginning of memory studies psychologists recognized that meaning can affect memorability. The first reaction to this was to try to study, as the German psychologist Hermann Ebbinghaus did, how memory worked for materials which were stripped of their meaning (Ebbinghaus 1885; 1913). A classic tactic was to ask subjects to remember lists containing endless different nonsense syllables, for example consonant–vowel–consonant sequences such as 'vum' or 'miv'. Other researchers, however, realized that studying memory in the absence of meaning was foolish because memory was designed to remember meaning. To do so was like trying to understand how quickly someone might run a hundred metres by making them crawl backwards along the track. They can do it, and they will get there in the end, but the performance is not particularly revealing of how they might run a race.

Frederic Bartlett was a key figure in the development of the study of meaningful remembering (Bartlett 1932), and he was the first to stress that memory is about the effort after meaning. See box 3.1 for a brief biography of Bartlett. By this he meant that both the act of first laying down a memory, and its subsequent recall, depended on the meaning associated with it. He believed that this view carried a number of important implications. First, memory should be studied not only in the laboratory but also as a naturally occurring phenomenon where the meanings are real and consequential for the people involved. He captured this point in the title of his book, which described 'remembering' as 'a study in experimental and social psychology'. The distinction referred to the two places where he believed memory should be studied, the laboratory and the social world, and not to two kinds of memory. Second, our pre-existing ideas and the way they are organized into what he termed a schema radically affect what we remember and how we recall it. He offered this notion as a result of his work on memory for stories. He found that when people remembered stories, they adjusted them to suit their own prior conceptions of what should be in them, and this affected their memory. Third, as our understanding of the world changes, there are consequences for what we remember, and the form our memory takes.

Since Bartlett's day, memory psychologists have made great progress in understanding the varieties and forms of human memory. An area of this in which there are a number of important and provocative findings for the social psychologist is in the study of autobiographical memory.

Autobiographical memory

Despite Bartlett's early recommendations, it is only since the 1970s or so that serious attention has been given to the study of memory as a naturally occurring phenomenon. This has been important in the study of individuals' memories of their own lives, and thus their memories of themselves. This work is now quite extensive, but two parts of it are of particular interest here for their attention to the structure of autobiographical memory, and the role of interpersonal perception in guiding memory.

At one level, autobiographical memory is about our memory of things which have happened in our lives, and our experience of them. These memories may be at many different levels of description, and Neisser argues that they are structured hierarchically, so that we might access the general from the particular, and vice versa. They are also temporally organized, so that we can move from time to time within layers (Neisser 1988). This overall structuring has many consequences for our actions. It allows for

Box 3.1   Frederic Charles Bartlett (1886–1969)

Frederic Bartlett was born in Stow-on-the-Wold in Gloucestershire in 1886. He began his academic studies by taking a distance-learning course with the Correspondence College of the University of London, where he was later appointed as a tutor in philosophy. The administrative centre of the Correspondence College was based in Cambridge and, shortly after his move to the city, he joined St John's College and gained a first in the moral sciences tripos. It was here that he met and married Mary Smith, an animal psychologist.

While studying at Cambridge he met the philosopher James Ward, the experimental psychologist C. S. Myers and the anthropologist W. H. R. Rivers. Each of the men had a strong influence on Bartlett's later ideas. After his appointment, by Myers, as an assistant at the newly established experimental psychology laboratory at Cambridge, he began to react against the associationist psychology which was dominant at the time. Associationists believed that human psychology consisted of discrete elements, such as sensations and responses, that became associated according to some universal law. Empirical work in this area used supposedly meaningless, nonsense material in an attempt to arrive at some understanding of these laws. Bartlett, however, under the influence of Rivers and Ward, used naturalistic material, such as pictures and folk tales, to explore the organization of perception, recognition and recall. In his key text *Remembering* (1932) he shows that perception and memory are best understood as active processes, heavily influenced by an individual's past experience. He used the term *schema* to refer to the flexible, dynamic organization of human cognition.

Bartlett also had a strong interest in industrial and applied psychology. During both world wars, he became interested in understanding human–machine interaction and, along with his colleague and one-time student, Kenneth Craik, developed a greater understanding of aircraft design and pilot training.

Strikingly, especially in the 1920s, Bartlett published substantial works on cultural or social psychology (see chapter 20) which are seldom acknowledged in summaries of his career. It is only recently that these interests of Bartlett have started to be redescovered (Saito 2000b).

Bartlett was professor of experimental psychology at Cambridge from 1931 to 1952. He became a fellow of the Royal Society in 1922 and subsequently received a knighthood. He died in 1969.

flexible access through a variety of routes which might be thought to relate to the demands we face in interacting with other people. It also encourages us to be confident if we forget some of the details of an event because the surrounding structure is still in place, and that in turn can encourage us to infer and genuinely believe we have a memory for something we have forgotten because it is consistent with all else we can remember.

At a second level, autobiographical memory is about ourselves, and there are good grounds for believing that we hold independently of our autobiographical memories a self-schema or mental representation of ourselves. This has been explored in a variety of ways, but all of them suggest that it derives from an integration of our many different experiences over time, with some occasions being understood by ourselves as being more or less representative of what we are (see chapter 2 on the self). The content of the self-schema has been explored in many studies, often by using quite simple tests such as the twenty questions one. In this, those taking part are given a sheet of paper with the question 'Who are you?' posed twenty times, with in each case a line beginning 'I am . . .' following it. The task is to fill in twenty different adjectives or phrases to complete the answer. This proves to be a far from simple challenge, and an analysis of the results from large groups completing this test shows that there is a measure of similarity in our views. For example, Rentsch and Heffner (1994) found that all their participants offered characterizations which placed themselves in different social groupings; described their interests and activities; reported their beliefs; listed their relationships to others; and offered idiosyncratic distinguishing features. While these components were common to all, an important aspect of them was that they reflected wider social norms in that subjects focused on what was distinctive. For example, if a respondent was gay, he or she would say as much, but heterosexuality was not typically commented on. Thus we understand and articulate our self-schema against a broad social backcloth, and do not include within it things which might be derived from that backcloth.

Our perception of others, and particularly our inferences and beliefs as to their intentions, can play a key role in guiding our memory, particularly when it is failing. This was shown in an interesting way in Ulric Neisser's analysis of John Dean's testimony at the Senate Watergate hearings, which led ultimately to the resignation of the US president Richard Nixon in 1974 (Neisser 1981). In Neisser's analysis, it was shown that Dean's memory was right with respect to the intentions of the other member's of Nixon's staff and Nixon himself. The correctness of his belief as to these other individuals' intentions made him unduly confident in his memory for a number of specific details, which was often wrong. This failing has been noticed elsewhere, and can severely compromise the value of eye-witness testimony if the witness has jumped to an incorrect conclusion as to the intentions underlying the actions which have been seen (Loftus 1979; Loftus and Ketcham 1991).

Recovered memories?

The veracity of a witness memory is a vital factor in any trial, and legal processes operate to test it in a variety of ways. Until recently, it was always assumed that the witness had a constantly available memory of the events in question. Any barrister who could get a witness to admit that he or she might have forgotten something and had now remembered it again would have effectively discredited him or her. However, in recent years, there has been much controversy associated with the claim by some victims of crimes, usually sexual or physical abuse, that they have been so traumatized by their experiences that they have repressed the memory of what was done to them. These victims' memories become available to them many years later, often in the course of psychotherapy, and in many instances, especially in the USA, have been the basis of criminal prosecutions. In one case, a woman recovered a memory of her father raping and killing a friend some twenty years earlier (Loftus and Ketcham 1996). As might be expected, these cases have caused enormous controversy and distress to many people, but do we have reason to believe that individuals can completely hide from themselves a memory so meaningful but so awful?

Answering this question, which has produced a very polarized debate in the scientific and popular literature, has proved extremely difficult. At the outset, the picture is complicated by the one clear finding in this area, which is that people can believe they have a memory of an event which has never happened. Loftus and Ketcham (1996) cite the case of a sniper attack on a school where even students who were not present reported vivid memories of an event they had not witnessed. The same case report also revealed that all the students who were present remembered the event quite clearly even if there were levels of inaccuracy in their recall.

These two facts, which are supported by numerous other studies, encourage a degree of scepticism about the claim of recovered memory, as do Loftus's observations on the ways in which the circumstances of psychotherapy can be well tuned for the creation of false memories. However, these facts alone do not themselves force the conclusion that such potent memories cannot be repressed, as many writers have been keen to point out. The picture is further clouded by the fact that even those who have not forgotten awful memories may nevertheless be extremely reluctant to report them to anyone. In these cases, the distinction between deliberate suppression of a memory and its unwitting repression can become very blurred. Furthermore, the experience of telling someone else, for the first time, the details of something awful which has happened to oneself may bring forth the emotions and feelings associated with the original trauma, which will make the experience of the actively recalled memory very different from the private and partly suppressed memory of which we have always been aware.

These findings have led to much greater scepticism on the part of juries and courts about claims of recovered memories. In the absence of independent corroboration, they are no longer accepted as a sound basis for a prosecution, and many convictions which were based on such testimony have been overturned. The way in which individuals might be biased by their selective access to memories is taken up later in the book when considering person perception (chapter 11).

Information or connections?

Our discussion of memory so far has assumed that memory is to be understood in terms of propositions, concepts and images, and that we can analyse it without paying attention to the underlying anatomy and physiology of the brain. There is an alternative view, however, which describes the operation of many psychological processes in terms which reflect those biological characteristics. This is the basis for what are known as the parallel distributed processing or connectionist models of cognition (Rumelhart, McClelland and the PDP Research Group 1986; Smolensky 1988). These models are motivated in part by the fact that the brain operates a large number of processes simultaneously, and has no problem integrating the results of many different cognitive activities. Connectionist accounts build from this base and seek to deny the role of symbolic representations in the operation of our thinking. Information is represented not as individual images or symbols, but as a set of connections between independent processing units in a vast and extensive network of units that mimics the organization of neural structures. None of these units has a symbolic character by itself. This system operates in both perception and learning by building or reducing the strength of the connections between individual units. Memories are thus formed through experiences which jointly activate parts of the network and strengthen the links within it, and recall occurs when some element is stimulated, thereby causing those parts associated with it to be reactivated.

This kind of account has seen its greatest success in models of perceptual and low-level cognitive processes, including learning (e.g. Dell, Chang and Griffin 1999; Proto-papas 1999; Seidenberg and MacDonald 1999). Social psychologists have been wary of adopting these models to date, because the symbolic character of social cognition is very important in our existing theories. Nevertheless, some papers have begun to appear in the literature where there is an attempt to use connectionist accounts to address social psychological matters. Some of these have attempted very grand proposals for linking cultural experience directly through to brain plasticity (e.g. Kennepohl 1999). Others have been more cautious, and have focused on more limited issues such as mental representations of self and others (e.g. E. R. Smith, Coats and Walling, 1999) and aspects of social reasoning and social behaviour (e.g. Read and Miller 1998). The uses within social psychology to date have been somewhat metaphorical, but some research-ers have begun to elaborate in quite productive ways on that metaphor; for example, Thagard and Kunda's (1998) development of their parallel constraint satisfaction model operates a connectionist-like system over networked symbol sets, which represent con-cepts and memories of other persons and types of person. It is unclear as yet what the prospects are for connectionist accounts in social psychology, but even within cognitive psychology there has been scepticism as to their value for the modelling of anything other than opaque and automatic processes for which there can be no conscious control (Baddeley 1990).

Judgement and reasoning

When we look carefully at how humans perform when reasoning about states of affairs and solving problems, they can often seem to be illogical, unable to understand num-bers, and blind to the significance of important details. They cannot achieve the standards of *Star Trek*'s Mr Spock, or Conan Doyle's Sherlock Holmes, let alone the numerical and logical precision of the supercomputers which are often present in science fiction stories these days, and seem rapidly to be becoming science fact as shown by, for example, the chess-playing successes of IBM's 'Deep Blue'. Even though such machines are a human creation, most people find themselves unable to learn or even understand the logic of their operation, let alone match the rigour of their reasoning. These failures and successes of our reasoning and problem-solving capacities have always been, within both psychology and those parts of philosophy from which it developed, a subject of considerable importance. Indeed, a curious feature of that history is that many of the formalized reasoning systems which we often find hard to learn were, in fact, attempts by philosophers to capture the structure of our thinking (Devlin 1997). All of this interest has given rise to a substantial psychological literature (J. R. Anderson 2000), but for our purposes here the important elements concern certain apparent failings in the way we make judgements about states of affairs and probable future outcomes, rather than our successes,

There are many reasons why people think in the way that they do, and why they sometimes make incorrect predictions and judgements. Interestingly, there are good reasons to believe that those failures are due to our using strategies in our thinking which in many circumstances are normally helpful. Many of the problems we confront in everyday life are ill-defined and open-ended; for example, deciding what to buy a friend for a birthday present, whether or not you can trust a friend enough to lend her your new car, which courses you should take at university, and so on. As we will see later in this book, in chapter 11 on person perception, some of the most difficult problems of this type which we face arise when we make judgements about other people and their actions. This in itself may sound an odd observation because we seem to make such judgements very easily, but that ease can be deceptive. If we try to specify fully our grounds for making the judgements, or indeed provide a computer with the capacity to make the same judgements as we do (Johnson-Laird 1988), then it becomes very clear that there is tremendous complexity underlying that apparent simplicity. This is handled in a variety of ways, and one of them involves a reduction in that complexity by using our existing knowledge of the world to create a number of rules of thumb, mental short cuts, or heuristics, as they are often called. These heuristics prove to have a number of characteristics which recur, and they seem to be a fairly reliable feature of human judgement and thinking in the face of uncertain circumstances and ill-defined problems. In the years since this area of work was initiated by Daniel Kahneman and Amos Tversky (Tversky and Kahneman 1974; Kahneman, Slovic and Tversky 1982), various heuristics have been identified and investigated, and amongst the more important ones for the social psychologist are the following.

Availability heuristic

A problem which faces any politician in an election campaign is the belief that mud sticks. If, for example, a candidate for office is repeatedly questioned by opponents as to the legality of some business deal in which she was engaged, the candidate will, especially if she is totally innocent, repeatedly deny the charges, but in hearing both the charge and its denial, voters will be inclined to think about the possibility of its being true. Previously they might not have thought about the possibility of the candidate's being involved in shady deals at all, but now they have an image available of her being so. Even if the charge is publicly acknowledged by all concerned to be completely false, she will still worry that the voters' view of her will be affected. This is a rational fear on her part, because of the operation of the availability heuristic. The operation of this heuristic leads people to believe that events which they can easily recall from memory and bring to mind are more likely to have happened in the past and to happen again in the future. In many instances, this heuristic yields reasonably accurate results, but often not. For example, ask yourself whether there are more words in the English language which begin with an 'r' or have 'r' as the third letter. Most people find it easier to think of words beginning with an 'r' than with 'r' as the third letter and so conclude that the former are more prevalent, but this is not the case.

Judgements as to the proportions of particular kinds of words in a language are rather peculiar, but there are several studies which report the existence and operation of this heuristic in a wide range of realistic cases. Researchers have, for example, examined the ease with which people can bring awful events to mind, and their corresponding judgements as to the likelihood of these happening (Lichtenstein, Slovic et al. 1978; Plous 1993). Typically they overestimate the probabilities of someone dying in a plane crash, being murdered or being burnt to death in a house fire, and underestimate the probability of death by drowning, being struck by parts falling off a passing plane, or committing suicide. Similarly, various studies have argued that the presence in the media of certain kinds of story can heighten this effect, so that people who watch lots of fictionalized violence overestimate its prevalence and have a greater fear of crime, or that stories about the problems of drug use can lead to a similar overestimate as to the scale of the problems it presents (Eisenman 1993). The effect of this heuristic has even been manipulated experimentally by Schwartz et al. (1991). They asked groups of subjects to think of themselves as having acted assertively on either six or twelve different occasions in the past. Most people find it relatively easy to think of six occasions, but much harder to think of twelve. When subsequently asked to rate how assertive they were, those who had the easier task of recalling six instances were much more likely to rate themselves as assertive.

Representativeness heuristic

Imagine for a moment that you are about to meet for the first time a woman named Laura who had been a student activist while at university, had graduated with a first class degree in philosophy and was unmarried. Now suppose that you are asked to make a judgement about her which asks you the likelihood of her being a bank manager, a feminist, and a feminist bank manager. When Tversky and Kahneman (1983) posed tasks like this to participants in their studies, the majority of them thought that it was more likely that she would be a feminist bank manager than a bank manager, but this cannot be so. The class of all bank managers includes feminist bank managers, and so there must be a greater probability of her being a bank manager. This mistake, which is known as the conjunction fallacy, shows the operation of what is called the representativeness heuristic. This heuristic underlies our tendency to judge, for example, events as being more likely if they conform to a particular image or stereotype we have of a category. To give another example, which would you say is more likely in a room full of people: that a man has a heart attack, or that a man who smokes has a heart attack? Many people will say the latter because they believe that there is a causal link between smoking and heart disease, and make their judgements in a way which ties them more fully to their pre-existing beliefs. However, since there is a probability that a non-smoker will have a heart attack, then the group of all men is more likely to include a heart attack victim than is the subset of men who are smokers.

This desire to seek patterns, and assume the world is consistent with them, again reflects something akin to the processes of knowledge-driven perception, and because we are always seeking patterns we find it hard to act as if they are not there. This can be seen operating in everyday life in, for example, the numerous inferences we make about people on the basis of very limited knowledge (chapter 11). It can also be seen in what is known as the gambler's fallacy, where individuals believe a pattern is present in a run of events even though each event is separate and random. For example, many people think that they can guess better than chance on the outcome of the toss of an evenly weighted two-sided coin if they know how it has landed in previous tosses. If it has come up tails seven times in a row, many believe there is a greater than fifty-fifty chance of it being heads on the eighth toss.

Together with the availability heuristic, this factor can lead to what is known as the false consensus effect. Given that we have extensive knowledge of ourselves and people who are like us, and can easily call these details to mind, we have a clear tendency to overestimate the extent to which other people agree with us, even if we are in a minority position and know that to be the case. For example, smoking is on the decrease in most of Western Europe and North America, and although smokers know this, they still believe that more people smoke than actually do.

Anchoring and adjustment heuristic

Those first two heuristics reflect the impact on our judgements of our pre-existing knowledge of the world, in terms of both its ease of access in memory and its content and structure. This third heuristic is concerned with how ideas generated in the here and now can have similar biasing effects. The idea behind it is that when making judgements, the point at which we start our deliberations can have an anchoring effect, and that subsequent adjustments to that estimate are thereby constrained. Numerous studies have demonstrated this effect (Tversky and Kahneman 1981), and it is a key concern we all have when engaging in arguments and debates. As is often observed, any politician who sets an agenda is more likely to be successful in achieving something akin to his or her desired goals than one who is chasing the argument by seeking to challenge the agenda which has anchored the debate.

Confirmation bias

The heuristics we have examined so far suggest that we are essentially conservative (not in any way in the political sense of the term) in making our judgements and choices. We tend to assume that the future will be pretty much like the past, and for a whole variety of judgements this is not a bad operating principle. There is a further characteristic to our thinking, though, which reinforces this conservatism, and this is known as the confirmation bias. This refers to our tendency, when we hold a particular idea or theory about the world, to seek evidence which supports our view and avoid or discount the importance of any evidence which contradicts that theory. This is despite the fact that evidence which challenges our ideas is far more informative than that which is consistent with them. To understand why, consider a simple example. If I believe that all swans are white, then no matter how many white swans I see, my theory cannot be said to have been proved more right. If I have seen ten thousand white swans, and I see another one, my belief has the same status, whereas if I see one black swan, it has overturned that belief at a stroke.

Many studies support the existence of the confirmation bias, dating all the way back to Wason's earliest studies (e.g. Wason 1960; 1968), where his participants in the laboratory were asked to hypothesize and test the rules underlying various systems and states of affairs, and all revealed this tendency to focus on confirming evidence and not seek counterexamples to their views. It is a pervasive feature of our thinking which operates in many areas of everyday life. Tajfel (1969) argued that it could be a key mechanism underpinning the persistence of ethnic and other kinds of prejudice.

Universality and specificity

So far, we have paid little attention to the social and cultural circumstances in which people do their thinking, but there are reasons to think that these are highly consequential, especially for the social psychologist. Research has been directed to understanding how this might be so in a number of different ways, and it is to this that we now turn.

Situated cognition

Some of the phenomena we have considered when looking at studies of memory and judgement so far suggest that the cognitive phenomena in question are influenced by the circumstances in which they operate. Recognition of this has led many researchers to examine in much greater detail the way in which cognitive abilities are both tied to and supported by the circumstances in which they operate. This study of what is referred to as situated cognition and learning has been important in a number of applied fields, especially education (Lave 1988; Hutchins 1995; Resnick and North Atlantic Treaty Organization. Scientific Affairs Division 1997).

A good example of how the situation in which a cognitive activity is placed can radically effect its operation is to be found in the early work of David and Terezinha Carraher (Carraher, Carraher and Schliemann 1985; 1987). They were studying Brazilian schoolchildren in an impoverished district in the north-east of the country. These children were performing poorly in arithmetic tests in school, and one might think that arithmetic is arithmetic no matter where you do it. However, much to the Carrahers' surprise they discovered that the same children were working as very competent and successful vendors of fruit and vegetables in street markets. In the classroom they could not multiply 7 by 13, but if, for example, they needed to sell seven mangoes at thirteen cruzeiros each, they would have no trouble calculating that a customer would need nine cruzeiros' change from a one hundred cruzeiro note.

From one point of view, it appears as if these children are failing to generalize a skill from one context to another, but this ignores the fact that processes which appear identical in the abstract description offered by our theories might not be so for the individual who is actually enacting them. This is easily shown by comparing noughts and crosses, the British game, or tic-tac-toe, its US equivalent, with number scrabble. In number scrabble, two players are presented with a set of nine cards numbered one to nine and lying face upwards on the table. They take turns in taking cards from this set, and the winner is the first person to have three cards which when added together make a total of fifteen. This game is identical in form to noughts and crosses. This might not seem obvious but examine the grid, often called a magic square, in figure 3.4. Each winning line on the grid adds up to fifteen, and corresponds to one of the different ways in which three cards drawn from the pack in number scrabble might produce a winning combination. For each winning combination there is a winning line on the grid, and vice versa. Thus, number scrabble and noughts and crosses could be represented at an abstract level as identical games, but this would ignore the fact that most players find it much easier to play noughts and crosses than number scrabble, and for them the games are not identical.

In many respects, the ideas behind the study of situated cognition extend the considerations in the earlier part of the chapter. There we were considering how the content and meaning of what someone is thinking, their purposes and the context all affect the results of that thinking. This work takes that line one step further by examining how thinking is tied to and supported by the context. A classic example of how environmental factors can be used to support cognitive processes is provided by Lave, Murtaugh and de la Rocha (1984). In this study participants were asked to make $\frac{3}{4}$ of a recipe which itself required $\frac{2}{3}$ of a cup of cottage cheese. One participant, rather than calculating that a half a cup of cottage cheese was required (i.e. $\frac{2}{3} \times \frac{3}{4}$), simply took the $\frac{2}{3}$ of a cup of cottage cheese, made a flat circle of it on the table, and cut away one quarter, leaving the desired amount.

In social situations, the physical characteristics of the environment can be very important in guiding our thinking, but so too is the situation provided by other people. Understanding how the social situations do this, however, is not easily characterized, and depends greatly on how the language we use is interpreted (see chapter 5). How we support one another's cognitive processes for both social and other purposes is undoubtedly important in various activities ranging from education through to flying

8	1	6
3	5	7
4	9	2

Figure 3.4

jumbo jets. Analysing how this is so is difficult and this work is still very much in its infancy when compared to other areas of cognitive psychology. However, it holds within it many interesting challenges for the social psychologist, and is a key area where social and cognitive psychology can come together fruitfully.

Do they think like us?

Much of the literature we have considered so far has been based on studies of people in modern industrial societies with a particular kind of social organization and structure, but this form is not universal and the study of situated cognition raises the prospect that cultural variation could be very significant. This possibility has in fact been recognized for quite some time. Since the earliest days of collaboration between psychologists and anthropologists – for example, the Torres Straits expedition of 1898 (Haddon 1901; Herle and Rouse 1998) – there has been an interest in the possibility that people from different cultures might think and reason differently. Chapter 5 will examine the role of language as such, but there have been other studies which have tried to explore this issue. The typical form of these has been to take standard psychological tests which have been developed for use on the members of one society, and see how those from a quite different society answer them.

A good example of this kind of work is provided by some early studies conducted by Aleksander Luria during the 1930s. At that time, he worked for the Institute of Psychology at Moscow University, and the purpose of the studies was to examine the impact on rural peasants of the collectivization of farms. The prevailing ideology proposed that changing the economic relationship between the peasants and the ownership of the means of production would affect their mentality (Luria 1977). In one part of his study, Luria asked various Kashgar villagers to answer questions about simple syllogisms. One question he posed was: 'Cotton can only grow where it is hot and dry. In England it is cold and damp. Can cotton grow there?' While you, like Luria's controls from Moscow, may have no difficulty in answering this question, Luria found that a number of the peasants in his study were unable to provide the simple answer 'No', suggesting that they could not do this kind of formal reasoning. Luria tried a number of other tests on them involving concept formation, abstraction, perception and problem solving, and found similar results. The overall pattern led him to the conclusion that 'our investigations ... showed that as the basic forms of activity change, as literacy is mastered, and a new stage of social and historical practice is reached, major shifts occur in human mental activity' (Luria 1977, p. 161).

Similar studies on a variety of tasks and in other societies have demonstrated variation in performance on a number of tests. This suggests that culture can have a big effect, but answering the question of how it does so reveals that we need to retreat from any simplistic notion of either different peoples having different cognitive abilities or there being a simple link between tests and underlying capacities. Two key figures in developing this line of argument were Sylvia Scribner and Michael Cole, who conducted similar studies amongst the Vai of Liberia (Cole and Scribner 1974; Scribner and Tobach 1996). The basis of their argument can be seen in the transcripts which Luria provided of some of the tests he conducted, and his observation on the importance of literacy. Read the transcript in box 3.2 of the exchange between Luria (L) and Abdurakhm (A), a 37-year-old illiterate peasant from a remote Kashgar village where the effects of collectivization had not been experienced by all. Abdurakhm has just failed to give the right answer to the cotton syllogism above.

Apart from illustrating the difficulties of conducting experiments in the field, there are many things of importance in this exchange. First, while Abdurakhm does not provide the right answer, it seems that he knows what it is. Indeed, in his second turn at speaking he effectively gives it. Second, he is making plain the conditions on which he will and will not say something in his third to sixth turns at speaking in this conversation, and his views are not that unusual. In English courts, the same principle holds. A witness cannot offer what is called 'hearsay' as evidence, that is, anything which is not based on her or his own first-hand experience. Third, Abdurakhm is clearly concerned with real answers to questions, and while he can deal with hypotheticals, he does not take them as valid ways of knowing.

This last point was picked up by Cole and Scribner, who also explored Luria's ideas about the importance of literacy in changing the way we think. They would pose to Vai villagers similar tasks, for example, 'Everyone who owns a house in the town pays house

---

Box 3.2   An exchange between Luria (L) and Abdurakhm (A)

Abdurakhm has just failed to give the right answer to the 'cotton syllogism':

L: In the Far North, where there is snow, all bears are white. Novaya Zemlya is in the Far North, and there is always snow there. What colour are the bears there?

A: There are different sorts of bears.

L: – (repeats his first utterance) –

A: I don't know; I've seen a black bear, I've never seen any others . . . each locality has its own animals: if it's white, they will be white; if it's yellow, they will be yellow.

L: But what kind of bears are there in Novaya Zemlaya?

A: We always speak only of what we see; we don't talk about what we haven't seen.

L: But what do my words imply?

A: Well it's like this: our tsar isn't like yours, and yours isn't like ours. Your words can be answered only by someone who was there, and if a person wasn't there he can't say anything on the basis of your words.

L: But on the basis of my words – in the North, where there is always snow, the bears are white, can you gather what kind of bears there are in Novaya Zemlaya?

A: If a man was sixty or eighty and had seen a white bear and had told about it, he could be believed, but I've never seen one, and hence I can't say. That's my last word. Those who saw can tell, and those who didn't can't say anything.
   At this point a young Uzbek volunteered 'From your words it means that bears there are white.'

L: Well, which of you is right?

A: What the cock knows how to do, he does. What I know, I say, and nothing beyond that!

tax. Sam owns a house in the town. Does Sam pay house tax?' In response to this, many Vai people would say 'Don't know' or 'How can I say?' In exploring why they were being given this answer, Cole and Scribner would often be told stories about how people cheat on their house taxes, and that the villagers did not know if Sam was like that, and so how could they come to a conclusion. In other words what they were doing was using all their relevant knowledge, and concluding that they did not know enough to provide a valid answer. What they were not doing was taking part in a particular language game typically found in school-based education, where you consider a problem in isolation from all else you know, ignore the fact that your questioner apparently knows the answer to the question, and do not expect your answer to have real-world consequences in terms of the substance of the query.

In focusing on literacy, Luria was in part right, and many authors have argued that it has major and profound effects on our abilities. It was once famously described as 'the technology of the intellect' (J. Goody 1968). However, Scribner and Cole found that it was not just literacy, but literacy exploited for the purpose of the school, which produced this effect in these studies, and that there are different kinds of literacy as a consequence. The route through which it has the effects we have been discussing may, according to Olson (1995), be the way it enables our attention to be directed. This may also be an important way in which culture affects much of our mental activity. Essentially it provides a guide for the focusing of our mental resources and an account of what is important, generally and specifically in terms of other people's intentions. We mentioned the role of understanding others' intentions earlier when discussing the John Dean case, and there is an argument that the ability to do this is the result of much longer-term evolutionary pressure which reflects our social environment.

The evolved social mind

A curious feature of all primates, that is, humans, gorillas, chimpanzees, pygmy chimpanzees and orang-utans, is that they have very big brains for the size of their bodies when compared to other mammals. The chimp's brain is about three times bigger, and the human's is about nine times bigger, than one might expect by comparison to the mammalian average. Having a big brain is costly in that it consumes a lot of energy and therefore requires the individual to find more food, and for humans increases the likelihood of birth complications and death and requires the infant to be born in a relatively immature state. In evolutionary terms, these costs, if not counterbalanced by some benefit, would work against the success and survival as a species of the owners of this costly organ. Once upon a time, it was thought that the advantage it conferred lay in our increased ability to control the physical and technical world, but, since the early 1980s, the evidence has mounted in favour of the alternative claim that the value of our brains lies instead in our ability to understand other persons and cooperate or compete with them. The argument is that the environmental niche in which we developed our mental powers was that of society and social groups, and that the key requirement in that environment was the ability to think about other people as thinking agents with goals and plans, as well as to think about us thinking about them thinking about us, and so on.

Finding evidence for this claim is not straightforward, but there are several compelling lines which when taken together are hard to deny. First, there is the fossil record, which shows that our ancestors' brain size increased at a pretty steady rate over five million years, but that tool technology hardly changed at all until the last few thousand years. This speaks very strongly against the idea that human mental abilities developed to handle the physical and technical world. Second, an examination of our near genetic relatives shows that increasing brain size is associated with increasing social sophistication and social complexity. Third, that increased social complexity is matched by an ability to complete a variety of tasks which other creatures find impossible to do. This includes a number of tasks which require the individual creature, for example a chimpanzee, to have a level of self-awareness and an ability to empathize with others, and understand their intentions (Byrne and Whiten 1988; Byrne 1995; E. N. Goody 1995; Whiten and Byrne 1997).

An important additional line of evidence on this comes from work in developmental psychology on a specific pathology, autism, which argues for an important innate social ability that has clear social and cognitive components.

Autism: a cognitive and social deficit

Autism was first described by Leo Kanner in an article in 1943, but there is no reason to believe that it did not exist before that date. It affects between 0.16 and 0.22 per cent of the population and is three to four times more likely to occur in boys than in girls. A mild form of autism, Asperger's syndrome, is more common and affects between 0.3 and 0.7 per cent of the population. In its classic form autism is identified in terms of three features: (1) autistic aloneness, in that the child prefers to be alone and can seem quite oblivious of other people; (2) problems in using language and communicating with others; (3) a marked fondness for clear-cut routines, which often extends to habitual, stereotyped and repetitive behaviours. Those who are diagnosed as autistic do not all show the classic picture, and may have each of the three features in varying extents. They may also have other deficits, but about 15 per cent will fall within the normal range for intelligence, and some will have islands of great ability in doing such unusual feats as rapid mental arithmetic with large numbers, calendar calculations and so on (Frith 1989).

Given the diverse nature of autism, any explanation is bound to run into difficulties, but one of particular interest here is the claim that many autistics lack a theory of mind, in that they cannot understand someone as having a different and false belief when compared to their own. This failing was first noted in the context of the Sally-Anne task due to Josef Perner and his colleagues (Wimmer and Perner 1983).

In this, a child who is taking part in the experiment watches a sequence of actions. First, one character, Sally, places a marble in a box, and then leaves the room she is in. Next, Anne comes in, and takes the marble out of the box and puts it in a basket. She then leaves the room. Finally, Sally returns to get her marble. At this point children are asked where Sally will look for her marble. Most 3-year-olds say that she will look in the basket, whereas 4-year-olds will say that she will look in the box where she origin-ally hid it. The 4-year-olds can understand that Sally's knowledge is different from their own, and that she will act on the basis of what she believes even though the child knows it is an incorrect belief. The classic autistic child will fail to understand where Sally will look for her marble, and will fail not only at age 3, but at age 4 and beyond.

The inability to make these kinds of analyses of other people's beliefs will, of course, have a major impact on the child's social and communicative skills. As we will see in chapter 5, the ability to use language properly depends critically on the ability to understand other people's beliefs and intentions. If the child has various related failings at a very young age – and there is now evidence that various deficiencies are present in the autistic child's interactive style at 18 months (Charman, Swettenham et al. 1997) – this will have consequences for the child's ability in many domains, and he or she will become socially isolated, compounding his or her problems.

In terms of the evolution of these skills, there is evidence that there are different patterns of brain activity in autistic children when they are doing certain tasks asso-ciated with interpreting others' actions (Baron-Cohen et al. 1999). There is also evidence of a clear genetic basis to the condition, and several writers have proposed that there is a specialized part of the brain, a cognitive module, which is responsible for our capacities to understand other people's mental states (M. Anderson 1992; Baron-Cohen 1995). Furthermore, the parents of autistic children often show weaknesses on certain social perception tasks when compared to other adults with unaffected children (Baron-Cohen and Hammer 1997)

Conclusions

The ability of individuals to take part in social life depends on their ability to perceive, think, reason and speak. The loss of these mental functions through brain injury or disease destroys those capacities and the social life which depends on them. This chapter has briefly examined various characteristics of human cognition in this regard which are relevant to our social lives. The precise impact depends on the areas of social life which are being analysed, and many of the subsequent chapters in this book will reflect this.

It is also the case, however, that our social lives can have a major effect on the way we think and act. Our cognitive abilities have evolved to their current level as a function of our ancestors' sociality. The flexibility with which this has endowed human beings ensures that those abilities are deployed in many different ways, as a function of the lives we lead both with other people and in interaction with the material world around us. Our social psychological makeup cannot be reduced to non-social psychological capacities, and our social actions cannot be predicted from them, but equally, we cannot have that social psychological character without them.

RECOMMENDED READING

Kunda, Ziva (1999) *Social Cognition: Making Sense of People.* Cambridge, MA: MIT Press.
First, this is a good overview text which separates ideas of basic cognitive processes from their application in specific social cognition topics, while providing substantial coverage of both.

Parkin Alan, J. (2000) *Essentials of Cognitive Psychology.* Hove: Psychology Press.
There are a number of textbooks which have the subject of cognitive psychology in the title and which cover a broad range of issues of relevance to work in social cognition. The J. R. Anderson (2000) reference noted above has been a popular and successful text which has been through many editions, and many others do an excellent job. Choosing between them is not easy, but this volume is amongst the most up-to-date.

Stuart-Hamilton, I. (1996) *Dictionary of Cognitive Psychology.* London: Jessica Kingsley.
A good dictionary of a subject is always of value, and apart from Reber's (1985) Penguin dictionary of psychology, this is a useful specialist source.

Wilson Robert, A. and Keil Frank, C. (1999) *The MIT Encyclopedia of the Cognitive Sciences.* Cambridge, MA, and London: MIT Press.
This is a key reference work for those readers who might wish to take their interest in this subject further. It contains articles from a number of leading authorities in the field and covers the full range of the cognitive sciences. It also provides key references and suggestions for further reading.

4

Emotion

Introduction

Imagine yourself sitting in a lecture with a hundred or so other students. You are in your first year at university, and this is one of your first lectures. You know a few of the people around you, but not very well. Since arriving at the beginning of term, you have been, at different times, anxious, excited, happy, fearful and miserable. The lecturer, who is teaching a course on the psychology of emotion, asks the audience to put on a smile, and almost everyone eventually does. What do you think happens as a result?

Try shutting your eyes, think of yourself in that lecture and put on a smile. If your imagination is good, you may be able to sense that what happens is an interesting sequence of events. Initially, a number of tentative smiles start appearing around the room, and as the number grows each becomes more substantial. Cheesy grins start to follow, and very soon many in the room are laughing, some quite loudly. These expressions are accompanied by a changing set of feelings. Initially, you feel awkward and embarrassed at putting on a smile, particularly in this context, where it can make you feel somewhat foolish. You also feel physically a little different as the back of your scalp tightens, your cheeks change shape and your ears move backwards slightly. Then, as you look at others in the room, and find that they look a little foolish too, you may be amused, and so your smile takes on a different, more genuine aspect. You and they both start to chuckle, and before long you actually feel amused. Given the emotional pressure which everyone in the audience will have been feeling since the start of term, there might also be a fair degree of tension released by this laughter.

The mild amusement which can be generated in this way does not, of course, reflect anything more than a small part of our emotional experience. Nevertheless, this sequence of events – and if you do not trust the results of this thought-experiment, try actually doing it with a group of friends – captures many of the important elements we need to consider in understanding what constitutes our emotional life. On the one hand, there is a variety of intrapersonal elements to do with how our body seems to feel different when we smile and laugh, and our conscious awareness of this and understanding of what it means. On the other hand, there are the interpersonal and social components to do with how we express ourselves, the actions and reactions of the other people present, and our understanding of the wider context. Necessarily, the link between these interpersonal and intrapersonal sides of emotion is very important as each carries implications for the other, and both are understood in a broader social frame of the accepted significance of emotional expression in our culture. This chapter will consider how both sides have been investigated and analysed, and how we might draw them together in a way which links the intrapersonal, interpersonal and social elements of emotion. In doing so, it will clearly illustrate the close links between the cognitive and emotional bases of our social behaviour. It will then consider why we have emotions at all, and conclude with a brief examination of how certain emotional difficulties play a role in different psychopathologies.

The intrapersonal side of emotion

The beginning: William James

Contemporary psychological work on emotion is often dated to William James's classic paper, which was simply entitled 'What is an emotion?' (James 1884). (See box 4.1 for a brief biography of James and an outline of his theory of emotion.) While his answer to this question proved to be flawed in a number of ways, it nevertheless provided an important focus for a great deal of subsequent work, and much of it is essentially sound. In it, he gave a central position to our emotional feelings, especially the extent to which they are based on changes in our bodily state. Essentially, the starting point for his analysis was the proposition that those reports we give of our feelings – which might range from butterflies in the stomach, sweaty palms and the heart rising in the throat, through numerous more refined and literary descriptions, to rather less delicate descriptions of the effect of fear – were pointing to very real conditions and changes in our bodies. These, combined with our experience of our emotional expressions in our faces and our bodies, and the actions we take when behaving emotionally, constitute our emotions. In the absence of these, he argued, our emotional sense 'would be purely cognitive in form, pale, colourless, destitute of emotional warmth' (1884, p. 190). In other words, when you describe yourself as happy or angry or sad, you are referring to something inside of your body which is physically changing.

Put this way, his theory seems like nothing more than plain common sense to many people. James himself thought it so self-evidently true that he was certain that his theory was correct, and he was not alone in thinking this. Carl Lange, a physiologist, independently and simultaneously proposed an almost identical theory to the one James had offered (Lange and James 1922). However, while the James–Lange theory, as it subsequently became known, did accord well with one aspect of our common beliefs about emotion, it contradicted another.

The counterintuitive aspect lay in their proposal for the sequence which follows the perception of some event which results in an emotional state. They argued that the bodily changes which are at the centre of emotional experience follow directly from that perception, we then recognize these changes in our body, and this recognition is the emotion. In other words, our conscious perception of the emotional significance of an event follows rather than precedes these bodily changes. To make their point clear, consider an example. Imagine you are walking along the street and a car suddenly swerves off the road, mounts the pavement and heads straight for you. In describing such an experience, you might say that because you were frightened your legs turned to jelly, that you felt sick, and many other things besides. But according to James and Lange this description gets the order of events wrong. Their position was that because your legs turned to jelly and you felt sick, you knew you were frightened. See box 4.1 for a summary of this position.

Box 4.1   William James (1842–1910)

William James was born in New York in 1842. His father had inherited a large fortune and used it principally for travelling, socializing and educating his five children. As a consequence of his unconventional upbringing, William, along with his brother, the novelist Henry James, developed a wide range of academic, artistic, linguistic and social talents. Indeed, it was later said of the brothers that, while William wrote psychology like a novelist, Henry wrote novels like a psychologist. After numerous diversions into the fine arts and the sciences, William eventually decided on a career in medicine. He graduated from Harvard in 1869, where he later took up an academic post lecturing in physiology. Despite his many privileges and abilities, things were never easy for William, who often suffered bouts of severe depression; these became less frequent, however, following his marriage to Alice Gibbens at the age of 36.

His key text, *Principles of Psychology* (1890), explored the themes of choice, individuality and purpose. It was widely admired at the time of its publication and James enjoyed the fame the book brought him. He travelled widely throught his life and maintained a correspondence with many of the key intellectual figures of the day, including Sigmund Freud and Bertrand Russell, the famous Cambridge Philosopher and Peace Campaigner.

James raised many challenging issues for psychology in a vivid manner; his conceptualization of 'emotion', for example, is particularly interesting. Developing the work of the Danish physician C. G. Lange, he suggested that an 'emotion' is our perception of the bodily changes produced in response to particular situations. In other words, we 'grieve' because we cry, rather than crying because we grieve. The theory, known as the James–Lange theory of emotion, dominated psychological research in the area until the late 1920s, when W. B. Cannon published a critique of the position. Cannon noted, amongst other things, that emotions are still present even when the given bodily part associated with an emotion has been removed.

Plate 4.3 William James

That is, people without tear ducts can still grieve. Cannon did not present a viable alternative explanation to James's, however, and it was left to Stanley Schachter (see box 4.2) to resolve the conceptual issues that James had raised.

James's principal contribution to social psychology was to encourage debate and discussion. He established a laboratory for psychological experiment at Harvard in 1875, but he himself lacked the patience required for experimentation and measurement. He died in 1910 shortly after a trip to visit his brother Henry in England.

These two central propositions of the James–Lange theory, concerning bodily states and the primacy given to them over our higher cognitive abilities in the genesis of emotion, have lain at the heart of debates over the intrapersonal dimensions of emotion ever since. Curiously though, a critique of the theory by one of James's own students, Walter Cannon, was seen at the time to be so effective that it pushed the James–Lange account, and indeed the study of emotion more generally, to the sidelines for many years because it spoke so effectively for the common-sense view.

William Cannon

On the basis of his own physiological studies, and those of others, Cannon argued that internal bodily states simply could not be the basis of emotional experience, and so to the extent to which they were tied to emotion, it must be as a consequence of some other process in the brain (Cannon 1927). He offered a number of arguments in support of this claim, but these can be drawn together in two groups. First, he argued that many parts of the body which were said by James and Lange to be the source of emotional feeling, such as the various organs located in the abdominal cavity often called the viscera, could not possibly be so. They are too poorly supplied with sensory receptors, they do not change condition as quickly as our emotions do, and they do not vary in the changes they exhibit as much as would be needed to account for the range of emotions we experience. In other words, they were too numb, sluggish and undifferentiated to fulfil the role ascribed to them. Second, emotional behaviour occurs even when the central nervous system, through which we consciously perceive and understand the world, is isolated from the viscera, for example in cases of spinal cord damage, and by contrast if changes to the viscera are produced by drugs rather than real events the result is not a genuine emotional feeling.

The last of these points attracted much attention, and Cannon supported it by offering as evidence the results of a study reported by Marañon. In a study which nowadays cannot be replicated for ethical reasons (see chapter 19 on 'Research Methods'), he injected over 200 subjects with epinephrine without telling them what he was giving them or what the effect would be (Marañon 1924). The effect of epinephrine on the body is to produce changes in the sympathetic nervous system which result in raised blood pressure, heart rate, respiration rate and blood sugar levels, and altered blood flow to various parts of the body. We are subjectively aware of many of these, and we might also experience them as palpitations, flushing, tremors, breathing difficulties and so forth. These are the changes which James and Lange had claimed were important in feeling an emotion. If they were correct, then Marañon's subjects should have experienced an emotion as a result. Most of his subjects did indeed report feeling anxious or sad, but, importantly, the great majority said that it did not feel like a real emotion. They said it made them feel as if they were experiencing the emotion, and those who did report a genuine sensation also reported that it was linked to particular emotional thoughts. In other words, the claim that emotional perception and description was driven by a changing internal landscape was simply wrong. Cannon concluded as a result that the true sequence of events in feeling an emotion was as common sense held it to be, namely that knowing you were frightened was independent of and preceded any bodily feelings. This position was accepted for many years, but was to change in the early 1960s with a reappraisal and replication of Marañon's work by a social psychologist, Stanley Schachter.

Stanley Schachter

While Cannon used Marañon's results to argue against the James–Lange view, Mara-ñon's own analysis of them was somewhat different, and ultimately more sympathetic to that view. He was interested not only in the great bulk of his subjects who reported that their feelings were somehow not genuine, but also in the minority who did feel genuinely moved. He recognized in these cases the importance of the interplay between the feeling due to the changed bodily state, and a conscious understanding for oneself of a relevant and appropriate set of ideas, memories or beliefs which could account for feeling that way. In this, he was maintaining the James–Lange emphasis on the importance of inner states, but argued that a proper understanding by the individual concerned as to why an emotion was being felt was indispensable.

Schachter recognized the importance of Marañon's work and argued that the general lesson to be drawn from it was that whenever we experience changes in ourselves and the world around us, we seek explanations of them. The majority of the subjects who reported that they did not experience a genuine emotion did not do so because they had an explanation of why they felt different. Simply, the explanation lay in the fact that they had had an injection, and although they were not given any expectations as to the effect, it would be an obvious candidate for many people for explaining the change they experienced. They were, after all, not told that there would be no effect. Those who did report a genuine emotion had been thinking about something which made them feel a certain way already, and the changes merely propelled them along the same road, so they too had an explanation, but a different one.

This line of thought lead Schachter to what is known as the two-factor theory of emotion. This accepted Cannon's argument that internal bodily changes could not be the source of emotional differentiation, but also accepted the James–Lange view that they played a role in emotional experience, and could be generated independently of a full cognitive appraisal of some emotion-eliciting event. That appraisal was, however, necessary for a proper appreciation of a fully differentiated emotional experience.

To test this claim, he conducted, with one of his colleagues, a study which is now considered to be a classic (Schachter and Singer 1962). This experiment is described in box 4.2.

Subsequent analyses of Schachter and Singer's findings, and related studies, have made it clear that what is going on in this study is far more complex than Schachter and Singer presupposed (Marshall and Zimbardo 1979; Maslach 1979). It played a pivotal role in ensuring that the role of cognition and interpersonal factors would not be underestimated in future.

An important part of the complexity in the experiment lies in the fact that the subjects' experience of their changing bodily states and the situation evolves over time. This is allowed for by the two-factor theory, but the exact specification of how individuals explain for themselves how they are feeling is a complex cognitive process. If you did turn the thought-experiment at the beginning of this chapter into an actual exercise, this is what you would have witnessed. Your understanding of what is happening is not based on a single interpretation at a single point in time. Instead it evolves over time, and this is true for all events which trigger emotions. The importance of this point is reinforced by the fact that many authors believe that not only are cognitive processes influential for the processes of emotional experience, but also emotional processes are fundamental to the organization of our cognition, an issue to which we will return later in this chapter. For this reason and others, most theories of emotion are now extremely wary of arguing for anything other than a close interplay between the psychological and physical components of emotion.

Box 4.2   Two-factor theory of emotion

Stanley Schachter, a social psychologist working at Columbia University in New York, proposed that different emotions could arise from the same bodily arousal. He assumed that, given a particular state of arousal, a person would describe his or her feelings according to both contextual cues and personal memories. In other words, although physiological arousal is an important condition for any emotional experience (as proposed by William James; see box 4.1), the nature of the emotion will depend on an individual's personal perception of both the external world and her or his internal state. In 1962, Schachter, along with his colleague J. E. Singer, devised an experiment to test this hypothesis.

All participants were told they were taking part in an experiment to test the effects on their vision of a substance called Suproxin. In actual fact, the participants were injected with adrenalin. One group was told that Suproxin would raise their heart rate (a known consequence of adrenalin injections). A second group was told that they might experience symptoms such as numb feet and headaches (symptoms not associated with adrenalin). And a third group were told nothing at all about what they might experience.

The participants were then placed in one of two social contexts. Stooges (i.e. role-playing actors who were confederates of the experimenter) were introduced into each group, and their job was to encourage one of two reactions in participants: euphoria or anger. After the experiment, participants were asked to describe how they felt. Interestingly, the adrenalin seemed to have amplified the mood which the stooges had promoted. So those in the presence of an angry stooge became particularly angry. Likewise, those in the presence of a euphoric stooge became very happy. Those participants who had been misinformed, or not informed at all, of the consequences of the injection experienced the most extreme emotions. The results of the experiment show that complex interactions between social context and bodily states create an emotion. Today, however, it might be more difficult to conduct the study. Some would now consider lying to participants about what was going into their bodies, as Schachter and Singer did, to be unethical.

Another element in this complexity, which changes the nature of the demands being placed on those cognitive processes and emphasizes the interpersonal focus which Schachter introduced, lies in the fact that those concurrent bodily states are not so undifferentiated as Cannon, Schachter and others believed. In his original formulation, James was keen to emphasize that the expressive actions of the individual were intimately bound up in our emotional experience. A number of writers have been attracted to this idea, and the role of facial expression has been accorded a central role. It turns out to be a crucial link between the intrapersonal and interpersonal elements of emotion. The recognition that it might be so, however, predated James's original publication by more than a decade.

The interpersonal side of emotion

Darwinian beginnings

Not only was Charles Darwin a keen observer of the natural world and the variation within it, he was also a keen observer of human life. In the development of his ideas on the evolution of modern humans he became fascinated by the nature of human emotional expressions, their presence in children from a very young age (he studied his son William extensively), and the similarities and differences between humans and other animals in their expressive repertoires. He even conducted a survey of human facial expressions of emotions by writing to various missionaries and colonial officers in different parts of the British Empire to solicit accounts of how the locals expressed different emotions. As a result he argued that facial expressions of emotion are an innate feature of humans, and as such exist as a result of evolutionary processes (Darwin 1872).

While other aspects of Darwin's work on evolution have long been respected, this element of his work was often neglected, or even seen as quite mistaken. For the greater part of the twentieth century it was simply assumed that human communication, including non-vocal communication, was essentially conventional in its structure and very different in different societies. Thus there were no universals in human expressive and communicative behaviour of any significance or consequence. If there were similarities, they were due to the fact that all humans had essentially the same limited body structure, and in any case they were greatly outnumbered by the many differences between societies and cultures which had been discovered.

This orthodoxy failed to recognize that there are many different elements in human communication, as we shall see in chapter 5, and that what was true for one component might not be true for another. There is no necessary reason why the principles underlying the development of communicative hand gestures need be the same as those for body postures or facial expressions. The received wisdom was also based on evidence derived from the search for variety rather than similarity, and it is always difficult to find something for which you are not looking. As soon as evidence for universality was sought, it was discovered. Now there is every reason to believe that human facial expressions of emotion have, as Darwin believed, a universal basis in a shared human evolutionary history. This is not to say, however, that there are not important cultural differences too.

Paul Ekman

An important contributor to this development has been Paul Ekman. In a number of studies, he and his colleagues have demonstrated that even individuals from cultures which have been almost totally isolated from one another can recognize, with a high degree of accuracy, each other's facial expressions (Ekman 1994).

A good example of these findings is provided by an early study in which he and a colleague compared the judgements of various facial expressions by the Fore of the

Plate 4.1 The universality of facial emotions: are politicians' smiles the same the world over?

New Guinea highlands with judgements of the same by Californians (Ekman and Friesen 1971). At that time – and with the spread of global society it is debatable whether or not this study could be repeated nowadays – the Fore were a non-literate neolithic culture, which had had very little contact with the outside world. Consequently, there was absolutely no reason to believe that they had acquired any of their expressive habits or understandings from elsewhere. The format of the experiment was very simple, and avoided the problem of translating the emotional terms of one language into those of the other. Ekman and Friesen told a brief story to each participant, and then asked him or her to nominate one of three pictures as being the appropriate one for the person mentioned in the story. Each of the pictures was of a Caucasian face showing an emotional expression for which the Californians had been in agreement as to the emotion being shown. So, for example, a story would be told of a father whose child had died. The subjects were then shown three pictures, one of which portrayed sadness, and the other two would be randomly drawn from the rest of the set of photographs, which included pictures of happiness, anger, surprise and fear. When compared with the judgements made by Californians presented with the same task, it was clear that there was a very high level of agreement between them and the Fore.

In a quite different study (see Depaulo 1992), American and Japanese participants were shown a stress-inducing film and their facial expressions were recorded under two conditions. In one, they were sitting in a group in a room with the lights on. In the other, they were on their own in the dark with their faces being filmed by an infra-red camera. The thinking behind this experiment was that if there were differences between societies in the facial expression of emotion, and these differences were essentially produced by social rules which varied an innately derived basic form of the expression, then altering the social conditions would vary the impact of those rules. In this case, being in the dark should reduce their effect, and the US and Japanese subjects should have expressions which were more alike in this condition than in the group situation. The results supported this position.

On the basis of these and many other studies which have sought areas of agreement between cultures in the recognition of facial expressions, Ekman has argued, and many other writers agree with his view, that there are at least six basic facial emotional expressions – anger, disgust, fear, happiness, sadness and surprise – which are readily understood by all humans no matter what culture and society they are from (Ekman, et al. 1987). Furthermore, it has been argued that this endowment provides an essential component for developing the James–Lange theory. Just as facial expressions are easily distinguished by observers, they also provide very different sensations for the person who is expressing them. Again, remember the exercise with which this chapter began. The sheer act of smiling provides a changed sense of our scalp, ears and face. This is at the core of what became known as the facial-feedback hypothesis.

Facial feedback

The idea that the feelings associated with facial changes might play a role in emotional experience has been given strong backing in recent times by a number of ingenious experiments and individual neurological case reports.

A good example of the former is a study by Strack and colleagues (Strack, Stepper and Martin 1988). This was presented to those who took part in it as a study of disability, for which they were asked to do a number of tasks in unorthodox ways. One of these required them to use a pen by holding it in their mouth in much the same way as those who have lost the use of their arms may do. One group was told to do this by gripping the pen between their teeth. Another was told to do it by holding it between pursed lips. As a result, the former were altering the position of their cheek muscles in the way they would when smiling, and the latter were changing their expression to one more like that of surprise. The effect of this difference was measured by getting both groups to rate a number of cartoons as more or less amusing while they were holding the pen. The results revealed that those who held the pen between their teeth rated the cartoons as significantly funnier than did those who held it in their lips.

A striking example of a neurological case report which tells us something about facial feedback has been provided by Fried and his colleagues (Fried et al. 1998). They were mapping the cortex of a 16-year-old epileptic girl in an attempt to locate the area of her brain in which the seizures were based, prior to neurosurgery. This is done by stimulating areas of the brain with a small electric current, and asking the patient to do a variety of tasks at the same time. This is important as a prelude to surgery as it enables the surgeon to ensure that areas associated with critical functions such as language, memory and movement are not unduly affected. In this case, when a certain part of the patient's left hemisphere near the area associated with the production of speech was stimulated, she smiled. When the current was increased, she started giggling and laughing, and reported feeling that very many things in the room were very funny. In other words, she was behaving in just the way that William James proposed. The cortical stimulation had provided the feeling and the expressive behaviour, and she had provided for herself an account of why she was feeling so amused.

Cross-cultural differences

None of these findings should be taken to mean, however, that because there is an evolutionary basis to emotional expression – and presumably much else in our emotional experience – this has explained everything we need to know about emotion. Arguments from the evolutionary origin of human psychology can never do this. Ekman recognized this, and realized that he needed to explain why there is not uniform agreement between the participants in the many different cross-cultural studies which have been done. The Fore in the study mentioned above may have agreed very often with the Californians, but they did not do so always. For this reason, he has proposed that there are three culturally variable causes of variation in the expression of emotion.

First, there are display rules. These are general cultural conditions which might lead an individual to elaborate or diminish an expression, or even perhaps substitute one for another. For example, the Spanish and the Japanese vary quite considerably in the extent to which they display their emotions. The Spanish are much more expressive and offer a fuller display than the Japanese, who consider it inappropriate to display their emotions so fully. Second, societies may differ in what elicits different emotions. The British, for example, are often saddened or angered by the ill-treatment of animals which may pass quite unnoticed in another society. Third, on any specific occasion, we will be aware of the consequences of expressing our feelings at that point in time, and we can, for a variety of reasons, hold back our expressions. I might, for example, think it really quite funny that a close friend has made a complete fool of himself, but when he tells me about it, if I know he is really upset and unhappy, I will hide my amusement and do my best to sympathize with him.

Each of these elements, of course, not only produces cultural variation, but also emphasizes the importance of cognitive factors in the process of the instigation of emotional reactions, and the expressivity which follows, as we noted in the previous section. They also lead to a focus on the context in which emotions are experienced, and the things which they are about. Amongst the most important of these is the interpersonal context, and our shared experience of emotion. This is where the interpersonal and the intrapersonal come together in our experience of empathy.

Empathy

While our emotions are a personal and often quite private experience, our public emotional rapport with other people is very important to us too. This is true with respect both to understanding the situations in which we act – misjudging the emotional tone of the moment can lead to some of our most embarrassing experiences – and to understanding ourselves – knowing that other people feel the same way as we do about something is very reassuring. Analysing empathy is, however, extremely difficult. While we may have a strong sense of when someone is empathizing with us, and when we are successfully doing it ourselves, it is much harder to say what we are doing, and to specify how emotional factors enter into it. Recent studies have suggested that the expressive elements of our emotional life, including facial expressions, might play an important role.

The origin of the term 'empathy' is in a German coinage of the late nineteenth century, but it only came into English in the early part of the twentieth century. The German word was *Einfühlung*, which might reasonably be translated as 'in feeling with'. The original emphasis was not on the more cognitive elements of empathizing, such as sharing points of view and trying to see an issue from another's perspective, as we often understand the term in everyday use now. Instead it was on the matching of bodily movements and patterns of action, so that the focus was literally on feeling physically the same.

Such matching has been analysed in a number of studies which have revealed that there is every reason to believe that the expressive similarity goes with an emotional similarity, and thus serves an important communicative role (Bavelas, Black and Lemery, 1986; Bavelas et al. 1988). For example, when we are getting on well with somebody, and experience them as being in harmony with us and sharing our emotions, we are highly likely to be moving towards similar patterns of expression, posture and gesture. Other emotions may spread in a similar way, and the mimicry involved has been documented in children from a very young age (Meltzoff 1988; Meltzoff and Moore 1997). It is also quite easy to observe in everyday life. Next time you are sitting and talking with friends, pay attention to similarities in their postures, gestures and expressions. If you all laugh, notice how what each of you is doing is not independent, but is closely linked to what other people are doing, a point which becomes very clear if someone laughs either too much and too loudly or too little. Notice also how the emotion in a particularly involving film or play, or exciting sporting contest, is mirrored in the bodies and faces of those who are watching.

Elaine Hatfield and others have argued that this matching produces what they refer to as emotional contagion, and is an important part of how we understand and appreciate one another (Hatfield, Cacioppo and Rapson 1994). In keeping with this idea of empathy as literally 'feeling with', they argue that as we change ourselves to be physically active in the same way as someone else we begin to share his or her emotional experiences. Our recognition of what someone else is doing on an interpersonal plane leads us to alter what we are doing, and through that we might end up with the same intrapersonal experience. Equally, of course, the other person may well be doing the same, and we can recognize the convergence this produces. Such an understanding of emotions provide insights into many of the phenomena underlying relationships (see chapters 6 and 7).

Plate 4.2 How can social psychology explain the similarity of these girls' displays of emotion? Empathy, contagion, or simply the fact that they are all perceiving the same stimulus?

Why do we have emotions?

This link between the interpersonal and the intrapersonal elements of emotion is highly advantageous for a species which has evolved for living in cooperative social groups. As we noted above, Darwin was interested in this, particularly with respect to facial expressions, but this is not the only answer to the question of why we have emotions. It is also important to approach it from the perspective of the role that emotions serve for the whole person's psychological processes in daily life. The communicative benefits which follow from their role in interpersonal relationships is one answer of this type, but it has been proposed that they are also important for our cognitive processes, as was suggested earlier in this chapter.

Once upon a time this suggestion would have seemed vaguely foolish. In considerations of human nature in the past, emotion and passion have often been seen as diametrically opposed to reason and intellect. The role of reason in controlling our more primitive passions has been seen as the key to human progress towards a more civilized way of life. This view, however, assumes that our intellectual capacities are rather more extensive than they actually are, and as is discussed in the preceding chapter, our ability to understand the social world depends as much on assumptions and heuristics as it does on our ability to draw inferences and to reason. With these constraints in mind, Oatley has argued that emotions play a central role in guiding our thinking, and act as some kind of watchdog which guards our interests (Oatley 1992).

The watchdog element is most obviously present on those occasions either when something unexpected happens, or when we are uncertain about what is likely to happen next. Responding to the unexpected, or to our own uncertainties, is vital for our well-being and survival, but the range of unexpected events is so great that we could not monitor for all of them even if we devoted our entire mental resources to looking for them. If we did, then we would have no mental capacity left for doing anything else. The solution to this dilemma, according to Oatley, lies in our ability to monitor what we are doing at a subconscious level in terms of rather general goals we have set for ourselves, while the rest of our attention is directed towards the fine detail of accomplishing our current ambition. Any additional event which either furthers those goals or, more importantly, threatens them, and obviously this might include threats to our very existence, will lead the monitoring system to interrupt our attention. Once it has produced this interruption, our awareness and our actions are redirected by our emotional state. This monitoring system is, it is proposed, the basis of our emotions.

A related account for the role of the emotions has been offered by Damasio (1994). He accepts the view that bodily states play a key role in emotional experiences, but has argued that their significance can be learnt and remembered as what he calls 'somatic markers'. When we think of possible future actions and events these somatic markers become associated with our understanding of them. Bodily feelings and emotions are evoked as a result, and our decisions as to what to do are in part guided by how we feel at the prospect of those actions and events. A common experience of this is the butterflies we might feel in the stomach at the prospect of doing something threatening, for example a parachute jump, for the first time.

A third view of this type is provided by LeDoux (1993). His account is more concerned with the neurological underpinnings of the interplay between cognition and emotion, and he pays special attention to the role of the amygdala. This structure is found in a part of the brain known as the limbic system, which is found in mammals but not in reptiles, and is thus thought to be more recently evolved than those parts of mammals' brains which are also found in reptiles and birds. The amygdala is, however, older in evolutionary terms than many other parts of the mammalian brain. LeDoux argues that it plays a central role in emotional processing in that it can assess the broad emotional significance, in positive or negative terms, of both auditory and visual experiences, and can interrupt higher cognitive processes on the basis of that assessment in the way that Oatley argues for. It can also receive input from those higher cognitive processes, and provide the somatic markers proposed by Damasio in his account.

All three of these proposals argue that there is an important interplay between our cognitive and emotional processes, and that each may affect the other. This contention is supported by a number of other studies which have demonstrated the effects of emotional states on cognitive processes. For example, various studies have demon-strated that our ability to access different kinds of memory can be affected by the emotional state we are currently in – we are more likely, say, to remember a bad holiday when we are feeling sad (Bower 1982; Tobias, Kihlstrom and Schachter 1992). In a similar vein, it has been shown that our judgements as to the significance of an argument or some state of affairs can be affected by the mood we are in. Forgas and Moylan (1987) interviewed over 900 people going to and leaving cinemas showing films which were likely to evoke quite different emotional states. They asked them for their views on a variety of topics ranging from crime in the community to how satisfied they were with their own life. The results revealed no difference between those going in to see the different films, but clear differences between those leaving them.

Emotional pathologies

The account of emotions that we have considered so far attributes to them an important role both in our personal experiences and psychological capacities, and in our relation-ships with other people and the wider society. If this is correct, then any impairment in someone's ability to express his or her emotions, to feel them or integrate them with the rest of his or her psychological life, or to understand their expression and significance by and for other people will have severe consequences. This is exactly what we find, and a consideration of emotional pathologies is important, both in its own right for the insight it can give us into understanding and treating various psychopathologies, and for the potential it has for furthering our understanding of emotions. We have already seen how the study of a young epileptic girl undergoing brain surgery provided important evidence in relation to the facial-feedback hypothesis. Her experience is very rare, but the examination of the experiences and abilities of those who have suffered from various naturally occurring mental disturbances and afflictions has been of great value in the study of emotion.

There are a number of different psychiatric conditions where emotional changes and problems play an important role, both for the individuals affected and for the clinicians who wish to help them. These range from various personality disorders where there seems to be a distinct absence of emotional feeling and rapport; through psychotic conditions, such as schizophrenia, where the emotional feelings and responses may be inappropriate in both scale and character; to those conditions often known as affective disorders, for example depression, where the emotional difficulty is the very heart of the condition. (Some of these conditions are also discussed in chapter 17, 'Health and Illness'.)

Before we turn to a consideration of particular conditions, however, there are two important points to bear in mind when considering mental health. First, the description of any psychopathology is very difficult, and must be done with great care. It can be all too easy to describe someone as mad simply because we disagree with them, or dislike what they are doing. The history of psychiatry includes cases where psychiatric definitions and the power over other people which is given to psychiatric institutions have been abused. For example, people have been classified as insane because they held moral or political points of view or professed sexual preferences which were at odds with the wider society. This possibility must always be guarded against. Second, there is always the danger that when we read about these conditions, we think they apply to ourselves, and that therefore we are ill in some way. The fact that we can identify with the descriptions does not in itself mean that we are all insane. What it does illustrate is the continuity between the normal and the abnormal, and that those who are classified as psychiatrically ill may not be so very different from the rest of the community.

Psychopathy

Although the term 'psychopath' has wide popular currency, and has been enshrined in various pieces of mental health legislation, for example the UK Mental Health Act of 1983, many psychiatrists argue that there is a variety of personality disorders which for different reasons might place an individual under the scope of legal restrictions. In many of these, the individuals in question have an unusual emotional responsivity which underpins the personality disorder and which becomes most noticeable in the poor nature of their social relations. Amongst these disorders, the one which best fits the popular conception of the psychopath and is of most relevance to our consideration of emotion is usually referred to as antisocial personality disorder.

An individual who manifests this condition may well have a superficial charm and social skill, but the apparent emotional responsivity is not underpinned by any depth of feeling. He – for it is most usually a man – will be unable to form close loving relationships, and will quite readily act in a callous and cruel fashion in pursuit of a personal goal. In the extreme, such individuals can be quite violent and dangerous. He will also show a complete lack of guilt, will act impulsively, and will often be quite unable to learn from adverse experiences, so that the antisocial behaviour persists no matter what other people do to help or punish him. As a result, such individuals often have a weak social network and poor personal relations. In these cases, it is as if the emotional compass which guides other people, and which also gives meaning and value to their personal relationships, is not available (Cleckley 1988; Gelder, Mayou and Geddes 1999).

While the psychopath's condition might seem maladaptive, Mealey (1995; 1999) has argued that sociopathy, which for her is a broader term incorporating both the more and less extreme variants of psychopathy, is in fact a genetically based condition arising from the variety of social and reproductive strategies which can be found in human groups. It has persisted because social deception and manipulation can be successful on a limited number of occasions and providing not too many other individuals are doing the same.

This analysis of the link between emotional deficits of this type and moral and immoral behaviour suggests that emotions may have an important role in the establishment of many important norms and customs in human societies. This idea has been actively pursued by Frank (1988), who sees a basis within our emotions for phenomena as diverse as altruism, guilt, gratitude, hatred and obligation, and by Rozin et al. (1999), who have argued for clear links between three moral emotions – contempt, anger and disgust – and three moral codes – community, autonomy and divinity.

Schizophrenia

Of all the major psychiatric syndromes, schizophrenia has been amongst the hardest to define. The specific set of symptoms which any one patient shows may well be quite different from those shown by another. The common thread, though, is captured by the term itself, which derives from the Greek for splitting *(schizo)* and mind *(phrenic)*. The splitting refers to the splitting off of one mental function or process from another, and not, as many popular conceptions would have it, the splitting off of separate whole personalities, as is believed to be the case in multiple personality disorder. When the term was first coined the mind was conceived of as a collection of functions – for example, reasoning, seeing, hearing, talking, remembering, feeling etc. – which needed to be properly coordinated and integrated if the mind was to operate effectively as a whole. Nowadays, although the precise nature of the functions is viewed somewhat differently, the general conception is still supported. If the nature of emotion and its integration with other mental functions is as various theorists of emotion have proposed, then one would expect the emotional life of schizophrenics to be affected, and this is what is observed. In terms of the diagnosis of the condition, there are three ways in which a disturbed emotional life might reveal itself.

First, the schizophrenic might show what is called inappropriate affect. In this he or she will feel an emotion which is not in keeping with what one would ordinarily expect, and the presence of which can sometimes be disturbing for the person who is experiencing it. For example, the death of a loved one might be responded to with laughter. Second, there is what is termed a flattening of affect. This refers to a lack of emotional reaction of any kind. Finally, there might be enduring mood changes, where the individual shows a high level of anxiety, irritability or euphoria, or may be quite depressed. Depression, might, however, be a secondary effect consequent upon being diagnosed as schizophrenic and being hospitalized (Gelder, Mayou and Geddes 1999). (See chapter 17 for a discussion of other aspects of schizophrenia and depression.)

Depression

While psychopathy and schizophrenia are quite striking conditions, they are nowhere near as common as the class of affective or mood disorders of which depression and anxiety are two very important examples. Unlike schizophrenia and psychopathy, these conditions do not seem so distant from everyday experience, and most of us have an inkling of what it must be like to suffer in this way. For example, feeling unhappy in response to misfortunes and disasters is part of everyday life. Furthermore, from time to time, most of us have experienced the way in which a sequence of events or a collection of memories can repeatedly provoke the same emotion, so that it becomes an all-pervading depressed mood. From this we can have some sense of what being depressed is like. However, the step from a depressed mood to clinical depression is a large one.

Where one draws the line between a passing emotion and a persistent mood is not simple, as one blends into the other. For most of us, the distinction between the two is analogous to the difference between the weather we get on any particular day, and the seasons of the year. The step to being clinically depressed is, however, much greater and is akin to climate change of the scale one gets with the onset of an ice age.

What counts as clinical depression is a complicated matter, and there are various types of depression. In some cases, there are clear grounds for thinking that there is a strong biological factor which causes the individual to become depressed, but in many others there is a strong interplay between social, cognitive and emotional factors. In these latter cases, it has been found that the onset of depression often follows challenging or difficult life events such as the death of a loved one (G. W. Brown and Harris 1978; and see chapter 17).

It has been argued that the reason adverse life events have this effect is that they produce an emotional reaction which combines feelings of sadness and disgust. These in turn lead to a pattern of thinking which reinforces all the negative elements of the emotions, and an increasingly negative state is produced over time as the way of thinking and the way of feeling produce a vicious depressive spiral (Power and Dalgleish 1997). Indeed it has been argued by the same writers that many psychopathologies may involve damaging interrelationships of just this type between ways of thinking and different emotional states.

Conclusions

Despite having once been exiled from social psychology, the study of emotion is now very much a central issue. Many authors now adhere to what might be called a neo-Jamesian position. William James's belief that our emotions depend on a broad range of physical, cognitive and environmental factors operating both consciously and subconsciously is widely accepted. While much progress has been made in understanding the physical basis of emotion, its evolutionary origins, and the cognitive and social factors which combine to produce our emotional experiences, there are still many unanswered questions relating to its role in a child's development, its variation across people and cultures, and the part it plays in various psychopathologies.

RECOMMENDED READING

Jenkins, J. M., Oatley, K. and Stein, N. (eds) (1998) *Human Emotions: A Reader*. Oxford: Blackwell.
This gives a wide range of articles from both the contemporary and historical literature, and thus provides an easy way to access some of the original research papers.

Oatley, K. and Jenkins, J. M. (1995) *Understanding Emotions*. Oxford: Blackwell.
The study of emotions in psychology has expanded greatly in recent years, and there are now a number of books which provide good overviews of the literature. This is well written and readily available.

Palnalp, Sally (1999) *Communicating Emotion: Social, Moral and Cultural Processes*. Cambridge: Cambridge University Press.
This reading addresses the significance and role of emotions in everyday life with a distinctly social perspective.

Strongman, K. T. (1996) *The Psychology of Emotion*. 4th edn. Chichester: John Wiley.
Again, this provides a good overview of the literature, and is well written and readily available.

5

Language and Communication

Introduction

Human language and the ways in which we use it lie at the very heart of our social lives. It is through communication with one another that personal relationships, communities and societies are made and maintained, and it is through those social networks and relationships that we become who we are. Having the ability to talk – or sign if one is deaf, for these are equivalent abilities – to and with other people, and to do so effectively, is fundamental to every aspect of our life, from our psychological well-being through our personal relationships to our social and professional standing. If you doubt that this is so, try to imagine what it would be like to understand and relate to the people you know if you and they lost your capacity to use language. How would you gossip about your friends, think about what they say about you, plan an evening out with someone, take a course on social psychology, intimate a sexual interest, make a veiled threat, persuade someone to vote for you, tell a loved one that you still care about them but that you are really angry with them for smashing up your car, or even just pass the time of day, if you could not use language?

You could do some of these things, as other animals do, by using various grunts, postures and gestures, but you would not be using the subtle expressions we use every day. Grunts and gestures are useless for gossiping about a friend, thinking about what might happen at work tomorrow, or any of the many other things we do in our daily lives. Simply put, without our ability to converse with one another, there is no such thing as human society as we know it.

This stark proposition is the main reason why human language and communication has received so much attention throughout the humanities and the social sciences. As a result, social psychologists working in this area have drawn on a very wide literature in their work, and use theories and findings from a variety of other disciplines including linguistics, philosophy, sociology and anthropology. The sheer scale, diversity and, at times, technical sophistication of the work which has been used can make this area a rather forbidding prospect for the newcomer, but this need not be the case.

A good idea of what is important in language and communication for the social psychologist can be gained by examining three basic properties of it – variation, indeterminacy and reflection. These terms may not sound like basic descriptions, and it is certainly true that a full understanding of them and their consequences leads to many extremely complex issues at the heart of social psychology. Nevertheless, in essence they refer to relatively simple ideas which can be easily grasped, and which provide a sound base for understanding the extensive literature in this area. The first half of this chapter will be devoted to providing this base. In the second half, we will build on this base by examining the role language and communication plays in the construction of our ideas and experiences of being male and female.

Three basic properties

Variation

This first feature is one which has received a great deal of attention in sociological studies of language use and is, at heart, a very simple idea about a very common phenomenon. When we speak to one another, not only do we choose the ideas we wish to communicate, but we also choose the way in which we express them. The language system allows us to say what seems to be the same thing in very many different ways. For example, my native dialect is a version of British English in which the aitch sounds at the start of a word may be dropped. So, 'heaven' may be said as 'eaven', 'hope' as 'ope', and so on. But if I wish to say 'I hope I go to heaven when I die' I am not required to drop those aitches by the idea of going to heaven. I might drop neither of them, one or both, and which of these I do will lead to a different impression being formed in the mind of whoever is listening to me as to what I am like.

Variation in the way we speak is most easily described in terms of clear features such as accent, but its presence and importance throughout the linguistic system can be easily demonstrated. If I wish to ask a friend to buy me a drink, I can communicate the same request by saying '*Buy me a drink*', or '*Can you buy me a drink?*', or '*I'm terribly thirsty*', or '*It's your round*' or many other expressions. As with the dropping of my aitches, whichever variant I choose will get the same basic message (which is often referred to as the intended meaning) across, even though the simple literal meaning is different in each case. However, the choice will lead to a different impression on the listener. The first example is rather brusque, the second is more polite, the third is a light-hearted hint, and the fourth makes certain obligations clear. The impact of this kind of variation was interestingly demonstrated by an exercise which Harold Garfinkel once set his students (Heritage 1984). (Garfinkel was an American sociologist who argued for the study of social interaction and the actions through which individuals accomplish their status and identity in interaction. This focus gave rise to the term 'ethnomethodology'.) They were told that when they next returned to their parents' home, they should change the way they interacted with their family for between fifteen minutes and an hour, and observe if this made any difference to the way that they were treated. Specifically, they were told to be perfectly polite in the way that a well-mannered stranger to the household might be. So, for example, instead of Caroline Morris calling her mother 'Mum', she might call her 'Mrs Morris' instead. Or when asking her little brother to turn down his loud music, instead of saying 'Turn that noise down, you little brat', she might say something like 'Brian, I know you like listening to loud music, but would you mind if I asked you to turn it down a little'. Talking in this way, as a polite stranger might, could hardly be described as offensive. If you were to ask many parents if they would like their sons and daughters to be more polite, they would undoubtedly say yes, but as his students discovered, in this context being polite can cause great offence, difficulty and distress. There are ways of being who you are, and if you change your way of interacting, you have changed who you are.

This kind of variability is a key feature of our communicative system on which many social psychological phenomena rest. To put it simply, it allows a speaker to say and do more or less the same thing in many different ways, and this extends, as we shall see in a minute, to all levels of the system. As we speak, we make choices, and those choices create ourselves in others' eyes. If I say the same thing in one of two different ways, the option chosen says something to the listener. Dropping aitches, generally varying our accent, and choosing different ways of making a request are only part of how we talk to one another, but the opportunity to vary how you say something is present throughout the linguistic system, as we shall see soon.

The importance of this for the social psychologist lies in how that variation is exploited in both the long term and the short term. In the longer term, speakers can choose a way of speaking as a way of establishing their identity. For example, as we shall see, men and women tend to adopt different styles of speaking. Even though these styles have much in common, an individual man or woman, by how he or she chooses from within this range over time, can emphasize or moderate the expression of his or her gender identity (Graddol and Swann 1989; Coates 1993). In the shorter term, speakers can vary their way of speaking to someone else in the light of how that person is speaking to them as a way of demonstrating their attitude, feelings and the like towards that person and what she or he represents, or indeed the subject of the conversation. For example, in a conversation between two strangers where they find that they like one another, they reveal this by beginning to speak more like one another in terms of their accent, rate of speaking, and a number of other factors (Giles and Coupland 1991).

Both these long-term and short-term aspects of identity creation also have an important impact on the process of interpretation. The identity of a speaker plays a very important role in setting the context in which an utterance is understood, because of the indeterminate nature of conversation.

To summarize, variability is a key feature of our communicative system on which many social psychological phenomena rest. To put it simply, it allows a speaker to say and do more or less the same thing in many different ways. As we speak, we make choices, and those choices create ourselves in others' eyes. If I say the same thing in one of two different ways, the option chosen says something to the listener about myself and what I have said.

Indeterminacy

The use of the term indeterminacy to describe an important feature of human language refers to the fact that what we say rarely if ever fully determines how we are understood. Almost everything we say requires a context for its interpretation. Having just said that a distinctive feature of human language is the variation it permits and which enhances its expressive power, it can seem paradoxical to suggest that there is uncertainty in its use. Nevertheless, this is the case, and it is important for the social psychology of language.

When first considering how we understand one another when we speak, it can be tempting to think that the words we use when we speak correspond directly to the idea we have in mind, and that exactly the same idea will arise in the mind of someone who hears those words as a result. This is a misleading temptation, however, because utterances depend on the context in which they are said for their proper interpretation This can easily be demonstrated.

For example, if I say to you 'Can you lift your arms?' this can be a genuine question about your ability, if I am a doctor who is treating you after an accident where you have damaged your shoulders. It can also be a request for you actually to raise your arms in the air, if I am a tailor measuring your chest size. The words alone do not determine whether this utterance is simply a question about your ability or the same question being used to make a request. If the communication was successful in both cases then there is necessarily an important degree of correspondence in our understandings of the conversation, but this is due to our shared understanding of the context as well as what was said. Also, there can be areas of difference. In the case of the doctor's genuine question, the focus is on the injury, but the patient may find that the focus on the injury evokes all sorts of other memories and thoughts which the doctor cannot predict.

In some cases, this indeterminacy is something to which we are very sensitive, and indeed exploit. For example, if I have a good relationship with a colleague at work, and would like to develop it outside of working hours, I might wish to do so without jeopardizing that working relationship. The flat refusal which might follow a direct proposal could lead to all kinds of embarrassment and difficulty. However, an indirect approach where I inquire about his or her out-of-work interests leaves open the possibility that the conversation will develop to the point where an invitation to meet after work can be obviously the next step or not. If it does seem to be the obvious next step, then I can usually take it with a fair degree of certainty that the invitation will be accepted. In most cases, conversationalists recognize that the early part of the conversation has a subtext which relates to that final invitation, and that, depending on the twists and turns the conversation takes, different outcomes can result. (See chapter 7, figure 7.2, for an example of how the analysis of language can be used to understand the development of relationships.)

In other words, how you understand what I say (or even what I have written in this chapter) depends on the context in which you understand it, and while I have control over the words I use, I cannot control the context you have in mind. While we can make good guesses about what the context of understanding is when we speak to someone, we cannot guarantee it, and this leads to uncertainty and indeterminacy in human communication. It also leads to a number of important implications for how we conceptualize language use.

First, it means that how we understand one another depends on the assumptions we make about what each other knows, and what each of us is seeking to achieve in the conversation. These assumptions are intimately bound up with the stereotypes we hold of other people, and the attributions we make in interpreting their actions. When we consistently make the right assumptions, everything goes smoothly, and it can seem that we understand the other person much more than seems possible from the words alone. When we make the wrong assumptions, all sorts of personal disaster can follow. Importantly, the way in which we exploit the variation we considered in the last section to create our identity and attitudes can make an important contribution to those assumptions.

Second, it means that the understanding of any one contribution to a conversation is not simply dictated by that single utterance. When we say something, we hope to be understood in a particular way, but it is not guaranteed. How the next speaker responds necessarily reveals something about her or his understanding of what we have said, and what we say next after that reveals our understanding of what she or he said, and so on. In this to and fro of conversation we can qualify the way we have been understood, show how we understand others, and generally create a sense of coherence and mutual understanding. Those who have worked in the conversation analysis tradition within sociology (see Heritage 1984, ch. 8, for an introduction) were amongst the first to emphasize this point. It follows from this that any analysis of a speaker's utterance which does not pay full attention to the way in which the conversational context defines its meaning is inevitably flawed.

Concern for context and the other person are not inevitable, but their absence is quite noticeable, as when, for example, a politician or some other public figure is being interviewed on television or radio. Frequently, the aim of the interviewee is to get his or her prepared message across no matter what has been asked. He or she is often successful, but the cost is usually a grumpy exchange and a sense in the public mind that such figures do not listen, are arrogant or duplicitous or even worse.

Reflection

These twin features of variation and uncertainty will be central to our later discussion, but it is worth noting that their importance is amplified by a third feature of human language use, reflection, in both the long term and the short term.

A noticeable feature of all human languages is that they contain a wide vocabulary for talking about talking. English is no exception and the range of words we have for describing what we say and how we say it is very large, and reflects some fine discriminations. We distinguish between threats and promises, requests and orders, subtle hints, clear hints and suggestions, and so on. It is also noticeable that we spend a large amount of time talking about what we have said and done, or might say and do. When we speak, we are aware that what we say and how we say it can be the subject of a later conversation, and that we can be held to account for what we have said and its impact on our resulting social relations. This ensures that the potential offered by the inherent variability and indeterminacy of language, which we have just discussed, is recognized and exploited. These features in turn ensure that there can be much debate and dispute over what someone actually meant.

It is worth noting at this point the connection between these concerns and work in the discourse analysis tradition (Potter and Wetherell 1987; Potter 1996), which is covered in chapter 19. In many ways, that work focuses on talk about talk and the consequences which follow for social psychology if it takes psychological terms, such as 'attitudes', out of their context of use, and does not properly understand the ways in which talk about talk is contextualized and understood.

If talk about talk reflects a long-range reflection on what we say, it is also the case that we reflect in the short term, and continually adjust and modify what we say as we are speaking. The ways in which this is done have been most closely studied by writers in the conversation analytic tradition which was mentioned above. Their focus has been on the phenomenon of repair (Schegloff, Jefferson and Sacks 1977; Schegloff 1992). This refers to the ways in which speakers and hearers modify what they say. Sometimes this is done by a speaker in the course of an utterance. For example, if I mispronounce a word, I might say it correctly almost immediately; if I get into a grammatical tangle, I can do likewise; and if I see that my choice of words is not being understood I can change them too. On other occasions a repair might be made by a speaker in response to a query from a listener who did not understand what was said. In some cases, the original speaker's utterance might even be modified by a listener who, for example, can remember a name the speaker does not know, or who knows the correct pronunciation of a word the speaker has just mispronounced.

The structure of human communication

When we are with one another, either in person or at a distance, for example, via telephone, email or letter, we communicate in many different ways. The variety of ways in which we can do this is, of course, much greater when we are face to face than when we are physically apart, and there are important consequences which follow from the reduction in the number of communicative options available when we are not physically together (D. R. Rutter 1984; 1987; J. L. Locke 1998). Nevertheless even in those cases, the messages and the communication are structured, and there are many layers to what we are doing. If we take the case of face-to-face conversation it includes many things ranging from the pronunciation of individual words, and the precise words we choose to express our ideas, to the way we smile or gesture, and can even extend to the way we dress, decorate our bodies and cut our hair. This range can be broken down in many ways, but a useful distinction is often made between the range of things we do with our voices when we use our language in having a conversation, and the various elements of non-vocal communication which accompany conversation. Such cues are central to the processes of perceiving and understanding others, described in chapter 11.

The structure of language and conversation

Human language has been described and analysed in greater detail, and for far longer, than any other kind of human behaviour. It was being analysed in classical Greece in the fifth century BCE, and there are good grounds for believing that it was studied by Vedic scholars in India at an even earlier date. Unsurprisingly, in the time since then, various detailed and sophisticated descriptive systems for and theories of language have been developed. The use which social psychologists have made of these systems can make life difficult for the newcomer to this part of the discipline because of the unfamiliar technical vocabulary, but it is important not to be deterred by this. The ideas behind the terms are usually straightforward, and their meaning can be easily clarified by reference to a relevant dictionary (see Crystal 1997 for a good example). Furthermore, the full extent of the contributions of other disciplines does not need to be understood before we begin an examination of the social and psychological consequences which follow from the ways that structure is used. It is, however, useful to be familiar with some of the basic ideas and terminology with respect to claims as to the structure of language.

A common move in examining structure is to divide language into a number of related levels. There are many ways of doing this, but for our purposes, we might simply identify four basic ones: the sound system of the language, its grammar, its meaning, and conversational organization. The first captures the structure of the language in relation to the medium in which it is expressed. In this case, it is the vocal-auditory channel which links the speaker's mouth to the listener's ear. The second is concerned with the internal structure of the language, and how different parts of it relate to one another. The third concerns linguistic structure in terms of the relation between the language and the world. Box 5.1 summarizes some key linguistic terms.

The sound system At the most basic level, when we speak we merely produce patterns of energy in the air. Any sound is nothing more than changes in air pressure at different frequencies, and it is only a sound when those changes are interpreted by a human listener. The changes travel as do the ripples on a pond when a stone is thrown into it. The listener's tasks in perceiving what was said are to relate those patterns of energy, first, to the basic sounds of the language, and, second, to the patterns into which those sounds can be organized. The analysis of how the changes in the air relate to the basic sounds and what the speaker and hearer are doing in producing and perceiving them is called phonetics. The different sounds are the fundamental basis through which we distinguish between the different meanings we wish to communicate.

Box 5.1   Key linguistic terms

Terms related to sounds

Phonemes   The basic sound units which the speaker produces.
Phonetics   The analysis of how the changes in the air relate to the basic sounds and what the speaker and hearer are doing in producing and perceiving them.
Phonology   The more general study of the rules under which phonemes are combined.

Terms related to grammar

Morphemes   The basic meaningful units in the language, often corresponding to words, though not always.
Morphology   The way in which morphemes are combined to produce different forms.
Syntax   How words and morphemes can combine to make the sentences of a language.

Terms related to meaning

Semantics   Generally speaking, literal meanings in language. It can loosely be taken as the relationship between the words and the world which they describe. Semantics focuses on the meaning of individual words and the meanings of sentences and groups of sentences in longer discourses.
Pragmatics   The way people use language to achieve a particular aim, for example persuading or showing off. In other words, it shows how language is used to achieve pragmatic ends.

For example, the words 'bin', 'din', 'fin', 'gin', 'kin', 'pin', 'sin', 'tin', and 'win' all have different meanings which are communicated by their different initial sounds. The second task for the hearer is to understand which sequence of sounds has been uttered so that the speaker's words can be identified. Here, the task facing the listener is eased by the fact that there are constraints on which sounds can follow which other sounds. The rules of combination are considered under the heading of phonology, and this constitutes a second major component in the analysis of the sound system.

Phonological analysis considers the organization of what are called phonemes. These are considered to be the basic sound units, but when we actually produce them, there are many causes of variation in the precise form they take. For example, a speaker of English from the London area will produce an /r/ sound in a way which is quite different from someone from Aberdeen. This kind of variation, and its interrelationship with phonological rules, means that there are a very large number of options in the way that something might be said. This means that the language, even at this level of detail, provides many options for the speaker to exploit.

Grammar   The second level describes the internal structure of the language and how the elements of it are related to one another and might combine. At one level, it examines how the basic sound sequences combine to make what are called morphemes. Morphemes are the basic meaningful units in the language and often correspond to words, but not always. The word 'fly' is both a morpheme and a word in that it can stand on its own. The morpheme '-ing' cannot stand on its own and is not a word, but can be combined with words to produce different forms, such as 'flying'. This level of structural analysis is often referred to as morphology.

At another level, grammar examines how those words and morphemes can combine to make the sentences of a language. This is often referred to as syntax. The study of grammar, especially the study of syntax, has become a very technical subject, but the important element for our consideration here is that, as with the first level, it permits a great deal of variation so that the choices the speaker makes, even for expressing what seems to be the same idea, can reveal something more. For example, 'Lee kissed Alex', 'Alex was kissed by Lee', 'It was Lee who kissed Alex' and 'It was Alex who was kissed by Lee' all express, at one level, the same basic proposition, but in the different ways the information is organized, much more is revealed. The last two place a different emphasis on Alex and Lee so that each is emphasized as the important element in the utterance. As with the choices an individual makes in the way the basic sounds are expressed, grammatical choices can be read as indicating many things about the speaker, his or her attitudes, intentions and much more.

Meaning   What counts as meaning is an extremely difficult issue, as is clear even from the many different ways in which we use the term in everyday speech. Analyses of meaning in language usually draw a distinction between literal and non-literal meaning. The former can be loosely taken as the relation between the words and the world which they describe, and is what is usually called semantics. It focuses on the meaning of individual words and the meanings of sentences and groups of sentences in longer discourses. To know the meaning of words such as 'cup' or 'chair' is to know what kinds of things can be referred to by them. Similarly, to know the meaning of even simple sentences, such as 'I'm thirsty', is to know under what circumstances this sentence can be said to refer accurately to some state of affairs.

Non-literal meaning is concerned with how the use of those literal meanings by a speaker on a particular occasion can give rise to other meanings. For example, if I say 'Do you have the time?' to a friend, and he and I are both just standing around doing nothing, and it is clear to both of us that he is wearing a watch, that friend will answer by telling me the time. The answer to the literal question would simply be 'yes', but we both know that the literal question is redundant, and that by implication I am asking him for a different reason. In a different context – for example, imagine the friend has just offered to help me clear up after a party – the interpretation of the same utterance would be very different. The relationship between literal and non-literal meaning is very complex in language, and is even more difficult when we try to understand what is meant by meaning in our other actions. This area of meaning is called pragmatics. It is of major concern to social psychologists because it is about the relationship between literal meaning and the social world.

When we examine non-literal meaning in terms of either words or sentences, again the linguistic system provides great variety which the speaker can exploit. The same non-literal meaning can usually be expressed by many different words and sentences. For example, if I want you to buy me a cup of coffee, I can say 'Get me a coffee', or 'I'd love a coffee', or 'Can you buy me a coffee?', or 'I bought the coffees last time we came here' and so on. The literal meaning of each of these sentences is different, but they are all orienting towards the same goal of getting the listener to provide the speaker with a cup of coffee. Importantly, though, the different ways in which they do it also achieve other effects which can be socially consequential. The first of these coffee examples suggests a degree of familiarity with or power over the addressee, the third seems more polite and respectful, and the fourth can be something of a complaint.

Conversational organization   The highest level of organization in language is at the level of the relationship between individual sentences. We have already considered the impact of different utterances in a conversation on the interpretation of each of them when examining the issue of indeterminacy, but there is more to the organization of conversation than that. This aspect of language has been studied more within the sociological field of conversation analysis mentioned above than within linguistics. This work has revealed that there is a high degree of order in how we take part in conversations, and that this produces a variety of structures. Examples of this include the regularity found in the way conversations are begun and ended; how decisions are made as to who speaks and when in a multi-party conversation; the way question–answer sequences are structured; how compliments, assessments, agreements, disagreements and apologies are delivered and responded to; how stories are told; and so on. Again, the way in which these different arrangements are exploited by the participants in a conversation provides them with a key resource for achieving their conversational goals.

The structure of non-vocal communication

The study of non-vocal communication (NVC) does not have as long a history as the study of language, and it has not developed the same elaborate and technical schemes and vocabulary. Where attempts have been made to develop such schemes, they have invariably failed even though they have at times seemed quite impressive; see for example the work of Ray Birdwhistell (Birdwhistell 1970). There are probably many reasons why this is so, but it is certain that NVC is not as structured or as powerful in its communicative potential as language itself.

The social psychological literature on NVC is very large, and it includes two different approaches to the subject matter. Some research has focused on the functions to which it is put by speakers, for example how emotion is expressed (see chapter 4), but the great bulk of it has taken observable non-vocal behaviour (NVB) as its starting point. Amongst the principal elements which have been considered under this heading are facial expressions, gaze, gestures, proxemics (which is concerned with the distance we maintain between ourselves and others), posture and touch. For each of these, different researchers have examined how variation in the specific type of NVB is related to variation in the characteristics of the speakers, the hearers, other non-verbal behaviours, the context in which they are talking, and a particular outcome.

For example, an early and important study (Argyle and Dean 1965) examined the relationship between mutual gaze, which is two people looking at one another's eyes at the same time, and intimacy as an outcome. As part of their analysis, they looked at how changes in amounts of mutual gaze were related to both the level of intimacy in the conversation, and other behaviours including facial expression (how much they were smiling), proxemics and the topic of the conversation.

The relationship between language and NVC has always proved difficult to unpick. In all probability, they interrelate in a number of different ways depending on what kind of interaction is taking place. At one time, there was a strong tendency amongst those who characterized NVC primarily in functional terms to treat it as being quite distinct in its role from the language which it accompanied. One idea which seemed attractive to some is to see NVC as being bound up with the communication of feelings and emotions, and language as being concerned with simply the communication of information. While some elements of NVC are central to the expression of emotion, such as facial expressions, it is quite clear that not only do these elements of NVC also serve to communicate more than just emotion, but also we can readily express emotion through language, in what we say and the way that we say it.

In considering NVC, the important point to bear in mind for our discussion here is that it too contains a variety of options for the speaker to exploit, and how and when these are exploited can have important consequences for how the speaker is understood. If you doubt this, it is quite easy to demonstrate the importance, for example, of the ways in which we look at one another. Next time you have a conversation with a friend, try altering the way you look at him or her. Instead of scanning his or her face as you usually do, look only at his or her left ear, and see what effect doing this has on both of you. You will probably find that he or she will start moving leftwards, and that the flow of the conversation becomes rather disturbed. This disturbance will be present in both your (by now slightly worried and bemused) friend's speech and your own.

Summary

In this first part of the chapter, we have considered three important features of language use – variation, indeterminacy and reflection – and the structure of the communicative system in which they are realized. In that structure, there are important distinctions between vocal and non-vocal communication, and in the former between the analysis of language in terms of sound, grammar and meaning. We now turn to a consideration of one area of human life of considerable personal, psychological and social significance in which the uses of language play an important role, and in which these features and structures are significant.

Gender, language and interaction

In daily life, we understand one another in terms of all sorts of social categories. This is by no means the limit to our understanding, but the ways in which we see people as similar or dissimilar are crucial to the picture we form of them and of ourselves. These categories are more than simple labels, and the psychological substance to which they are tied matters greatly for how we feel and think about ourselves and others, as we shall see in a number of subsequent chapters. The way that speakers use their language is very important in this categorization process. Research in this area has examined language in relation to a number of key social categories, for example ethnicity and class (see Fasold 1984; Hudson 1996; Romaine 1994), but work on gender provides some of the more interesting examples of this so far.

Studies of the differences between men and women, and between boys and girls, have been a subject of research in social psychology for some time (e.g. Maccoby and Jacklin 1974; and see chapter 6, 10 and others in this book). Early social psychological studies of gender differences in social interaction tended to focus more on asking individual male and female participants to judge what other men and women were saying and doing rather than analysing the interactions or the language directly. This changed with the publication in the mid-1970s of Robin Lakoff's book *Language and a Woman's Place* (Lakoff 1975). Although written from a linguist's point of view, her book made a number of claims important for the social psychologist. First, it analysed how language is used in different ways by men and women when they speak, and how in turn this creates and structures their identity and their social standing. Second, it focused on how the language itself can be used to describe their roles and activities in different ways, and how these descriptions can lead us to think about men and women very differently. Since this book first appeared Lakoff's claims have been challenged in a variety of ways, but the areas and issues which she identified have remained important.

Gendered speech

Lakoff's argument that men and women speak differently was not new. Popular views as to these differences have been around for a very long time. They typically portray women as talking too much, being rather more polite and refined than men, liable to engage in too much small talk and gossip, and being unable to be clear, logical and direct. Such views have undoubtedly been tied to and derived from broader negative stereotypes of women. While denying the contention that the broader stereotypes did reflect the true nature of women, Lakoff did not simply disagree with these common views as to the nature of women's speech. Instead she argued that women did indeed use different ways of speaking that were weak and inconsequential, but that they were constrained to do so by the nature of existing social relations.

In making this case, she sought to pinpoint the different linguistic forms which constituted this weak and relatively powerless way of speaking. If we combine her analysis with the many other findings in the field, it is clear that men and women do use the variation the language system permits differently, and they do so at every linguistic level we considered earlier (Coates 1993; Romaine 1999). However, the story is not so simple as to allow us to say that there is a woman's language as distinct from a man's. This is clearly illustrated if we look at the sound system of the language, and the various features of grammar and vocabulary which Lakoff believed led women to appear hesitant and unsure of themselves.

The sound system   There are many aspects of how we use the sound system of the language which depend on the gender of the speaker. One element of this, the pitch of the voice, is dictated by biological factors, but interestingly it is not dictated to the extent which is commonly believed. We all know that men have deeper voices than women, and that this deepening occurs after the boy's voice has broken at puberty. Because men are, on average, larger than women this will make their voices deeper too. However, it is a mark of the importance of gender to our social identity that men and women often accentuate the difference, with many women speaking higher and men lower than simple physical factors would dictate (Graddol and Swann 1989). This is possible because the acoustic characteristics of the vocal tract can be changed by altering the tension of the different muscles which operate on it. Thus biology specifies a range of possibilities for the pitch of a speaker's voice, and individual speakers exploit that range for different purposes. Given this, it would also be possible for men and women to speak more like one another than they do, and there have been notable cases of women lowering their voices to achieve a distinctive effect. During her time as leader of the Conservative party in Britain, Margaret Thatcher is reported to have been advised to lower her voice so that she sounded less strident and more serious.

The ways in which the specific sounds of a language are used also reveal the influence of gender. Many studies of accents have reported that women are less likely to show the more extreme forms of a regional accent than men. For example, in his study of the Norwich accent, Peter Trudgill found that the working-class women he studied showed fewer of the local accent features in their speech while taking part in a variety of linguistic tasks than working-class men did. Interestingly, both the men and the women were very sensitive to this difference, and indeed when asked about it, they overestimated the degree to which it was present (Trudgill 1972). Trudgill and others have interpreted this as indicating that women seek to speak in a more conventional way, almost as a cautious 'safety-first' strategy, and by contrast men speak in a more distinctive way, reflecting their greater assertiveness. At first glance, both of these results would seem to suggest an important relationship between gender and language, but the story is more complicated than this, and is so in a way which adds further interest for the social psychologist.

The first point to make is that the above findings are based on the average performances of the men and women studied, and this ignores the fact that there is great variation in speech style in each group across different occasions. Other factors affect how we speak at each moment, and importantly this includes our changing relationship to those to whom we are speaking. Considering this factor in a wide variety of circumstances led Howard Giles to develop accommodation theory. In its simplest form, this proposed that as two people speak to one another their speech styles will converge or diverge, and that they do so for a variety of reasons. For example, if the concerns of the two speakers are mainly interpersonal, and they are being friendly, then the speech styles will converge. Conversely, if they are wishing to mark out their group membership in a way which distinguishes them from one another, then their speech styles will diverge (see Giles and Coupland 1991).

The other important point to make concerns the findings from a study by Lesley Milroy. She studied the speech of three working-class areas of Belfast: Ballymacarret, Clonard and Hammer. She found that the speech of the women, in their use of the local accent, varied when compared to local men not simply as a function of their gender, but also as a function of the extent to which they were integrated into social networks. The greater the degree of their integration into dense networks, the more they displayed the local accent, and thus the kind of gender difference which Trudgill found in Norwich disappeared (Milroy 1980). The precise mechanism which produces this outcome is unclear, but it is likely to depend upon the conjoint understanding of a shared group membership and social position by both women and men.

These two observations do not deny a relationship between gender and language, but they do illustrate that a person's gender is entwined with other personal characteristics and circumstances, and that separating it from them in our analysis of the data can mislead us. Those circumstances can be of a general kind such as the social networks studied by Milroy, or they can be the immediate ambitions, aspirations and desires of the type considered by Giles. The importance of the immediate moment is emphasized when we consider gender and linguistic variation at the level of grammar and vocabulary.

The grammar and vocabulary of uncertainty   Lakoff, perhaps reflecting her background in linguistics, paid great attention to this aspect of women's language. She proposed that women often used a wide variety of constructions which were more convoluted than they needed to be, and which were as a consequence less forceful. Furthermore, she argued that women were coerced in more or less subtle ways into using these forms rather than the stronger ones which men use.

A good example of the various grammatical devices to which she paid attention were tag-questions. She saw these as an important way in which women would typically undercut the strength of any assertion they might make. So, for example, a man who wanted to comment on bad weather might say 'It's a rotten day.' In contrast, a woman, according to Lakoff, would say something like 'It's a rotten day, isn't it?', where the addition of the tag-question 'isn't it' immediately reflects back on and queries the validity of the assertion just made, thereby immediately undercutting its force and the standing of the speaker. This weaker stance in women's speech was also revealed, she argued, in the kinds of vocabulary which men and women use. This is most striking in the case of swearing. Whereas a woman who knocked a cup of coffee over might say something quite mild such as 'Oh, damn', a man can happily say something much stronger.

Superficially, Lakoff's account can seem quite sensible, but more detailed research has again discovered that the various linguistic forms which she saw as typical of women are not peculiar to them, and indeed on many occasions there are no differences between men and women in their use (Graddol and Swann 1989; Coates 1993; Romaine 1999). However, these mixed results of the testing of her hypotheses have once more led to analyses which are of even greater interest to the social psychologist. These depend on a consideration of the language in terms of the uses to which it is being put rather than simply by reference to the structures which are used. This change of emphasis is easily illustrated in the case of tag-questions.

The apparent strength of a speaker's commitment to the truth of an assertion is challenged by the addition of a tag, but whether or not this amounts to an undermining of oneself depends upon the reasons and motivation for adding the tag, and how one is generally seen. For example, if you were the owner of a night-club, and an unexpected and seemingly violent male visitor to your office said 'I've got some very clumsy friends. You wouldn't want them to have any accidents while they were visiting your nice club one evening, would you?', it is unlikely that you would take the addition of the tag-question as indicative of any weakness or uncertainty on his part. If anything it contributes to a menacing and demanding tone. The literal meaning of the words do not, in themselves, convey a threat. The threat which is in the utterance is an implication and part of the pragmatics of what is said in that context. In recognizing this implication, you would consider not only the words said, but also what else you might understand about the speaker's mentality and attitudes and thus his likely intentions. By pairing these you can draw an inference, but there is no guarantee that you have drawn the right one.

Conversational style   This last example challenges the idea that we can link any linguistic form to a single interactional function. This challenge has led many writers to focus more on pragmatic aspects of meaning, and consider the broader dynamic of a conversation. In studies of this it has been argued that women take a more supportive role, interrupt less, and in general adopt a more cooperative and collaborative style than men. Support for this comes from an early study by Fishman (1978), who found that in the couples she studied, women would give more positive feedback than men through using brief interjections, such as 'uh huh, mhmm, yeah', while a man was talking, and by continuing the topic he had raised. Typically, men would only offer a brief acknowledgement at the end of a turn, and then shift the topic.

This idea has been pursued by a variety of authors with a fair measure of support for the idea that there are cooperative and competitive speech styles, and that women are more likely to use the former and men the latter, particularly when talking in single-sex groups (Coates 1993). In a cooperative style, the speakers and hearers are more likely to help each other get their message expressed and understood through a variety of conversational manoeuvres; for example, by a speaker following the topic initiated by a previous speaker, and by an absence of interruptions which deflect from that topic. A competitive style does the opposite.

Some have argued that this leaves men and women talking to each other at times in ways which they do not recognize as being fundamentally distinct and that this leads to many unrecognized misunderstandings (Tannen 1990). Others have argued that the roots of this difference lie deep in the different developmental pathways which are followed by boys and girls, and that the linguistic styles are the result of fundamental psychological differences in how we relate to and understand other people (Gilligan 1993).

Overall, there is a variety of differences between men and women in how they use language. Both exploit the variation which language permits, and exploit its indeterminacy to convey meanings above and beyond the specific words spoken. How we infer what those meanings are depends on our understanding of many factors to do with the context in which something is said, and which other persons are taking part in the conversation.

Sexist language?

The second focus in Lakoff's book was on the language used to describe men and women in their various roles and activities. She claimed that the language used to describe women was loaded so as to represent them in a negative way, and that this language was important in creating and maintaining the subordinate position of women. This idea has also been pursued by a number of other writers, including Dale Spender in her 1980 book *Man Made Language*. There are many features of English which support this claim, and they are to be found in all other languages which have been examined from this point of view.

For example, the pairs of terms in English used to describe corresponding male and female roles or activities usually cast the female version in a less positive light. Just notice what comes to mind when you read the word 'master' as opposed to the word 'mistress', or 'bachelor' as opposed to 'spinster'. If you consider a number of these pairs where the female half does not seem to come off so negatively, such as 'actor–actress', 'poet–poetess', 'sculptor–sculptress', notice also that the female version is often marked out through the lengthening of the word by, for example, the addition of a suffix, and that the male and female version can often be referred to jointly by use of the male term, but not the female one.

This use of the male term to include the female has received much attention in the cases of so-called generic 'he' and 'man'. Traditionally, it was proposed that these 'generic' words could be taken to refer to all people, both male and female, or could just refer to the males. This traditional view proved to be very contentious, and many argued that the use of generic terms did indeed hide women. Both sides in the dispute were making important psychological claims, and, interestingly, both had sound reasons to believe that they were right. The difference between them lay in what they were right about, and is centred on work on what has been called the Sapir–Whorf hypothesis.

The Sapir–Whorf hypothesis   This hypothesis derives its name from the work of two American linguists, E. E. Sapir and B. L. Whorf, who worked on native North American languages. Box 5.2 reviews their key ideas. They were struck by how the structure and vocabulary of these languages led to descriptions of events and objects which seemed radically different in their conceptualization from that which was present in English. For example, whereas a user of English might describe a falling stone by saying 'The stone is falling', a speaker of Nootka would say the equivalent of 'It stones downwards.' These differences led a number of psychologists to explore the extent to which a language could determine the perceptions of the world a speaker of it would have. They did this by examining the ability of the speakers of different languages in many different sensory and conceptual domains, but the most significant work focused on the ability to perceive and remember different colours.

The evidence against the Sapir–Whorf hypothesis listed in box 5.2 would suggest the claim that generic terms such as 'he' would not affect the way women are thought about, but there is an important twist in the tale. To understand this twist, read the following story, and see if it makes sense to you. If it does not, give yourself a few minutes to ponder why before reading on:

A man was driving his son to school one day. The road was icy, and as they approached a sharp bend, a large articulated lorry going in the opposite direction went out of control and crushed the car against the wall of a house. The man was killed instantly, but his son was not. He was rushed to the hospital for emergency surgery. The casualty team prepared themselves, but when they entered the operating theatre the surgeon took one look at the boy and said 'Oh my god, I can't operate on him, he's my son.'

Box 5.2 Sapir–Whorf hypothesis

Edward Sapir (1884–1939) was a linguist and anthropologist at Columbia University. His idea that the vocabulary and grammar of a language may influence the way the speaker perceives the physical world was developed by his pupil, Benjamin Whorf (1897–1941), a fire prevention engineer who studied linguistics and native American languages in his spare time.

Their most significant studies focused on the ability to perceive and remember different colours. The languages of the world vary greatly in the colour vocabulary they offer speakers. English has eleven basic colour terms (black, white, red, green, yellow, blue, grey, brown, pink, purple and orange) whereas Dani, which is spoken by the Dani people of the New Guinea highlands, has only two (black and white). If our language can affect the way we see and remember the world then comparing English and Dani speakers should reveal differences in their ability to see and remember colours. Unfortunately for the hypothesis, this does not seem to be the case, and the Dani are unaffected by the small size of their vocabulary (Rosch 1977).

While it is widely agreed that most people perceive the physical world around them in the same way, recognition of social categories does seem to vary depending on our past experiences and cultural background. The cultural connotations of an expression can lead us to evaluations which go beyond the simple meaning of the words. For example, terms used in English to describe corresponding male and female roles or activities sometimes cast the female version in a less positive light. The value attributed to the term 'virile' as opposed to 'effeminate' illustrates this process.

On first hearing this story many people find it to be nonsensical. They correctly observe that a dead man cannot do an operation, and then they start speculating that the father who died in the crash was not the biological father, but was known as the father because of some complicated adoption, divorce or sperm donation. The one thought that is hard for them to access is that the story is perfectly sensible because women can be surgeons, and the surgeon is the boy's mother.

In the surgeon riddle, no one who gets caught by it has any trouble admitting that there are female surgeons. Their problem lies in remembering this in the moment of interpreting the story. This failure emphasizes the fact that when we use a language, we cannot consider all the possible meanings of the things which someone says. We only consider what they are likely to have meant, and what is plausible, because to consider all the possibilities is an almost endless task. This plausibility is greatly affected by what the language used places in the foreground, particularly via the associated thoughts or connotations provoked by the specific words used. This is affected in turn by our knowledge of the structure of our social world, and the whole process of understanding has this character because of the uncertain and indeterminate nature of the language as used, which we considered earlier.

Further examples of the ways in which the connotations of a word or expression can lead us to interpretations which go beyond the simple meaning are to be found right across the modern world. They are the staple resources of ad-men and spin-doctors because certain ways of saying things are more comforting and blind us to the other aspects of what is being described. In recent wars, press spokesmen for different governments have been very keen to use expressions like 'smart bombs', 'surgical strikes' and 'degrading enemy capacity' when the actions in question often involve the violent slaughter of human beings. This idea has been around for many years, and was a matter of great concern to the novelist George Orwell (1949), who parodied the spin-doctors of his day with his characterization of 'newspeak', a language in which revolutionary thoughts could not be expressed.

A final consideration on the question of the power of a language is the much-derided issue of political correctness, and the associated idea that linguistic reform to remove certain expressions from the language is of any consequence. As Cameron (1995) points out, this is a debate which really has generated more heat than light, and operates most usually on naive assumptions as to how language and thought relate. As we have seen already, what is meant by any word, phrase or sentence is a complex mix of denotation and connotation, supposition and inference. Using politically correct language does not in itself change anything. What it can do, if used appropriately, is to raise awareness of the negative and denigrating connotations of certain terms and expressions, and to show concern for another's position in the world.

Conclusions

The study of language and communication is central to the concerns of social psychology. It matters because, as we shall see in part II, individuals construct and maintain their identities in the world as they interact with one another, and we understand who we are by witnessing ourselves living our lives with each other. Our interactional system – that is, our language and our non-linguistic communication – provides each of us with rich resources for doing this, both in the moment of action and in reflection subsequently. In those reflections we have a system of description which allows for negotiation, contains a collected record of our beliefs, and gives us a route by which we can simply tap into our own and others' ideas and representations. These features can be seen easily in our creation and interpretation of gender. Ways of speaking can emphasize or diminish the significance of a person's gender identity; our understanding of another person's gender can affect the way we interpret what she or he says; and the language we use to describe one another can lead us to think about our gendered selves in many different ways.

RECOMMENDED READING

Coates, J. (1998) *Language and Gender: A Reader*. Oxford and Malden, MA: Blackwell. There are many books on the relationship between language and gender, but this provides one very useful collection of edited readings and overviews.

Foley, W. A. (1997) *Anthropological Linguistics: An Introduction*. Cambridge, MA: Blackwell.

Fromkin, V. and Rodman, R. (1998) *An Introduction to Language*. 6th edn. Fort Worth, TX: Harcourt Brace.
A good place to start is a book which provides access to the wide variety of issues which are relevant to the study of language. Encyclopaedias such as *The Cambridge Encyclopedia of Language* and dictionaries of linguistic terms can be very helpful in this respect, but they do not achieve the integration which a good text provides and which is essential in this area. Both of these books do this, one from a more anthropological and the other from a linguistic perspective.

Hoffman, E. (1989) *Lost in Translation: A Life in a New Language*. London: Heinemann.
Finally, in the academic study of language, it is easy to lose track of the full sense of what language means to people. Reading good novels is the clear antidote to this, and this provides an excellent one which explores the way a language creates meaning in our lives, and how the loss of that language by living in a new society with a new language can be so devastating.

PART II

Social Interaction and Relationships

6

The Development of Social Relationships

- Introduction
- The emergence of interaction
- Links between early social experiences and later social relations
- Others than mother
- Conclusions
- Recommended reading

Introduction

Humans are fundamentally social. We spend our lives dealing with others – with strangers, acquaintances, family members and friends. Our daily encounters range from a fleeting exchange of glances to sustained conversations or disputes. As people spend time together, they construct relationships, and the nature of their relationships then constrains the possibilities for future interaction. All human social life – family ties, friendships and rivalry, workplace organization, the political process – all of our endeavours as social creatures take place within the relationships we form throughout our lives.

This chapter examines how social relationships develop from infancy through young adulthood. The study of social development requires both a clear description of how social relations change over time and an analysis of possible causal influences on individual development. To do this, we need to describe general developmental trends but also try to predict individual differences; a focus on differences amongst individuals usually means looking for continuity in social relations over time and an effect of experiences in one relationship on later ones.

The emergence of interaction

Readiness for interaction

Human infants are born with a fascination with the social world. The ability to interact is fostered by infants' perceptual biases in favour of other members of their species. Infants are particularly sensitive to sounds in the range of the human voice; their attention is caught by the properties of the human face, especially the eyes (Slater and Butterworth 1997). Newborns are naturally somewhat short-sighted, and they can focus best on an object about 8 inches from their face – the sort of distance between their own eyes and the faces of adults who hold them. Thus, amongst all the sights and sounds that confront the human newborn, other people are particularly salient.

Sensitivity to the social world begins even before the infant is born. For example, the sense of hearing begins to develop before birth, and newborns have shown some rudimentary recognition of a sound they heard in the womb, the mother's voice. This was demonstrated by DeCasper and Fifer (1980), who asked whether newborns would actually work for social stimulation – suck on a nipple that brought them not milk but the sounds of a human voice. In the event, the infants worked to hear the familiar sounds of their own mother's voice but not the voice of a stranger.

Newborns are not just interested in the face as a whole but seem particularly sensitive to facial expressions that, for adults and older children, convey social meaning. Mouth movements are especially salient: the one social act that newborn infants reliably imitate is a gesture that in many societies is later considered rather rude, sticking one's tongue out at another person (Meltzoff and Moore 1992). There are also reports that newborns imitate various facial expressions of emotion (Field et al. 1982). Thus infants' early perceptual biases focus attention on other people's communicative signals. Imitation in the first months of life may be limited but it is not just a series of reflexes; infants show effort and correct their attempts to copy another person's action (Reddy et al. 1997). Furthermore, the experience of imitating a model may serve to highlight the parallels between a companion's facial expression and the infant's own inner experience whilst producing that expression. The infant's interest in mouth movements and ability to copy them might also eventually contribute to language acquisition.

It is not simply infants' attraction to the social world that equips them for interaction; they also show rhythmic patterns of action that provide a framework for conversation-like exchanges with other persons (Reddy et al. 1997; see also chapter 5). They act, and then they wait, and it is relatively easy for adults to insert their own actions into the infants' pauses; thus the natural rhythms of infants' behaviour create opportunities for contingent reactions from other people. As the months go by, infants take a more active role in these interactions. By 3 months of age exchanges are seen in which infants and other people coordinate their gaze and vocalizations.

Mutuality in infancy

When can it be said that interaction is truly mutual? The infant's contribution to social interaction is revealed in various ways, including when the adult companion's behaviour is limited or changed. For example, in a number of studies, the adult (usually the mother) has been asked to stop communicating with the infant for a brief time and instead show a still face, with neutral expression of emotion. This procedure upsets infants considerably, which suggests that the infant's usual behaviour in an interaction with the mother is not produced by chance but is sensitive to the mother's actions and expressions of emotion (Cohn and Tronick 1983).

Additional evidence for mutuality of interaction is found in studies of infants' interactions with equally unskilled companions, namely other infants. By 6 months of age, it is clear that infants influence each other's behaviour. If an infant cries, and if that distress is prolonged, another infant's own tendency to fuss or cry is greater than would be expected by chance (Hay, Nash and Pedersen 1981). And mutual influence can also be detected in 6-month-olds' tendencies to touch each other and touch toys they each are holding (Hay, Nash and Pedersen 1983).

Clinical studies of depressed women and their infants have also highlighted the mutuality of early social interaction. Experimental manipulations (see chapter 19)

Plate 6.1 A striking example of mutuality in infancy

have demonstrated that infants respond to their mothers' simulation of depression with distress and confusion (Cohn and Tronick 1983). Observational studies (see chapter 19) of infants with their depressed mothers have demonstrated that the mothers are often sluggish in their responding to their infants, irritable, and less likely to talk about what the infant is doing (Murray 1992). The infants of depressed mothers in turn show more distress than other infants and begin themselves to act in a 'depressed' manner, even when they are cared for by other caregivers (Field, Healy and Goldstein 1988). Most disturbingly, the caregivers looking after these babies themselves start acting in a depressed way. Again, if infants' early social interactions were purely random events, they would not be so sensitive to their mothers' expression of emotion and mental states.

The beginnings of cooperation and conflict

Over the course of the first year of life infants take on an increasingly active role in interaction with their companions, and their interactions reveal early signs of both cooperation and conflict. The ability to cooperate emerges in the context of the conventional social games, such as peek-a-boo and give-and-take, that infants play with their companions. These games qualify as cooperative because they demonstrate mutual engagement, repetition of action that constitutes a *role* in the game, and alternation of turns (Ross and Goldman 1977). Younger infants' role in such games is often just to laugh, but, between 6 and 12 months of age, they initiate the games – for example, when an infant covers up her father's face with a flannel and says 'peek-a-boo' rather than simply allowing her own face to be covered. Infants' clear understanding of the 'rules' underlying these cooperative games is shown when for one reason or another the flow of interaction stops and the game breaks down. In an experimental study, adults engaged 12-month-old infants in cooperative games and then, after the game had continued for some time, failed to take their turns (Ross and Kay 1980). The infants waited for the adult to resume the game and then signalled and tried to force toys into the adult's hands so that the game could continue.

Clear instances of social conflict when one person objects to something another has done can also be discerned in the second year of life, with parents (e.g. Belsky, Woodworth and Crnic 1996), peers (Caplan et al. 1991) and siblings (Perlman and Ross 1997). Contrary to social stereotypes, very young girls and boys do not differ in their rates of conflict with peers or their use of force within those conflicts. Indeed, when small groups of 1- and 2-year-olds are observed, groups with a majority of girls are more likely than those with a majority of boys to engage in conflict and to use force when they do so (Caplan et al. 1991). Gender differences in aggression do not emerge until later in the preschool years (Keenan and Shaw 1997).

Links between early social experiences and later social relations

We have seen that infants' interactions with their companions are mutual and in many ways resemble the cooperative and conflictual relations of older people (see chapters 7 and 9). We may now ask: are these earliest social experiences critical for later social life? Do infants learn critical lessons about how to relate to others in the earliest years of life? If so, does that mean that infants who are deprived of care in the early years never completely recover?

The study of early social experiences emphasizes the importance of emotion in social interactions at any age. If infants are severely deprived or abused, can they ever come to understand or regulate their own emotions, or mesh with the emotions of others? But the study of early experiences also points to the importance of cognitive aspects of social interaction. In particular, Bowlby's (1969) attachment theory has placed great emphasis on infants' working models of social relationships. Such models can be seen as a particular form of emotionally-laden social representation (Bretherton 1985) that guide and could obstruct all future social interactions. (See chapter 14 for a detailed account of social representations.)

Attachment theory

Within contemporary psychology, the study of the impact of early social experiences is most often taken up with reference to the concept of attachment, as set forth by the British psychoanalyst John Bowlby (1969) and elaborated by his follower Ainsworth and her colleagues (Ainsworth et al. 1978). Bowlby described his theory of attachment as an explicitly ethological theory ('ethology' refers to the study of animal behaviour), and drew heavily upon contemporary research on biologists' studies of parent–offspring relationships in birds and mammals, in particular the detailed observations of infant–mother interaction in macaque monkeys done by Robert Hinde (1974).

Plate 6.2 John Bowlby

At the same time, Bowlby was trained as a psychoanalyst, and his theory was stimulated by clinical observations of young criminals (Bowlby 1944) and by his clinical work with children who had been separated from their parents during and in the aftermath of World War II. Bowlby's thinking about attachment relationships owed much to Sigmund Freud's (1938) characterization of the bond between mother and child. In his earlier writings, Freud placed emphasis on love between mother and child as almost an afterthought, a secondary product of the infant's love of food, that is, the milk that was delivered by the mother's breast. In contrast, in his later writings, Freud appeared to recognize that the love between mother and infant had its own role in the child's development, apart from its association with basic nutrition. In a final statement, Freud characterized the relationship between mother and infant as 'unique, without parallel' and acknowledged its causal force by describing it as 'the prototype of all future love relationships' (1938, p. 188).

Bowlby's theory initially focused on several attachment behaviours, such as sucking, clinging and following a parent figure, and he argued that these behaviours had been selected for in the 'environment of evolutionary adaptedness' to protect the infants from predators. It is clear, however, that each of these basic social responses can be used with companions other than the mother, and that each has multiple functions. For example, in an unfamiliar experimental situation, when 9- to 12-month-old infants were given the chance to follow their mothers or an unfamiliar woman, half followed each; when they were given the choice to follow their mothers or a novel toy, propelled across the floor by means of an almost invisible string, all but one of the infants crawled or toddled away from their mothers, in pursuit of the toy (Hay 1977). It would seem that, if infants in the environment of evolutionary adaptedness had happened on a rather attractive predator, they might well have followed the predator rather than their own mothers!

In Bowlby's later writings, he went beyond this initial attempt to identify unique attachment behaviours, describing instead more complicated attachment systems and the cognitive dimensions of infants' and caregivers' perceptions of their relationships. His thinking along these lines was very much influenced by advances in cognitive psychology in the 1950s and 1960s, in particular a set of ideas known as control systems theory. He no longer concentrated attention on particular discrete actions, like clinging or following, but rather focused on the infant's growing ability to use the attachment figure as a secure base from which to explore the world, and on the way the mother–child relationship might help infants regulate their own emotion in the face of untoward events. In particular, in the language of cognitive psychology, he proposed that infants constructed working models of their relationships with their attachment figures that guided their dealings with the world at large.

Throughout these discussions, Bowlby was at pains to say that he was discussing the importance of a mother figure in the infant's life, who would usually be, but need not be, the biological mother. Later work drawing upon Bowlby's ideas has tended to emphasize the importance of the mother's biological tie to the infant, but this was not a necessary part of Bowlby's theory. Bowlby argued that human infants were monotropic; that is, in his view, they possessed an inborn tendency to form a focused attachment with one particular figure, with other attachment relationships less common and less intense. However, his theory did not require that that figure necessarily be the woman who had given birth to the infant.

Bowlby's notion of a working model was elaborated upon by his colleague Mary Salter Ainsworth, who operationalized, or made concrete, Bowlby's ideas and started an extensive programme of research. Working models of any relationship might be described along a number of dimensions. The dimension on which Ainsworth concentrated attention was one she had studied earlier, in the context of adult love relationships – the *security* felt in a particular relationship. In her earlier work in Canada, Ainsworth had focused upon security as a central construct in personality formation. The preoccupation with security as the hallmark of attachment relationships represents Mary Ainsworth's particular contribution to attachment theory.

Measuring the security of attachment

Ainsworth's initial descriptive studies of infant–mother attachment relationships focused on families in two cultures: urban and suburban families in Baltimore, Maryland, in the USA, and infants in traditional Ganda families in Uganda (Ainsworth 1967; Ainsworth et al. 1978). She studied infants' use of the mother as a secure base from which to explore the world. Bowlby had discussed this as a general phenomenon in human life that had been selected for in the course of evolution; however, his clinical studies suggested that things could go badly wrong in the attachment process, with major implications for children's later social relationships.

Ainsworth sought to devise a method that would highlight differences amongst mother–infant pairs in the security of their attachment relationship, which would then provide a basis from which to study its long-term consequences. To do so, she devised the experimental procedure known as the Strange Situation (Ainsworth et al. 1978), which is reviewed in box 6.1 over the page.

The Strange Situation derives from two observations made in psychoanalytic studies of the formation of the attachment relationships, namely that, as infants near their first birthdays, they become both wary of strangers and distressed upon separation from their mothers (Ribble 1944; Spitz 1946). These changed patterns of interaction are taken as evidence of a more focused attachment to the mother and a consequently less generally positive view of the rest of the social world. Other investigators demonstrated the fact that infants had multiple attachment relationships (Schaffer and Emerson 1964) and that reactions to strangers and separation varied considerably, depending on how much control over the situation infants had and how the strangers were acting (Rheingold 1969a; Rheingold and Eckerman 1973). However, Ainsworth introduced a confrontation with a stranger and two forced separations from the mother into a brief experimental procedure designed to reveal differential levels of security in infants' attachment relationships. The procedure took place in an unfamiliar environment and consisted of a very unusual sequence of brief encounters (none more than three minutes in duration). It thus fully deserves the title of a Strange Situation.

Ainsworth's aim was to upset the infants enough to reveal different levels of security in their attachment relationships but not so much as to cause psychological harm. The accumulating set of strange experiences revealed differences in the mother–infant relationships that might not be apparent if infants and mothers were observed interacting under pleasant circumstances.

Box 6.1   The Strange Situation

Mary Salter Ainsworth's particular contribution to attachment theory was to devise a method that would highlight differences amongst mother–infant pairs in the security of their attachment relationship. This method is known as the Strange Situation.

In the simplest version of the Strange Situation, mother and baby enter a room. The baby is given 3 minutes to explore this new environment, and thus secure-base behaviour can be assessed. A stranger then comes in and chats to mother and baby for 3 minutes. The mother then leaves the room, leaving the baby in the care of the stranger, for 3 minutes or until the infant breaks down in tears. The mother returns, the stranger leaves, and the mother and baby stay together for another 3 minutes. The mother then says goodbye once more, leaving the baby alone in the room for 3 minutes or until the infant becomes severely distressed. The mother returns, attempts to comfort the baby if he or she is distressed, and their reunion is observed.

The Strange Situation has been criticized because of its artificiality and lack of experimental control (e.g. Masters and Wellman 1974). However, Ainsworth was intent not on devising a controlled experiment but rather on inventing a psychological test that highlighted variation in attachment relationships. She characterized three types of attachment relationship: one which was secure (which she called Type B), and two which were insecure, known as Type A (avoidant) and Type C (ambivalent). The avoidant children showed relatively little interaction with their mothers and seemed not bothered at all by either the presence of the stranger or the two separations. In contrast, ambivalent children were highly distressed by the separation, but showed ambivalent behaviour when the mother returned; they seemed angry and unwilling to greet her pleasantly and engage in positive interaction. Other researchers have found that there is also a 'disorganized' type of attachment, sometimes associated with the infants' experience of abuse at the hands of their parents.

Ainsworth and her colleagues have argued that the Strange Situation did not unduly distress secure children because they felt secure in the relationship and understood that their mother would return. The other two groups, however, did not feel this security. Other researchers have found that security of attachment in infancy predicts security at 6 years of age; it can also predict the quality of children's relationships with peers.

Researchers continue to debate the extent to which these patterns are attributable to the quality of children's early relationships or to the innate temperament of the individual child. In all likelihood, it is probably some combination of the two. Simple determinism, in terms of either genetically determined characteristics or the effects of early experiences with the mother, is not enough to account for the vagaries of social development. The human being is social from the moment of birth, if not before, and important experiences accrue throughout the life span.

Is the Strange Situation a reliable and valid measure of an attachment relationship? If it is reliable, it should produce consistent results over time. If it is valid, it should predict later outcomes for the child and should be explained by prior causal influences. The particular attachment behaviours, such as looking at, touching and following the mother, are not consistent over time (Masters and Wellman 1974). However, the overall patterns of organization described by Ainsworth do endure over different administrations of the procedure and over the second year of life (Ainsworth et al. 1978; but see Belsky et al. 1996).

Ainsworth characterized the majority of infants in her sample as secure. Secure infants explored the strange environment with interest, showed some wariness of the stranger but not undue distress, might become somewhat distressed when the mother left the room, but could be comforted by the friendly stranger and warmly welcomed the mother when she came back. In contrast, there were two types of insecure attachment relationships revealed in her study, known as Type A (avoidant) and Type C (ambivalent), with a secure relationship referred to as Type B.

Later studies have found that there are some children who cannot be so easily classified into these three categories and whose attachment relationships are characterized as disorganized (Main and Solomon 1990). Disorganized attachment is sometimes associated with the infants' experience of abuse at the hands of their parents (see Belsky and Cassidy 1994).

Many other researchers have used the Strange Situation and found that security of attachment in infancy predicts security at 6 years of age (Main and Cassidy 1988) and also predicts the quality of children's relationships with peers (Fagot 1997). These predictive relationships can be described as a basic social competence shown in different ways, with different companions, over the years of childhood (Waters and Sroufe 1983). This might imply that really there are enduring traits of individual children, particular features of their temperaments, that contribute to all the different relationships that they have. If that were the case, security of the relationship with the mother would be seen as one sign of a child's equable temperament, not a cause of the child's subsequent social adjustment. The attachment researchers have been at pains to deny that this could be true, arguing that security of attachment derives from the mother's sensitivity in the early months of the child's life (De Wolff and van Ijzendoorn 1997), not the child's own pre-existing temperament (Sroufe 1985). To support their argument they note that the same infant may be secure with the father but insecure with the mother, or vice versa (Fox, Kimmerly and Schafer 1991). If security of attachment were simply a function of the infant's own temperament, rather than a characteristic of relationships, such discrepancies should not exist. Other investigators, however, have stressed the fact that infants' temperaments affect interactions with their caregivers and may thus play an important role in the attachment process (Dunn 1993).

Effects of early experiences: a gradient of privation

Is the mother–infant relationship as unique and without parallel as Freud claimed it to be, and, more importantly, does it serve as a 'prototype for all future love relationships'? Many case studies and correlational studies have sought links between the quality of a child's earliest social experiences and his or her later social relationships. These experiences vary along a continuum of privation, from the complete absence of contact with other human beings to insecurity of attachment with one's parents.

At the extreme end of the gradient of deprivation are the case studies of children who were found roaming alone in the forests, having been abandoned by their families and uncared for by any other human companions. Reports of such 'wild children' have been chronicled since medieval times, and stories about children reared by animals have been told for millennia, at least since the myth of Romulus and Remus and the founding of Rome. The earliest detailed scientific account of such a wild child was made by Itard in 1801, who studied and attempted to rehabilitate Victor, the so-called 'Wild Boy of Aveyron' (Itard 1801/1962). Recent studies in this tradition focus on children who spent their early years in conditions of terrible neglect or abuse, such as small children living in the Nazi death camps (A. Freud and Dann 1951) or children forced to live in cupboards or attics, shut off from most human contact (Curtiss 1977).

Most of these children could be characterized as virtually asocial and almost inhuman when they were found, particularly if they were discovered late in childhood or in the early adolescent years. For example, Victor, the wild boy found in the forests of France, and Genie, a girl who had been virtually imprisoned for years in the back recesses of her California house, walked on all fours and had no human speech. Both were taught to speak, but neither developed adult-like fluency in their languages. Indeed, neurological tests showed that Genie's language depended on processing in the right side of her brain, not in the usual language centres in the left hemisphere (Curtiss 1977). Children who have been rescued from such complete deprivation also show distinctive ways of relating to others that do not conform to the usual modes of relating in the culture at large; however, many of these children appear to develop attachments to the people who have rescued them (Itard 1801/1962). Some children seem more resilient than others in the face of such extreme privation.

Anna Freud's classic study of concentration camp orphans (Freud and Dann 1951) drew attention to the fact that children can provide some care and nurturance to each other, even in the absence of adult attachment figures. A group of six young children were found at the end of World War II. They had lost their parents but somehow remained together, in conditions of extreme privation. Presumably they had had contacts with other adults in the camps, but none of their parents had survived and no consistent adult caregivers had remained with them. The children demonstrated an extreme attachment to each other, and showed extreme distress if any member of the group was separated from the rest. Their intense love for each other and their disdain for adults seemed odd and indeed pathological to the adults who rescued them. Freud saw, however, that their behaviour could be viewed as a successful adaptation to a terrible set of circumstances, and not just as a sign of pathology in the absence of a mother figure. It is important to note that the children studied by Freud and Dann (1951) had language and behaved as human children, albeit ones with a trust in each other and not in adults. With time, the children grew more secure on their own and formed emotional ties with adult caregivers. The children were adopted, most by surviving relatives in North America. Unpublished case notes suggest that they managed to enter the world of work and to form their own families in adulthood (Rutter, personal communication). Although they were presumably affected in certain respects by their terrible early experiences, their relationships in childhood and adult life were within the normal range of human experience. Thus, even children can provide social experiences for each other that compensate in some way for the absence of a mother figure.

Studies of somewhat less deprived children, those raised in institutions such as orphanages and children's homes, have shown reasonable rates of recovery from deprivation in the early years, although that depends on the length of time spent in institutional care. Tizard and Hodges (1978) studied two groups of children who had been in institutional care in early childhood: those who were eventually returned to their biological families and those who were adopted into other, usually more affluent families. These children were compared with a third group of children who had never experienced institutional care. In terms of social disadvantage, their families were comparable to the biological families of the first group. The institution-reared children in this sample had received reasonably good physical care in the institutions, but, since staff turnover was very high, they had met an enormous number of adult caregivers and had not really had the opportunity to form enduring attachments. If there is really a critical time in development in which attachments can form, these children should not have been able to form new attachments later in childhood. However, the children who were adopted did become attached to their new parents, just as some of the extremely deprived 'wild children' have been reported to form new attachment relationships late in childhood.

There are some indications, however, that institutionally reared children have difficulties in their subsequent relationships. For example, the children studied by Tizard and Hodges were characterized as showing an 'institutionalised syndrome' in adolescence (Hodges and Tizard 1989). A close reading of the evidence shows that this was expressed mainly in terms of attention-seeking behaviour with teachers and a tendency to prefer group interaction rather than intimate, confiding relationships with peers. Although these tendencies could be seen as a pathological outcome of the failure to form attachment relationships in the first years of life, they could also be seen as sensible social adaptations to life in group care. Children who had not been able swiftly to engage in interaction and establish even a fleeting relationship with others might not have received the care they needed from the paid caregivers, and they might have been less likely to seek the attention of prospective adoptive parents or encourage their biological relatives to take them back. Once the children have returned to a nuclear family situation, these social skills are characterized as pathological 'overfriendliness'. None the less, the excessive friendliness shown by children who have spent time in institutions can be very worrying for their adoptive parents, who have concerns that the children's interest in strangers and willingness to follow them might lead the children into dangerous situations.

It has also been suggested that children who did not receive one-to-one maternal care in infancy will not be able to relate effectively with their own children. A sample of women reared in children's homes (Quinton, Rutter and Liddle 1984) interacted with their young children in problematic ways. It is unclear, however, whether problems shown in the later lives of children reared in institutions are due entirely to their early experiences in group care. For most of these children, their later years are not easy and the milieu in which they rear their own children is often characterized by unemployment, poverty and family difficulties. Social support in adulthood can mitigate the effects of deprived early experience, but circumstances in the lives of women reared in children's homes set up a chain of events that make it very difficult for such support to be acquired (Quinton et al. 1993). It appears to be rather easier for men reared in institutional care to find supportive women than for the women to find supportive men (Rutter, Quinton and Hill 1990).

Similar issues arise when we consider children who have been abused by their parents and their tendencies to abuse their own children. These two populations of children with problematic early experiences overlap considerably, of course, because children who are abused by their parents are likely to be taken into care. When examining the effects of multiple caregivers in infancy, through a series of foster placements or stints in children's homes, it is important to note why the children were not in fact being cared for by their biological parents and what characteristics of children and parents might have led to the institutional care arrangements. Longitudinal studies of children who were themselves maltreated in childhood show that most do abuse their own children; however, a substantial minority do not, suggesting that factors other than 'working models' must be taken into account (Egeland, Jacobvitz and Sroufe 1988).

In general, investigations all along the gradient of privation in children's lives suggest that the extent and quality of interactions children have are of enormous importance for social and intellectual development, but that their effects are not restricted to a narrow time window. Important experiences take place after the second year of life. Furthermore, even within the early years, children interact with persons other than a primary caregiver, and those early relationships themselves have an important influence on development.

Others than mother

In the context of Bowlby's strong claim about the human infant's tendency to monotropy, care by persons other than the mother figure might be seen as forms of mild deprivation along the gradient just described. For example, care of infants by paid childcare workers is seen by some attachment theorists as a public health risk (Belsky 1990), although analyses of a representative sample of over 1,000 North American mothers and infants suggest there is no simple, main influence of day care on children's capacities to form secure attachments with their parents (NICHD Early Child Care Research Network 1997). Furthermore, longitudinal studies of Swedish children show that high-quality day care has a positive influence on cognitive development (Broberg et al. 1997). However, at the same time as attachment theory has had an almost dominating influence on the study of social development, others have drawn attention to the fact that most human children live in complex social worlds and that a variety of early relationships have direct and indirect effects on development. To illustrate this alternative perspective, we now examine some studies of children's relations with their fathers, siblings and peers.

Fathers

The preoccupation with motherhood in theory, policy and clinical practice has obscured the father's role in families, now and in the past. Indeed, fathers have mainly been studied in their absence, either in terms of the impact on children of the father's absence from the home due to the demands of his job or military service or in the many contemporary studies of families undergoing separation and divorce. In common English, 'father', used as a verb, refers to the biological act of procreation. In contrast, 'mother', used as a verb, refers to a set of caring, nurturant acts that could, theoretically at least, be shown by any person to another. In other words, children can be 'mothered' by substitute caregivers but can be fathered only by their biological sires. Does this mean, then, that the father's role is a simple, biological one, pleasurable but soon over? If not, what contributions does the male parent make to the business of rearing the young? And how is the father's role in the family negotiated with the mother?

It is often thought that fathers are more likely to become strongly attached to their infants if the fathers are present during the births, but there is no clear evidence to support this view (Palkowitz 1985). Infants form strong attachments to their fathers as well as their mothers (Fox, Kimmerly and Schafer 1991). Both relationships are important: children are advantaged if they have a secure relationship with both parents, not just one of them (Pipp, Easterbrooks and Harmon 1992). Nevertheless, infants' attachments to their fathers may derive from somewhat different factors from those that create attachment between mother and child. A father's sensitivity to his infant's needs predicts a secure relationship between father and child, but the relationship between sensitivity and security of attachment is not so strong for fathers as it is for mothers (De Wolff and van Ijzendoorn 1997). When spending time with their children, fathers do different things from those that mothers do. Mothers spend more time caring physically for their infants and doing the work of the household; fathers spend more time playing with their children (Lamb 1977). Although both parents discipline their children, mothers are more likely than fathers to try to induce toddlers to conform to household rules (T. G. Power and Parke 1986). Even in very early life, infants have different experiences with their fathers and mothers. Mothers are much more likely than fathers to sing to their infants, though, if they can be induced to sing to their babies, fathers are as likely as mothers to do so in an exaggerated, high-pitched tone of voice (Trehub et al. 1997). Fathers smile playfully while engaging in rough-and-tumble play with their infants, whereas mothers are likely to smile in that way while reading stories (Dickson, Walker and Fogel 1997). There are some indications that father–infant interaction is complex and idiosyncratic, whereas mothers are more likely to interact in simple ways, using conventional games and nursery songs (Lamb et al. 1982; Trehub et al. 1997). Fathers are more likely to be very active whilst playing with their children, whereas mothers spend more time simply watching their infants try to do things on their own (Dickson, Walker and Fogel 1997). The distinctive quality of father–child interaction does not depend on the extent to which fathers take on the role of primary caregiver (Lamb et al. 1982).

Much research suggests that divorce is associated with problems for children, and that these problems do not disappear if a parent remarries; rather, newly created families face a new set of problems. It is difficult, however, to determine whether the negative effects of divorce are due to the absence of the father (for the overwhelming majority of children remain in their mother's custody) or rather are due to the other financial and social costs incurred in the divorce itself. There is considerable variation amongst families who have undergone divorce, and the outcome for children depends on parenting style as well as family structure (Hetherington and Stanley-Hagan 1999).

Furthermore, when family life is stable and family income is adequate, children who grow up in families without fathers, such as the children of lesbian couples, are not necessarily disadvantaged (Golombok, Tasker and Murray 1997). Even in very disadvantaged families, such as those headed by poor, single African-American women in the rural South of the United States, consistent parenting and family routines, as well as the mother's own self-esteem, mitigate the effect of poor incomes (G. H. Brody and Flor 1997). Thus, in general, this complex literature would suggest that children are affected deeply by their close relationships, and their fathers are important to them, but that, likewise, many different family structures can lead to good as well as unfortunate outcomes for children.

Siblings

A similar point can be made about another important family relationship. Siblings make very important contributions to each other's lives, but children without siblings are not necessarily critically disadvantaged. Recently the study of 'only children' has generated acute interest amongst Chinese psychologists, as a consequence of the 'one child' policy in contemporary China (e.g. Yang et al. 1995). At the other end of the spectrum, some children have siblings who are exactly the same age – with increased use of fertility treatments, there are many more multiple births, so triplets, quadruplets and even quintuplets are no longer seen as being as remarkable as they once were. Psychologists have long capitalized on the phenomenon of twin births to study the contribution of nature vs. nurture to child development (e.g. Hewett et al. 1998). This debate is outlined in box 6.2. More recently psychologists have focused on the quality of the twin relationship and the extent to which the development of twins differs from that of children who are born one at a time (see Rutter and Redshaw 1991).

Psychologists have long been interested in the importance of a child's ordinal position in the family (Levy 1939; Koch 1960). Sulloway (1996) cites evidence suggesting that subsequent children are by nature risk-takers whilst firstborns are conservative high achievers, and argues that this pattern explains much about the history of science and, indeed, global politics. None the less, despite the long-time interest in ordinal position, it is only since the early 1980s that developmental psychologists have focused on the quality of the sibling relationship in its own right.

In a longitudinal study of Cambridge children (Dunn 1993), firstborns were observed before and after the birth of a sibling. Most of the children reacted to this 'life event' with equanimity, but some became highly distressed. When children were extremely upset by the sibling's birth, they were likely to behave negatively towards the younger sibling and, eventually, the sibling behaved negatively towards them. Firstborn girls who were especially close to their mothers had difficulties adjusting to siblings, and thus there was an inverse relationship between the quality of the mother–child relationship and that of the relations amongst the siblings. Other investigators have obtained contradictory findings, suggesting that children who are securely attached to their mothers are also more likely to be attached to their siblings (e.g. Teti and Ablard 1989).

Box 6.2   Nature and Nurture

In developmental psychology, there is an ongoing debate about the relative influence of *genetic* factors (nature) and *enviromental* factors (nurture) on human characteristics, such as intelligence and personality.

Early debates were characterized by extreme positions. At one end of the spectrum were those who believed that genetic influences were responsible for all individual and social differences. Such ideas influenced the work of Francis Galton (1822–1911), who pioneered the study and measurement of intelligence. (He also coined the term 'eugenics' to describe his belief in the 'rational improvement of human evolution' through selected breeding.) At the other extreme were those who believed that genetics had absolutely no influence on human behaviour. This position was adopted by J. B. Watson (1878–1958), the founder of behaviourism. He claimed that any infant could be conditioned (i.e. rewarded for desirable behaviour) to become any kind of specialist, for example a doctor, musician or writer.

Such sharply opposing viewpoints delayed the understanding of the interdependence of genetic and environmental factors. Today, behavioural geneticists (those who study the genetic basis of psychological characteristics) make the distinction between a *genotype* (the basic set of genetic instructions) and a *phenotype* (the genotype's final expression in a particular environment).

The best-known method of studying the influence of genes and environment on human behaviour is the *twin study*. Twins can either be identical (monozygotic, MZ) or fraternal (dizygotic, DZ). The hypothesis is that differences within MZ pairs, who are genetically identical, arise only from environmental differences, whereas differences between DZ pairs are a consequence of both genetic and environmental factors. Studies of MZ twins separated at birth (by adoption, for example) and brought up separately (and, supposedly, in different environments) provide information on the influence of environmental factors on genes. In general, the results show that environmental influences can vary a lot without influencing fundamental similarities between MZ twins. Twin studies are often criticized, however, because they do not fully control the effects of environment, and, in fact, tend to underestimate the similarities of the environments of separated twins, as dictated by the criteria of adoption agencies, for example.

Although behavioural geneticists are more likely to acknowledge the impact of environmental factors than they were in the past, there is still disagreement about the actual extent of influence, with figures ranging from 0 to 90 per cent (see Gould 1992; Plomin 1989).

Much theoretical attention has focused on the phenomenon of sibling rivalry, a topic that has exercised the human imagination at least since Cain felt he was unfairly treated in comparison to his brother Abel. Sibling conflict has been discussed in many theoretical traditions. Psychoanalytic writers drew attention to sibling rivalry (e.g. Levy 1939), whilst social learning theorists examined how fighting with siblings contributes to the development of aggression (Patterson 1986). More recently sibling rivalry and the 'niche-choosing' strategies rivalrous brothers and sisters take to avoid overt conflict have been examined from the perspective of evolutionary biology (Sulloway 1996). Similarly, behavioural geneticists draw attention to siblings' attempts to distinguish themselves from each other, which may help create unique environments within families; experiences not shared with siblings are thought to have a greater impact on individual development than do the general features of family life (Dunn and Plomin 1990). Finally, within cognitive psychology, the sibling relationship is thought to contribute to social cognition and moral understanding (Dunn 1988; H. S. Ross et al. 1996).

Conflict between siblings is a normal part of growing up. It is not in itself a sign of family pathology; indeed, in families where the mother is depressed or suffering from bipolar mental illness, siblings are *less* likely, not more likely, to quarrel (Hay, Vespo and Zahn-Waxler 1998). At the same time, there are important links between the parent–child relationship and sibling conflict. Maternal rejection promotes aggression in the sibling relationship, which in turn promotes aggression with peers (MacKinnon-Lewis et al. 1997). Mothers' interventions in sibling quarrels actually reduces the level of aggression and promotes resolution of the conflict (Perlman and Ross 1997). Indeed, the way parents approach quarrels between siblings provides important lessons in justice; in line with Gilligan's (1982) theory about gender differences in moral reasoning (see chapter 10), mothers tend to resolve conflicts by focusing on people's feelings, whereas fathers focus on issues of fairness and justice (Lollis, Ross and Leroux 1996).

Dunn (1988) has pointed out that sibling conflict and indeed other forms of interaction between siblings provide an important impetus to cognitive development. By negotiating their points of view with each other, siblings come to understand psychological processes. Support for this claim is provided by studies in Britain and Japan that show children with older siblings do better on standardized tests of social cognition in which they are asked to say what a story character understands or believes (Ruffman et al. 1998).

Sibling relationships, of course, are not invariably rivalrous. Sisters and brothers play together and sometimes look after each other's needs. The extent to which children provide care for their sibling varies considerably across cultures. A great deal of responsibility for the care of siblings is sometimes seen as pathological in Western culture, but is the norm in many other societies. Boys as well as girls are sometimes expected to care for younger siblings, although that depends on the work adults do within a given society (Whiting 1983).

Peers

Peer relations begin in early infancy. Even at 3 months of age, infants show different sorts of behaviour in the presence of their peers and of adults (Fogel 1979). By the end of the first year infants share toys with their peers and engage in conflict with them (Caplan et al. 1991). Familiar peers facilitate each other's exploration of the environment (Ispa 1981), and, under unusual circumstances, as we have seen, very young peers form deep attachments and nurture each other (A. Freud and Dann 1951).

Much attention has been focused on children's relations with the peers they meet in play groups, nursery schools, daycare centres and school classrooms. Even in the earliest years of life, infants prefer to interact with particular peers (Howes 1983), and these tendencies become marked in preschool groups, where children show preferences for peers who show prosocial actions (Denham et al. 1990). In many studies children have been asked to give their opinions about their classmates, using a technique known as sociometrics, first introduced by Moreno in 1943. The sociometric technique can be used to identify particular, mutual friendships and, indeed, cases where children are mutual enemies. It is also commonly used to classify children into five groups: popular children, who are liked by many peers; rejected children, who are actively disliked by many peers; neglected children, who are neither liked nor disliked by their classmates; controversial children, who are liked by some but actively disliked by others; and average children, that is, everybody else (e.g. Coie, Dodge and Coppotelli 1982).

Many investigators have sought to understand why some children are rejected by their peers. Dodge and his colleagues have identified links between peer rejection and aggression, but the process is a complicated one, linked to cognitive factors (Crick and Dodge 1996). Dodge has argued that highly aggressive children have a specific social cognitive deficit: they tend to misconstrue neutral or friendly overtures by others as aggressive, and react accordingly. Their defensive reactions are perceived as aggressive by the initially friendly or neutral peer, who reacts in kind. Eventually a self-fulfilling prophecy arises, so that aggressive children are targets of aggression from others. Children who bully other children are often victims of bullying themselves (Perry, Kusel and Perry 1988). Peer rejection itself makes the initially aggressive child more likely to show aggression, and more likely to turn to other aggressive children for companionship (Cairns and Cairns 1994). Such difficulties in peer relations may arise in children's earliest encounters with familiar peers; toddlers who are especially suspicious of peers' intentions are also more likely to exhibit proactive, physical aggression against their peers (Hay, Castle and Davies 2000).

When children's peer relations are assessed using sociometric methods, the children are often asked to talk only about same-sex peers. This is because, in the primary school years, children's peer relations show gender segregation: boys tend to play with boys and girls with girls. Eleanor Maccoby (1988) has argued that this tendency to seek out the company of one's own sex, which she believes to be based on innate preferences for particular forms of activity, serves to create almost completely separate worlds in which girls and boys socialize themselves to conform to gender stereotypes. Maccoby argues that boys tend to spend their time in active play, in larger peer groups, whereas girls are more often spending time with one or two 'best friends', conversing, sharing secrets and indulging in quieter, less action-packed endeavours. She believes that these experiences in childhood give females and males rather different expectations of social life that come into conflict when, in adolescence, they meet up again and attempt heterosexuality.

Tests of Maccoby's theory would need to go beyond observation of children in classrooms or on school playgrounds; more is known about sociometrics in the classroom than about children's personal friendships. However, in contrast to Maccoby's view, it has been shown that girls' relations with peers are not always as harmonious as they might appear at first glance. Girls sometimes report acts of violent aggression that have escaped the attention of teachers or parents (see Cairns and Cairns 1994). When girls and boys were both fitted with miniature microphones, allowing recording of peer interaction at some distance from the observer, girls were as likely as boys to engage in verbal and physical aggression with peers; the difference was, that girls did it at some distance from adult supervisors (Pepler and Craig 1995).

As children make the transition into adolescence, larger groups of peers become particularly influential. Some adolescents join gangs. Indeed, sometimes the first positive peer experiences an initially rejected child has are with other delinquent individuals in a gang (Cairns and Cairns 1994). Peers certainly influence the many decisions adolescents make in the transition to adulthood. Both the peer group as a whole and particular close friends influence adolescents' experimentation with smoking, alcohol and illegal drugs (Urberg, Değirmencioğlu and Pilgrim 1997).

Conclusions

As we have seen, from infancy onwards, children relate to many different people These relationships do not exist in isolation from each other; rather, there are many links across the different sort of relationships in which children engage. The study of children's social development has been much influenced by the theoretical and clinical perspectives of family systems theory (Cox and Paley 1997). Furthermore, increasing attention is being given to social networks, neighbourhoods and communities, as well as the broader historical and cultural context in which children grow up (Elder, Modell and Parke 1993).

A family systems or community-oriented approach means that psychologists are beginning to formulate somewhat different questions about the social influences on children's lives. For example, we may ask not whether the father or the mother is the critical influence on later development, but how the two parents' own relationship affects and is affected by each parent's relationship with the child. Recently investigators have focused attention on spillover from the marital relationship. Conflict between the parents induces each to act with more hostility to the child, which in turn is linked to behavioural problems in the child (Harold et al. 1997).

Another example of a family systems approach is the current interest in differential treatment of siblings by their parents, and, what is even more complex, the alliances that each parent forms with particular children in the family. Differential treatment is associated with children's psychological problems (Dunn, Stocker and Plomin 1990).

Family relationships also affect and are affected by the children's relations with others outside the family. The spillover from marital conflict affects the sibling relationship, which in turn is linked to aggression with peers (MacKinnon-Lewis et al. 1997). The way 6-year-old children argue with their friends can be predicted from the nature of their conflicts with mothers and siblings three years earlier (Herrera and Dunn 1997).

In all these more complex accounts of social relations in childhood, the child's own role must be taken into consideration. In the 1960s, Bell (1968) and Rheingold (1969b) drew attention to the power children have over the lives of others; in Rheingold's words, infants turn adults into parents. More recently, children's contributions to their own social lives were emphasized by behavioural geneticists, who wished to draw attention to the role of children's own genetically determined attributes in the experiences those children have. In this view, 'people make their own environments' (Scarr and McCartney 1983). Yet an emphasis on an active child, engaging as a key player in complex social relations with others, need not reduce to a behavioural genetics argument. As was stated in box 6.1, simple determinism, in terms of either genetically determined characteristics or the effects of early experiences with the mother, is an inadequate account of the vagaries of social development (see also box 6.2). Rather, as we have seen throughout this chapter, the human being is social from the moment of birth, if not before, and important experiences accrue throughout the life span. Social life is already complicated in infancy, and remains so. We do not take our place in human society only at childhood's end. Children, and even infants, are full and serious participants in any human society.

RECOMMENDED READING

Campbell, A. and Muncer, S. (1998) *The Social Child*. Hove: Psychology Press.
This is an edited collection of contemporary and controversial articles about important issues in the study of children's social development.

Damon, W. (ed.) (1998) *Handbook of Child Psychology, Vol. 4*. Chichester: John Wiley.
This edited volume provides an encyclopaedic account of current research on social development.

Durkin, K. (1995) *Developmental Social Psychology: From Infancy to Old Age*. Oxford: Blackwell.
This textbook is designed to integrate basic developmental research into the domain of social psychology.

Schaffer, H. R. (1995) *Social Development*. Oxford: Blackwell.
This textbook in developmental psychology summarizes important theoretical and applied issues in social development.

7

Interpersonal Relationships

- Introduction
- What is a relationship?
- Describing relationships
- Dimensions of interpersonal relationships
- The dynamics of relationships
- The diversity and complexity of relationships
- Conclusions
- Recommended reading

Introduction

For most if not all of us, personal relationships are the most important issue in our lives. Surprisingly, however, the systematic study of relationships in adulthood was largely neglected by psychologists until the 1970s. Before then, attention was focused on aspects of individual functioning or on the behaviour of individuals in group situations. The rapid development of the study of relationships has been due in large measure to two factors. First, it was realized that a relationship between two individuals has properties that are simply not relevant to an individual on her or his own. For example, the extent to which each partner reveals herself or himself to the other is an important aspect of their relationship, but irrelevant to the behaviour of an individual in isolation. Second, and following from this, the behaviour of each partner in a relationship depends in part on the other, so study of relationships must take account of what goes on between the partners.

This chapter considers first the nature of relationships. The next two sections are concerned with description, for if we are to have an ordered body of knowledge about relationships it will require a descriptive base. Chemistry became a science when the periodic table provided a means for classifying the elements, biology when the theory of evolution by natural selection provided a basis for the work of taxonomists and systematists. Only with an adequate descriptive base can we specify the limitations of the generalizations we reach.

But relationships are never static, and the subsequent section focuses on the various psychological factors and processes involved in the dynamics of relationships. Many of these are treated in other chapters in this book, and they will be mentioned only briefly here. Beyond that, we need to know in what sort of relationship, and how, each of these processes operates. As an example, the processes operating in the development of close heterosexual relationships are reviewed briefly: data on other types of relationship – mother–child, marital, peer, employer–employee and so on – are summarized by Auhagen and von Salisch (1996).

What is a relationship?

Interactions and relationships

First we need to specify what we mean by a relationship. In this chapter an interaction implies an interchange of strictly limited duration: at a minimum, individual A shows behaviour X to individual B, who may respond with behaviour Y. In the first instance a relationship implies a series of such interactions between two individuals who know each other, such that each interaction is affected by preceding ones and usually by the expectation of future ones. It will be apparent that the distinction between interaction and relationship is a blurred one, but that need not detain us here. And of course behaviour is not all: every relationship has emotional and cognitive aspects that continue between interactions and contribute to its persistence (Hinde 1997).

As used in this way, 'relationship' refers to what goes on between two individuals. For example, research on relationships may involve the analysis of conversations, where each partner is continually affecting the other. But the term 'relationship' is also used in another sense to refer to aspects of each partner's involvement. Thus it is sometimes essential to distinguish A's relationship with B from B's relationship with A: for instance, A may be committed to a relationship with B when B is not committed to a relationship with A. Here each relationship is not between the two partners, but inside their heads. Even then, however, it is a relationship characteristic, because how committed A is depends in part on B.

The self-system

What do we mean by 'inside their heads'? A concept useful here is that of the self-system. We behave somewhat differently according to the situation we are in or whom we are with, and we change as life goes on, and yet we see ourselves as the same person. As we have seen in chapter 2, we account for this continuity in our lives by postulating a self, and we assume that other people have selves too. We can equate a person's self with the manner in which she or he describes herself or himself. Thus you might describe yourself by giving your sex, your age, your religious and political views, your occupation, your relationships, your attitudes and idiosyncracies and so on. Since individuals describe themselves as having different characteristics in different situations, details of those situations must be included in, or readily available to, the self. For that reason it is preferable to refer to the 'self-system'. A's relationship with B can be seen as part of that self-system.

As argued in chapter 2, discussion of the self-system may seem to belong with individual psychology, but paradoxically it is a basically social matter. How one sees oneself is based on how one perceives others to perceive oneself. And one tends to behave in a way that maintains the consistency of the self-system, and to interpret the behaviour of others in a manner that supports its integrity (Backman 1988). We shall see that reference to the self-systems of the participants is fundamental for many issues arising in the study of relationships.

Levels of complexity

Interactions and relationships refer to two levels of social complexity which are part of a series – intra-individual systems, individual behaviour, interactions, relationships, groups and societies (Hinde 1997) (see figure 7.1). As already noted in the case of individual behaviour and relationships, each of these levels has properties that are simply irrelevant to the level below. And partly for that reason, each successive level tends to require new explanatory concepts. Thus the occurrence of an aggressive interaction between brothers may be explained in terms of temporary moods, for example 'they are tired', or of short-term precipitating factors, for example that one child took the other's toy; but an aggressive relationship between brothers may be explained in terms of longer-term traits or, for instance, family factors such as sibling rivalry.

Furthermore, there are two-way relations between the successive levels of social complexity. The characteristics of a relationship depend on the nature of its constituent interactions, and the course of each interaction is affected by the relationship of which it forms part – for instance, by memories of previous interactions or expectations of future ones. And the nature of a relationship affects and is affected by the family or group of which it forms part.

Each of these levels of social complexity may also affect, and be affected by, the physical environment and, more importantly, the sociocultural structure. The latter is a shorthand term for the system of beliefs, values, myths, conventions and institutions, with their constituent roles, shared by most or all members of the society, group or dyad. Indeed these beliefs, values and the like merge with those idiosyncratic to individuals. For instance, parents are influenced in how they treat their children by current social conventions, including beliefs about how children should be brought up

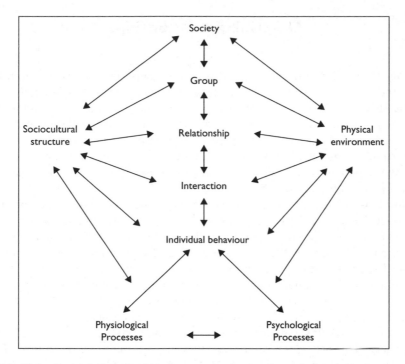

Figure 7.1 Dialectical relations between successive levels of social complexity

and values about how children should behave, and also by their own past experience. Because the various beliefs and values influence each other, they must be seen as forming a structure. But because this sociocultural structure constantly influences and is influenced by individuals, relationships, groups etc., it must also be regarded as a dynamic process. Indeed not only the sociocultural structure but also all the levels of social complexity are to be seen not as entities but as processes, constantly influencing each other. Thus the behaviour of a courting couple affects and is affected by their families, and by cultural conventions about how couples ought to behave, and how couples actually behave affects the conventions about how they should behave. The manner in which the self-system influences how an individual behaves in relationships, and the reciprocal influence of the relationships in which one is involved on one's view of oneself (the self-system), are just one example of these mutual influences.

Thus relationships cannot be studied in isolation. It is useful to distinguish the levels shown in figure 7.1 for the sake of discussion, but it is essential to remember their dynamic nature and the two-way relations between them. This leads one to the view that individuals, interactions and relationships are to be seen not as entities but as processes being created, maintained or degraded through these mutual influences between the levels of social complexity.

Describing relationships

Describing relationships involves a number of problems. The first is common to every scientific endeavour: description of any phenomenon can never be complete, and must always be selective. Thus we cannot describe every nod, wink and utterance, every action, every wish and every feeling of the two partners in a relationship: selection must be made with reference to the problem in hand. Furthermore, description can never be 'pure': it is likely to be contaminated by theories or hunches thought to 'explain' the phenomena with which we are concerned. But we must at least try to be conscious of the criteria by which we select.

This brings us to a second problem: the level of complexity at which description should be attempted. Should we focus on the details of interactions – the nods and winks, the words exchanged – or should we go for more global properties? Kelley et al. (1983) took the former course, going for the actions and subjective phenomena within interactions. They described relationships in terms of the interactions between the temporal chains of two individuals' affect, thought and action, specifying (1) the nature of the events in each chain that are interconnected; (2) the pattern, (3) the strength and (4) the diversity of interconnections; (5) the extent to which the interconnections facilitate or hinder the chain of actions; (6) their symmetry or asymmetry; and (7) the duration of the interaction or relationship. This provides a valuable framework for analysing the course of interactions, as illustrated in box 7.1 and figure 7.2. The authors emphasize that each interaction may influence the causal conditions for subsequent ones, but the emphasis is on the analysis of interactions rather than relationships.

In this chapter, a somewhat more global approach is preferred. This involves selection, at any rate initially, of the level of analysis at which we habitually talk about relationships, and aspects of relationships that appear to us to be important in everyday life. This might appear unduly subjective, but can be justified by the view that we have become adapted, biologically and/or culturally, to be reasonably good at understanding the dynamics of relationships. Of course it remains possible that we are not conscious of the things that really matter, or that such a procedure will miss crucial details. However, it is in no way incompatible with the more detailed approach advocated by Kelley et al. (1983), seeing that as a possible next step. It has the advantage of tackling directly aspects of the patterning of interactions that are specific to the level of relationships.

Box 7.1   Interconnected chains of events

Kelley et al. (1983) provide a possible example for the sequence shown in figure 7.2 as follows: a young woman, P, compliments a young man, O, on his appearance, who blushes. At the same time P thinks about what she has said and considers whether it was appropriate. But P observes O's blush and concludes that he welcomed her compliment. She smiles. Simultaneously O becomes aware of his blushing and, seeing P's smile, concludes that P has noticed his blushing, and blushes even more. And so on.

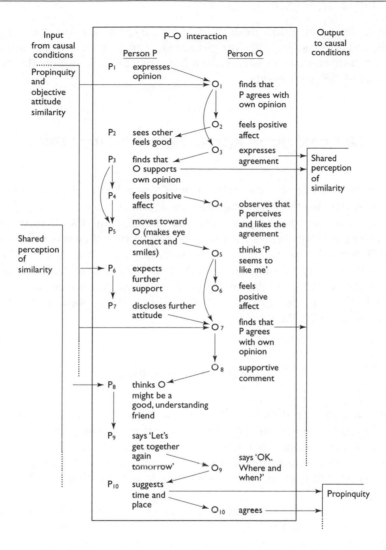

This illustrates an interaction process that closes the causal loop by which
initial causal conditions (propinquity and objective attitude similarity) are
sustained or strengthened and lead to a new causal condition (shared
perception of similarity). The interconnected chains of events for the two
persons are shown in the centre. Input from the causal conditions to the
interaction is shown by arrows leaving to the right. Interaction closes the
causal loop by including direct or indirect connections between those events
affected by the input and those events responsible for the output.

Figure 7.2 P–O interaction (Kelley et al. 1983)

A third problem is more specific to the study of relationships. Much work on social
behaviour concerns interactions rather than relationships. For instance, the circumstances in which prosocial behaviour occurs may be studied by accumulating instances
in which one individual helps another, and deducing generalizations. Relationships,
however, involve properties concerned with the patterning of interactions (see below).
Thus generalizations about relationships cannot be made directly from generalizations

about interactions, and a full description must concern not just the properties of interactions, but also the way they are patterned. And of course behaviour is not all: the course of each interaction and relationship depends crucially on the perceptions and intentions of the participants.

Dimensions of interpersonal relationships

If you start to think about your own relationships, you will immediately become amazed by their complexity, by the confusing mass of detail that comes to mind. What one needs, therefore, is a means to pigeon-hole what is important about relationships. The following scheme involves twelve categories of dimensions: they move from categories principally concerned with the interactions to issues more relevant to relationships, from more objective to more subjective aspects, and from characteristics of the relationship between the partners to relationship characteristics over which the partners may differ and which lie 'in the head' of each (e.g. Hinde 1997). Reflect about your own relationships as you read them.

Content of interactions

We usually categorize relationships in terms of what the individuals concerned do together. A teacher–pupil or an employer–employee relationship implies certain types of interaction. Usually a range of types of interaction is implied, only some of which are essential. Thus teachers must teach, but may also play games with their pupils. Married couples are expected to live together: couples who do not may be referred to as 'married only in name'.

What the individuals do in a relationship reflects their motivations: individuals are likely to stay in a relationship to the extent that it satisfies their needs (using the term 'need' in an everyday sense). Thus a classification of relationships in terms of the content of the interactions may also be one in terms of the needs that the relationship satisfies or attempts to satisfy.

One important type of relationship is not defined in terms of content – namely friendship. Friendship in fact defies easy definition, in part because no particular content of interaction is specified and in part because friendships are so heterogeneous. Auhagen (1991) defines friendships as involving a dyadic, personal, informal relationship, which involves reciprocity and mutual attraction, is voluntary, long-lasting and positive, and does not involve explicit sexuality. This definition implies that the behaviour involved is freely selected. Many other definitions have been suggested: intimacy, not explicitly required in Auhagen's definition, is required by some, and many would not rule out sexuality (see also Hays 1988).

Another category of relationships which does not depend on the content of the interactions is that of kin relationships. One's aunt is one's aunt, whatever the nature of the interactions in the relationships.

Table 7.1 Rules and friendship

Cluster	Rules
Exchange	Seek to repay debts, favours or compliments, no matter how small Share news of success with the other Show emotional support Volunteer help in time of need Strive to make him or her happy while in each other's company
Intimacy	Trust and confide in each other
Coordination	Respect privacy Do not nag
Third party	Do not criticize other in public Stand up for the other person in her or his absence Keep confidences Be tolerant of each other's friends Do not be jealous or critical of other relationships

Source: Argyle and Henderson (1985)

Relationships that are defined by the roles that the participants occupy, for instance teacher–pupil or doctor–patient relationships, imply particular contents in the interactions. Each role has certain rights and duties associated with it: thus a teacher is entitled to some respect, and there are some things a teacher must do. The actual behaviour shown by the participants is thus influenced both by the nature of their role and by the specifics of the situation, their own idiosyncracies and so on.

More generally, one can also consider each type of relationship as governed by rules whose neglect is likely to lead to a deterioration in the relationship. Rules in this sense grade into the conventions and norms which are less crucial to the continuance of the relationship but nevertheless influence its detailed course. The rules relevant to a number of types of relationships, as revealed by questionnaire methods, have been reviewed by Argyle and Henderson (1985), basing their conclusions on studies of several different societies. The rules for friendship, and the clusters into which they fall, are shown in table 7.1. Rules, of course, are not necessarily obeyed, but their abrogation may lead to a deterioration in the relationship. They may, however, serve as a goal: married couples may strive to attain a societal ideal of married bliss, and parents attempt to follow the current advice on how relationships with children should be conducted. In addition, rules about how the participants should behave may affect how outsiders treat them.

Diversity of interactions

A related characteristic concerns the number of different things the participants do together. Thus a teacher–pupil relationship may or may not extend outside the classroom, and married couples vary in the variety of the interactions in which they participate. Some relationships may revolve around one primary type of interaction (uniplex relationships) – for instance, tennis partners.

Of course this diversity of interactions depends in part on the level of analysis employed: a mother–child relationship could be regarded as multiplex, involving bathing, feeding, playing and so on, or uniplex, as involving only maternal–filial interactions. But diversity is important because the more things individuals do together, the more can interactions of one type affect those of another, the more shared experience is possible, and the more facets of their personalities are exposed (e.g. Hays 1985).

Qualities of interactions

A greeting can be warm or distant, a discussion friendly or competitive, a meal together harmonious or acrimonious, a kiss tender, passionate or dutiful. The qualities of interactions are one of the most important properties of a relationship, and yet one of the most difficult to assess. However, as we have seen in chapter 5, a number of sources of evidence are available – the content of speech, its intonation, stress and the supporting gestures that accompany it, and non-verbal signals (e.g. Noller 1987). A classic example is the use by G. W. Brown, Birley and Wing (1972) of an index of expressed emotion, assessed from the amount of criticism, hostility and emotional overinvolvement expressed by the relatives of schizophrenics released from hospital. Fifty-six per cent of patients from homes with a high index, but only 16 per cent of those from homes with a low one, relapsed within nine months (see also Vaughn and Leff 1976; and chapter 17). In addition, the extent to which the behaviour of each partner meshes with that of the other is often a crucial issue, though it must be remembered that while friends behave harmoniously, rivals may know exactly how to needle each other.

In all those cases it must be remembered that a given quality may refer to only some or to all the interactions in a relationship, and to the behaviour of one or both participants. In the former case, A's relationship with B may have a quality different from B's with A.

Relative frequency and patterning of interactions

A relationship is not simply the sum of its components, but depends on their interrelations. Several issues are involved.

Covariance of properties   Descriptions of a relationship as loving, competitive, sensitive and so on usually depend on the content and quality of many types of interaction. For instance, we would perhaps be more prone to call a relationship affectionate or loving if the partners did a number of different things together, strove to be close, liked to do things that were conducive to the welfare of the other, meshed well with each other, were willing to reveal themselves to each other, felt anxieties relieved when in each other's presence, and saw their relationship as durable – though there are no implications that all these properties are necessary, that additional ones may not also be important, or that some of these are not also characteristic of relationships of other types. It is the coincidence of some of them in one relationship that is important. Of course few relationships are uniformly of any one quality, but such labels have a special importance in that the ones deemed appropriate by the participants may affect the relationship's future course.

Ratio and derived measures   What matters in a relationship is often not how often the partners do something, but how often they do it relative to the frequency with which one or both participants initiates or wants to initiate interactions of that type. Thus how often a mother picks up a baby, and the proportion of times when the baby is crying to be picked up and the mother does so, measure two different properties of the mother–baby relationship. In the former case the mother might be picking up the baby when it was better left to sleep; in the latter she would be responding to an expression of its needs.

Relations between interactions of different types   Some properties of relationships depend on both the absolute and the relative frequencies of different types of interaction. For instance, if a mother often initiated contact with her baby and seldom rejected the baby, we might call her warm: if the opposite were the case we might call her rejecting. If she often did both, we would call her controlling, and if she seldom did either we might call her permissive. Such labels applied to a relationship can influence its future course, especially when they are used by the participants.

The relations between two dimensions of parental behaviour have proven predictive value for child behaviour in another context. The dimensions concerned can be very roughly labelled as '*strong control*' and '*warmth*'. Baumrind (1971) identified three groups of parents: authoritarian parents, who exercise control rigidly and show little warmth; authoritative parents, who exercise control with sensitivity and are moderate or high on warmth; and permissive parents, low on both. A fourth group, of indulgent parents, are high on warmth and low on control. (This represents a considerable simplification of her categories.) Baumrind found that children with authoritative parents had the most favourable outcomes on a number of dimensions. A more recent study (Hinde, Tamplin and Barrett 1993a) found that those 4-year-olds who showed least aggression in preschool were those whose mothers provided a balance between control and warmth (figure 7.3).

This approach suggests the importance of studying the structure of relationships, in the sense of the relations between the frequencies of different types of interaction. Figures 7.4 (a) and (b) compare the structure of the relationships of a sample of 4-year-olds with their mothers and teachers. (In the latter case, it will be noted, the relationship is with a category of others rather than an individual.) The items consist of the total frequency of interactions and the frequency of each type of interaction relative to that total. A number of differences between the two structures will be noted. In the mother–child case there were distinct groups of positive and negative items, but the teachers showed positive responses primarily in response to child dependence. The more mother and child interacted, the more likely were their interactions to be positive, whereas frequent teacher–child interaction was linked to the negative group. Children who often initiated interactions with their mothers often received initiations, whereas children who often initiated to teachers received answers but not necessarily frequent initiations. In

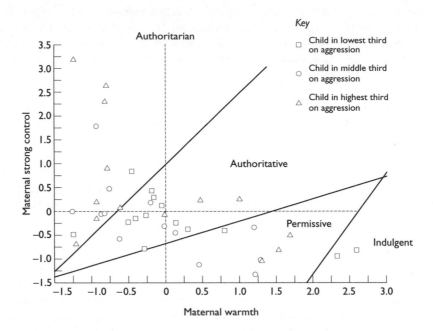

The less aggressive children tend to lie in the authoritative area, with a few in a fourth area labelled 'indulgent'. Maternal warmth and control were assessed from observational data.

Figure 7.3 Relations between aggressive behaviour of 4-year-olds in preschool and mother–child relationship (Hinde, Tamplin and Barrett 1993a)

this way study of the structure of relationships can show up important differences between relationships of different types: the study of individual relationships which do not conform to the structural norm is also made possible (Hinde, Tamplin and Barrett 1993b).

Sequencing of interactions   Sometimes the sequencing of interactions is of crucial importance. A pat on the back after four put-downs means much more than a pat on the back followed by four put-downs (e.g. Sigall and Aronson 1967).

Reciprocity in interactions

Sometimes the two participants in an interaction are doing effectively the same thing, as in a conversation between two friends or an evenly matched game of tennis. Such interactions are known as reciprocal (or symmetrical). By contrast, in complementary interactions, discussed below, the partners do different but functionally related things: a mother feeding a baby or a teacher instructing a pupil would be examples. Of course, as in other cases, the distinction depends to some extent on the level of analysis employed.

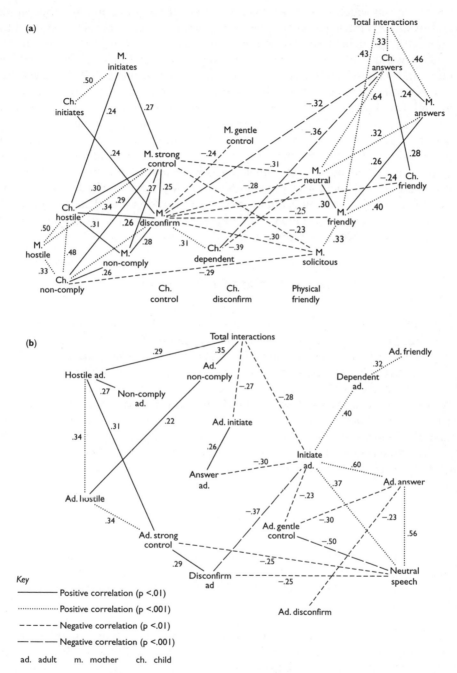

Figure 7.4 Structure of (a) child–mother relationships and (b) child–teacher relationships of 4-year-olds (Hinde, Tamplin and Barrett 1993b)

Relationships in which all interactions are reciprocal are probably rare, though some relationships between friends, colleagues and sports partners approach that condition. They normally occur between partners who are similar to each other in the relevant ways. There is considerable evidence for the importance of similarity in interpersonal attraction and mate-selection (see reviews by Buss 1999; Hinde 1997). However, long-term relationships depend on more than initial attraction, and the characteristics over which similarity matters may change with the stage of the relationship. For instance, Duck and Craig (1978) followed twenty male and twenty female students living in the same campus residence over eight months. At one, three and eight months they reported their friendships and completed three personality tests – one providing a gross personality profile, a second concerned with less easily available information about value systems, and a third dealing with ways of thinking. While the first test had been found to predict friendship choice on acquaintance, it did not do so at these test times. The second and third tests, which could be said to probe successively more deeply, predicted friendship choice at three and eight months respectively.

Complementarity in interactions

Relationships involving primarily complementary interactions are more common than relationships that are primarily reciprocal, because many relationships involve partners differing in age, sex or status; because, even when such differences are absent, individuals tend to strive for status; and because in long-term relationships individuals are likely to have some needs which can be satisfied only by someone different from themselves. In practice most close relationships involve a complex and idiosyncratic patterning of reciprocity and complementarity. Complementarity may involve dominance/subordinance, nurturance/succourance, security/anxiety, teaching/learning and many other dimensions. Of course, as in other cases, the distinction depends to some extent on the level of analysis employed.

Conflict

Some degree of conflict is virtually inevitable in every relationship. It is not necessarily a bad thing as, if resolved, it can be constructive and lead to greater mutual understanding. But many conflicts in close relationships involve one or more of four basic issues (Baxter 1990):

1   *Autonomy vs. relatedness*. People need to feel autonomous – that is, that their actions and feelings emanate from themselves and are their own. But a relationship implies mutual interdependence, and depends on each partner making some concessions for the sake of the other, and thus forgoing some autonomy.
2   *Openness vs. privacy*. Relationships depend on communication, and that involves exposing the self-system. Exposure, however, increases vulnerability, and permitting oneself to become vulnerable demands trust in the partner. Furthermore, a degree of privacy may be important for the integrity of the self-system.

3 *Predictability vs. novelty*. The essence of a close relationship involves knowing the partner, but knowledge of the partner involves predictability. Complete predictability can lead to boredom.
4 *Jealousy*. This destructive emotion is usually based on one or more of four types of perceived loss: loss of equality in the relationship, loss of self-esteem, loss of specialness, and (threatened) loss of the partner (Buunk and Bringle 1987).

In the short term, behaviour in a conflict situation may involve an attempt to leave the relationship, waiting and hoping that things will improve, ignoring the partner, or attempts to solve the issue in question (Rusbult and Zembrodt 1983). While the principle of tit-for-tat may produce a tendency to reciprocate negative behaviour, the recipient may value the continuation of the relationship more than his or her immediate *amour propre*. A satisfactory relationship makes a constructive reply more probable (Rusbult et al. 1991). A common pattern in heterosexual relationships is for women to use emotional appeal strategies, while men tend not to deal with conflicts openly, but to withdraw (Christensen and Heavey 1993). In poorly adjusted couples conflicts may be exacerbated by poor communication, leading to a vicious circle (Noller 1987).

In the longer term the partners may take a decision as to where their priorities lie and go for one pole or the other (e.g. complete connectedness, abandoning autonomy); seek for achievement of each pole but only for some of the time or over some issues (e.g. autonomy during the week, connectedness at weekends); opt for partial achievement of both poles (e.g. one spouse might agree that the other should go off and play golf on Saturday afternoons, but only nine holes); or reframe the issue so that it is no longer a problem (e.g. if each spouse agrees, as part of their connectedness, that the other has the right to do his or her own thing, then the autonomy/connectedness issue has been reframed). Reframing is the most cognitively complex solution, and is probably used primarily in long-term relationships (Baxter 1990).

Power

Power can be defined in terms of the extent to which one individual can affect the quantity or quality of another's actions or rewards, and is an aspect of complementarity. It is, however, extremely difficult to measure, for a number of reasons. First, power is seldom absolute, one partner having power in some contexts and the other in others. Second, in exchange theory terms, the nature of power varies with the resource exchanged: we shall return to this later. Third, the means by which power is asserted are often extremely subtle – for instance, the complaining of the hypochondriac, the 'I'm upset' routine, the nurturant care which cannot be refused without offending convention. Even loving may be a source of power, for it can create an obligation for connectedness. Fourth, it is often difficult to know what level of analysis to use in measuring power. Thus in one study of power distribution in marriages the issue was addressed in a number of life areas (e.g. money, household chores, decisions about holidays), but it was found necessary in each case to distinguish between three levels: executive (e.g. who buys the tickets for the family holiday), executive decision-making (who decides where to go), and how responsibility for executive decision-making is decided (i.e. who decides who shall decide) (Collins et al. 1971).

But however difficult power differentials may be for the outsider to assess, the fact is that many individuals in close relationships do feel controlled by their partners, and it is what they feel that matters. Such feelings stem in part from the fact that social norms have long assumed male control in many aspects of heterosexual relationships, and men continue to subscribe to these norms, while the growth of feminism has allowed women to resent and challenge them. Another issue may be that women feel a greater need for connectedness in close heterosexual relationships, and are therefore less willing to rock the boat, but feel that their autonomy is thereby constrained. There is some hope that the force of both these issues is on the decrease. Social norms are changing, albeit too slowly, and women have more opportunities for independence, reducing their need for connectedness.

Self-disclosure

This refers to the extent to which a partner in a relationship reveals herself or himself to the other cognitively, experientially, emotionally and/or physically. A need to share experiences, ideas and feelings with others is virtually ubiquitous, and inadequate opportunities to meet this need lead to feelings of loneliness (Kelvin 1977; Peplau and Perlman 1982). On the other hand, most people need to defend areas of privacy, and denial of privacy, for instance in the army, is conducive to establishing conformity to group norms (Burgoon et al. 1989).

Self-disclosure involves costs because it increases vulnerability. For that reason, self-disclosure in a close relationship demands trust in the partner. Self-disclosure to a stranger may be easy because vulnerability to someone who will never be seen again does not matter.

Some individuals reveal themselves more readily than do others. This applies especially to relatively superficial matters: with high-intimacy topics the amount of disclosure is characteristic of the relationship (L. C. Miller 1990). In some relationships, like that of patient to doctor, self-revelation is one-sided. This may also be the case even in close personal relationships: nevertheless self-disclosure in A's relationship with B is a characteristic of the relationship between A and B, because what is disclosed depends on the partner.

Interpersonal perception

For participants in or students of interpersonal relationships, a major issue must be the way in which the partners think about each other. Is their vision of each other biased or clouded? Do they understand each other? Do they feel understood? How closely does the partner approximate to their ideal? These seemingly nebulous issues can be translated into concrete form in terms of specific questions:

1   Does A see B as B really is?
2   Does A see B as B sees B? (Understanding)
3   Does B feel that A sees B as B sees B? (Feeling understood)
4   Does A see B as close to A's ideal partner? (Satisfaction)

Table 7.2 An instrument used to assess interpersonal perception

Husband's protocol	Respondent asked to describe	Wife's protocol
A	Myself as I am	B
A^1	My spouse as I see him or her	B^1
A^2	Myself as I think my spouse sees me	B^2

Source: Drewery and Rae (1969)

The most frequent method for tackling those questions consists in asking each partner to fill in a questionnaire from more than one stance. For instance, a respondent might be asked to describe herself, her spouse, her spouse's view of her, and her view of herself and her ideal spouse. Comparisons between these and her spouse's answers would provide answers to the above questions. As an example, the instrument used by Drewery and Rae (1969) is shown in table 7.2. Comparison $A–B^1$ would show whether the husband sees himself as his wife sees him, $B–B^2$ whether the wife feels understood.

Considerable data has been gleaned by the use of such methods. Thus Drewery and Rae showed that alcoholic outpatient husbands were unlikely to see themselves as their wives saw them, but self-perception and wife's perception was positively correlated for controls. There is considerable evidence to show that married or engaged couples tend to see themselves as more similar to each other than they really are (Murstein 1972).

On the whole, people like to be seen by others in a good light, and try to behave in a way that will be acceptable to others. Sometimes, however, it is preferable to be seen as one really is, perhaps because it is then possible to interact with the partner in a more straightforward and honest manner. The balance between these two depends on the nature of the relationship. Thus one study found that satisfaction in members of dating couples was greater the more positive the partner's appraisal of self. However, in married couples satisfaction was less if there was a large discrepancy between the individual's self-view and that of the partner, even if the partner's view was more positive than the self-view (Swann, de la Ronde and Hixon 1994). Occasionally individuals deliberately try to lower the opinion that others have of them: thus anxious individuals, doubtful of their own abilities, may perform poorly in order to lower the expectations of others to coincide with their own self-view (e.g. McNulty and Swann 1994; Swann 1987).

Satisfaction with the relationship

How an individual behaves in an interaction depends in part on his or her satisfaction with the relationship in which that interaction is embedded. The participants' perceptions of a relationship may be inaccurate and may or may not agree, and misperception and disagreement may help or hinder a relationship according to its nature. However, satisfaction depends both on the difference between the participant's perception of the relationship and his or her norm or ideal for the relationship in question, and on the availability of alternatives (Murstein 1972). If commitment is low, satisfaction with a partner may be reduced by the appearance of a third party.

Commitment

'Commitment' refers to the extent to which a partner in a relationship strives to ensure its continuation or optimize its properties. In some cases the emphasis may be primarily on continuity, in others on optimization of properties, and in yet others on both. Commitment is strongly linked to issues of intimacy, trust and cooperation.

Commitment can be enforced from outside, as in arranged marriages, or it may arise as the relationship develops. In many societies, commitment to marriage initially develops gradually but comes to involve outside pressures as it becomes public with formal betrothal and marriage ceremonies: public recognition can act as a powerful glue to a relationship.

If personal commitment is acknowledged, it can have a profound influence on future behaviour. Of almost equal importance is belief in the partner's commitment. In exchange theory terms (see below), if a partner provides resources in the expectation of

Plate 7.1 They seem pretty satisfied, but are they committed?

future returns, he or she relies on continuity. Similarly the growth of intimacy involves an increase in vulnerability and thus faith in the partner's commitment. And since personal growth may demand changes in relationships, it may require faith in the partner's commitment to continuity if the relationship in question is important: a parent who threatens to disown a child may be inhibiting the latter's development.

A number of studies have assessed the factors making for commitment. Current satisfaction and the costs that would arise if the relationship were terminated are of course important issues. One study found that what the participants feel they have put into a relationship, and their perceived commitment to it, are better predictions of continuity than the rewards they feel they are getting or how much they feel they love each other (Lund 1985).

The dynamics of relationships

We have seen that we must recognize the multifaceted and dynamic character of relationships, and be able to describe the characteristics of particular relationships. The twelve categories just considered are offered as a first step towards the latter goal. But we must also attempt to specify the psychological factors and processes that affect the course of their dynamics. Since many of these are treated elsewhere in this volume, they are referred to only briefly here.

Individual characteristics

It need hardly be said that the course of a relationship depends on the characteristics of the participants, though it must be remembered that, as was seen in chapter 2, the cross-situational consistency of personality traits tends to be low, and individuals behave differently in different relationships.

One example from a classic study by Newcomb (1961) goes a step further in exploring the manner in which the psychological characteristics of the participants affect the dynamics of a relationship. Students newly arrived at Bennington College tended to form friendships with others with attitudes similar to their own, and attitude similarity increased as friendship deepened. However, the way in which this happened depended on the personalities of the individuals. Non-authoritarian students became friends with others who genuinely agreed with them. Authoritarian students, tending to interpret the world in terms of their own preconceived notions, believed that those with whom they associated had attitudes that were more similar to their own than was actually the case.

Dissonance and balance

The issues here, concerned with the degree of consistency between the beliefs, attitudes and values that individuals hold, will be discussed in detail in chapter 13. While it is perfectly possible to hold simultaneously views that are inconsistent or contradictory, on the whole we feel happier if there is harmony in our heads. If we perceive that there is not, we are likely to take steps to remove the sense of dissonance by restoring balance. For instance, if A is fond of B but discovers that B disagrees with him strongly on an issue that he holds dear, A is likely either to try to convert B, or to cease to like B, or to change his own opinion on the issue, or to refuse to believe that the discrepancy exists (Kenny and Kashy 1994; Newcomb 1961).

While consistency theory provides insight into many aspects of relationships, its application is complicated in real-life situations. For instance, it depends critically on the relationship involved: if Joe loves Ann, and Harry loves Ann, the theory would predict that Joe would like Harry: this is not necessarily so. Again, agreement with someone we do not expect to meet again matters less than agreement with a friend.

Attribution

Individuals tend to attribute causes to personalities or events; this will be discussed in chapter 11. The course of a relationship will be influenced by the attributions that individuals make, which in turn will depend on their personality, their circumstances, and so on. For example, partners in a relationship are prone to explain problems in terms of the personal traits and attitudes of their partners. Where the conflict arises from unsatisfactory behaviour by one partner, the individual who perceives himself or herself to be wronged tends to attribute the blame to personal characteristics of the partner, while the latter may attribute blame to external circumstances, people or objects, to an aberrant and temporary state, or to more pressing and important issues (Kelley 1979).

Most attributions involve much more than postulating a cause for an event. For instance, responsibility for the event may be assigned, meanings attached to the actions of those involved, and a new narrative of the past constructed (Fincham and Bradbury 1992; Planalp and Rivers 1996).

Exchange and interdependence theories

Exchange and interdependence theories imply that each individual in a relationship seeks to maximize the rewards obtained and minimize the costs incurred. In some earlier versions (Homans 1974), it was supposed that individuals expect to receive rewards commensurate with the costs they incur and profits in line with the investments they bring to the relationship. What counts as an investment might be culture-specific, but age, maleness, seniority, wealth, beauty and skills often contribute. The subjective value of the rewards and costs may be less important than the public perception of their extent.

Other approaches emphasized the interdependence of the two parties in a relationship (Thibaut and Kelley 1959; Kelley and Thibaut 1978). The rewards and costs experienced by each partner depend not only on what she or he does, but also on what the partner does. The stability of the relationship depends on the relations between the outcomes (ratio of perceived rewards to perceived costs) of each partner, what each thinks that she or he deserves, and the alternatives available.

However, the goals of the partners may differ according to the nature of the relationship. Thus in close relationships each may strive to maximize their joint rewards, but in competitive ones to maximize the difference between her or his own rewards and those of the partner. Equity theorists (e.g. Walster, Walster and Berscheid 1978) suggest that individuals perceive relationships to be equitable, provided their reward/cost ratios are comparable to their partner's. If an individual perceives a situation to be inequitable, he or she may attempt to redress the balance or experience guilt, depending on whether he or she sees himself or herself as under- or overbenefited.

All exchange and interdependence theories must face the difficulties of measuring rewards and costs in real-life situations. It is also necessary to assess what the participants will consider as fair: should each get equal shares, or rewards in proportion to their costs, or rewards according to their needs? In practice, different principles operate in different relationships. A further important issue concerns the nature of the rewards. While early exchange theorists assumed that all rewards had similar properties, Foa and Foa (1974) pointed out that that is not the case. For instance, if I give you money, I have less. If I give you information, I have lost some power to influence you but may gain in understanding. If I give you love, I may have even more to give – or at least I may perceive myself as a loving person and thus as having more to give. Distinguishing the properties of the several types of resource exchanged in relationships has permitted a considerable extension of theory (see also Foa et al. 1993).

Attachment

As we saw in the previous chapter, a sensitive parent, or other primary caregiver, forms a secure base from which the young child can set out to explore the world, and to which he or she can retreat if worried, frightened, tired or hungry (Bowlby 1969). However, children differ in their temperaments, and parents differ in their sensitivity and their parenting techniques (Stevenson-Hinde 1991), so that parent–child relationships are diverse, as we saw revealed by the Ainsworth Strange Situation.

It is supposed that the child forms an internal working model of the relationship with the parent, which is incorporated in the self-system and influences subsequent relationships (Bretherton 1990), though of course the model may also be influenced by subsequent experience.

A number of techniques have been developed for assessing the internal working models held by adults regarding their relationships. The Adult Attachment Interview depends on a complex coding procedure which takes account not only of what the interviewee says but also of how she or he says it, a procedure which requires extensive training, but has proved to have considerable predictive validity (van Ijzendoorn 1995). A very simple questionnaire (Hazan and Shaver 1994) has also yielded correlations with a number of aspects of adult behaviour, but seems to be much influenced by the current relationship context of the interviewee. A scheme yielding two dimensions – positive/ negative models of self and of others – and thus four attachment styles, shows considerable promise (Bartholomew and Horowitz 1991).

Positive and negative feedback

The course of relationships may be affected by processes that can be described as involving positive and negative feedback. Thus if A loves B, and B perceives A to love B, then B may be more prone to love A and A may then love B more. As another example of positive feedback, intense or persistent anger by one partner will diminish the affectional bond, giving more cause for frustration and thus more anger. However, anger can lead to negative feedback: mild anger invoked by separation from a loved one can assist in the overcoming of obstacles to reunion and discourage the partner from going away again.

Social and other extra-dyadic issues

The course of a relationship may be influenced by many issues external to it. We may list some of the more important ones.

The physical environment   The physical environment can affect the course of a relationship. For instance, proximity can aid the formation of relationships, but crowding can engender or augment negative feelings. Barker (1978) cites a study of boys in a community which showed that there was more variation on the hostility/friendliness and dominance/passivity dimensions in the behaviour of the same boys in different settings than there was with different individuals in the same setting.

Social roles and norms   Some relationships involve incumbents of particular roles in society, and their behaviour is affected by the rights and duties associated with those roles. Thus some of the behaviour of husbands and wives is prescribed by societal expectations of behaviour appropriate to a marital relationship. Such rights and duties may be obligatory, or merely expected. The more the former is the case, the more probable are sanctions to be applied for transgression.

Other norms are not attached to particular relationships (see chapter 8 for a discussion of norms). For instance, in many Western societies parents expect boys to be assertive and outgoing, while shyness may be expected or acceptable in girls. Such norms influence parent–child interaction, which may in turn affect the course of personality development. In one study, 4-year-old boys who were at the shy end of the normal range got on less well with peers, teachers and mother than those who were not shy, but 4-year-old girls who were shy got on better than those who were not. The difference was related to parental norms: it is seen as good for little girls to be shy, but not little boys (Stevenson-Hinde and Glover 1996).

In practice, individuals bring to their relationships expectations derived not only from the society as a whole but from each of the overlapping groups to which they see themselves as belonging – women, the younger generation, liberals, middle class, football fans, and so on. In addition a couple may elaborate its own rules and norms and denigrate outsiders, in a manner similar to that which occurs in groups. As we have seen, the effects are two-way, the behaviour of individuals in due course affecting the societal norms.

Third parties   A's relationship with B may be influenced by B's relationship with C: the impact of jealousy was mentioned earlier. As we saw in the previous chapter, studies of relationships within families have shown that the marital relationship is related to the parent–child relationship (Cowan and Cowan 1978), that the mother–firstborn relationship may be profoundly affected by the birth of a sibling (Dunn and Kendrick 1982), and so on (Hinde and Stevenson-Hinde 1988). Such relations are likely to depend on two-way influences.

The diversity and complexity of relationships

Human relationships are astonishingly diverse. As we have seen, it is usual to classify them, in terms of the content of the interactions, into such categories as 'parent–child', 'teacher–pupil', and so on, with others being characterized by kinship ('sibling', 'aunt'), and friendship by more intangible properties. Many different psychological processes operate in each case – probably more than have been listed in the preceding section. Furthermore, such processes operate over time, each interaction being affected by previous ones, by memories, thoughts and feelings which have been experienced in the absence of interactions, and by influences from outside the relationship. To exemplify the issues, we may summarize briefly the processes involved in the development of close relationships, in the light of research on heterosexual relations. It must be remembered, however, that the several processes mentioned may operate simultaneously rather than sequentially.

Perceived similarity is likely to play an important part in the early stages of inter-personal attraction – at first similarity in relatively superficial characteristics, but in progressively more fundamental aspects of the personality as the partners get to know each other better (Huston 1974). Individuals may also be attracted by qualities that they see themselves as needing in a partner, such as protectiveness. In general, in choosing a partner, men in the Western world tend to be more romantic and erotic than women, women more pragmatic (Hendrick et al. 1986; Buss 1999). But in both cases the important characteristics are likely to change as the relationship progresses.

As the two individuals get to like each other better, they will tend to spend more time together, and positive feedback will operate. The quality and diversity of the interactions will increase. One may give the other a present, with expectations of reciprocal exchange, though not necessarily in the same currency: a material gift may be associated with hopes for affection (Foa and Foa 1974). There will be some differences of opinion, with one finding that issues he or she deemed important are irrelevant to the other: attempts to restore balance in one or other of the ways described above will follow, and the resolution of minor conflicts may augment interpersonal perception (e.g. Kelley 1979). Each will attribute characteristics to the other, characteristics which may or may not resemble their real nature (Murstein 1972). One would hope, however, that the perception of each partner by the other would become more accurate. Each will create a personal narrative of the course of the relationship which will affect future interactions.

Each will also compare her or his perception of the partner with other possible partners, and with a notion of an ideal partner. If the comparisons are satisfactory, the relationship will deepen (Murstein 1972). The resources exchanged may progress through information and goods to expressions of status (liking) and eventually to love (Foa and Foa 1974). Each will become more and more willing to make sacrifices for the relationship, and to become more and more committed to it. They will begin to share their possessions and time more and more, and to guide their behaviour in accordance with the good of the partner and/or of the partnership (Kelley 1979). Such expression of a private pledge may lead in due course to a public pledge and ultimately to marriage.

It will be apparent that this brief sketch does scant justice to the complexity inherent in a close personal relationship. And the course of any relationship, and the extent to which the several psychological processes operate, will depend on the personalities of those involved. For instance, earlier we saw differences in the manner in which authoritarian and non-authoritarian individuals perceive their friends. Indeed 'love' itself has many facets; these are described in box 7.2.

Box 7.2   Types of Love

Defining love has fascinated scholars and philosophers for millennia. The idea that we can experience different types of love was explored in the ancient Greek text the *Symposium*, written by Plato around 399 BCE. Plato made a distinction between feelings of intense physical attraction and those of deep friendship, and this basic idea has been developed by contemporary academics. For example, Hendrick and Hendrick (1986), factor analysing questionnaire data, distinguished six styles of loving:

Eros   Physical; intense emotion; strong commitment
Ludus   Love as a game; little depth of feeling; manipulative; no commitment
Storge   Love as friendship; solid, down-to-earth, with little passion
Pragma   Rational, calculating
Mania   Emotional, irrational, involving uncertainty but intense feelings
Agape   Altruistic, non-demanding

The love relationships of young adults mostly involve mixtures of these elements. With older and married individuals love means something rather different; more comfortable, affectionate and trusting, with a deep sense of friendship (Grote and Frieze 1994), and with a rational apprehension of the needs, virtues and failings of the partner (Tweedie 1979).

Conclusions

An exciting body of research is now yielding a much deeper understanding of relationships than was the case a few decades ago. Systematic research involving description, specification of the psychological processes involved in interpersonal relationships, and delineation of the relevance of each could lead, in the future, to greatly increased knowledge by social psychologists, and to personal fulfilment more widely.

RECOMMENDED READING

Ashmore, R. D. and Del Boca, F. K. (eds) (1986) *The Social Psychology of Female–Male Relationships*. Orlando: Academic Press.
This surveys discussions about gender differences.

Auhagen, A.-E. and von Salisch, M. (eds) (1996) *The Diversity of Human Relationships*. Cambridge: Cambridge University Press.
This multi-authored book discusses a wide range of relationships – not only familial loving and friendly relationships but also neighbours, colleagues etc.

Duck, S. (1997) *Handbook of human relationships*. London: Sage.
This is an important multi-authored book with articles on a wide range of relationship issues.

Hinde, R. A. (1997) *Relationships: A Dialectical Perspective*. Hove: Psychology Press.
This single-authored book attempts to review much of the current literature in a manner which could provide a basis for an ordered body of knowledge about relationships.

8

Interaction in Groups

- Introduction
- What is a group?
- Describing social influence processes in groups
- Explaining social influence in groups
- Conclusions
- Recommended reading

Introduction

In this chapter we shall extend the scope of our study of interaction and relationships by examining some aspects of interaction processes in groups of people, especially the operation of social influence processes in small groups. We shall examine five different sets of influence phenomena and four alternative theories of social influence. But rest assured, we will draw a conclusion about how best to understand social influence in small groups.

What is a group?

The word '*group*' can be used very broadly to cover vast social categories such as 'Americans', 'women' or 'conservatives', intermediate-sized groupings like the members of a university or factory or church congregation, and handfuls of people such as a family, committee or group of friends. That very generous usage of the term can be justified if we accept that a group exists when a set of individuals perceive themselves to be members of the same group, a definition which could apply to each of those examples. But we would hardly expect exactly the same processes to operate in large-scale social categories such as nations or genders as in small, face-to-face groups like families or teams. This chapter will examine interaction processes in small groups, which are extremely common and very influential in the lives of virtually all of us. The study of small group processes is often called group dynamics.

How small is 'small'?

First, in fact, let us briefly ponder: how big is 'small'? In terms of number of members, what is the upper limit of a small group? That is a question that is difficult to answer precisely, but the American sociologist R. F. Bales (1950) offered a helpful rule of thumb. In a small group, 'each member receives some impression or perception of each other member distinct enough so that he (or she) can . . . give some reaction to each of the others as an individual person' (1950, p. 33). Thus, a class of schoolchildren could count as a small group but a lecture hall of university students would not. In practice, the upper limit is about thirty, but we will mostly be considering smaller groups than that.

The lower limit offers a choice between three and two. Are we justified in modifying the old adage to read, 'two's a dyad, three's a small group'? That certainly appeared to be the view of the early German sociologist Georg Simmel (1950), who helpfully pointed out that in marriage 'the decisive difference is between monogamy and bigamy, whereas the third or twentieth wife is relatively unimportant for the marriage structure'. (Presumably the same argument applies to the number of husbands.) Simmel also observed that 'a marriage with one child has a character which is completely different from that of a childless marriage, but it is not significantly different from a marriage with two or more children' (1950, pp. 138–9). To justify his distinction between two-person and larger groupings, Simmel argued that in larger groups, unlike dyads, the removal of one member does not necessarily mean the disappearance of the group, coalitions and subgroups become possible, and complete unity of mood and feeling is very unlikely to exist.

On the other hand, there are some similarities between at least some types of dyads and small groups. Certain dyads, especially married couples and stable partnerships, like many groups, play a part in defining their members' social identities; a couple become 'the Snodgrasses', a pair become 'an item' in the eyes of their friends. Further-more, some dyadic relationships can show the general defining characteristics of a small group, which we are just about to consider.

So, in studying small groups, we will be considering groups of from three to about thirty people, while recognizing that sometimes the study of dyads, as in the previous two chapters, can also be informative. But size is not everything in deciding what is and is not a small group.

Defining characteristics

Every bus queue and doctor's waiting room of patients is not necessarily a group. A small group is likely to have a number of defining characteristics which distinguish it from a collection of people who happen to be in the same physical space. The following six are probably the most commonly invoked defining features of groups:

1   *Self-perception.* The members perceive the group as 'real' and themselves as members of it.
2   *Interaction.* Group members interact with one another. Their behaviour and ideas become mutually influencing and interdependent.

These two basic features themselves generate others:

3   *Shared goals.* Even if the group was established in response to externally imposed purposes or goals, it will have to interpret and perhaps re-interpret those, and it is likely to add shared, self-generated goals.
4   *Internal norms.* Over time, norms internal to the group will arise. The members will act and expect each other to act in standard ways, and members disregarding the norms will lay themselves open to disapproval and the exercise of sanctions by other group members. The concept of 'norm' will be discussed in more detail below.
5   *Roles.* Sets of norms are likely to come to differentiate positions within the group, such as mother, chairperson, organizer, and the group will have developed a set of roles.
6   *Affective relations.* Group members need not all have positive feelings about each other but they are unlikely to be emotionally neutral or indifferent. A distinctive set of feelings is likely to develop.

This set of defining characteristics of small groups has several relevant consequences for us.

The 'reality' of groups   The defining characteristics allow us to argue for the reality of groups. An issue which surfaces from time to time is whether groups are something more than the individuals in them or just the sum of the characteristics and behaviours of the individuals who make them up. I, and many other social psychologists, would argue that shared goals, internal norms, roles and affective relations are emergent properties of the group, not simply the sum of individual characteristics. They emerge through the interaction that results from perception of a shared group identity; they are not carried into the group by its members. Furthermore, groups are likely to be particularly characterized by their emergent properties, such as their distinctive goals and norms, which can persist long after the founding members have left. Committees, youth clubs, and families can sustain purposes, norms and ethos despite marked changes in membership. Thus, groups have a reality which amounts to more than the particular individuals who make them up (cf. Jacobs and Campbell 1961).

Differences amongst different types of groups   The defining characteristics allow us to see readily some systematic differences in the ways in which different types of groups function. Work groups, families and friendship groups all have shared goals, but they are likely to vary in how task-related they are. At one exteme, the primary goals of a committee are likely to relate to achieving tasks external to the committee itself, while, at the other, the only major goal of a set of friends may be the maintenance of the group itself. In families, the role structure may be obvious and marked; for example, father, mother, daughter and son may all be expected to act in rather different fashions; whereas informal roles in groups of friends, such as social organizer and group comedian, may be limited and quite hard for an outsider to detect. Different types of groups appear to end in different ways; work groups tend to be wound up or disbanded in an orderly fashion, friends drift apart and the group collapses, but many families seem to go on forever.

Laboratory groups   These tend to be temporary groups of strangers, often students. They meet for an hour or so to do what an experimenter tells them to do, then go their own ways, never to meet again. Are they really social groups? Do they possess the defining characteristics of small groups? Fraser and Foster (1984) have argued that initially they do not, but that they might be thought of as groups at an early stage of group formation. It is hard to ignore such groups, not only because they have been so popular in social psychology, but also because some of the most thought-provoking lines of research on small groups have been conducted largely with laboratory groups. But since there is some evidence of systematic changes in group functioning over the lifetime of a group (Tuckman 1965; Levine and Moreland 1994), we must be cautious in generalizing from laboratory groups to fully fledged social ones. (See chapter 19 for a discussion of the external validity of, or generalizing from, laboratory experiments.)

Describing social influence processes in groups

The study of social influence processes is a good example of thought-provoking research done mainly in the laboratory. The notion of 'social influence' could of course be seen as virtually synonymous with 'social psychology', since it could apply to much of child rearing, dyadic interaction, attitude acquisition and change, the impact of the media and many other issues. But for social psychologists, the term 'social influence' most commonly refers to changes in views and/or actions of group members as a result of being exposed to the views and/or actions of other group members. Furthermore, the members are usually equals within a group. The study of social influence processes within small groups does not consider marked differences in power or authority, of the kind, for instance, that may distinguish formally appointed leaders from other group members.

Norms

Some influences within a group may be unpatterned or between only two or three members. Let us focus, however, on influence processes operating within a group as a whole, that is, on the emergence, maintenance and change of group norms. At least four points are worth bearing in mind regarding norms:

1   Norms can be thought of as having two, not always closely related, components: a descriptive or behavioural one and a prescriptive or expectational one. In the United Kingdom, unlike much of the rest of the world, we have a norm that we drive on the left-hand side of the road, and fortunately the behaviour of the overwhelming majority of drivers matches the prescription. But we also have a norm that books borrowed from friends and teachers should be returned; how many are I do not know, though sometimes it seems to be very few. Widespread and marked slippage between expectations and behaviours is often a sign of social changes and accompanying anxieties, as with, for example, sexual practices, the permanence of marriages, and drug taking.

2   In small groups, norms may be externally or internally derived. External norms can be thought of as norms which operate on a wider scale and which each member carries into the group setting from outside the group. Many are general cultural prescriptions, about honesty, for example, or consideration for others or not wearing your underwear on top of your outerwear. Internal norms are norms developed by the group members themselves as a result of the group's own functioning. The study of social influence and norms in small groups has overwhelmingly been the study of internal norms, and it is these that we shall be concerned with.

3   Group norms serve a number of important functions for both individual members and for the group:

    (a)   For an individual member, they act as guides to what is expected and acceptable. As such, they can be particularly important and helpful to a new member of a group.

    (b)   For the group, they provide means of coordination and control. A committee with well-established procedures for taking decisions can rattle through an agenda much more rapidly than one where there is little agreement on how they should proceed.

    (c)   For both individuals and group, group norms act as markers of group identity. Some markers, such as distinctive features of dress, may be made obvious to one and all; others may be supposed only to be known to members of the group, such as greeting rituals among freemasons.

4   When members accept the norms of a group they are said to be conforming to the norms. Conformity is often felt to be a bad thing, and later we shall get some insight into when it seems undesirable and when it does not. For the moment, however, we should be prepared to accept the idea of conforming to norms as a neutral description and not as a negative value judgement.

Now we are ready to examine some of the best described phenomena of social influence amongst relative equals, before subsequently considering several attempts to explain social influence.

Norm formation

In 1935, Muzafer Sherif took a standard phenomenon from the study of individual perception, the autokinetic effect, and used it to produce a classic series of demonstrations of how a norm can be formed when none existed before. An individual taking part in one of Sherif's studies sat in a completely darkened room and attempted, over a number of trials, to judge the direction and amount of movement shown by a pinpoint of light. If he was alone, after a few trials he would settle down to a fairly constant estimate of the movement, which for some was an inch or two but for others could be substantially greater. If he was then joined by one or two other participants and they had to announce their judgements in turn, their initially divergent answers would converge over trials and an internal group norm would emerge. If members of dyads and trios, having converged, were then separated and required to respond on their own, they would tend to stick to their previous group norm (Sherif 1935; 1936).

The perceived movement in the autokinetic effect is entirely an illusion! The pinpoint of light is quite stationary and appears to move only because the completely dark room removes all cues regarding the light's position. Sherif found that, if participants knew they were observing an illusion, norm formation did not occur, an issue elaborated on by Alexander, Zucker and Brady (1970). They demonstrated that the effects obtained by Sherif and others were dependent not just on the internal features of the experiment but also on assumptions carried into the laboratory by the particpants. When they had the situation explained to them in advance, participants tested individually did not settle on stable responses and pairs of participants did not converge on common answers. Does social influence, then, only operate when the task is ambiguous or even misleading, as with the autokinetic effect? Apparently not, as Solomon Asch strikingly demonstrated.

Maintaining norms through majority influence

Asch's (1951; 1952) research studies, which have had continuing impact in social psychology and beyond, are outlined overleaf in Box 8.1, which you should read now.

One potentially important consideration which merits more attention than it has received so far is the likelihood of systematic cultural variations in the power of majority influence. A plausible expectation would be that, at least on some issues, members of a society with strong collectivist values, such as China or Japan, would be more ready to accept majority influence than people who live in a society with much stronger individualistic values, such as the USA or Britain. On the basis of a very systematic review of research, Bond and Smith (1996) have in fact found that in studies using the Asch procedure there have been higher levels of conformity in countries whose values have been shown to be more collectivist than in countries with more individualistic values. Before you – probably a reader from a more individualistic culture – jump to the conclusion that that must be a weakness of more collectivist cultures, you should remember that, depending on the context, refusing to conform may not be a sign of intelligent commitment to the truth but rather an indication of unthinking bloodymindedness and lack of consideration for others.

Solomon Asch, though living in what is now seen as a highly individualistic society, was interested in how to reduce conformity rather than how to increase it, an issue which may have been of even greater concern than it would be today to a liberal social

---

Box 8.1   Asch and majority influence

Asch (1951; 1952) devised a task in which a participant had to say which of three comparison lines was most similar in length to a standard line, all four lines being simultaneously presented for inspection. In a control condition in which participants performed the task on their own, they achieved a high degree of accuracy, making errors on less than 1 per cent of the trials; that is, the perceptual judgements were relatively simple and unambiguous. In experimental conditions, participants gave their answers after five or six others had replied. These 'others' were collaborators of the experimenter and on twelve of the eighteen trials they gave unanimous but wrong answers. On those trials, genuine participants on average agreed with the obviously wrong answer just over one third of the time, with about 75 per cent of those participants making at least one error.

Asch (1951; 1952; 1956) conducted a series of studies to explore what led to variations in the frequency of conformity and resistance to conformity. He found, for example, that the size of the majority made a noticeable difference. In his set-up, virtually maximum effects were obtained with a unanimous majority of only three; larger majorities produced little more conformity. Other investigators using other tasks have found that conformity does increase with majorities larger than three, although each additional member of a majority has less effect than the previous addition (Latané 1981). Asch also explored the impact of breaking a unanimous majority by having at least two people out of step. He found that a genuine participant's conformity to the majority was markedly reduced by either having one other person agreeing with the participant or by having one person who disagreed with the majority and with the genuine participant. Such issues were fruitfully elaborated on by Allen (1975). Asch also showed that ambiguity of the task is by no means irrelevant to the amount of conformity, finding that the more ambiguous the materials used, the greater the conformity.

---

scientist in the USA of the immediately post-World War II era, with manifestations of illiberality such as anti-left-wing 'witchhunts' (see Bond and Smith 1996 for some relevant evidence). Asch himself emphasized that two-thirds of the time his participants succeeded in resisting unanimous majority influence. But his studies have usually been seen as demonstrations of the great influence of a majority, and overgeneralizations and unjustified extrapolations have often been made from them. Social influence research has been invoked in support of the likelihood of irresistible group pressures, of the victory of majority thinking over the ideas of a minority, and of continuing conformity to a dominant status quo. If those were the only outcomes of social influence processes, it is hard to see how new ideas could ever become accepted by a group, how individual members could succeed in changing the views of a group, or how a group could become a force for innovation and change. Yet the French social psychologist Serge Moscovici was convinced that those were all important features of influence processes within groups and that they were particularly likely to reflect the influence of minorities within groups.

Plate 8.1 In one of Asch's experiments, a genuine participant, number 6, looks anxious in the light of others' false replies.

Changing norms through minority influence

The initial innovative research by Moscovici and his colleagues on the influence of minorities within groups is summarized in Box 8.2 over the page.

Perhaps the most dramatic subsequent claim regarding minority influence was initiated by an ingenious experiment performed by Moscovici and Personnaz (1980). They wished to show that minority influence not only changes overt behaviour and verbal responses, which could be merely superficial compliance, but also alters underlying beliefs, which has come to be called conversion. They also wished to demonstrate that minority influence is actually more effective than majority influence in producing conversion. To do this, they made use of a well-established feature of our perception of colours, the chromatic after-image. If you stare at a square of a single colour, then quickly focus your eyes on a plain white surface, you are likely to see the complementary or 'opposite' colour to the one you were originally looking at. If the original square was blue then you should see the complementary colour yellow; if the original was green then you should see red. Moscovici and Personnaz reasoned that if minority influence was really changing the way in which members of the majority were seeing the world by modifying their underlying beliefs, then a powerful demonstration of the point would

---

Box 8.2   Moscovici and minority influence

In 1969, Moscovici, Lage and Naffrechoux virtually stood Asch's majority influence procedure on its head. Their six-person groups each consisted of a majority of four genuine participants and a minority of two confederates of the experimenters. The groups were shown a series of blue-coloured chips and each participant had to describe the colour of each chip. Not surprisingly, at first genuine participants almost invariably described them as 'blue'! But the collaborators insisted they were 'green'. By the end of this and other studies, however, some participants were indicating hesitancy and doubt, provided that both collaborators agreed consistently that the chips were 'green'. The size of the effect of minority influence was noticeably smaller than that of Asch's majority influence, but the existence of any significant effect at all was quite thought-provoking, given the lack of subtlety or even plausibility of the minority's position. Moscovici (1976) emphasized the importance of behavioural consistency in producing minority influence; to bring about change, a minority must really stick to its views repeatedly (see also Maass and Clark 1984). Since then our understanding of what is associated with influence by a minority has become more sophisticated. Nemeth, Swedlund and Kanki (1974) and Mugny (1982) have shown that a minority is likely to be more effective if it demonstrates not only consistency in expressing its position but apparent flexibility or reasonableness in doing so. It also appears to be the case that minority influence works more slowly than majority influence. At first there may be little evidence of the minority having much effect, but over time some members of the majority come to show signs of doubt and unease and slowly come to accommodate their views to those of the minority.

---

be to show that not only would some participants agree that blue was green but they would also report that when they then focused on a white surface they saw red not yellow. (And remember, most people do not know about complementary colours and chromatic after-images, unless, of course, they have been reading psychology text-books!) That is what they found. In addition, they found that a change in the complementary colour reported was more likely if a genuine participant was told that 'green' (in response to a blue chip) was the answer of a minority of participants than if told it was the answer of the majority.

The intriguing notion that in such studies some participants were really markedly changing the way they saw the colour chip has come to be doubted for a number of methodological and theoretical reasons (Martin 1994; 1995). Moscovici and Personnaz (1991) themselves have come to believe that an apparently deviant minority answer encourages at least some of a majority to look more closely at and pay more attention to the stimulus or issue, in order 'to see whether the deviant responses might contain a grain of truth' (1991, p. 102). Since the chip used in their study was not a pure blue but a blue with some green hues in it, increased attention would result in taking more note of the greenish elements than would be the case with an initial first impression of 'blue', and this increase in attention might account for the effects of minority influence revealed by the reports on the colour of both the chip itself and the after-image. Their additional claim that the after-image procedure can be used to show that minority influence is more effective than majority influence in bringing about real changes in beliefs has also run into controversy. Doms and van Avermaet (1980) found evidence of conversion following both majority and minority influence. And doubts have been raised as to whether merely telling a participant that a particular response is usually given by a majority or a minority of respondents really is an adequate way of comparing the impact of Asch-like majorities and Moscovici-like minorities (Martin 1995).

Nevertheless, Moscovici's ideas and research have led to productive disagreements about whether the same explanations can be offered for social influence by majorities and by minorities or whether two different types of explanations are necessary, and we shall consider that later. Even more importantly, it must be recognized that the controversies concerning minority influence reflect disagreements about how best to explain such influence, not about whether minority influence exists or not. That is now taken for granted by social psychologists, as is the notion that an understanding of social influence involves a great deal more than explaining conformity to majority pressures. Both Asch and Moscovici created extreme cases of social influence, whereby their groups were prestructured in terms of majorities and minorities, and confederates were 'programmed' to exert influence by telling blatant lies. Complex social influence processes, however, have also been studied in groups without confederates or a predetermined structure and where participants argue about quite complex issues.

Group decision-making and group polarization

The term *group polarization* describes the finding that in laboratory settings small groups commonly come to more extreme consensuses on problems than might have been expected from a knowledge of the initial individual positions of the members of the groups. What usually happens in a group polarization study is that, first of all, five or six participants are independently asked to consider a series of issues or problems and to write down their own personal positions or views. Then they are asked as a group to discuss each item in turn until they arrive at unanimous group decisions. Finally, they are often asked to reconsider each item on their own and write down their current personal answers.

Contrary to common assumptions in lay and management circles that groups tend to be cautious, middle-of-the-road decision-makers, numerous studies have found that, in general, group decisions tend to be more polarized than the average of the initial individual decisions of group members. That is, a consensus becomes more extreme than the average of the individual starting points by moving further in the direction that the individuals, or at least a majority of the individuals, were already inclining towards. In the late 1960s, for example, French *lycée* pupils tended to have moderately favourable attitudes to their president, General de Gaulle, and mildly unfavourable attitudes towards Americans. Small groups of pupils arrived at consensuses that were more favourable towards de Gaulle and more anti-American than the averages of the attitudes of the group members (Moscovici and Zavalloni 1969). Furthermore, when individuals offer post-consensus individual decisions, they retain much, though not all, of the polarization that occurred during group discussion. That is, the average of the final individual decisions is usually more polarized than the average of the initial individual decisions, but not quite as extreme as the group consensus.

Interestingly, what came to be recognized as group polarization had earlier, following a study by Stoner (1961), been misidentified as 'the risky shift', in which groups supposedly took riskier decisions than the average of the individuals who made them up (Kogan and Wallach 1967). It gradually emerged, however, that on some issues groups took more cautious, less risky decisions than the individual average (Stoner 1968; Fraser, Gouge and Billig 1971). Fraser, Gouge and Billig (1971) showed that, in general, shifts to risk or to caution occurred where the average of initial individual decisions was on one side of a neutral or mid-point, and the group decision moved further towards the already preferred pole. This strongly suggested that risky shifts and cautious shifts were cases of the more general group polarization processes demonstrated by Moscovici and his colleagues (Moscovici and Zavalloni 1969; Doise 1969) using topics that had nothing to do with risk-taking. It is now accepted that the so-called 'risky shift' had little or nothing to do with risk. Group polarization has been shown to occur with a wide range of different types of issues and problems (Fraser and Foster 1984; Isenberg 1986) and is held to result from the operation of influence processes generally found in small groups, as we shall subsequently see.

It is not yet clear, however, how readily group polarization occurs outside the laboratory. In the lab, it has been demonstrated not only in numerous ad hoc lab groups taking unfamiliar, hypothetical decisions but also when such groups take decisions with some real consequences, and even with naturalistic, 'real-life', groups taking somewhat unfamiliar decisions. Outside the lab, Walker and Main (1973) compared decisions on civil liberties cases where the hearings had been conducted by single US federal judges or by trios of such judges. They found that more extreme judgements were given by the trios, which might be interpreted as group polarization, if one assumes that the nature of the cases and other features were comparable for the single judges and the trios. It could also be argued that jury decisions are typically examples of group polarization (R. Brown 1986). Individuals' views may initially be rather mixed and indecisive, but in the great majority of cases juries end up with a unanimous or near unanimous decision of one kind or the other. But none of the above – probably not even trios of judges – represent well-established groups taking the types of decisions they normally take according to the procedures they normally use.

The very limited study of such groups has failed to detect group polarization. Semin and Glendon (1972) found that a trio of civil servants, who had first individually evaluated the same jobs and then met to achieve agreement, consistently averaged. Celia Gouge and I studied the decisions of nine trios of university examiners, one clinical team in child psychiatry, and two student union committees taking financial decisions. None of the three types of groups polarized. The examiners and the clinical team averaged; the financial committees became less extreme, that is, they awarded slightly smaller sums of money than the individual members, on average, had been inclined to do (Fraser 1973).

Numerous differences between the decision-making processes of lab groups and well-established committees could be pointed to, such as the practical constraints which limit many committee decisions, and major role differences, frequently obvious in committees but rarely represented in lab groups of equals. But the key difference may lie with the fact that lab groups, being at an early state of group development, will not have developed the shared internal norms possessed by an established decision-making group. It is possible that group polarization is particularly likely to occur prior to a group's developing a set of norms for taking one particular type of decision. Thus, group polarization would appear in lab groups. It could also occur in established groups taking decisions of a novel or one-off kind, or even, perhaps, taking decisions of a familiar kind but following unfamiliar procedures. Furthermore, if group polarization does cease to be apparent in well-established groups, that may be because members take account of group norms in arriving at their own initial views; their group decisions could still be more extreme than the averages of sets of unacquainted individuals.

Groupthink

One distinguished researcher into group processes who was fascinated by really major policy-making groups was Irving Janis (1972; 1982). Using published reports, historical records and the like, he carried out detailed analyses of a number of what he regarded as major policy 'fiascoes', including President Kennedy's invasion of Cuba at the Bay of Pigs in 1961, the defencelessness of Pearl Harbor early in World War II, and prime minister Chamberlain's policy of appeasement in the 1930s. Subsequent episodes which could well have attracted Janis's attention might have included President Nixon's administration and Watergate, prime minister Thatcher's government's decision to introduce the 'poll tax', and the Russian political and military figures responsible for the conduct of their first war in Chechnya. Janis concluded from his analyses that a crucial set of small group processes could be identified as having taken place in each of the groups studied. He called those *groupthink*, which was short for 'a mode of thinking that people engage in when they are deeply involved in a cohesive group, when the members' strivings for unanimity override their motivation to realistically appraise alternative courses of action' (Janis 1972, p. 9). Janis's own studies have received support from analyses of other naturalistic decision-making bodies (e.g. Hart 1990; Hensley and Griffin 1986).

It is very tempting, and up to a point plausible, to regard cases of groupthink as particularly dramatic examples of group polarization. The group decisions usually do appear to be extreme, at least in retrospect when it is clear they did not work, yet presumably all the group members did not start from those positions. But in thinking about how to understand groupthink, we should bear three qualifications in mind.

First, in attributing major political events to a particular pattern of small group processes we are in danger of espousing a psychological, or social psychological, explanation of history and thereby ignoring institutional, political and economic forces which almost certainly played major parts. Second, although descriptive studies

Plate 8.2 Did Margaret Thatcher's Cabinet agree on the poll tax because of groupthink?

of real-world policy-making groups have appeared to support Janis, analytic laboratory studies have been less supportive. In particular, they have failed to find consistent effects associated with variations in cohesiveness amongst groups (e.g. Flowers 1977; Callaway and Esser 1984). Of course, whether what is accepted as cohesion in short-lived lab groups is really similar to cohesiveness in well-established groups of policy-makers can be argued over, but the doubts raised by the laboratory studies have had the beneficial effect of encouraging the formulation of alternative explanations of groupthink and related phenomena (see Hogg 1992; Aldag and Fuller 1993). Third, if we accept that group polarization is at least part of groupthink, we must remind ourselves that so far group polarization itself has been used only as a description of what can happen in small groups. We still have to explain what the processes are that bring about group polarization and the other influence phenomena we have described.

Explaining social influence in groups

There have been numerous attempts to explain the operation of social influence processes in groups, including explanations limited to particular aspects of social influence such as minority influence and group polarization. Let us confine ourselves to examining four sets of ideas which can be applied broadly in helping us understand social influence in groups.

Social comparison processes

Festinger (1950; 1954) argued that individuals are continually concerned to evaluate both their abilities and their opinions. As far as abilities are concerned, physical yardsticks are often available; a runner's improvement, or lack of it, can be assessed by a stopwatch. When such a yardstick is available, we are likely to use it. In the absence of physical yardsticks, we use social ones. We compare ourselves to others, particularly to relevant, similar others, claimed Festinger. As far as our opinions are concerned, in order to validate our views of the world we usually have to compare them to those of others. In doing so, we are particularly likely to be influenced by a social consensus, which can appear to imply a 'correct' way of viewing things. So, group members will be inclined to accept majority views. Indeed, groups and their members will tend to attempt to create and maintain uniformity of views, an argument strikingly illustrated in a classic study by Schachter (1951), who showed how a deviant member of a small group is likely to be ignored and excluded from discussion by other group members.

Festinger's social comparison ideas point to the commonness of social influence and imply a general tendency in groups towards conformity. But perhaps they are too general for our purposes. It is not clear how readily they can handle details of the range of phenomena we examined. For example, people are supposed to prefer physical yardsticks if they are available. Why then, about one-third of the time, did Asch's participants reject them in favour of social ones? If, despite that point, Festinger's ideas are most readily applicable to conformity via majority influence, how will we explain competing influences, in minority influence or group polarization? Perhaps Festinger's ideas set the scene for thinking about social influence processes rather than explain them in detail.

The law of social impact

At the opposite extreme of apparent explicitness about how social influence operates are the ideas of Latané (1981). He proposed that the intensity of social impact, or, if you prefer, the strength of social influence, can be captured by the following simple equation:

$$I = f(sin)$$

which does not assert that influence is some form of sin, but that the intensity of social impact (I) is a function of the combination of the strength (s), the immediacy (i) and the number (n) of the sources of social impact which are operating. 'Strength' refers to the power of each source of influence, which could be derived from the status of the individual or from control of rewards and sanctions or from a variety of other characteristics of a person. Thus, other things being equal, the strength of influence of a high-status communicator will be greater than that of a low-status one (see chapter 13 on changing attitudes by persuasive communication). 'Immediacy' refers to the degree of physical presence of the influencing agent. Any barrier between the source and intended recipient of social influence will reduce the amount of influence. For example, in Milgram's (1974) very famous series of studies on obedience to authority, the degree to which a participant administered electric shocks to another supposed participant was noticeably reduced if the experimenter issued his orders over an intercom from another room instead of from the same room as the person being ordered to give the shocks. 'Number' refers to how many sources of influence are operating. We know, for instance, that majority influence increases with the size of the majority, although each additional member of the majority seems to add a decreasing additional amount of influence. Both of those features are captured by a second, more technical equation of Latané's which attempts to specify to what degree each additional influencer will increase influence (see Latané 1981).

Latané's Law of Social Impact, then, is an explicit, relatively simple formula which claims to be applicable to a wide range of social influence phenomena, including both majority and minority influence. As such it can play a part in integrating our thinking about social influence. There are, however, certain technical difficulties with the formula. The equation which specifies the effect of the number of influencers cannot be automatically applied; part of it has to be calculated afresh for each situation examined. Also, one can question whether simply multiplying the three key terms together is necessarily the optimal way of relating intensity, strength and number of influencers. More importantly, perhaps, it can be argued that by identifying three key variables and relating them in a simple way, the Law of Social Impact appears to describe the operation of social influence rather than explain it. We are left without a clear picture of the processes of influence and why they have their effects. We may also feel that Latané's law is particularly useful as a description of how one individual is influenced by others. It is much more difficult to see how to use it to calculate the overall outcome when there are contrary patterns of influence within a group, as in group polarization. But Latané's work does encourage us to attempt to find one framework which would explain a variety of aspects of social influence in groups rather than resorting to different explanations for each different set of phenomena.

Normative and informational social influence processes

Let us return briefly to groupthink. Janis (1972) drew a strong contrast between a desire for unanimity in a cohesive group and concern for obtaining information from a variety of sources. Such a distinction between being concerned with relations with others and being concerned with task-related information has been drawn, one way or another, by a number of social psychologists (e.g. Jones and Gerard 1967, pp. 309–15). Deutsch and Gerard's (1955) version of that distinction has come to dominate thinking about influence processes in groups, such that it has been dignified with the title of the 'dual-process model' of social influence (see Turner 1991). They differentiated between 'normative social influence' and 'informational social influence', following a series of studies they conducted in order to try to explain what had accounted for conformity in Asch's studies. They defined normative social influence as 'influence to conform with the positive expectations of another' (and many would add 'or to avoid sanctions from another'). They continued, 'positive expectations . . . refer to those expectations whose fulfilment by another leads to or reinforces positive rather than negative feelings, and whose non-fulfilment leads to the opposite, to alienation rather than solidarity'. Informational social influence was defined as 'influence to accept information obtained from another as evidence about reality' (p. 629).

The key to grasping this distinction is to recognize that you can be influenced by others either because you are concerned about your relations with them or because you are concerned with getting from them the best answer to the task or problem you are working on. That is, you are likely to agree with them because you want to be liked or because you want to be right. Unfortunately, the words *normative* and *informational*, which have come to be used to label the distinction, can be more of a hindrance than a help, because both are somewhat misleading. Both processes can lead to the formation of group norms, so in that sense both can be seen as 'normative'. Both involve the transmission of information. The difference lies not with the presence or absence of information but with the nature of the information: is it focused on the interpersonal relations in the situation or on the task that is being tackled? Those, after all, are the two key potential focuses of concern in any interaction, whether in dyads or in groups. Unfortunately, everyone interested in influence in groups soldiers on with the standard unsatisfactory terms, so, reluctantly, we too will conform to the norms, but you can think of 'normative influence' as interpersonally focused influence and 'informational influence' as task-focused influence.

How then does the dual-process model help us understand the various sets of phenomena we examined earlier? Let us begin by thinking about what may be happening in the minds of participants who find themselves in Sherif and Asch situations. With Sherif's autokinetic effect, a participant is in an unfamiliar situation about which she knows very little. She probably has less than complete confidence in her perception of the amount of movement shown by the seemingly unstable light and in her ability to translate her perception into inches. Her feelings towards a fellow participant may well be, 'Your guess is as good as mine!' This other guess, then, would be regarded as conveying some useful information about the task. Thus, the willingness of participants to move towards one another's judgements is understandable in terms of mutual informational social influence processes.

The genuine participant in the Asch situation may well be thinking rather differently. He can see quite clearly that the correct answer is, say, line C but to his surprise and dismay he hears everyone else agree that it is line A. Something strange is happening! He can stick to his own judgement and be the odd man out, and that is what happened on average about two-thirds of the time. But he might feel that he does not want to continue to appear an oddball, with the other participants following the experimenter's instructions to indicate, by means of disapproving exclamations, headshakes and the like, that they regard him as strange when he does disagree. So the simplest thing to do is to say 'A' instead of 'C'. Here the genuine participant is more concerned with his relations with the others than with finding the best answer to the problem and, as a result, is succumbing to normative influence.

Yet it is conceivable that even in the Asch setting informational influence might also be occurring. A baffled participant, in trying to make sense of what was happening, might reckon that it was extremely unlikely that five other people would make the same silly mistake. There must be a sensible explanation. Perhaps his own position in the room was producing a distorted view of the stimuli, or maybe he had missed or forgotten some part of the instructions. In fact, the agreed judgements of five others might be a better guide to the right answer than his own impression. So he would say 'A'. To complete the possibilities, we probably should concede that some concern with getting on with the others in the Sherif situation and appearing sensible in their eyes could have been operating.

In short, both Sherif's studies of norm formation and Asch's research on majority influence can be understood in terms of a combination of informational social influence processes and normative social influence processes, with Sherif's results depending more on informational influence and Asch's more on normative influence. One piece of evidence which can be used to challege this interpretation of Asch's findings is the fact that when Asch subsequently questioned participants as to why they had conformed to the majority, they gave reasons which more often suggested informational influence than normative influence. But, of course, claiming that you agreed with others because you thought they were right is likely to be seen, particularly in a university setting, as much more acceptable and socially desirable than admitting you did it to get in their good books even though you thought they were wrong. Asch's participants may have been tending to rationalize rather than to explain. Furthermore, if Asch's participants had conformed because they thought the others were right, then, presumably, they would have tried to stick to those answers if, later, they were shown the stimuli again in the absence of the others. There is not good evidence that that is a strong effect in Asch situations, although in Sherif settings participants do tend to stick to the group norms if they subsequently perform the task on their own. Those findings do lend support to the suggestion that, with Asch, participants tended to change their overt behaviour, but not their minds, because of normative influence, whereas with Sherif the behaviour changes were more likely to reflect changes of mind as a result of informational influence.

One benefit from recognizing the difference between normative social influence and informational social influence is that it helps us understand our mixed feelings about conforming. Commonly, our first reaction is one of distaste, for 'conformity' can seem to imply a lack of independence and integrity, yet we may also have an uneasy feeling that it is not always blameworthy. Now, however, we can see that when conformity results from informational influence it really is quite acceptable. Indeed, we can see it as a praiseworthy attempt to come to a rational conclusion on the basis of the best infomation available. Thus what we see as distasteful is conformity resulting from normative influence, especially if we are saying things publicly that we do not really believe in order to curry favour or avoid criticism. But even normatively based conformity will be seen by many as perfectly acceptable when it is engaged in for the sake of tact. What is to be gained from insisting that Joe Bloggs was nasty minded and a fool when in the company of his family grieving his recent death? And we should remember that there are still many cultures which place considerably more emphasis on tact and respect for the views of others than some Western ones do.

According to Moscovici (1976; 1980) minority influence is the case *par excellence* of changes of mind and not just of behaviour. Indeed, in attempting to maximize the differences between minority influence and majority influence, he has claimed that whereas the former entails 'conversion' to new ideas the latter only consists of 'compliance' in overt behaviour, and hence the two require quite different explanations. Others, of course, disagree and argue that similarities between the two types of influence justify us in trying to explain both within a common theoretical framework (e.g. Latané and Wolf 1981; Kruglanski and Mackie 1990).

My own sympathies lie with the latter approach. In majority influence, normative processes may often outweigh informational ones, and the reverse is usually very clearly the case in minority influence, but there are good grounds for trying to place both within the same dual-process normative/informational framework. Minority influence as demonstrated in the 'blue–green' and other laboratory studies seems to depend overwhelmingly on informational influence processes which lead at least some members of the majority to wonder, in the light of the unexpected, unfamiliar views of the minority, if there is not a better view of reality than the one they had unthinkingly taken for granted. Moscovici himself has attempted to spell out the processes of intellectual disruption and reconsideration that he believes underlie minority influence. He has labelled his own accounts as a 'genetic model' and as an analysis of 'behavioural style'. They can be seen as quite detailed accounts of what informational influence processes involve in this context. The impact of minority influence is unlikely to depend on the minority's exerting much normative influence, but that is one reason the minority effects are usually rather limited; the informational influence of the minority has to make headway not only against the contrary informational influences emanating from the majority but also against the normative influence of the majority. Notice, however, that the implausibility in these lab studies of the minority being able to exert much normative influence does not mean that minorities in other contexts need lack normative influence, particularly if we introduce the possibility of examining externally acquired and ascribed normative influence. A leader, for instance, can often be thought of as a minority of one who can exert considerable normative influence.

Group polarization occurs fairly consistently on problems on which the overall average of initial decisions is already clearly tending towards one pole rather than the other. That means that the distribution of all the participants' initial views is likely to be skewed; that is, they will tend to be piled up towards the generally favoured end of the scale with a tailing off towards the non-preferred pole. In turn, that means that the majority of the members of a typical group discussing a problem will, to varying degrees, already favour one alternative, with one or two members either being neutral or inclining towards the other extreme. Thus group polarization appears to be a rather messy variant on majority influence. As such, we would expect both normative and informational influences to operate, and there is substantial evidence that they both do. If, for example, participants are not permitted to engage in discussion but are confined to comparing their own positions with those of other members of the group, then some polarization still occurs (e.g. Sanders and Baron 1977; Cotton and Baron 1980), which suggests a form of normative influence. On the other hand, in a series of studies Vinokur and Burnstein (e.g. 1974) demonstrated the major role played in group polarization by 'partially shared relevant arguments', which suggests informational influence. Unfortunately, much of the subsequent theoretical debate attempted to establish which of the two was right. Eventually, Isenberg (1986) concluded that they both were, but in different circumstances. That possibly is justified if we are looking at variants of contrived laboratory studies of group polarization. However, if we imagine real-life groups discussing a problem at some length in order to achieve a consensus, then, as Fraser (1971) argued when first proposing the dual-process model as an explanation of group polarization, the obvious expectation is that both types of influence process would normally be operating simultaneously.

A very reasonable assumption is that the positions argued for and the information transmitted by members of a group will bear some relation to the positions originally held by the members. Thus, in a group which initially is more inclined to go to a Chinese restaurant than a Greek one, with, say, three members favouring the former, one preferring the latter and one indifferent, discussion is likely to be dominated by arguments favouring sweet-and-sour rather than Greek salads. At the same time, it seems unlikely that normative influence would be entirely absent. The enthusiast for Greek food would realize he was out of step. The others might decide to exert normative influence fairly crudely by pressing the still mildly recalcitrant salad-lover to accept the majority view before they all starve. They would urge forcefully, without presenting any fresh arguments; the deviant would screw up his face, shrug and reluctantly agree. Fraser (1971) indicated how an analysis in terms of both normative and informational influences can account for many of the fine details of group polarization research. A number of subsequent studies have shown that in fact both types of influence do operate and that the effects of informational influence are usually greater than those of normative influence (e.g. D. G. Myers, Bach and Schreiber 1974; Isenberg 1986). That is probably a fair reflection of the relative importance of the two types of influence processes in the laboratory situations which have usually been studied.

Finally, you may remember that Janis (1972, p. 9) described groupthink as occurring when people 'are deeply involved in a cohesive group, when the members' strivings... override their motivation to realistically appraise alternative courses of action'. If we accept that groupthink is, at least in part, a form of group polarization and if we accept Janis's description of it as accurate, then it should be fairly obvious to you that we are looking at a style of group polarization that depends very heavily on normative social influence resulting from the concern to maintain group unanimity at all costs. According to Janis, that in turn was often the case because the most readily attainable consensus amongst group members was also the favoured position of a powerful group leader, another source of normative pressure.

So the dual-process model appears to help us understand all five sets of influence phenomena with which we have been concerned. Is that it then? Has social influence in groups been completely explained? Not quite. The normative/informational distinction does have some problems associated with it. In practice, it can be difficult at times to separate them and be confident that it is one or the other rather than a combination of the two that is having an effect. A number of the variables which cause one to vary also cause the other to vary in the same direction; an increase in the size of a majority, for instance, is likely to increase the potential for normative influence and for informational influence. Conceptually, it is at times difficult to distinguish them. Is influence from an expert, for example, normative or informational influence? Another problem highlighted by both Paicheler (1988) and Turner (1991) is the tendency for implicit biases to become associated with the two terms. Normative influence tends to be seen as clearly 'social' and coming from other group members, and especially in Asch's and Janis's work, it can seem irrational and unhealthy. Informational influence as 'evidence about reality' is usually seen as rational and healthy, but because 'information' can come from anywhere it can seem almost asocial. But is not the question of who provides the information likely to be very relevant to whether it proves influential or not? That was an issue, amongst others, taken up by Turner (Turner et al. 1987; Turner 1991) in his critique of the dual-process model and his development of an alternative theory.

Self-categorization theory

Turner pointed out that information is not intrinsically convincing or unconvincing. For it to carry influence it has to be seen as valid. What, then, validates information for an individual? Turner's answer is that it is the information's relationship to a group that is crucial, together with the individual's desire, or lack of it, to be a member of the group. Self-categorization theory is Turner's (Turner et al. 1987) modification of Tajfel's social identity theory (e.g. Tajfel 1974; Tajfel and Turner 1979). Social identity theory was originally developed to explain relations between groups, usually large groups or social categories, and the theory is presented in some detail in chapter 15. Turner modified the theory in an attempt to explain what happens within groups, usually small ones. According to Turner, a key decision for an individual with regard to any particular group is whether or not to categorize oneself as a member of that group. Do the group members seem similar to you? Do you want to be similar to them? If you do perceive – that is, self-categorize – yourself as a group member, then you search for the norms of the group and you attach those norms to yourself. The greater the salience, or importance, of that group identity for you, the greater your acceptance of the group norms.

So far that may seem to you to be something akin to normative influence, as in group-think for example. But Turner argued that those processes also applied to the validation of information. Whether information seems valid or not depends on whether its source can be seen as being part of one of the groups in which you have categorized yourself. For example, how much informational influence would you feel yourself subjected to in a Sherif-type autokinetic experiment if it dawned on you that the other participants were all blind? Or if exactly the same message were delivered to different groups of markedly prejudiced whites by either a black person or a white one, it would not be surprising if it were more persuasive when delivered by the fellow white (Boyanowsky and Allen 1973). So Turner argued that both what had been called normative influence and what had been called informational influence operated in very similar fashions and depended on perceptions of group membership. Indeed, he argued for abandoning the normative/informational distinction in favour of what he called referent informational influence, that is, informational influence which was dependent on the nature of the reference group from which it came. Concern with interpersonal relations and concern with a task were united in this one general type of influence.

Turner's arguments regarding the importance of group membership in social influence are very plausible. It is naive to ignore the nature of the source of information in considering its persuasiveness. The views of an expert may be ignored precisely because she is perceived as having nothing in common with her listeners, whereas arguments of non-experts can carry a great deal of weight because they come from people you know and trust. Nevertheless, it is premature to abandon a distinction which has proved useful on many issues and which did help our understanding of the various facets of social influence in groups. The fact that sometimes it is difficult to draw the distinction readily and clearly does not mean it has no value, and we may have doubts about social influence being invariably dependent on self-categorization. Sometimes the rewards and sanctions of normative influence do seem to be all important, including instances when they are being wielded by people with whom one feels little or no affinity. On other occasions, certain lines of argument and information from opponents may strike you, on reflection, as so much more convincing than those being offered by your nearest and dearest that you find you are convinced despite yourself. An all-encompassing referent informational influence may have thrown the babies out with the bathwater.

The best way in which to understand how social influence operates in small groups may well be to add the importance of group identity to what we learned about normative and informational influence processes. Often those latter two types of influence processes will occur together. Some phenomena, such as conformity when it is compliance, and groupthink, result mainly from normative influences; minority influence depends overwhelmingly on informational influences; in group polarization, both types of influences are typically present. Normally, though, the magnitude of both types of influence will be affected by the salience of the self-categorization or group identity of the participants with regard to the group they are currently participating in. What was the dual-process model should now be recognized as having three major components.

Conclusions

We have seen that a small group is a set of from three to about thirty people who see themselves as a group. As a result, various other defining characteristics will emerge which will mark them out as a group. A major set of activities in any group will be the operation of social influence processes centred on group norms. Norms will be formed. Sometimes they will be maintained, usually through majority influence. Sometimes they will be changed, often through minority influence. In attempting to arrive at a common position through argument and discussion, a group might polarize or resort to group-think. Both Festinger's social comparison theory and Latané's Law of Social Impact do throw some light on how social influence operates. It was concluded, however, that the most illuminating framework is the dual-process analysis in terms of normative and informational social influence processes, particularly if it is supplemented by the idea that both types of influence processes are closely tied to the sense of group identity of the group members. You, of course, are welcome to disagree with that conclusion, particularly if you can see even the outline of a better one!

RECOMMENDED READING

Baron, R. S., Kerr, N. and Miller, N. (1992) *Group Process, Group Decision, Group Action*. Milton Keynes: Open University Press.
This is an American review of a broad range of issues regarding small groups.

Brown, R. J. (2000) *Group Processes*. 2nd edn. Oxford: Blackwell.
This is a British review of a broad range of issues regarding small groups.

Janis, I. (1982) *Groupthink: Psychological Studies of Policy Decisions and Fiascoes*. 2nd edn. Boston: Houghton Mifflin.
You can read this for its political analysis or for its small group analysis or, preferably, for both.

Milgram, S. (1974) *Obedience to Authority*. New York: Harper and Row.
This is not really about small groups and it deals with authority and obedience rather than social influence, but it remains a thought-provoking book about the extreme effects that some people can have on others in certain circumstances.

Paicheler, G. (1988) *The Psychology of Social Influence*. Cambridge: Cambridge University Press.
This is a French account of a range of issues regarding small groups and social influence.

Turner, J. C. (1991) *Social Influence*. Milton Keynes: Open University Press.
This is a sophisticated, detailed analysis of social influence, especially in small groups, but not quite as tough going as Turner et al. (1987).

9

Altruism and Aggression

Introduction

Some of the fascination of social psychology lies in its ability to explain aspects of human behaviour which surprise us. For example, why do people not help others in distress? Part of its radical impact derives from its capacity to challenge what we normally take for granted; for instance, the popular belief that humans inevitably behave violently. In this chapter we shall examine some evidence which helps to explain puzzling behaviour and consider some theories which challenge commonly held ideas.

We will focus mainly on social psychological studies of altruism and aggression. Questions about human nature and whether humans are selfish or selfless have been debated for centuries. One of the very first textbooks in social psychology discussed altruistic motivation (McDougall 1908), but helping behaviour has only been researched in a major and sustained way since the 1960s (Batson 1998). Until recently, the voluminous literature on aggression greatly exceeded that on prosocial behaviour and altruism. For example, aggression was included in the 1928 volume of *Psychological Abstracts*, whereas altruism did not merit this status until 1968.

Problems of definition

There is remarkable diversity in the definitions of altruism and aggression used by social scientists. There is also a conspicuous lack of agreement in the way terms related to altruism are defined.

Prosocial behaviour   The term 'prosocial behaviour' describes a broad range of actions including helping, rescue and altruistic behaviour. Essentially, prosocial behaviour is behaviour that is positively valued by the individual's society as generally beneficial to other people and the ongoing social system. This definition emphasizes that what is considered to be prosocial is a social judgement which depends on time and place. For instance, when a nation is at war, violent acts (normally defined as antisocial behaviour) may be considered by a particular society to be prosocial behaviour (attacking the enemy).

Helping   Helping is 'an action that has the consequences of providing some benefit to or improving the well-being of another person' (Schroeder et al. 1995, p. 16). As you might expect, with hundreds of different studies of diverse kinds of helping, there are conflicting views about both appropriate terminology and research methods. Some of the conceptual difficulties faced by researchers trying to investigate and draw distinctions between helping and altruism will now be described.

There are many subjective aspects of helping. Whether an act is judged helpful may depend on who is doing the judging. The same act may be helpful to one person and unhelpful to another. For example, intervening to prevent a crime may be helpful to the victim but not to the offender. In order to help someone, it is desirable to know what the other person wants. There may be a difference between intentions and consequences. Problems of definitions can arise with behaviour which is intended to help but which does not, and with behaviour which is helpful but which is not intended to be. It is very difficult to establish someone's intentions. As helping is generally considered to be socially desirable behaviour, people may deliberately present a false picture of themselves to an interviewer (Batson 1998). What people say cannot necessarily be relied on as a true reflection of their mental processes (Nisbett and Wilson 1977). People are usually not conscious of all the factors that influence their behaviour; at best, they can offer a more or less plausible explanation for it.

Altruism   One influential researcher, Batson (1998), argues that altruism is a motivational concept. 'Altruism is motivation to increase another person's welfare' (1998,

p. 282). Thus, we should focus on the motivation for the helpful act rather than its consequences for the helper when seeking to distinguish between helping and altruism. For Batson (1991; 1998) the key contrast is between self-serving, egoistically motivated helping which has the primary goal of benefiting oneself (e.g. 'If I help, it will make me feel good and look good to others') and altruism. Altruistic behaviour is conduct intended solely to benefit someone else rather than in order to benefit the helper (e.g. 'I intend to help this person avoid further suffering'). This emphasis on motivation will be discussed later in the chapter when we describe the egoism vs. altruism debate.

Aggression   For contemporary social psychologists (R. A. Baron and Richardson 1994; Geen and Donnerstein 1998), the term 'aggression' is defined by the perpetrator's motive. Similarly, we will define aggression as behaviour intended to harm a victim who is motivated to avoid the infliction of such physical and/or psychological pain. The notion of acts intended to cause psychological hurt includes behaviours which do not necessarily involve physical injury; for example, behaviours such as verbal abuse or spreading malicious rumours about other people. While most psychologists would agree that aggression is intended, they differ in their accounts of the goals of aggressors.

Instrumental aggression   Social psychologists often distinguish between instrumental and hostile aggression. Instrumental aggression occurs when there is an intent to injure, but the aggression is mainly a means towards achieving some other, non-injurious goal, for example to win social approval or to gain money. Robbery normally involves instrumental aggression. For instance, Walsh (1986) concluded from his interviews with convicted robbers that the skill attached to armed robbery relates principally to the ability to control a victim through the threat of violence. The object is to create incapacitating terror. Typical responses were:

> 'Doing proper robbery you go in there to scare people obviously . . . if they're really scared, they never make a move, if they're not scared they are likely to fight.'
>
> 'Main idea is to frighten the hell out of people.'
>
> 'Sometimes they're really frightened . . . almost too happy to hand over the cash.' (1986, p. 93)

Hostile aggression   Hostile aggression occurs when the aggressor's primary intent is to harm the victim. Berkowitz (1993) argues that people are most likely to display hostile aggression when they are emotionally aroused and especially when they are angry. Some sadists, however, have learnt to find aggression pleasurable, even when they are not necessarily angry; for example the serial killer (Levin and Fox 1985; Duclos 1998) and a substantial number of sex offenders (Toch and Adams 1989; Baumeister and Campbell 1999). Such a sadist's incapacity for empathy may be extreme:

> The offender attacks a patient suffering from cerebral palsy, abandons him in freezing weather, and steals his wheelchair. His comment to the victim . . . is, 'Good-bye, sucker.' (Toch and Adams 1989, p. 135)

Both altruistic and aggressive behaviours are complex and shaped by many interrelated factors. It is possible to explain these behaviours from each of three levels of analysis. At the group level, psychologists study biological origins emphasizing genetically determined behaviour patterns shared by a species. They also study cultural groups, such as national and religious ones, and how they influence behaviour. At the individual level, psychologists study how the characteristics of people (such as personality and competence) and certain aspects of situations (e.g. the characteristics of victims who need help or the number of people present in an emergency situation) interact to determine behaviour. At the third and most microscopic level, psychologists are becoming increasingly interested in clarifying more fully the potential interrelationships among affective influences (e.g. anger and empathy) and cognitive processes (e.g. moral reasoning and attributional processes), and the effect of these interactions on altruistic and aggressive behaviour. A complete understanding of the causes of these behaviours will involve all three levels.

As you read this chapter, it would be useful to consider, even in cases where the precipitating factor for a particular act may seem apparent, whether or not there are other important contributing factors which are less obvious. For example, the Los Angeles riots of 1992 were allegedly triggered by a jury verdict which acquitted white policemen of severely beating an unarmed black motorist. But probably there were other contributing factors as well which were less obvious. The severe recession in California in the early 1990s may have led to the social frustration of many black people in Los Angeles. People who during the affluent 1980s had come to expect improved conditions were now experiencing a relatively sharp reversal of their economic fortunes. With this notion of multiple causation in mind, let us turn to a more detailed discussion of human helping and human aggression.

The chapter opens with the altruism vs. egoism debate. We shall then consider helping behaviour mainly from the helper's perspective. A central theme is the powerful influence of situational factors on helping. This is exemplified by reviewing some of the classic work on helping in emergencies, as well as by presenting some of the latest work on sustained long-term helping.

The immediately following discussion on aggression will start by reviewing some major theories. Next, we shall focus on personal and situational factors, especially in close intimate relationships. We shall then emphasize the wider influence of social structures and consider examples of institutional violence. Finally, we examine the ultimate in human destructiveness, the phenomenon of genocide.

Are people genuinely altruistic?

In advanced capitalist societies, like the United Kingdom and the United States, it is commonly assumed that the real motivation for human action is self-interest. This assumption has influenced the approach of psychologists to prosocial motivation.

The majority view: helpers profit from helping

Most theorists who are centrally involved in the current egoism vs. altruism debate originally claimed that helping is exclusively motivated by the prospect of obtaining some benefit for ourselves. Prosocial acts are really selfishness disguised. For example, they might consider that students who give money to the homeless on the streets of London or New York are doing so more to reduce their own personal distress (feelings of discomfort, anxiety and upset) at being faced by a victim than because they genuinely care about the welfare of others.

The arousal–cost–reward model　The majority of social psychologists believe that people are more likely to help if their costs are minimized and their rewards are maximized. For example, the arousal–cost–reward model (Dovidio et al. 1991; Piliavin et al. 1981) proposes that emotional arousal generated by and attributed to a victim's plight is unpleasant and the potential helper is motivated to reduce his or her own personal distress. In so doing, the person is likely to choose to respond in a way that will most rapidly and completely reduce adverse arousal (distress), incurring in the process as few perceived net costs (costs minus rewards) as possible. Usually one efficient way of reducing this arousal is by helping to relieve the other's distress.

The potential helper's perceived costs of helping can be physical (e.g. risk of being hurt or killed) or economic (e.g. money) or psychological (e.g. possible disgusting experiences). There can also be costs of not helping (e.g. self-blame and perceived censure from others). Many different types of rewards are possible. Benefits of helping include praise from one's self, victims and others, and a benefit of not helping could be a continuation of other activities. The relative importance of these considerations may differ from individual to individual. The major problems in testing this kind of theory are that some costs and benefits may be too intangible to measure, and it may be hard to compare the magnitudes of quite different types of rewards and costs.

The negative-state relief model　One of the most contested issues concerns Cialdini and his colleagues' (1973; 1990) negative-state relief explanation for the motivation to help evoked by empathy. (Empathy includes both the cognitive process of taking the perspective of another and the emotional result of experiencing events and emotions in the way that person experiences them.) The negative-state relief model proposes that a selfish form of motivation accounts for empathic helping. It suggests that adults experiencing negative states, particularly guilt and sadness, are motivated to find ways to relieve their negative mood simply in order to make themselves feel better. The reason that adults are more likely to help when they feel bad is because they have learned through socialization that they can reward themselves for helping and so feel better. But acting to obtain the inner affective rewards that are associated with helping is just one possible way to alleviate negative moods; other mood-improving opportunities can also serve this purpose. (In the section below on 'Mood and helpfulness' you will find a related discussion of empirical work.)

The dissenters' view: helping for the sake of helping

Opposing this portrayal of selfishly motivated helpfulness are several psychologists who have devised some ingenious experimental ways of testing the different predictions of alternative theories. Batson and Oleson (1991) tentatively claim to have shown that some, but by no means all, helping is genuine altruism, motivated by the sole purpose of reducing the other's suffering (the empathic-concern hypothesis). In other words, when people feel empathic concern for another (feelings of warmth, tenderness and compassion caused by taking the perspective of someone in need), they will sometimes help even when it is not in their own best interests to do so. Batson (1998) emphasizes that any self-benefits (e.g. social and material rewards) that result from helping a person for whom we feel empathy may be unintended consequences of the helping action. If so, as long as the helper's sole intention is to help another, Batson argues that the act should be considered altruistic.

Tests of the empathic-concern hypothesis   Recent experiments have tested the empathic-concern hypothesis indirectly, that is, they have tested whether an alternative form of selfish motivation can account for the empathy–helping relationship. For instance, it has been shown that at least under some conditions, helping behaviour fostered by empathic concern for a victim cannot be easily dismissed as an attempt to reduce personal distress, avoid punishment such as the feelings of guilt associated with failure to help, minimize personal sadness that often accompanies empathy, or obtain the empathic joy one experiences when observing that another person's needs have been met (Batson and Oleson 1991).

Although the hypothesis has survived some tests of alternative selfish motivation, this still means that other forms of such motivation continue to be possible explanations. Additional research is necessary to test predictions derived directly from the hypothesis, before some opponents (e.g. Cialdini and his colleagues) will concede that genuine human altruism exists. Nevertheless, there is a growing recognition among some leading researchers that considerable empirical support for Batson's position now exists (Piliavin and Charng 1990; Schroeder et al. 1995).

The social context of helping

Why do people not help?

A classic example of failure to help is the murder of Kitty Genovese. In 1964, around 3 a.m., Kitty was knifed to death as thirty-eight of her law-abiding neighbours watched from the safety of their New York apartments. At first, her screams, struggles and the flash of bedroom lights drove the killer away, but he soon returned to stab her again. No one telephoned the police during the attacks, even though it took over 30 minutes to murder her.

This incident generated an explosion of unprecedented empirical activity (E. E. Jones 1998) aimed at answering the question, 'Why don't people help?'

Latané and Darley's decision model   Latané and Darley (1970; 1976) have developed a five-stage decision model of emergency intervention (box 9.1 over the page). It describes several preliminary decisions that an individual must make before offering help. Unless an appropriate choice is made at each point no help will be given. For intervention to occur

Box 9.1 The decision process of bystander intervention and non-intervention

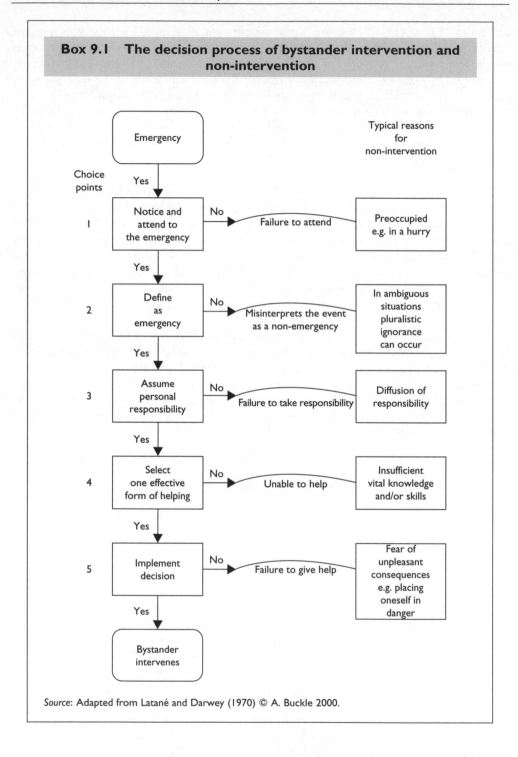

Source: Adapted from Latané and Darwey (1970) © A. Buckle 2000.

Plate 9.1 Some people do not help. Why not?

a potential helper must: (1) notice the emergency; (2) define it as an emergency; (3) take responsibility; (4) decide on a way to help; and (5) implement this action. The researchers suspected that in the Genovese case witnesses made inappropriate choices at points 2 and 3.

The presence of other bystanders

The bystander effect   To test their ideas, Latané and Darley conducted some dramatic experiments on the bystander effect: that is, the tendency of a person to be less likely to help (and slower to respond) when in the presence of others than when alone. This phenomenon is now one of the most reliable findings in social psychology.

What causes the bystander effect? Often explanations based on apathetic, indifferent bystanders and the impersonality of city life are exaggerated. Rather, the causes lie in human errors of social judgement and lack of communication. Latané and Darley argue that the presence of others can affect a bystander's response in three ways. First, the belief that others can intervene may allow an individual to diffuse feelings of responsibility, guilt and blame for failure to help. Second, information provided by the reactions of other witnesses may strongly affect a person's response to an emergency. Third, the behaviour of the other people present can affect the bystander's perception about what behaviour they feel is appropriate, which in turn can influence the bystander's own choice of action.

Diffusion of responsibility   Latané and Darley's (1970) experiments on intervention in emergencies show that people tend to be inhibited from helping in the presence of others because they fail to see themselves as being personally responsible for helping. This process is called diffusion of responsibility. Each person believes that responsibility for helping is spread (diffused) equally among all bystanders. As a result, all are likely to feel less responsible than they would if they were alone.

Focusing responsibility on a specific person should lead to an increase in helpfulness. For example, in a field experiment carried out on a beach in New York City, the experimenter's confederate asked one of the sunbathers, 'Would you watch my things?' He then left the scene, leaving his belongings: a portable radio on a beach blanket. Later, a thief (another confederate) picked up the radio and started to walk away. In this condition, 95 per cent of the sunbathers who had agreed to accept responsibility tried to stop the theft. In the control condition, the first confederate simply asked sunbathers, 'Do you have a light?' He did not ask anyone to take personal responsibility for his belongings. When the thief picked up the radio only 20 per cent of those talked to but not singled out for responsibility intervened (Moriarty 1975).

In some circumstances the competence of a bystander can overcome diffusion of responsibility among multiple bystanders. Registered nurses will give aid to an accident victim even when a bystander is present (Cramer et al. 1988).

Ambiguity and pluralistic ignorance   Social influence processes that affect a bystander's interpretation of the incident are stronger in ambiguous emergencies than in obvious emergencies, where there is less need to depend on the reactions of others to be convinced that there really is an emergency. In the previous chapter we saw how Asch (1952) found that ambiguity in the situation increased the amount of social influence exerted by others. In ambiguous emergencies, pluralistic ignorance can easily occur. This is a state of affairs in which a group of people misinterpret each other's perceptions and then use this misinterpretation as evidence about what must be true. For example, in our culture we are expected to be calm in an emergency. This may result in everyone pretending to be calm in such circumstances, and then falsely concluding from one another's unconcerned behaviour that nothing urgent is happening. Latané and Darley argue that Kitty Genovese was a victim of pluralistic ignorance. The onlookers misread each other's passive behaviour as a sign that other people did not view the situation as an emergency, and so influenced each other to believe that there was no crisis.

Experiments (Shotland and Straw 1976) show that when a man attacks a woman and she attempts to attract help in various ways, she is more likely to be successful when her behaviour reduces the degree of ambiguity in the situation. In one study (Shotland and Stebbins 1980), more subjects exposed to a message of 'Help, rape!' sought help for the victim than did those exposed to other messages which were less clear.

Who helps?

Are certain people more likely to be helpful than others? In this section, we will discuss three areas of research that examine some of the personal characteristics which might affect people's willingness to help. We will first consider the way in which variations in our mood influence our helpfulness. Next, we will examine male–female differences in helping. Finally, we will ask whether there is an altruistic personality.

Mood and helpfulness

Moods are generalized positive or negative feeling states. Many laboratory and field experiments have found that happy people are helpful (Salovey, Mayer and Rosenhan 1991; Forgas 1998a). Indeed, one of the most consistent findings in all psychology is that being in a good mood leads to a greater likelihood of helping. For example, R. A. Baron (1997) predicted that shoppers in a shopping mall would be in a better mood when a pleasing fragrance was present than when it was not, and that this positive effect on emotions would lead to helpful behaviour (giving change for a dollar). As predicted, helping was considerably more likely to occur near a pleasant-smelling shop (bakery or coffee shop) than near a relatively odourless clothing store. Nevertheless, under some specific conditions, being in a positive mood can decrease the likelihood of helping; for instance, whenever potential helpers anticipate that unpleasant consequences might ruin their good mood (Isen 1984). One explanation for the findings that positive feelings motivate helping is that when people are in good moods, they are more likely to recollect and attend to the positive, rewarding aspects of life (such as rewards for helping). They also think less about the costs (Isen et al. 1978).

In contrast, people who are in bad or sad moods focus on their own problems and are much less likely to help someone in need (Bierhoff 1988). But, undoubtedly, one negative mood that is consistently likely to motivate helping is guilt (Tangney 1991). The influence of negative moods on helping is more complex than for positive moods. As we have noted earlier, in discussing the egoism vs. altruism debate and the negative-state relief model, Cialdini and his colleagues (1973; 1990) argue that adults are more likely to help when they feel bad. This is because they have learned that they can reward themselves for helping and so make themselves feel better.

In support of this negative-state relief hypothesis, the researchers found that under-graduates who had been put into a bad mood, because they had either accidentally hurt another person or witnessed another person being hurt, were more likely to offer help by volunteering to make phone calls for a worthy cause than were students who were not experiencing a negative mood. In contrast, when other students who were in bad moods for the same reasons received praise or money preceding the opportunity to volunteer, they did not help more. Thus, according to the negative-state relief model, the basis of their motivation to help appears selfish, depending on the anticipated personal, emotional consequences. Once the students' negative moods were relieved by another mood-improving event, praise or money, they no longer needed the self-rewards that come from helping.

Contrary to these findings and the negative-state relief interpretation, other studies (Schroeder et al. 1988; Dovidio, Allen and Schroeder 1990) suggest that it is at least occasionally possible for individuals to act altruistically. For example, Batson and his colleagues (Batson et al. 1989) led some undergraduates who were experiencing high levels of empathic concern – that is, feelings of sorrow and compassion – to expect that they would soon watch a video programme that would improve their moods. But others were not led to anticipate this mood-improving event. The result was that expecting a mood-enhancing opportunity did not lead those students high in empathic concern to be less helpful. Whether or not their own moods would shortly be lifted, they showed high levels of helpfulness. Apparently, their primary motivation was altruistic; they were concerned to increase another person's welfare.

Overall, the experimental research on the impact of mood on cognition and behaviour is complex and has produced a mixed pattern of findings.

Gender differences

When Maccoby and Jacklin (1974) published their classic book on the psychology of sex differences, methods for summarizing the literature were largely subjective (Eagly 1995). Since that time there has been a welter of findings and of sophisticated quantitative procedures for evaluating them. Distinctions have also been made between gender and sex. Gender is one's socially constructed identity as male or female. It may or may not be identical to one's biological sex characteristics (Woehrle 1999).

But research has found few consistent gender differences in helping. Those that do exist match Western stereotypes of socially desirable behaviour. In high-risk situations, males are more likely to act in chivalrous ways (Eagly and Crowley 1986), while women are more likely to be helpful in long-term caring relationships (Belanksy and Boggiano 1994; A. M. McGuire 1994). More critically, Eagly and Crowley (1986) also found that in private situations, men are no more likely to help than women. Eagly and Crowley's findings are based on a systematic review of the results of studies that had found sex-related differences. Deaux and Lafrance (1998) point out that Eagly and Crowley's use of quantitative meta-analytic procedures (see chapter 19) allowed them not only to assess the size of sex differences but also to examine the moderate differences that are found. They stress the advantages of meta-analytic procedures in enabling us to gain vital insight into the influence of context and the highly flexible nature of gendered behaviours. They persuasively argue that a complete understanding of the subtle influence of gender must take account of the larger social system in which gender is enacted. Culture, social structures, power inequities, social roles and status must all be considered.

It has also been argued by D. M. Buss and Kenrick (1998) that evolutionary psychology provides an alternative perspective for understanding gender. It proposes that acts of helping will be far from randomly distributed across helpers and recipients. For example, Burnstein and his colleagues (1994) investigated certain hypothesized powerfully evolved rules to help kin. They presented American and Japanese subjects with some hypothetical opportunities to help. One prediction tested was that helping females should decrease more steeply with increasing age than does helping males. This prediction is based on the fact that the reproductive value of females decreases more steeply with age than does the reproductive value of males. The prediction was supported in a hypothetical life-or-death situation. In this condition, participants were presented with a scenario in which a house was rapidly burning and they had time enough to rescue only one of three persons. It was stressed that only the person who received help would survive. As predicted, people reported more willingness to help women young enough to bear children than to help women past menopause.

Evolutionary thinking strongly suggests that the greater the genetic similarity between two people (genetic relatives), the more likely it is that one will help the other when such help is needed in order to secure gene survival in the next generation. Evolutionary psychology has usefully suggested some possible circumstances under which natural selection might promote certain forms of genetically based helping. But concerns about human beliefs and intentions are beyond its range. It defines altruism as 'any act that increases the fitness of others while simultaneously decreasing the fitness of the actor' (Fry 1999, p. 17), where fitness (or genetic fitness) is the average number of offspring contributed to the next generation of a population by people with a specific genetic constitution, relative to the contributions of people with other genetic constitutions.

There is substantial evidence of a link between genes and helpfulness. Genetic influences probably operate indirectly by enabling individuals to respond empathically (Hoffman 1990) and/or by giving them the capacity for effective emotional communication (R. Buck and Ginsburg, 1991). A comprehensive review of gender differences in empathy and related emotional responses (Eisenberg et al. 1989) found that different measures of empathy differ in what they tap. There were large differences favouring females for self-report questionnaires but no gender differences in facial and physiological measures. It seems that when people can easily control their responses, they often attempt to present themselves in ways that are consistent with gender stereotypes concerning sympathetic and nurturant behaviour.

In later work (Eisenberg et al. 1992) there is evidence of slight gender differences. Females are slightly more likely than males to show both sympathy and personal distress in reaction to empathy-inducing stimuli. It is unclear whether these slight gender differences are due to different socialization experiences or biological factors. Most probably, they are due to both. Certainly, humans differ considerably in their ability to experience empathy. Women (but not men) who report growing up in homes high in positive emotions and submissive negative emotions were especially likely to report responding emotionally to sympathy-inducing and distressing films.

To summarize, there are sex-related differences in helping. It is likely that genetic differences operate indirectly, for example by giving people the capacity to respond empathically. Although men and women may be genetically predisposed to be helpful and the physical differences between them – men on average being larger and stronger than women – may facilitate some kinds of helping, such differences are unlikely to account solely for sex-related differences in helping. An understanding of the broad social and physical context in which the act of helping occurs seems essential. Any natural propensity to empathize and help is moderated by learning experiences. One consistent finding is that people tend to offer the types of help that are appropriate for their gender roles.

The altruistic personality

Several studies (e.g. Savin-Williams 1987; Oliner and Oliner 1988) show that some prosocial tendencies are stable across situations and long periods of time. There are two approaches which attempt to identify the combination of individual characteristics or traits that make up the prosocial, or even altruistic, personality.

One approach focuses on the relatively enduring characteristics of a small number of exceptional individuals. The aim is to discover what makes these apparent altruists different from ordinary people. For example, several studies (London 1970; Oliner and Oliner 1988) have interviewed people who saved Jews from Nazi extermination, in an attempt to identify characteristics of the altruistic personality. London's (1970) study of Christian rescuers identifies a spirit of adventurousness and a strong identification with a parental model of high moral standards as relevant.

Oliner and Oliner's (1988) study is a fascinating comparison of the stories of 150 rescued survivors, 406 rescuers and 126 non-rescuers of Jews in Nazi Europe. Not surprisingly, the rescuers were higher on social responsibility and more emphathic than non-rescuers. Rescuers also displayed a capacity for 'extensive relationships' (stronger feelings of attachment to and responsibility for others, including non-family and non-friends). Rescuers' motives for their first act of rescue varied. Some (37 per cent) were aroused by empathy for the victim. For example, a Polish woman begged by an escaped concentration camp inmate for shelter recalled: 'He was shivering, poor soul, and I was shivering too, with emotion' (Oliner and Oliner 1988, p. 189). Others (11 per cent) were moved to respond by their concern that fundamental principles, such as justice and care, were being violated. But the majority (52 per cent) felt obliged to act in response to social pressure from members of their social circle.

One methodological problem with this type of study is that the rescuers may have answered the interview questions merely in a socially desirable way that they believed was appropriate to their status as public heroes. Although the rescuers were certainly helpful people, it is not entirely clear whether their motives were altruistic. Batson (1988) argues that primarily selfish motives such as avoiding guilt or maintaining one's positive self-concept remain possibilities. Nevertheless, he accepts that there might well be sources of altruistic motivation other than empathic emotion.

A second approach to studying the altruistic personality focuses on a few traits that may be present in any individual, as discussed in chapter 2. The aim is to study relatively large groups of people in order to discover the personality characteristics that make some individuals consistently more helpful than others. Interestingly, the combination of traits identified by this approach also include the traits identified by Oliner and Oliner (1988). For example, Bierhoff and his colleagues (1991) identified traits which included dispositional empathy, a sense of social responsibility and low egocentrism. Such similar findings suggest that we can be more confident that there really is a prosocial, or altruistic, personality.

Clearly, personal influences on helpfulness can include both personality traits and mood states. But it is important to remember that they do not operate independently of the situation in which the helping occurs.

Encouraging long-term helpfulness

One value of recent work is that researchers have examined constructs derived from laboratory experiments for their generalizability to everyday life. In turn, their new findings also contribute to developing and refining established social psychological theories. The forms of helping that are being explored include some which are unique to relatively recent years. For example, volunteering to assist AIDS patients was unheard of until 1981. Similarly, advances in medicine have created opportunities to help by donating a kidney (Borgida, Conner and Manteufel 1992).

These types of helping also differ from those studied in the early laboratory experiments in that offering help probably results from a planned decision, is of longer duration and may be very costly. In contrast, the earlier studies, such as the classic example of the bystander intervention situation (Latané and Darley 1970), focused on situations in which potential helpers encountered unexpected opportunities to help that required snap decisions and usually entailed no future contact between the helper and the recipient. The assistance was also not particularly costly.

Non-spontaneous helping: researching voluntary work

Several researchers (Clary and Snyder 1991; Clary et al. 1998; Snyder and Cantor 1998) have advocated the study of helping in non-spontaneous situations – situations in which the helpers have time to decide when and how to help. They argue that voluntary work, especially if it involves a regular commitment, is one such area worthy of study from the perspectives of both psychological theory and social policy. They point out that because non-spontaneous helping requires more planning and matching of personal capabilities and interests with the type of helping, it is likely that personality theorists should find dispositional factors exerting a much stronger influence than in spontaneous situations, where their influence has been generally weak. Another reason for choosing non-spontaneous helping situations is that they appear to be a promising area for investigating neglected motivational questions about volunteers' decisions to seek out conducive helping opportunities and to sustain their helpfulness for a long time without obligation.

Helping people with AIDS

One study of sustained and potentially costly helping without obligation is Snyder and Omoto's (1992a; 1992b; 1995) investigation of who volunteers to help people with AIDS (PWAs). This is an example of action research: research carried out with the aim of achieving an understanding of phenomena that leads to practical applications and solutions of social problems. The researchers aimed to find out what the consequences of volunteering are not only for volunteers themselves, but also for the recipients and for society.

They have developed a three-stage model of the volunteer process (antecedents, experiences and consequences) to guide their research. As shown in table 9.1, the first stage focuses on antecedents, that is, 'Who helps and why?' The second stage examines experiences of volunteer–PWA relationships for both parties and the effects on PWAs'

Table 9.1 Stages of the volunteer process

Level of analyses	Antecedents	Experiences	Consequences
Individual volunteer	Personality Demographics Personal history Motivations Psychological functions	Relationship development	Satisfaction Commitment Increased knowledge Attitude change
Broader social Influences	Recruitment of volunteers	Effects on PWAs Treatment process	Social diffusion Public education

Source: Snyder and Omoto (1992b)

general treatment and coping processes. The third stage explores the consequences of volunteering and seeks to identify changes in volunteers' attitudes and behaviour as well as the broader consequences for AIDS voluntary organizations. The researchers are keen to use the volunteers to educate non-volunteers and fight 'AIDS hysteria' (prejudicial attitudes based partly on scant or incorrect information; Herek and Glunt 1988). They hope that by using the AIDS volunteers as credible sources of AIDS-related information they may be able to influence the social diffusion of knowledge about AIDS.

Snyder and Omoto (1992a; 1992b) identified five main types of motives that lead volunteers to do AIDS volunteer work (see figure 9.1). For example, some volunteers were mainly fulfilling needs for knowledge (e.g. 'to learn about how people cope with AIDS') and the expression of personal values (e.g. 'because of my humanitarian obligation to help others'). Paradoxically, though, the volunteers whose motives were apparently most selfish were those who were most likely to continue in such work for a long time. 'Continuing volunteers could be distinguished from quitters not so much by their community concern and humanitarian values, as one might expect, but by their more "selfish" desires to feel good about themselves and to learn about AIDS' (Snyder and Omoto 1992b, p. 232).

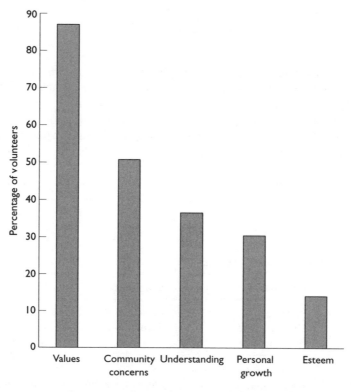

Figure 9.1 Percentages of volunteers choosing each type of reason (Snyder and Omoto 1992b)

Future directions

Snyder and Omoto's work is illustrative of certain promising lines of new developments in research on helpfulness.

Practical applications   A notable aspect of Snyder and Omoto's work is that they have been careful to make explicit its practical implications. This is becoming increasingly common in social science research, and this and related issues are pursued in more detail in chapter 18 on 'Social Psychology and Policy'. Like other studies of voluntary work (e.g. Clary and Snyder 1991; Clary et al. 1998), their findings have implications for recruiting more volunteers. For example, the finding that different people perform the same helpful acts for different reasons suggests that the best way to persuade volunteers to become involved is to highlight various attractive reasons for volunteering. Like many other researchers (e.g. Batson 1998; Penner and Finkelstein 1998; Schroeder et al. 1995), they also observe that the helper may profit from a helpful act. From a practical point of view, perhaps what matters most is the effectiveness of the help rather than the social desirability of the reasons given for helping.

What is most striking about Snyder and Omoto's work is its scope and multi-level analysis. The authors sketch out the connections between an individual's helpfulness and its potential influence on other small groups. They also draw our attention to the possibility of altering certain aspects of societal organization both to facilitate helping and to influence society's collective response to AIDS. These are vast interdisciplinary tasks, but they are ones to which social psychologists can make a central contribution.

The context of personal relationships   Snyder and Omoto (1992a; 1992b; Omoto and Snyder 1995) recognize the importance of the context of personal relationships in understanding differences in helping in different settings. They are investigating the relationships that develop between PWAs and volunteers to determine the form of these relationships and their consequent effects on both parties, bearing in mind that these are relationships which take place against a backdrop of stigma and chronic illness. They emphasize that the propensity to help another is strongly affected by the pre-existing character of the relationship between the helper and the recipient of help. Their work is innovative in that, unlike the standard experiment where the help-demanding event arises during a fleeting encounter between strangers, their work allows for measurements of some of the ways in which both the helper and the recipient are altered by all their encounters. This broader perspective can throw light on the reasons why a person who gives help once may or may not do so again.

Research emphasizing the consequences of providing help for the helper is flourishing. One tradition has examined continuing care to family members suffering illness (e.g. Williamson and Schulz 1995). See also chapter 17 for a consideration of social support in illness. Midlarsky's (1991) field studies on helping by older adults and by siblings of children with disabilities show that helping may alleviate helpers' psychological distress and enhance their well-being. But not all consequences of helping will be positive. Nadler (1987; 1991) points out that the offer to help may be refused. This is especially likely when the realization that they need help is damaging to the recipients' self-esteem (Searcy and Eisenberg 1992; Schneider et al. 1996). Theorists who emphasize the power of reinforcements or rewards might expect that this would make similar offers from the rejected help-offerer less likely in the future.

This focus on the ongoing interdependence between people involved in the helping process is a welcome new trend which raises important basic and applied questions to pursue in future research on helping. Now, let us turn to current ideas about aggression.

Theories of aggression

Aggression has always been a topic of special interest to social psychologists and we now know a great deal about the answers to the question: 'Why and when are people aggressive?' Certainly, popular beliefs in Western societies that humans inevitably behave violently are too pessimistic. Most psychologists and contemporary biologists (Bateson and Martin 1999) agree that human violence is not inevitable. Fears of war and violent crime undermine our sense of security, but victimization surveys show that many public fears of violence are disproportionate to the actual risks. For example, Dowds (1994) showed that fears of street violence markedly exceeded the actual risks, and B. Jones and colleagues (1994) described a survey of 10,000 women in the UK which had found that 20 per cent felt 'very unsafe' when walking out at night, even though less than 1 per cent had in fact been attacked in the last year. To the extent that our actions are based on erroneous beliefs, we are likely to be ineffective in reducing aggression. As you will see, psychological research can offer new insights into the nature of aggression and suggest a more adequate basis for eradicating conditions conducive to both individual and collective violence.

Why do psychologists reject traditional notions (S. Freud 1930; Lorenz 1966) that human aggression arises from innate tendencies – more specifically, that aggression stems from an inborn and spontaneously generated urge that constantly drives the person to attack others? This idea has been discredited for several reasons, including lack of empirical support. In contrast, alternative evidence shows that many different influences can determine whether one person will attack another. Also, as we shall see in this chapter, there are various forms of aggression and it seems inappropriate to identify one common, innate primary source.

Additional evidence of flexibility in aggressive behaviour is provided by the great cross-cultural variation in forms of human aggression (Fry 1999). Cross-cultural evidence also shows that not all human cultures are violent but that a continuum exists ranging from peaceful cultures to violent ones. For example, among the peaceful Semai of Malaysia physical aggression is so rare as to be virtually non-existent (E. Goody 1991), whereas at the other extreme, the Waorani of Ecuador were until recently extremely aggressive, with probably the highest homicide rates of any society (Robarchek and Robarchek 1996).

Further evidence of the importance of sociocultural factors, and the enormous potential for human cultural change, is shown by numerous instances of cultures supplanting violent practices with less violent ones, sometimes with rapid and dramatic results. For example, the Waorani managed to reduce their high homocide rate by more than 90 per cent over a few years. Such instances of behavioural flexibility in aggression conflict with a view that humans are solely or largely genetically programmed for physical aggression. Nevertheless, psychologists do acknowledge that genetic factors may exert some influence on a person's readiness or capacity to engage in violence. There is also increasing interest in how potentially important biological processes may be in influencing the expression of aggression. This will be shown subsequently in the section on 'Gender differences in aggression'.

Now let us review some of the most influential and modern conceptions of aggression. We will begin by considering various theories of instrumental aggression before turning to hostile aggression.

Aggression as coercion

Some psychologists (Tedeschi and Felson 1994) maintain that often the aggressor's primary aim is to influence – that is, coerce – the victim. Tedeschi (1983) emphasizes that it is best to view aggression as coercive power, a form of social influence involving the use of threats or punishments to gain compliance.

Patterson's social learning account   Other exponents of coercion (Patterson 1979; 1986; Patterson et al. 1989) observed aggressive children's behaviour at home. The researchers recorded how the family members continually influenced and were influenced by each other. Apparently, the children displayed a wide variety of coercive behaviours in attempts to control the behaviour of other members of the family. Often, the child's coercion was aimed at ending the target's annoying behaviour. A typical coercive sequence occurred when a young boy was teased by his sister. If the boy retaliated by hitting her in an attempt to stop the annoyance, usually the sister would cease to be annoying. Thus, the boy learnt that coercive behaviour paid; it produced a rewarding outcome. More generally, Patterson has shown how coercive behaviour in families is increased and maintained by its consequences in the form of terminating unpleasant treatment or gaining attention.

Power and dominance

A number of researchers have extended this position, maintaining that aggression may involve more than coercion. They interpret aggressive behaviours as primarily attempts to reassert or establish power and dominance over others.

Domestic violence   A representative American study (Finkelhor et al. 1990), concluded that much physical abuse of wives is caused largely by power differentials. The husband's traditionally accepted dominance, and greater economic and physical power, enabled him to assault the weaker members of his family when they did not comply with his wishes.

Another version of this power analysis is that violence arises not from power differentials but from a struggle for power and dominance. Renzetti's (1992) study of partner

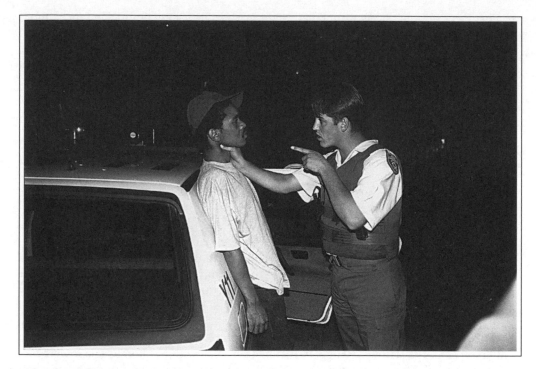

Plate 9.2 A policeman cautions a suspected criminal – coercion or dominance?

abuse in lesbian relationships (lesbian battering) found that batterers tended to be individuals who felt powerless and used violent coercive behaviours as a means to achieve power and dominance over their partners. Batterers were intensely dependent on their victims, and this was a central element in an ongoing struggle in these relationships. As batterers became increasingly dependent, their partners attempted to exercise greater independence. This, in turn, led to the batterer trying to tighten her hold on her partner, often by using violence. In most cases, the batterer finally succeeded in cutting her partner off from friends and all activities that did not include the batterer herself.

L. E. Walker and Meloy (1998) note that a considerable number of batterers follow, harass, watch and frighten their partners or ex-partners, engaging in what functionally can be called stalking. Research on stalking is at an early stage, but it is likely that the primary motivation of some stalkers is to control or dominate their victims. Indeed, Tjaden and Thoennes's (1997) study of stalking in America found that the most commonly perceived motivation for stalking by its victims was control. The relentless harassment associated with stalking can even be carried out across cyberspace. The Internet presents easy opportunities for stalkers to communicate with their victims to threaten implicitly or explicitly or to induce fear (P. E. Mullen, Path and Purcell 2000).

Impression management

Other writers (Felson 1978; Toch 1969) focus on the use of aggression as primarily an attempt by some aggressors to manage a desirable conception of themselves in their own and others' eyes. Toch (1969) concluded from a series of interviews with violent men that violence on their part could result when another person was seen as a threat. Aggression was a means of impression management, which restored one's threatened identity. Many offenders were 'self-image promoters' whose fights were intended to impress the victim and the audience with the belief that the offenders were formidable and fearless.

Box 9.2 over leaf gives Luckenbill's account of homocide, in which impression management and saving face play a central role. Savitz, Kumar and Zahn (1991) estimate that 60 per cent of homicides in their Philadelphia, USA, study matched this analysis.

The cognitive neoassociationist view

One classic theory of aggression, derived from both the psychoanalyst's couch and animal learning experiments, assumed that its main cause was frustration. Berkowitz (1993; 1999) argues that this frustration–aggression relation is just a special case of a more general relation between unpleasant stimulation and aggressive inclinations. His cognitive neoassociationist view is that unpleasant stimuli, such as unpleasantly hot weather, generate negative affect, that is, unpleasant feelings such as that of annoyance. These feelings automatically activate tendencies towards both aggression and flight, as well as physiological reactions and memories related to such experiences by associative networks.

Whether aggressive behaviour or escape follows hinges on several factors, as individuals assess their predicament. This can involve examining their feelings, weighing the appropriate alternative reactions and making efforts to control their annoyance. Berkowitz stresses that this assessment has a secondary rather than a primary causal role and may be short-circuited, especially when infuriated. Thus, he denies that emotion is a consequence of the person's appraisal of the situation. In his view, anger accompanies rather than creates the instigation to aggression. Nevertheless, the conditions which arouse anger remain controversial, although there is an acceptance that anger is neither wholly rational nor entirely non-cognitive. There is a substantial amount of evidence which supports Berkowitz's theory. People who have been exposed to unpleasant stimuli tend to attack appropriate or relevant targets, even when they know their aggression cannot reduce the unwanted stimulation.

Berkowitz (1993) also presents some controversial experimental evidence that certain scenic details, associated by the person with aggression and/or pain and suffering in the past, make it both additionally and automatically more likely that anyone who has already been angered or otherwise made ready to aggress will either display aggression or express it more intensely. These aggressive cues may be objects, such as the person's souvenir gun, or other stimuli, such as violent pictures on television (Jo and Berkowitz 1994). Cues are merely at the scene and remind the person of aggression. In a recent

---

Box 9.2   Luckenbill's Analysis of Homicide

A classic example of impression management, where the aggressor, and in many cases the victim, are primarily concerned about saving face, is Luckenbill's (1977) analysis of the interactions between offender and victim in the time just before the act of homicide. In keeping with the symbolic interactionist (see chapter 2) view of violent encounters as a sequence of moves and countermoves between protagonists, he portrays murder as the outcome of a dynamic interchange between an offender, victim and, in many cases, bystanders, as they continually respond to the actual and anticipated behaviour of others.

The sequence typically begins with the victim offending the antagonist. This opening move may be a belittling remark or some physical act such as flirtation. It can also be a refusal to comply with the other's wishes, which often occurs before child murder.

In stage two, the offended party tries to confirm that his or her interpretation of the other's behaviour is correct. Sometimes this clarification results from consulting onlookers, and sometimes it derives from the history of the relationship, as when a husband who has experienced past fights with his wife now reflects that the present situation is similar. It can also be inferred from the victim's continuation of the behaviour. For example, a child's continued screaming confirms refusal to obey the command to stop.

Stage three involves decisions about how to react. The aggrieved individual may initiate defusing moves, such as excusing the behaviour as a joke. But if such face-saving techniques do not work, or are inappropriate, the person must either retaliate or back down. Retaliation is the path chosen in homicide situations and those in which someone is seriously injured. Usually, this retaliation is verbal, but occasionally it is physical and injury or murder occurs at this stage.

Otherwise a fourth stage is entered and counter-retaliation by the victim takes place. Onlookers may now take sides in the dispute, further escalating the conflict.

At stage five, both parties are unable to back down without showing weakness or losing face. Often, weapons at hand are used and the offender may kill the victim in a single shot, stab or rally of blows. If not, the battle rages, with one or both parties eventually falling.

In the sixth and final stage, the killer may voluntarily wait for the police or be restrained by onlookers or simply flee.

---

commentary, Berkowitz (1999) again emphasizes that this kind of influence is dependent on the meaning that cues like weapons have for the people seeing them. For example, weapons will not have an aggression-facilitating effect if they are only associated with sport and recreation, and are not regarded as having an aggressive meaning as instruments of violence. Direct evidence that weapons prime aggression-relevant cognitions is provided in a study by C. A. Anderson, Anderson and Deuser (1996).

The presence of cues associated with aggression is just one of the many input variables in a general affective aggression model developed by C. A. Anderson and his colleagues

(1996; 1998). The model incorporates new ideas derived from many contemporary research programmes. It proposes that aggression is elicited by many immediate situational and individual difference variables which influence arousal, affect and cognitions. The model is briefly mentioned here because its obvious breadth and complexity illustrate an increasing trend in modern theories of aggression. This trend is to integrate theoretical processes at different levels of analysis, from the physiological to the social, in order to appreciate more fully the processes by which social and environmental variables, such as temperature, operate via internal states to lead to overt aggression.

Assessment of the theories

All theorists emphasize the importance of situational influences on aggression. But they differ in their accounts of how acts of aggression are provoked. Theorists in the behaviourist tradition, like Patterson and Berkowitz, typically stress conditioned responses to stimuli in the surrounding situation, whereas interactionists, such as Felson and Luckenbill, see aggression as an interaction steered mainly by the actual and anticipated behaviour of others.

Several theorists have argued that we cannot make sense of aggressive acts unless we understand their meaning for the participants. Often, these theorists have focused on aggression as a calculated act to gain expected benefits. Such interpretations have highlighted the wide range of participants' reasons for engaging in aggression. In contrast, Berkowitz draws attention to other, relatively neglected, impulsive aspects, providing us with a more complete picture of different kinds of aggression.

Individual differences

Some individuals, for example school bullies, are much more aggressive than others (Farrington 1993; Randall 1997). In this section, we will consider some of the most important individual variables in aggression.

The consistency of aggression Aggressiveness is a relatively stable disposition over time and situations (Loeber and Hay 1997). Prospective longitudinal research, such as Farrington and West's (1990; 1994) study of 411 mainly white, working-class London males, shows stability in highly aggressive patterns of conduct from childhood to adulthood. But it is important to realize that although a majority of those who are violent in adulthood have been identified as aggressive in childhood, only a minority of aggressive children go on to be seriously aggressive. Whether the remainder continue to be aggressive in more subtle ways remains unknown. Similar studies of both sexes (Stattin and Magnusson 1989; Eron et al. 1987) have found the same pattern. These studies also show that unusual aggressiveness is often just one aspect of general antisocial behaviour.

Hostile attributional bias Huesmann (1998) notes that research investigating social cognitive processes in aggressive behaviour has made a major impact on developmental social psychology. For instance, there is evidence that aggressive people search for and perceive fewer social cues than non-aggressive people (Dodge 1986; Crick and Dodge 1994). They are also more likely to interpret actions in a hostile way (Slaby and Guerra 1988; Dodge 1997). For example, aggressive children often misperceive other children's actions: 'They want to take my toys'; 'That child doesn't like me' (Stefanek et al. 1987). In short, hostile attributional bias, which is the tendency to attribute hostile intentions to ambiguous actions by others, is an important trait promoting aggression in both 'normal' and 'abnormal' people. (Attribution making and attributional biases are discussed in more detail in chapter 11.)

Type A behaviour   Have you ever met people whom you could characterize as excessively competitive, often in a hurry, and aggressive? Probably you have. Most probably they are Type A personalities, whose characteristics puts them at risk of stress diseases including heart disease (see chapter 17). Such individuals are especially likely to show hostile aggression when they believe that they are threatened or are under stress (Carver and Glass 1978; Strube et al. 1984; Strube 1989; Bushman and Anderson 1998). Not surprisingly, they are also more likely than Type Bs (their opposite type) to be prone to conflict with others in work settings (R. A. Baron 1989; 1997; Neuman and Baron 1997).

Irritability and rumination   European research (Caprara et al. 1994) has found that certain traits related to aggression, such as irritability and rumination (a tendency to retain or augment feelings of anger over time following provocation), are linked to two of the 'big five' dimensions of personality (Costa and McCrae 1994) discussed in chapter 2. The two are agreeableness and emotional stability. Highly aggressive people are at the disagreeable and unstable ends of these two dimensions.

Gender differences in aggression   Psychological, anthropological and criminological literature suggests that, cross-culturally, males tend to be more frequently and more severely physically aggressive than females (Fry 1999). For example, men tend to commit more homicides than women (M. Wilson and Daly 1985). But there is a lack of consensus about why these patterns exist. There is also some disagreement about the conditions under which males are generally more physically aggressive than females, and the nature of the cognitive and affective processes that mediate this finding.

Maccoby and Jacklin (1974) argued that sex differences strongly reflect biological differences as well as culture. More specifically, they noted that aggression is related to levels of sex hormones. Biological influences on gender differences in aggression are also suggested in recent research on hormone activity. But no simple causal relationship exists between levels of male sex hormones and aggression in human males (Geen 1998b). Nevertheless, levels of hormonal activity may help to determine the type and magnitude of a person's responses to provoking situations. For example, in one self-report study (J. A. Harris et al. 1996) people were asked to report on both their tendencies to behave aggressively and their tendencies to behave prosocially in different situations. In addition, participants' level of testosterone was measured. Sophisticated analysis indicated that, for both men and women, higher incremental levels of testosterone seemed to cause increased tendencies to behave aggressively and decreased tendencies to behave prosocially.

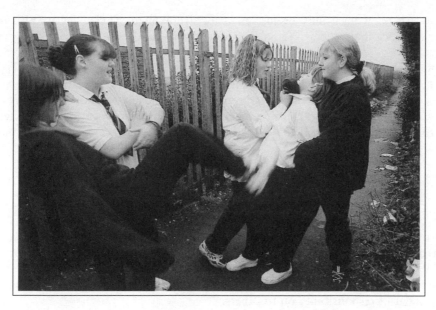

Plate 9.3 It is not only males who can be physically aggressive.

Later reviews (Frodi, Macaulay and Thome 1977; Eagly and Steffen 1986) concluded that differences between men and women in aggression were partly a response to social expectations and beliefs. For example, most studies showed that both sexes are less likely to inflict harm on a woman than on a man (Frodi et al. 1977). Women also consider aggression a more inappropriate response, and experience guilt or anxiety about their own aggressive behaviour. This mix of cognitive and affective processes may lead to the inhibition of aggression. Interestingly, Eagly and Steffen (1986) conclude that men and women's beliefs about the negative consequences of aggression become most divergent under circumstances involving physical aggression. This might explain the typical finding that men are more physically aggressive than women, and why the differences are reduced if more psychological forms are included. For instance, there are many cross-cultural examples of both sexes acting in verbally aggressive ways (Burbank 1987). But the subtleties of usage have still to be explored.

Research in several different countries, including Finland and the United Kingdom, suggest that women may make more frequent use of indirect aggression than men (Osterman et al. 1998). Indirect aggression involves using other people and/or other covert means to enable the aggressor to inflict harm on the victim, perhaps without ever being detected, by, for example, spreading malicious gossip about the victim or arranging for others not to associate with him or her. Indeed, females are more prone to use indirect forms of aggression from age 8 onwards (Osterman et al. 1998; Green, Richardson and Lago 1996).

One review (Bettencourt and Miller 1996) emphasizes that men are especially more likely than women to assault victims who have not provoked them. Also, specific types of provocation lead to different outcomes. Threats to self-esteem have little effect on women's aggression, unlike men's, but under the intense provocation of insults or physical attacks women may be just as aggressive as men. The reviewers also found further evidence that gender differences are reduced when verbal or written aggression are involved.

While biology is implicated in human aggression, we are the only species capable of male–female differences in aggression because of the beliefs we hold. Males and females differ principally in the ways in which they aggress. Men are more physically aggressive than women, but in circumstances of intense provocation this difference tends to become a fine one. Females tend to use indirect aggression more than males.

Institutional violence

So far our discussion has centred on personal violence. But large-scale violence such as war involves institutionalized violence. Institutions can promote violence in a number of ways. We shall focus on three notions which help to explain how people's restraints against aggression can be lowered: deindividuation; dehumanizing the victim; and displacement of responsibility on to others.

Deindividuation and aggression

Both experimental (Zimbardo 1969; Prentice-Dunn and Spivey 1986) and naturalistic studies (Mann 1981; B. Mullen 1986) have shown that deindividuation can lower inhibitions against aggression. Deindividuation is a process whereby normal constraints on behaviour are weakened as persons lose their sense of individuality. This tends to lead to an increase in forms of impulsive and/or deviant behaviour. Deindividuated people are more likely to be aggressive because their attention to their public self (how one wishes others to evaluate one's actions) is reduced. Factors which contribute to deindividuation and subsequent (but not inevitable) aggressive behaviour include anonymity, group unity and activities that arouse and distract. An example of institutionalized deindividuation is military service, which creates anonymity by identical uniforms and emphasizes group immersion and activity, such as drills and hierarchical ranking. This reduced self-awareness makes it less likely that soldiers will act against military discipline and disobey orders.

The Stanford prison experiment   An often-cited study which exposed the predominance of situational factors in promoting institutional violence is the Stanford prison experiment (Haney, Banks and Zimbardo 1973). This bleak study demonstrated that normal college students randomly assigned to adopt the role of guards in a mock prison showed cruelty towards other students randomly assigned as prisoners. The experiment had to be discontinued prematurely because of the escalating brutality of the 'guards' and the increasingly demoralized state of the 'prisoners'. The researchers concluded that the explicit social norms established by them in the experiment, together with the participants' previous knowledge of the roles of prisoners and guards had powerfully shaped the participants' unusual behaviour.

It is important to note that the 'prisoners' pointed out that it was only some 'bad guards' who instigated much of the brutality. Their disproportionate influence can be explained by the phenomenon of pluralistic ignorance. The silence of the 'good guards' about the brutality may have influenced the 'bad guards'' behaviour by fostering the illusion that the 'good guards' found it acceptable.

Aggression and dehumanization

Throughout the study, the deindividuated 'prisoners' were clothed only in smocks and nylon caps, and were allowed no personal belongings; the aim being to weaken their sense of individuality, power and control of the self. The degradation and dehumanization of the 'prisoners' also made it easier for the deindividuated 'guards' to treat them brutally. If victims are stripped of dignity and so made less human, aggressors do not feel empathy for them and are less restrained about inhumane treatment. The effectiveness of dehumanization has been shown in other experiments too. For example, in a typical laboratory experiment on aggression, college men who had learnt to see the victims as 'animals' were much more punitive than other participants who were induced to have a positive attitude to victims (Bandura, Underwood and Froms on 1975). Military discourse is a particularly pervasive way of dehumanizing victims. Terms like 'targets', 'collateral damage' (C. Cohen 1987) and 'ethnic cleansing' are grim examples. The Nazi concentration camps revealed just how horrifyingly effective dehumanization can be in disinhibiting aggression.

Obedience and aggression

The compelling power of authority to produce aggression was shown in a classic series of experiments by Milgram (1974). He demonstrated that a majority of ordinary people were obedient to a legitimate authority figure, the experimenter, who instructed them to deliver what seemed to be dangerous, even potentially lethal, electric shocks to a protesting victim. In fact, the participants were deceived about both the experiment's purpose and the victim's pain. No shocks were actually received, although the victim, an experimental accomplice, gave off signs of mounting distress.

Fortunately, Milgram (1965) found that obedience was substantially reduced in some circumstances; for example, when 'fellow subjects' defied the experimenter and refused to continue in the experiment. But in real life, disobedience can be dangerous. In the armed forces, immediate obedience to instructions is expected and disobedience is punished. Such military socialization increases the likelihood of acts which prior to military service might have appeared unthinkably aggressive. The process can be facilitated by the gradual increase of aggressive behaviour, lack of direct contact with the victim, and the approval of superiors for aggression in response to orders.

At the Nuremberg trials, the Nazi defendants pleaded that they were only acting in obedience to orders. Later, the Nuremberg Accords established that subordinates cannot be excused for inhumane actions, even when the orders come from the highest authorities. But as Milgram has shown, it is all too easy to manipulate situational

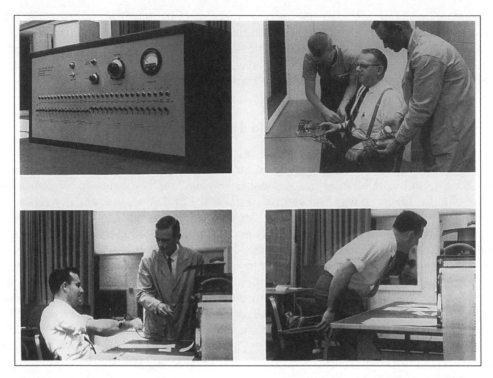

Plate 9.4 (a) The shock generator used in the experiments. Fifteen of the thirty switches have already been depresssed. **(b)** The learner is strapped into the chair and the electrodes are attached to his wrist. Electrode paste is applied by the experimenter. The learner provides answers by depressing switches that light up numbers on an answer box. **(c)** A participant receives a sample shock from the generator. **(d)** A participant breaks off the experiment.

factors to produce a behaviour which in specific circumstances is free of the moral restraints which ordinarily inhibit aggression.

These controversial studies raise important methodological and ethical issues (Darley 1999). Perhaps the most telling criticism is that the experimenters did not establish that the participants had no doubt that their actions would seriously harm their victims. Regarding ethics, researchers defended themselves on the grounds of their contribution to understanding behaviour. For example, Zimbardo (1980) attempted to justify the prison experiment by pointing out that the findings could not have been established in another way, and that they had a substantial impact on prison organization in America. Like other social psychologists discussed in this chapter, he was keen for psychologists to be in the vanguard of campaigns to bring the findings of applied psychology into public debates, with the aim of bringing about social reform.

Genocide

How can people deliberately engage in attempts to exterminate, in whole or in part, other racial, ethnic, religious or political groups? This is a question which Staub, a survivor of the Holocaust, seeks to answer in his account of the psychological and cultural origins of genocide. He uses a multi-level analysis: the psychology of individuals, of groups of perpetrators and of the whole society. The theory is illustrated by four case studies, including one of the Holocaust.

Hard times

Staub (1989; 1996; 1999) sees the origin of genocide in severe, persistent difficult life conditions such as depression, war, and its aftermath of national humiliation, widespread political violence and social disorganization. These conditions, when combined with certain sociocultural characteristics involving strong respect for hierarchical authorities, tendencies to devalue outgroups like Jews, and a history of aggressiveness as a way to deal with conflict, lead to a willingness to defend the self physically and symbolically and to harm others. Not only do all these preconditions make people more likely to denigrate, dehumanize and brutalize other groups, they also make perpetrators more likely to follow an authoritarian leader, to idealize their group over others, and to justify their cruelty and killing.

The continuum of destruction

Staub emphasizes that the whole process is one of escalation but not inevitability. Gradually, less harmful acts against the victims change the perpetrators and the norms of the whole society and make more harmful acts increasingly probable and acceptable. The perpetrators progress along a psychological continuum of destruction, which may evolve into genocide. The behaviour of internal bystanders – that is, members of the society who are not directly involved – and external bystanders – that is other nations – can either inhibit or facilitate this evolution.

Evaluation of Staub's analysis

Staub's analysis is an example of societal psychology (see Himmelweit and Gaskell 1990) that identifies a multiplicity of factors and their interrelation, which form a pattern of intertwined 'roots of evil' that predispose society to genocide. The strength of his theory lies in both its breadth and its dynamism. He applies many empirically established concepts to explain the changing beliefs and behaviour of both perpetrators and bystanders, such as obedience to authority, conformity to role expectations, diffusion of responsibility and pluralistic ignorance, to name but a few. Most importantly, he notes how a society's values both influence and are influenced by the changing behaviour of its members. The successive levels of social complexity that he identifies – that is, individuals, groups and the whole sociocultural structure – are viewed as processes in continuous creation. Another strength of his account is the importance he attaches to the potential power of bystanders in deterring genocide.

Major criticisms of Staub are that he has overgeneralized the preconditions. Difficult times, given the variety of his indicators, have been prevalent in many non-genocidal societies. What is needed is a more precise account of how actual life conditions, at particular times, create the preconditions for genocide. Another limitation of his analysis is that it does not cover the kinds of genocides that have occurred against indigenous peoples in democratic states such as Australia and the USA, viz. genocides where the perpetrators were not necessarily enduring particularly hard times, but could have been doing better had the victims not been there. Nevertheless, the scope of his theory is impressive and the criticisms really point to the need for interdisciplinary studies of genocide.

Summary

We have seen that whether or not a person or an institution will be aggressive depends on a large array of individual and situational factors. It would be difficult, but not theoretically impossible, to eradicate both individual and collective forms of violence altogether. First, it is easy to learn that aggression can be rewarding and, second, although we can change the way unpleasant experiences influence our actions if we stop to think, it is sometimes difficult to avoid acting impulsively. But we live in a time of possibilities. Recent treatment programmes designed to foster new ways of behaving in individuals have had some success in reducing anger, hostile attitudes and aggression as well as increasing alternative prosocial skills (Feshbach 1989; Goldstein 1989; Hollin and Howells 1997; Gross and McIlveen 1998). Similarly, the focus of world attention has encouraged some successful demands for democracy in authoritarian and totalitarian states, despite its relative impotence in quickly stopping warfare in Bosnia, Kosovo and elsewhere in recent years. In order to deter both individual and collective violence, the conditions for doing evil need to be understood better. Social psychology has a vital role to play in explicating these conditions. More optimistically, as we have seen, it is also already contributing to an analysis of the conditions for doing good.

Future research is likely to continue the current trend of focusing on controversial social issues linked to helping and harming behaviour as well as investigating particular kinds of such behaviours. This recognition of diversity and subtypes of behaviour is likely to result in less overgeneralization from original concepts. Similarly, the trend towards exploring the potential interrelationships among affective and cognitive influences is likely to grow, together with a sensitivity to the extent to which these processes are qualitatively distinct.

All these tasks are going to necessitate more multidisciplinary and multi-method research. The trend is towards more naturalistic research methodologies exploring the real lives and natural habits of humans and other animals. But there is still a pressing need for prospective longitudinal studies of altruistic behaviour similar to those which have already been conducted on aggression. Finally, all this research activity will require an open-mindedness on the part of both researchers and students of psychology, so that they are receptive to new ideas and carefully evaluate alternative points of view.

Conclusions

Both altruism and aggression are complex and multiply determined. They have been defined in many different ways, which reflect differences in underlying theories as well as problems of measurement. Theorists have attempted to explain these behaviours at many different levels, which are not exclusive but intertwined. Helpful and aggressive behaviours have much in common at the biological and cultural level, but at the most microscopic level of the interrelationships among cognitive and affective influences they tend to be far more distinct. Since the early 1990s, there has been increasing interest in clarifying these interrelationships. We now know a great deal about the influences of transitory states and situational factors on helping and harming behaviours.

Early empirical research on helping behaviour considered why and when people help spontaneously. Recently, attention has been focused on longer-term motivations for and consequences of helping. Some of the most consistent findings are that happy people are helpful and that aversive events heighten people's hostility. Prosocial behaviour and aggression are especially likely to occur in those rewarded for performing these behaviours or those who have learned such behaviours from role models. Some self-report evidence suggests that there is a prosocial personality.

There is substantial longitudinal evidence that aggression is a relatively stable disposition over time and situations. But, contrary to popular beliefs, violence is not inevitable. Many aggressive actions are largely a reaction to external events. People are not innately driven to violence because of pent-up urges inside them. The nature of aggression changes as we shift from individual aggression through group aggression to war and genocide. The role of intergroup relations themselves, and the perpetuation of outgroup stereotypes, are important factors maintaining group conflict and the institution of war. Cross-cultural studies show that violence is not inevitable. It is possible for at least some groups to live peacefully.

RECOMMENDED READING

Batson, C. D. (1998) Altruism and prosocial behaviour. In D. T. Gilbert, S. T. Fiske and G. Lindzey (eds), *The Handbook of Social Psychology, Vol. 2*. 4th edn. New York: McGraw-Hill.
This is a scholarly, state-of-the-art review of altruism and prosocial behaviour by one of the most eminent researchers in the field

Berkowitz, L. (2000) *Causes and Consequences of Feelings*. Cambridge: Cambridge University Press

One of the most distinguished social psychologists in the world presents a lively summary of what is known about the causes and consequences of good and bad feelings. The book contains a penetrating discussion of feeling effects on aggression and helpfulness.

Geen, R. G. and Donnerstein, E. (eds) (1998). *Human Aggression: Theories, Research and Implications for Social Policy*. San Diego: Academic Press.
Well-known researchers provide a comprehensive and rigorous survey of theory and methodology in the study of human aggression.

Jack, D. C. (1999) *Behind the Mask: Destruction and Creativity in Women's Aggression*. Cambridge, MA: Harvard University Press.
This exploratory interview study illuminates the many facets of women's aggression. The author indicates why the net effect of aggressive behaviour can often be constructive rather than destructive.

Miller, A. G. (guest ed.) (1999) *Special Issue: Perspectives on Evil and Violence, Personality and Social Psychology Review*, 3(3), 176–275.
This special issue is an accessible and critical review of a variety of conceptual and empirical perspectives on sustained harm-doing. Contributors include internationally renowned experts such as Baumeister, Berkowitz and Staub.

Schroeder, D. A., Penner, L. A., Dovidio, J. F. and Piliavin, J. A. (1995) *The Social Psychology of Helping and Altruism: Problems and Puzzles*. New York: McGraw-Hill.
Finally, this is a very readable and authoritative overview of this vast research literature. The book raises many fascinating questions for future research.

PART III

Understanding the Social World

10

The Development of Moral Reasoning

Introduction

Morality is an important aspect of our relations with others – in fact, some would argue it is the most important aspect. Morals are systems of social rules that shape our interactions and guide our behaviour. Our sense of right and wrong can influence our feelings of altruism (chapter 9) or prejudice (chapter 15), can affect our daily lives and relationships with friends or at work, and can even, although perhaps not often enough, have a bearing on social policy (chapter 18). One important social question is how we come to behave in moral or immoral ways. Obviously, part of this question depends on how attitudes or reasoning connect with moral behaviour and action (see chapter 12 for a more detailed discussion of this general difficulty in social psychology). But another part, which is at least as important, concerns how we come to understand or reason about these rules themselves. It is this latter part, the development of moral reasoning, that forms the focus of this chapter.

Learning morality from others

The child's moral development involves a gradual immersion in the world of adults' rules and principles. But quite how do we conceptualize this process? For example, is moral development a matter of straightforward socialization – the simple learning of an adult morality? Social learning theorists argue that it is, and that it is the mechanics of that learning which need to be understood by theorists.

Social learning theories

Aronfeed (1968) suggested that children gain an understanding of morality through a form of social conditioning. When children behave in a particular way they may receive feedback on their actions from others. Parents or caregivers occupy a very important role for the child's development, since support or encouragement for any particular form of behaviour will increase the chances of a child repeating that behaviour later. Conversely, criticism or punishment will decrease the chances of that behaviour being repeated since it entails negative consequences for the child.

According to this social conditioning model it is through adults' reinforcement of certain forms of behaviour that the child comes to behave in a way which is deemed morally appropriate or inappropriate. For Aronfeed, moral thought is therefore the consequence of a process of association; the child associates his or her behaviour and the feedback to that behaviour with the thoughts that preceded it.

A further social learning approach has been suggested by Bandura, who argued that children's moral development comes about through the more indirect process of observational learning or vicarious conditioning. Bandura and McDonald (1963) found that children who observed an adult 'model' making moral judgements tended to give more mature responses themselves in a subsequent post-test. On the other hand children who had seen no adult model, but whose own responses had been reinforced whenever they reflected more mature forms of reasoning, showed no such improvement. Bandura concluded that an important mechanism for the child's moral development is the mimicking or imitation of adult behaviour.

According to Bandura (1977; 1986) the child observes, internalizes and then replicates the moral judgement and behaviour of adults. As these observations increase in both depth and scope the child comes to grasp some of the complexities, and perhaps vagaries, of more mature moral thought. Aronfeed's and Bandura's theories share a sense in which children absorb morality from those around them. Yet whilst Aronfeed sees the adult as the direct conditioning agent in the child's moral development, Bandura views development of the child's judgement as rather more detached from immediate features of the relationship between adult and child.

Although social learning accounts appear empirically robust, the theoretical simplicity of the approach has its difficulties. For a start, there is an abiding concern that social learning theories tend to relegate children's lived experiences to a behaviouristic plane, where the personal significance of social relationships is of little importance. There is also an ethical worry for Aronfeed's social conditioning model. If punishment is a key to preventing immoral behaviour and thought, then it would seem that the greater the degree of punishment the more effective the moral 'education'. This, in turn, leads to a rather odd conception of morality, since the rightness or wrongness of an action is determined by the strength, perhaps physical, of reactions to it (Patterson 1982).

A further difficulty for Aronfeed's theory is that children may learn to exhibit 'moral' behaviour only in the presence of those who are able to enforce punishments. Away from the watchful gaze of an adult, the child might feel no constraints on producing behaviour that would not be sanctioned if an adult were present (Walters and Grusec 1977). Indeed, children can be well aware of the differences between interaction with peers and with adults and can act differently in each separate context (Corsaro 1990).

Aspects of Bandura's approach also need clarification. If moral development is a product of the child's modelling of others' judgements, it needs to be established whether all 'models' are equally effective in promoting development. For example, is one parent more influential than the other as a model for the child's behaviour and judgement?

Lastly, it is certainly debatable whether all children grow up simply reproducing the moral rules and norms of adults. In this sense, it would appear that the notion of the 'socializing agent' requires rather more elaboration than either Aronfeed or Bandura give it.

Parents and moral development

Perhaps the most prominent influence a child receives, certainly in the early years, is that of the parents or caregivers. Parents not only provide the child with protection, support and basic material needs, but in most cases also act as the principal figures who enforce moral and other rules.

Sigmund Freud (1930) proposed that our sense of moral duty arises from our relationships with our parents. The importance of this relationship is a result of the parents' role as principal caregivers and as sources of comfort, support and security – or, as Freud puts it, as love objects. However, when a child does something that his or her parents disapprove of, the child is punished. This punishment leads to feelings of frustration and anger in the child and parents become objects of hate.

In the early years punishment acts as an external form of control exercised by parents. Over time this external form of control becomes internalized. However, the child does not usually enforce this internal form of control by means of self-punishment. Rather, when a child does something wrong he or she feels guilt, which acts as the principal mechanism for internalized self-control. To avoid guilt, or self-punishment, the child is motivated to act morally and in accordance with the mother's or father's moral standards. Identification with the punitive parent therefore leads the child to adopt the moral standards and principles of that parent – the parent's superego. Thus moral rules move from external to internal forms of control, and a child adopts the moral standards of his or her parents.

The psychoanalytic approach (see chapter 2), like social learning theories, places an emphasis on punishment as the principal motivator of moral development. Freud, however, presents us with a more sophisticated account of the means by which external processes of control become translated into internal processes of self-regulation. Also, by introducing the notion of identification, Freud's theory allows us to conceptualize how different individuals may have a qualitatively different influence upon the child's development.

However, Freud's theory has, generally, been criticized not only for the lack of empirical evidence but also because many aspects of the theory are difficult to test. For example, Freud claims that external control leads to feelings of guilt which, in turn, motivate the child to act morally. Yet it would seem difficult to distinguish between a child who refrains from certain behaviour because of guilt and one who does so, to adopt a social conditioning theory explanation, through fear (see, for example, Kochanska 1993). Thus, whilst evidence has generally supported the proposition that children reflect the moral values of their parents (e.g. L. J. Walker and Taylor 1991), it is difficult to determine whether Freud's account, or other socialization accounts, are the best for explaining this process.

Hoffman (1989) has described how different forms of parenting might influence a child's moral reasoning. Hoffman and Saltzstein (1967) identified three different styles of parenting through interviews with parents, and then observed how others rated the behaviour of these parents' children in real-life situations. The first parenting style, love-oriented discipline, involves the parent withholding affection or approval when a child behaves badly. According to Freudian theory this would be an effective form of moral education. However, the children of parents who used predominantly love-oriented forms of discipline did not show benefits over and above other children in their rate of moral development. Parents who employed predominantly power-assertive disciplinary techniques used a variety of punitive measures to enforce their rules, or simply gave their position of power or authority over the child as a justification for preventing the child from acting in a certain way. Results indicated that a consequence of this parenting technique is that children tended to respond only to the threat of sanction. Thus, away from adult supervision children showed little sense of how to behave appropriately. With the third parenting style, inductive discipline, parents explained to their children the reasons behind a particular moral prohibition. Pointing out the consequences of certain forms of behaviour and the reasons for not acting in a particular way was the most effective in ensuring children developed a moral sense for themselves.

Hoffman's work suggests that moral development is promoted when children are given rationales for their moral behaviour and judgments. Similar work by Baumrind (e.g. Baumrind 1991) has also indicated that combining parental authority with justifications for the rules that parents enforce is the most effective form of helping children to attain social competence and avoid deviance up to adolescence (Smetana 1995).

There are, however, problems in establishing a link between parenting styles and development. The relationship between a child and his or her parent is something that researchers can only ever hope to capture briefly, or second-hand from either self-reports or reports from others involved with the child and parents. Such reports may be subject to some inaccuracies, if not all participants in the research judge by the same criteria when reporting behaviour, or fail to present themselves to researchers in an entirely candid fashion. Moreover, the work of Baumrind and Hoffman provides evidence of only a correlation between parenting styles and children's reasoning or behaviour. For example, it may be that authoritative or inductive disciplinary techniques are more prevalent amongst parents from middle-class backgrounds, and so there is at least a possibility that different, overarching social factors might also have a causal role in the positive outcomes associated with inductive or authoritative parenting styles.

Society and morality

Children's parents have an important influence upon their moral development. Yet an emphasis upon parents and other adults as the principal socializers of a child runs the risk of neglecting the role of the wider social context in a child's development. The eminent sociologist Emile Durkheim suggested that a sense of moral duty arises from a feeling of connectedness to society: 'we are moral beings only to the extent that we are social beings' (Durkheim 1961/1925, p. 64). What binds individuals together is the recognition that 'society' is something more than the sum of the individuals who make it up. It is the source of all moral knowledge and the authority by which morality can be held to be legitimate (Durkheim 1974/1906).

For Durkheim, morals possess power because they regulate behaviour between people as a sort of social bond or contract. Mature moral reasoning therefore reflects an awareness of the importance of maintaining our social relationships. In spite of the sociological basis of Durkheim's theory, the consequences of his theory for moral education are rather similar to traditional social learning accounts. In order to understand morality, Durkheim argued, the child must come to understand the rules which preserve social relations. Moral development can therefore only come about through the imposition of these rules by the adult upon the child.

Moral education, according to Durkheim (1961/1925), requires that the child form a 'spirit of discipline' in respect to his or her moral thought and conduct. The spirit of discipline is principally instilled when the child goes to school. At home, family feelings of altruism and solidarity can obscure the need for hard and fast rules. At school, on the other hand, the child has his or her first experience of a more formal, social institution which, in turn, demands a more rigorous adherence to collective rules. The teacher possesses social authority and acts as an intermediary between society and the child.

A strength of Durkheim's theory is that it allows a conceptualization of morality as a social process: moral judgments possess a power because they locate an individual in a society or social group which shares certain practices and rules. However, an at least tacit implication of Durkheim's theory is that to act morally is nothing more than to conform to the rules of society. Thus there is little room for any meaningful development in social morality beyond the status quo.

A second difficulty lies in Durkheim's claim that all morality is imposed upon the child by the group or, in the case of the teacher, by a representative of society. It is important to remember that this imposition of morality does not function in quite the same way as it does for social learning theories. Durkheim's conception of 'society' allows us to invoke an idea of morality as something more than, in its strictest sense, self-interest. Yet how far can the notion of an imposed morality go? What is right might not always correspond with what the majority, or authorities, in society impose.

Piaget's theory

Jean Piaget (1896–1980), of the University of Geneva, studied the cognitive development of children for most of his lifetime, and his ideas have had important influences on developmental and social psychology. Piaget complained that Durkheim too readily equated adult morality with *the* morality and neglected the ways in which children develop for themselves a sense in which moral rules are legitimate. In his book *The Moral Judgement of the Child* (1932), Piaget outlined his own theory of moral development.

Plate 10.1 Jean Piaget

The rules of the game

Piaget's investigations began by exploring how children from Geneva and Neuchâtel in Switzerland understood the rules of a game. Amongst the children the boys' preferred game was 'marbles' and the girls' preferred game was 'hopscotch'. The rules of these games, argued Piaget, were handed down from one generation of children to the next, a little like the ways in which moral standards are handed down from adults to children. Piaget employed a structured, clinical interview to gauge the underlying form of a child's thought.

Piaget stated that children's reasoning about rules could be summarized in three stages, through which the child's thinking progressed. For the very young child up until around 3 years, motor rules allow the child an understanding of the concept of regularity. The notion of regularity can come about either through the rituals imposed by parents (e.g. going to bed or eating at a certain time and place), or through the habits that the child develops for itself by manipulating the marbles.

A sense of obligation begins when the child starts to appreciate that rules are coercive. Of course, in one sense, the rituals imposed upon the child by parents in the early years are also coercive. But what distinguishes the second stage is that the child can begin to appreciate the social nature of a rule. In fact, Piaget denies that coercive rules are properly 'social' in nature. Only the rational rules of the third stage, based on mutual respect, show fully socialized thought. With this unilateral respect rules are sacred and cannot be changed; they possess their power precisely because they are seen as things which are imposed upon the child from without. Coercive rules are similar in origin and function to the rules of society that Durkheim envisaged, since both the rule and the reasons for following it come from an authority figure.

Amongst the older children, from roughly 10 years, Piaget noted that rules were still seen as binding because they allowed children to play with one another in a meaningful and regulated way. However, changing the rule to make a new game or improved version of the game was acceptable so long as everyone else playing appreciated and agreed with the change. Piaget claimed that this more mature understanding reflected an awareness of rational rules. Rational rules were not imposed by an authority figure. Instead, a mutual respect for one another allowed children to change rules until they found the best (or most 'rational') ones.

Piaget then went on to explore how children developed an understanding of more specifically moral problems. Piaget asked children some general questions about morality – for example, what a lie is, or what purpose punishment fulfils. To complement his findings from more general questions, Piaget presented children with moral stories or vignettes. These vignettes typically contrasted the behaviour of two children in a range of situations. Piaget's interviewees were usually asked to judge whether one of the two protagonists was naughtier than the other, and then to justify their selection (see box 10.1 for some examples).

Younger children tended to regard the material consequences of action as the crucial determinants of right and wrong. Thus, for these younger children, the greater the amount of material damage done, or the greater the threat of sanction from an adult authority figure, the more morally reprehensible the action was. Older children, on the other hand, tended to base their judgments more on the characters' motivations and

Box 10.1   Piaget's moral vignettes and interviews with children

The stories of the broken cups

A.   A little boy called John is in his room. He is called to dinner. He goes into the dining room. But behind the door there was a chair, and on the chair there was a tray with fifteen cups on it. John couldn't have known that there was all this behind the door. He goes in, the door knocks against the tray, bang go the fifteen cups and they all get broken!

B.   Once there was a little boy whose name was Henry. One day when his mother was out he tried to get some jam out of the cupboard. He climbed up on to a chair and stretched out his arm. But the jam was too high and he couldn't reach it and have any. But while he was trying to get it he knocked over a cup. The cup fell down and broke.

Children's responses in interview

GEO (6): Have you understood these stories? – *Yes.* – What did the first boy do? – *He broke 11 cups.* – And the second one? – *He broke a cup moving roughly.* – Why did the first one break the cups? – *Because the door knocked them.* – And the second? – *He was clumsy. When he was getting the jam the cup fell down.* – Is one of the boys naughtier than the other? – *The first is because he knocked over 12 cups.* – If you were the daddy, which one would you punish most? – *The one who broke 12 cups.* – Why did he break them? – *The door shut too hard and he knocked them. He didn't do it on purpose.* – And why did the other boy break a cup? – *He wanted to get jam. He moved too far. The cup got broken.*
CORM (9): [Which boy is naughtiest?] -*Well, the one who broke them as he was coming isn't naughty, 'cos he didn't know there was any cups. The other one wanted to take the jam and caught his arm on a cup.* – Which one is the naughtiest? – *The one who wanted to take the jam.* – How many cups did he break? – *One.* – And the other boy? – *Fifteen.* – Which one would you punish most? – *The boy who wanted to take the jam. He did it on purpose.*

The stories of the roll and the ribbon

A.   Alfred meets a little friend of his who is very poor. This friend tells him that he has had no dinner that day because there was nothing to eat in his home. Then Alfred goes into a baker's shop, and as he has no money, he waits till the baker's back is turned and steals a roll. Then he runs out and gives the roll to his friend.

B.   Henriette goes into a shop. She sees a pretty piece of ribbon on a table and thinks to herself that it would look very nice on her dress. So while the shop lady's back is turned (while the shop lady is not looking) she steals the ribbon and runs away at once.

Children's responses in interview

SCHMA (6): [repeats the stories]. Is one of these children naughtier than the other? – *The boy is, because he took a roll. It's bigger.* – Ought they to be punished? – *Yes. Four slaps for the first.* – And the girl? – *Two slaps.* – Why he did take the roll? – *Because his friend had had no dinner.* – And the other child? – *To make herself pretty.*

GEO (6): Which of them is naughtiest? – *The one with the roll because the roll is bigger than the ribbon.* [And yet Geo is, like the other children, perfectly aware of the motives involved].
CORM (9): [tells the two stories correctly]. What do you think about it? – *Well, the little boy oughtn't to have stolen. He oughtn't to have stolen it but to have paid for it. And the other one, she oughtn't to have stolen the ribbon either. –* Which of them is the naughtiest? – *The little girl took the ribbon for herself. The little boy took the roll too, but to give to his friend who had no dinner. –* If you were the school teacher, which one would you punish most? – *The little girl.*

Source: Piaget (1932, pp. 118, 119, 120–1, 127–8)

intentions. Thus, an ill-intentioned act was judged to be morally worse than one that was the result of clumsiness.

Piaget then explored the judgments of children in another area of morality – lying. Once again Piaget found two broadly distinguishable forms of thinking. In general, younger children's judgments as to the severity of a lie were not based upon the intention of the liar to deceive. Rather, for these younger children, to tell a lie was 'to commit a moral fault by means of language' (1932, p. 138). Moreover, the further the departure from the truth the worse a lie was deemed to be, regardless of whether it was intended or not. Once again, for the older children the severity of a lie was judged according to the liar's intention to deceive.

Heteronomy and autonomy

For Piaget, the two types of moral reasoning were indicative of two fundamentally different ways of thinking about the source of morality. Younger children, in general, reasoned in a way which Piaget described as heteronomous. Not only did younger children's moral judgments focus on the material features of a situation; they were also strongly influenced by the potential responses of an authority figure, invariably an adult or an older child, who determined what was right or wrong for these younger children. And, importantly, it was not that the younger children were unable to understand an actor's intentions, as some have argued (e.g. Constanzo et al. 1973; Imamoglu 1975). Indeed, Piaget went to some lengths to point out how well the younger children understood the motivations of the protagonists in his stories.

Piaget argued that heteronomous reasoning is egocentric; in making moral judgments the egocentric reasoner cannot appreciate that others may see the situation differently, or from a different perspective. As a consequence, authority figures possess an almost magical quality for the child, since they have the ability to impose punishments and to enforce the moral law by virtue of their position of relative power. So the greater the amount of material damage the greater the child perceives the adverse reaction of the authority figure will be, and hence the worse the consequences (in terms of punishment) for the child.

Amongst the older children, however, Piaget noted that reasoning was more autonomous in character. The older children's moral thought was based on notions of intention and motivation. For older children morality was not something that was seen to be determined by authority figures.

As with the rules of the game (where, for the older children, rules could be changed if everyone agreed), moral rules are determined not by an authority figure but through an appreciation of others' perspectives. Autonomous thought allows the child to understand that others have different moral perspectives from her or his own. The child's thought is no longer egocentric, and this allows her or him to construct an understanding of morality with others. With autonomy, moral rules can only be changed through mutual consent. Autonomy allows, more than anything, a method for the construction of new moral values and for the improvement of existing ones through rational processes (Moshman 1994; 1995).

Clearly the shift from heteronomy to autonomy – what has been called the two moral worlds view (Youniss and Damon 1992) – is of developmental significance. But although most children under 8 years of age reason with heteronomy and the majority over 10 years can reason with autonomy, strict age limits to the different forms of reasoning should be treated cautiously, for at least two reasons. First, different domains of a child's thinking may shift from heteronomous to autonomous at different times. Second, the shift in moral thought correlates with a new orientation to morality – with a changed conception of the social relation or bond which morals regulate. An adult can still reason heteronomously under relevant conditions (see the account of the previous chapter) (Milgram 1974).

Finally, Piaget turned to examine how children thought about justice. Younger reasoners equated justice with retribution, which served an expiatory function, and a punishment was just precisely because it was severe. Older children, and more autonomous reasoners, viewed justice as more a question of reciprocity – putting right what had been wrong. With distributive justice (for example, the share each child received of a cake), whilst the younger children thought that a fair (or just) share was whatever an adult authority figure decided, older children (roughly 8–10 years) tended to prefer a more egalitarian distribution. Children who were over 10 years tended to prefer forms of distribution in which equality was tempered by need or deservingness. Piaget also noted how the notion of collective responsibility developed as children matured. Whilst the younger ones had little willingness to accept that all members of a group should take a share of the blame if one of them did something wrong, older children felt that in certain circumstances members of a group should share some of the responsibility.

Social relations

Heteronomous or autonomous reasoning colours how we think about social relations. The authority figures of heteronomous thought make the relations between individuals unidirectional or asymmetric. Autonomous thought, by contrast, makes morality seem more consensual – produced by a symmetric relation based on equality.

Piaget argued that this change in the way a child thinks about social relations correlated with a growing recognition of the social and interpersonal nature of moral duties and obligations. And by imposing their authority over children adults actually maintain the child's egocentricity, moral heteronomy and a morality of constraint.

For children to develop an understanding of the true function of morality, they had to engage in relationships which were not governed by the pressure of authority and the need to conform to an authority figure's wishes. Such an understanding could only come about through interaction with peers, in a context in which the child's moral thought was not constrained. With peers children could cooperate to develop a sense in which moral duty was a social contract made on an equal (or equitable) and rational basis. Thus it was through peer relations of cooperation that children could learn a sense of right and wrong for themselves.

As was seen in chapter 6, a number of researchers have explored whether social interaction, and in particular peer and adult–child interaction, influences development. Youniss (1980; Youniss and Volpe 1978) suggested that parents and peers have a qualitatively different role in the child's moral development. Parents, as authority figures, tended to act as a source of moral knowledge for heteronomous reasoners. Peers, on the other hand, provided the possibility of the construction of new knowledge for more autonomous reasoners.

Kruger (1992) explored, more explicitly, the differential effects of adult–child and peer relations on children's moral development. Kruger paired 8-year-old children with either a peer or an adult. These children were then asked to discuss a moral dilemma together with their conversation partner. During the conversation, those children who were paired with a peer were more active participants in the conversation than those who were paired with an adult. Moreover, in a subsequent post-test children who had been paired with a peer demonstrated higher 'levels' of moral reasoning.

However, in adult–child interaction many different aspects of authority, such as physical power, knowledge and the ability to impose punishment, are compounded. Leman and Duveen (1999) studied children's (8 to 10 years) discussions amongst their own peer group about one of Piaget's moral stories. Whilst children using autonomous forms of justification were better able to persuade their peers, conversations were profoundly influenced by the gender of the two children interacting. Leman and Duveen suggested that, depending upon the context or task, gender could act as a source of authority, deriving from the social roles and attributes associated with different gender groups.

A number of researchers (Kohlberg 1963; 1984; Damon 1977; Turiel 1983) have argued that Piaget's claim that heteronomous reasoners see adults as infallible authority figures is simply incorrect. Laupa and Turiel (1986) argue that young children do not show unilateral respect for adult authority figures. For example, when asked whether an immoral action would be acceptable if an adult condoned it, young children often said that it would not (Laupa 1991). However, Laupa's results did show some of the features of heteronomy, and in particular the non-differentiation of adult authority attributes, amongst the younger children in her studies.

A further criticism of Piaget's theory is that it incorporates an ethnocentric and gender-specific conception of morality. For example, for Weinreich-Haste (1982), Piaget's conception of morality is based too much on concepts of rules and rationality that are more in keeping with 'male' notions of morality. In a similar vein, Buck-Morss (1975) argues that Piaget's emphasis on questions of epistemology and the developmental process runs the risk of neglecting the importance of social and cultural influences in development. Authority and social relations are so important in Piaget's theory that these social aspects of moral development do indeed merit more scrutiny than Piaget gave them.

Cognitive-developmental theory

After Piaget, Kohlberg (1963; 1981; 1984) cultivated a theory of moral development which shared with Piaget's a sense in which moral reasoning is fundamentally a cognitive process. The term cognitive-developmental is Kohlberg's, not Piaget's. Piaget described his general theory of cognitive development as 'genetic epistemology' (Piaget 1970). Like Piaget, Kohlberg conceptualized morality as a system of social rules. However, whilst Piaget saw moral reasoning as grounded in the social relations which exist between individuals, Kohlberg (1963) argued that our moral understanding is independent of social relations. For him, a sense of moral understanding developed specifically through resolving cognitive conflicts within the child's mind. These conflicts were a consequence of an individual's reflections on 'everyday' moral dilemmas.

Kohlberg's theory

Kohlberg's moral dilemmas (see box 10.2) invariably involved contrasts between two different moral rules. For example, the classic 'Heinz and the druggist dilemma' contrasted one moral rule 'It is wrong to steal' with another, 'It is right to preserve life.' Kohlberg and his colleagues then interviewed children's responses to the dilemmas and coded their responses according to a scale devised by the researchers.

Box 10.2   Examples of Kohlberg's dilemmas

Heinz and the druggist

In Europe, a woman was near death from a special kind of cancer. There was one drug that doctors thought might save her. It was a form of radium that a druggist in the same town had recently discovered. The drug was expensive to make, but the druggist was charging $2,000, or ten times the cost of the drug, for a small (possibly life-saving) dose. Heinz, the sick woman's husband, borrowed all the money he could – about $1,000, or half of what he needed. He told the druggist that his wife was dying and asked him to sell the drug cheaper or let him pay later. The druggist replied, 'No, I discovered the drug, and I'm going to make money from it.' Heinz then became desperate and broke into the store to steal the drug for his wife.

Should Heinz have done that? Why or why not?

The tickets to the rock concert

Judy was a 12-year-old girl. Her mother promised her that she could go to a special rock concert coming to their town if she saved up from babysitting and lunch money to buy a ticket to the concert. She managed to save up the $15 the ticket cost plus another $5. But then her mother changed her mind and told Judy that she had to spend the money on new clothes for school. Judy was disappointed and decided to go to the concert anyway. She bought a ticket and told her mother that she had only been able to save $5. That Saturday she went to the performance and told her mother that she was spending the day with a friend. A week passed without her mother finding out. Judy then told her older sister, Louise, that she had gone to the performance and had lied to her mother about it. Louise wonders whether to tell their mother what Judy did.

Should Louise, the older sister, tell their mother that Judy lied about the money, or should she keep quiet? Why?

The tailor and Valjean

In a country in Europe, a poor man named Valjean could find no work, nor could his sister and brother. Without money, he stole food and medicine that they needed. He was captured and sentenced to prison for six years. After a couple of years he escaped from prison and went to live in another part of the country under a new name. He saved money and slowly built up a factory. He gave his workers the highest wages and used most of his profits to build a hospital for people who couldn't afford good medical care. Twenty years had passed when a tailor recognized the factory owner as being Valjean, the escaped convict whom the police had been looking for back in his home town.

Should the tailor report Valjean to the police? Why or why not?
   Does a citizen have a duty to report an escaped convict?
   If Valjean were reported and brought before the judge, should the judge send him back to jail or let him go free?

Source: Kohlberg (1984, pp. 640–51)

Kohlberg claimed that interviewees in his own research did not provide justifications for their moral choices that suggested different moral worlds for adult–child and peer morality. For example, in another dilemma similar to 'The tickets and the rock concert dilemma' (see again box 10.2), a boy disobeyed his father, his father having reneged on an earlier promise to allow him to go out, and the boy went out anyway. The boy's brother found out about the disobedience and Kohlberg asked his interviewees what they thought the brother should do – tell his father or keep quiet. One of Kohlberg's interviewees, a 10-year-old boy, argued that it would be right to tell the father because he might get 'beaten up' if he did not, but simultaneously wrong because his brother would beat him up if he did (Kohlberg 1984, p. 182)! Kohlberg argued that this demonstrated that children were motivated to judge moral issues in ways that cut across the level of symmetry or asymmetry in the social relation. He proposed that we develop an understanding of morality only by appreciating that some forms of moral reasoning are necessarily superior to and more logical than others (Kohlberg 1971).

From his observations Kohlberg (1984) developed a three-level, six-stage theory of moral development which extended through to adult life (see box 10.3). An individual's moral thought progresses through these stages in order – with level 3, stage 6, constituting if not the endpoint, then the limit of development. There is a change from one level to the next in orientation to moral rules in terms of society's rules and norms. Stages constitute 'refinements' of the form of the reasoning within each level. Pre-conventional reasoning (stages 1 and 2) is governed by a socially egocentric perspective. Stage 1 reasoning reflects the orientation to authority that Piaget described as heter-onomous thought. Stage 2 reasoning constitutes an advance upon stage 1, since it is not orientation to authority but an individual's self-interest which governs moral judgment. However, stage 2 thinking is still egocentric, according to Kohlberg, since such reason-ing still does not concord with society's conventions.

Box 10.3   Kohlberg's stages of moral development

Level 1   Pre-conventional

Stage 1: Heteronomous morality	Avoidance of breaking rules backed by punish-ment. Obedience for obedience's sake.
Stage 2: Individualism, instrumental purpose and exchange	Acting in accordance with individual interests – fairness is an equal exchange based upon motivations of self-interest.

Level 2   Conventional

Stage 3: Mutual interpersonal expectations, relationships and interpersonal conformity	Living up to what is expected of you. Mutual relations of trust and respect should be main-tained provided they conform to your expected social role.
Stage 4: Social system and conscience	Rules are to be upheld except when they conflict with other social duties. Right is con-tributing to society and fulfilling social duties.

Level 3   Post-conventional

Stage 5: Social contract or utility and individual rights	Awareness of the social contract between individuals, but also of the different moral perspectives of others. Some individual rights, however, transcend the different perspectives of others and therefore should be upheld.
Stage 6: Universal ethical principles	Following self-chosen ethical principles. When such principles conflict with existing moral standards, these principles should be upheld regardless of the majority opinion.

Source: Kohlberg (1984)

With the final stage (6, 'Universal ethical principles'), reasoning is post-conventional, although for research purposes, Kohlberg compounds stages 5 and 6 (Colby and Kohlberg 1987). Society's rules and norms are no longer the source of moral legitimacy and the individual can reason in a principled manner which is independent of any social or historical context. Such reasoning, according to Kohlberg, is rare – indeed, so rare that he provides a list of 'moral exemplars' to describe the stage. These exemplars include Socrates, Abraham Lincoln and Martin Luther King. These individuals, argued Kohlberg, demonstrate the principled and autonomous thinking which represents the pinnacle of development in moral thought.

A distinctive feature of Kohlberg's theory is that moral development continues in adulthood. Indeed, Colby et al. (1983) observe significant development in the reasoning of men over 30 years of age in their longitudinal sample. Studies have claimed to identify both decline and development in reasoning amongst elderly adults (see Pratt, Golding and Hunter 1983; Walker 1986).

Over time Kohlberg's model has, in response to new findings and criticisms, become even more complex. In addition to the six stages there are also transitional stages (for example, between stages 2 and 3, or 3 and 4) in which reasoning reflects some of the qualities of both stages. Kohlberg also introduced the notion of two substages, which resembled Piaget's characterizations of heteronomy and autonomy, in which judgments may be made either descriptively or prescriptively (Kohlberg 1984, p. 183).

According to Kohlberg, each successive stage is more 'adequate', since it is better for resolving moral conflicts than those that precede it. Thus, in development, children (and adults) progress through stages, although not all people will develop fully and reach stage 6. Successive stages also complete the social perspective of the stages which precede them (Selman 1971). For instance, at stage 3 ('Mutual interpersonal expectations, relationships and interpersonal conformity') the conventional reasoner possesses a social perspective in which the scope of the moral world is limited to a few, close personal relationships. At stage 4 ('Social system and conscience') the scope of judgment is based on a recognition of the self as a fully fledged member of society – although the motivation for moral thought is still a deference for social conventions. With progression through the stages the scope of an individual's moral world (the number of events and people about which the individual reasons) widens, although the motor of development remains private mental reflection.

The logic of moral development

At a first glance Kohlberg's stage theory of moral development presents us with more variation in reasoning than Piaget's 'two moral worlds' model. A further, important aspect of Kohlberg's theory is that it covers development beyond the age of 15 years: Kohlberg (1969) observes development up until middle age. Yet the stage theory also makes some very specific claims.

Perhaps the crux of these claims lies in Kohlberg's insistence upon a logical sequence for the stages of development. From a cognitive-developmental perspective, development is the construction of knowledge rather than the construction of just any old belief. And knowledge is derived from rational (or logical) processes. So if thought proceeds in any manner which is not the same as Kohlberg's theory it cannot count as development, since it is 'illogical'. As we shall see, one problem for Kohlberg is that he claims to identify this logical sequence, and hence *the* moral sequence.

A second claim is that individuals cannot skip stages as they develop. Each new stage builds and improves upon the previous one, and to conform to the logic of development requires that reasoning develops in a particular way. Third, an individual's thought cannot undevelop; there can be no regression to previous stages.

Fourth, any judgement at a particular time is a consequence of the whole of an individual's reasoning, not just part of it. So, for example, someone cannot demonstrate stage 2 reasoning in response to one dilemma and stage 4 reasoning in response to another. Finally, since Kohlberg's stages correspond to *the* developmental sequence, the order of progression through the stages must be universal. Of course, it would be perfectly possible for someone not to advance all the way up the scale. But the sequence must remain the same for everyone, regardless of the cultural, social or historical context in which he or she lives.

The demands and conditions for moral development within Kohlberg's model seem rather stringent. Yet in many respects the theory has proved remarkably robust in terms of empirical findings. The largest, longitudinal study of moral reasoning was conducted by Colby et al. (1983), who found patterns of development which were very similar to those predicted by Kohlberg's theory. Colby et al. found that their all-male, American cohort (starting at 10 and finishing at 36 years of age) showed increases in the higher stages and correlating decreases in lower stages of reasoning over time – just as Kohlberg's theory would have predicted. Moreover, Colby et al.'s results indicated that very few subjects skipped a stage, and also that few regressed from a higher to a lower stage of reasoning over the course of the study.

However there were rather more equivocal results regarding whether or not individuals, interviewed at a particular time, occupied just one stage of reasoning. Although only 9 per cent of subjects showed reasoning that was two or more stages apart (e.g. stages 1 and 3), 50 per cent showed reasoning across two adjacent stages (e.g. stages 3 and 4). Colby and Kohlberg claimed that these results could be explained by short-comings in the coding system. Yet in spite of further refinements to the coding system (Colby and Kohlberg 1987; Rest 1983), Kohlberg and his colleagues seem rather better at using the coding system than others (Siegal 1982).

Another problem is that Kohlberg's initial sample was all male. Kohlberg did aim to make amends later by studying women's moral reasoning, and these results showed that women tended to reason at slightly lower levels than men (Kohlberg and Kramer 1969). Further sources of variation have been found in wider investigations of Kohlberg's model. In Kohlberg's own study, boys with higher IQs tended to progress faster up the stages, and IQ correlated strongly with progress to the higher stages of reasoning. There was also a correlation between a subject's level of reasoning and his socioeconomic status. And Kohlberg found a very strong relationship between educational experience and final level of reasoning; no one reached stage 4 unless he had attended college.

A final problem stems from the theoretical requirement that the developmental sequence is universal. Results from cross-cultural studies of moral development give ambiguous results. Snarey (1985) finds some support for Kohlberg's arguments for a universal developmental sequence. However, Western cultures have far greater proportions of higher-stage reasoners (i.e. stages 4, 5 and 6) than others. In some tribal cultures any reasoning higher than stage 3 is conspicuously absent.

All these social and cultural variations in moral development indicate that one of two things is happening. First, if Kohlberg's model is correct, moral reasoning in Western cultures is simply more advanced than elsewhere, men's reasoning is more advanced than women's, and the further your educational career extends, the more advanced your reasoning will be. In short, Western, educated males think more 'morally' than anyone else. But a second explanation could be that Kohlberg's model is ethnocentric – reflecting male, liberal, Western, 'rationalist' values and failing to tap into any conceptions of morality which might resist a Kohlbergian interpretation (Emler 1987).

Moral and conventional rules

If morals are universal, then we should be able to identify them. The identification of universal moral rules, as distinct from other social rules, has been the focus of the work of one of Kohlberg's colleagues, Elliot Turiel. Turiel (1983) argued that whilst social conventions are relative, and vary across time and cultures, moral rules are not. Rather, moral rules are universal – they are true for all people at all times regardless of the social or cultural context in which people live (Helwig, Tisak and Turiel 1990). Evidence for this distinction between moral and conventional rules comes, argues Turiel, from rule contingency studies.

In rule contingency studies (Tisak and Turiel 1988; Turiel 1978), children are presented with dilemmas or stories which describe the actions of an individual performing a moral transgression. Children are asked whether the actions of the protagonist are wrong, and whether they would still be wrong if there was no rule prohibiting it. In general, findings reveal that children even as young as 4 years believe that certain forms of behaviour (e.g. hitting, stealing or deceiving) are unacceptable at all times whereas other social rules (e.g. addressing a teacher by her first name) are situation- or context-specific (Turiel 1983, p. 41).

Turiel argues that moral development involves 'separating out' conventional from moral rules. The process of differentiation is accelerated by the child's familiarity with certain events or situations (Davidson, Turiel and Black 1983), although even children as young as 3 years can make basic distinctions between moral and conventional rules (Smetana 1981). Children recognize that moral rules are not arbitrary and not contingent, argues Turiel, 'through abstractions from the experience itself (either as an observer or a participant)' (Turiel 1983, p. 43).

Rule contingency studies have been seen as casting doubt upon Piaget's assertion that heteronomous reasoners view adults as authority figures who act as the source of moral knowledge. However, it is important to remember that since, for Piaget, it is the social relation that governs the form of moral reasoning, there are no strict age limits to reasoning that is heteronomous or autonomous. Thus a child could reason with heteronomy in the presence of an adult and with autonomy amongst peers at a certain stage of development (cf. Leman and Duveen 1999).

Additionally, Turiel and his colleagues' moral stories are presented to the child in the third person: in most rule contingency studies children are asked about their reactions to the behaviour of a fictitious protagonist and, in the case of adult authorities issuing commands, fictitious adults. Thus the pressure an authority may exert upon an individual's moral reasoning is removed from the immediate features of the testing environment. Turiel's conception of moral development as a process of differentiating domains of social thought has nevertheless been very influential in recent research. As with Kohlberg's theory, cross-cultural studies of moral and conventional rules have produced some evidence for the universality hypothesis (Turiel and Wainryb 1994).

Moral development in a cultural context

Cognitive-developmental theories claim that moral rules are universal. Of course, this does not mean that everyone, everywhere, will abide by these rules. But it does mean that the same issues – causing harm to others, cheating, lying – will be regarded as immoral across all cultures. However, there are those who have argued that, contrary to cognitive-developmental theory, culture plays an important role in our moral reasoning.

Culture and morality

Shweder, Mahapatra and Miller (1987) explored the distinction between morality and convention amongst Hindu children in India. The researchers asked both Indian and American children to rate rules in terms of how serious it would be to transgress them. Rather than finding a common set of moral rules which were distinct from conventions, Shweder found that amongst the Indian sample the boundaries between morality and convention were less clear cut than amongst the Americans. For example, many of the Indian children believed that having a haircut and eating chicken after the death of your father was an extremely serious moral transgression. Similarly, a woman playing cards whilst her husband cooked rice was rated as wrong. Such transgressions were rated as either trivial or not moral transgressions at all by the Americans.

Shweder's findings bring into question Turiel's claim that the distinction between morality and convention is universally recognized. At the very least, there are subtleties in moral reasoning in different cultures that the cognitive-developmental theory fails to consider as relevant forms of reasoning. Shweder (1990) suggests that there may be many different moral realities that are the products of different cultures, their traditions and histories. He argues that Kohlberg's and Turiel's methods by their nature under-estimate the importance of culture to an individual's sense of the world (Shweder 1991; Shweder and Much 1987).

In a similar vein, Miller and Bersoff (1992) suggest that the motivations for following moral rules might differ in complex ways across cultures. From their study they argue that Hinduism emphasizes issues relating to interpersonal expectations over 'Western' notions of justice and rationality, which can, sometimes, lead to subtle differences in the sorts of judgments individuals will make.

It seems almost self-evident that culture and social context play some part in our moral reasoning. Yet identifying that role is not as straightforward a matter as it might, at first, appear. Moreover, Helwig, Tisak and Turiel (1990) dispute the notion of moral reasoning as 'culturally determined' – arguing that most people feel a sense of moral outrage at, for example, torture or racism regardless of the cultural or historical context in which it occurs. Yet whilst, in an ideal sense, it might be true that we tend to regard morality as universalizable, cross-cultural studies provide grounds for questioning the assumption that any one system of morality is universal.

Women's moral voice

Cross-cultural work highlights one source of variation in moral reasoning. Carol Gilligan's work on variation within a culture has been very influential, and is summarized in box 10.4.

Box 10.4   Carol Gilligan (1936–)

In 1982, Carol Gilligan, professor of human development and psychology at Harvard, argued that different forms of moral reasoning can be found within a culture. Gilligan, noting that Kohlberg's theory was developed initially from an all-male sample, argues that women reason in a different way from men.

Gilligan explored women's moral reasoning by interviewing twenty-nine American women who were pregnant. These women faced a real-life choice as whether to continue with the pregnancy or have an abortion. From her interviews she identified three levels of reasoning which bore some similarities to Kohlberg's levels, moving from pre-conventional (level 1) to conventional (2) and post-conventional (3) thought. However, whilst Kohlberg's levels had corresponded to notions of justice, Gilligan's were more concerned with elaborating a distinctly female moral voice – an 'ethic of care'. Level 1 reasoning was governed by self-interest, level 2 by self-sacrifice. Level 3 reasoning involved a sense in which care for others was a universal obligation.

Gilligan claimed that male and female 'voices' stem from the different forms of socialization and upbringing that boys and girls receive. In Western society, according to Gilligan, boys are generally expected to develop a sense of independence. Girls, in contrast, are seen as nurturers, carers and less independent. These gendered expectations lead men to adopt a more detached and independent view of morality, which focuses on issues of justice and abstract moral principles. Women's path of socialization leads to a more care-oriented, interpersonal view of morality, which is concerned with others' welfare over and above abstract notions of justice. For Gilligan, an ethic of care constitutes an alternative orientation to morality, which Kohlberg and others fail to recognize.

Although Gilligan's initial study was conducted solely on women (reversing the bias in Kohlberg's methodology but, in another sense, repeating the mistake), in subsequent research (Gilligan and Attanucci 1988) she has claimed to find a greater incidence of justice-oriented reasoning amongst men and care-orientation amongst women. However, a number of other studies have failed to support Gilligan's claim when rather more rigorous methods are used (e.g. L. J. Walker 1984; M. R. Ford and Lowery 1986).

An abiding concern regarding Gilligan's model is that it merely reproduces stereotypical notions of male and female roles (J. Sayers 1986). Of course, this reproduction of stereotypes is not theoretically damning in itself, but at least two further worries arise. First, if we consider gender roles, attributes and expectations as social constructions (e.g. Lloyd and Duveen 1992), we must also accept that these roles, attributes and expectations are not fixed but change as society changes. Similarly, different cultures invoke rather different notions of gender and of the roles and expectations of men and women. In other words, it is not clear whether Gilligan's ideas can endure across cultures and time.

Second, in theoretical terms Gilligan's account of the developmental process is rather thin. Whilst it is doubtless true that boys and girls are subjected to very different socialization influences from the start of their lives, there could be at least some instances where boys are socialized to nurture and girls to be independent. Such individual differences in the process of socialization would blur the boundaries between women's and men's moral voices. Sochting, Skoe and Marcia (1994) found that sex-role orientation – that is, a tendency to behave in more stereotypically masculine or feminine ways – was better than gender group membership *per se* at predicting the type of reasoning an individual will use.

Conclusions

Parents, peers and wider society clearly have an important role to play in the child's moral development. According to Durkheim, our moral thought is necessarily social. But whilst the social context is clearly important, theorists such as Kohlberg and Turiel argue that it is not the be all and end all of our moral reasoning. For cognitive-developmental theorists, moral thought is not wholly the product of our social environment. Rather, moral reasoning is a matter of how we, as individuals, make sense of that environment. In this sense, cognitive theories allow us to conceptualize moral reasoning as a truly autonomous process. We can, after all, make moral choices: we can change our own sense of morality, and we can persuade others to change theirs through argument and debate.

However, a potential problem for cognitive-developmental approaches is that they underplay, or perhaps even ignore, the importance of the social crucible in which moral thinking and action happen. And whilst autonomy is clearly an important aspect of morality, studies from a variety of cultures and even within cultures point to significant and consistent social variations in moral reasoning. Any theory of moral development needs to account not only for the cognitive changes that can be observed in the child, but also for those social aspects that give our moral judgements a social meaning.

It seems plausible to suggest that our moral reasoning is a result of both social and cognitive forces and influences. Indeed, since morality is to do not just with our understanding of rules but also with our relationships with others, it is hard to make sense of moral thinking outside of any social context. Consider again Kohlberg's stage 6 moral exemplars – Socrates, Abraham Lincoln and Martin Luther King. According to Kohlberg these individuals articulated the universal ethical principles which represent the pinnacle of moral thought. In one sense, each of them can be said to have reasoned in a way which was un- (or post-) conventional. Yet in another sense, each of these individuals' moral reasoning was very much a consequence of the world in which he lived.

RECOMMENDED READING

Gilligan, C. (1982) *In a Different Voice: Psychological Theory and Women's Development*. Cambridge, MA: Harvard University Press.
In a classic book which sought to redress the 'male bias' in research into moral reasoning, Gilligan offered what was, in its time, a fresh methodological as well as theoretical perspective on moral development. A matter of some debate is how successfully Gilligan's ideas have stood the test of time.

Kohlberg, L. (1976) Moral stages and moralization: the cognitive-developmental approach. In T. Lickona (ed.), *Moral Development and Behavior: Theory Research and Social Issues*. New York: Holt.
In what is perhaps the most accessible statement of his position, Kohlberg outlines the basic principles and findings from his theory.

Moshman, D. (1995) The construction of moral rationality. *Human Development*, 38, 265–81.
Moshman provides a thoughtful account of how Piagetian theory might be developed in the light of contemporary research on moral reasoning.

Shweder, R.A. (1991) *Thinking through Cultures: Expeditions in Cultural Psychology*. Cambridge, MA: Harvard University Press.
Shweder offers a cross-cultural perspective on moral development and moral reasoning and in doing so highlights many of the problems associated with cognitive-developmental theories.

Perceiving and Understanding People

Introduction

There is nothing so engrossing as other people. Much of our social life is spent trying to understand better the people that we come into contact with. Indeed the fascination with other people is so great that many of us spend a considerable amount of time and effort in attempting to understand the lives of people we will never meet; American film stars or the British royal family, for instance. In fact, to be interested in other people is something that most of us consider a prerequisite for any 'normal' person. And there are many people for whom being able to form accurate impressions of others is one of the most important parts of their job; police officers, psychiatrists and interviewers are good examples.

Yet this is a very complex task which we set ourselves. There are numerous ways in which we can go about finding out about others, many of them far from straightforward. We might, for instance, want to rely on our direct observation. Yet the only things that we can directly observe are other individuals' actions, what they do and what they say. But when we claim to understand other people we do not mean that we simply know how they typically behave; we want to know *why* they behave in that way. In other words, what *type* of people are they? What causes them to behave in the way that they do? This leap from observing someone's behaviour to attributing a reason for that behaviour has been a central focus of psychology. That is, to make useful judgements about others we not only have to consider information about them, but we also need to go beyond that information and make inferences about the sort of person they are. You will recall, however, from the discussion of cognition in chapter 3 that in order to make complex inferences, individuals usually need to take short cuts, or use heuristics, to make the task manageable, which leads them to be less than perfectly rational in their assessments of other people.

This chapter will start by considering some early evidence on impression formation from lists of adjectives describing hypothetical others. Then attribution theory, explaining the processes by which we infer the causes of other people's behaviour, will be outlined. Some of the circumstances where people are seemingly most error-prone in making attributions will then be described. Next, a number of criticisms of attribution theories will be discussed, before we move on to consider other processes involved in person perception, such as biases we have in our representations of others in memory, and the ways in which we use our socially derived knowledge to categorize others and make inferences about them on the bases of those categorizations. Finally, the way in which initial impressions of others can influence interpersonal interactions between perceiver and perceived will be considered.

Simple impression formation

A founder of the field of person perception was Solomon Asch, whose work on conformity was described in chapter 8. His early experiments on impression formation consisted of presenting participants (often called perceivers in this field) with lists of adjectives about another person (the target). For instance, they would be presented with the words 'intelligent', 'skilful', 'industrious', 'warm', 'determined', 'practical', 'cautious'. It became clear to Asch that, rather than simply adding together these molecules of information, perceivers were constructing a holistic image of a person. Furthermore, there were some central traits which, if changed, would change the whole impression formed by the perceivers – for instance, if the word 'warm' in the above list were changed to 'cold' it did more than just change that one part of the perceiver's judgement of the person; it changed the whole pattern (Asch 1946). Other traits, such as 'polite–blunt', did not have this overall effect, and were labelled peripheral traits. Another key finding was a primacy effect, whereby adjectives placed earlier in the list were more influential than ones placed towards the end. This was taken to mirror the process by which we might be overinfluenced by our first impressions of a new acquaintance. There was a prolonged debate over the exact rules which were used by perceivers to combine the information – whether, as Asch claimed, it was a holistic or gestalt-type process, or, as N. H. Anderson (1965) argued, an additive or averaging, algebraic-type process. But eventually the focus of the person perception debate turned away from the simplistic and artificial use of lists of adjectives to the use of tasks which were thought to be closer to the actual processes used in understanding people, such as attributing causes to observed behaviours.

Attribution theories

In social life we are continually confronted by the behaviour of others. But behaviour in itself is often not particularly informative, because the same behaviour could have many different causes, and therefore we do not know how to interpret it. For instance, if we notice that a politician is on her way to church on a Sunday, there is more than one way in which we could interpret that information. It may be that she is deeply religious, or it may be that she thinks that she will attract more votes if she is seen to go to church.

Similarly a manager may notice that the new receptionist on trial placement in the sales department was very aggressive when dealing with a telephone query from a customer. Was this because the receptionist is a very abrasive person? Or perhaps that particular customer can be so frustrating that all the receptionists in the department are always unpleasant to her? Or was the receptionist just having an off day, because he was in an uncharacteristically bad mood due to a hangover?

Both of the above scenarios require the observer to make inferences, to go beyond the behaviours and assess the causes of those behaviours. Attribution theories are concerned with how individuals attribute cause to the actions of others. As with many things people do, there are a large number of ways of approaching the same problem. Thus we need to consider not only how it is logically possible to make these attributions, but how and when people actually use those options open to them.

Heider's book *The Psychology of Interpersonal Relations*, published in 1958 and representing the work of a long and learned career, is commonly acknowledged to be the foundation of attribution theory. In a break with both psychoanalytic appproaches and group-based social psychology, Heider was interested in understanding the cognitive processes by which individuals come to understand each other. Furthermore, Heider was insistent that it was more useful for psychologists to understand these processes in the same way as lay people understood them, rather than to assume that they were the outcomes of deep or unconscious processes fuelled by complex motivational forces associated with, for instance, sex or death. Attribution theory was further articulated and developed by E. E. Jones and Davis (1965) under the title correspondent inference theory (CIT). The focus of CIT was whether an observed behaviour corresponds to a personal disposition of the target (that is, the person being observed) or to some other cause, such as an attempt to show that he or she is a socially acceptable and desirable person. For instance, in the case of the politician going to church, if we found that she only went to church when she thought that she was being watched by the media, we would conclude that it was unlikely to reflect a deeply held disposition of religiosity on her part. However, if the behaviour was not socially desirable – gambling, for instance – we would have little hesitation in attributing it to a disposition on her part;

she could not be doing it for impression management purposes (i.e. to manipulate the impression that observers form of her).

Others have since produced other frameworks from which individuals' attributional processes can be described and understood. Perhaps the most attention has been paid to Kelley's covariation theory or attribution cube model (1972). Kelley hypothesized that in seeking to decide why an actor behaved in a certain way, observers would want to know three things about that particular behaviour:

1 variability across people (e.g. receptionists, to return to our previous example), or consensus;
2 variability across entities (customers), or distinctiveness;
3 variability across time and contexts (phone calls, or perhaps days), or consistency.

Box 11.1   A Summary of some of the main Attribution Theories

Author	Name	Summary of theory
Heider (1958)	Naive psychology	Individuals attempt to understand the cause of other people's behaviour. In particular, they attempt to determine whether the cause for a behaviour was internal – e.g. personality, mood, attitude etc. – or external – e.g. due to the influence of others, the situation that they were in, luck etc.
E. E. Jones and Davis (1965)	Correspondent inference theory	Individuals attempt to judge whether an observed behaviour corresponds to a personal disposition of the target. To do this, they take into account the social desirability of the action.
Kelley (1972)	Covariation theory or attribution cube	To judge whether a behaviour is caused by the situation or by a permanent or temporary disposition of the individual, individuals take into account three types of information: consensus, distinctiveness and consistency.

Different combinations of variability of the behaviour across people, entities and time should lead us to make different attributions as to the cause of the behaviour. Let me continue with the example of the receptionist being rude to a customer. If the other receptionists were rarely rude to that customer (low consensus), and if the new receptionist was rude to all customers (low distinctiveness) and always rude to that customer (high consistency), then we would probably conclude that the new receptionist was a rude sort of a person; this is called an internal attribution, as the cause is seen as internal to the person. If, however, all receptionists were rude to that customer, the new receptionist was never rude to other customers and always rude to this one customer (high consensus, high distinctiveness and high consistency), then we should conclude that our explanation of the rudeness should centre on something to do with the customer; an explanation external to the receptionist. Other combinations of variability on these three dimensions should lead to other conclusions, such as someone being in an atypical mood or there being some peculiar dynamic between the two people involved. (See R. Brown 1986 for a systematic exploration of what he describes as the calculus of attribution making.)

Kelley's covariance model is, then, assuming that people are subjecting the information that they gather concerning several facets of a scenario to some rather complex analysis (in fact the analysis that Kelley is suggesting as appropriate is modelled on the analysis of variance that psychologists and statisticians use on sophisticated experimental designs). Some critics of attribution theories have expressed surprise at the diversity of models that have been put forward to explain attribution processes. (The CIT and covariance models described above are not the only ones that have been proposed. Another very influential model was proposed by Weiner (1979) for the attributions given to success or failure on a task. See Hewstone 1989 for a wider discussion of attribution theories). Others have claimed that the models formulated by Jones and Davis, Kelley and others will eventually be integrated because, although they appear to be different, they have the same conceptual core (Medcof 1990).

These attribution theories demonstrate the complexity of the inferences that have to be made if people are to interpret the actions of others correctly. This leads to several further, perhaps more interesting, questions. First, if attributing causes to the behaviour of others is so complex, and given (as was argued in chapter 3) that human reasoning cannot be considered to be perfectly rational or optimal, how often do people get it wrong and systematically misattribute or misunderstand the causes of the behaviour of

Plate 11.1 Person perception is a two-way process. Who is making attributions about whom here?

others? Second, perhaps it is implausible that people spend much of their everyday lives attempting these very complex calculations; in which case is there another, rather more straightforward way in which we interpret the behaviour of others?

Biases in attributions

Much social psychological research has been interested in the mistakes that people are prone to make in attributing the causes of other people's behaviours. But some types of bias have been noted so repeatedly that they are worthy of detailed consideration.

The fundamental attribution error

The fundamental attribution error is considered to be the most important of these biases; hence its name. As the examples in the previous section suggested, one of the central goals of people perceiving others is to decide whether an action was primarily caused by people's dispositions (i.e. an internal attribution) rather than the situations that they find themselves in (i.e. an external attribution). For instance, if we notice that a person is often late to classes, the fundamental attribution error would predict that we would be more likely to conclude that the lateness was caused by dispositional factors (for example absent-mindedness or poor motivation) rather than by situational factors (for example poor public transport or the previous lecturer overrunning). This is not to say that people are incapable of making such judgements well, but rather that when people do make attributional errors they are more likely to err towards dispositional attributions than to situational ones. As a test of this you might like to examine your own judgements next time you consider the cause of another person's behaviour. How readily do you invoke 'personality' characteristics? Or next time you read a popular newspaper or magazine, you might notice that it is full of dispositional attributions for why people did the things that they did, be they pop stars helping the needy or vicars behaving badly. You might like to question whether there are situational explanations that are missed by the journalists and that may be more plausible than the dispositional explanations which are so readily given.

Two types of explanation have been proposed for the fundamental attribution error. The first, and most commonly cited, focuses upon the individual's cognitive processes and suggests either that individuals are more salient for us than situations, or that explanations concerning people are simpler and more concrete, and thus easier to generate, than explanations concerning situations, which are rather more complex and abstract. The other type of explanation for the fundamental attribution error is centred on the values and assumptions of our culture. One of the central and taken-for-granted assumptions of our capitalist and Christian traditions is that individuals are primarily responsible for their actions, and thus we tend to look for dispositional explanations of actions more readily than situational ones. This is a difficult theory to test, but there are other cultures, perhaps ones that emphasize the power of natural or supernatural forces, where the fundamental attribution error is overturned and individuals preferentially

---

Box 11.2   A Summary of some general attributional errors

Error	Tendency
Fundamental attribution error	To emphasize the influence of personal dispositions and to discount situational influences when attributing causes to the behaviour of others.
Actor–observer error	To emphasize the influence of the situation and to discount the influence of personal dispositions when attributing causes to one's own behaviour.
False consensus error	To judge one's own behaviours as being more common than is actually the case, and to judge behaviours that are not one's own to be less common.
Ultimate attribution error	To generalize negative attributions regarding an outgroup member to a whole outgroup, and positive attributions of an ingroup member to the whole ingroup.
Self-serving bias	To assign internal causes for one's own successes or positive outcomes, and to blame external, situational factors for failures or negative outcomes.

---

seek situational rather than dispositional explanations (Furnham and Lewis 1986). However, this latter, cultural type of explanation has received little attention in the attribution literature. But there are other facets to this complex attributional error too. For instance Forgas (1998b) has added affect into the equation, and found that if experimental participants were induced into a happy mood, this exacerbated the fundamental attribution error, but a sad mood reduced dispositional attributions for others.

The actor–observer error

The second attribution error that will be described here could be described as the antithesis of the fundamental attribution error when making attributions about oneself. The actor–observer error (labelled, perhaps more accurately, the self–other error by D. Watson 1982) is the term given to individuals' tendency to emphasize the influence of the situation, and to discount the influence of personal dispositions, when attributing causes to their own behaviour. To go back to my observations regarding the explanations people give for lateness in the section above, I have also noticed that whenever latecomers give a reason for their own late arrival, they almost never mention their own personal dispositions, but rather give explanations solely in terms of situational factors. You can probably think of numerous other situations where we explain the behaviour of others in terms of their dispositions, and ourselves in terms of the situation. Why is this?

In this particular example, we might wonder whether it is a self-serving bias (sometimes referred to as a motivational bias) – an attempt to bolster our image to others or to ourselves by portraying positive outcomes as having causes internal to ourselves and negative outcomes as being caused by other people or by the situation. However, the actor–observer bias has been observed to operate for positive and neutral outcomes as well as for negative ones, so this cannot be the only explanation of it (L. Ross, Bierbrauer and Polly 1974). Like many of these phenomena, it does not operate under all circumstances (S. E. Taylor et al. 1979) and probably can have more than one cause. But one of the best-supported theories as to the cause of the actor–observer difference was proposed by Storms (1973), who suggested that the effect was caused by the different attentional perspectives that we have on our own and others' behaviour.

Storms was investigating 'getting acquainted' conversations between pairs of strangers in a laboratory setting. Following the interactions, each participant was asked which one of the pair had been more influential in shaping the conversation. Typically, and consistently with the self–other bias, participants attributed more responsibility to the dispositions of others than to themselves. Storms claimed that this was caused by the fact that they could see the behaviour of the other, it was central and salient in their visual field; in contrast their own behaviour was not seen as being so influential because people could not see it – for example their own facial expressions – and thus were not so aware of their own influence. This was confirmed by the ratings of two other participants involved in the experiments, in the role of observer. Each observer stood behind one of the interacting pair with screens erected such that they could observe only the participant opposite them. Observers tended to rate the participant that they could see as having a greater influence on the conversation than the one that they could not see, again supporting the notion that those things which are observed and salient are more likely to be seen as important causes of behaviour than the unobservable. As a final demonstration, the participants of the conversation were video-recorded, and at the end of the experiment were shown the videotape of either themselves or their partner in the conversation. Participants who saw the videotape of the other person (i.e. the same view that they had during the conversation) were, if anything, more adamant that the other person had been influential in the conversation. However, a complete reversal in attributions occurred for those participants who were shown the videorecording of themselves during the conversation. They could now see their own behaviour in a way that is not usually available to us in our day-to-day conversations. This produced a quite dramatic change in their perceptions of their own role in the conversations, and they rated themselves as being far more influential than they had before being able to see themselves.

This led Storms to a conclusion which, like that for the fundamental attribution error, relies on the differential salience of information. He argued that we weight more heavily the dispositional influences on the behaviour of others and the situational influences on our own behaviours because those influences are simpler for us to see and notice. (See chapter 3 for a description of the effect of the availability heuristic.)

It should be noted, however, that (perhaps like many laboratory-based experiments) these 'points of view' effects have not always been exactly replicated (S. E. Taylor et al. 1979). Other explanations of the actor–observer differences in attribution have claimed that the social rules for language use lead individuals to use general and abstract adjectives (linked to dispositions) when referring to others (e.g. 'He is an extrovert') but more specific observations emphasizing the concrete situation when referring to themselves (e.g. 'I was really enjoying that party') (Semin and Fiedler 1989). Yet another approach was taken by Nisbett et al. (1973), who claimed that the bias may be a function of the greater knowledge we have about ourselves than others. For instance, as familiarity with another person increases and people know more about her or him, they tend to make more situational and less dispositional attributions about the person (i.e. attributions about familiar people become more like self-attributions).

Motivational biases

The explanations for biases in the way in which we perceive and interpret the actions of others have so far been explained in purely cognitive terms – people attempting to interpret the information correctly but failing due to their faulty cognitive processes. This is at odds with another commonly held view: in the words of an old saying, 'People see what they want to see'. This view is not only widely held by people in Western countries, but is central to many schools of thought in psychology. For instance, Freudians often assume that people repress information which may be painful to them, interpret information so as to bolster their own self esteem, and project their own faults onto others (see chapter 2). A central question is the extent to which biases in person perception are caused primarily by motivational as opposed to cognitive processes. Or are both processes so interdependent that the dichotomy is false, and it is impossible for one to function without the other?

Early research in the attribution of success and failure seemed to support the view that people were making attributions in either ego-defensive or self-esteem-boosting manner; they would attribute their success to internal causes but failure to external causes. For instance Johnson, Fiegenbaum and Weiby (1964) set-up an experiment whereby they could manipulate whether a pupil would succeed or fail a particular test. When the pupil passed, the teachers attributed this to their own good teaching, but when the pupil failed, his or her inadequacies were blamed.

Research into the attributions of group members following success or failure at an achievement task arrived at similar findings. When a group succeeds, people tend to emphasize their own contribution to the team. When the group performs poorly, other members of the group are seen as having been more influential. (See D. T. Miller and Ross 1975 for a review of this literature.)

However, more recent literature has called into doubt these motivational explanations of bias in person perception and attribution. This challenge has come about partly because the same phenomena can also be explained in terms of the information available to the perceivers, in the way that Storms (1973) explained the actor–observer error. In fact, by manipulating the information available to participants in these experiments, L. Ross, Bierbrauer and Polly (1974) managed to invert the usual findings such that participants blamed themselves for failures but attributed successes to causes external to themselves. Short of claiming the existence of a 'counter-defensive bias' (i.e. the opposite of a normal ego-defensive bias), they concluded that such errors were more plausibly the result of information-processing errors. Findings such as these also led to a questioning of why members of a species which prides itself on its intelligence should deliberately fool themselves into misinterpreting their own social world so as to maintain a false impression of their own worth – what could possibly be the evolutionary role of such a psychic mechanism?

The case that all error and bias in person perception were caused by information-processing deficits was put both forcefully and plausibly by Nisbett and Ross (1980). However, subsequently this cold cognition approach to person perception has been questioned. Many researchers and theorists in this area have been unhappy with such a cold or affect-free model of social cognition. Not only is it totally at odds with the emotional people we see around us in everyday life, and with many other psychological theories and meta-theories from cognitive dissonance (see chapter 13) to psychoanalytic approaches, but also further theorizing has suggested strongly that such an approach to cognition is not even internally consistent (Wicklund and Frey 1981). It is clear that both our information processing and our memory about other people are profoundly affected by both the thinker's mood at the time and the emotion connotations of the material being processed (Forgas 1992). This new approach to person perception has been given ever greater importance by writers in social cognition since the early 1980s, but paradigms which include both cognition and emotion are emerging only slowly (see chapter 4 for a more detailed account of the role of emotion in social behaviour).

Whether caused by cognitive shortcomings or by emotional or motivational problems, it is clear that the impressions we form of others can be erroneous at times. But typically how often are we right and how often are we wrong? You would get very different answers to that question depending on whom you asked.

At one extreme, perhaps, are Nisbett and Ross (1980), who cite many experiments showing human inference to be quite erroneous, and they even go on to argue that people are typically performing at their best in the psychology laboratory, and are even less accurate in their everyday lives. Funder (1987) takes the opposite view, arguing that many laboratory experiments are deliberately set-up to maximize the errors that people make, and that those errors would not arise in everyday life. Funder also argues that experimenters often misunderstand what their participants are trying to achieve, and therefore misinterpret their very sensible behaviour as being 'irrational'.

Another position in this accuracy debate takes a compromise position between these two extremes, labelling people as 'good enough' perceivers (S. T. Fiske 1992). Fiske and others (e.g. Hilton and Darley 1991) argued that people have to be considered as pragmatic in their orientation, forming impressions of others with particular ends in mind, for instance social interaction. Therefore, she asserts, if we do not understand the goals that people set themselves, we will not be able to make any sense of what they actually do. Achieving accuracy may be a secondary goal to achieving trust or establishing an appropriate level of intimacy on which an interaction can proceed. Put another way, would you rather be seen by your friends as someone who always analysed situations perfectly logically, or as someone who was fun to be with? The laboratory experiments measure and report only on the former.

Other critiques of attribution models

Several researchers have voiced concerns about attribution models, which, whilst coming from very different perspectives, all find those models to be implausible as explanations of the way in which individuals make decisions about others.

For instance, some theorists have questioned whether the search for the cause of other's behaviour is really so ubiquitous. Rather, they have proposed that the rhetoric of everyday life is more generally characterized by the attribution of blame: whose fault it was, the need to justify and make excuses, and the specification of what ought to have been done; the rhetoric of a naive moralist or lawyer rather than a naive scientist (Fincham and Jaspers 1980; Billig 1987). (See chapter 10 for a discussion of how individuals engage in moral reasoning.)

In evaluating models of human cognition it is important to note that two processes can give the same outcome, but have very different underlying structures. For instance, the way in which computers process possibilities in a game of chess is very different from the way in which human players think about the game. Yet, simply observing the moves one would not usually know if the player were human or machine. Is it possible that attribution models are nothing more than elegant algorithms which often produce results which are not dissimilar to those produced by humans, but bear little relationship to the ways in which people actually think?

Kruglanski has argued that a mistake with attribution models has been to accept them as *the* way in which individuals make causal attributions, rather than as one example of how a particular type of problem may be approached by some people (Kruglanski 1980; Kruglanski and Ajzen 1983). He argues that attributional models are just one example of what he terms lay epistemology – how people actually think. This lay epistemology consists, he asserts, of a series of logical propositions which are tested against the available information, and attribution models might provide a framework within which useful propositions might be generated for testing. In other words, individuals would generate propositions such as 'If the receptionist was blunt with that woman because he is a rude person, then he will have been rude to other customers; if he has never been rude to other customers I'd better consider whether it was the customer's fault', and a search for consistency would begin. Once this had been completed, and the possibility that the act was highly atypical of the actor had been dismissed, then the distinctiveness of the act could be investigated, and so on.

Others have argued that the 'disinterested logic' of attribution theories misses the human element of cognition concerning other people. Unlike cause and effect in the physical environment, it is difficult to imagine that we can understand the actions of another human being without sharing some of the same needs, emotions and thoughts as that person. 'Putting yourself in another person's shoes' or empathizing with them is a pervasive characteristic of our thoughts about others, which is not captured well by attribution models (Bruner 1990).

Another type of criticism concerns the complexity of attributional models. Langer, for instance, published a paper in 1978 which argued that much human inference was 'mindless' inasmuch as individuals engaged in little thought and made the decisions spontaneously, relying on habit or well-learned 'scripts' (Abelson 1981), rather than undertaking complex analyses to determine causal relationships (see also Langer 1989a;

1989b for a reconsideration of her position). Weiner's (1985) detailed review of the evidence finds support for the view that causal attribution is not ubiquitous, suggesting that perhaps more thoughtful processes occur only when unexpected events occur or a goal is not attained.

Zajonc (1980) has gone further and argued that our most instantaneous judgements are affective rather than cognitive. His experimental findings lead him to the rather surprising conclusion that within a fraction of a second of being presented with an object people know whether they like or dislike it, and only later know why that is. This, Zajonc concludes, suggests that the process by which we decide whether we like or dislike something may be quite independent of our cognition about that thing. Indeed cognitive therapists hope to explore that spontaneous emotion and reframe it, so that the affect, which may have been based on faulty beliefs about the social world, becomes more appropriate to the actor's situation.

There are other ways in which we make snap judgements about others too, such as by relying on non-verbal cues. As we have seen in chapter 5, there is a significant body of literature addressing the ways in which we are influenced by, for instance, people's language use and intonation. There have been a number of studies that suggested people used cues which they were not even aware of, such as the amount of eye contact of a conversation partner (Thayer 1969). And the possibility that we can get a truer picture of someone by observing their non-verbal 'leaks' has been of particular interest to everyone from jealous lovers to police interrogators; we have less control over our non-verbal behaviour than over our choice of words. However, a detailed consideration of these findings is beyond the scope of this chapter; see D. J. Schneider, Harstorf and Ellsworth (1979) or Hinton (1993) for a more detailed consideration of non-verbal cues in person perception.

Another criticism of attribution theories concerns the need to be aware that the process and content of person perception may well vary between cultures. For instance, 'supernatural' attributions (e.g. 'It was God's will' or 'The evil spirits were working through him') are very rare in Westernized societies but common in many others (Howitt et al. 1989). Shweder (1991) has criticized psychology for ignoring the possibility that an important characteristic of individual cultures is a particular representation of what it is to be human. He argues too that cultures influence the way in which individuals think about other people and their relationships with them. There are few areas within social psychology where this is more relevant than the field of person perception.

This discussion of attribution theory has, I hope, given some indication of the extensive breadth and depth of interest that the theory has been responsible for. The diversity of approaches is not trivial; there is little consensus even about when or how often attributions are made. But while attribution research may not have provided us with simple answers to issues of interpersonal perception, it has proved a rich and flexible theoretical framework which has stimulated and guided a great quantity of research over several decades.

Memory and recall for information about people

So far we have only considered the situation in which all the information concerning the target is available to the perceiver just before the judgement is made. This may be highly atypical of most social judgements we make about others. Often we draw on our memory to answer questions such as who would be trustworthy enough to ask a favour of, or whom to ask to a party. Or a directly observed behaviour might be evaluated in terms of the knowledge we have gained from past experiences of the target. In these cases we need to use information already stored in our memories. One of the assumptions that is made about memory and recall is that there is far too much information available in our social world to be able to keep it all in our memories; there has to be some selection or filtering in the mechanisms we use to store and retrieve the information, so that we can, hopefully, retain most of the useful information we observe but forget the irrelevant items. Several early studies in the field of social cognition specifically tested to see what sorts of information were more likely to be recalled. For instance, Rothbart, Evans and Fulero (1979) gave participants an expectancy (for instance that the group that they were going to receive information about were unusually friendly) before presenting them with some information that was consistent with that (e.g. 'Jo invited friends to a potluck dinner at his house') and some that was inconsistent ('Jo avoided introducing himself to a new neighbour'). Their results showed that events that were consistent with their expectancies of the groups were more likely to be recalled than events which were inconsistent with those expectancies. Rothbart, Evans and Fulero therefore concluded that we are more influenced by evidence that supports our preconceptions than by evidence that challenges them. This, they conjecture, might lead to the self-perpetuation of social stereotypes: once we expect individuals to act in a certain way we will preferentially recall confirmatory evidence and thus, even if that initial stereotype were erroneous, individuals' beliefs in it could still be maintained over time.

Also in 1979, Hastie and Kumar published the results of an experiment that seemed to demonstrate exactly the opposite to be true; person-memory was better for information that was *in*congruent with initial expectations. Throughout the 1980s data supportive of both camps was found in approximately equal proportion, suggesting that something rather more complex was going on than was initially assumed. A meta-analysis, using sixty published and unpublished papers in this area, attempted to find the variables that sometimes favoured schema-consistent results and sometimes schema-inconsistent ones (Rojahn and Pettigrew 1992). Overall, a slight advantage of schema-inconsistent information over schema-consistent information was found, but it was dependent on the way in which the experiments were conducted. Processing demands, length of exposure, delay between presentation and recall, proportion of inconsistent items, order of schema presentation, degree of inconsistency and importance of categories to participants were all found to be important moderator variables. More recently the degree to which counter-stereotypic cases deviate from the norm has been demonstrated to be yet another relevant variable. Extremely deviant examples may be discounted as being so extraordinary that they do not generalize, and can sometimes even add to the stereotype through what Kunda and Oleson (1997) call a 'boomerang effect'. As an example of this they suggest that possibly the reason that Margaret Thatcher did little to counteract stereotypes of women was because she was too far removed from the category. But one thing that is clear from a review of these studies is that schemata operate as focusing mechanisms, and information that is seen as irrelevant to the schema is less likely to be remembered than information which is either consistent or inconsistent with it.

Categorizing people

One common way in which we judge other people is by categorizing them, sometimes into categories rooted in the physical characteristics of the person (such as gender, age or ethnic group) and sometimes into categories which are entirely constructed within our social worlds (e.g. hippy or yuppy). Indeed, our predisposition to categorize others has lead some to assert that 'categorisation is endemic to us' (Wilder 1981, p. 250). Wilder considers the times when perceivers are more likely to see and judge a person as a member of a group rather than as an individual. Stereotypes of groups can be used to make inferences about members of that group in the absence of other information or as a cognitive short cut. It is relatively simple, and probably very common, to identify a 'target' as being of a particular group or 'type' and thus assume that he or she has the supposed characteristics of that group or type. This is not to say that individuals fall neatly into non-overlapping sets, and clearly even in a group or type, some members are going to be more prototypical than others, displaying more of the defining features of the group.

This simple categorization can have dramatic consequences. For instance, in several recent episodes it has become clear that many police officers immediately categorize others by race, and make assumptions about them based upon that categorization. For instance, in the Steven Lawrence murder in London in 1993, the initial assumption was that a black person at the scene of a crime is probably the perpetrator of the crime rather than the victim. (See chapter 15 for more discussion of prejudice.)

There has been considerable debate over how this knowledge of the categories into which we place people is stored in our minds. Are the categories defined by prototypes or by lists of features that a target needs to possess and not possess in order to be ascribed membership? For instance, to be seen as a sporty type in student circles, you might not only need to wear trainers, exhibit a certain physique and discuss sports a lot, but also *not* to be too interested in your studies or student politics and *not* to be seen to read even the most basic of textbooks.) However, evidence from both cognitive psychology and artificial intelligence suggests that the prototypes are more characteristic of our commonly used categories. Forgas has conducted several studies which show how widespread and shared these types of categorizations are. For instance, students readily talk about certain 'types' of student, such as sporty types, quiet loners, trendies and intellectuals (Forgas 1985). The high degree of consensus shown between different students demonstrates that these stereotypes are clearly not individually generated, but are widely shared knowledge.

This is a very important point. Most recent work on social cognition uses the word 'cognition' as being synonymous with individual information processing. However, Forgas argues forcibly that cognition is inherently social in as much as most of the knowledge that we use in our thinking is socially created (1983). Indeed, much of the knowledge we use in the categorization of people is so widely held and with such high consensus that it might best be described as a social representation (Moscovici 1981; 1984; see also chapter 14). Furthermore, this socially created knowledge probably serves many functions, affective and motivational as well as cognitive, in identifying out-groups, bonding ingroups and maintaining identity and self-esteem as well as in aiding impression formation (Tajfel and Forgas 1981). These normative and expressive roles of person categorization may have been seriously underestimated in the field of person perception.

A central question that we must ask is the extent to which people make judgements about others using depth processing models such as attribution theories, or rely on pre-existing knowledge such as stereotypes. Weiner (1985) concludes that it is partly a function of whether the information is consistent with our knowledge-base and partly a function of how salient those categories are. S. T. Fiske and Neuberg (1990) have proposed a more complex model that also recognizes that motivation may play a role in the depth and type of processing used in person perception. If, for instance, a person is highly motivated to produce an accurate impression of the target, then care may be taken to consider the individual attributes of the target. If, however, the accuracy is deemed to be of relatively little importance to the perceiver, she or he may simply rely on category membership in impression formation, and make judgements on age, sex, ethnicity and so on. Indeed, many impressions of others are probably based solely on the most visible and salient of categories, and would not require any further processing of information about the target. Whilst this might be cognitively economical, it can of course lead to erroneous judgements and a whole host of socially undesirable outcomes, such as intergroup hostility and discrimination. This sort of simple categorizing is what Langer called mindlessness, and in her more recent works she has confronted the issue of how to persuade perceivers not to rely on such simplistic methods for impression formation (Langer 1978; 1989a; 1989b). But since then Lepore and Brown (1997) have argued that categorization does not inevitably lead to prejudice: low-prejudice individuals could categorize on black–white racial stereotypes just as readily as prejudiced individuals, but without overlaying the stereotypes with negative features.

So far targets have been considered to be passive players in person perception. Indeed, in some cases there is little they can do to prevent themselves being labelled according to, for instance, age or sex stereotypes. But in many ways we are very active in providing categories for others to label us with; for instance by the clothes, jewellery, hairstyle and badges we wear.

Other knowledge structures used in person perception and categorization

Besides stereotypes, there are other types of knowledge which we also bring to person-perception tasks, including causal schemata, personae and narratives. Perceivers do not come to attributional tasks with only the covariation evidence to use; they also come equipped with knowledge about what kinds of cause are typically associated with what kinds of effects. For instance, we might expect success in simple tasks to be explained by a single cause (e.g. 'He found his way to the party because he knew the back streets well') but success in a difficult task would need several causes (e.g. 'He found his way through the Australian Bush because he was well prepared, had good maps and a good sense of direction, and was trained by experts in the local terrain'). We might also have hunches about what sort of behaviours are caused by luck, mood, situation, motivation, ability and so on. Kelley (1972) describes these as causal schemata: general conceptions that people have regarding how types of causes interact to produce a specific kind of effect. He suggested that causal schemata were more likely to be used to make causal attributions than covariance or CIT models when there was little information about the target available. In those cases the perceiver has to rely on previous knowledge of the type of behaviour displayed rather than calculations of consensus, consistency and distinctiveness.

Personae or person prototypes (Nisbett and Ross 1980) can be described as shared representations of types or characters. They often originate in literature, film, soap operas, mythology, legends, psychological theories and so on, but become more widely known and detached from their original portrayal. Examples are the 'rebel without a cause', the 'dumb blonde', the 'anal retentive' and the 'prostitute with a heart of gold'. Targets can either be assigned directly to one of these personae (e.g. 'She's a real *femme fatale*') or compared to one (e.g. 'He's got a bit of the gentle giant in him at times'). They are not dissimilar to Forgas's 'middle-level' categories (such as types of students) discussed above.

Narratives, 'stories for doing' (S. T. Fiske 1992) or scripts (Abelson 1981) are more difficult to conceptualize, and have only recently been considered as important in social cognition and person perception, but are nevertheless important sources of knowledge about our social world. They embody and share knowledge for many different purposes, including giving accounts of how events usually unfold, creating scenarios or imagined future events to show how things are or how things might have been if alternative lines of action had been taken. They differentiate the possible from the impossible in our social lives, and help us in the mental simulations we use in planning the future and making sense of the past. These narratives are one of the features distinguishing one culture from another. They enter our lives from diverse sources (such as our first story books as children, television and film, literature and conversation) and exercise a persistent influence. They give us powerful indications as to what to expect from others, and person perception is an expectancy-led process.

The outcomes of person perception

The impression that one gets from much of the person-perception literature is that the field is about one-off judgements unrelated to either the past or the future. This is highly atypical of the times when it is important to us, in our everyday social lives, to make judgements about others. For instance, little person-perception work is conducted within the realm of intimate, family or long-term relationships. But in those realms we might not only make judgements about others, but also act upon those judgements, for instance in deciding on the warmth or intimacy that we wanted to show in the relationship. One might ordinarily suppose that if we do misperceive or misinterpret the actions of another in those circumstances the outcome would not be so dire, as we would be able to correct our judgements on future occasions. Unfortunately, however, research suggests that errors in person perception might be magnified rather than extinguished in the interactions that follow.

Take, for instance, the case of judgements based on racial stereotypes. The literature on self-fulfilling prophecies in social interaction suggests that, even if there were no basis in fact for those stereotypes, they could be pivotal in shaping future interactions. For instance, Word, Zanna and Cooper (1974) studied what happened when white interviewers interviewed white and black job applicants. In the first instance, they observed closely the behaviour of just the interviewers, and found that when they were interviewing a white job applicant they would, on a number of different measures, behave in a generally more informal manner, even though the experimenters had trained the black and white applicants to respond in a standardized way. In a subsequent experiment interviewers were trained to behave in a manner resembling either the formal style used with black applicants or the informal style used with the white applicants in the first study. This time the applicants were all white, and were naive to the interviewer's training or the experimental objectives. The results showed that the applicants treated like the black applicants in the first experiment were judged to perform less well in the interviews, and responded with more reserved demeanours, finding the interviewers to be less friendly. As well as highlighting the difficulties faced by black job applicants in societies where racism is prevalent, the experiment also shows how the interviewers' initial perception of the respondent shaped their subsequent interaction, leading to the initial perception becoming self-fulfilling. Similar results have been found concerning our stereotypes for physical attractiveness; if you expect an attractive person to be more interesting or rewarding to talk to, you are likely to be nicer in the way you talk to them (Andersen and Bem 1981). This, in turn, is likely to make the person more animated and interesting in the conversation, which will lead you to think that your initial impression, based solely on the 'what is beautiful is good' stereotype, was correct all along. Conversely, unattractive individuals may often not be given the chance to prove that they are also interesting to talk to.

The extent to which this phenomenon will occur is likely to be a function of, among other things, the belief system of the perceiver. Using telephone conversations under laboratory conditions and false photographs to manipulate the perceived attractiveness of the other, Andersen and Bem found that they could even reverse the effect in some pairing; for instance, they found that women rated as androgynous on a sex-type questionnaire formed more positive impressions of other women if they were shown a less attractive photograph of them. (This is an excellent example of the characteristics of the perceiver, rather than the perceived, being profoundly influential on perceptions. See D. J. Schneider 1973 and Hampson 1984 for this implicit personality theory conception of person perception. It is perhaps in part through these sorts of effects that enduring differences between the interactional styles of individuals can be shaped. For instance, if one is physically attractive then others, particularly members of the opposite sex, will tend to be friendlier in conversation. This may well explain why physically attractive people have been found to be 'objectively' more socially skilled and more likeable (even in telephone conversations with strangers, where their physical attractiveness was not known to their conversation partners; Goldman and Lewis 1977). It is therefore not surprising that physically attractive people rate the quality of their interactions, particularly with members of the opposite sex, more highly (Reis, Nezlek and Wheeler 1980). This is exactly what sociologist Robert Merton (1957) described as a self-fulfilling prophecy; an initial false definition of a situation can influence the situation and make it become true. Thus, rather than first impressions being trivial and soon overturned once we get to know someone better, those first erroneous impressions can shape all future interactions to make the perceiver believe that those initial impressions were indeed true. Thus person perception needs to be seen as the crucial first step in many interpersonal phenomena.

Conclusions

There are issues which, from reading the rest of this book, you may have expected to be covered in this chapter but are not – for instance the development of person-perception skills through the life cycle. Doise and Mackie (1981) have argued that we cannot understand adult cognition without seeing it as an outcome of a socially driven developmental process, but unfortunately our knowledge of how children acquire social knowledge and skills in their development of the understanding of others has, at the time of writing, hardly been integrated into the literatures covered in this chapter.

And although the social and shared nature of much person perception has been emphasized, one important part of the process which is only just starting to get attention is the ways in which knowledge about people and categories is negotiated and communicated between individuals (Wigboldus, Semin and Spears 2000). And McFadyan (1992) found that negative information about some outgroups (e.g. the unemployed) was communicated very carefully so the speakers could ensure that they were not branded as bigoted or uncharitable because of the way in which they put down others.

It is always difficult to predict the future direction of a field, but an exciting new theme in social cognition is starting to make an impact on the person-perception literature. The early models of cognition were founded on symbolic models that assumed that our thought processes were based on a logic not dissimilar to the sort of formal logical rules used by computers. A more recent line of thought suggests that we should stick closer to the actual way in which the brain operates, as a neural network of nodes that get stimulated as nerve connections between them fire. Simulations using these connectionist models are starting to be able to replicate many of the person-perception and attributional phenomena noted in this chapter (see, for example, E. R. Smith and DeCoster 1998; Van Overwalle 1998). There is much optimism that connectivism will clarify and give a unifying framework to some of the diverse phenomena described in this chapter.

But we need always to remember the full complexity of the social world that will never be reduced to individual cognition. For instance, it is clear that we do not make social judgements just to be able to predict what targets will do or to satisfy our curiosity; they play an important social function. One of the important ways in which we communicate the sort of person we are is through our likes and dislikes of others, be they other students or politicians, actors or musicians. If I tell you that I worship Nelson Mandela and folk music, and hate the royal family and all-girl bands, I do so not to tell you anything about either of them, but to tell you something about me!

Recommended reading

Fiske, S. T. and Taylor, S. E. (1991) *Social Cognition*. 2nd edn. New York: McGraw-Hill.
This book gives an overview of a North American perspective on person perception.

Hewstone, M. (1989) *Causal Attribution: From Cognitive Processes to Collective Beliefs*. Oxford: Blackwell.
Hewstone's book gives a detailed account of the attribution theory literature.

Hinton, P. R. (1993) *The Psychology of Interpersonal Perception*. London: Routledge.
Hinton gives an easy-to-read and interesting introductory overview of the field.

Pennington, D. (2000) *Social Cognition*. London: Routledge.
Pennington considers the way in which humans interpret, analyse and remember information about the social world. The book covers attribution, social schemas and social representations, prejudice and discrimination.

12

Attitudes and Actions

- Introduction
- Might attitudes be irrelevant?
- Conceptions of attitudes
- Attitudes, actions and behaviour
- Conclusions
- Recommended reading

Introduction

More than sixty-five years ago, the distinguished Harvard psychologist Gordon Allport (1935, p. 798) asserted that 'The concept of attitudes is probably the most distinctive and indispensable concept in contemporary American social psychology'. Since then major social psychologists have, from time to time, virtually repeated Allport's claim (e.g. Fishbein and Ajzen 1975; W. J. McGuire 1985). It could be that these views represent a form of intellectual imperialism, whereby all academics wish to convince their readers that their, the writers', interests are the most crucial issues in their discipline. But in the case of the study of attitudes the claim does have some independent justification. For the notion of attitude has been the key concept used by social psychologists to tackle three major sets of questions of fundamental importance, not just to social psychology, but to the social sciences in general as well as to lay people. These three questions will be examined in turn in this and the following two chapters.

First, there is the issue of to what extent our internal mental activities relate to our overt behaviour. How, if at all, do our views of the world connect to our actions in the world? Social psychology usually refers to that as the 'attitude–behaviour problem'. Second, there is the issue of to what degree individuals have their views of the world internally organized. Are our positions on one set of concerns quite independent of our views on other topics or are they systematically related? And, whether they are well organized or not, how best can we change someone's views on one topic or another? That has been thought of as the study of attitude organization and attitude change, and will be examined in the next chapter (chapter 13). Third, we can ask why, at least some of the time, so many people have similar views on particular issues. Historically, that was the first of the three sets of questions to be tackled by the study of attitudes, especially by Thomas and Znaniecki (1918–20), and it has been pursued through concerns with widespread prejudices and stereotypes. More recently, however, the study of shared attitudes and widespread beliefs (see Fraser and Gaskell 1990) has been more actively investigated as part of the study of social representations and related ideas, which will be the focus of chapter 14.

Might attitudes be irrelevant?

In this chapter we will concentrate on the first of the three big issues, attitude–behaviour relations, after we have examined some of the alternative ways of conceptualizing attitudes. But for the moment let us make do with our commonsensical assumptions about what our attitudes are. You, I am sure, take it for granted that you do have attitudes on all sorts of topics. If I asked you what your attitude was towards, say, your parents or the EU or gender equality or Prince Charles, I imagine you would have no great difficulty in telling me, provided you felt like doing so. It is very unlikely that you would begin by saying, 'I don't know what you mean by "attitude".' And if I asked you to try to tell me what, in general, your attitudes consist of, you might, on reflection, say that they seem to be some kind of mixture of what you know about the attitude object and what you feel about it. (At this point you might stop to ask yourself if you agree with what I have just claimed, and if you can be any more precise about the nature of your own attitudes, before I get round to telling you how social psychologists have conceptualized them.)

Like the early social psychologists who studied attitudes and people at large, you probably take it for granted that there are relatively consistent – though not perfect – relations between your attitudes and your behaviour. You probably assume, for instance, that your attitudes towards your parents bear some relation to how you act towards them. Furthermore, a commonsensical assumption seems to be that our attitudes in some way determine or cause our actions.

If it could be demonstrated that, in fact, there are no consistent relations between our views of the world and our behaviour, we would certainly be taken aback. If knowledge of someone's attitudes told us absolutely nothing about how that person might act, it is hard to imagine that social psychologists would continue to invest in the study of attitudes the time and effort that they have done. Understanding attitudes would be seen as about important as understanding day-dreaming; an interesting little topic, but hardly the most indispensable one in social psychology. Yet, the absence of relations –

certainly the absence of strong relations – between attitudes and behaviour has some-times appeared to be what social psychology has discovered. The classic and extreme example of this is the unsophisticated but intriguing study by LaPiere (1934), which is summarized in box 12.1.

Box 12.1   LaPiere and contradiction between attitudes and behaviours

R. T. LaPiere was an American social psychologist who, in the early 1930s, travelled extensively in the USA with a young, married Chinese couple. At that time in America there appeared to be widespread, though moderate, negative attitudes – that is, prejudice – towards and discrimination against Chinese and other Far Eastern people. Altogether, LaPiere and his companions requested service at a total of 251 restaurants and hotels, and LaPiere kept a systematic record of whether or not they were served. To examine the relation between the actions that occurred and attitudes, six months later, without indicating that he had already visited them, he sent all the establishments a brief questionnaire which included his key question, 'Will you accept members of the Chinese race as guests in your establishment?'

LaPiere's striking findings, the details of which are in the table shown here, was that the overwhelming majority of the hotels and restaurants which did reply to his enquiry indicated, via their policies, strong negative attitudes to serving Chinese people, despite the fact that, with only one exception, all of them and all of the establishments which had not replied had, in fact, served the Chinese couple. Attitudes and actions were almost completely contradictory.

LaPiere's Findings

Behaviour/attitude	Yes	Depends	No
Behaviours (Did they serve?)	250	0	1
Attitudes (Would they serve?)	1	9	118

LaPiere's apparently baffling findings puzzled social psychologists for decades. Some tried to explain away the results as being due to methodological shortcomings of what was a very early and rather simple study. For example, the attitudes were collected well after the behaviours had been observed; perhaps there had been a change in views towards Asians in the period in between. But there was no good evidence that prejudices towards them had worsened across America. Again, perhaps the people replying to the written enquiry were not the people who had served and accommodated the Chinese couple. That was in fact quite possible in many cases, but it only explains the results if we assume that the basis on which the entire American catering industry was organized in the early 1930s was that in order to work as a receptionist or waiter it was necessary to like Asians, whereas anyone who disliked Asians was restricted to formulating and communicating policy from backstage. Hardly likely. Both the above are relevant methodological criticisms, but they do not convincingly explain away LaPiere's findings.

Much the same holds for attempts to handle them by means of conceptual critiques. It has been argued, for instance, that LaPiere had not actually investigated attitude–behaviour relations because he had not measured attitudes. The written replies, some claimed, were a second measure of behaviour. Others argued they should be regarded not as measures of attitudes but as indicators of intentions to behave. So, depending on which of these lines of criticism you favoured, you could claim that LaPiere had demonstrated contradiction between one set of behaviours and another or between intentions and behaviours but not between attitudes and behaviours. If you accepted either of those claims, though, you should still have been puzzled. For surely the two behaviours, or the intentions and behaviours, would have depended on very similar underlying attitudes towards Asian people, so how could the blatant contradiction between the two have emerged? Before trying to solve that puzzle, let us backtrack a little in order to tackle the question implicitly raised by this paragraph: just what is an attitude?

Conceptions of attitudes

The most frequently quoted definition of attitude is the one offered many years ago by Gordon Allport (1935, p. 810): 'An attitude is a mental and neural state of readiness which exerts a directing influence upon the individual's response to all objects and situations with which it is related.' In that definition, Allport states that attitude is not overt behaviour but a disposition which influences behaviour. In insisting on not just the mental basis but the neural basis of attitudes – for which he had even less evidence then than we have now – Allport was very strongly asserting the 'reality' of attitudes; they really are there, inside us...somewhere. He was insisting on what has become the overwhelmingly dominant view of social psychology that an attitude is a real, underlying disposition or latent process, as opposed to the then contrary probabilistic conception of attitudes offered by adherents of behaviourism. For behaviourists (see chapter 20), psychology was confined to observing and theorizing about overt, observable behaviours. Postulating unobservable processes and states, such as attitudes, was claimed, on the basis of a misguided view of science, to be unscientific and hence unacceptable. Thus, if a behaviourist used the term 'attitude' at all it was merely as a convenient shorthand to describe the probability that an individual would produce certain behaviours. Saying that someone had a favourable attitude towards religion, for example, simply meant that she frequently went to church, prayed regularly and the like. For the minority of social psychologists who espoused behaviourism, an attititude was nothing more than 'a syndrome of response consistency' (Campbell 1963). But the dominant view remains that an attitude is a relatively stable, psychologically real, latent process. Social psychologists have offered a number of slightly different ways of elaborating on that conception. Let us look briefly at three alternative latent process views of attitudes, each of which currently has its proponents. They can be conveniently distinguished in terms of the number of components of attitudes that they postulate. Together with the probabilistic view, that gives us four conceptions of attitudes:

Zero components   The probabilistic view
One component   Attitude as general evaluation
Two components   The belief–evaluation or expected value analysis
Three components   The tripartite conception

One component

An attitude is always an attitude towards something, such as a person or group or idea, and that 'something' is conventionally referred to as the attitude object. A simple and easily measured view is that an attitude towards an attitude object is an individual's general evaluation of that object, where the evaluation is an affectively or emotionally loaded judgement about how the individual feels towards the object. Overall, how well disposed or ill disposed is the individual towards it? How much does he like it or dislike it? How strongly is she for it or against it? This view can be readily and quickly measured. But is that all our attitudes involve, our general feelings of 'pro' and 'con'? Is there not also some more specific contents, such as things that we take for granted as true or false about attitude objects?

Two components

That notion is, in fact, a key part of the two-components approach, the belief–evaluation or expected value conception practised, as we shall see, by Fishbein and Ajzen (1975; Ajzen and Fishbein 1980) and others. This conception says that a person's attitude on an issue is a combination of a number of key beliefs or expectations about the attitude object and the corresponding evaluations or values of the beliefs. The beliefs are thought of by the person in terms of 'true' or 'false' and the evaluations, as we saw with the one-component analysis, in terms of 'good' or 'bad'.

For example, both a financially hard-pressed farmer and a nature-loving environmentalist may believe, rightly or wrongly, that it is completely true that using a particular pesticide kills off all caterpillars. That in itself does not give us much of a clue about their respective attitudes towards pesticide use. But if we ask them to evaluate the belief in terms of how good or bad killing off all caterpillars is, then the farmer might evaluate it as 'very good', because that would leave him with an unblemished crop which would fetch a good price, whereas the environmentalist might regard it as 'very bad' because of what it would do to caterpillars. Thus, in the light of their different combinations of belief and evaluation, different attitudes are beginning to be apparent. If, in response to another six or seven pairs of belief statements and corresponding evaluations, we observed from the farmer and the environmentalist consistently different belief–evaluation combinations, then we might well be able to conclude that the former had a very favourable attitude towards pesticide use whereas the latter's attitude was very unfavourable.

So, according to this approach, attitudes are a combination of particular beliefs and affectively laden evaluations. But what of the common assumption that our attitudes in some way facilitate or direct or cause our actions? Should that not be explicitly built into our conception of attitudes?

Three components

That idea is made explicit in the three-component approach, the tripartite conception (e.g. Rosenberg and Hovland 1960; Breckler 1984). This argues that an attitude has three distinguishable parts to it. One is the cognitive component, which consists of what, rightly or wrongly, we believe to be the case regarding an attitude object, that is, our cognitions. A second is the affective or emotional component, that is, our feelings on the matter. Do we like or dislike the person, group or idea? The third component is the trickiest to formulate. In the past, it was called the conative component, where 'conation' was a term, little used nowadays, referring to the exercise of the 'will' or striving to achieve. Sometimes (e.g. Breckler 1984) it is described as the behavioural component, but it is misleading to imply that part of an attitude is behaviour when, as we have seen, an attitude is distinct from behaviour. Currently the most convenient way to describe this third part is as the intentional component. That is, the cognitions and feelings we have are accompanied by intentions to act in certain ways towards the focus of our attitude. In practice, of course, intentions may not be acted on. Hence this formulation, while strongly implying that attitudes are likely to be correlated with actions, does not claim that the two need be perfectly related.

The tripartite conception, then, asserts that to assess someone's attitude fully it is necessary to measure all three components. These components are likely to be significantly but less than perfectly intercorrelated; if they were uncorrelated with one another they could hardly be described as three parts of the same thing; if they were perfectly correlated they might just be exactly the same thing three times over. For at least ninety years or so, a number of social psychologists have espoused a tripartite conception of attitudes, but surprisingly few of them have bothered to subject it to direct empirical examination. But over the years a few people have attempted to examine the cognitive, affective and intentional components of an attitude as independently as possible (e.g. Ostrom 1969; Breckler 1984), and in general they have found what the tripartite view implies: that the components are significantly but less than perfectly correlated with one another.

The tripartite conception is the most comprehensive of the views of attitudes which we have considered and as such is the one which, henceforth, I will assume gives the best analysis of what an attitude is. Does that mean that the one- and two-component views are completely wrong and to be ignored? Not necessarily. The belief–evaluation analysis can be thought of as one specific way of implementing, or operationalizing, the cognitive and affective components of a tripartite view. Furthermore, as we shall see, two-component practitioners such as Fishbein and Ajzen do include intentions as major predictors of behaviour, but they treat them not as parts of attitudes but as separate from them. So the two- and three-component analyses are not so different. The one-component general evaluation analysis obviously overlaps with the evalution component of the belief–evaluation approach and the affective component of the tripartite analysis. In fact, it can be thought of as one way of measuring the feelings which are a central part of all the conceptions of attitudes and often taken to be the main motivator or driving force of our attitudes. Thus, although something of an over-simplification, a one-component analysis offers a quick and easy way of measuring one key component of our attitudes. Since different components are themselves significantly intercorrelated, this 'cheap and dirty' way of measuring attitudes is likely to agree moderately well with more elaborate assessments.

Zero components

The only really contradictory analysis of attitudes that we have encountered has been the behaviouristic one. The behaviourists avoided conceding any internal existence to attitudes. So, with tongue in cheek, we might suggest that that can be thought of as a zero-component analysis!

Attitudes, actions and behaviour

Are attitudes and behaviour unrelated?

LaPiere's (1934) study was by no means the only early piece of research which posed problems for the common assumption that our attitudes determine our actions. Wicker (1969) reviewed much of the research which up to that time had attempted to relate attitudes to behaviour. He offered some very sobering conclusions. 'Taken as a whole, these studies suggest that it is considerably more likely that attitudes will be unrelated or only slightly related to overt behaviours than that attitudes will be closely related to actions' (1969, p. 65). 'The present review provides little evidence to support the postulated existence of stable, underlying attitudes within the individual which influence both his verbal expressions and his actions' (1969, p. 75). It should be recognized that Wicker's conclusions, in certain respects, overstated the material he reviewed. He had, in fact, found quite marked variations amongst studies in the size of attitude–behaviour relations reported, including some quite strong relations. Furthermore, some of the low or zero relations probably reflected badly designed studies rather than the real absence of attitude–behaviour connections. Nevertheless, Wicker's conclusions came as something of a shock to social psychologists interested in attitudes. Some developed doubts about the value of the concept, but others treated the review as a challenge to engage in more sophisticated thinking about attitudes and to improve methods of studying them.

It came to be accepted that attitudes are only one set of determinants of behaviour, rather than the whole explanation. The nature of the situation in which behaviour is likely to occur is also important; in some situations it is easier to act on one's attitudes than in others. In trying to make sense of LaPiere's surprising results, a sophisticated methodologist, Donald Campbell (1963), argued that if, as was likely at the time, many restaurant and hotel staff did harbour prejudice against Chinese people, they would have found it much easier to express their negative attitudes in a letter to an unknown other than when face to face with two very presentable, Westernized individuals. The situational 'hurdle' or barrier to be jumped in order to act on their attitudes was lower in the former case than in the latter. What would have been really baffling would have been if the staff had 'jumped' the high hurdle and refused service face to face but had not got over the low hurdle of being discouraging by letter. That, Campbell claimed, would have been real attitude–behaviour inconsistency rather than the understandable 'pseudo-inconsistency' which LaPiere had found. In addition, it came to be recognized that social pressures, whether from the situation itself, from other people to whose views of you you pay attention, or, more generally, from societal norms, including legal ones, are powerful influences on our behaviour which sometimes can override the influence of our attitudes.

It was also recognized that considerable care had to be paid to the adequacy of measures of both attitudes and behaviours. A one-question measure of an attitude was likely to have very limited reliability, which in turn would reduce the possible size of correlations with other variables. Conceptually more sophisticated measures and more elaborate multi-item scales were much preferable. And single-item measures of behaviour were also likely to be inadequate. In addition, a major methodological and conceptual improvement resulted from Fishbein's (e.g. Fishbein and Ajzen 1975) insistence that both attitudes and behaviours should be measured at the same level of specificity or generality. Many early studies, including LaPiere's, had attempted to assess fairly broad attitudes and had hoped they would predict a very specific piece of behaviour, but all too often those hopes had been dashed. Suppose you are sufficiently interested in the general attitudes of the members of one ethnic group in your home town or locality towards the members of another ethnic group to conduct an attitude survey of the former. Would you then expect that variations in those attitudes would strongly predict whether or not members of the first group would shop in a particular department store which employed an above-average number of sales staff from the second group? Is that really the question you should be asking? If you were interested in the behavioural consequences of the general attitudes, it would make more sense to attempt to assess the behaviours towards the second group just as broadly, that is, measure a variety of different behaviours towards the second group. On the other hand, if you were really interested in predicting the behaviour of shopping in a specific store, then you should try to measure a relevant and comparably specific attitude. You might think of measuring people's attitudes towards the store, but even that could be a little too general. Some people might have a favourable attitude towards the store itself but a not very favourable attitude to shopping there, because it is on the other side of town or because the bus service to it has been discontinued. The comparably specific attitude to assess would in fact be people's attitude to shopping in the store. Once it came to be generally accepted that attitudes and behaviours should be measured at the same level of generality or specificity, then, as we shall see, the size of the relationships reported increased substantially.

Yet other complications and elaborations of attitude–behaviour relations came to be acknowledged. Behaviour might result not from a single attitude but from a number of attitudes. Perhaps staff in the LaPiere study were influenced by the need to make money whenever possible and by the desire not to create a scene and risk offending other customers. In addition, and as we shall see when we come to look at 'cognitive dissonance', behaviour may come to determine attitudes as well as attitudes determining behaviour. Sometimes, for example, we may adopt attitudes which help justify behaviour which we have already produced. On occasion, our attitudes may be rationalizations rather than causes of our actions.

You may well feel that each of the above points is a plausible elaboration on how attitudes and behaviour are related, and combining a number of the points helps to make LaPiere's results much less baffling than they originally seemed, especially the importance of situational and social pressures, the need to assess attitudes and behaviours at the same level of generality, and the possibility of multiple attitudes influencing behaviour. At the same time, you may have an uneasy sense that, although they are all good points in principle, in practice the attitude–behaviour issue has become very complicated. In fact, is it still possible to do manageable studies of how our attitudes influence our actions? One very influential framework which has convinced social psychologists that the answer to that question is a resounding 'Yes' has been the theory of reasoned action (Ajzen and Fishbein 1980).

The theory of reasoned action

The theory of reasoned action (TRA) is outlined in figure 12.1 and in box 12.2.

Guided by the TRA, many attitude–behaviour studies have succeeded in finding very substantial relations amongst the key terms in the theory. Ajzen (1988, p. 119)

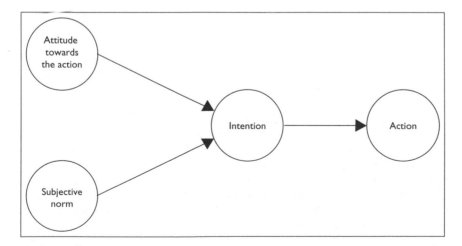

Figure 12.1 The theory of reasoned action in outline

Box 12.2 The theory of reasoned action (TRA)

As depicted in figure 12.1, Ajzen and Fishbein (1980) argued that the immediate determinant of an action A is an intention to perform A. If all you wish to do is to predict whether or not people will perform A, then you should ask those people if they intend to do A or not. Particularly if there is not much of a time lapse between measuring the intentions and the actions, the prediction is likely to be pretty accurate. But if you wish to understand why the people hold the intentions and perform the actions that they do, then you have to examine two, but only two, sets of determinants: their attitudes and their perceptions of normative or social pressures. Their attitudes are held to derive in part from their beliefs about the attitude object, which is usually the action in question. Fishbein and Ajzen measured attitudes themselves via a two-component belief-evaluation technique, as described earlier in this chapter. So, the attitudes are assessed as a combination of the beliefs multiplied by the corresponding evaluations of the beliefs.

A somewhat similar pattern holds for subjective norms. People's perceptions of social pressures regarding particular behaviour derive in part from their normative beliefs. These are beliefs that individuals and groups whose views matter to them think that they should or should not perform the behaviour, whether it be giving up smoking, applying pesticides, voting Conservative or whatever. But, according to Ajzen and Fishbein, those normative beliefs only become perceptions of subjective norms when they are combined with motivations to comply with the beliefs. You may well believe that your parents think you should give up smoking, but if you have decided you are not at all inclined to go along with their views on that particular matter then that normative belief will not exert social pressure on you.

The TRA accepts that the relative influence on actions of attitudes and of subjective norms varies. With some actions attitudes are likely to be more influential, with others social pressures will have more impact. For example, on matters which we regard as issues of principle we would expect our own attitudes to be crucial, but on many occasions when politeness is the norm we usually are quite prepared to act pleasantly – at least for short periods of time – towards people who we prefer to avoid because we dislike them. Ajzen and Fishbein try to capture these variations by, in each study, statistically calculating the optimum weights to assign to attitudes and to subjective norms in order to obtain the best combined prediction of intentions.

A final point to note is that we should imagine an arrow from 'Action' going all the way back to the beginning of the model, to indicate that an action at one point in time can influence future beliefs and/or normative beliefs and hence end up having some effect, in this mediated or 'indirect' way, on future actions. If, for example, a woman, under pressure from her partner, has sex without contraception and there are no undesired consequences, that may cause her to modify her beliefs about unprotected sex, which in turn could influence her attitudes and intentions and make her more likely in future to act in a similar way.

summarizes the results of ten studies, which on average found the following correlations:

Attitudes–Intentions   = +0.72
Subjective norms–Intentions   = +0.65
Combined attitudes + Subjective norms–Intentions   = +0.80
Intentions–Behaviours   = +0.83

Ajzen, however, did not explain why he selected the ten studies he did select. Perhaps they were his all-time favourites because they worked best! If so, they at least indicate what is possible in attitude–behaviour research. But very systematic reviews also reveal that substantial relationships, approaching those magnitudes, have consistently been demonstrated in studies making use of the TRA (see Manstead and Parker 1995, p. 71). Our grasp of attitude–behaviour relations has improved considerably since Wicker (1969) claimed that attitude–behaviour correlations were usually nearer 0.0 than +0.3.

The theory of reasoned action, however, is not perfect. It has probably always been more convincing as a useful predictive device than as a source of fully justified understanding, because a number of unresolved conceptual problems have lurked within it. Its creators have been committed to measuring attitudes as two-component combinations of beliefs × evaluations despite claiming that attitudes are our general feelings of being for or against the attitude objects, which would be more appropriately assessed by a one-component general evaluation measure. Over the years the normative side of the model has been chopped and changed and some researchers still feel that an improvement would be to restore a measure of personal moral norms, that is, what the respondent thinks is morally right. The assumption that our own attitudes and our sense of social pressures are independent of each other does not seem altogether justified. On reflection, are they not likely to have influenced each other in a number of ways so that they are to some degree correlated rather than independent? And the fact that there is, as yet, no principled theoretical way of predicting when attitudes will be more influential than social pressures, and vice versa, means we have to find out statistically study by study.

Above all, the bold assumption that the whole of our past lives directly affects our current behaviour only via our current attitudes or our present perceptions of subjective norms is a challenge to all and sundry to show that that is an oversimplification. For example, Fisher (1984) found that a measure of values regarding sexuality, which tapped views more broad and general than specific attitudes, significantly improved the prediction of students' reported contraceptive behaviour if that measure was used as well as assessments of attitudes and perceptions of subjective norms regarding contraceptive behaviour. Or again, in several studies (e.g. Parker, Manstead and Stradling 1995) it has been shown that the prediction of antisocial driving behaviour can be improved by adding to the usual predictors a measure of 'anticipated regrets'; that is, people who, in advance, think that they would regret violating driving norms are less likely to cut in, weave recklessly and overtake on the inside. Eagly and Chaiken (1993, pp. 177–93) review a number of attempts to show that the predictors of behaviour are more numerous than Fishbein and Ajzen would have us believe. Many of those studies found specific additional predictors for specific types of behaviours. But there have also been developments of more general theoretical significance.

The theory of planned behaviour

In 1979, Bentler and Speckart produced what looked like a substantial difficulty for the TRA. In reporting three studies involving smoking and drug use, they confirmed, by means of sophisticated mathematical modelling, some aspects of the TRA, including the indirect effect of past behaviour, which can influence future behaviour by first influencing current attitudes and/or perceptions of subjective norms. But they also showed that past behaviour could have a direct impact on future behaviour. The more you have done something in the past, the more likely you are to do it again, whether or not your attitudes or perceptions of social pressures change. Past behaviour as a third general predictor of our actions was not a part of the TRA. How big a problem was that for the theory?

One view was that, because of the types of behaviours involved, Bentler and Speckart's (1979) findings did not seriously threaten the TRA. To explain why not, let us backtrack just a little. So far, we may have seemed to have used the terms 'action' and 'behaviour' interchangeably. There is, however, a sensible distinction that can be drawn between them, and sometimes is. 'Actions', it can be claimed, are thoughtful, intentional behaviours which we are consciously in control of. But some behaviours do not have those characteristics. We can behave with little or no thought or no voluntary, or volitional, control. We do things 'mindlessly' or out of habit or because external influences force us to. We have tics and funny little habits; we stumble over our feet and we accidentally knock things over. None of those, it can be argued, is really an 'action', and actions are what the theory of reasoned action claims to be about. What about the behaviours studied by Bentler and Speckart? Are smoking and using drugs really thoughtful, intentional actions? Are they not more like habitual behaviours over which people have lost control? If you believe the latter, then Bentler and Speckart showed that there are some behaviours which can be directly influenced by their having been engaged in previously, but the TRA is not interested in them because they are not 'actions'. Bentler and Speckart (1981) did attempt to close this escape route for the TRA by applying their mathematical analyses to different behaviours which were unquestionably actions, but those findings proved to be quite messy and we will not pursue them here.

Someone who has tackled some of the issues raised by Bentler and Speckart has been Ajzen (1988), no longer working as Fishbein's junior partner. Ajzen's *theory of planned behaviour (TPB)* is presented in figure 12.2 and in box 12.3.

Having got to grips with the TPB, let us briefly consider two other lines of advance, both of which, amongst other things, can help our understanding of the relative impacts on behaviour of attitudes and subjective norms.

Attitude accessibility

So far we have assumed, implicitly, that if people have attitudes on a topic then their attitudes are likely to have some effects on their behaviour regarding the issue. But might the attitudes of some of those people not be more salient or more readily called to

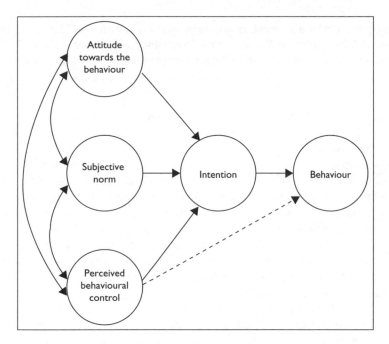

Figure 12.2 The theory of planned behaviour (Ajzen 1988, p. 133)

Box 12.3   The theory of planned behaviour (TPB)

Icek Ajzen (1988) argued that it was possible to extend the TRA to include some at least of the behaviours hitherto excluded. Tics, trips and reflexes would remain beyond a theory of the influence of attitudes and subjective norms, but behaviour such as smoking, which can be planned even if smokers may feel they cannot control it, could be accounted for if an appropriate third general predictor were included, *perceived behavioural control*. With that third predictor added, the TRA became the somewhat more general TPB, as summarized in figure 12.2.

Let us apply the TPB to a reluctant smoker. The smoker's own attitudes may be in favour of giving up. He may well know that his partner, friends and parents all want to see him quit and he would like to comply with their wishes. Unless it avoided the issue by insisting that smoking is not reasoned action and thus could not be commented on, the TRA would seem to have to predict that the smoker would give up smoking. But we know that many smokers with those attitudes and subjective norms are still smoking months and even years later. So does the TPB. It recognizes that however favourable the smoker's attitudes and subjective norms are towards stopping smoking, if he believes that he completely lacks control over his smoking behaviour then he is likely to continue puffing away. There is evidence (Ajzen 1991; Madden, Ellen and Ajzen 1992) that on a range of issues the TPB does a moderately, but significantly, better job than the TRA in predicting behaviour. The TPB still

> contains most of the conceptual problems which apply to the TRA, as outlined above, and Manstead and Parker (1995) have added a few more of its own, but conceptually and empirically the TPB does represent some additional progress.

mind by them than would be the case with other individuals? If an attitude is to have an effect on an action, is it not likely that that attitude has to be seen by the actor as relevant to the possible action?

Those questions have been tackled by Fazio and his colleages in terms of attitude accessibility or availability (Fazio 1986; 1989; Fazio and Zanna 1978). The more accessible or readily called to mind an attitude is in a given context the more likely it is to have an effect on behaviour in that context; that is, the greater the accessibility of an attitude the greater the likelihood of attitude–behaviour consistency. What, then, makes an attitude more or less accessible? Research has already detected a number of determinants which increase accessibility. They include: direct or first-hand rather than indirect or second-hand prior experience of the attitude object; the opportunity to 'consolidate' a newly formed attitude, for example by getting a good chance to enter this new view into your memory; and having a greater rather than a lesser range of information about the attitude object (see Rajecki 1990, ch. 4). An understanding of when and why attitudes will or will not be readily accessible is one step towards understanding when our behaviour will be strongly influenced by our attitudes and when it is more likely to be the result of other factors such as subjective norms.

Self-monitoring and personality differences

In general, for an individual attitudes are likely to vary in their accessibility from situation to situation. But could there be some individuals for whom attitudes are usually relatively accessible and other people for whom other considerations tend to loom larger than their own attitudes? That is more or less what research on self-monitoring seems to imply. Snyder and colleagues (e.g. Snyder 1979; Snyder and Monson 1975) have been claiming for some time that a dimension of personality along which people vary is the degree to which they monitor, or consciously pay attention to, the appropriateness of their own behaviour for the particular situation they are in. Rather than describing this monitoring as 'situation-monitoring' or even (see chapter 2 on the self) ' "me"-in-situation-monitoring', Snyder chose to label it 'self-monitoring'. Some people find that quite confusing, perhaps because they feel that the concern of high self-monitors to do the right thing in the situation means that they are exactly the people who will not be 'true to themselves'. So, let us settle for writing about high and low monitors.

There is some evidence that high monitoring and attitude accessibility are inversely related (Kardes et al., 1986), as the immediately preceding arguments have implied. More directly relevant to our concerns, there is rather more evidence that variations in monitoring are related to variations in attitude–behaviour consistency (Synder and Tanke 1976; Zanna, Olson and Fazio 1980). Doubtless you will have already worked out that high monitors, who would seem rather concerned about appropriateness and social norms, tend to show less consistency between attitudes and behaviour than do low monitors, who appear more willing to act on their attitudes.

'Self-monitoring' is one of a cluster of related notions – others include objective self-awareness and self-consistency – which have been shown to be relatable to attitude–behaviour consistency. Chapter 2 raised doubts about the degree to which such supposed personality traits really apply across a multitude of situations, and that issue has been raised specifically about 'self-monitoring' (Briggs and Cheek 1986). But it is necessary to recognize that part of a comprehensive analysis of the relations between attitudes and behaviour will inevitably involve personality differences amongst people, and variations in monitoring are likely to prove to make up some of those differences.

Conclusions

It is useful to think of progress in understanding attitude–behaviour relations as having involved three phases. In the first, the commonsensical and early social psychological assumption that our attitudes are powerful, perhaps all-powerful, determinants of our actions was seriously called into question by social psychologists from LaPiere to Wicker. Those doubts were largely allayed in the second phase by the work of Fishbein, which, particularly in the form of the theory of reasoned action (Ajzen and Fishbein 1980), dominated and focused research during that phase. In the present third phase, research and thinking are more disparate but can be seen as constructive attempts to go beyond the TRA. There can be little doubt that substantial progress has been and continues to be made in tackling the attitude–behaviour problem, and this is likely to remain an area of major concern for social psychology.

RECOMMENDED READING

Ajzen, I. and Fishbein, M. (1980) *Understanding Attitudes and Predicting Social Behavior*. Englewood Cliffs, NJ: Prentice-Hall.
This is the major presentation of the theory of reasoned action.

Eagly, A. H. and Chaiken, S. (1993) *The Psychology of Attitudes*. San Diego: Harcourt Brace Jovanovich.
This is probably the most authoritative and systematic textbook on attitudes.

Manstead, A. S. R. and Parker, D. (1995). Evaluating and extending the theory of planned behaviour. In W. Stroebe and M. Hewstone (eds), *European Review of Social Psychology, Vol. 6*. Chichester: John Wiley.
This summarizes both TRA and TPB and discusses some subsequent developments.

Rajecki, D. J. (1990) *Attitudes*. 2nd edn. Sunderland, MA: Sinauer.
This is another helpful textbook on attitudes.

13

Attitude Organization and Change

Introduction

Attitude change, if it is being attempted deliberately and systematically, can have sinister overtones, especially if the onlooker dislikes the goals of the change. Sometimes, with brainwashing techniques or some forms of advertising, our distaste is fully justified. But when we recognize the range of domains within which attempts at attitude change are routine, we see that many of them are benign, or even essential if we are not to be accused of irresponsibility. Here is something of the range of efforts, from the laudatory to the reprehensible, that can be made to change attitudes:

Socialization of children: education: conversation: mass media: advertising: brainwashing

If parents resolutely refused to offer concepts and ideas that their children lacked, or declined to attempt to explain the world around them, they would lay themselves open to charges of irresponsibility and even neglect. Yet much of what they are expected to do as good parents involves attitude change. Formal education, from nursery school to university, also incorporates numerous attempts at attitude change, as do everyday conversations with relatives, friends and even temporary acquaintances. In so far as efforts at change through socialization, education and everyday interaction appear to be undertaken in the interests of the child, student or attentive friend, they are usually assumed to be desirable. If the self-interests of the parent, teacher or persuasive friend become apparent, then we may start to feel suspicious. The obviousness of self-interest in parts of the media, in much of advertising, and in regimes and cults which practise the extremes of attitude and behaviour change known as brainwashing gives those efforts at changing attitudes negative connotations of varying degrees.

It is hard to think about changing attitudes without wondering how and to what extent existing attitudes are organized or interrelated. If each attitude is held, as it were, in a completely separate box or pigeon-hole then attempts at change can be focused on one attitude at a time. But if our attitudes are usually highly organized, such that knowing people's attitudes on a couple of issues gives a good clue to their attitudes on other issues, then perhaps the task of changing one particular attitude becomes trickier. Would all the attitudes have to be changed simultaneously? On the other hand, if a way could be found to modify one specific attitude, that change could have knock-on

Plate 13.1 Some people work very hard at changing other people's attitudes

effects on related attitudes, which might produce more extensive changes than would be the case if our attitudes are unorganized and unrelated to one another.

Although it would seem to make sense to study attitude organization and attitude change simultaneously, that has not in practice tended to happen. In this field social psychology's initial focus was on attitude change. It then largely switched to attitude organization in terms of cognitive consistency. Currently, it is mainly back on theory and research on attitude change. This chapter is organized in terms of those three phases of research and theory.

The emergence of interest in attitude change

Research on attitudes really got into its stride in the 1930s in the USA. Initially much of that research consisted of descriptive studies of the views of large samples on current issues of the day (Newcomb 1937). But also in the 1930s there emerged commercial public opinion polling organizations, which, with greater economic resources, could more easily do large-scale descriptive attitude surveys than could university researchers. Meanwhile, academic social psychologists were raising their scientific sights, feeling that their task was to analyse and explain rather than merely describe attitudes. In the late 1930s too there was an increasing general awareness of the apparent power and possibilities of mass communication, both as a benign tool for social engineering and as a source of political influence. That awareness was heightened by the advent of World War II, during which an impressive array of social scientists was encouraged to carry out research for the US Armed Forces (Stouffer et al. 1949). One major focus of that research was how best to communicate with the troops with a view to 'managing' their morale and their attitudes on relevant issues. In the light of those developments of the 1930s and 1940s, it is no surprise that in the immediate post-war period the primary interest of attitude researchers was the study of attitude change and how it could most effectively be achieved.

As we have seen, the contents and contexts in which attitude change could be studied were potentially very wide-ranging. Also, in addition to the obvious strategy of using persuasion, a number of other general strategies for attempting change could have been examined, as we shall see later. But if the potential scope was enormous, the actual research was much narrower. It concentrated on attitude change via persuasive communication, involving adults, frequently students, in relatively benign settings. Typically this was studied within the framework of a very simple communication model, in which a source (or sender) transmitted a message to a receiver in an attempt to change the receiver's attitude on a particular issue. The aim was to find out which features of source, message and receiver were most likely to bring about change in the receiver's views (e.g. Hovland, Janis and Kelley 1953; Jaspars 1978). Studies started to accumulate on, amongst other things, the impact of features of the source, such as the sender's attractiveness or expertise; the structure or form of the message, such as whether it was a one-sided message which ignored counter-arguments or a two-sided one which recognized their existence; and characteristics of the receiver, to see if some people were more persuadable than others.

Much of the research was careful, painstaking but piecemeal, with a small part of the whole being studied at a time. This probably contributed to the emergence of a number of apparent contradictions in findings. Sometimes, for example, one-sided messages were found to be more effective in changing attitudes than two-sided ones, but sometimes the opposite results were found. This initially annoying contradiction was resolved when the message variable was related to the receiver variable, in terms of how well informed on the issue the receiver already was. It transpired that better-informed receivers were more likely to be persuaded by two-sided messages, whereas one-sided messages were more effective with receivers who knew little about the topic (McGuire 1969). Progress, however, seemed slow and, despite the efforts of thinkers such as Hovland and McGuire, was largely atheoretical. By the late 1950s, the study of attitudes seemed to require a major input of theory. This need was met by one relatively simple idea developed and elaborated in slightly different ways by a variety of different theorists.

Attitude organization as cognitive consistency

A simple idea

The simple but very general idea that seemed to hit many social psychologists at about the same time was that we like our views of the world to be organized and consistent. We like 'good' to go with 'good' and 'bad' to go with 'bad'. If I like Jean and I like John, then I expect them to like each other. If I like Emily but cannot stand Ernest, then I expect them to dislike each other, and so on. If our views of the world are consistent, then supposedly everything is fine. We are in a state of what can be called *equilibrium*. We can relax and feel no need to put our mental world to rights. We can more or less stop thinking. But if there is inconsistency, things are quite different. We are uneasy and it is then that we will feel obliged to think about the inconsistencies in order to reorganize our thinking and restore consistency.

In the late 1950s and early 1960s a number of different attempts to elaborate on this general idea emerged. They differed amongst themselves in fine details, in explicitness and in what they called the desired state of equilibrium. The most explicit model, which attempted to make very precise predictions, called it *congruity* (Osgood and Tannenbaum 1955). A number of somewhat less precise models talked of *balance* (Heider 1958; Newcomb 1953; Abelson and Rosenberg 1958). The analysis which subsequently attracted most attention and which has lasted best was the least precise but most flexible, and it described the desired state as *consonance*. This was Festinger's (1957) theory of cognitive dissonance. A very readable exposition and comparison of several of these models of cognitive consistency is contained in R. Brown (1965).

Festinger's Theory of Cognitive Dissonance

For the core ideas of Festinger's theory, read box 13.1 before proceeding further.

Box 13.1   Leon Festinger and the theory of cognitive dissonance

Leon Festinger was a major figure in the emergence in North America, in the decades following World War II, of what Farr (1996) has called 'modern social psychology' (see chapter 20). Festinger was a creative thinker, formulating in the early 1950s both a theory of social communication in small groups and a theory of social comparison processes. The latter continues to influence the study of how and with whom we compare our opinions and abilities. However, the set of ideas probably most readily associated with Festinger is dissonance theory.

For Festinger (1957), anything that was represented in a person's mind was a cognitive element, whether it was a specific belief, or a general assumption, or an awareness of particular past behaviour, or whatever. Three types of relationships could exist amongst pairs of elements. They could be irrelevant to each other, such as 'I like lager' and 'I study psychology.' They could be consonant, such as 'I like lager' and 'I drink lager when I get the chance.' Or they could be in a dissonant relationship, such as 'I drink lager whenever I get the chance' and 'I think alcohol is bad for my health.' For Festinger a dissonant relationship between any two cognitive elements, A and B, exists when A implies not-B. Note that 'A implies not-B' is not a strict logical relationship but a more general, less precise 'psycho-logical' one; if two elements seem even somewhat contradictory to the person who holds them then they are dissonant and inconsistent. Festinger claimed that if people detect that they are harbouring such cognitive inconsistency, they feel uneasy, that is, they experience dissonance. This uncomfortable 'gut feeling' is unpleasant and they will attempt to remove or at least reduce dissonance.

Dissonance theory suggested a number of techniques that can be used in different circumstances, but did not systematically indicate which techniques would be used when and by whom. The simplest technique would seem to be to change one or other of the dissonant elements by, for example, telling yourself lager is pretty tasteless stuff which is hard to like or by questioning the assumption that alcohol necessarily damages your health. A slightly subtler possibility is to introduce a third reconciling element. You might tell yourself that only certain types of alcohol, but not lager, damage health, or that damage to health requires higher levels of alcohol consumption than you normally engage in. Alternatively, it might be possible to reduce the strength of dissonance by finding more arguments or opinions of friends in favour of one of the dissonant elements rather than the other; dissonance is held to be strongest when the two contradictory elements are felt to be equally convincing. If none of these techniques is available and effective, your best hope of reducing dissonance may well be to try to forget about the issue. Do not think or talk or read about it, and hope that your sense of unease will fade away if you do your best to ignore what was bothering you.

The notion of dissonance itself together with the techniques for its reduction gave rise to an array of ingenious lines of research. One major study which strictly speaking predated dissonance theory but contained many of its key ideas was reported in a fascinating book by Festinger, Riecken and Schachter (1956). They were interested in what people do when beliefs which they strongly hold appear to be disconfirmed. That is an obvious situation in which they should experience what Festinger was to call *dissonance*. The book reports what Festinger and his colleagues found when they infiltrated a doomsday cult who believed that their leader, a medium called in the book 'Mrs Keech', was in touch with the 'Elders of the Planet of Clarion'. Mrs Keech claimed that the Elders had informed her of the exact date on which a natural disaster would wipe out large parts of North America, prior to which a space ship from Clarion would rescue Mrs Keech and her followers.

This study was a very unusual one for social psychology, not just in content but also methodologically in that it combined participant observation with a natural experiment, that is, a field experiment where the contrasting conditions are created by forces other than the experimenters (see chapter 19). The key contrast lay with the fact that some of the cult members were going to face events together in the presence of Mrs Keech while others were going to be dispersed individually across the United States. Since Festinger's main prediction was that the absence of social support was likely to lead to the abandoning of beliefs in the face of disconfirmation, whereas the presence of social support would facilitate making sense of the apparent disconfirmation so that the beliefs could be not just retained but actually strengthened, you can see why this appeared to be a 'natural experiment'.

Fortunately for many millions of people in North America, friendly spacemen did not knock on Mrs Keech's door and disaster did not strike. Although Festinger and colleagues were able to report that their far from obvious prediction had been supported, their conclusions were subsequently seen as being open to dispute for methodological and theoretical reasons. Their ingenious piece of research has not lead to a subsequent body of work in the way that other aspects of dissonance theory have. Let us look briefly at just two of those.

According to Festinger (1957), any time someone takes a decision between at least two competing alternatives, dissonance is likely to be aroused. Think of consumer decisions where thought and information about pros and cons of alternatives have preceded the decision-taking. If the decision is to buy a new Ford, that means the Volkswagon and the Renault which were being considered will be rejected, although presumably they had a number of appealing features. How then does a decision-maker handle the unease connected with a tricky decision that could turn out not to have been the best one? Festinger proposed that decision-making was likely to be followed by selective exposure to information. In short, you are likely to avoid exposing yourself to information about the rejected options while still being happy to hear, read and learn about what you have chosen. Some confirmatory evidence was found for selective exposure to information following a decision, but other studies failed to find support for the idea. Festinger (1964) subsequently pointed out that that was likely to be because dissonance theory would predict that selective exposure operated even more selectively than was being assumed. For example, someone who was very confident about her decision might well willingly expose herself to apparently contradictory information, happy in her assumption that she could 'deal with it' or explain it away, thereby confirming to herself that she had made the right decision. Selective exposure to information need not follow decision-making, but is likely to do so when it would help to reduce dissonance caused by the decision. Subsequent study of this issue has continued to attempt to specify more exactly when selective exposure to subsequent information is likely to follow decision-making (Frey 1986).

Probably the best-known line of research inspired by dissonance theory has been the study of attitude change by eliciting counter-attitudinal behaviour, that is, behaviour contrary to what the individual really believes, which should of course create dissonance. This line of research was started by a rather elaborate experiment by Festinger and Carlsmith (1959), the gist of which is as follows. One at a time participants completed two deliberately boring tasks. A participant was then told an untrue cover story which ended with him being asked if he would greet the next participant and tell him that the task was interesting. In return for doing so he would be paid. Some were told they would be paid $1, others were told $20. Once they had misled the next supposed participant, they were then asked to rate the interest of the original, boring experiment. The main point of the study was to see if the different magnitudes of the bribe to act counter-attitudinally would lead to different amounts of attitude change.

Intuitively, you may feel that paying someone handsomely to tell a lie would have greater effects than paying very little. It might, for instance, make him feel more positive towards the generous experimenter, and when asked about the original tasks the participant might reciprocate by deciding that they were not really that bad. Festinger and Carlsmith, however, argued that dissonance theory predicted the exact opposite. Knowingly lying about the boring tasks was likely to create dissonance, but being offered what was then the substantial sum of $20 provided a justification for the lie. Participants could tell themselves, 'For that money, anyone would have done the same, after all it wasn't a serious lie. . . . ' So, in so far as dissonance was created at all, it would be easy to reduce it. But, they argued, it is hard to use a measly bribe of $1 to explain your behaviour. You told a lie and you cannot explain it away so readily in terms of external pressures to do so. Dissonance will arise. How is it to be reduced? The investigators suggested that the most likely way in this case was to change your attitude towards the boring task. If you told yourself that 'on reflection, it wasn't that boring; in fact it was actually mildly interesting', then you had not really lied when you had told someone else that it was interesting. And what they found was compatible with their predictions. On average, people who were offered $1 rated the tasks as moderately interesting while those offered $20 rated them as very slightly boring. For the latter group, just a little dissonance reduction may have occurred, because they did not rate the experiment as quite as boring as did a control group who were spared the deception and lying.

The general point to hold on to is that if you hope to change someone's views by getting him or her to act contrary to them, then the less overt pressure you appear to be exerting in eliciting the behaviour the greater the chance of attitude change. Strangely, this topic was often described as the study of forced compliance; it makes much more sense to think of it as demonstrating the power of (apparently) *un*forced compliance. Nowadays, parents, educators and politicians often seem to have grasped that point very well. It is only unreconstructed authoritarians who order about children, students or the electorate. Enlightened 'agents of change' assure them that if they do what is being suggested they will be doing it for their own good.

The research on attitude change through evoking counter-attitudinal behaviour led to considerable theoretical debate about how best to explain the findings. Self-perception theory (Bem 1965; 1972) offered one alternative, based on a quasi-behaviouristic analysis, whereby it is claimed we infer our own attitudes from observing our own behaviour, just as others infer our attitudes from our observable behaviour; for example, 'I must like brown bread because I eat a lot of it.' Another alternative explanation of the findings was offered by impression management theory (e.g. Schlenker 1982), which emphasizes that when people behave in front of others they 'manage' the impression that they want the others to gain of them. (This should remind you of the ideas of Goffman 1959 from chapter 2.) Current wisdom is that no single theory has emerged as the outright winner. Both self-perception theory (Fazio, Zanna and Cooper 1977) and impression management theory (Tetlock and Manstead 1985) can be used to complement rather than contradict dissonance theory, the different theories being best able to handle different aspects of phenomena in different contexts.

A reformulation of dissonance theory

Criticisms and refinements of dissonance theory emerged not just from competing theorists but from within research on dissonance theory itself. Initially claims about perceived inconsistencies generating feelings of dissonance which we would feel obliged to try to reduce were seen as applying very widely. But sceptics pointed out that few, if any, of us appear to be the near perfectly consistent beings that dissonance theory, and the other consistency theories, proposed. Instead, we seem quite happy to live with at least minor inconsistencies between the attitudes we hold and what we do, and between what we say and do one day and what we do and say the next. Certainly if people were as consistent as the consistency theorists wanted them to be, the attitude–behaviour relations we were studying in the previous chapter should have been even stronger than they were.

Much of the study of dissonance over the subsequent thirty years can be seen as the gradual delimiting or narrowing of the scope over which dissonance reduction is likely to occur. It came to be recognized, for example, that for inconsistency to create dissonance it was necessary to feel a sense of commitment to the attitudes and actions involved. For example, if after making a decision you retain the feeling that you could reverse it at any time, you are unlikely to feel dissonance. Again, if you have to make a choice between alternatives or if you find yourself acting counter-attitudinally, it is necessary for you to feel you have been in a position to exercise volition, to have decided or acted from your own choice, for dissonance to develop. As the compliance research implied, if you believe you had no choice but to behave or decide inconsistently, then you can live with the inconsistency. One reason for that is that if factors beyond your control force you to be inconsistent, the inconsistency is not likely to reflect badly on you, at least in the eyes of those people who understand the circumstances. A feeling of dissonance is likely to require a sense that you have had personal involvement in the inconsistency, and as a result your self and self-worth may be called into question; that is, inconsistencies are most likely to lead to dissonance when they carry with them aversive or negative consequences for the self. Thus, we are more likely to ignore inconsistencies that only we know of.

Instead of a detected inconsistency automatically arousing dissonance and attempts to reduce it by trying to restore consistency, even keen proponents of dissonance theory became willing to concede that we are content to be only partially or moderately consistent beings. This view of inconsistency and dissonance is best captured by the substantial revision of dissonance theory by Cooper and Fazio (1984), who argued as follows. If someone detects cognitive inconsistency on her part, and if she perceives the inconsistency as having likely aversive consequences for her, and if she accepts personal responsibility for the inconsistency, then dissonance will be aroused. However, an initial dissonance arousal must be sustained if it is to function as dissonance motivation powerful enough to encourage her to do something about the inconsistency; a fleeting sense of unease is not enough. If the dissonance arousal is labelled negatively by her and if she accepts responsibility for the negative arousal, then she will experience dissonance motivation, and only then will she engage in some form of attitude or behaviour change in an attempt to restore cognitive consistency. The two views of the relation between inconsistency and dissonance can be shown as follows:

1   An early interpretation of Festinger (1957)
Cognitive inconsistency → Dissonance → Attempted restoration of consistency

2   Cooper and Fazio (1984)
Cognitive inconsistency → Aversive consequences → Personal responsibility → Dissonance arousal → Label arousal negatively → Attribute to responsibility acceptance → Dissonance motivation → Attempted restoration of consistency

Together with arguments amongst dissonance, self-perception and impression management theories, the contrast between views 1 and 2 succinctly conveys the extent to which the study of attitude organization in terms of consistency has become a sophisticated area with a choice of alternative, complex theories.

The contrast also makes clear that the idea of consistency has not led to a neat answer to the question: are our attitudes coherently and consistently organized or are they inconsistent and unorganized? (See Eagly and Chaiken 1993, ch. 3.) It transpires that the safest, if unexciting, conclusion is that they seem to be moderately organized, but we will often tolerate inconsistencies. (In chapter 15, you will find a similar conclusion about attitudes being moderately coherent, following our discussion of the classic study on the authoritarian personality.) That conclusion suggests that the foray from the study of attitude change into theories of attitude organization as consistency was unlikely to provide a single, neat, tidy theory to structure the piecemeal findings of research on attitude change. The consistency theories, including dissonance, do have some helpful implications for change. The most general one is that for change to be a possibility, some form of inconsistency or conflict must be created and brought to the attention of the receiver. Dissonance theory suggests a number of conditions, such as volition and commitment, and a number of techniques, such as unforced compliance, which are likely to be associated with effective changes of attiudes. But consistency theories have not been developed in such a way as to become general theories of attitude change.

As things have worked out, however, that has not proved a great disappointment, for the continuing study of attitude change itself increasingly became theoretically more adept, and the past two decades have produced not one but two theories which, individually or jointly, may result in the general theory of persuasive communication that attitude researchers were longing for immediately prior to the advent of theorizing about cognitive consistency. Before examining those major developments and some of their precursors, we should pause to recognize that social psychologists do realize that changes in attitudes – and for that matter in behaviour – can result from processes other than explicit attempts at persuading people to change their minds.

Methods of attitude change other than persuasion

Sometimes attitudes change with increasing direct experience with an attitude object. There is considerable laboratory evidence (Vanbeselaere 1983) that increasing familiarity with relatively simple stimuli tends to increase our liking for them. This is what Zajonc (1968) called the *mere exposure* effect. A much more complex, socially relevant variant on that idea has been the continuing interest of social psychologists in exploring whether relations between ethnic groups can be improved by increasing contacts between the groups (Hewstone and Brown 1986). We shall examine that contact hypothesis in chapter 15. Attitudes, and behaviour, can also change through what can be thought of as increasing indirect experience with an attitude object via what social learning theorists such as Bandura (1986) call *modelling*. That involves watching the reactions of another and then copying the reactions of the model. Modelling is usually held to involve both indirect experience of the attitude object and indirect, or vicarious, experience of another's reward or reinforcement. You might, for example, decide to risk trying an unfamiliar food if you see someone else obviously enjoying it. Parents sometimes appear to have a touching faith in the power of modelling. 'Oh, yum yum, that's good!' lies the desperate parent, forcing down a spoonful of mush when confronted with a recalcitrant infant who refuses to touch the stuff.

Yet another way of attempting attitude change is directly to offer rewards, or threaten sanctions, in order to change people's attitudes and actions. That strategy is often called incentive-induced change. Advertisers seem increasingly keen to offer us free gifts if we will just agree to try their products. Governments attempt to encourage us to do some things, such as engage in certain forms of savings or investments, and try to discourage us from other activities, such as smoking, by manipulating taxation of one kind or another. Whether it is parents using positive incentives as bribes to get children to act 'properly', or legal systems using negative incentives as sanctions to discourage us from sexual and racial discrimination or burglary or murder, incentive-induced strategies are usually targeted directly at behaviour, with the hope that attitude change will follow. As we saw in the previous chapter and in our discussion of 'compliance' and dissonance, attitude change can sometimes arise through first changing behaviour, and towards the end of this chapter we shall return briefly to the relation between attitude change and behaviour change.

These additional possibilities of attitude change obviously extend the scope of the topic beyond its traditional and current core. One view might be that the study of persuasive communication was, as we saw, already so piecemeal and full of contradictory findings that providing additional possibilities for confusion is hardly a great step forward. That, however, is far too pessimistic a view, given the encouraging, quiet progress that was achieved in understanding attitude change, despite most attitude researchers having switched their attention to attitude organization and consistency.

Theories of attitude change

McGuire's information processing model

W. J. McGuire (1968; 1969), building on a distinction between 'reception' and 'acceptance' of a message which had been drawn originally by Hovland, clarified a number of apparently inconsistent earlier findings relating to characteristics of receivers. Would you expect people who are less well informed, less well educated, less 'intelligent' and with low self-esteem to be more persuadable than people who score much more highly on all of those attributes? You might, but you would not be quite right, because . . . it depends. McGuire showed that it depends on the complexity of the message and the fact that to be persuaded you have both to receive or understand the message and to accept or yield to it. If it is a simple persuasive communication, everyone should be able to understand it, but individuals who are better informed, better educated and the like are able to be more critical of it and hence less likely to accept it. If it is a complex message, however, the better informed are more likely to understand it and so more of them may be in a position to accept it. Indeed, as McGuire pointed out, sometimes the very ill informed will not understand a contentious message at all and so will not be persuaded by it, while the very well informed will understand it only too well and will reject it, so the most likely to be persuaded will be receivers of intermediate knowledge, intelligence, self-confidence and the like. In addition to resolving earlier contradictions, McGuire (1968; 1969) developed the reception vs. acceptance distinction into a five-stage information processing model:

Attention → Comprehension → Yielding → Retention → Action

(By 1985 it had become a twelve-stage model but, like me, you may feel that a good thing can be carried too far.)

McGuire proposed that, first, a persuasive communication has to be attended to. If the receiver's attention is gained, then comprehension of the message may occur. If comprehension does take place, the receiver might yield to the message, that is, change his attitude. If he does so at that time, that attitude change may be retained rather than subsequently forgotten about. If the changed attitude is retained, then it may be acted on, which after all is usually what the source of the message was aiming at all along. Notice that the first two stages, attention plus comprehension, correspond to reception, and yielding is the equivalent of acceptance.

In addition to allowing him to resolve the receiver-related contradictions just discussed, McGuire's fairly simple analysis helps to reveal why in practice expensive advertising and media campaigns can often have only limited consequences. It is not enough for such a campaign to grab the attention of large numbers of people. It has to carry them successfully through each of the following four stages too, but at each stage some of those whose attention was grabbed will almost certainly drop out. McGuire's model also throws light on why laboratory studies often appear to provide stronger effects than do more naturalistic field studies. That is the case not only with regard to persuasive communications but also in contentious areas such as the impact on viewers of observing violence in the media (Berkowitz 1993). Laboratory studies usually confine themselves to stages 1 to 3 of McGuire's model – that is, they look for short-term or even almost instantaneous effects – whereas field studies are more likely to try to locate evidence of longer-term behavioural consequences, which would presuppose effects which work their way through all five stages.

McGuire's information processing model provides a helpful, simple description of what might be necessary for effective persuasive communication, but it does not give a convincing explanation. Presumably the key thing to be explained is what brings about acceptance of or yielding to the message. McGuire seems to imply that it is getting the content of the message adequately understood by the receiver but, as Eagly and Chaiken (1993) have concluded, there is not convincing evidence that the more accurately you remember a message the more likely you are to change your attitude to agree with it. There are a number of reasons why that initially plausible-seeming assumption does not work, including the point that if getting the message straight was enough to persuade you, you would find yourself utterly unable to resist the injunction, 'Drink Duff's Beer – It Makes You Drunk.' So, if understanding the message does not explain attitude change, what might?

Greenwald's cognitive-response model

Greenwald (1968; 1981) argued that what was crucial was not working out what the message contained but how you reacted or responded cognitively to the communication. His cognitive-response model envisaged a more active, thoughtful and evaluative receiver than did McGuire's model. The focus was not on getting the content of the message right but on how hard the receiver thought about the message, and how favourable or unfavourable the content of the thoughts were that the receiver produced in response to the message. Greenwald's approach led to a substantial body of research on how receivers' cognitive responding to persuasive messages was influenced by the quality of message arguments, the amount of distraction, repetition of messages, and other variables likely to affect the favourability of thinking about a message, and there were encouraging signs of support (e.g. Petty, Wells and Brock 1976; Eagly and Chaiken 1993).

Nevertheless it was possible to see Greenwald's model as just one of an interesting array of cognitive mini-theories of persuasion which appeared over the next decade and a half (see Eagly and Chaiken 1984) and in at least moderately sophisticated ways explored particular sets of phenomena within the general topic of persuasion. Eagly and Chaiken (1984) pointed out that there was still no general framework for explaining persuasive communications. Yet Chaiken herself (1980) had possibly already prepared the ground for the emergence of more general theories by drawing a distinction between 'systematic' and 'heuristic' processing in connection with persuasion and attitude change.

Systematic and heuristic processing

So far all of the approaches to persuasion that we have examined, including those of both McGuire and Greenwald, assume that attitude change occurs through receivers assiduously paying attention, processing information, and thinking hard about arguments and counterarguments; in short, engaging in systematic processing in which they do careful cognitive work on the detailed content of the message. That view has no place for reactions such as 'I don't really follow what that nice man's saying, but he's usually right so I'll go along with him' or 'If it's good enough for her, it's good enough for me!' That is, people often seem to take short cuts in making up their minds or changing their behaviour. They may accept a message not because they have considered it carefully but because it vaguely rings a bell, or because they like the source of the message or approve of the group that the source comes from. In those circumstances they are engaging not in systematic processing but in heuristic processing. It is worth noting that this important qualification to the idea of people as immaculate cognitive processors and evaluators of information, which Chaiken (1980) emphasized in the study of attitude change, was also being recognized in a number of other areas of social psychology that had threatened to be wholly dominated by overly rational cognitive analyses (see chapter 3). We earlier saw that dissonance theorists came to accept that people were not wholly consistent in their thinking. Similar other developments included Kelley's (1972; 1973) extension of his theory of attribution processes, Langer's work on 'mindlessness' (Langer, Blank and Chanowitz 1978; Langer 1989a; 1989b) and the 'rediscovery' of emotion (see chapter 4).

The elaboration likelihood model

R. E. Petty and Cacioppo (1981; 1986) developed a distinction similar but not identical to Chaiken's in their elaboration likelihood model (ELM). In so far as it considers not only a broad range of reactions from the receiver but also a variety of types of message contents and even some features of the source, the ELM can be seen as an important and very interesting move towards a more comprehensive theory than hitherto existed. Petty and Cacioppo postulate two routes to persuasion: the central route and the peripheral route. The central route involves the careful, thoughtful consideration of message content that most previous work presupposed, and probably conjures up in our minds images of carefully prepared pamphlets or written articles that merit attentive pondering. If such a central route were the only route to persuasion then television advertisers would be spending a great deal of money pointlessly. For what careful messages are contained in scenes of cars bursting through sheets of flames or racing along winding mountain roads? Presumably very few viewers think they are being told that if they buy a new Peugeot 406 it comes complete with a suave, sexy male driver, whereas if they want a beautiful but fey young woman they should get a Renault Clio. Television advertising is not pointless but, in general, aims to go down the peripheral route. It tries to grab your attention, before you disappear to the lavatory, and then create favourable feelings towards cars, soap powders and perfumes by means of attractive associations, prestigious sources and one or two punchy ideas that can be conveyed very quickly. The ELM's peripheral route depends on simple cues, such as an attractive source, and is a broader concept than Chaiken's heuristic processing. The latter confines itself to short cuts in cognitive processing, whereas the former adds to those the operation of affective and motivational processes too.

Plate 13.2 Were these fuel protesters taking the central or the peripheral route to persuasion?

The key to understanding which route a message will take is the likelihood of the receiver elaborating on the message (hence, the elaboration likelihood model). High elaboration – that is, careful attention and thought being paid to the message content – indicates the central route, while low elaboration points to the peripheral route. High elaboration requires that the receiver has both the motivation and the ability to process the message carefully, and so the message needs good content. Low elaboration is likely in the absence of motivation and ability, and so the message requires effective, easily processed cues, such as attractiveness or similarity. The ELM has led to substantial research designed to test its predictions. In particular, numerous studies have been done involving the impact of distraction. You might think that any distraction is likely to reduce the impact of a persuasive communication. But the ELM predicts that that should only be the case if persuasion depends on careful processing of a coherent message, that is, if the central route is being followed. If the message is going down the peripheral route and relying on a few dramatic cues or the quick arousal of positive affect, then anything which distracts the receiver from noticing the flaky nature of the argument might well enhance persuasion. There is substantial evidence supporting those predictions and others from the ELM (see R. E. Petty and Cacioppo 1986; Eagly and Chaiken 1993; R. E. Petty, Priester and Wegener 1994).

Note that it is unlikely that the two routes are necessarily mutually exclusive. Elements of both may well be present simultaneously. Is there any reason, for example, why a carefully constructed, detailed argument should not be presented by an attractive and credible source? It may be that, in describing the core of their carefully constructed theory as a simple, striking contrast between 'two routes to persuasion', Petty and Cacioppo were themselves making use of elements of the peripheral route. A less concrete or catchy alternative might have been to propose that persuasive communications can be thought to lie along a dimension, at one extreme of which is the 'pure' systematic message and at the other the 'pure' heuristic one, with a great range of combinations of the two being possible between the extremes. But however one thinks of the relation between the two 'routes', evidence indicates that attitude change achieved via careful processing of well-prepared messages is more persistent, more resistant to change and more predictive of behaviour than attitude change which results from the effective manipulation of particular cues.

The heuristic-systematic model

As a general theory of attitude change via persuasive communication, the ELM has a major rival in the not altogether dissimilar HSM, which is short for the heuristic-systematic model of Chaiken and her colleagues (Chaiken 1980; 1987; Bohner, Moskowitz and Chaiken 1995). Like the ELM, the HSM contrasts two types of processing of messages. If receivers are motivated to process messages they engage in detailed bottom-up systematic processing, which requires ability and cognitive resources as well as motivation. If unmotivated, they follow a principle of least effort, which leads to top-down heuristic processing. Heuristic processing is held to be the 'default state', that is, what you do unless you are specifically motivated to put some effort into considering a message. Balance between heuristic and systematic processing occurs through the operation of the sufficiency principle, whereby a person engages in enough systematic processing so that his actual confidence in a judgement matches his desired level of confidence. If his desired level of confidence is higher than his actual confidence, then an unpleasant dissonance-like state results which the person will try to reduce.The two types of processing can co-occur in additive or in interactive ways because, in the HSP, they are regarded as endpoints on a continuum. It is argued, though, that there will be a major asymmetry in the co-occurrence; when you are engaging in systematic processing you can also use heuristic elements, but when you are being heuristic, you will not also do a great deal of systematic processing. Clearly, much of this is similar to the ELM, with some differences in emphasis and in details, and much of the evidence which can be used in support of one of the models can also be used to support the other. But there are interesting differences between the two.

As has been pointed out, ELM's peripheral route encompasses more than does HSM's heuristic processing. In other respects, however, HSM has come to be even more ambitious than ELM. Now it regards itself not merely as a theory of persuasive communication but as a very general account of the two broad informational strategies through which 'people construct their social knowledge' and 'understand the social world' (Bohner, Moskowitz and Chaiken 1995). Furthermore, unlike the assumption of ELM and most of the prior work on persuasion, HSM argues that what motivates the manner in which we process information is not necessarily a concern for truth or accuracy. Accuracy motivation – that is, the desire to establish one's beliefs as valid – is held to be one major motivation guiding our information processing, but it is only one of three major types of motivation. Sometimes our primary concern in processing a message will be defence motivation, which is our concern to safeguard or defend our current self-concepts (see chapter 2). At other times, impression motivation may be our primary aim; we may be processing information to see how it can help us project a particular situationally relevant impression or self-image. Thus, HSM is creating points of contact between, on the one hand, issues and processes traditionally confined to the study of attitude change and, on the other, an array of additional phenomena and theories. We have already pointed to links with dissonance, self and impression management theories; the chapter by Bohner, Moskowitz and Chaiken (1995) offers quite detailed demonstrations of plausible relations between HSM and both attribution theories (see chapter 11) and models of minority influence (see chapter 8).

Time will tell whether the very wide-ranging HSM or the, as yet, more narrowly focused ELM will develop into the better general theory of attitude change. It may be that instead of research in the immediate future being focused on choosing between the two, research and constructive thought may be devoted to synthesizing them, given the substantial overlap of their basic concepts.

The previous sentence might have made a reasonable conclusion to this chapter, had I not had a nagging worry about attitude change and its relation to the previous chapter, which, of course, was on attitudes and behaviour.

Attitude change or behaviour change?

Why should we be interested in attitude change, unless it can be shown to lead to behaviour change? Early in chapter 12 it was pointed out that if there were no substantial relations between our attitudes and our actions, then neither social psychologists nor lay people would be overly concerned with inconsequential attitudes. The same can be said of attitude change. Social policy experts, advertising executives, attitude theorists and parents all show a great deal of interest in changing attitudes because they hope that as a result they will be encouraging desired behaviours. Why then should we not just focus on changing behaviour, especially since some might argue that, if we did, we would concentrate on incentive-based strategies rather than persuasive communication? Some of the most dramatic and general behaviour changes are, after all, achieved by governments changing laws and manipulating taxation (e.g. Fhaner and Hane 1979; Stroebe and Jonas 1996).

In fact, simply aiming at behaviour change, while ignoring attitude change, has a number of major limitations. It is very hard to achieve on a large scale unless it is done by a government or a powerful institution with a high level of control over its members. Fortunately, few of us have the power to issue an order and watch it being jumped to by others who actually object to it. As we saw earlier in this chapter, unless behavioural compliance is produced in an apparently unforced way, attitude change is unlikely to follow. Using the terms of chapter 8, behaviour change will remain mere compliance and will not become conversion, in which case, if freed from the pressures and surveillance which initially produced the changed behaviour, people are likely to revert to their previous actions. That in turn indicates that, for behaviour change to be maintained in the absence of attitude change, a system of regular surveillance and control is likely to have to be established. It is, for most people and purposes, much preferable for changes of behaviour to be internalized as attitude change and to be voluntarily maintained by self-monitoring. So attitude change usually is necessary. But so is behaviour change, a point that much of the study of attitude change has not taken seriously enough.

Imagine that a campaign to encourage young smokers to stop smoking is claimed to have been highly successful. Thousands of people's attitudes have been changed in the direction of being in favour of stopping. How many of them will actually stop? The theory of planned behaviour (Ajzen 1988), which we examined in the previous chapter, would suggest that only some of them will. Those whose favourable attitudes towards stopping are accompanied by both perceived normative pressures in favour of quitting and perceived behavioural control of their smoking would definitely be expected to stop. Those whose friends and colleagues generate normative pressure against giving up might or might not quit, depending on the relative strengths of the attitudes and the normative pressures, and, whatever the attitudes and normative pressures may be, those who believe they lack the requisite behavioural control would carry on smoking. In the light of that, it is tempting to suggest that every theory of attitude change needs a theory of attitude–behaviour relations tacked on to the end of it.

In this chapter, we have seen how substantial progress has been made from the early piecemeal studies of source, message and receiver to the present potentially comprehensive accounts of attitude change. In the previous chapter, we saw substantial progress from the initially baffling findings of LaPierre (1934) to the current sophisticated analyses of relations between attitudes and behaviour. One further challenge facing the study of attitudes is to integrate the two lines of advance by embedding theories of attitude change within theories of attitude–behaviour relations.

Conclusions

In this chapter, we have examined both attitude change and attitude organization or consistency. Since the two issues have tended to be studied rather separately, we have taken an informal historical approach, in order to see the relations between the study of the two topics and to appreciate the progress made in understanding attitude organization and change. Three phases of study were identified. First there were the origins, in the 1930s, of interest in attitude change, leading to largely empirical research in the 1940s and 1950s on persuasive communication in terms of features of source, message and receiver. The second phase, of the 1960s and 1970s, was characterized by a switch of focus to understanding attitude organization in terms of the maintenance of cognitive consistency. That came to be dominated by the ideas of dissonance theory, which over a thirty-year period were elaborated and refined to produce a detailed account of when we would strive to maintain an organized view of our world by trying to restore cognitive consistency and when, instead, we would be prepared to live with inconsistency. In the third and current phase, of the 1980s and 1990s, the agenda has again been dominated by inquiry into attitude change, still predominantly, though not exclusively, via persuasive communication. Discrete progress made during the second phase, in the form of resolving apparent contradictions in findings and producing an array of cognitive mini-theories of aspects of persuasion, has blossomed into ambitious attempts, in the form of the ELM and the HSP, to produce much more general theories of attitude change through persuasion. A challenge for a future fourth phase will be to convert theories of attitude change into theories of attitude change which produce behaviour change.

RECOMMENDED READING

Bohner, G., Moskowitz, G. B. and Chaiken, S. (1995) The interplay of heuristic and systematic processing of social information. In W. Stroebe and M. Hewstone (eds), *European Review of Social Psychology, Vol. 6*. Chichester: John Wiley.
This is an ambitious extension of the HSM account of attitude change.

Brown, R. (1965) Ch. 11 in *Social Psychology*. New York: Free Press.
This is a lucid and entertaining, if dated, summary and comparison of three models of cognitive consistency.

Eagly, A.H. and Chaiken, S. (1993) *The Psychology of Attitudes*. San Diego: Harcourt Brace Jovanovich.
This authoritative work offers more accounts of attitude change than most people would wish to have.

Festinger, L., Riecken, H. W. and Schachter, S. (1956) *When Prophecy Fails*. Minneapolis: University of Minneapolis Press.
Festinger L. (1957) *A Theory of Cognitive Dissonance*. Stanford, CA: Stanford University Press.
The first of these two readings is a unique study of impending doom, and a prelude to the second.

Petty, R. E. and Cacioppo, J. T. (1986) *Communication and Persuasion: Central and Peripheral Routes to Attitude Change*. New York: Springer-Verlag.
This is probably still the best version of the ELM account of attitude change.

14

Social Representations

- Introduction
- Characteristics of social representations
- The dynamics of social representations
- Reified and consensual universes
- The development of social representations of gender
- Social representations as organizations of meanings
- Conclusions
- Recommended reading

Introduction

Look at the outline map of Europe on the oppsite page. You will see the cities of Vienna and Berlin marked on it, Vienna close to the centre and Berlin to the north. Where would you then locate the cities of Prague and Budapest?

For most people who have grown up since the end of World War II both of these cities belong to the Eastern division of Europe, while Vienna belongs to the West, and consequently both Prague and Budapest should be to the east of Vienna. But now look at a map of Europe and see the actual locations of these cities. Budapest, to be sure, lies further east, downstream along the Danube from Vienna. But Prague in fact lies to the west of Vienna.

This small example illustrates something of the phenomenon of social representations. Our image of the geography of Europe was reconstructed in terms of the political division of the Cold War, in which the ideological definitions of East and West came to

Figure 14.1 Where are Prague and Budapest?

substitute for the geographical. We can see in this example how patterns of communication in the post-war years influenced this process and stabilized a particular image of Europe.

As well as illustrating the role of communication and influence in the process of social representation, this example also illustrates the way in which representations become common-sense. They enter into the ordinary and everyday world which we inhabit and which we discuss with our friends and colleagues, and which circulate in the media that we read and watch. In short, representations sustained by communication and influence constitute the realities of our daily lives and serve as the principal means for establishing the affiliations through which we are bound to one another.

The concept of social representations was introduced into social psychology in 1961 by Serge Moscovici through the publication of his research on everyday ideas about psychoanalysis. (For a brief biography of this important figure in European social psychology, see box 14.1.) We shall see more of this work later in the chapter, but at the outset it is important to recognize that a focus on collective or shared representations is associated with a distinctive perspective in social psychology, one which embraces what chapters 1 and 20 described as the wider 'societal' frame for social

Box 14.1   Serge Moscovici (1925–)

Serge Moscovici, one of the most influential social psychologists in recent times, was born into a poor Jewish family in Romania. Growing up in the years which saw the rise of Nazism and the spread of anti-Semitism, he spent part of World War II as a forced labourer in the factories of Bucharest. After the war he left Romania, and eventually settled in Paris in 1948 (in 1997 he published an account of these experiences in his autobiography, *Chronique des années égarées*, or *Chronicle of Stray Years*).

From the 1950s onwards he has produced a series of works across an extraordinarily wide range of social psychological interests and concerns. In 1961 he published his study of the way in which psychoanalysis has both been interpreted by different social groups and also influenced common-sense and everyday thinking, a work which introduced into social psychology the theory of social representations, the theory with which he has continued to be most closely associated. This work, *La Psychanalyse, son image et son public* (1961/1976), unfortunately remains untranslated into English, but he has recently published a collection of his essays and papers related to the theory under the title *Social Representations: Explanations in Social Psychology* (2000) (see also chapter 17).

His work on group processes has also had a significant influence in social psychological research (see chapter 8). With his colleagues in the Laboratoire de Psychologie Sociale at the Ecole des Hautes Etudes en Sciences Sociales in Paris, he undertook a series of experimental studies of social influence processes which explored the conditions under which minorities can influence social groups. This work challenged the existing pattern in the study of social influence processes, which had been centred on the idea of conformity, by emphasizing the necessity of also studying processes of innovation in groups. He presented an overview of this work in his book on *Social Influence and Social Change* (1976), and the study of minority influence has become a significant concern in contemporary social psychology. His interest in group processes also led him to undertake an historical study of social psychological conceptions of the crowd (*The Age of the Crowd*, 1985). In addition to his earlier work on group polarization (see chapter 8) he has, more recently, produced a book on decision-making in groups (*Conflict and Consensus*, with Willem Doise, 1994).

As well as producing such an impressive body of research and theory, he played a leading role in creating the European Association of Experimental Social Psychology, and in fostering dialogues with social psychologists in Eastern Europe during the years of the Cold War. He has also been a leading participant in discussions between European and American social psychologists (for several years he taught at the New School for Social Research in New York in addition to his work in Paris).

Throughout his career he has been concerned with the nature of social psychology and its relationship to broader social theory, a concern which led to his work on *The Invention of Society* (1996), for which he received the European Amalfi Prize for Sociology. In addition to his work in social psychology he has also published original research in the history of science and a series of studies on the changing human conceptions of nature, an interest which led him to an active participation in the formation of the Green movement in France.

> The range and breadth of Moscovici's contributions have made him one of the most celebrated – and sometimes the most criticized – of social psychologists. A sense of the diversity and originality of his work can be found in the long interview with Ivana Marková included in his recent collection of essays on *Social Representations*.

psychology, and one which is also sharply critical of a social psychology built around the analysis only of the psychological activities and interactions of individuals. We can appreciate this point more clearly by remembering what chapter 5 told us about the process of communication and the role of language. All communication assumes some shared frame of reference between the actors involved, and language itself is always a property of a community of language users for whom words function as conventional signs allowing meanings to be articulated and exchanged. In a similar way Moscovici's theory of social representations assumes that knowledge of the world is not an individual property but, rather, is organized as collective structures which express the understanding of a community. A focus on the collective nature of knowledge and its role in the organization and elaboration of meaning is not unique to the theory of social representations (see e.g. Farr 1996).

There is a long tradition of such thinking in the history of psychology (cf. Moscovici 1998; 2000), but one which for most of the twentieth century was marginalized by more dominant forms which have taken the individual as the unique centre of psychological processes, and which has seen the aim of social psychological research as the analysis of these processes in a formal, abstract and decontextualized way. Moscovici's work, in fact, formed an important element in the emergence of a more critical perspective in social psychology in the 1960s and 1970s, particularly in Europe (see for example, Israel and Tajfel 1972; chapter 2). Today the theory of social representations continues to be an important aspect of social psychological research and theory not only in Europe but also in Latin America, and is even becoming better known in the United States (e.g. Deaux and Philogene 2000). At the same time the critical spirit in social psychology has produced a number of versions of constructivist (e.g. Gergen 1999), discursive (e.g. Harré and Gillett 1994; Potter and Wetherell 1987) and rhetorical (e.g. Billig 1987) theories (for a recent discussions of some of these perspectives see Danziger 1997; Flick 1998; Ibanez 1997). Nevertheless, and perhaps because it has been an active focus of social psychological research since the 1960s, the work on social representations retains a distinctive vitality and importance in contemporary debates in social psychology.

Characteristics of social representations

If the theory of social representations is associated with a distinct perspective in social psychology, this is not because it introduces either new facts or new methodological techniques to the discipline, although it may have some claims to make on both these counts. Rather, its novelty and significance lie above all in the conceptual framework it introduces. To appreciate this perspective it is important to consider some of the key characteristics which Moscovici associates with the idea of social representations.

One way to approach this is to consider what each of these two words, 'social' and 'representations', indicates and what is meant by bringing them together in a single concept.

Let us begin with 'representations'. In its broadest sense representation refers to anything which stands for, or represents, something else. In psychology the idea of representation has been used to refer to the ideas we form of the world around us, the mental images we construct. In fact there has been some debate as to whether representations are primarily images in the sense of pictures or whether they are better described as propositional in the sense of a linguistic or logical description of the world we inhabit. Whether we think of representations as images or propositions is less important for the moment than recognizing the important function which representations play in psychological processes, for it is above all through our representations that we make sense of the world we inhabit, and it is these representations which orient our action in the world around us and our interactions with others.

We can find a good example of the functional role of representations in the developmental psychology of Jean Piaget, aspects of which we have encountered in chapter 10. In his studies of infancy, for example, Piaget demonstrates that when an object which a young infant of 6 months or so is reaching out for is suddenly hidden, the infant loses all interest in the object. Even though by this age infants have developed the capacity for coordinating hand and eye, in these circumstances it as though an object which they can no longer see is no longer an object in their world. Another example can be taken from Piaget's work with older children, around the age of 5, who will argue that the amount of water is changed when the water is poured from one shaped container to another. Children at this age do not appear to grasp the idea of conservation in a way which they can articulate. In both of these instances, children produce forms of action or argument which might appear to contain characteristically childish 'errors' from an adult perspective. But Piaget considers these not as 'errors', but rather as indications of the way children's thought and action are structured at different levels of development. In each case, their action reflects the way in which they construct, or represent, their world, and both of these examples illustrate the way in which the world which we know consists of the representations we form of it.

This idea of representations has long been a central feature of psychological thought, even if it was eclipsed during the pre-eminence of behaviourism in the first half of the twentieth century (see chapter 20), but it has most commonly been taken as indicating ideas about the world elaborated by individuals through their action and experience. If Moscovici's work presents a distinctive perspective in social psychology it is largely because of his insistence on the social character of representations. In talking about *social* representations, Moscovici emphasizes that representations are not simply individual constructions, but rather refer to collective, shared organizations of meaning through which a community aims to sustain a particular view of some aspect of the world. Indeed, the adjective 'social' introduces a number of different nuances to the idea of 'representation':

1   Representations can be considered as social since, as we shall see, they emerge within the context of social relations and social interaction, and it is through social processes that they become organized as particular structures or one structure is transformed into another. Moscovici has often used the image of the café to

illustrate this process – as people sit around the table and talk, a certain collective way of understanding or conceptualizing the theme of the conversation takes shape.

2   These representations are always concerned with aspects of the worlds we inhabit, or as Moscovici (1984) expresses it, social representations are always the representation of something. This insistence on attending to the content of representations is one of the ways in which Moscovici's work is distinctive in contemporary social psychology. For the most part cognitive theorizing has focused on the information-processing aspects of cognition and largely ignored the significance of what is being thought about.

3   Representations always have a symbolic value for people; to think in one way rather than another, to believe one thing rather than another, always locates a person within a social system. Again, Moscovici (1984) expresses this in his characteristic way by asserting that representations are always representations of someone or some collective. Further, this symbolic aspect of representations is also bidirectional. When people identify someone else as a communist, or a racist, they not only place that person at a certain point within their mental world, but in so doing they also reveal something of their own position within broader frameworks of cultural meaning.

These points provide a social matrix within which to consider the structure and functioning of representations. The focus of work on social representations has been on the way in which collective ideas are elaborated, communicated and changed, as well as on the role which such collective ideas play in social psychological processes. As my example of representations of Europe illustrated, social representations are concerned both with the way in which realities are conceived or defined and with the way in which they are communicated. Both of these elements are combined in Moscovici's characterization of social representations as:

> system(s) of values, ideas and practices with a twofold function; first, to establish an order which will enable individuals to orient themselves in their material and social world and to master it; and secondly to enable communication to take place among the members of a community by providing them with a code for social exchange and a code for naming and classifying unambiguously the various aspects of their world and their individual and group history. (Moscovici 1973, p. xiii)

The dynamics of social representations

This characterization of social representations describes their functional role in social psychological processes. In doing so it answers one kind of question about why we form representations, by describing the purposes they serve in our collective life. But we can also ask a different kind of question about why we form representations, which is concerned not so much with their functional role as with our motives for forming them. Here Moscovici argues that 'the purpose of all representations is to make something unfamiliar, or unfamiliarity itself, familiar' (Mosocvici 1984, p. 24). Unfamiliarity, in fact, has often been seen as a key element promoting social psychological activity.

Moscovici emphasizes how unfamiliarity introduces a dynamic in which we achieve familiarization and establish representations through the processes of anchoring and objectification (Moscovici's analysis can also be usefully compared to Bartlett's ideas about social conventionalization; see Saito 2000a).

Anchoring is a process which draws the unfamiliar into existing social psychological categories, thereby locating the strange or foreign within the familiar. It is essentially a process of classification and naming. For instance, in his own study of representations of psychoanalysis Moscovici (1976; 1984), observed that among Catholics it is often anchored in the familiar setting of the confessional. But, of course, the precise character of the familiar categories in which the unfamiliar is anchored also generates a set of meanings for this unfamiliar object, a set of meanings which may emphasize some aspects of an object while obscuring others. Thus, while the representation of psycho-analysis as a form of confessional certainly familiarizes this object for a Catholic community, Moscovici also observed that their accounts of psychoanalysis tended to omit or ignore any reference to the libidinal or erotic aspects which are at the core of psychoanalytic theories.

How something becomes anchored is thus central to the representation which emerges, and, not surprisingly, the process of anchoring provides a group with a means of stabilizing a representation of something unfamiliar in such a way as to protect or sustain their existing patterns of thought and belief, even their own identity. An example of this process at work can be seen in De Paolis's (1990) study of repre-sentations of psychology and psychologists among other professional groups. Psychi-atrists anchored the psychologist in the category of a vocation, emphasizing the psychologists' capacity for establishing human relations with their clients. The psychia-trists saw psychologists as making contributions that were intuitive and reflected their personal qualities. In this way, of course, the psychiatrists were also protecting their own position by denying that psychology had any scientific knowledge or professional expertise to bring to their work with disturbed patients. In contrast, De Paolis found that teachers emphasized precisely the professional quality of psychologists. Indeed, they saw psychologists as offering support and assistance for their problems and difficulties in the classroom on the basis of their scientific training and expertise. In the years since De Paolis undertook her study, which was originally completed as a PhD thesis in Paris in 1986, things may have changed considerably. Psychiatrists may have become tolerant and accepting of the professional role of psychologists, while teachers may be more suspicious of psychologists' claims to offer scientifically based solutions to classroom problems. Nevertheless this study illustrates clearly the significance of anchoring in the establishment of representations.

Objectification refers to the way in which representations are projected outwards into the world, so that they constitute the reality we experience. At the heart of every representation is what Moscovici describes as a figurative nucleus, 'a complex of images that visibly reproduces a complex of ideas' (Moscovici 1984, p. 38). As this phrase indicates, what Moscovici is referring to here is not simply a sense of an image as a pictorial reproduction, but, rather, the way in which an image draws together a complex set of meanings which include values and attitudes as much as knowledge, the image serving to give concrete shape and form to this cluster of abstractions. Much of our sense of the world we inhabit reflects the role of such images, so that it is more often the case that we see what we know rather than that we know what we see.

A strong sense of images as the figurative nucleus of social representations can be found in studies which have sought to generate graphical images as the basic data for analysing representations, as for example in Milgram's (1984) study of inhabitants' representations of the city of Paris, or De Rosa's (1987) use of images to investigate social representations of mental illness. Other empirical studies of the process of objectification have generally been concerned with the analysis of such images and their role in perception and action. D'Alessio (1990), for example, explored images of childhood and development by asking adults at what age they thought children would be able to solve some intelligence test items. By comparing these estimates with the standardized ages at which most children can actually solve these problems, she was able to demonstrate that adults' images of children overestimate the intellectual competence of young children while underestimating that of older children. In other words, these adults responded in terms of their image of the 'normal' developmental path of children, an image which is at some variance with the realities uncovered by research on the development of intelligence. Another study, by Molinari and Emiliani (1990), investigated the images which mothers held of their own young children and compared these images with the styles the mothers adopted in reading a picture-book with their children. They found that mothers who emphasized intelligence and autonomy as central characteristics of their children, rather than imagining the child as obedient and dependent, tended to engage with their children through a narrative style in which the mothers emphasize and control the re-telling of the picture story, rather than a more dialogical style where the story which emerged from the pictures reflected more of the child's own reactions.

It is both useful and important to distinguish these two complementary processes in the construction of social representations. Nevertheless, anchoring and objectification are interdependent processes in the dynamic elaboration of social representations. A representation can become securely anchored to the extent that it is also objectified, and objectification would not be possible unless a representation were anchored.

Reified and consensual universes

I have already referred briefly to some elements of Moscovici's own study of the social representations of psychoanalysis in France in the 1950s. One reason why this theme attracted his attention was his recognition of the extraordinary speed with which psychoanalytic ideas spread in the early years of this century. When Sigmund Freud published *The Interpretation of Dreams* in 1900, he was an obscure Jewish Viennese neurologist who had achieved more notoriety than recognition among his medical colleagues. Yet by the 1920s and 1930s he had become a public celebrity whose treatment by the Nazis after the annexation of Austria in 1938 was a source for concern among several Western governments. However, it was not so much Freud's personal fame which attracted Moscovici's attention as the way in which his ideas about our psychic lives had entered the popular imagination, providing not only an image of the structural organization of the mind with its division between conscious and unconscious processes, but also a language for dealing with psychological events and human relationships. In part of course, the rapidity with which these ideas entered common sense and popular culture can be analysed in relation to shifts and changes at an ideological level in the nineteenth century, in which industrialization and the rise of the market economy also produced dislocations at a psychological level.

The rapid spread of psychoanalytic ideas was also of interest for Moscovici in so far as it provided an example of the way in which ideas which emerged first in the world of science became part of the ordinary and everyday world of common sense. Indeed it would not be too much to say that Moscovici originally elaborated his ideas about

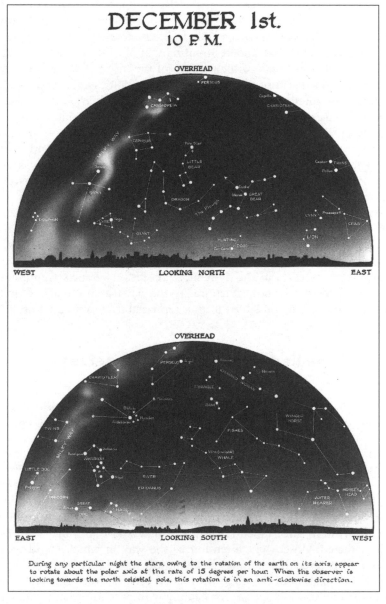

Plate 14.1(a) Astromomy: part of the reified universe

Plate 14.1(b) Astrology: part of the consensual universe

social representations precisely in order to study this process, so that a study of social representations of psychoanalysis should be a study of how these scientific ideas were transformed as they passed into the realms of common sense. For Moscovici, these two, science and common sense, constitute two distinct forms of knowledge, which he refers to as the reified and consensual universes. Where science attempts to proceed experimentally through the construction and testing of hypotheses, common sense relies more on intuition, suggestion, or what the anthropologist Lévy-Bruhl described as 'participation'. (There is again here a reminder of Moscovici's debt to Piaget. Many of the characteristics which Moscovici associates with common sense are similar to those which Piaget had found in his studies of the mentality of young children). Where the reified universe is always open to the lessons of experience, the consensual universe is constrained by the power of belief. In drawing such a sharp distinction between the reified universe of science and the consensual universe of common sense, Moscovici argues that it reflects a powerful representation of knowledge in our modern era, in which science has displaced religion as the source of legitimation (cf. Moscovici 1982; 1984; 1998; and also Duveen 1998). In this way social representations, as the characteristic form of collective thought in the age of modernity, are also seen as historically distinct from forms of collective thought in earlier epochs.

Moscovici's distinction between the reified and the consensual universes has certainly been one of the more problematic aspects of his theory. It is clearly intended not as a distinction between individual persons, but rather between the different patterns of thought and communication in each case. The same persons may engage in both modes of thought. Its origins certainly lie in his interest in the ways in which scientific knowledge become part of the every day world (cf. his interview with Ivana Marková in Moscovici 2000). But it can also be argued that the world of science has been just as much influenced by everyday notions of common sense, as can be seen in the history of the study of intelligence (cf. Carugati 1990) or personality (cf. Semin 1990). Whatever the difficulties may be in providing an adequate account of this distinction, from the point of view of the circulation of knowledge in everyday communication there is clearly an important difference according to whether something is claimed to be the product of scientific investigation or simply common sense.

The development of social representations of gender

The introduction to this chapter suggested that the originality of the theory of social representations lies in the conceptual innovations it has bought to the study of social psychological phenomena. In what ways, then, can the concepts outlined in the preceding sections help to structure specific research studies, and how, if at all, might these be different from more conventional social psychological studies? The first of these issues is addressed in this section through a review of one set of studies of the development of social representations of gender, while the second issue will be considered further in the concluding section. Before looking at this case study of gender, it is important to note that a wide diversity of research methods has been employed in studies of social representations. Quantitative as well as qualitative methods, questionnaires as much as ethnography, even experimental methods have been used (see Flick 1998; Doise, Clémence and Lorenzi-Cioldi 1993 for overviews of the various methods employed). Moscovici himself has always defended the idea that social psychology should be governed by a 'methodological polytheism' (Moscovici 1982) in which particular methods are selected because they are appropriate to a specific inquiry, rather than accepting that any one method should be given priority in all circumstances. (For further discussion of the range of methods employed by social psychologists, see chapter 19.)

This case study explores children's development from the perspective of social representations. Earlier sections of this chapter emphasized the significance of social representations for social life in general. But how do people become participants in this social world? This question can be taken in various ways. We could consider how adults come to take on new representations as they engage with different social groups. But we can also consider this question by asking how children come to be participants in the social worlds in which they grow up. Here the issue concerns not only how children come to acquire the representations which are characteristic of their community, but also how these representations influence children's own development. Through a focus on the development of social representations of gender, we can trace something of this complex process.

It is tempting to think about this development as beginning with the birth of a new baby, but in fact we need to consider the context in which this baby is born. Even before their birth children are the objects of the hopes, fears and aspirations of their parents, and within this context expectations related to the gender of the child exercise a powerful influence. The parents, of course, are themselves participants in social groups which share particular representations of gender, representations which circulate around the expected child and help to structure the parents' responses to the child once it is born. In a famous study Rubin, Provenzano and Luria (1974) asked the parents of newborn children to describe their babies. Even when there were no differences in birthweight, birth length or the babies' initial reactions to stimulation, these descriptions varied systematically as a function of the biological characteristics of children's external genitalia. At this point in their lives these children had literally done nothing, and yet their very physical form served as signifiers for others to project a gender identity on to them. In doing so the parents also located the child within a social world, that is, they extended a social identity to the child. The development of social representations of gender is a process in which children progressively internalize this extended social identity. As we shall see, by the age of 4, this process enables children to establish themselves as independent actors in the field of gender (Lloyd and Duveen 1990; 1992).

In the first eighteen months of children's lives their gender identity is regulated by the actions of others. Observations of women who were themselves the mothers of young children playing with 6-month-old infants illustrate some of the ways in which this occurs. In these studies (C. Smith and Lloyd 1978; C. Smith 1982) the women had not previously met the babies they were asked to play with, and the children were presented to them dressed and named stereotypically as either girls or boys. In fact half the time these children were cross-dressed and cross-named. Regardless of the biological sex of the child, the first toy offered to them for play was usually one which carried a gender marking consistent with the child's apparent gender. Thus a child presented as a girl was usually offered a doll, while a child presented as a boy was more likely to be offered a hammer. Even more striking was these women's reactions to these infants' gross motor activity. Such activity is not itself an indicator of gender, being a feature of the behavioural repertoire of both girls and boys. However, when this activity was produced by a child dressed and named as a boy the women offered both verbal and motor encouragement, stimulating further activity. The same behaviour produced by a child dressed and named as a girl was viewed by the women as a sign of distress, to which they responded by soothing and calming the child. The structuring activity of the adult was also evident in a later study of women playing with their own 13-month-old infants (C. Smith 1982). At this age children's spontaneous play with toys showed little clear differentiation, either in terms of their preferences for toys of particular gender marking or in the way they used toys. However, the entry of the mothers into the observation room amplified and sharpened children's activities. With their mothers present, boys engaged in more gross motor activity (such as banging the hammer), while there was a slight tendency for the manipulative play of girls to increase. While these differences were small, they nevertheless illustrate the consistent effect which the mothers introduced into their children's play, effects which themselves served to emphasize a differentiation between the genders.

From these studies we can see how social representations of gender expressed through the actions and practices of their parents come to structure the child's world in terms of gender. For the young infants, toys and other objects of material culture do not carry any clear gender signification. It is the actions of others which recognize the marking of objects and connect these meanings with the 'facts' of the child's gender. Around the age of 18 months there is a profound shift in children's psychological development as a capacity for representation emerges, which implies not only that children begin to engage in representational activities such as language, but also that they become capable of regulating their activity in terms of these representations. (Piaget described this development as the emergence of the semiotic or symbolic function see Piaget and Inhelder 1969.) As a consequence, children also begin to take on a more active role in controlling and regulating their expression of gender.

The emergence of children as independent actors in the field of gender can be seen in two observational studies of children playing in pairs with familiar peers of the same age (these studies are reviewed in Lloyd and Duveen, 1989; 1990). In the first study, children aged 18 months to $3\frac{1}{2}$ years were observed as pairs of either two boys, two girls or a girl and a boy. In the second study, with children aged 3 to 4 years, the design was changed so that a single target child was observed once playing with a girl and once playing with a boy. All of these observations took place in a room furnished with a variety of toys with known gender markings as either feminine (e.g. dolls, saucepans, shopping bags) or masculine (e.g. guns, trucks, briefcases). Each time a child picked up a toy, therefore, their choice could be identified as being either congruent or incongruent with their own gender. Analyses of these toy choices showed a strong and asymmetrical pattern. Boys made far more congruent than incongruent toy choices, whereas girls tended to choose more evenly between both congruent and incongruent toys. Among the younger children in the first of these studies, these patterns were modulated by the gender of the child's partner, so that boys playing with girls made more incongruent choices than boys playing with boys, and girls playing with boys also made more incongruent toy choices. Amongst the slightly older children of the second study, the asymmetric pattern of choices was more firmly established, and less influenced by the gender of the child's play partner.

The asymmetry between boys and girls evident in their play with gender-marked toys contrasted sharply with these children's performance on a range of cognitive and linguistic tasks, in which they were asked to sort pictures of people and toys according to gender, or to identify appropriate gender-marked words. Although children's knowledge of these different codes for gender marking increased as they developed, few differences were found between girls and boys. The differences observed between girls and boys in their use of toys, therefore, could not be attributed to any difference in their knowledge of how these objects were marked for gender. Rather, it seems that even at this young age children are using their knowledge to construct different identities. For the boys in these studies, the material culture of toys seems not just to carry particular significations of gender, but also to provide an arena in which the boys express a clearly differentiated identity. The girls, by contrast, while not oblivious to the gender marking of toys, do not use this material culture as a resource for expressing a differentiated identity. In this sense, the social identity of being a girl or of being a boy can be seen as different positions within the same overall representation of gender.

In speaking of identity here, the emphasis is on the relationship between identities and representations. As Duveen and Lloyd (1986) have argued, identity can be considered as the internalization of a social representation. In the context of the analysis given here, this usage of the term 'identity' is distinct from the sense it has sometimes been given in conventional cognitive accounts of gender development. There it is taken to refer to children's ability to categorize themselves as male or female, an ability which is held to be a key moment in the development of a wider understanding of gender (cf. Ruble and Martin 1997; Golombok and Fivush 1994; Archer and Lloyd 1985). Such definitions are rather more restrictive, since they focus on the children's knowledge of their membership of a gender group. Consistent with the definition of social representations given earlier, the usage employed here takes identity to refer to the values, ideas and practices associated with gender. Thus identity in the sense used here encompasses children's activities as much as their talk, so that what children do is seen to be as much an expression of their social identity as what they say. Of course, such young children may not yet be able to articulate clear or sophisticated ideas about gender, but their activity is already structured by representations of it, an important phase within a more extended developmental process.

Their emerging social representations of gender not only serve to provide children with a means for regulating their choice of toys, but are also linked to the emergence of wider patterns of knowledge about the social worlds they inhabit. One way of exploring this knowledge is through the study of children's pretend play, which begins to emerge in young children with the emergence of the semiotic function itself. By the fourth and fifth years pretend play is established not only as a social and collective form of activity in which children evoke and recreate aspects of the world they inhabit, but also as a forum in which their understanding of this world can be given structure and organization. Of course many different aspects of their worlds are recreated by children in their pretend play (see, for example, the studies by Furth 1996; Corsaro 1990), but gender as a theme is frequently evoked, as Box 14.2 over the page illustrates.

This example is transcribed from videorecords of children during free play in the reception classroom of an ordinary infants' school (Lloyd and Duveen 1992). One of the boys, Oscar, is chased for some time by the girls, but once he is kissed by Christine, perhaps somewhat to his surprise, he proclaims in turn (16) that he is going to marry her. Children create a simple world in which physical contact between sex group members is construed as sexual and involves marriage.

This episode provides us with a glimpse of children's understanding of family life. It is based upon a view of adult sex group membership which offers little role choice or variability. Sexuality for these young children is heterosexual and (as other episodes indicated more specifically) procreative. Central to the social representations of gender in this extract is a reproductive metaphor which offers an image of gender in terms of the bipolar opposition of the masculine and feminine. This is the image or *figurative nucleus* at the centre of their social representation of gender, and appears to be an image which children acquire very early in their lives. In their play, children evoke sexuality as the union of bipolar opposites, and once established it is celebrated through the rituals of marriage and domestic life. Indeed for these children there is a form of fusion of sexual relations, the institution of marriage and the complementarity of gender roles in

---

Box 14.2   Extract from a conversation among children

1.	Edith:	...and Lulu kiss, uhm, Oscar. Go on.
2.	Christine:	I'm not playing now.
3.	Edith:	Go away, then
4.	Lulu:	No, you kiss Oscar and I kiss Darren
5.	Edith:	I know. Look. You (Joan) kiss him Darren
6.	Lulu:	And I'll kiss Oscar.
7.	Edith:	Joan kiss Oscar.
8.	Edith:	Joan kiss Darren, and Oscar kiss...you!
9.	Joan:	(Starts for Darren, who runs) Hey!
10.	Edith:	Come here. (Grabs Lulu and moves her towards Oscar, not unwillingly) No, kiss! Kiss her on the lips. Kiss her on the lips. Come on!
11.	Lulu:	No way!
12.	Edith:	Go on. Kiss her. Kiss her.
13.	Christine:	(Makes a dash for Oscar) I kissed him.
14.	Oscar:	I kissed HER!
15.	Edith:	Oooh!
16.	Oscar:	(Points at Christine) I'm going to marry her.
17.	Edith:	(With Lulu, no longer struggling, very close) Kiss her.
18.	Oscar:	I'm going to marry her.
19.	Sally:	(Also closing in on Oscar)
20.	Oscar:	All right (But which one should he kiss?)
21.	Sally:	Kiss me. (They kiss)
22.	(All laugh. Oscar throws himself back on sofa)	

domestic life. The structure of a bipolar opposition is the connecting thread between these different elements, each of which implicates the others, so that when one element is evoked in play it can lead to the evocation of the others.

The figurative nucleus of bipolar opposites also supports a conceptualization of social life in terms of two complementary but exclusive categories. This conceptual structure influences how children interpret the world around them, while their participation in collective life provides a scaffolding which confers further legitimacy on this conceptual structure. Box 14.2 is taken from a study of the ways in which social representations of gender develop through the first year of children's schooling (Lloyd and Duveen, 1992). Many of the familiar patterns of division and separation between the genders were observed in this study, in terms of both whom children chose to play with, and what games and activities they chose to engage with. These patterns were observed to emerge more strongly through the course of the year, and again to be more strongly marked among boys than among girls (although important variations were also observed *among* girls and *among* boys). However, observations in reception classrooms also showed that even when teachers attempted to exercise a more egalitarian influence on the children it was resisted by the children themselves (Maccoby 1998 records similar observations). For example, on one occasion a teacher happened to be passing by a table where a boy was attempting to prevent a girl from sitting down, and suggesting that this was a 'boys' table' and she should sit at a 'girls' table'. The teacher intervened strongly telling the boy that in this classroom there were no such things as 'boys' tables' or 'girls' tables', but that children could sit wherever they wanted. The expression on the boy's face as he listened to the teacher showed a sense of confusion. He seemed to understand that he was being told off, but not to comprehend what he had done wrong. And indeed, later that day and on successive days he was observed again attempting to separate boys' and girls' tables (albeit when the teacher was not present).

An analysis of children's social representations of gender structured around a figurative nucleus of a bipolar opposition suggests some reasons for children's conservatism. As an image, a bipolar opposition offers a degree of clarity and simplicity which is also consistent with children's limited capacity for any cognitive elaborations which might require greater sophistication. Children's resistance to any influence of an egalitarian voice in representations of gender is also a resistance to losing this clear and sharp image of the world. The image of bipolar opposition crystallizes for the child a state of understanding which fuses the form of knowledge (its categorical structure) with the content of knowledge (the separation between things masculine and things feminine). All things masculine tend to cohere together and to separate from things feminine. The ethnographic observations in this study showed that separation along these lines can come to characterize the pattern of interaction in the classroom, and once established in this way the dynamic interplay of activity and understanding is capable of sustaining such moments over extended periods of time. Within this context, the gender identities which children construct are most clearly visible at the points where they resist the influence of alternative representations (cf. Duveen 2000).

Thus we can see how the social representations of gender circulating in the communities into which children are born initiate a complex developmental process in which these social representations enable children not only to sustain a stable sense of themselves and the world they inhabit, but also to form identities through which they can participate in this social world. From this developmental perspective the relationship between social representations and social identities can be seen very clearly, but it is a relationship which is not limited to growing children. Wherever representations are internalized they are linked to a process of identity formation, with significant consequences for the forms of social activity which follow. For these young children the most immediate consequences are in terms of which other children they play with, and what games or toys they choose. In the longer term, gender identifications linked to these social representations exercise a powerful influence not only on the educational careers of these children but also on their wider social lives.

Social representations as organizations of meanings

The distinctive perspective of social representations is its concern with the ways in which meanings become organized and structured, and the role of these structures in all forms of communication. This raises the question of the relationship between the idea of social representations and the concept of attitudes (see chapter 12). Clearly both these concepts bear on similar issues, and M. Jahoda (1988) in fact suggests that Moscovici's introduction of the term 'social representations' has added nothing of substance to the more familiar social psychological concept of attitude. Yet there is an important distinction to be made between these two ideas, though it is one which is confused by some aspects of the history of social psychology through the twentieth century; indeed, the history of the concept of attitude is itself a confused and tangled one (cf. W. J. McGuire 1986).

One important source for the concept of attitude in social psychology was the work of the Chicago sociologists W. I. Thomas and F. Znaniecki (1918–20), who, as Jaspars and Fraser (1984) point out, considered attitude as the reflection of the social world within the individual. From this point of view, attitudes were considered as being collective in nature and as providing an essential link between individuals and the social groups to which they belong. However, as the idea of attitudes was taken up more generally it was also transformed. The social or collective aspect of the term was displaced by a focus on attitudes as more or less permanent psychological states of individuals. This transformation corresponds to what Graumann (1988) has described as the 'individualisation of the social' in the history of social psychology, and reflects both the impact of behaviourism in social psychology and the pervasive influence of an ideology of individualism (cf. Farr 1996; 1998). Thus, where the idea of attitude originally proposed a confluence between social and psychological processes, contemporary theories of attitudes emphasize the psychological ones at the expense of the social. Not only has the collective origin of attitudes been lost in this transformation, but so too has a sense of their symbolic significance in establishing the basis for membership in social groups. As Jaspars and Fraser (1984) observe, attitudes in the sense that Thomas and Znaniecki used the term differentiated between social groups rather than between individuals within a group, which is how the concept has come to be applied.

The sense that something important in social psychology has been lost in the transformation of the meaning of attitude is not unique to the perspective of social representations. It can also be seen, for instance, in the work of Tajfel and others on social identity theory. However, the theory of social representations has offered some distinctive contributions to this discussion. Fraser (1994), for instance, has suggested that the two concepts can be brought back into relation with one another by considering social representations as structured and widely shared sets of social attitudes. Central to Fraser's argument is that while attitudes have come to be seen as very specific predispositions to action in contemporary social psychology, in fact they do not necessarily exist as isolated psychological forms. Rather, specific attitudes commonly appear in a structured or organized group with other attitudes, although the interrelationships between them has rarely been the focus of investigation. If we do focus on the structures which hold groups of attitudes together we find that, according to Fraser, they correspond to what Moscovici has described as social representations. Fraser's suggestion has not been welcomed by some other writers on social representations (see the comments by Doise, Clémence and Lorenzo-Cioldi 1994; Gaskell 1994; Farr 1994), who have seen his argument as confounding once again social and individual processes. If social representations are collective processes they should be understood as underlying specific or individual attitudes, that is, particular attitudes can only be understood if they are considered as elements within more general forms in which social meanings are organized.

If we do consider social representations as more general forms in which meanings are organized, two further points emerge. First, it is important to distinguish between central (or core) and peripheral aspects of social representations. At the centre of social representations is a core of values and attitudes which provide the structure for the representations and which, consequently, are resistant to change. In empirical research these aspects are reflected in the regularity with which they are expressed by different individuals and in different circumstances. At the periphery of social representations are other elements which are more loosely connected to the core, and which, consequently, will be more influenced by the particular circumstances and situations in which they are expressed. This distinction has been elaborated by a group of French researchers based in Provence, who have also suggested empirical techniques through which core and peripheral elements of representations can be distinguished (Abric 1993; Guimelli 1993; Moliner 1994). In this conception of the structure of social representations it is the relations between the elements which provides the structure of a representation which are important, and within a particular structure different elements have different weights.

The second point which emerges from a consideration of social representations as organized structures of meanings concerns the role of practice or action. The focus on attitudes as individual psychological constructs has tended to separate the psychological aspects of attitudes from actions or behaviours, and indeed in recent social psychology this relationship has come to be a major focus (cf. chapter 12). However, Moscovici's definition of social representations as 'systems of values, ideas and practices' suggests a different perspective, in which the same underlying organization of meaning can be seen as being expressed through what we do as much as through what we say (see Wagner 1994 for a more extended discussion of this point). At times, of course, we may say one thing and do another, but such inconsistencies are often the consequence of specific situational influences, although they may also reflect ambiguities or paradoxes within the organization of representations themselves. Contemporary theorizing about attitude–behaviour relations also recognizes the significance of situational influences in generating inconsistencies. However, such theories seem to remain oriented to a principle of consistency in a way that social representations theory does not. In his work on psychoanalysis, Moscovici (1976) introduced what he termed a hypothesis of cognitive polyphasia, by which he meant that different representations could coexist side by side, even if they were mutually contradictory, giving rise to ambiguities or paradoxes which appear as inconsistencies between what is said and what is done, or between what people say at different times. Wagner et al. (1999) have explored this theme in relation to representations of mental illness in contemporary India, where people articulate both traditional Indian conceptions and ideas derived from the Western medical tradition. The researches suggest that such polyphasia can be seen as an indication of changing structures of representations.

While theoretically the sense that practices can be structured by the same underlying organization of meanings as values and ideas may be clear enough, there has been little empirical research in the field of social representations which has included a consideration of practice as well as values or ideas. The work on the development of social representations of gender is one exception, though one which also reflected the limitations of undertaking more common paper-and-pencil forms of research with young children. The best example of the inclusion of practice is in Denise Jodelet's (1989/1991) pioneering study of social representations of madness among the inhabitants of a French village, which for many years has been part of a programme in which the mentally ill from local asylums have been lodged in the homes of ordinary villagers. This study is described in chapter 17, where it will be seen that the villagers' action towards the patients were tightly regulated by their social representations of madness.

As I mentioned at the beginning of this chapter, Moscovici's theory of social representations has not been the only attempt in recent social psychology to move beyond the limitations of individual cognitive perspectives. Recent years have seen the emergence of both constructivist and discursive social psychologies. While all of these approaches share a commitment to analysing the ways that people think and act in terms of the meanings they construct, the theories differ in the way they understand what this process of construction is and how it operates. For Moscovici, construction can be taken in at least two senses. First, there is the construction of social representations themselves through processes of communication within society. Second, for the individual there is a construction of meaning which is achieved through the use of such representations. Discursive psychology has placed less emphasis on such a distinction, preferring to consider representations themselves as objects constructed through the talk and the texts which people produce (cf. Potter 1996; Potter and Edwards 1999). Where the study of social representations has been concerned with the structure of collectively organized bodies of meaning, discursive psychology has focused more on the performative process through which meanings are achieved (although as Danziger 1997 observes, different versions of discursive psychology have diverse views about the extent to which any reality can be apprehended beyond the discursive). These differences have given rise to debates which have been quite sharp at times, with discursive psychologists frequently objecting that social representations theory has been insufficiently critical of the mainstream of social psychology (cf. Potter and Edwards 1999; Moscovici 2000). This seems an extreme or exaggerated position to take. What is the case is that both strands of thought have introduced a critical spirit into contemporary social psychology, which has challenged the mainstream assumption that social psychological processes must always be located within an individual mind by exploring the social and collective character of human thought and interaction.

Conclusions

This chapter has emphasized that what is most characteristic of the theory of social representations is the distinctive perspective on social psychology it provides. Not surprisingly, then, the theory has also been the focus of critical attention and debate. Indeed, some critics have suggested that Moscovici's own contributions are too vague and imprecisely defined to serve as the basis of a scientfic theory (see for example M. Jahoda 1988; Smedslund 1998; but see also Duveen 1998 for a critical evaluation of these arguments). Nevertheless, the theory has been sufficiently clearly presented to engender both a wide range of empirical research and a continuing series of theoretical arguments. In establishing the theory, Moscovici (1984; 1998; but see also Deutscher 1984; Farr 1998) drew on the concept of collective representations formulated by one of the founders of the discipline of sociology in the nineteenth century, Emile Durkheim. For Durkheim, the idea of collective representations was elaborated in contrast to that of individual representations, which not only served to distinguish the object of socio-logical inquiry from the province of psychology, but also was part of a more general view which resisted any attempt to explain sociological phenomena in terms of psycho-logical ones. Social facts could only be explained in terms of other social facts and not reduced to the consequences of individual psychological processes. While accepting much of Durkheim's argument, Moscovici also sought to shift the focus of attention away from what he saw as the rather static characterization of collective representations in Durkheim's conception, and towards an emphasis on the way in which representa-tions are formed and transformed. Hence his preference for the term 'social' to char-acterize representations. Where Durkheim's questions are always concerned with what it is that holds societies together, Moscovici's interest has always been in how things change. It is this dynamic perspective which examines the interrelationship of represen-tation and communication, which was the point of departure for the theory of social representations, and which has shaped its central concerns with the ways in which meanings are organized, communicated and transformed.

RECOMMENDED READING

Duveen, G. and Lloyd, B. (eds.) (1990) *Social Representations and Development of Knowledge*. Cambridge: Cambridge University Press.
This collection includes a range of developmental studies undertaken from a social representations perspective.

Flick, U. (ed.) (1998) *The Psychology of the Social*. Cambridge: Cambridge University Press.
As well as providing an interesting collection of texts on various aspects of social representations theory, this book also includes important contributions related to discursive and constructionist approaches.

Jodelet, D. (1989/1991). *Madness and Social Representations*. Hemel Hempstead: Har-vester Wheatsheaf.
This book provides the best major study of social representations available in English, and makes an important contribution to the field in its own right.

Moscovici, S. (2000) *Social Representations: Explorations in Social Psychology*. Ed. G. Duveen. Cambridge: Polity.
This collection includes most of Moscovici's key texts on social representations avail-able in English. The interview with Ivana Marková in the final chapter of the book also offers a more wide-ranging account of his work in social psychology.

PART IV

Social Issues

15

Prejudice and Intergroup Relations

Introduction

The commonness of prejudices

Many English people appear to dislike the French. They call them 'Frogs' and assure you that 'Wogs begin at Calais.' Scots seem less inclined to share that specific dislike, though their liking for the English themselves can be rather limited. As a Scottish working-class lad growing up in Aberdeen, I was assured, on occasion, that wogs actually started at Stonehaven, the first place of any size south of Aberdeen. That claim was not made very often and did not seem to be altogether serious, but it did capture some not uncommon feelings in the area. Obviously, the very best people were from Aberdeen itself! Almost as good were Scots who lived north of us; they were Highlanders and so were real Scotsmen; Scotswomen did not figure prominently in these sweeping generalizations. The further south you went from Aberdeen, however, the more doubts you had about the people who lived there, and when you got to London and southern England, lots of those people were believed to be effete, stuck-up and too hypocritical to be trusted.

It is not just in Britain that such prejudices flourish. If you stick a pin into any part of the map of the world you are very likely to find traditional or current animosities of varying strenths (see Simpson and Yinger 1985); Chinese and Indians, Vietnamese and Cambodians, Argentinians and Chileans, Greeks and Germans, and so it goes on. Hostilities between groups are not by any means defined only in terms of nationality. The single largest body of systematic empirical evidence regarding prejudice has emerged from study of intergroup relations within the USA. Most research has focused on white Americans' attitudes towards black Americans and other minorities in the USA, but there are smaller bodies of work demonstrating prejudices towards whites and between minority groups themselves. In recent decades, events in Rwanda and the former Yugoslavia have provided further illustrations but of a far more horrific kind. In addition, gender, sexual orientation, religion, social class, disability and age all describe large-scale group or social category differences which are now recognized as providing bases for prejudices.

Thus prejudices between groups are very common, appear to exist world-wide and can occur between a variety of different types of groups. In this chapter we shall focus primarily on intergroup relations, including prejudices, between ethnic groups. It is worth noting that there is good evidence (e.g. Dovidio and Fazio 1992) from opinion polls and research on stereotypes that the public expression of blatant ethnic prejudices in a number of countries, including America and Britain, has declined detectably in recent decades. Unfortunately, it is possible that 'old', crude and direct prejudice is being replaced by 'new' prejudice expressed in more subtle, indirect ways (see R. J. Brown 1995; Pettigrew and Meertens 1995).

Definition of terms

I shall write of ethnic groups rather than 'races', partly because 'ethnicity' is a broader concept than 'race', and partly because, for practical purposes, I do not know what a race is. In theory, a race is a set of people from the same gene pool. But gene pools have, over millennia, become substantially mixed and it is very difficult to say how many races there now are in the world. Assigning individuals to races involves a strange mixture of biology and social convention, with the latter taking priority in many cases. In numerous countries, for example, what decides whether you are regarded as 'black' or 'white' is not whether most of, say, your great-grandparents were black or white. You are 'black' if even one of them was black and you are only 'white' if every one of them was white. Those classifications may seem arbitrary and illogical but they are the social conventions which determine which 'race' you belong to and are seen as belonging to by others

An ethnic group, however, is explicitly defined as a set of people who share a common cultural background. The common culture may be associated with certain common.

Plate 15.1 Prejudice and discrimination can be blatant

biological characteristics, such as skin colour, but it need not be. Thus, for some purposes, the English, Scots and Welsh can be described as being three distinguishable ethnic groups, but to claim they are three separate races sounds strange.

Intergroup relations is a very broad term which covers a number of related issues, including prejudice and discrimination. According to Sherif (1966), intergroup relations refers 'to relations between two or more groups and their respective members. Whenever individuals belonging to one group interact, collectively or individually, with another group or its members *in terms of their group identification* we have an instance of intergroup behaviour' (1966, p. 12). The groups we are considering here are not the small, face-to-face groups of Chapter 8, but large groups or social categories, such as nations and majority and minority groups within nations. But a concrete example of intergroup relations can involve only two persons, one from each of two different groups, provided they interact not as two unique individuals but in terms of being members of two different groups, that is, if they are aware of their contrasting group identifications as they interact. In principle, an exhaustive account would consider a great variety of types of intergroup relations, including positive ones such as cooperation, friendship and helping. In practice, most attention in this area has focused on negative relations.

Prejudice is the most commonly studied aspect of intergroup relations. Sometimes definitions of prejudice emphasize pre-judging, that is, the making of premature judgments based on inadequate information, or they stress the irrationality of prejudice. I have considerable sympathy for both of those points but I do not feel that they lead to a very suitable definition. For if faulty information and irrationality define our prejudices, does that mean that our other sets of beliefs, including political and religious convictions, are based only on sound information and complete rationality? I might be tempted to claim that of my own beliefs but not of everybody else's! So I suggest that prejudice should be thought of as a negative or unfavourable set of attitudes towards a group and its members. One necessary qualification is that some prejudices are actually positive. For instance, whatever groups we ourselves belong to, we all tend to think well of nurses. Furthermore, some subordinate groups may come to accept the views of a dominant group so completely that they appear to hold positive attitudes towards the dominant outgroup. But the most common forms of positive prejudices are directed towards groups that we ourselves belong to. Despite these examples of positive prejudices we shall follow the standard practice whereby prejudice is assumed to be negative unless indicated otherwise.

Discrimination refers to overt behaviour towards a group and its members. Usually it refers to negative, unfavourable behaviour, although, as with prejudice, in a minority of instances there can be positive, favourable discrimination, usually towards members of one's own group. It can be helpful to recognize that prejudice versus discrimination is an example of an attitude/behaviour distinction. From what we have learned in chapter 12, we would expect the two to be quite strongly associated with each other but not so closely as to have a one-to-one relation. Prejudices may be covertly held by individuals without always resulting in overt discrimination, and acts of discrimination can occur for reasons other than underlying prejudice. Discriminatory behaviour might result, for example, from social pressure to discriminate rather than from negative attitudes.

Racism, sexism, ageism and other -isms are terms usually used to describe a combination of prejudice and discrimination which has become institutionalized in an organization or society. Racism would include systematic segregation of ethnic groups or discriminatory legislation regarding immigration.

Intergroup conflict can take far more virulent forms than those we have considered so far. It can be blatant and extremely violent. The terms 'prejudice' and 'discrimination' are quite inadequate to capture the extensive, systematic horrors of events in Rwanda, East Timor or the former Yugoslavia.

In fact, such overt, large-scale aggression has rarely been studied by social psychologists, though Ervin Staub (1989) has been an honourable exception (see chapter 9). The primary focus in the study of intergroup relations has been prejudice and that will be the main, though not exclusive, concern of this chapter.

Four types of theories

Currently in social psychology there are numerous different theories which attempt to explain some aspects or other of intergroup relations. No theory can claim to offer a really comprehensive analysis. These theories are hard to organize in a simple way. Different ones seem to address somewhat different issues, and theories which are clearly contrasting in some important respects can be similar in others. In the past, some experts (e.g. Tajfel 1978b) have classified theories as offering either individualistic or social explanations. Although some theories do lean in one direction or the other, supposedly individualistic analyses, such as psychodynamic or Freudian theories, usually also have social elements, and some social analyses, such as Tajfel's own social identity theory, also make powerful assumptions about psychological processes in the individual.

Of four currently influential theoretical approaches, or types of theories, which will be considered, historical priority has to be granted to Freud's analysis which, thirty years later, gave rise to the single most influential of the Freudian-inspired theories in this field, the theory of the authoritarian personality. Partly in opposition to the psychodynamic approach, which its critics regarded as overly individualistic and reductionist (see chapter 2), more avowedly social accounts emerged in the form of socialization theories of the acquisition of prejudice by children and of Sherif's realistic group conflict theory of intergroup relations. The increased dominance of cognitive ideas in social psychology in recent decades (see chapters 3 and 20) has not only led to a resurgence of interest in individualistic mechanisms, but has also resulted in acquisition and intergroup theorists, most notably Aboud and Tajfel respectively, attempting to integrate social and individual psychological mechanisms in their explanations. So, let us briefly examine in turn: the relatively individualistic and affect-based theories of Freud and the authoritarian personality theorists; current somewhat piecemeal individualistic cognitive analyses; two acquisition theories, in the form of the older socialization approach and the more recent social-cognitive developmental theory of Aboud; and two intergroup theories – Sherif's realistic group conflict, or competition, theory and Tajfel's social identity theory.

Psychodynamic theories

Freud's theory

Like much of Freud's thinking, his account of the relations between groups, particularly in *Group Psychology and the Analysis of the Ego*, published in 1921, leant heavily on his theory of the psychosexual development of the child, especially his ideas regarding the Oedipus complex, the name of which invokes the Greek hero who unknowingly killed his father and married his mother. (See Chapter 2 for a fuller account of some of Freud's ideas.) Freud claimed that young children are very strongly attracted to their opposite-sex parent in a broadly sexual, or sensual, way. This creates inevitable tensions amongst parents and child. One major consequence of these largely unconscious processes is that children inevitably harbour feelings of ambivalence towards their parents, that is, a mixture of love and hostility. The affection can be expressed but, it is claimed, much of the animosity has to remain in the unconscious. For Freud, the link between these powerful feelings towards specific individuals and the relations between large groups such as nations is the figure of the leader. A powerful, charismatic leader of an army, church or country, in Freud's theory, evokes similar feelings to those experienced towards parents. The leader is a form of father for the group members. The unity of a group such as a nation derives from the members' each internalizing the leader as part of their superegos or, to simplify somewhat, their consciences, and thus sharing common feelings towards the leader and, by extension, towards the group. But, of course, these feelings will be ambivalent, a mixture of love and hate. The positive feelings, according to Freud, will be directed towards the leader but the negative ones will be handled by displacing them onto some external group and its leader. Freud claimed that cohesion can always be created within a group provided that an external 'enemy' can be found to act as the target for the hostilities of the group members; an astute observation which, unfortunately, has also occurred to cunning political and national leaders from time to time, especially when their popularity is declining.

It is fair to say that Freud's theory of intergroup relations has not been widely accepted in social psychology. In part, this is because of its extreme reductionism, whereby hostility between two nations is reduced to the feelings of individual citizens towards their parents. In part, it is because of specific doubts about specific features of the theory, such as its possible overemphasis on very hierarchically organized groups. But in addition Freud's analysis has been largely ignored for the same very broad reasons that academic psychology claims to be justified in rejecting psychoanalytic thinking in general, namely that the theory is imprecise and inconsistent and that reliable empirical evidence available in support of it is very limited. These claims, of course, are strongly contested by proponents of psychoanalytic ideas. Suffice it to say here that, although Freud's own theory of relations between groups is not currently regarded by most social psychologists as a plausible account, it has had considerable influence on the thinking of some subsequent theorists, such as the frustration–aggression theorists (Dollard et al. 1939: Berkowitz 1962; 1969), who borrowed limited elements of Freud's theory, such as the defence mechanisms of displacement and/or projection. These are two of a number of ways in which it is claimed individuals can defend themselves against having to acknowledge unacceptable or personally threatening emotions.

Of the various analyses in this field influenced by Freud, one stands out particularly clearly: the theory of the authoritarian personality. Not only did this theory borrow extensively from Freud but its ideas have persisted in one way or another (see for example Sherwood 1980; Bethlehem 1985; Ahrendt and Young 1994).

The authoritarian personality

The very influential book which gave rise to the study of authoritarianism and its relation to prejudice appeared in 1950 in the name of four major authors, Adorno, Frenkel-Brunswik, Levinson and Sanford, and several other co-authors. The main authors' names were listed alphabetically; the work is not primarily Theodor Adorno's. The collaborative theoretical and empirical enterprise was carried out in the USA in the late 1940s as a response to events in Germany and Europe during the immediately preceding decades, culminating in the Holocaust. The investigators' hope was that an understanding of what led to prejudice and authoritarianism would help reduce the possibility of such events ever recurring. They believed that variations in individuals' acceptance of a widespread prejudiced ideology or belief system were due to personality differences. In their own words: 'The research...was guided by the following major hypothesis: that the political, economic and social convictions of an individual often form a broad and coherent pattern, as if bound together by a "mentality" or "spirit", and that this pattern is an expression of deep-lying trends in his personality' (1950, p. 1).

They pursued their hypothesis in two distinct ways. First, they attempted to locate relevant variations in attitudes and personality by devising attitude and personality scales, administering them to large samples of respondents and analysing the resulting data quantitatively. Second, having identified to their satisfaction what they believed were the crucial differences amongst people in personalities and related beliefs, they attempted to explain how those differences come about by studying in some detail, through interviews, tests and qualitative techniques, a relatively small number of people. R. Brown (1965) gives a very readable and quite detailed summary, and critique, of both aspects of their work.

In the first part of their research, the investigators developed, in turn, measures of three sets of attitudes – anti-Semitism (A-S scale), ethnocentrism (E scale), politico-economic conservatism (PEC scale) – and one personality characteristic – authoritarianism, or the potentially fascistic personality. They found that the A-S scale, that is, prejudice specifically towards Jews, and the E scale, that is, prejudices towards a range of minorities other than Jews, correlated highly, with correlations up to about +0.80. The E scale correlated significantly with the PEC scale, though noticeably less highly than with anti-Semitism. The fourth measure, frequently labelled 'the F scale', where 'F' stands for 'fascistic personality', was intended as a measure of the hypothesized personality trait (see chapter 2) of authoritarianism. This trait was regarded as being a broader internal disposition than any particular set of attitudes, and its formulation was substantially influenced by psychoanalytic thinking. Someone scoring highly on the F scale agrees with items indicating undue respect for authority, high levels of conformism, punitiveness, sexual repressiveness and other associated characteristics. The F scale was found to correlate highly with the A-S and E scales.

At first sight, then, apart from the 'hiccup' concerning politico-economic conservatism, the investigators appeared to have demonstrated remarkable coherence of attitudes and personality. Indeed, they appeared to have demonstrated greater consistency than was revealed in our examination of attitudes in chapters 12 and 13. But that first impression has to be qualified. Because of several methodological shortcomings, the correlations obtained almost certainly exaggerated the real relationships (see R. Brown 1965). With more sophisticated methods, the authors probably would have found that prejudices towards a wide variety of minority groups are moderately correlated and these prejudices in turn are moderately correlated with the trait of authoritarianism. What causes the correlations is what the second half of the research aimed to discover.

To do that the authors studied in some detail eighty extreme scorers, either highly prejudiced and authoritarian or very non-prejudiced and 'democratic'. Each of these respondents was interviewed at length and given a number of tests, including projective tests of a kind often favoured by psychoanalytically inclined researchers but viewed sceptically by others. The conclusions drawn from the detailed analyses of all the evidence showed similarities to Freud's analysis.

The key differences, it was claimed, between the authoritarians and the non-authoritarians could be traced back to the types of families in which they had grown up. The families of the former had been much more likely to practise rigid disciplining of their children and the giving of affection conditional on the obedience of the children. Markedly different rules for acceptable behaviour applied to parents and to children; an embryonic ingroup/outgroup distinction thus operated within the family itself. The parents were status conscious, concerned about social acceptability and respectful of authority. Their children in turn were expected to be respectful of authority, especially that of their parents. The children were forced into a surface submission to parental authority and found it difficult to express feelings of hostility or aggression towards their parents. The ambivalence of feelings which Freud had emphasized was certainly present. The children were almost obliged to make a show of their love and respect but they could in virtually no circumstances reveal any signs of hate. Instead, the strong negative emotions were displaced on to safe targets, usually low-status minority groups. The markedly non-authoritarian children, so it was argued, grew up in much more relaxed, open and democratic households, where some expression of negative feelings towards parents was possible and even tolerated. As a result, those children could cope with their feelings of ambivalence without having to engage in unrealistic idealization of parents and denigration of minority groups.

Clearly, this account owes a lot to the ideas of Freud. But at least two differences are worth noting. First, Freud's analysis, which argued for the universality of ambivalent feelings towards parents and hence the likelihood of the universality of outgroup prejudices, has been turned into the basis of an explanation of individual differences in prejudice. Second, because Freud's somewhat unconvincing analysis of the role of the leader was played down, it is no longer clear why feelings originally aroused by one or two individuals, the parents, should be displaced on to entire ethnic groups possibly numbering tens of millions.

In fact, a number of criticisms of the ideas of the authoritarian personality theorists have come to be recognized. Some of these are directed at details of the methods used, in what, at its time, was pioneering and very ambitious research, and such methodological criticisms have been well summarized by Roger Brown (1965) and the unrelated Rupert Brown (1995). Other criticisms, though often containing methodological elements, have cast broader doubts on the adequacy of the approach. For example, what light does the idea that authoritarians are likely to be highly prejudiced cast on the fact that socially and politically important prejudices in a society are usually quite widespread, being held to some degree by many people who would not be thought of as having authoritarian personalities? By only attempting to explain in detail the emergence of prejudice or its absence in small samples of extreme cases, the theorists rather left us in the dark about what underlies the prejudices of most of us. That the authoritarian personality theory might not tell us a great deal about the operation of widely held prejudices was strongly implied by some classic studies by the doyen of American social psychological race relations experts, Thomas Pettigrew (1958). He studied anti-black prejudices amongst whites in South Africa and the USA and in different white groups within those countries. He showed that though there were marked differences in strength of prejudice between countries and between groups, these group differences were not systematically accompanied by average differences in authoritarian personality scores. Furthermore, critics would suggest that if individual differences in being prejudiced really do bear some relation to having an authoritarian personality, the relation could be explained in a relatively simple and straightforward way. Adorno et al. (1950) found that scores on their A-S, E and F scales were correlated. From interviews with some of their respondents they concluded that the parents of authoritarian and prejudiced people were themselves authoritarian. Should it not follow that the parents would also have been prejudiced? In which case, why not assume that, deliberately or otherwise, authoritarian and prejudiced parents directly transmit their authoritarian and prejudiced views of the world to their children? An apparently straightforward socialization explanation would render the more complex psychoanalytical analysis unnecessary. How convincing apparently straightforward socialization explanations are will be considered below as part of 'Acquisition theories'.

We end then in a position of substantial scepticism concerning the importance of authoritarian personalities in helping us understand widespread prejudices and hostile intergroup relations. The evidence suggests (e.g. Bethlehem 1985; R. J. Brown 1995) that there is some relation between something like an authoritarian type of personality and the likelihood of holding prejudices against other groups, though there is contradictory evidence about just how strong that relation is. The explanation of the relationship is even less clear and, at best, the relationship seems to have only a limited role to play in enlightening us about prejudices. However, the psychodynamic emphasis on complex emotions inculcated in childhood underlying hostility towards outgroups might turn out to have some part to play in accounting for the views of bigots. All of us appear to hold prejudices of one kind or another. But few of us build our lives around them. It is tempting, though perhaps too comforting intellectually, to tell ourselves that extremists, such as those who gun down members of a group they dislike, must have been subjected to emotional pressures that the rest of us were fortunate enough to escape.

Cognitive analyses

In recent decades, especially in the United States, social psychology has been dominated not by the study of strong emotions, but by the detailed study of cognitive processes. That emphasis has become apparent in the analysis of prejudice, with serious attempts being made to demonstrate how normal, general features of cognitive processing, including its major limitations and biases, can account for at least some of the phenomena of prejudice. In so far as such attempts can claim successes, these have lain with the study of prejudices in individuals' minds rather than with an understanding of intergroup relations more broadly.

One concept at the heart of such endeavours is categorization (see chapter 3 of R. J. Brown 1995; and chapter 11 for categorization in person perception). Many distinguished psychologists (G. W. Allport 1954; Bruner 1957; Tajfel 1981) have long argued that one of the most basic yet most important of universal, human, cognitive processes is our propensity to organize large numbers of, in certain respects unique, actions, events and people into much smaller numbers of categories or classes of partially similar actions, events and people. Imposing categories on the world around us appears to be inevitable.

It is commonly argued that we could not cope with the world if we tried not to categorize but to treat every action, event or person as unique. We would be swamped by unorganized details. Thus, it is argued, the organizing of people into broad categories – as men or women, black or white, members of ingroups or outgroups – which is a constant feature of prejudices, is simply an inevitable result of the way the human mind works.

But of course there is more to prejudice than the recognition of distinguishable categories. I am pleased to say I can usually manage quite easily to recognize the difference between men and women, but that in itself does not make me prejudiced against one sex or the other. Prejudice would only exist if I believed that in general the two categories were not of equal worth, that men were 'better' than women or vice versa. What then might introduce such a differential evaluation? When we come to the intergroup theory of Tajfel (1974; Tajfel and Turner 1979) we shall see that he proposed a primarily affective, motivational mechanism, a need for positive self-esteem. But can additional cognitive processes turn categorization into prejudice? One area where that has been claimed is the study of stereotypes.

A stereotype can be thought of as a relatively stable set of shared generalizations about the supposed characteristics of the members of a group, a simplified 'picture in the head' of what a set of people are claimed to be like. Since a classic study by Katz and Braly (1933) and its near replication almost twenty years later by Gilbert (1951), social psychologists have been aware of the commonness and resistance to change of national and ethnic group stereotypes. If such stereotypes were generally accurate descriptions, then we might think of them as useful if simplified guides to groups of people. If they tended to err in positive directions, we might not be too critical of their shortcomings. In fact, we have to be cautious in making general claims about the accuracy or inaccuracy of stereotypes. Some particular stereotypes almost certainly can be without foundation. Others, though, may well have at least a kernel of truth to them, especially if we recognize (see McCauley and Stitt 1978; McCauley, Stitt and Segal 1980) that when people invoke a stereoype, they may be claiming not that all members of the group display the features of the stereotype, but that members of the group are more likely to have the characteristics than members of other groups. What accounts for the particular characteristics included in a particular stereotype is virtually impossible to say, but there is considerable evidence (R. Brown 1986) that one recurring set of influences which helps determine the general nature of a stereotype as positive or negative is the political relations between the groups involved. Far from being a neutral description or mildly flattering assessment, a stereotype held by a dominant or majority group about a subordinate or minority group is usually negative. In all probability that is likely to tell us more about the current relations between the two groups than about actual characteristics of the minority (Oakes, Haslam and Turner 1994).

Exponents of cognitive analyses of prejudice, however, would wish to argue that relatively simple cognitive mechanisms can also throw light on negative characteristics of stereotypes of minority groups. One such mechanism commonly invoked is that of illusory correlation, which can arise because of an apparent cognitive tendency to associate unduly strongly in our minds two sets of phenomena which are relatively rare or infrequent, especially if one set involves negative behaviours (Hamilton and Gifford 1976; Hamilton and Sherman 1989). If a member of a majority group is reported to have committed a murder, we are unlikely to attach as much importance or pay as much attention to the fact as we would if a minority group member did such a thing. Then, it is claimed, we read much more into it. We tend to establish a false or illusory correlation between the infrequent event and the relatively small group of people, which results in a generalization about minority group members being relatively likely to commit murder. In this way, it is argued, creating assumed shared distinctiveness via illusory correlations can help establish negative stereotypes. Once established, such stereotypes can be maintained via assumed shared distinctiveness and illusory correlation, which create expectations regarding the minority group members. These expectations then distort our cognitive processing of subsequent information through selective attention, perception and recall. We tend to notice and remember information which fits our expectations, including our stereotypes, while tending to ignore and forget evidence which is not consonant with our preconceptions.

Numerous other supposedly common cognitive processes have also been invoked to help account for the ease with which we can establish and maintain prejudices and stereotypes of minority groups. Quatrone and Jones (1980) proposed that the establishment of such stereotypes would be facilitated by the phenomenon of outgroup homogeneity, as opposed to ingroup variability. That distinction refers to the findings of a number of empirical studies (Quatrone 1986) that we are more likely to see greater similarities amongst outgroup than ingroup members and hence are more willing to generalize from the behaviour of a single outgroup member than from one member of an ingroup. The maintenance of an already established stereotype, on the other hand, is likely to be assisted by the typicality of exemplars. It is claimed that we attach a great deal of importance to what we believe to be typical examples of a group or category. If, on the other hand, we see an individual member of a group behaving in what we think is an atypical fashion, we tend to ignore that. In fact, we need lots of examples of the supposedly atypical before we are willing to allow the contradictory evidence to change our minds. In other words, we can ignore lots of examples that do not fit our stereotypes.

Cognitive analyses, then, have encouraged us to examine more closely some everyday underpinnings of prejudice. As a result stereotypes may seem less ludicrous, more understandable. Prejudices become reflections of cognitive limitations, inaccuracies and biases, with no apparent need to postulate the powerful, near unfathomable emotions of psychoanalytic theory. Prejudices acquire an almost mundane, even banal quality. They exist because 'that's the way the mind works'. If that were so, presumably the processes would be universal, perhaps biologically determined and, perhaps most worryingly, inevitable. Of course, universal phenomena can reflect social processes, not just biological ones, but cognitive analyses in this field appear to avoid broader social analysis. They say little about material or historical relations between actual groups. Although these analyses are offered by their proponents as an enlightened, liberal approach to the study of prejudice, critics might accuse them of being implicitly conservative. A more balanced view may be that as yet they are a piecemeal set of analyses in the study of prejudice. They draw our attention to interesting psychological mechanisms in the individual that eventually will have to be incorporated into more comprehensive theories that also take account of larger-scale social processes.

Where might we find these more comprehensive social analyses? At present there are two sets of theories that are usually seen as being more socially oriented than the theories we have examined so far: the acquisition theories and the intergroup theories.

Acquisition theories

Socialization analyses

How do children acquire prejudices? That is a question that some, though not very many, social scientists have been attempting to answer from at least the 1920s. One of the early answers came from Lasker (1929). He believed that a child is 'certain to have his mind canalized, even before he starts going to school, into habitual acceptance of the prevailing racial attitudes of the group within which he lives . . . the average child is made to notice outer differences and to accept them as signs of inner differences in value' (1929, p. 127). That assertion – with its emphases on having his (or her) mind canalized into acceptance and being made to notice and to accept – appears to be an example of a socialization analysis rather than a developmental analysis. That distinction is a rough and ready contrast but nevertheless is a useful one to be aware of. Any attempt at explaining children's acquisition of important sets of ideas about the society around them is virtually bound to acknowledge the importance of both social influences external to the child and the child's own current internal capabilities and limitations. A socialization explanation is one which, at the end of the day, places primary emphasis on the influence of others in producing changes in the child, whereas a developmental explanation, at least in this context, sees the child as the main determinant of changes.

Until relatively recently, socialization analyses have dominated this topic (see, for example, Milner 1975; Duckitt 1992). Their main focus has been the attitudes of white children, in America and to a lesser degree in the UK, towards blacks. Their fundamental claim has been the attractively commonsensical idea that chidren become prejudiced because they are 'taught' to be prejudiced. Widespread existing prejudices are transmitted to children by parents and other socializing agents. The 'teaching' and transmission may sometimes be explicit. Some parents or peers may deliberately tell children what the supposed shortcomings of outgroup members are, but much of the teaching is likely to be rather more subtle, perhaps even unintentional. But, explicitly or implicitly, current attitudes towards a variety of ethnic and other groups will be conveyed to young children from a variety of socializing agents.

It has usually been assumed that parents are particularly influential, but numerous other sources of prejudiced views have also been held to be relevant. Children may bring home from school authoritative opinions from teachers or racist jokes from peers. Educational materials and the media may transmit stereotypes and prejudices. It is not so long ago that primary school reading books might well have had illustrations of Jenny, with apron on, 'helping Mummy do the dishes' and Tommy, in dungarees, 'helping Daddy fix the car'. And from time to time the tabloids clearly demonstrate, with attacks on 'froggy French' and others, the media's transmission of prejudices. Common views within the neighbourhood may be picked up by a child. So, a traditional socialization analysis emphasized that in a variety of ways a variety of socializing agents would transmit to the next generation current widespread prejudices. That, it was claimed, explained how it could be that from the age of about 3 onwards some white children in the USA, and in Britain, would manifest signs of anti-black sentiments, with the percentages of such children increasing with age, and the prejudicial views becoming more elaborate and more adult-like from the age of 6 or 7 onwards (see, for example, Aboud 1988; R. J. Brown 1995).

Such an approach seems to have much to commend it, in addition to its easily accepted, almost commonsensical basis. It appears to account for the persistence of many prejudices over generations. It can throw some light on the tricky question of the choice of targets for prejudice by dominant groups by arguing that in stratified societies low-status groups are commonly devalued and derogated. Potentially it can handle variability in strength of prejudice within a group by pointing out that different children are exposed to different combinations of socializing agents and different degrees of consistency among their socializing agents with regard to prejudice. Perhaps above all, it emphasizes that widespread shared prejudices are not mysterious phenomena but are the result of the transmission to the next generation of widespread shared social beliefs and values.

It should be noticed, however, that socialization theories of prejudice normally make no real attempt to explain why current widespread prejudices came into being in the first place. Critics, such as Aboud (1988), have pointed to other limitations of socialization theories, which she called 'social reflection theories', because they treated children's prejudices as straightforward reflections of existing social views. Such theories would appear to imply that the older children get and the longer they are exposed to sources of prejudice the more prejudiced they will become. But as we shall see, that does not actually happen. Socialization analyses also tend to overestimate the similarities of children's views to those of their parents. Some major studies, such as Davey (1983), have found unexpectedly limited similarities. Above all, Aboud argues that social reflection theories treat children as far too passive. They do not simply soak up adult ideas willy nilly. They may have views of their own or fail to understand what they hear. Younger children certainly have cognitive limitations which make it very unlikely that they could internalize adult ideas in forms identical to the adult originals. Aboud (1988) offered a theory which attempted to overcome what she regarded as the weaknesses of social reflection theories.

A social-cognitive developmental theory

Aboud (1988) did not deny the importance of socializing influences in the child's environment. The exact contents of particular prejudices and the choice of targets for prejudice on the part of a group will be conveyed to the child through socialization processes. But, according to Aboud, an age-related, non-linear structuring of the acquisition of prejudice, which cannot be explained by socialization theory, is explained by two overlapping sequences of development which themselves are underpinned by Piaget's general and supposedly universalistic account of cognitive development, which we encountered in passing in chapter 10. Aboud distinguished between a sequence of different types of processes – from affect to perception to cognition – which she claimed dominates the child's experience, and a sequence of changes in the primary focus of the child's attention – from self to group to individual. See table 15.1.

Table 15.1 Aboud's two sequences of development

Dominant process	Age	Primary focus	Age
Affect	Up to c.5–6	Self	Up to c.6–7
Perception	c.6–8	Group	c.7–8
Cognition	c.8 and above	Individual	c.8–9 and above

Aboud argues that the two sets of changes combined should have predictable consequences for the development of prejudice in children. The combination of affective experience and inability to recognize alternative possibilities will make young children prefer familiar, comforting others who are like themselves and be suspicious of unfamiliar, dissimilar others. Those tendencies will be strengthened by increased concern with perceptual similarities between ingroup and outgroup members. But such tendencies should become diminished, at least in part, by the increasing abilities to decentre and differentiate from the age of 8 or 9. In other words, the child's own cognitive limitations should lead us to expect that young children will manifest intergroup prejudices and that these prejudices will become stronger up to the age of 8 or so. But then, contrary to what a socialization analysis would predict, childhood prejudices normally should cease increasing and start to show signs of declining somewhat as children's cognitive capacities develop. And that is exactly what Aboud's (1988), and others', careful reviews of studies of the attitudes of white children show. Their prejudices do not increase in a straightforward linear fashion. At first sight, that looks like powerful confirmation of Aboud's emphasis on the contribution of the child's own cognitive capacities and limitations to the emergence of prejudice. But caution is required.

It should be noted that the two sequences of development which Aboud postulated are much less well established than is Piaget's account of cognitive development. Indeed, it would be desirable if Aboud's framework were spelled out in considerably more detail than it has been. In particular, it may be that lurking behind the claim that prejudices emerge from positive feelings towards familiars and fear of strangers are implicit assumptions about inborn propensities to like similar and dislike dissimilar others, an apparently commonsensical notion accepted by many lay people. Similarity is a slippery concept to use as an explanation, because there are so many grounds for things being regarded as similar or dissimilar and it is rarely made clear why one or two of those grounds are crucial and the rest irrelevant. Why skin colour should be the one visible element that overrides everything else, as is often implied, is rarely, if ever, made clear.

In addition to such conceptual reservations about Aboud's theory, there is a crucial body of empirical evidence which calls part of it into question. Her theory, as we have seen, handles the evidence from white, majority-group children very well. But as Aboud herself makes clear, a smaller number of studies of children of American minority groups – black Americans, Hispanics and Native Americans – have revealed a rather different pattern of development. The minority-group children in general show less prejudice against the white majority than white children reveal against minorities, from the onset of such signs at 3 or 4 right up until the age of 8 or so. Then from about the same age at which the hitherto ever-increasing prejudice of the white children starts to level off and then decline, the minority-group children start to show increasingly positive ingroup evaluations together with strengthening anti-white prejudice. In view of that, Aboud's theory, which wishes to explain the emergence of prejudice in terms of universal processes of cognitive development, is in trouble, for how universal can the processes be if they cope well with the first body of evidence they encounter but fail to cope with the second? Despite that, Aboud's general argument that what is required is an integration of socialization processes with an account of the child's own capacities and limitations is surely correct in principle, even if her own social-cognitive theory is inadequate.

Intergroup theories

Realistic group conflict theory

The ideas and research of Muzafar Sherif (Sherif and Sherif 1953; Sherif 1966) explicitly assert a very important view of negative intergroup relations, including prejudice; hostility between members of different groups has to be understood as a consequence of relations between the groups in general, and not because of characteristics of group members or interpersonal relations. Intergroup relations become negative when two groups come into competition with each other because of real conflicts of interest. A variety of realistic group conflict theories have been espoused in other social sciences and beyond (D. T. Campbell 1965).

Sherif provided striking evidence for such a position, not by analysing national or superpower hostilities, but by studying boys in summer camps (Sherif and Sherif 1953; Sherif et al. 1961). Some details of these studies are presented in box 15.1

Box 15.1   Sherif's Three Summer Camps

In different years, Sherif and his colleagues conducted three different field experiments under the guise of running fairly small-scale camps during summer holidays. The procedures in the three studies were not identical, so what follows is a brief synthesis of what happened across the studies.

There were about two dozen 11- or 12-year-old boys in a study, divided into two more or less equal-sized groups. They were normal, healthy, stable boys without obvious personality or family problems, who were oblivious to the fact that they were participants in a field experiment. Four phases can be identified in the research, phases 1, 2 and 3 being present in the first two studies and 2, 3 and 4 occurring in the third.

In phase 1, all the boys were allowed a couple of days to get to know each other, without systematic interventions by the investigators. Some signs of personal friendships started to emerge.

In phase 2, the boys were divided into two distinct groups, with separate accommodation and distinctive names such as the Bulldogs and the Red Devils. The purpose of this phase was to permit ingroup identity and cohesiveness to develop. There was no contact between the groups in this phase. As far as the boys were aware, the allocation to groups was done at random. In fact, Sherif and his colleagues had stacked the odds against themselves slightly by deliberately separating friends. During this phase no explicit competition between the groups was introduced by the investigators.

In phase 3, overt competition was introduced. Over several days, the two groups were required to compete with each other in a series of sports events, such as tug-of-war, and other tasks, including cleaning the cookhouse, and prizes were awarded on a group, but not individual, basis. For Sherif, this was the crux of the research. If the key determinant of intergroup hostilities was group conflict of interest due to overt competition, then, in phase 3, clear signs of hostility should become apparent from members of each group towards members of the other. And that was what the investigators reported. Not only did name calling and the exchange of insults occur but teams raided the other teams' bases and took or destroyed possessions. Groups of pleasant, stable young boys had, almost too easily, been turned into enemies.

Phase 4 was designed to try to undo that disturbing development. From parts of his first two studies Sherif had concluded that well-intentioned efforts to reduce the hostilities by subsequently encouraging friendly interaction amongst the members of the two groups had been fairly ineffectual. By the time of the third study he had decided that the most likely way of countering the hostility engendered by competition for resources was to provide for the two teams common or superordinate goals, the benefits of which could only be attained by everyone working cooperatively. Thus in the final phase, the boys in both teams found that the only way to move the camp wagon out of clinging mud, to unblock the communal water tank and to raise enough money for something very desirable was for everyone to pitch in together and work cooperatively. Following active pursuit of these superordinate goals, there were clear signs that hostilities between members of the two groups had declined substantially, although they had not been totally removed.

All in all, Sherif's studies seem to provide strong evidence for the argument that negative intergroup relations can be created by overt competition involving real conflict of group interests, and subsequent studies, both in the laboratory (e.g. Doise 1978; R. J. Brown 1988) and in the field (e.g. Struch and Schwartz, 1989) provide further support. Some qualifications, however, are in order.

Sherif's ideas are often applied to relations between large-scale groups, including nations, but his evidence comes from rather small groups of children. His studies may be thought of as small-scale simulations of much larger-scale phenomena, but we should be cautious in generalizing from his evidence. Caution in generalizing also applies to the success he had with superordinate goals. R. J. Brown (1978), for example, did not find the hoped-for effects of superordinate goals in a field study of relations between different sections of a factory workforce. Are superordinate goals always as readily perceived and then accepted as legitimate as in Sherif's study, where he as the experimenter virtually had the power to impose unambiguous shared goals on small numbers of children?

More importantly for present purposes, is overt competition a necessary condition for prejudice and discrimination? Sherif himself, as well as subsequent writers such as Tajfel and others, acknowledged that in the summer camps there were limited indications of intergroup hostilities, such as name calling and insults against the outgroup, before

Plate 15.2 Perhaps De Klerk and Mandela did achieve superordinate goals

overt competition was introduced in what is described in box 15.1 as phase 3. In fact, such indications were apparent in phase 2 of all three of Sherif's summer camp studies, which implies that realistic group conflict, though probably powerful when it does occur, is not the whole story, as Henri Tajfel emphasized.

Tajfel's social identity theory

Almost twenty years before social identity theory emerged, Tajfel was interested in the effects of categorization. From studies of judgments of arrays of inanimate stimuli, such as coins, lines and blocks of wood, he had concluded that classifying stimuli of varying sizes or lengths into two separate categories or groups appeared to have a number of detectable consequences. In particular, people tended to underestimate variations within each group while overestimating differences between the groups (Tajfel 1959; Tajfel and Wilkes 1963). Tajfel was aware of the possible implications of such findings for prejudice and stereotyping (e.g. Tajfel 1969).

In the late 1960s, Tajfel and colleagues embarked on the studies of categorization which led to his formulation of social identity theory. Tajfel's initial idea seems to have been that, in the laboratory, he would establish groups by means of a neutral or pointless distinction which would generate no intergroup prejudice or hostility, and then he would explore what additional elements of intergroup relations had to be added to the neutral categorization in order to discover the minimal conditions for intergroup hostility to emerge. Tajfel's initial findings, however, forced him to rethink, because, hard though he tried, he could not devise 'neutral' distinctions that had no consequences. For convenience sake, he worked with sets of 14-year-old boys from the same school, so that there was no pre-existing group distinction between them. In each study the boys were divided randomly into two groups, but told they had been divided according to a supposed difference between them; a difference which the experimenters assumed was about as pointless a distinction as possible. In one study boys were solemnly assured that they had been found either to overestimate or to underestimate large numbers of black dots exposed exceedingly briefly on a screen. In another study, again at random, half the boys participating were told that they had been found to prefer the paintings of Klee to those of Kandinsky and the other half were told the reverse, when in fact it was unlikely that many of the boys had much liking for either. Towards the end of each study the boys were asked how outgroup and ingroup members, other than themselves, should be paid for participating in the study. Surprisingly, despite the apparent silliness of the distinctions, both studies revealed clear evidence of ingroup favouritism and outgroup discrimination (Tajfel et al. 1971). Supposed dot overestimators, on average, wanted dot overestimators to be paid more than dot underestimators, and vice versa, and similarly for the supposed admirers of Kandinsky and Klee.

Why would this occur? One possibility might have been that the participants made the assumption that the trivial difference that they had been told of could point to other, more important differences between the two groups. To check if this could account for the rather unexpected outcomes, Billig and Tajfel (1973) deliberately carried to its apparently ridiculous extreme what has come to be called the minimal group paradigm. They let participants in the study know that they were being divided into groups X and Y purely by chance. The experimenter, with no trickery whatsoever, tossed a coin in front of each person and allocated him to X or Y accordingly. Despite this unambiguous demonstration of the arbitrariness of being an X or a Y, by the end of the study members of group X were discriminating in favour of Xs and against Ys and the reverse was true for members of group Y. Not surprisingly, Tajfel's conclusion from these studies – and the basic findings have been replicated in numerous studies since (Brewer and Miller, 1996) – was that the act of categorizing people into different groups, that is, categorization *per se*, appeared to be sufficient to elicit ingroup preferences and outgroup discrimination. Overt competition, as claimed by Sherif, might be a sufficient condition for creating intergroup hostility but it was not a necessary one.

Social identity theory emerged (Tajfel 1974; 1978a; Tajfel and Turner 1979) as a way of explaining these and other findings, such as the evidence of incipient hostility in phase 2 of Sherif's studies, and the fact that prejudices can exist towards groups where overt realistic conflict is hard to discern. The originator of social identity theory and its key concepts are briefly described in box 15.2, which you should read now.

That box presents the heart of Tajfel's social identity theory, although, of course, there is more to it than that. For example, before his premature death, Tajfel had started to develop a framework for understanding the possibilities of change for members of low-status groups by contrasting an individualistic strategy of individual mobility or 'passing' into a higher-status group versus a strategy of group-based activism aiming at real social change (Tajfel 1978a; Tajfel and Turner 1979). After Tajfel's death, his close collaborator John Turner (Turner et al. 1987) formulated a variant of social identity theory called self-categorization theory, which we encountered in chapter 8. That theory

Box 15.2   Henri Tajfel and social identity theory

Henri Tajfel (1919–82) was a man whose academic achievements and crucial life experiences were particularly intertwined. He was born in Poland and was Jewish. At the start of World War II, he was a student in Paris and then a soldier in the French army. From 1940 to 1945, he was a prisoner of war in Germany, where he passed as a non-Jewish Frenchman, for fear that if his real ethnic identity were discovered he would suffer the fate of his family in Poland, who perished in the Holocaust. At the war's end, he worked for a period for organizations attempting to achieve the rehabilitation of war victims. Subsequently, he moved to Britain where, having trained in psychology, he had a distinguished career as a social psychologist. For the fifteen years before his death, he was professor of social psychology at the University of Bristol. He played a major part in the emergence of social psychology in Europe (see chapter 20), while attempting to understand, in a spirit of striking magnanimity, stereotyping, the consequences of social categorizations, and intergroup hostilities, all issues which had so forcefully affected his own life. One of his major achievements was the development of social identity theory, which we have already briefly encountered in several earlier chapters.

Social identity theory was constructed around three key concepts: social categorization, social identity and social comparison. We are all members of a variety of social groups or categories which have greater or lesser importance in our lives. There is no escaping category memberships, many of which, such as gender, class, nationality, ethnicity, religion and the like, reflect powerful organizing principles of the societies in which we live. As we have seen, category membership is likely to carry with it some very general consequences, like underestimating similarities within a category and overestimating differences between categories. But as was argued when we considered stereotyping, that in itself is not enough to generate prejudice and hostility between members of different groups. What has to be added to categorization to produce the assertion, 'We are not only different from them, we are better than they are'? According to Tajfel, it was a combination of social identity and social comparison.

He proposed that people's sense of who they are (see chapter 2 on the self) can be thought of as their identity, and that identity consists of two components, personal identity and social identity, with the latter, for Tajfel, being the more important. Personal identity is made up of purely personal, even idiosyncratic, features of an individual. As such it is hard to see what can be said systematically about these highly variable features of different individuals. What can be studied is a person's social identity, which is an integration of the various category- or group-based identities that are important to that individual. For most of us, our gender, ethnicity, class and age all contribute to our sense of identity, together, perhaps, with our feelings of belonging to a particular family, doing a specific job or being a student at one university rather than another, and the like. Such group memberships tell us who we are not only by providing guidelines about how we should act but also by determining how we are valued by others. In that latter regard, a very important assumption of Tajfel's is that normally individuals attempt to maintain a positive sense of self, which, of course, depends on the groups which are important to their identities being positively valued. For members of a high-status group that should pose little or no difficulty. They can point to how much better educated, paid, housed etc., etc., they are than the members of numerous other groups. But what about members of a low-status group? How do they defend the value of their group, and hence themselves?

Tajfel proposed that they, like high-status individuals, attempt to sustain a positive esteem by engaging in selective social comparisons in such a way that their group is likely to emerge from the comparisons looking good. A low-status group can compare itself favourably against even lower-status groups, which may help account for the evidence from America and Britain that prejudice against non-white minorities is usually particularly strong amongst poor white working-class individuals. In practice, however, a low-status or minority group is unlikely to be able to avoid comparison with the ever-present majority completely, in which case the minority can engage in comparisons on dimensions of their own choosing. At the very beginning of this chapter I suggested that male Scots tend to compare themselves favourably against the English in terms of honesty and masculinity. And not wholly dissimilar dimensions seem to be invoked by working-class individuals regarding the middle class. If the working class were to attempt achievement-related comparisons, they would lose. Thus, according to social identity theory, it is not surprising that a common working-class view is that, ultimately, people should be judged not on superficial features such as money or size of house or car but on fundamental characteristics such as honesty, integrity, friendliness and willingness to help others in need. And guess which class is deemed to come out better on those dimensions of comparison! So through a combination of categorization, identity and comparison, a group strives to sustain positive group distinctiveness and hence positive self-esteem for its members. If that positive group distinctiveness is challenged or threatened, the group and its members are likely to attempt to enhance group distinctiveness, which may well result in increased prejudice and hostility to selected other groups.

was designed to extend Tajfel's intergroup analyses to intragroup ones and has resulted in important theoretical and empirical studies of social influence processes (Turner 1991) and cohesion (Hogg 1992) in small groups, as well as of stereotyping (Oakes, Haslam and Turner 1994).

Important aspects of social identity theory, however, remain to be clarified. For example, one reasonable expectation from it is that there should be a systematic relation between strength of group identification and strength of prejudice and hostility towards relevant outgroups, with the obvious prediction being that the most prejudiced groups and individuals within a group should be those with strongest ingroup identification. Also, it seems to follow from the theory that there should be an inverse or negative relation for groups and individuals between self-esteem and prejudice, with low self-esteem being associated with high intergroup hostility. In fact, the empirical evidence is inconsistent with regard to identification and prejudice (e.g. Hinkle and Brown 1990) and self-esteem and prejudice (e.g. Hogg and Abrams 1990).

Another set of puzzles relates to our 'choices' of particular group identities and particular comparisons. We are all members of many groups and social categories. What determines which of those loom large in a particular context? When is gender or ethnicity or family or even some combination of group memberships crucial? Social identity researchers assert that different contexts or situations make salient or relevant different group memberships. But an analysis of what determines this overused notion of salience would be very helpful. In addition, what determines the choice of particular outgroups for comparison? Social identity theory does suggest that they will be groups against which the ingroup can be made to look good, but that is only a limited part of what is likely to turn out to be a complicated answer.

Let us pose just one further set of complex questions. Most research on social identity theory has examined only one aspect of social identity at a time, but how are our separate group identities integrated into an overall sense of identity? Do we just add up our perceptions of the evaluations of the different groups that are significant for us? That seems too mechanical and simple. And, if one group-based identity is challenged, with a resulting loss of self-esteem, what happens to the other parts of our identity? Do they remain unaffected? In addition to the above qualifications and criticisms, more systematic evaluations and critiques of social identity theory can be found in R. J. Brown (1995, ch. 6) and Rabbie, Schot and Visser (1989).

Social identity theory, however, is proving to be a valuable framework for helping us understand the ubiquity of intergroup hostilities and prejudice. It does not deny Sherif's argument that overt conflict of interest is a powerful determinant of intergroup hostility but rather extends his intergroup approach by explaining how, in the absence of such overt competition, salient group categorizations can themselves be sufficient to generate intergroup rivalry. Social identity theory and realistic group conflict theory should be seen as complementary, not contradictory.

Some conclusions from the theories

The different types of approaches make different assumptions and invoke different concepts and hence might seem to be in flagrant disagreement. Some of them emphasize group or social mechanisms while others highlight features residing in an individual. Some stress cognitive mechanisms and others focus on affective ones. What might we do to avoid a conclusion that we are left with irreconcilable contradictions? Perhaps the main step is to recognize the partial nature of each of the theories. As yet, none can be offered as a really comprehensive account of all the facets of prejudice and intergroup relations which have attracted the attention of social psychologists. Each approach appears to be asking rather different questions and, in general, one approach is not very helpful in providing answers to another approach's queries. It is as if we have assembled many jigsaw pieces but are not quite sure if we yet have all the bits we need, or if some of the pieces we have will turn out not to fit this puzzle.

To try to begin to assemble the full picture, we might start with the intergroup theories. Both overt conflict of interest and categorization *per se* appear to be sufficient conditions to generate hostility and, in practice, each will often reinforce the other.

Social identity theory already incorporates some important cognitive mechanisms and might be extended to handle others while still insisting that intergroup hostilities are underpinned by more than just normal everyday cognitions. Despite Sherif's summer camp studies, the intergroup theories have not usually been regarded as acquisition theories, but cognitive limitations of and external social influences on children do not seem incompatible with intergroup analyses, and attempts to fuse such concepts, like Milner (1996), are desirable. Psychodynamic pieces, especially those supplied by Freud himself, may well prove to be parts of some other jigsaw. But intergroup theories have tended to treat groups as homogeneous and to ignore substantial variations in prejudice within a group. Socialization analyses in terms of exposure to variations in socializing agents could help to fill that gap, and, who knows, it may even be necessary to incorporate notions of emotionally based personality characteristics in order to understand the thoughts and actions of bigots. As Duckitt (1992) has attempted to demonstrate, if we are to understand the complexities of prejudice and intergroup relations we are likely to require a complex theoretical integration.

What can be done?

For many people studying these issues, the aim is not just to understand the world of prejudices but also to change it, by finding means of reducing prejudice and improving intergroup relations. Let us briefly consider in two rather different ways what social psychology has to contribute to the possibility of beneficial change. First we will examine some of the implications of the theories we have encountered. Then we will look at the most substantial body of empirical evidence on the matter, research conducted to test the contact hypothesis.

Implications of the theories for change

We can ask two distinguishable questions of the theories we have examined. Are intergroup prejudices and hostilities inevitable? Can they be, at the very least, reduced? Note that a theory might argue that prejudice is inevitable but, despite that, it can be reduced. What do the various theories seem to imply? Space permits only some broad and possibly contentious suggestions.

For Freud, intergroup hostilities were inevitable. Presumably though, in principle, they might be reducible via universal psychoanalytic therapy – something very hard to imagine in practice. For authoritarian personality theorists, prospects may seem a little more tractable; only authoritarians need be subjected to psychotherapy. If society could find ways of breaking the claimed cycle of authoritarian parents rearing authoritarian children, then at least the problem of bigots might disappear. Cognitive analyses, as well as social-cognitive developmental theory, appear rather depressing because their emphasis on normal cognitive development and adult cognitive functioning being at the heart of the emergence and maintenance of prejudice appears to imply an inevitability, based on supposedly universal cognitive processes which are likely to be hard to change. Perhaps the most optimistic of the theories is the traditional socialization approach. It bypasses the issue of inevitability by not indicating what produces particular prejudices in the first place, but contents itself by arguing that if existing prejudices are 'taught' to children the next generation will sustain the prejudices. Thus if social means can be found not to teach prejudices, prejudices should disappear. Clearly, it is no easy task, in practice, to specify how a society, already accepting of certain prejudices, can come to succeed in not passing them on. Presumably the goal of rearing societies of children who have not been taught to be prejudiced, or who have been taught to be non-prejudiced, will take many generations of efforts. None the less socialization theory, in principle, seems to hold out hope that improving intergroup relations is quite possible.

The intergroup theories of Sherif and Tajfel appear to imply pessimism with regard to inevitability but some optimism concerning reduction. Can we envisage a world containing no realistic group conflicts whatsoever? I cannot. But unless such a halcyon condition is possible then, according to Sherif, competition will continue to lead to intergroup hostilities. If Tajfel was right in offering favourable group comparisons with selected outgroups as the only mechanism for the maintenance of positive individual and group esteem, then at least selective intergroup prejudices seem inevitable. Both theories, however, do hold out hope for the amelioration of specific intergroup hostilities. Sherif demonstrated that the successful creation of cooperation through superordinate goals can reduce prejudice. One strategy that can be derived from social identity theory for reducing intergroup rivalries has been dubbed recategorization, and although recategorizing groups might take a variety of forms, the one that has attracted most attention has been that of encouraging two groups to recategorize themselves as one superordinate group (e.g. Gaertner et al. 1993). Sherif and social identity theory may be saying similar things. Instead of merely getting two distinct groups to accept certain limited common goals, perhaps Sherif had gone some of the way towards encouraging both sets of group members to regard themselves as belonging to a common group of campers.

A second technique from social identity theory for improving intergroup relations has been called decategorization. A likely feature of marked intergroup hostility is that the intergroup boundary will be very salient. The differences between the groups will be continually emphasized. The possibility of changing groups will be minimized. Without attempting a more ambitious recategorization, some diffusion of hostilities might be possible simply by playing down the boundaries and ignoring markers of group differences.

A third, somewhat more complex possibility is criss-cross categorization. If two salient categorizations, such as ethnicity and gender, can be crossed, there is laboratory evidence (e.g. Deschamps and Doise 1978) that intergroup discriminations can be reduced. For example, women in one ethnic group may recognize some common interests with women in another, and similarly for the men. There is of course a danger in practice of such a strategy backfiring. If for example the women in the two groups were to reduce inter-ethnic prejudices more markedly than the men, the result might be worsened gender relations in both ethnic groups. Some of the complexities of criss-cross categorizations in action can be seen in Vanbeselaere (1991) and Hewstone, Islam and Judd (1993).

We also should note one aspect of Henri Tajfel's (1978a) thinking which unfortunately has subsequently received only limited attention. He offered an analysis of the conditions necessary for a change in the position of low-status groups for whose members individual mobility via 'passing' into a higher-status group is not possible. Of those necessary conditions the most crucial was that, collectively, the group members must challenge the legitimacy of the prevailing majority–minority relations. Of course, forcefully challenging the legitimacy of the prevailing status quo may not, in the short run, improve intergroup relations, but it is likely to be a necessary precondition for moving towards greater equality of the groups, which, as we shall shortly see, is itself a necessary condition for improving intergroup relations by means of increasing intergroup contacts.

The possibilities for reducing hostilities which can be derived from the intergroup theories clearly require very careful implementation but none the less are welcome. Like virtually all the constructive implications of the theories, however, they offer hope of reducing specific intergroup prejudices and hostilities. Probably none of the theories, with the possible exception of rather simple socialization analyses, pictures a future where all prejudices and hostilities can be removed.

Empirical evidence: the contact hypothesis

Limited optimism can be derived from the theories. That is also the case with empirical research deliberately attempting to improve intergroup relations. We have already seen that Sherif and his colleagues had detectable success. Some other efforts have been less effective. A sense of the possibilities and difficulties involved in attempts at constructive intervention in this field can be obtained by a brief examination of the single main focus of such attention over the years, the contact hypothesis. The idea that in some way relations between two hostile groups should improve if their members have more contact with each other has a plausible ring to it. But if any kind of contact would do, then there would have been far less black–white prejudice in apartheid South Africa or the southern states of the USA. than in Denmark or Scotland. So there must be particular conditions under which intergroup contact will be beneficial.

An early, very influential summary of what those conditions might be came from the Harvard psychologist Gordon Allport (1954), who concluded his analysis of 'the effect of contact' with this summary:

> given a population of ordinary people, with a normal degree of prejudice, we are safe in making the following general prediction . . . : Prejudice . . . may be reduced by equal status contact between majority and minority groups in the pursuit of common goals. The effect is greatly enhanced if this contact is sanctioned by institutional support . . . and if it is of a sort that leads to the perception of common interests and common humanity between members of the two groups. (1954, p. 267)

Subsequent investigators have proposed additional conditions, including the development of intimacy (Amir 1976) and high acquaintance potential (Cook 1978). Many research studies have been conducted (see Hewstone and Brown 1986; Miller and Brewer 1984), and reviewers of the field have sometimes managed to come to markedly different assessments of the efficacy of contact (see W. S. Ford 1986 vs. Pettigrew 1998).

Plate 15.3 Contact itself is not enough

The latest review that I am aware of is particularly authoritative and encouraging. It comes from Thomas Pettigrew and colleagues at the University of California at Santa Cruz. They are conducting a very ambitious, very detailed meta-analysis (see chapter 19) of over 200 studies of the contact hypothesis. Put simply, a meta-analysis is a very systematic statistical analysis of a large number of related studies which permits the results of different studies to be summed together. It is a powerful technique for finding the clearest overall patterns where there have been some contradictory findings. Although the final and full results of the meta-analysis have not yet appeared, a number of clear findings have already emerged (Pettigrew and Tropp 2000) and these include the following:

1   More than 90 per cent of 203 studies analysed found an inverse or negative relationship between contact and prejudice. That is, face-to-face interaction between members of different groups is importantly related to reduced prejudice.
2   The association between contact and reduced prejudice generalizes beyond the specific outgroup members actually encountered to the outgroup as a whole.
3   The size of the relationship between contact and reduced prejudice varies with different types of outgroups.
4   The more rigorous the study, the bigger the relation between contact and reduction of prejudice.

In short, under the types of conditions specified by Allport (1954), intergroup contact does work.

For the future, the hope must be that social psychology will prove able to contribute substantially more to the improvement of intergroup relations. Steps in that direction would include the development of better-integrated, more comprehensive theories of intergroup relations, greater focus on aspects of intergroup relations other than prejudice, and a greater willingness on the part of social psychologists to attempt to apply to real-world conflicts the understanding that they feel they have gained from systematic surveys and laboratory experiments.

Conclusions

Intergroup relations can take a variety of different forms, but usually only the negative ones have been examined by social psychologists. These include discrimination, racism and overt conflict, as well as the much-studied prejudice. Four theoretical approaches have underpinned a great deal of the work. Psychodynamic theories depend heavily on the ideas of Freud regarding powerful parent–child emotions. Cognitive analyses attempt to explore the part that normal cognitive processes play in creating and sustaining prejudice. Aquisition theories focus exclusively on children's acquisition of prejudices. Intergroup theories emphasize the relations between the groups, rather than features of individuals, as the primary way of understanding prejudice and discrimination. The different types of theories appear to be studying different parts of the whole. Overall, these theories are not markedly optimistic about the prospects for reducing intergroup hostilities. But there are just sufficient positive indicators both from the theories and from research on the contact hypothesis to encourage optimists to sustain their optimism.

RECOMMENDED READING

Allport, G. W. (1954) *The Nature of Prejudice*. Reading, MA: Addison-Wesley.
This is a classic, which remains impressive.

Brewer, M. B. and Miller, N. (1996) *Intergroup Relations*. Buckingham: Open University Press.
This is a useful, slim, overview.

Brown, Rupert (1995) *Prejudice: Its Social Psychology*. Oxford: Blackwell.
This gives a good, clear, well-organized review of the topic.

Foster, D. and Louw-Potgieter, J. (eds) (1991) *Social Psychology in South Africa*. Johannesburg: Lexicon.
Chapters 2, 6 and 9 remind us that this is not just an academic issue.

Taylor, D. M. and Moghaddam, F. M. (1994) *Theories of Intergroup Relations*. 2nd edn. Westport, CT: Praeger.
This provides expositions and critiques of most of the theories in this chapter, and a few others besides.

The World of Paid Work

Introduction

People retiring today from full-time professional or white-collar careers are likely to have spent about 100,000 hours – that is, about 45 hours × 45 weeks × 45 years, or twelve entire years of their lives – in paid work. The only activity that most men spend more time on is sleeping. Many women, though, may spend even more of their lives in unpaid domestic work than on paid work. What the future holds can only be guessed at. Gender differences regarding paid and unpaid work may well continue to diminish, even if as yet the latter have not decreased as much as is often assumed. The average time spent in paid work may, in the longer term, continue to drop, despite recent developments, at least in Britain – such as raising women's retirement age, weakened trade unions, and decreased job security – which, in the shorter run, seem to point in the opposite direction. Though hours of work are, on average, falling in Europe, there is no sign of such a decline in the UK or the USA. For jobs in general, Handy (1984) claimed that over the previous generation, the hours in the average working life more or less halved. With that shortening came arguments concerning the 'collapse of work' and 'the flight from work', that is, claims that paid work no longer has the centrality for society and the individual that it once did. In our view, however, employment remains of central concern to most individuals and families and to the societies they live in. No other institution has arisen to replace paid work as the basis of economic and social structures or as the justification, rightly or wrongly, for differences in rewards and statuses (see Sayers 1988).

This chapter will focus on the world of paid work, or employment, and its impact on individuals. Two sets of issues will be examined. The first relates to the meaning and nature of paid work for those who are in work and can assume that they are likely to remain in work, that is, the securely employed. About them we ask the questions, 'What might individuals hope to get from their jobs?' and 'What do they get from them?' In the second set of concerns, we examine what life is like for people who usually long to have secure employment but do not. They may be in insecure employment or currently unemployed.

Why do we work?

The two most obvious answers to that question – 'because we have to' and 'because we want to' – were, more or less, the answers offered by that still influential pessimist Sigmund Freud and that currently discredited optimist Karl Marx. For Freud, work was an unpleasant necessity for survival, and it is true that necessity plays a major part in the motivation to work of virtually all of us. For the great majority of people, pay is the main source of the material necessities, and the luxuries, of our lives. At times most of us probably have fantasies of not having to work at all, yet, fantasies notwithstanding, the majority of people claim that, if given the chance, they would go on working even if it were not financially necessary. Warr (1982) found that 64 per cent of his sample said that they would, although only half of those would wish to continue working in their current jobs.

So, we work in part because we have to, but for other reasons as well. Work is, as Freud asserted, a necessity, but need it be an unpleasant one? Might we not also be working because we want to? That was what Marx argued should be the case; work was potentially a creative, integrating process which linked people to the products of their efforts and to their fellow beings, and such work was essential to an individual's well-being. If we think of men and women in the professions – doctors or architects or even underpaid academics – in challenging jobs that offer considerable autonomy, it is easy to assume that, at least in part, they are working because they want to do what they are doing. If we imagine semi-skilled workers being ordered to perform a limited set of repetitive tasks, we are likely to be much less sure. In acknowledging that we work for a mixture of extrinsic rewards, especially pay, and intrinsic ones such as the interest of the work itself – together perhaps with some sense of social obligation – we have to recognize that the balance between the two varies markedly from one set of employees to another. To pursue these issues further, let us examine a few of the ways in which psychologists have theorized about what people might get out of paid work. What should lead employees to a sense of well-being and satisfaction with their jobs?

What might employees get from their jobs?

Probably the best-known theory of what leads employees to be motivated to work and to feel satisfied is Herzberg's two-factor theory of job satisfaction (Herzberg, Mausner and Snyderman 1959; Herzberg 1966). Herzberg argued that employees have needs for security and for self-realization or growth and that different aspects of the job meet these different needs. Security needs are met by extrinsic factors such as pay, interpersonal relationships and working conditions, whereas personal growth needs require intrinsic factors, including interest in the work itself and feelings of achievement, recognition and responsibility. Herzberg's most distinctive claim, however, was that having the extrinsic factors met – he called them *hygiene* or *maintenance factors* – prevented negative feelings of dissatisfaction, whereas having the intrinsic factors met – he called those *motivators* – led to positive feelings of satisfaction with the job. In other words, job satisfaction and dissatisfaction were not opposite ends of one and the same continuum; they were the extremes of two separate dimensions, both of which ran from neutral. Good pay and good working conditions would not produce satisfied workers; they would only result in employees who were not disgruntled and dissatisfied. Satisfaction depended on intrinsic motivators.

Unfortunately for Herzberg's theory, the majority of subsequent studies which have examined it using techniques of assessment other than the very particular technique used by Herzberg himself have failed to confirm the clear separateness of determinants of satisfaction and dissatisfaction (Landy 1989; E. A. Locke and Henne 1986). Largely as a result, Herzberg's theory has been virtually abandoned by academics interested in job satisfaction, although it still lingers on in some management circles. But its current neglect may be as overdone as its popularity in the 1970s. The main weakness of Herzberg's theory may have been that it was overstated rather than that there was no truth in it. If he had been content to make the more modest claims that the bases of job satisfaction and dissatisfaction *tend to be* different, and that it is *difficult* to produce high degrees of satisfaction through hygiene factors alone because high satisfaction *usually* requires motivators as well, then his position would have been much more defensible. Certainly, we should continue to assume that employees might hope to obtain from their jobs not only extrinsically based satisfactions relating to pay, conditions and colleagues but also intrinsic satisfaction with the work itself and with feelings of achievement, recognition and responsibility that follow from it.

There have been numerous other theories of both job motivation (the antecedent conditions for work) and job satisfaction (the consequences of work) (see Landy 1989; E. A. Locke and Henne 1986; Judge and Church 2000). In principle, both sets of theories should help us understand what employees might expect from their jobs. Unfortunately, most reviewers agree that, as yet, empirical evidence has not shown any of the theories to have a high degree of empirical validity. So let us look elsewhere for further guidance on what we might hope to get from paid work.

Box 16.1 Marie Jahoda (1907–2001)

Marie Jahoda was born, one of four children, into a prominent Viennese family in 1907. Her father, Carl, was an engineer and businessman. Her mother, Betty Probst, was a committed pacifist. Rampant inflation had decimated the family's fortunes.

The Austrian revolution and consequent establishment of a temporary socialist government took place when Jahoda was 11, and she was politically active from an early age. She was an active member of the Socialist Youth Movement, chairperson of the Federation of Socialist Secondary School Pupils, and co-editor of *Schulkampf*, all whilst still at school.

Jahoda went on to study psychology under Karl and Charlotte Buhler, to work with Gustav Icheiser, to work with Otto Neurath in the Museum of Social and Economic Affairs, and to undergo psychoanalysis with Heinz Hartmann. She was acquainted with Anna Freud and met Sigmund Freud socially.

Plate 16.1 Marie Jahoda

Fieldwork in the unemployed community of Marienthal took place in 1931–2 and the work was published in 1933. This methodologically innovative research focused on a community rather than on individuals. It was problem-driven rather than method-, theory- or literature-driven. The researchers strove for atheoretical, substantive, 'social book-keeping' rather than hypothesis-testing and theory-building. Problem definition was collaborative rather than expert-dominated. Working practices were heterarchical and participatory rather than hierarchical and bureaucratic. The research team formed alliances that transcended disciplinary and professional boundaries, and cultivated and utilized the potential of collective political and ideological commitment, rather than aspiring to illusory political and ideological neutrality. Empirical research, sense-making and writing were simultaneous rather than sequential (Fryer 1987; 1992; M. Jahoda, Lazarsfeld and Zeisel 1972).

In November 1936 Marie Jahoda was taken into custody for 'illegal political activities'. As a Jewish Austro-Marxist intellectual she was in double jeopardy at a time of escalating anti-Semitism and fascism. After eight months' detention she was sentenced to three months' gaol and one year of preventive arrest, but in 1937, following appeals at the highest level from France, she was released from prison, deprived of Austrian state citizenship and given twenty-four hours to leave the country.

Jahoda took sanctuary in England and between 1937 and 1944 worked for the Ministry of Information and the Foreign Office, was an active member of the London Bureau of Austrian Socialists, became director of 'Austrian Self-Help', and broadcast coded messages into Austria to assist the resistance via Red Radio Vienna. She also found time to do more classic community fieldwork in Wales (Fryer 1987) and to take up a Pinsent-Darwin Studentship at Cambridge University.

In 1945 Jahoda moved to the USA, where she worked at the Columbia Bureau for Applied Social Research. She was central to the most influential explanatory account of what it is about being unemployed which causes social and psychological problems: the manifest and latent function of employment account, an account which has been vastly influential but also subject to extensive criticism (Fryer 1986; 1995). This account is often wrongly assumed to have emerged from the *Marienthal* fieldwork but actually was not developed until 1948–9, when Jahoda worked with Robert Merton in New York. She was deeply influenced by Merton's article on manifest and latent functions (M. Jahoda 1995; Merton 1949).

In 1949 Marie Jahoda was appointed professor of social psychology at New York University and became director of the Research Centre for Human Relations. She subsequently held chairs at Brunel and Sussex universities and received many distinctions, including a CBE, the Kurt Lewin Award, the Award for Distinguished Contribution to Psychology in the Public Interest, and honorary higher degrees. She has also worked in and made major contributions to many areas in addition to employment and unemployment (mental health, authoritarianism, Freudian studies, methodology, attitudes etc.). Until her death at 93, Jahoda was an active contributor to social psychology from her home in Sussex.

This box was kindly written by David Fryer, Community Psychology Group, University of Stirling, Scotland. David Fryer is grateful to Professor Jahoda for correcting an earlier version of this piece. Sadly, Marie Jahoda died on 28 April 2001, a few months after this box was written.

Marie Jahoda's research on employment and unemployment spanned a very large part of the twentieth century; box 16.1 contains a brief biography of her life and work from the 1920s to 2000. One of her many lasting contributions is a simple framework for understanding at least some of the things that we might expect to get from employment as an institution (M. Jahoda 1982). Using the Freudian distinction between manifest and latent functions, she stated that the obvious or manifest function of paid work is to provide financial benefits to employees. Having acknowledged that crucial function, Jahoda wrote little more about it. Instead she focused attention on the less obvious, latent functions of employment, which may only start to become apparent to the individual in atypical circumstances, such as being made unemployed. According to her analysis, paid work normally serves five important latent functions for an individual:

1 It enforces activity; you cannot sit around for long doing nothing.
2 It structures your time; certain things have to be done at certain times.
3 It forces you to share common goals; you cannot be entirely self-concerned.
4 It inserts you in a social network; you are rarely a complete isolate at work.
5 It conveys status and identity; in part, you are defined by your job.

As we shall see, this has been an influential framework in thinking about what happens to people who become unemployed. As an analysis of employment, however, it has one strange gap. Apart from the mention of 'activity', it says nothing about a manifest function of employment that may have been so obvious it was not noticed, namely that of providing 'work' and all of the elements that go with that, such as the opportunity to exert physical effort, to use work skills, and to obtain a variety of types of intrinsic satisfactions from your efforts. A useful distinction to note at this point is the difference between *work* and *job*. 'Work' can be used to refer to the content of what an employee does; 'job' includes the work itself but many other things too, such as colleagues, pay, work conditions etc. 'Work' refers to the intrinsic elements; 'job' captures both the intrinsic and extrinsic ones. Jahoda's framework emphasizes some of the things individuals may get out of their *jobs*, such as companionship, identity and shared goals, but it says little about what might be gained from *work*. So, let us consider one more framework that encompasses many of Jahoda's ideas as well as important features of work itself.

Warr (1987) was interested in the relations between, on the one hand, employment and unemployment and, on the other, mental health or psychological well-being. After an extensive review of relevant research, he concluded that there were nine different sets of determinants of whether both employment and unemployment led to better or to worse mental health, and they are listed in box 16.2, in a slightly different order from Warr (1987). For the moment, let us focus on the relevance of his analysis for the employed; its implications for the unemployed will be discussed later. If we can specify

---

Box 16.2 Warr's vitamin model

Environmental features (categories)	As vitamins → (processes)	Mental health
Availability of money	Constant effects	i Affective well-being
Physical security	(*non-toxic*)	(= job satisfaction)
Valued social position		ii Competence
Opportunities for control		iii Autonomy
Opportunities for skill use	Additional decrement	iv Aspiration
Externally generated goals variety	(*toxic*)	v Integrated functioning
Environmental clarity		
Opportunities for interpersonal contact		

how these nine features of work lead to positive psychological well-being, it seems reasonable to argue that these are elements that, in an ideal world, all employees should get from their jobs. (Twelve years later, Warr 1999 suggested adding a tenth vitamin, supportive supervision.)

A first thought, then, might be that workers should receive as much as possible of each of these nine features. Take, for example, 'availability of money'. Low pay is associated with worse mental health, and higher pay with better mental health. To maximize well-being, should not everyone receive as much pay as possible? 'Fat chance of that', you might think, and you would be right. But that obviously unrealistic suggestion also runs into other difficulties. It makes the common assumption that systematic relations between two variables are likely to be linear, that is, an increase in one is accompanied by an increase in the other over the entire range of the variables. But an important feature of Warr's model is that he argues that none of the nine relations between features of the job and mental health is linear.

In the case of pay, for example, Warr argued that the evidence shows that, in general, increases in pay will lead to increases in well-being up to a point, but thereafter, other things being equal, well-being will remain more or less constant. Thus, the extraordinarily high salaries of some very senior executives are no guarantee that they will be happier than their junior management colleagues, but very low wages may well buy misery.

'Opportunity for control', another determinant of well-being, operates in a rather different way. Little or no opportunity to control what you do is harmful to mental health, and well-being increases as individuals increasingly feel that they can exert some control over their jobs. After a point, additional control does not bring greater well-being, and, unlike pay, with extremely high levels of control well-being actually begins to decline again. If you have a sense of complete control over absolutely every element in your job, where does spontaneity or creativity or challenge come from? Too much control can start to be harmful.

Pay and opportunity for control illustrate the two patterns which Warr identified and which can also be seen in box 16.2. Ingeniously, Warr proposed that these two slightly different patterns are similar to the ways in which two different sets of vitamins affect our physical health. With all vitamins, too few of them is harmful, so if we have been deprived of vitamins it is beneficial to increase our intake of any and all of them. An optimal state is reached, other things being equal, well before high consumption is reached. For some time at any rate, further increases in vitamin intake will neither further improve nor damage our health. For some vitamins, such as vitamins C and E, that continues to be the case no matter how high the intake, that is, they continue to have *C*onstant *E*ffects. But with other vitamins, such as A and D, too high intakes become poisonous, that is, they result in harmful *A*dditional *D*ecrements. Warr claims that vitamins in the 'constant effects' block (box 16.2) are non-toxic and vitamins in the 'additional decrements' block are toxic. The hypothesized differences in the relations between level of intake and level of well-being is depicted in box 16.2.

Warr's vitamin model is the most extensive and systematic analysis we have of the relations between paid work and well-being, but we should not accept it uncritically. The list of nine determinants seems somewhat arbitrary; other analysts might have drawn up slightly different lists. It is primarily, though Warr argues not exclusively, a situational analysis; nine sets of features of the work situation, admittedly as perceived by the employee, are held to determine work-related mental health, and there is little consideration of the psychological processes which might mediate between situation and mental health. Any model containing nine key non-linear relationships will be difficult to test in its entirety, although sets of two or three determinants, and the interactions amongst them, might just about be grappled with in a single investigation. Perhaps the closest that an individual investigation has come to testing Warr's model was DeJonge and Schaufeli's analysis of Dutch healthcare workers (1998). They did indeed find non-linear relationships between several of the 'vitamins' and psychological well-being, exactly as predicted by Warr.

Nevertheless, the vitamin model encourages us to argue that, ideally, we should all be obtaining from our jobs at least intermediate levels of: pay; physical security; social status; control; skill use; external goals; variety; clarity; and interpersonal contact. Many employees in high-status, middle-class occupations are likely to be experiencing most, if not all, of these desirable features. In so far as their jobs diverge from the ideal, it may well be because of additional decrements, in, for example, goals, variety and interpersonal contact. But many manual workers are not as fortunate. How much control, skill use and variety is available to many production-line or service industry workers? And there is little need to reassure semi-skilled machine minders or super-market checkout staff that enormous salaries will not damage their mental health.

Having seen what employees might gain from paid work, let us now try to find out what they feel they do in fact get from their jobs.

What do employees get from their jobs?

Studies have not yet been conducted which would permit us to give you a neat account of which workers receive what vitamins from their jobs. But there have been many studies of employees' satisfaction and dissatisfaction, often with their jobs in general and sometimes with particular facets of their jobs, and job satisfaction is part, though not all, of what Warr means by mental health or psychological well-being at work. Reports of job satisfaction and dissatisfaction are the most accessible way of judging how much, and sometimes what, workers feel they are getting from their jobs.

We regard job satisfaction (and dissatisfaction) as a set of attitudes towards one's job in general and towards particular facets of one's job. These attitudes will contain a marked affective or emotional component, but in line with the discussion in chapter 13 of the tripartite model of attitudes, they will also contain cognitive beliefs about one's job and action-oriented intentions regarding it.

Surveys of job satisfaction

As one typical set of findings, let us look briefly at the degrees of satisfaction and dissatisfaction reported by Berkowitz et al. (1987). They studied a random sample of the male full-time labour force in and around Madison, the state capital of Wisconsin. How typical the results are likely to be of other workforces, and especially women, will emerge shortly. Each of the approximately 250 respondents was asked to rate his satisfaction with a variety of facets of his job, and finally with his job in general, on a series of 10-point scales, where 1 was 'completely dissatisfied' and 10 was 'completely satisfied'. Table 16.1 represents the results. We could, for the sake of simplicity, lump together scores between 10 and 7 as (more or less) 'Satisfied' and 1 to 4 as (more or less) 'Dissatisfied'.

We can now see that more than three out of four members of this random sample of the male, full-time labour force claimed to be satisfied with their jobs in general, and not quite 5 per cent described themselves as dissatisfied. With the marked exception of feelings about promotion prospects, high levels of satisfaction are apparent for virtually all facets of their jobs. Are these results obtained from one relatively thriving Midwest American town in the early 1980s atypical? Apparently not. In recent decades, surveys have consistently reported high levels of job satisfaction. Indeed, Staw (1984) concluded from a review of the evidence that over the years the percentages reporting satisfaction had been increasing; in the USA by the early 1980s, typically between 80 and 85 per cent of respondents did so. And those high levels appear to have continued in many countries, including the UK (Guest and Conway 1999). Curtice (1993) reported findings from an international survey, conducted in nine European countries plus Israel and the USA, in which respondents were offered seven answers ranging from 'completely satisfied' to 'completely dissatisfied'. Curtice concluded that: 'dissatisfaction is rare among nearly all workers. In line with other surveys of job satisfaction . . . between 80 and 91 per cent of workers in all countries except Hungary claim to be at least *satisfied* with their job' (1993, p. 105).

Before we are tempted to conclude that the great majority of workers must be getting from their jobs most of what they might be getting, there are at least a couple of sets of critical questions we should ask. First, amidst this mass of apparently contented employees, are there not pockets of relative dissatisfaction? Where are we most likely to find unhappy workers? Second, can we accept the consistent survey evidence at face value? Is the world really full of very happy workers?

From the earliest systematic surveys of job satisfaction onwards, it has been clear that the main differences between groups lie with social class-related variations in occupational level or status, rather than with other major demographic divisions such as gender, ethnicity or age. In an early study, Hoppock (1935) reported findings from a small community in Pennsylvania. Virtually all the workers in the community were interviewed, resulting in a sample of 268 respondents. Simplifying somewhat, if we translate Hoppock's findings on to a seven-point scale where 7 is 'extreme satisfaction' and 1 is 'extreme dissatisfaction', the mean scores at different occupational levels would have been:

Unskilled manual	4.0
Semi-skilled	4.8
Skilled manual and lower white-collar	5.1
Supervisory, managerial and professional	5.5

A survey conducted in Britain in 1978, which asked respondents, 'Do you enjoy the work you do a lot, a little or not at all?', found that 'a lot' was the answer offered by 81 per cent of managers, 73 per cent of skilled workers, and 66 per cent of unskilled

Table 16.1 Data on job satisfaction (percentages)

Completely satisfied true	Dissatisfaction/ satisfaction in general with job	Work interesting	Hours good	Pay good	People pleasant	Physical surround- ings pleasant	Job security good	Opportunity for own abilities	Promotion good	Supervisors treat me well	Fringe benefits good
9–10	28.6	52.8	50.2	36.7	46.8	32.7	46.4	47.6	15.3	42.7	42.8
7–8	48.7	28.7	19.8	30.2	37.9	35.1	24.2	26.6	19.4	31.1	28.2
5–6	17.4	8.8	17.3	19.8	10.9	19.4	19.3	13.7	24.2	8.8	13.4
3–4	3.2	5.2	6.4	6.8	2.8	8.4	5.2	3.6	9.2	2.8	5.2
1–2	1.6	4.4	6.4	6.4	0.8	3.6	4.8	7.6	21.4	2.8	7.6
Completely dissatisfied/false Don't know, not asked etc.	0.4	0	0	0	0.8	0.8	0	0.8	10.5	11.7	2.8

Source: Berkowitz et al. (1987)

workers. That pattern of a detectable, but usually not dramatic, decline in reported satisfaction as occupational status or prestige decreases has been consistently reported in many studies. But there is evidence that this may be changing. As professional and white-collar workers are being subject to increasing job insecurity and having to work much more intensively than they did in the past (Burchell et al. 1999), their privileged position in the labour market may be eroded.

Other demographic variables in general reveal less marked, less consistent differences. Increasing age, on balance, tends to have a modest positive association with increasing job satisfaction (e.g. Berkowitz et al. 1987) and particularly with overall job satisfaction. Evidence regarding possible ethnicity differences comes almost entirely from studies of blacks and whites in the USA. It is relatively consistent in showing small differences in job satisfaction favouring whites (Weaver 1977; 1980). Given the history of marked job discrimination against black people in the USA, and elsewhere, it may seem surprising that the differences found are usually only small.

Like many ethnic minorities, women have been and continue to be discriminated against in the labour market. Overall, women tend to have less prestigious and less well-paid jobs than men and, even within the same occupation, they are still likely to experience worse conditions of employment than men. We might, in general, expect women fairly consistently to express lower levels of job satisfaction than men, but that is not the case. Findings regarding gender differences tend to be inconsistent, and when they do appear they tend to be relatively small. Some reported differences, especially of lower satisfaction on the part of women, are likely to disappear if occupational level and other confounding variables are controlled for or partialled. Not infrequently, women actually appear to be slightly more satisfied than men. For example, in the eleven-nation study described above (Curtice 1993), job satisfaction scores were available for both men and women in full-time jobs in ten of the countries. If we look at those respondents with high job satisfaction – that is, 'completely satisfied' or 'very satisfied' – more men than women were highly satisfied in two of the ten; there was no difference in another two; and in six of the ten more women than men were highly satisfied. Of course, in some countries many women work in part-time jobs, which tend to have lower status, worse pay and poorer working conditions than full-time jobs (O'Reilly and Fagan 1998). If we average across the ten nations the percentages reporting high job satisfaction, we get the following slightly unexpected results:

Men in full-time jobs	Women in full-time jobs	Women in part-time jobs
40.4%	42.9%	46.7%

Women in part-time work are more likely than women or men in full-time work to find their jobs highly satisfying. Evidence such as Curtice's (1993) and Agassi's (1982) suggests that interesting gender differences in this area still have to be explained adequately. It may be that slightly greater satisfaction despite worse conditions and prospects reflects lower expectations of work by women, but, to be honest, as yet we do not really know. Hakim (1996) has suggested that these patterns of gender differences can only really be understood if one accepts that only a minority of women prioritize employment in their lives, and that most are firmly family-focused. Women are therefore a much more heterogeneous group than men. In any case, it would be surprising if the attitudes towards and the meanings of paid work of men and women were near identical, given the real differences that have existed and still do exist for the sexes concerning the role of paid work in their lives. It may be that surveys of job satisfaction do not tell us everything about the meanings of paid work to individuals or to categories of employees.

Let us turn then to our second set of critical questions. Can we really accept at face value survey evidence about general levels of job satisfaction in a workforce? There are several lines of argument that justify some scepticism. One of these relates to apparently contradictory evidence. A number of intensive studies of specific groups of workers in a variety of countries have made strong claims of marked dissatisfaction (e.g. Beynon 1984; Haraszti 1977; Nolan, Wichert and Burchell 1999). Does the incidence of strikes and disputes, and management concern about absenteeism and labour turnover, really fit with such high levels of satisfaction?

A second set of arguments relates to the assessment of satisfaction through surveys. Virtually any direct enquiry about 'satisfaction' – whether it is job satisfaction, pay satisfaction, life satisfaction, marital satisfaction, sexual satisfaction or some other form of satisfaction – produces reports of high levels of satisfaction. Might they not be spurious, in part at any rate? If people are confronted by an unknown other, such as an interviewer, who asks them about 'satisfaction', they might feel obliged to engage in positive self-presentation and not create a first impression of being a 'moaner'. Admissions of 'dissatisfaction' might be threatening to the self-esteem of respondents. Could they tackle the possible next question, 'Well, what are you going to do about it?', especially if they would have to admit that their current jobs are about as good as they are likely to get? In which case, for some people, a claim of being satisfied is tantamount to saying that they are making the best of a not-too-good job, whereas for others it may mean that they really enjoy their work.

Being 'satisfied' can have at least those two different meanings; it can mean reluctant acceptance and adjustment or it can mean real, positive pleasure. If we wish to use reported job satisfaction as an indicator of whether or not employees are getting from their jobs what they could conceivably be obtaining, we need to be able to get at the notion of satisfaction as pleasure.

Indirect questions in surveys of job satisfaction

One way of attempting to focus on satisfaction as positive pleasure is to ask not direct questions such as 'How satisfied are you with...?', but more indirect, hypothetical questions which free the respondent from pressures to give socially desirable responses and from threats to their self-esteem. Two such questions which have been asked in a few surveys (e.g. Agassi 1982) are 'If you had your time over again, would you still want to do your present job?' and 'Would you recommend your job to your son/daughter/ best friend?' If people who say they are 'satisfied' are really pleased with their current jobs, you might expect them to answer 'Yes' to both questions. Many do, but many do not. If such questions are accepted as indirect measures of job satisfaction, then the overall level of reported job satisfaction drops quite markedly compared with what is found with direct questions. In addition, the modest differences in satisfaction associated with occupational status which are found with direct questions become much more marked. Thus, although typically only about 15 per cent of Canadian blue-collar workers claim dissatisfaction in response to direct questions, usually less than half of them say 'Yes' to indirect questions (Archibald 1978). He reports data from an American study in which different occupational groups were asked 'What type of work would you try to get if you could start all over again?'. The following percentages said they would choose similar work again: company lawyers, journalists, scientists, university professors – over 80 per cent; skilled printers – 52 per cent; skilled steelworkers, skilled car workers – 41 per cent; unskilled steelworkers – 21 per cent; unskilled car workers – 16 per cent.

It is likely that the indirect questions are better at tapping 'satisfaction as pleasure' than are the direct ones, and that the size of the difference in reported satisfaction between the direct and indirect questions is an indication of the extent to which a group of employees is putting on a good face in response to direct questions. Agassi (1982) found that that gap was higher for manual than non-manual workers, for women than men, for older than younger workers, and for employees with an 'instrumental' attitude to their jobs than for those without. Thus it seems that the usual surveys of job satisfaction systematically overestimate the extent to which a labour force is getting from their jobs what they might be getting, and that overestimation is greater the lower down the occupational hierarchy one looks. It transpires, for example, that the dissatisfaction of production-line car workers which emerged from Beynon's (1984) intensive study of a single car plant is not contradicted by surveys of car workers which use indirect questions regarding satisfaction.

It should be noted that there are other possible methods for trying to assess job satisfaction, ranging from intensive direct observation or even participant observation (see chapter 19 for a discussion of such methods) in particular firms or plants to the use of aggregate statistics relating to labour turnover rates and to absenteeism rates. But, for a variety of reasons, surveys using both direct and indirect questions regarding job satisfaction are likely to prove the most practical way of assessing what workers are and are not getting from their jobs.

Consistently high levels of reported job satisfaction indicate that, by and large, high-status professionals and senior managers feel that their jobs are serving them very well, but such extremely positive attitudes become progressively less common the lower the status and prestige of a job. Particularly with the use of indirect questions, considerable dissatisfaction with many facets of their jobs can be found among semi-skilled and unskilled manual workers. Need such dissatisfaction exist?

Methods of increasing job satisfaction

There have been a number of systematic management techniques which have been used in efforts to increase the productivity of employees. In the earlier days of industrialization the main attempts to do this were through careful studies of the flow of work in factories, and trying to find more efficient ways of accomplishing tasks, such as the use of conveyor belts and production lines. More recently, management has concentrated more on the work attitudes of employees as the main route to increased productivity and competitiveness. The umbrella term for this school of management thought is human resource management (HRM). Unfortunately, the term has come to mean very different things to different people. For some, it means a careful consideration and manipulation of organizational climate and management practices to generate a strong and healthy psychological contract between managers and employees, whereby employees will be committed to the organization, and respond willingly and flexibly to its demands. In return managers look after employees' interests and show themselves to be trustworthy and caring. Often HRM is associated with employees working more autonomously, or in teams, rather than being closely supervised by managers, and being flexible in their responses to changes, rather than sticking rigidly to the tasks listed in their job descriptions (see, for example, Guest and Conway 1997).

Others, more sceptical of the motives of employers' see HRM as yet another way of exploiting the 'human resources' in the organization as effectively as the other resources, such as money and machinery. This is achieved by creating the convenient illusion that 'bosses and workers are on the same side', so that employees work themselves harder for longer hours and do not see the need to be protected at work by trade unions.

Why, you may ask, do organizations not improve the job satisfaction of their employees by doubling their pay? The answer, of course, is very obvious. There are limits to management's concern with worker satisfaction, and a doubling of salary costs is one very clear limit indeed.

A more sensible question to ask is, 'How effective is increasing pay in generating higher levels of job satisfaction?' Certainly pay dissatisfaction appears to be a common feature of job dissatisfaction and of industrial action, such as strikes, and the most obvious way of reducing pay dissatisfaction would seem to be to increase pay. But the evidence, and the theories, tend not to provide as strong support for the link between level of pay and pay satisfaction, let alone job satisfaction, as might readily be assumed.

Motowidlo (1982) has pointed out that, typically, the correlation between amount of pay and degree of pay satisfaction reported in empirical studies set in developed countries is quite modest; he cited correlations varying from $+.13$ to $+.46$. Berkowitz et al. (1987) found that although measures of material benefits, including pay, were one set of predictors of pay satisfaction, they were not the most powerful predictors, which were measures of the perceived fairness of respondents' pay.

This empirical demonstration of the centrality of fairness of pay fits well with theorizing about pay satisfaction, much of which (e.g. Adams 1965) argues that if you think your pay is fair you are satisfied with it, and if you do not you are dissatisfied. In recent decades, the most commonly used analysis of pay satisfaction, that of Lawler (1971), has been couched in terms of fairness. It is summarized in slightly simplified form in figure 16.1. Lawler claimed that if people felt that their actual pay was about equal to what they believed they deserved they would be satisfied, but if they perceived themselves as deserving more or deserving less than they were receiving then they would feel dissatisfied in the first case and guilty in the second. What an individual perceives as the amounts that are being received and should be received are themselves determined by a variety of considerations, as can be seen in figure 16.1.

Thus, there is considerable agreement that increased satisfaction with pay is even more likely to be achieved by increasing people's sense of the fairness of their pay than

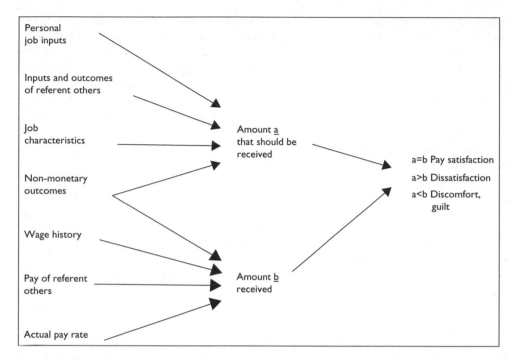

Figure 16.1 Lawler's model of pay satisfaction

by simply increasing the pay itself. That seems like good news to employers but not to trade union officials or even employees' families.

Job satisfaction and performance

It is not just employees who are interested in how satisfying or unsatisfying they find their work. Employers often have an interest in the issue too. If they are enlightened employers they would like their workers to enjoy their work. But, in addition, from the human relations approach of the 1930s through to today's HRM, employers have frequently been interested in employees' job satisfaction because of the common assumption that satisfaction leads to high productivity. It may seem obvious that the happy worker will be the productive worker, but that does not necessarily follow. It is possible to work hard and effectively when you feel you have to – to avoid the sack, for instance – even if you are pretty dissatisfied. It is also conceivable that if satisfaction with your job is strongly related to the enjoyment you derive from your colleagues, then your satisfaction might be even higher if you could only eliminate the time and effort you expend on the boring work which gets in the way of your socializing!

In other words, it is by no means inevitable that productivity and satisfaction will go together, and reviews of empirical studies consistently reveal surprisingly modest correlations between the two. Doubts about satisfaction being the royal road to productivity mounted in the 1960s with reviews such as Vroom's (1964), which, across a substantial number of studies, found an average satisfaction/performance correlation of only +.13. According to Staw (1984), when the problematic nature of relations between satisfaction and productivity came to be recognized by management and by management-oriented academics, research interest in job satisfaction dropped markedly in the 1970s, suggesting, of course, that the large volume of previous research had not been conducted just out of concern for the well-being of workers. The fact that interest in studying job satisfaction started to increase again in the 1980s could be taken to imply that researchers and management began to feel that the assumption of minimal relations between satisfaction and performance may have been too pessimistic.

A helpful way of understanding the changing views regarding satisfaction and performance is to note the parallel with the attitude–behaviour problem, discussed at some length in chapter 13. In both cases, at first it was naively assumed that strong, simple, unidirectional relations existed between attitudes and behaviour and between satisfaction and productivity. Critical reviews in the 1960s of early empirical studies appeared to cast severe doubt on these hitherto taken-for-granted assumptions. The resulting shocks gradually led to more sophisticated thinking and more careful research on the problems. In the case of satisfaction and productivity, it has been recognized that the psychological state of the workforce is far from being the only determinant of output. Many major factors external to the employees, such as the organization of the production system, the effectiveness of management and the state of the labour market, are also likely to be important. Indeed, if you think of semi-skilled workers on a highly mechanized production line performing simple and repetitive tasks with a minimum of autonomy or control, you may wonder how their level of satisfaction or dissatisfaction could have any effect whatsoever on output, short of their literally dropping spanners in the works to gain temporary respites while the machines are fixed (see Beynon 1984). Thus, the question we should ask is 'Under what conditions is the level of employee satisfaction most likely to have consequences for outcomes?'

A key advance in studying attitude–behaviour relations was recognition that both elements should be measured at the same level of generality or specificity. If, as has frequently been the case, satisfaction is assessed as overall satisfaction with the job in general, why should that be a powerful predictor of an arbitrary and specific indicator of behaviour on the job, such as a count of number of units produced in a given time? Rather than focusing exclusively on such limited measures of productivity, should not outcomes be assessed by a much wider set of indicators of performance? Table 16.2 indicates what a broad view of performance indicators might include.

Detailed reviews of the empirical evidence, by E. A. Locke (1984), Podsakoff and Williams (1986) and others, reveal varying amounts of evidence for and varying strengths of the different relationships, although all of the relations have been found by at least one or two studies. For example, a moderate relationship between dissatisfaction and quitting the job – that is, turnover – has been demonstrated in many studies and that is also, in general, the case with absenteeism, although there the consistency of the correlations has tended to be just slightly lower. Far fewer studies, however, have explored how dissatisfaction relates to time-keeping on the job.

Studies that directly relate measures of satisfaction to measures of productivity typically find positive relations, not all of which are large enough to be statistically significant. In the light of extensive reviews by Iaffaldano and Muchinsky (1985),

Table 16.2 Some possible effects of job dissatisfaction on performance

Effect	Indicator
1. Physical withdrawal	Turnover
	Absenteeism
	Timekeeping
2. Psychological withdrawal	Disinterest
	Alcohol, drugs
3. Aggressive responses	Sabotage
	Stealing
4. Attempts at change	Joining trade unions
	Industrial action
5. Less good citizenship	Less helping others
	Less care of resources, equipment
6. Effects on productivity	Indirect effects, via 1–5 above
	Direct effects, quantitative and qualitative

Podsakoff and Williams (1986) and others, the average correlation appears to be just below +.20. The general picture which emerges, then, is not of one overwhelming type of satisfaction/performance relation but of an array of relations, which, modest though they are, have non-negligible implications for management.

But what is the direction of cause and effect? So far, we have assumed that satisfaction is likely to help determine performance, but is the reverse not also plausible? Just as our behaviour can change our attitudes, might our performance determine satisfaction, rather than the other way round? If work is going well, are we not likely to feel more satisfied with our jobs than if it is going badly? Most satisfaction/performance studies have only assessed the relations by means of correlations which do not permit us to be sure about cause and effect. Clegg (1983), though, did use a research design which justified him in claiming that, in his study at least, dissatisfaction did cause increased turnover. M. M. Petty, McGee and Cavender (1984) also found modest support for satisfaction influencing performance. Thus, it seems very likely that some of the commonly found relations between satisfaction and performance do result from variations in the former bringing about variations in the latter.

For many people, the idea that high satisfaction with a job leads to high productivity seems like obvious common sense. We have seen, however, that, like many other instances of common sense, that assumption conceals a complex set of relationships. And our understanding is by no means complete. Perhaps satisfaction has more influence on the performance of employees in complex and highly skilled jobs that carry at least some autonomy than on relatively unskilled workers whose noses can be kept to the conveyor belt or checkout computer by close supervision. Perhaps satisfaction will be shown to have even more impact on less commonly studied qualitative aspects of performance, such as 'good citizenship' behaviours like showing consideration for workmates and taking good care of tools and resources, than it does on quantitative measures of productivity. Even with our incomplete understanding, however, it has become clear that employers, as well as employees, do stand to gain by increasing job satisfaction.

Employees in relatively secure jobs that give them little satisfaction deserve our sympathy. But they may be relatively privileged compared both to workers who know that their jobs could disappear tomorrow and to those who wish to work but have no jobs at all. How satisfied or dissatisfied are the insecurely employed and the unemployed? That is what we will examine in the remainder of this chapter.

The psychological effects of unemployment

Unemployment has been a major problem for most industrialized countries since the mid-1970s, and few experts predict a simple or quick solution. Having large numbers of willing and able workers idle is an illogical or absurd situation from many perspectives. Economically it is a wasted resource; idle workers do not contribute to the output of the nation, do not pay taxes and do consume welfare benefits. Socially it is seen as unjust, and exacerbates a variety of social problems including crime (Hagan 1994), homelessness and divorce (Lampard 1994) to name but a few. And many of the individuals who experience unemployment themselves suffer problems of poverty and poor physical and psychological health. It is psychological health which will be considered here, although it will be argued that one cannot understand well the psychological effects of unemployment without also understanding the social and economic correlates of employment and unemployment.

In the next section of this chapter the various sources of evidence concerning the psychological health of individuals in the workforce are discussed. Then the reasons why individuals seem to depend on employment to maintain their psychological well-being will be considered, before looking at the ways in which the labour market can have widespread effects on the psychological health of people other than the unemployed themselves.

Unemployment and psychological health: the evidence

The social scientist and lay person alike generally accept that unemployment can be psychologically damaging. Arguments to the contrary have occasionally been made; for instance, by the extreme left, who see unemployment as a liberation from capitalist control, or from the far right, who have argued that the unemployed are content in their idleness (see M. Jahoda 1988). But psychological and socioeconomic studies have found that neither of these claims receives any significant support. Unemployment at the beginning of the twenty-first century seems to be just as harmful as it was in the Great Depression of the 1930s.

The rapid global rises in unemployment in the 1970s and 1980s spawned many psychological studies of the impact of unemployment. They will be considered briefly according to the type of research design used.

Cross-sectional studies The simplest type of evidence has involved the collection of an indicator of psychological health from matched groups of employed and unemployed individuals. For instance, Warr and Payne (1982) reported the results of interviews with a large random sample of adults in England, Scotland and Wales, in which respondents were asked about their feelings on the day prior to the survey. Six per cent of men in jobs and 9 per cent of employed females reported high levels of emotional strain, compared to 16 per cent of unemployed men and 21 per cent of unemployed women. This pattern of results has been replicated many times over in Britain and elsewhere, demonstrating conclusively that the psychological well-being of the unemployed is, on average, worse than that of those with jobs. This finding is of course open to alternative causal explanations – for some of those unemployed individuals there may have been chronic low levels of psychological well-being which had made it difficult for them to find work. It is also difficult to control for prior variables, such as the social class, level of work ethic etc. of employees and the unemployed, using this research design.

Longitudinal studies   A superior design for determining the impact of unemployment on mental health is to follow the same individuals as they move into and out of employment. A number of studies have done this; for instance, Warr and Jackson (1985) and Payne and Jones (1987) reinterviewed men who were unemployed at the time of an earlier survey. (Many of the earlier studies tended to focus only on male unemployment, perhaps reflecting sexist assumptions on the part of researchers. Where men's and women's experiences of unemployment are considered together, little evidence of gender differences has generally been found.) Whilst those who remained unemployed at the time of the reinterview continued, on average, to have high levels of psychological distress, those who became re-employed in the time between interviews tended to improve in their psychological health.

The other logical possibility for a longitudinal design is to examine changes in the psychological health associated with the inflow into unemployment. As the rate at which a representative sample of employees becomes unemployed is so low, inflow studies have instead focused on plant closures and mass redundancies. However, findings from this type of study (e.g. Kasl and Cobb 1982) have typically been confounded by the fact that the anticipation and fear of impending unemployment may be as stressful as unemployment itself, if not more so.

Qualitative studies   A number of researchers have collected more detailed information about individuals' reactions to unemployment using less structured interviews. For instance, Fineman interviewed a number of white-collar workers who were made redundant in the late 1970s, and revisited them a couple of times later, during which time some became re-employed and some remained unemployed or alternated between temporary employment and unemployment (1983; 1987). By letting them relate their own narratives, a more complex set of accounts emerges. For instance, one feature that is not revealed in many quantitative studies is that a minority of individuals enjoy many features of unemployment, such as spending more time with their families or escaping from what was a stressful or unpleasant job. But for most the experience of unemployment is not only stressful, but continues to affect their attitudes to work long after their re-employment. Furthermore, if that re-employment is into a job which is perceived as inferior to the job that they lost, for instance in the level of skill required or the prestige of the job, then that too can be a continuing source of discontent.

Aggregate studies   A number of researchers have attempted to monitor the way in which the economy effects psychological health through time-series analysis. Brenner (1973) pioneered this field, using data from New York state covering a period of up to 127 years. His main indicator of economic prosperity was the number of individuals employed in manufacturing, which he found predicted the number of psychiatric hospital admissions after a two-year time lag. Brenner replicated this technique using British data, and arrived at similar conclusions (Brenner 1979). However, these aggregate studies are problematic in interpretation because of artifacts in the measurement of indicators such as admissions and suicide rates (Dooley and Catalano 1986). But whatever their findings, these studies still tell us little about the psychological, social or economic mechanisms by which employment and mental health are related. Is it possible, for instance, that during times of high unemployment even those in work experience lower levels of psychological well-being (perhaps because they worry that they too will become unemployed)? This question will be addressed after considering the mechanisms by which employment affects psychological well-being.

Why does unemployment affect psychological well-being?

Several models have been put forward as to why unemployment is so damaging to an individual's psychological health. Three of these theories will be discussed here, two emphasizing the impoverished environment of the unemployed compared to the employed, the other focusing on the way in which individuals cope (or fail to cope) with unemployment.

Environmental vitamins and latent functions

A number of psychological theories postulate that paid work provides a healthier environment for the individual, and that the unemployed person, without the benefits which commonly accrue from such an environment, will suffer psychological ill-health. Warr's vitamin model (1987), described earlier in this chapter and in box 16.2, provides a detailed example of such a theory. This model is similar in its type of explanation of the psychological effects of unemployment to another very influential model, M. Jahoda's latent functions or deprivation model (1982), also described earlier in this chapter. Perhaps the most important difference between these theories is that Jahoda assumes that virtually all jobs provide access to her five 'categories of experience', whilst for Warr a major aim of his model is to differentiate between good employment and bad employment, and good and bad unemployment. However, both attribute the poor psychological health found among the unemployed to their lack of access to the good things about employment. Although Warr's model was largely derived from systematic reviews of empirical evidence, neither of these theories' capacity to explain the psychological effects of unemployment has been subject to a rigorous direct test, but Gershuny's empirical investigation of Jahoda's model provided some support.

  Gershuny (1994) tested Jahoda's theory of the latent consequences of employment and found broad corroboration for it among both employed and unemployed samples, inasmuch as the more individuals had access to Jahoda's categories of experience, the better their psychological health. However, even those unemployed individuals who had access to all five categories of experience had worse mean levels of psychological well-being than employees, so it could not account for anything but a small part of the differences between the employed and unemployed.

Personal agency

An alternative model to account for the psychological effects of unemployment portrays individuals as attempting to construct their own futures, rather than being acquiescent recipients of 'vitamins' from their environments. Agency theory asserts that, rather than being primarily passive, individuals are active and striving, making decisions, initiating and planning, future-oriented, purposeful, organizing and structuring, in short pro-active rather than reactive (Fryer 1992; Fryer and Fagan 1993). However, not all environments are conducive to those sorts of activities. It is, according to this theory, the frustration of agency that causes poor well-being in unemployment. Unemployment is commonly a threatening, inhibiting and restrictive environment characterized by inadequate resources, low social power and an uncertain future. Support for this theory comes from three types of observation.

Fryer's first evidence came from very detailed case studies of eleven carefully selected individuals who were very well adapted to unemployment in most ways (Fryer and Payne 1984). These highly atypical individuals had in common an ability to structure and fill their own lives and work towards goals that they set themselves. Fryer and Payne concluded that a small proportion of the population have got the personal resources to continue to identify and pursue goals of personal significance outside of normal paid employment, and thus protect their psychological health through such activity.

Further evidence of the nature of the psychological environment that allows people to be able to undergo periods without paid work, but to avoid harmful psychological consequences, comes from a study that compared groups of men from two factories that were facing falling order books (McKenna and Fryer 1984). One group were made redundant and the other group were (following trade union negotiation) temporarily laid off on a rolling basis. The data were collected in one period where one group of men, because of the coincidence of lay-off, holidays and maintenance shutdown, went for approximately twelve weeks without work. The two groups of men, redundant and laid-off, were thus both without work, claiming benefit and in other objective ways in a similar position. The groups differed greatly, though, in their adjustment to workless-ness. The laid-off workers planned in advance how they would spend their spare time, for instance decorating their homes, repairing cars, gardening, taking up new sporting activities and going on holidays. They typically bought in the materials that they needed in advance of their lay-off, and were usually successful in carrying out their plans before their return to work. Five weeks after the lay-off these men were, if anything, slightly better in their self-perceived health than a control group of men who had remained at work in the factory.

By contrast, the men who had been forcibly made redundant had considerably worse reported health. Due to relatively large redundancy payments they did not have immediate financial problems (it should be noted that this made this group atypical; the vast majority of people in the UK who become unemployed do so with very little or no redundancy money). However, they typically spent much of their time watching television and reported feeling bored. When interviewed, fear of uncertainty about their future was mentioned frequently as one of their main worries; they did not know whether they would be working or still unemployed in a few weeks' or months' time. The researchers concluded that it was the inability to plan for the future that caused the problems for the redundant group, not the lack of a job *per se*.

A third type of evidence that demonstrates the importance of agency to good psychological functioning comes from studies of employees. Several studies have demonstrated that insecurely employed workers suffer many of the same problems as the unemployed. For instance, Burchell (1994) found that unemployed men who returned to work in insecure jobs, where they still felt threatened by unemployment, showed no gain in psychological health. Burchell and Rubery (1990) found that the most vulnerable and insecure employees scored as badly in terms of psychological health as the unemployed, and many other studies of the insecure workforce have reached similar conclusions (see Wichert, Nolan and Burchell 2000 for a review). Similarly, Dooley, Catalano and Rook (1988) found that the psychological health of a representative sample of US employees fell as the aggregate levels of unemployment rose, presumably as they felt the threat of unemployment. Fineman's (1983; 1987) qualitative surveys and follow-ups with white-collar males who had suffered redundancies (referred to above) found some instances of men who seemed to cope better with unemployment than with employment under very adverse labour market positions. For instance, in one telling quotation a mathematics graduate who had experienced a number of insecure jobs between spells of unemployment finally decided that life was less stressful in unemployment than in such unsatisfactory and unpredictable jobs: 'I've done absolutely nothing about finding work. Since unemployment my life has been much more pleasant' (1987, p. 273).

Agency theory has thus widened the debate about unemployment and poor psychological health. Unemployment can be seen as only one way in which individuals can be disadvantaged or made vulnerable by the labour market. There is much evidence that the changes in the British labour market since the 1970s have left many more employees (particularly white-collar employees) feeling insecure (Felstead, Burchell and Green 1998); the unemployed themselves may be just the tip of the iceberg in terms of the poorer psychological health brought about by high unemployment and 'flexibilization' of the workforce (Burchell et al. 1999; N. Buck et al. 1994).

It may, of course, be that both environmental and agency accounts of unemployment are equally valid and complementary; it is unlikely that we will find a simple, unidimensional explanation to a complex, multifaceted problem like unemployment. Like many problems in social psychology a simple nature–nurture, environment–individual or external–internal debate is a false dichotomy. We need to be able to look at both the individual and the situation, as well as the relationship between the two.

Unemployment, poverty and social exclusion

A discussion of the effects of unemployment would be incomplete without a consideration of the poverty that goes hand in hand with unemployment. Researchers in the 1930s tended to give much emphasis to the economic plight of the unemployed and the strains that this put on them, but more recent researchers have tended to emphasize more the psychological effects of unemployment and downplay the role of poverty *per se*. While it is true that the absolute level of poverty of the unemployed in the 1930s is much more acute than that in the 1980s and 1990s, Fryer (1992) has argued that poverty is nevertheless an important source of the misery and distress that accompanies unemployment in modern times. Fraser (1981) suggested that whereas in the 1930s the children of unemployed parents often went barefoot, nowadays they wear second-hand shoes. Surveys of the unemployed consistently find that the financial difficulties of surviving without a wage are emphasized more than anything else. Difficulties in paying bills and having to go without essentials such as food and heat are perhaps even more difficult to bear when there is so much conspicuous consumption in our affluent society. And whilst the unemployed of today may possess consumer durables like washing machines and video-recorders which would have been beyond the imaginations of the unemployed in the 1930s, their relative poverty still excludes them from activities and statuses which are considered the norm.

It is that exclusion from society (a society in which consumerism and material possessions play a great part) that is felt in a very real sense by the unemployed (Townsend 1979; Rodgers 1994). Telling teenagers that perfectly warm and functional clothes can be purchased from second-hand shops is cold comfort if their peers derive so much identity and esteem from dressing in the latest designer styles and fashions. As Kelvin and Jarrett (1985) emphasize, one of the benefits of employment is the identity it gives (see chapters 2 and 15 in this volume for discussions of the centrality of social identity in our lives). Not only does unemployment rob people of this identity, but it also denies them access to another important form of identity in our lives in the form of symbolic consumption (McGhee and Fryer 1989). There is an increasing body of evidence that, as some individuals within a society come to have much greater wealth than others, this inequality leads to a range of individual and social problems, ranging from poor health to a lack of social trust and an increase in crime (Wilkinson 1996).

The psychological health of dependants of unemployed people

It is not only the unemployed themselves who suffer; their dependants have been found to be affected too. For instance, Elder used North American cohort studies started in the 1920s and 1930s to establish a link between the psychological well-being of children and the extent of the economic losses that their families suffered during the Great Depression. Worse psychological health was caused at least in part by the worse parenting styles which seemed to occur when families suffered the most extreme loss of income (see, for example, Elder and Caspi 1988). Moser, Fox and Jones (1984) demonstrated convincingly, using the a major government longitudinal study, that the wives of unemployed men also suffered increased levels of mortality. Fagin and Little (1984) found depression in wives of unemployed men, particularly if they did not work themselves, and also found some evidence of psychological problems amongst the children, including disturbed feeding habits, minor gastrointestinal complaints, sleeping difficulties, proneness to accidents and behavioural disorders. These studies serve as a reminder that even those who are not in the workforce themselves can be victims of economic recession. Thus in order to understand the full psychological effects of recession we need to understand the nature of the social support structures (such as families) in which individuals are embedded (Burchell 1992b).

Conclusions

This chapter has covered some of the principal interests that social psychologists have in the world of paid work.

We started by considering why people worked, and concluded that people worked in part for pay and in part for other social and psychological benefits to be gained from employment. Next we surveyed the literature on job satisfaction, and tried to understand the paradox of why such a large majority of employees claim to be satisfied with their jobs, even though much of what we know about the quality of jobs, and many of the behaviours of employees, are seemingly inconsistent with this claim. To understand what people mean when they say that they are satisfied with their jobs is a complex task, but careful research has allowed us to understand some of the complexities of job satisfaction. These complexities have not stopped many attempts to increase job satisfaction by new management methods, perhaps because employers believed that a satisfied workforce would be more productive. However, there is surprisingly little evidence of really strong links. Perhaps the benefits of a satisfied workforce are felt in more subtle ways, such as lower absenteeism and turnover.

Pay satisfaction has also been studied in considerable depth, and again the relationships between objective conditions and satisfaction are not simple. Pay satisfaction appears to be more closely tied to perceptions of fairness of pay than to the absolute levels of pay *per se*.

The final section of the chapter has considered the effects of unemployment. In the same way as money is not the only good reason for working, the lack of a wage is not the only way in which the unemployed suffer. We considered both environmental and agency explanations proposed to explain what it is about employment and unemployment that gives employees a much higher level of psychological health than the unemployed.

Perhaps the most difficult thing for a psychologist to come to terms with is that the world of paid work is constantly changing as management styles, technology, laws, politicians, attitudes to work and the economy all change. The challenges of employment in the new millennium may be rather different from the challenges that psychology has reacted to in the past, even if the impact of unemployment remains depressingly similar to the effects that were documented during most of the twentieth century.

RECOMMENDED READING

Beynon, H. (1984) *Working for Ford*. 2nd edn. Harmondsworth: Penguin.
This is a thought-provoking, in-depth study of a far from satisfied workforce.

Feather, N. T.(1990) *The Psychological Impact of Unemployment*. Springer-Verlag.

This is a comprehensive overview of the literature on psychology and unemployment.

Furnham, A. (1997) *The Psychology of Behaviour at Work*. Chichester: Taylor and Francis.
This gives overview of the organizational psychology literature.

Warr, P. (1999) Wellbeing and the workplace. In D. Kahnemann, E. Diener and N. Schwartz (eds), *Wellbeing: The Foundations of Hedonic Psychology*. New York: Sage.
This restates and updates Warr's vitamin model.

17

Health and Illness

Introduction

This chapter is about aspects of the social psychology of mental and physical illness. It focuses primarily on mental health problems such as depression and schizophrenia, although a variety of other health problems will also be referred to. The main purpose of the chapter is to present a selective review of social psychological theory and research that has contributed to our understanding of health-related topics, with an emphasis on research on the distribution, manifestation and course of mental health problems. The chapter begins with a brief review of the range of perspectives in social psychology from which health-related topics have been approached. Following this, we look at recent research into the social distribution of health problems, and then predisposing factors that are known to increase an individual's vulnerability to particular health problems. The fourth and fifth sections look respectively at the impact of life events and of social support. We then review research on the role of family and marital interactions in depression and schizophrenia. The next section focuses on public attitudes to mental health problems and their impact on the lives and social integration of people with mental health problems. Finally, we review research that investigates lay concepts of health and ill-health before drawing the chapter together by offering some general conclusions.

As a starting point, it is useful to remind ourselves of certain basic issues that shape any research into health and illness. First, when considering 'illness' we are dealing with a huge range of phenomena that are somehow problematic, abnormal or disruptive of daily functioning. Second, although the majority of this chapter focuses on forms of mental illness, the psychosomatic nature of many health problems makes it difficult to distinguish neatly between mental and physical illness. Third, as research in medicine, para-medicine and the social sciences adds to our understanding of the bio-psycho-social nature of illness, we must recognize the multiple aetiologies and manifestations of all illnesses. As a consequence, the studies presented in this chapter should be seen as one of several possible ways of understanding these health problems rather than as definitive accounts.

Social psychological perspectives on health and illness

The wide range of contributions and approaches to the topic of health and illness by social psychologists reflects the diversity of modern social psychology. Thus we find theoretical perspectives on health and illness within social psychology ranging from the impact of cognitive style to cultural conceptions of 'health', and a similar diversity in the range of methods used, from large-scale surveys to in-depth qualitative analyses. Researchers working within a social-cognitive framework tend to focus on the health behaviour of individuals, investigating for example why particular individuals or social groups succeed or fail in changing health-related behaviours such as smoking or condom use (Abraham et al. 1992; Eagley and Chaiken 1993). Those positioned at the more sociological end of the spectrum of social psychology are more concerned to understand how societies conceptualize forms of illness, and how the health behaviours of individuals are shaped by the sociocultural norms of the communities of which they are a part (e.g. C. Campbell 1997; Gervais and Jovchelovitch 1998). In addition, an increasing body of research conducted by other health researchers investigates the role of social factors in determining who gets ill, why and how. Arguably, this work makes less use of social psychological theories, but its empirical focus on how social factors interact with psychological and biological ones in shaping the health of individuals who have different psychosocial experiences contributes to developing ever-more sophisticated bio-psycho-social models of various health problems.

As well as having different foci of research, social psychologists and others investigating social factors in health and illness also vary in their basic assumptions about the nature of health and illness. Generally speaking, social psychologists who work within a social-cognitive framework adopt an epistemological position in which the validity of depression or schizophrenia as meaningful psychological constructs is taken as a given and not questioned. This is also the case for other researchers interested in the role of various social factors in the development and course of health problems. At the risk of being selective, this chapter focuses primarily on research at this more cognitive and individual-oriented end of this spectrum: the majority of studies reviewed in this chapter adopt this position. On the other hand, social psychologists working within more sociological or social constructionist theoretical frameworks view 'health' and 'illness' as social and cultural notions that cannot be distinguished from the collective practices and belief systems within which they emerge and are lived out. Rather than viewing notions such as 'depression' as fixed and universal psychological states, these research-ers would take a more sceptical view of these constructs as socially shaped problems that vary from society to society, over time, and according to the gender, ethnicity or social status of the person to whom they refer. The final section reviews research on lay notions of illness that is conducted from this theoretical perspective.

The social distribution of illness

One of the most striking facts about all forms of illness is that they are not evenly distributed in the population. The distribution of illness in the community, and the investigation of reasons for its uneven distribution, is known as epidemiology. There are some very reliable findings about the uneven distribution of illness, but explanations for these findings are more a matter of debate and controversy. Various psychosocial explanations often suggest themselves, but it is important to weigh the evidence care-fully, and not to jump to conclusions. In this section (and those that follow) we will use two forms of mental ill-health – depression and schizophrenia – to illustrate how social psychology can provide at least partial accounts of the uneven distribution of these disorders. Because some readers may be unfamiliar with the nature of these mental health problems, it is useful to begin with some background descriptive information about depression and schizophrenia.

Depression is the most commonly reported psychological problem in developed countries as well as being a component of many other mental health problems. At any one time up to 15 per cent of the adult population may be suffering from mild forms of depression. The principal symptoms of depression are sadness, pessimism, low self-esteem, and loss of interest and motivation. Depression has a broad network of effects. Basic biological functions are disturbed. For example, depressed people often have poor sleep and show loss of appetite and libido. Mood and emotion are affected: depressed people usually feel sad, but may also experience anger, guilt and anxiety. Thought processes are also affected. Though depressed people remain in touch with reality, they characteristically have a distorted negative view of things. Beck has talked about the 'negative triad' of depressive thinking, that is, negative views about the world, the self and the future (Beck et al. 1979). Finally, behaviour is affected. Depressed people are slow and withdrawn and do much less than when they are not depressed.

Plate 17.1 Depression is the most commonly reported psychological problem in developed countries

Our second illustrative (mental) health problem, schizophrenia, is a so-called psychotic disorder that affects one in one hundred people in their lifetime. The term 'psychosis' refers to a collection of severe mental health problems in which experiences are arguably qualitatively different from normal experience, and sufferers lose contact with consensual reality and may have reduced insight into their problems. Not all people with schizophrenia have the same symptoms, but some characteristic features are hallucinations (hearing voices, which are often hostile in what they say), and holding fixed, delusional beliefs (often of a paranoid or suspicious kind). Occasionally, the stream of thought and of speech is seriously disordered, illogical, and incoherent. As a consequence, people with schizophrenia are often also seriously impaired in their ability to perform everyday tasks and social roles.

Women and depression

Demographic variations in the rate of psychiatric problems have been consistently reported. Across all forms of mental ill-health, women, people in lower social classes, the unemployed, and people who are separated or bereaved show higher rates of psychiatric distress (Bebbington et al. 1981; Dohrenwend and Dohrenwend 1969). One very well-established finding is that the rate of depression in women exceeds that in men in the adult population by a ratio of more than 2 to 1 (D. Goldberg and Huxley

1980; S. K. Myers et al. 1984; Weissman and Klerman 1977; Weissman and Olfson 1995). This finding holds up whether the focus is on clinically diagnosed cases of depression, or on individuals' own reports of depressive feelings in community surveys. It also seems clear that higher levels of depression in women are not just due to their being more likely to report depression and seek help for it. This may be one factor, but the hypothesis that women are more likely to seek help for depression than men has not been consistently supported (e.g. Amenson and Lewinsohn 1981).

Though higher rates of depression in women than men have been found in a variety of different countries, it is important to note that there are some non-modern cultures in which the finding has not been replicated, such as rural Iran. One of the most interesting studies of depression in a non-modern culture is of the Old Order Amish, a strict religious sect in Pennsylvania which maintains a closed society, cut off from the modern world. J. A. Egeland and Hostetter (1983) found low levels of depression generally, and an equal sex ratio of depression in this unusual culture. The fact that there are cultures in which sex bias in depression is not found is of theoretical importance. If the sex bias were attributable entirely to biological factors, it should be found in all cultures, with no exceptions. There is thus good reason to look for psychosocial explanations, and there is now a large body of relevant research. Three such explanations will be considered briefly: (1) the way women and girls are socialized, (2) the kind of roles women have as adults, and (3) women's cognitive style.

1 *Socialization* Women learn 'helplessness' in their upbringing, and this predisposes them to depression as adults.
2 *Social roles* The social roles of women are less satisfying than those of men, and make them more vulnerable to depression.
3 *Cognitive style* Women are more likely to ruminate on negative life events in a way that prolongs their effects and leads to depression.

Explanations in terms of female socialization have taken as their starting point the hypothesis that depression is equivalent to a form of learned helplessness (Seligman 1975). This term, which is associated with a programme of empirical research by Seligman and colleagues, refers to a state of apathy that is induced by an experience of lack of control over unpleasant stimuli. It is also associated, in experimental research on animals, with an inability to initiate new learning. There are parallels between the behavioural and cognitive components of learned helplessness and of depression. Applying this to female socialization, women and girls may be more likely to be ignored, may have more difficulty in getting their contributions taken seriously, and may be less likely to be able to act in a way that achieves their goals. Certainly there is some empirical evidence consistent with this. For example, Le Unes, Nation and Turley (1980) found that female college students were more susceptible to learned helplessness in a laboratory situation than their male counterparts. Maccoby and Jacklin (1974) reported that, while the behaviour of boys is likely to be praised or criticized, girls are much more likely to be simply ignored. The 'learned helplessness' that girls acquire through such socialization practices may result in a higher level of depression in adulthood. While there is a degree of plausibility in this hypothesis, researchers have yet to test it directly. In addition, there is more to depression than the sense of helplessness that females may acquire through socialization.

The social role explanation lends itself to empirical investigation in a more satisfactory way. For example, it can be argued that in our society marriage or cohabitation is a less satisfying and more stressful social role for women than for men, and that this makes them more vulnerable to depression. There is evidence that in many homes women bear a disproportionate share of responsibility for housework and child care (Wu and DeMaris 1996). The theory has been advanced with various different emphases, for example that women have less status and power within a long-term intimate relationship, or that the traditional housewife role is relatively boring and unrewarding (Gove and Tudor 1973). Evidence suggests that employment outside the home may act as a buffer against depression by increasing self-esteem, social status and social support (Nolen-Hoeksema 1990); see chapter 16 for a more detailed description of the relationship between employment and mental health. The strength of this theory is that it fits in well with one of the important facts about the sex ratio in depression, namely that it is particularly among married people that women are more prone than men to depression. This suggests that there is something about the social role associated with being a married woman that makes people vulnerable to depression. However, Cochrane (1983) suggests that marriage may make women particularly vulnerable to hospital admission for depression, but that it may not be so relevant to the actual incidence of depression in the community.

A third cognitive explanation for why there is more female depression has been advanced by Nolen-Hoeksema (1987) in relation to how men and women respond to brief episodes of unhappiness. Her data shows that men are more likely to distract themselves when something happens to make them unhappy, whereas women are more likely to explore the reasons for their depression. In other words, men tend to be more action-oriented, while women are more state-oriented. Nolen-Hoeksema suggests that this leads to a ruminative cycle in which women maintain depression by ruminating about it. Certainly, this is consistent with the 'vicious circle' cognitive theory of depression that has been advanced by Teasdale (1988) and others. When people are depressed they are more likely to think unhappy thoughts and retrieve unhappy memories. These thoughts and memories in turn make them more depressed. Another cognitive factor that may increase women's vulnerability to depression is attributional style (see chapter 11). Research suggests that women are more likely to adopt a self-blaming pattern of thinking, in which they blame failure on their own lack of ability and success on luck. This attributional style has been linked to depression (Wolfe and Russianoff 1997).

Finally, it has been suggested that the very concept of depression is gendered. Busfield (1996) argues that as disorders are known to be more common in one gender than the other, gender itself plays an increasingly important role in constructing what we assume that disorder to be. For example, a woman showing low self-esteem, withdrawal and anxiety may be readily given a diagnosis of depression, whereas a woman with gender-atypical alcohol-related problems may be ignored. The reverse may be occur for men (Ussher 1991). The possibility that gender may actually play a part in the diagnosis and construction of mental disorders challenges the principles of universalism on which psychiatric diagnosis rests. It suggests that even an apparently simple task of deciding whether someone is depressed may be bound up with cultural notions of gender, race, age and so on.

Social distribution of schizophrenia

Another example of the uneven distribution of mental illness is the relationship of schizophrenia to social class. There is no doubt that schizophrenia is found more commonly in people of lower socioeconomic status (Murphy 1983). Again, the question arises of why this should be. There are two main possibilities. The first is that the stresses of life in the lower socioeconomic groups make people more vulnerable to schizophrenia. This cannot be ruled out, but there is no direct evidence for it. The other possibility is what has been called downward drift, in which people are thought to move down socioeconomic levels as a result of the gradual development of schizophrenia. One way of testing this is to look at the social class distribution of the parents of people with schizophrenia. E. M. Goldberg and Morrison (1963) did this and found a relatively normal social class distribution in the parents. There is thus some clear evidence for downward drift, though it may not be the whole story.

Another robust finding about schizophrenia is that married people with schizophrenia are likely to be discharged from hospital sooner and to have a better outcome (see Watts 1983, pp. 300–1). Again, various explanations arise. Married people may do better because their marriages are helpful in recovering from schizophrenia. Alternatively, there may be some other factor, such as a generally good capacity for adjustment, that results in some people being more likely to both marry and to recover better from an episode of schizophrenia. There is some evidence to support this idea: using school records as an index of sociability (a measure that is free from retrospective bias), Rosen, Klein and Gittleman-Klein (1971) found that recovery from schizophrenia could be predicted just as well from childhood sociability as from current marital status.

Predisposing factors

Variables such as gender, marital status and socioeconomic status provide convenient markers that can lead to investigation of the psychosocial factors that predispose towards mental or physical illness. However, it is also possible to approach this issue more directly by investigating psychological variables, such as patterns of early experience or personality dimensions, as predisposing people to forms of ill-health. In this section we look at the evidence for childhood experiences and attributional style as predisposing factors for depression, and at 'Type A' personality characteristics as a predisposition for heart disease.

Childhood experiences and adult depression

Sigmund Freud suggested that adult depression may have its roots in early childhood experiences and, in particular, in real or imagined loss. This idea that early experiences of loss, separation or rejection may predispose the person in later life to depression, anxiety, anger or sadness forms the basis of Bowlby's attachment theory (Bowlby 1980), which was discussed in some detail in chapter 6. One way of testing these ideas empirically is to investigate whether people who lose one of their parents through death as children are vulnerable to depression as adults. On first consideration, one of the methodological attractions of investigating a variable such as parental death is that it is very clear cut: there is no measurement problem, no matter of fine judgement about whether or not it has occurred. However, as with much research on health and illness, arriving at definitive conclusions about the relationship between parental loss and depression is harder than it first appears.

There is considerable support for the idea that the rate of parental loss in childhood is higher amongst people who become depressed in adulthood than amongst non-depressed people. For example, G. W. Brown, Harris and Copeland (1977) found that 23 per cent of depressed people in a community sample had suffered the death of their mother when they were children, compared to only 6 per cent of a non-depressed sample. Among women, loss of the mother before the age of 11 appears to have the most serious impact (G. W. Brown and Harris 1978). However, it is possible that depressed and non-depressed people may differ in a variety of other ways. For example, the depressed sample might be of lower socioeconomic status. Given that there tends to be a somewhat higher parental death rate in lower socioeconomic groups, this could provide an alternative explanation of why there might be an apparent association between adult depression and death of a parent in childhood. However, in studies that have controlled for variables such as age and social status, the relationship between parental death and depression still seems to exist, although evidence is not entirely consistent (Crook and Eliot 1980). Research suggests that the death of a parent does not always increase the risk of depression, and that this link appears to depend on the quality of care provided when the parent dies (T. Harris, Brown and Bifulco 1986). Of course, poor parenting can arise in many other contexts. For example, mothers who are themselves depressed tend to provide poor parental care, rendering their children more vulnerable to depression themselves when they grow up (Goodman and Gotlib 1999). For a good review of the evidence on poor care in childhood and adult depression, see Gotlib and Hammen (1992, ch. 7). From the opposite point of view, there is evidence that some factors may reduce a person's vulnerability to depression: having a job, an intimate relationship with a partner, not being overburdened with child care, and having a strong religious belief were all identified by G. W. Brown and Harris (1978) in their community survey of working-class women as factors that reduced the likelihood of adult depression.

Dimensions of personality as predisposing factors

Personality variables have also been used to predict whether people develop health problems. For example, Beck et al. (1979) predicted that people with a negative style of thinking would be vulnerable to developing depression. One component of negative thinking is how causality for events is attributed (see chapter 11 for an explanation of attribution theory). A negative attributional style is characterized by the tendency to attribute successes to factors external to oneself (such as chance) and/or to factors that are specific to situation or to time. Conversely, a person with a negative attributional style will tend to attribute failure to factors that are internal, global and/or stable (e.g. 'I failed my exams because of lack of ability/my personality'). Despite the plausibility of the hypothesis that this style of thinking may predispose a person to depression, the evidence for this is not strong. For example, Brewin (1985) has reviewed the evidence on the relationship between depression and a negative pattern of attributions. There is no doubt that such negative attributions are a symptom of depression. They are also probably a guide to the prognosis of an episode of depression. However, there is very little evidence that they predict the onset of depression. In fact, the most compelling evidence on the role of personality variables in predicting illness relates to physical illness.

One of the most robust findings in this domain is that people's risk of having a heart attack can be predicted from their personality style. Reliable measures have been developed of what is called 'Type A' personality, characterized by extreme competitiveness, a sense of time pressure, aggressive tendencies and ambitiousness. The most reliable measures are those based on standardized interviews, in which people's behaviour can be observed and taken into account, as well as their answers to questions. One of the best prospective studies of Type A personality as a risk factor for coronary heart disease (CHD) was conducted by Rosenman and colleagues (Rosenman et al. 1975; Carmelli et al. 1991). Over 3,000 working men with no previous history of CHD were studied longitudinally. The risk of heart attacks was 2.2 times as high in Type A personality men as in others, and this was relatively independent of other physical risk factors such as weight, smoking etc. (see figure 17.1). The findings suggest that in the population at large, a predisposing factor of a psychological nature should be added to the other physical risk factors in predicting the likelihood of heart disease.

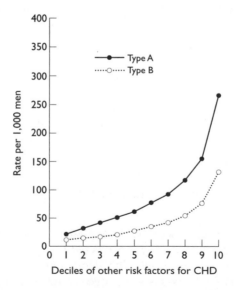

Figure 17.1 Percentages of Type A and Type B personalities aged 39–49 sustaining heart attacks, in terms of increasing levels of other risk factors

Life events

So far, we have considered the background circumstances that predispose people towards illness. In this section we will consider the role of specific events in the period immediately preceding an episode of illness. This has also been a fruitful area of research in relation to a variety of different mental and physical conditions. Life events can range from death of a spouse or being fired from one's job to more minor, but nevertheless significant, events, such as a close friend moving abroad or a child starting school. The basic assumption of this research is that life events are associated with varying levels of psychosocial stress. While there has been a large programme of research on life events over many years, gradual methodological refinements have made the findings from this research increasingly secure and specific:

1 checklists replaced by interview measures of greater reliability;
2 objective measures of illness response;
3 'threat' of event considered;
4 'independent' vs. 'non-independent' events distinguished;
5 formative vs. triggering aspects of aetiology distinguished.

Early research in this field simply used a checklist of possible life events, and asked research participants to indicate which events had occurred to them within the specified period. However, this kind of checklist method is open to reporting bias. In addition, early research used a self-report measure of the extent to which people had been ill. This too was vulnerable to reporting bias, with the result that an association between reported life events and reported illness might be explicable entirely in terms of people's tendency to report having problems in their lives. More recent research, pioneered in Britain by George Brown (see below), has used a structured interview measure (the Life Events and Difficulties Schedule). Respondents are systematically asked about what has occurred in different areas of their lives over the months preceding an episode of illness, and account is taken of the number of life events, and their significance for the individual within the context of the person's wider life. It has been shown that this kind of interview-based measure can produce highly reliable indices of life events, which can be combined with careful clinical diagnosis of the extent to which people have suffered from mental or physical illness to ensure that data is as valid as possible. Box 17.1 shows an extract from a typical life events inventory.

Depression

Pioneering work on the association between life events and depression was conducted by G. W. Brown and Harris (1978). The basic finding of this research is that people who become depressed experience considerably more life events in the months preceding depression than do comparable control subjects. Brown and Harris called these 'provoking agents', and noted that, in a sample of working-class women in London, they were often events that involved some sort of loss or threat of loss. The assessment of the

---

| **Box 17.1   Life events inventory** |

Instructions: Below is a list of events that might bring about changes in a person's life. Think about the past twelve months of your life and check off 'yes' or 'no' to show whether the event was present in your life during that time. In the blank next to each item, describe how you are coping with that particular item (e.g. relying on friends, family member(s), doctor(s), spiritual leader, medication, figured out who to blame, denial, still mourning, working through it, over it, celebrated, etc.).

		Yes	No	*How you are coping*
1	Became disabled or incapacitated			
2	Loss of sense of self			
3	Loss of personal mobility			
4	Loss of previous capacities and capabilities			
5	Sexual problems			
6	Infidelity			
7	Divorce or separation			
8	Social isolation			
9	Death of a spouse, lover or other family member			
10	Became a parent			
11	Mortgage or loan foreclosure			
12	Moved to new town			
13	Long-term illness, injury or disability			
14	Broken up with a friend due to conflict			
15	Had a law suit brought against you			

---

severity and significance of these events represents an interesting methodological challenge. Again, it is best not to depend simply on people's tendency to regard certain events as threatening. Brown and Harris trained independent observers to make reliable ratings of how severe each event was in the particular context in which it occurred. Events given the highest severity ratings were those that involved long-term losses, whether of a person, a role or an idea. This would include, for example, redundancy from a job held for many years, finding out that a close friend or family member has a life-threatening illness, or discovering a spouse's infidelity. There was a particularly high incidence of events rated as severe in the period preceding an episode of depression. Subsequent work by Brown and his colleagues has specified even more precisely the kind of loss-related or threatening life events that are likely to lead to depression. For example, life events that are related to areas of prior difficulty, and that correspond to areas of prior personal commitment, are particularly likely to lead to an episode of depression (G. W. Brown, Bifulco and Harris 1987).

Although these findings suggest that certain life events are causal in the onset of depression, it is possible to argue that the relationship between life events and depression is not what it appears. It is not always easy to tell exactly when an episode of depression begins. Might it not be that the life events that appear to occur in the period preceding depression in fact represent the early impact of the gradually developing episodes of depression? To investigate this, Brown and Harris separated life events into those which were clearly independent of a developing episode of depression, and those which might have been the result of developing depression. The fact that there was a high rate of clearly independent life events preceding depression makes it virtually certain that the events led to depression, rather than the depression accounting for the life events.

Schizophrenia

Life events also have a role in the precipitation of schizophrenia, though the nature of their impact seems to be different. G. W. Brown and Birley (1968) found that the rate of life events in the three weeks preceding an episode of schizophrenia was about three times higher than that found in a control sample. Looking further back over a three-month period, there was no evidence for an increased rate of life events. In addition, Brown and Birley found that whereas depression was preceded by a high rate of specifically threatening or unfavourable events, schizophrenia was preceded by a high rate of events of all kinds, ranging from the threatening to the trivial. Exciting or arousing events such as being promoted or winning the lottery may have a similar impact to that of negative life events in precipitating an episode of schizophrenia. However, as we will see in the section on 'Marital and family interactions', the nature of family interactions is also important in the development, onset and relapse of schizophrenia.

Despite the apparently clear-cut nature of these findings, establishing the nature of the relationship between life events and the onset of illness is harder than first appears. It is questionable in the Brown and Birley (1968) study whether life events always preceded the development of schizophrenia: some of the patients included in the study had shown milder symptoms of schizophrenia in the weeks preceding the beginning of a more florid schizophrenic episode, and the majority of patients in the study had established illnesses and were experiencing a relapse rather than a first episode of schizophrenia. A review of five more recent studies of life events and schizophrenia (Bebbington and Kuipers 1988) suggests that, although there is some evidence that life events independent of the illness may precede an episode of schizophrenia, results are clouded by methodological problems associated with the long-term nature of schizophrenia and the difficulty of defining 'onset' of the illness. It is also worth bearing in mind that a considerable body of research evidence suggests a genetic component in vulnerability to schizophrenia (Gottesman 1991). Studies of adopted children that attempt to separate out genetic inheritance from the family environment (e.g. Tienari 1991) provide the most robust evidence that genetic inheritance makes a contribution to a person's vulnerability to schizophrenia. It seems that the impact of life events is different in depression and in schizophrenia: life events may have a formative role in relation to depression and a triggering role in relation to schizophrenia.

Social support

So far, we have considered factors that can contribute to mental or physical illness. Social factors can also help to protect people from illness. The best example of this is social support. The basic finding is that when people have a good level of social support they are less likely to develop either physical or mental illness. However, this finding warrants closer examination. There are different kinds of social support, and they have different effects on the likelihood of illness.

First, there is an important distinction to be made between social integration (i.e. the extent to which people have a good range and frequency of social contacts) and social support of a more intimate and subjective kind (see S. Cohen and Wills 1985). The most commonly used index of this latter kind of support is having someone in whom you can confide. Second, there are two main hypotheses about how social support affects the risk of illness. One, the direct effect hypothesis, suggests that lack of social support has an across-the-board relationship with illness, increasing the risk of it regardless of other factors such as how stressful life may be. This could occur because belonging to a large or supportive social network provides a set of socially rewarding roles, enhances self-esteem, or, in some cases, may encourage people to have a more healthy lifestyle. The other hypothesis proposes a stress-buffering role for social support. Social support may show its impact in helping to protect or buffer people against the adverse effects of stressful life events. One implication of this is that there will not be a particularly close relationship between social support and illness amongst those who are not experiencing stressful life events. It is those who experience both stressful events and a lack of social support who will be vulnerable to illness.

The research literature provides support for both these hypotheses, although it depends which kind of social support is being considered. Social integration tends to show a direct relationship with health, that is, one that is independent of whether or not people are coping with stressful life events. For example, using a measure of the number and frequency of social contacts, Williams, Wase and Donald (1981) found a direct relationship between social integration and general mental health that was not dependent on whether people had experienced stressful life events. On the other hand, more subjective and intimate kinds of support, such as having a confidant, seem to be particularly important in stress buffering. Strong evidence for this comes from G. W. Brown and Harris's (1978) study of women in south London. They found that, among those who had both experience of stressful life events and no confidante, 41 per cent were depressed. In contrast, with just one of these, but not both, the rate of depression was 10 per cent or less. More recently, Sherbourne, Hayes and Wells (1995) have found that people who are isolated and lack social support or intimacy are more likely to suffer from depression when under stress, and to remain depressed for longer, than those who have supportive relationships with a spouse or friends.

Evidence for the stress-buffering effects of social support can also be found in relation to other health problems. For example, following a traumatic event, people with inadequate social support are particularly vulnerable to developing post-traumatic stress disorder (PTSD) (S. Perry et al. 1992). Perceived lack of social support at the time of a trauma has also been shown to predict the severity of post-traumatic stress up to six years after the trauma, regardless of initial symptom levels (Dalgleish et al. 1996). Nuckolls, Cassel and Kaplan (1972) looked at the frequency of physical complications in childbirth. While childbirth complications may both produce and be produced by stress, the researchers' findings suggest support for the latter relationship. Among those who had experienced major life change, and had no social support, the frequency of complications was 91 per cent. In contrast, rate of complications in women who had just one of these, or neither, was 49 per cent or less (see table 17.1).

Recent research in the area of psycho-neuro-immunology sheds new light on how social support may have a stress-buffering impact upon an individual's health status via its effect on the immune system. Psycho-neuro-immunology is the study of how psychological processes affect the immune system via neurophysiological pathways. There is a growing body of evidence to suggest that stress can lead to illness via its effect on natural killer cells in the blood that protect against viruses. Esterling, Kiecolt-Glaser and Glaser (1996) investigated people who experienced chronic stress associated with caring for a relative with Alzheimer's disease. They found that levels of natural killer cells were higher among those carers who had good emotional and tangible social support networks than among carers with less social support. These findings highlight the bio-psycho-social nature of health and illness issues, and add to our understanding of the specific processes through which social interactive experiences may impact positively or negatively on the individual.

However, the relationship between social support and illness is complex. As is often the case when looking at health and illness in their social context, an empirical relationship is explicable in a variety of ways. Determining the exact causal relationship is much more difficult than establishing the association in the first place. In many cases, declining physical or mental health may result in reduced social integration and support. Thus, levels of social integration may sometimes be the consequence rather than the cause of poor health. For example, the association of premature retirement with increased mortality is probably explicable almost entirely in terms of existing illnesses which lead to the retirement, rather than in terms of the reduced social integration that accompanies retirement. Another possibility is that people who are socially isolated may not be good at looking after their health and may be more reluctant than others to make appropriate use of medical services when they need it.

A further complication is that what seems to be important is not levels of social support *per se*, but the perceived adequacy of this support. For example, in a large-scale community study in Australia, Henderson et al. (1980) found a much stronger negative

Table 17.1 Percentages of mothers with childbirth complications as a result of recent life changes and social support (%)

Life change	High support	Low support
High	33	91
Low	39	49

Source: Nuckolls, Cassel and Kaplan (1972)

association between perceived adequacy of social relationships and neurotic symptoms, on the one hand, than between the availability of attachment and social integration and neurotic symptoms, on the other. While there is likely to be a relationship between the perceived adequacy and the actual availability of social support, these findings suggest that different people probably have different needs for support. Personality characteristics may contribute to an individual's coping ability, and these may also influence the person's likelihood of finding social support. However, this is difficult to test empirically, as personality factors may also influence a person's judgement and reporting of his or her social support and health status. An area of research on social support and health in which more conclusive findings have been produced is the study of the differing needs and experiences of women and men. A study by Bolton and Oatley (1987) on the role of social support in enabling men to cope with unemployment suggests that for men, social integration may be a more important protective factor than intimate support. Busfield (1996) suggests that, compared to men, women's typically closer relationships and more supportive roles with family members and close friends may make them more vulnerable to depression when members of their close network face adversities.

Finally, it is also clear that social support is not simply 'provided': it arises out of an interaction process. People elicit or rebuff social support by the way they behave. If depressed people receive inadequate social support, it may be at least partly because their ability to obtain appropriate support is inadequate or has reduced since becoming depressed, rather than because this support is not potentially available in their social environment (see Parry 1988). Social relationships are an important contributing factor in the onset of depression, and depression in turn can have a negative impact on both new and established social relationships (Teichman and Teichman 1990). The next section explores the role of these interactive processes in health and illness in more detail.

Marital and family interactions

Depression

Although social support is generally beneficial in its effects, family interactions are not necessarily supportive. There is a growing body of evidence that depression is intimately intertwined with problematic forms of marital interaction. (For a good review, see Gotlib and Hammen 1992, ch. 7.) The effects go both ways: the state of a marriage can affect depression, and depression in turn can affect the quality of a marriage:

Evidence that marriage affects depression:
1   Marital problems often precede onset of depression.
2   Marital problems and hostility increase the risk of relapse after treatment for depression.
3   Marital treatment can be effective in treating depression.

Evidence that depression affects marital interaction:
1 Marriages of depressed people have a negative style of communication.
2 A depressed partner is often regarded as a 'burden' and leads to low marital satisfaction.
3 Where one partner is depressed, the other is at risk of depression too.

Several strands of evidence support this conclusion. First, among those who are experiencing marital problems, there is a very high rate of depression. Rush, Shaw and Khatami (1980) found that, among couples with marital problems, at least 30 per cent had a partner who was clinically depressed. It is also clear that marital problems are an important predictor of relapse amongst those who receive treatment for depression (Hooley and Teasdale 1989). In addition, marital disputes are one of the most frequent life events that precede the onset of depression (Weissman and Paykel 1974).

These studies support the view that marital problems lead to depression and prolong it. However, there is equally strong evidence that depression leads to disturbances in marital interaction and communication. Given the pervasive impact of depression, it is not surprising that marital interaction should be disturbed while one partner is depressed. However, the available research suggests that depression may also have a more long-term effect on marital relationships. Bothwell and Weissman (1977) looked at marital interactions after recovery from depression, and found that the marriages of depressed women remained disturbed, even after they had recovered from depression. It is also noteworthy that, though many other aspects of their lives improved with recovery from depression, marital adjustment was the one area that did not show such improvement. People who are vulnerable to depression do not appear to have problems in all social relationships. It is probably close relationships, and long-term relationships with a sexual partner in particular, that are likely to be disturbed.

In exploring exactly what goes wrong, direct observation of marital interaction is a more accurate and objective measure than relying on people's report of their social interaction. A number of studies using this methodology have been carried out (for a review see Gotlib and Macabe 1990). These studies show that depressive marital interaction is characterized by less positive communications, smiling and positive facial expressions, and more negative communications, conflict and tension than interactions in which neither partner is depressed. Given this negative pattern of communication, it is perhaps not surprising that close interaction with a depressed person takes its toll on the partners. The spouses of depressed patients often report finding their partner a 'burden', and frequently regret having married. Coyne et al. (1987) found that 40 per cent of people whose spouses were depressed were sufficiently depressed themselves to justify referral to psychotherapy. There are two factors that may contribute to this. One concerns spouse selection; the other concerns the direct impact of a depressed person on a partner.

There is growing evidence (Hammen 1991) that the spouses of depressed people themselves have higher than normal levels of psychological problems that do not simply represent the impact of depression on the spouse. For example, Hammen and others have examined family histories and found that the spouses of depressed patients often come from families where there is a history of family discord and psychological problems. One way of investigating the second hypothesis, that being in a relationship with a depressed person has a direct impact on the partner, is to examine people who have not chosen to live together, but who simply find themselves brought together by circumstance. Hokanson and colleagues have conducted a series of studies on college room-mates (e.g. Hokanson et al. 1989). Sharing with a college room-mate who had transient depression was found to have no great impact. However, sharing living space with a college student who was consistently depressed resulted in a progressive increase in depression levels in the room-mates as well. Over time, the nature of the relationship was also affected by the depressed student becoming increasingly dependent upon the room-mate, and the room-mate became increasingly managerial. Not surprisingly, room-mates reported decreasing enjoyment of contact with their depressed colleagues, and increasing aggressive feelings towards them.

Depressed people may thus be the cause of problems to those around them; but they can also suffer from the impact of their relationships. There is evidence too that depressed patients suffer from adverse attitudes and behaviour in partners and family members. Certain families show higher than average levels of expressed emotion, a term used to describe the emotional flavour of typical interactions within families. The level of expressed emotion is measured by combining ratings of three factors: critical comments made by family members about the person and their illness; hostility, defined as negative emotions, or statements of resentment, disapproval, dislike or rejection; and overinvolvement, consisting of overconcern, overprotectiveness and excessive anxiety. Using what is now a standard and reliable methodology, Vaughn and Leff (1976) interviewed the families of hospitalized depressed patients in order to assess levels of expressed emotion, particularly of a hostile and critical kind, shown towards the depressed family member. Patients who were discharged to families with high levels of such expressed emotion were more likely to relapse during the following nine months than those from families with low expressed emotion. Levels of expressed emotion in family interactions have also been found to be related to relapse in schizophrenia.

Schizophrenia

People with schizophrenia are also vulnerable to unhelpful patterns of emotion in their families. Indeed, research on expressed emotion began with schizophrenia (G. W. Brown, Birley and Wing 1972). A carefully standardized interview was conducted with the families to which schizophrenic patients were to be returned. Patients whose families showed most expressed emotion in these interviews were significantly more likely to relapse and to need to return to hospital in the following nine months than those whose family members showed low levels of expressed emotion. These findings were replicated by Vaughn and Leff (1976), and have been followed by a series of studies producing essentially the same findings in a range of different countries, including Britain, the USA, India, Italy, Poland and Australia. For an overview of this research, see Leff and Vaughn (1985) or Kavanagh (1992).

Expressed emotion has also been found to interact with other factors. There appear to be two ways in which people with schizophrenia can survive relatively high levels of familial expressed emotion without showing relapse. The first is to have relatively little face-to-face contact with their family members. Vaughn and Leff (1976) found that when the amount of face-to-face contact averaged less than five hours a day, expressed emotion was less likely to produce relapse. The other factor is long-term medication. This study also found that expressed emotion in families was less damaging to patients who were taking neuroleptic medication. When the person with a schizophrenia diagnosis did not take medication following discharge from hospital, and had high levels of contact with her or his family, the risk of relapse for those in families with high expressed emotion was found to be 92 per cent. With low face-to-face contact and long-term medication, the relapse rate fell to 15 per cent (see figure 17.2). However, MacMillan et al. (1986) did not find evidence that medication reduces the likelihood of relapse for patients in families where expressed emotion is high.

Although research suggests that expressed emotion in families is a good predictor of outcome for people with schizophrenia, understanding why this might be the case is less straightforward. The effects of a person with mental health problems returning to the family environment may well disrupt family life and in turn make relapse more likely (Woo, Goldstein and Nuechterlein 1997). It is also possible that the high levels of expressed emotion observed in a research interview may be a marker of family pathology or of some other factor related to relapse (Kuipers and Bebbington 1988). Little research has been done on exactly what goes wrong in families with high expressed emotion, but family intervention programmes designed to lower expressed emotion have produced results suggesting that this can have a positive effect on prognosis. One of the largest studies of these interventions (Hogarty et al. 1991) randomly assigned hospitalized patients with a schizophrenia diagnosis and high levels of expressed emotion in the families to which they were returning to one of four groups: a control group receiving only medication and regular outpatient care, a group receiving weekly social skills training, a group in which patients and family members received weekly education about schizophrenia and interpersonal strategies, and a group that received both of the later two treatments. At both twelve-month and two-year follow-up points, the control group showed the highest rates of relapse and the combined treatment group the lowest. Education about schizophrenia and interpersonal strategies only marginally outperformed social skills training, although assessments of expressed emotion at follow-up suggested that reductions in relapse rate were found in families where expressed emotion

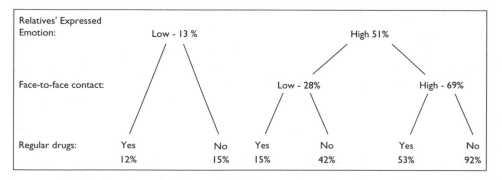

Figure 17.2 Percentages of schizophrenic patients showing relapse within nine months (Vaughn and Leff 1976)

had reduced. Overall, it is clear that a bio-psycho-social model recognizing the combined impact of genetic inheritance, life events and family interactions factors may be the most powerful in understanding the onset and course of schizophrenia.

Social integration and public attitudes

In this section and the one that follows we broaden our perspective to consider how the experience of illness is also determined by the beliefs, attitudes and social practices that surround forms of ill-health. As social practices and policies relating to mental ill-health have undergone such a radical shake-up in recent years, we will continue to focus our attention on these forms of illness. The study of public attitudes towards forms of mental distress has consistently shown that the general public regards mental illness and the mentally ill with fear, suspicion and distrust (for reviews of this work, see Bhugra 1989 or Miles 1987). For example, a British study using vignette descriptions of people with mental health problems found that lay people rated themselves increasingly less willing to engage in social activities with the person as the level of close interpersonal interaction involved increased (P. Hall et al. 1993). This effect was particularly strong when the person was described as having symptoms of paranoid schizophrenia. Across a range of studies conducted in several countries, public attitudes are generally negative and reflect rejection of and discrimination against the mentally ill. This negativity far exceeds the generally negative attitudes that Western societies hold towards illness in general. In a rational, individualistic society in which the mind is held to be the core of the person, it seems that there is something particularly fearful and threatening about the possibility of 'insanity'. Miles (1987) suggests that the mentally ill are commonly assumed by the lay public to be easily recognizable, potentially dangerous and very unpredictable.

The significance of these negative and rejecting public attitudes towards mental illness has risen substantially with the introduction of 'community care' policies. Since the early 1980s, the numbers of inpatient psychiatric beds has fallen consistently in Britain. This trend is mirrored across Europe and North America (Ramon 1996). For all but the most acute episodes of mental distress, hospital-based care has been replaced with outpatient treatments provided in smaller, non-residential mental health centres located within the community. Treatment programmes, provided by an increasing range of medical and non-medical practitioners, have developed a widening remit to include not only intra-psychic problems, but issues of daily living and social welfare.

As social integration has become a new ideal for mental health care, the horrors of institutionalization (Goffman 1961) have been replaced with new challenges. People with mental health problems have not only the difficulties associated directly with their illness to cope with, but the continued public prejudice and stigma associated with mental illness and the mentally ill. This can impact on all areas of life including work, housing, and new and existing relationships. A study of seventy-six long-term mental health service users living in the community found that although they reported being moderately happy with life, 61 per cent of the sample thought the public were unsympathetic to their problems, and 67 per cent thought members of the public were afraid of the mentally ill (Rose 1996). On a more positive note, Philo (1996), reviewing a series of public attitude studies in Britain, suggests that in some domains – particularly public views on employment of people with mental health problems – attitudes appear to have become more sympathetic since the early 1980s.

In recent years, social psychologists have also paid increasing attention to the role of the media in constructing public beliefs and attitudes. Not only is there a proliferation of media output of all forms, but many people, particularly children and young people, have little direct experience of mental illness, and may be disproportionately influenced by media output. The Glasgow University Media Group (Philo 1996) analysed a sample of one month of television news and fiction items with a mental health theme, and found that more than 50 per cent of items portrayed mental illness using themes associated with violence and harm to others. A similar study by Rose (1998) analysed British television news and drama programmes, and found that although the mentally ill were represented in a variety of ways, the most dominant themes were of danger, unpredictability and violence, whereas themes associated with success or coping were rare.

Lay notions of illness

In this section, we continue to focus on research on public perceptions. However, we turn our attention here to social psychological research on health and illness that adopts a more social constructionist perspective than the research presented so far. Within a social constructionist framework, 'health' and 'illness' are more than simply behavioural reactions to biomedical factors, or the attitudes of isolated individuals to their own or others' health status. Health and illness can also be understood as social constructs that are shaped and perpetuated by the collective practices and belief systems of the society, culture and historical period within which they emerge and are lived out. Moving away from a fixed biomedical conception of health, social psychologists working within this framework draw on other social sciences that chart the historical rise of the biomedical model (Foucault 1967; 1973), cross-cultural variations (Helman 1990), and the role of politics and ideology in shaping our health practices (Zola 1972). They study, for example, the collective practices and public discourses associated with certain health problems, such as institutionalization of the mentally ill and the recent shift towards community-based care (Morant 1998; Prior 1993). Another area that has become the subject of much research is how lay people make sense of health and illness (R. Brody 1987; Calnan 1987; Herzlich 1973; Joffe 1996; Radley 1994; Stainton-Rogers 1991).

One of the most fruitful theoretical frameworks for this form of research on health and illness is the theory of social representations. As we learned in chapter 14, social representations are common-sense theories or branches of knowledge about aspects of the social world (Moscovici 1984). Box 17.2 gives details of Jodelet's research on social representations of madness.

Also working within a social representations framework, Joffe (1996) used interviews with gay men in Britain and South Africa, and analysis of AIDS awareness campaigns in the media, to investigate the social representations of HIV/AIDS that circulated in the homosexual communities in these two countries. She argues that the representations she found reflect a collective defensive response of communities that were threatened and blamed by society for the rise of AIDS. Thus, each group accounts for the origins of AIDS in ways that exonerate the gay community and locate the causes of AIDS

Box 17.2   Denise Jodelet and social representations of madness

As we learned in chapter 14, social representations are common-sense theories or branches of knowledge about aspects of the social world. They exist both in individual cognitions and in the fabric of society, and are lived out in conversations, in the media and in social practices. Social representations serve the important function of helping individuals, social groups and societies to make sense of concepts and ideas (such as illness, science or gender) that are important in their social world.

Jodelet aimed to explore how madness is socially represented through a detailed study of a small family colony in rural France, where local inhabitants have acted as foster parents for some 1,000 psychiatric patients for over 100 years. The study was designed to investigate what happens when a community is faced with the challenge of integrating people with mental health problems into its midst, and is thus of relevance to many of the issues raised by recent 'community care' policies in Britain and elsewhere. Using a combination of participant observation, depth interviews with foster parents and hospital personnel, archival analysis of the history of the family colony, and surveys of the family homes where patients lodged, Jodelet was able to build up a picture of a community where massive but implicit exclusion of the mentally ill took place.

Although it appeared on the surface that the lodgers were well integrated into the daily life of the community, participant observation uncovered a range of taken-for-granted practices that served to control and marginalize the mentally ill. For example, foster parents meticulously separated their own and their lodgers' crockery and clothing for washing; they often built separate extensions to their properties to house the patients; and there were powerful taboos against sexual or romantic relationships with patients. In addition, Jodelet found evidence amongst foster parents of a complex typology of practical knowledge about madness and its causes and treatment. This body of lay knowledge made few references to modern psychiatric notions, and had more in common with the medieval theory of humours. Thus, by paying attention to the minutiae of social and symbolic life, it is possible to find traces of archaic pre-medical belief systems in lay understandings of mental illness. Jodelet suggests that the routine practices of this community betray a belief in, and fear that, madness might be contagious and communicated through bodily fluids.

---

elsewhere. For example, British gay men attributed the origins of AIDS to perverse sexual practices involving monkeys in Africa, whilst South African gay men attributed HIV/AIDS to an FBI plot to exterminate an undesirable black population. Joffe argues that these social representations of the origins of HIV/AIDS reflect both the moral condemnation of homosexuality in 'straight society', and an unconscious need to defend the ego against spoiled identity.

Recent research has also investigated how lay people conceptualize and understand states of physical health and ill-health more generally. Despite the fact that modern Western societies are dominated by biomedical knowledge, research on popular conceptualizations of health and illness detects complex belief systems which include pre-medical understandings. For example, among French people Herzlich (1973) found social representations in which health was conceptualized as an internal resource that was eroded by the demands of the outside modern world. Illness, on the other hand, was seen as originating outside the individual, and was associated with the demands of urban living. Other researchers have found a range of conceptualizations of health and illness (Brody 1987; Calnan 1987). Popular notions of health include health as an internal resource, the absence of illness, a capacity to do things, or a state that is determined by emotional and psychological well-being. Illness is conceptualized variously as an unpleasant experience that undermines personhood, the disruption of social roles and activities, enforced stillness, or the degenerating effects of maturation. In Western societies, where a belief in individual agency and responsibility prevails, there may also be an implicit suggestion in lay notions of illness that individuals who become ill are somehow at fault or responsible for their illness. The strength of these assumptions varies with the type of illness. For example, individual responsibility is imputed less for infectious diseases than it is for problems of a psychological nature (Radley 1994).

Overall, research on lay notions of health and illness highlights how communities construct understandings of health problems that are grounded within culturally specific belief systems about the world and about humanity. Lay models of illness often incorporate historical knowledge systems, are emotionally charged, and may relate to a community's need to protect or defend its own identity.

Conclusions

It will be clear from the above reviews that the social psychology of health and illness is a vast topic within which researchers have made diverse contributions from a range of different theoretical perspectives. We end this chapter by drawing together some of these threads.

The finding that forms of ill-health are unevenly distributed across the population and between cultures alerts us to the fact that social factors must play some role in the aetiology or manifestation of health problems. However, as is often the case, even an apparently robust empirical finding, such as the fact that women are typically twice as likely to suffer from depression as men, has many possible explanations. One of the key tasks for researchers is to design studies and develop theories that allow us to tease out and collect data on the various factors that might contribute to such a finding. This work allows us gradually to refine our understanding of the numerous factors involved in health and illness. For example, we now have models of depression that take account of both past and present psychosocial factors. Past psychosocial experiences, such as patterns of early upbringing, that occur long before an illness develops may leave people vulnerable to particular mental or physical health problems, or may be predictive of how well individuals fare once they become ill. Some of these vulnerability factors may be detectable as pre-morbid personality patterns (e.g. Type A personality or a negative attributional style). However, others may be less visible (e.g. childhood loss). A particular early experience may be a sleeper until an episode of illness at a later date.

We have also reviewed research that indicates that stressful or threatening events and social experiences often precede the onset of illness and may act as triggers to forms of ill-health. In addition, concurrent and ongoing social circumstances can impact on the development and course of health problems. For example, we have reviewed evidence to suggest that living with family members who display high levels of expressed emotion can be detrimental to those suffering from schizophrenia and depression. On the other hand, close and supportive social networks and relationships often act as a protective factor. In all of the above areas, what seems to be important is the subjective perceptions of the individual in judging, for example, his or her social networks to be psychologically supportive or a particular life event as stressful.

Social factors also contribute to experiences of ill-health in shaping how the sufferer is viewed by other people. Research shows that public attitudes towards mental ill-health and the mentally ill remain generally negative and rejecting, and that the media continues to perpetuate images of the mentally ill as dangerous and violent. These lay notions of mental ill-health sit uneasily with the policy of providing community-based mental health care and encouraging the social integration of people with mental health problems. This form of social psychological research reminds us that in order to develop a rounded understanding of phenomena associated with health and illness, we must consider both the psychosocial circumstances and experiences of the individual, and the value systems and social practices of the society and culture to which she or he belongs.

RECOMMENDED READING

Busfield, J. (1996) *Men, Women and Madness: Understanding Gender and Mental Disorder*. Basingstoke: Macmillan.
The first reading explores the gendered construction of mental disorder and reviews biological, psychological, feminist and social accounts of why people become mentally ill.

Cochrane, R. (1983) *The Social Creation of Mental Illness*. London: Longman.
This gives a careful analysis of what we know about the social distribution of mental illness.

Gotlib, I. H. and Hammen, C. L. (1992) *Psychological Aspects of Depression: Toward a Cognitive-Interpersonal Integration*. Chichester: John Wiley.
This provides an excellent review of psychological research on depression (especially chapters 6–7 for social aspects).

Marková, I. and Farr, R. (eds) (1995) *Representations of Health, Illness and Handicap*. Chur: Harwood Academic.
This reading contains a series of studies on social representations of AIDS, learning disabilities, mental illness and diabetes. It includes work on the media, professionals and lay people.

Murphy, E. (1991) *After the Asylum*. London: Faber.
This is a lively treatment of the currently much-debated topic of caring for the mentally ill in the community.

Stroebe, W. and Stroebe, M. (1995) *Social Psychology and Health*. Buckingham: Open University Press.
The final reading focuses on the health behaviour of individuals. Chapters 6 and 7 review the relationship between stress and health.

18

Social Psychology and Policy

- Introduction
- Objectives: what are we trying to achieve?
- Understanding social processes: the example of social capital
- Making judgements: if not rational, then what?
- The problem of individual differences in ability
- Conclusions
- Recommended reading

Introduction

This chapter is about the contributions that social psychology can make to mainstream policy-making. A brief examination of the strengths of psychology relative to those of economics or political science points to the form of contribution that the psychology can make. Four specific areas are then examined:

- *The objectives of policy*: what difference does it make if we set 'subjective well-being' – happiness – as a goal instead of economic well-being?
- *Social processes*: what insights does social psychology give us into the processes that underlie social problems?
- *How people think*: what are the implications for policy-making?
- *Individual differences in ability*: what are the problems and implications for policy-making?

When we think about what politicians and other policy-makers do, we do not tend to think of social psychology. Politics is the stuff that political scientists study. Maybe economics also comes to mind – after all, 'it's the economy, stupid!' as President Clinton's successful campaign of the early 1990s reminded us – but not psychology.

Having read this book this far, it should be clear to you that social psychology makes – or has the potential to make – contributions to many different specific areas of policy. Examples include: health psychology (chapter 17); the psychology of work (chapter 16); selection and assessment (see below); and race relations (chapter 15). We might think of such areas as applied social psychology. These contributions are important. But does psychology also have a role to play in the broader sweep of politics and policy?

Much politics, and policy, *is* about political and economic matters. There are clashes of interests between groups, such as between the haves and have-nots, between employers and employees, and sometimes between nations and ethnic groups. There are also technical issues of economic management and institutional design. Yet when it comes down to it, most policy is about trying to alter human behaviour. We want people to be more productive, to use their cars less, to commit less crime, to achieve their best at school, to be less prejudiced, to lead healthy lives, to provide better services and so on. This suggests that good policy-making must be based, at least in part, on a sound understanding of human thought and behaviour – a detailed model of the person and the way we interact with one another.

This detailed model of the person is clearly lacking in a world-view based only on economics and political science. A caricature of a seminar in economics goes along these lines: 'We have produced a great theory. It goes like this . . . our assumptions are that the individuals have equal abilities, have complete knowledge and act rationally.' Of course, these assumptions and the model of the person on which the theory is based are completely implausible – and often by the speaker's own admission. The question then is: would more psychologically realistic analyses lead to better models – and better policy in general? This is the main question that this chapter will address.

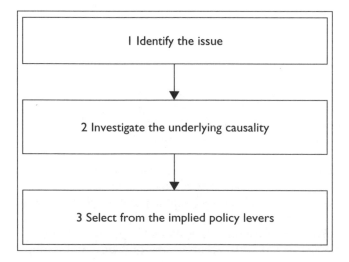

Figure 18.1 Evidence-based policy making: three basic steps

On the positive side, one can argue that there is a quiet revolution occurring inside the policy-making machines of many governments across the world. It is called evidence-based policy-making, and it is creating new opportunities for academics and specialists, including social psychologists, to make contributions to policy. The idea is simple: policy should be based on detailed empirical evidence both on what causes each particular problem and on what works in terms of reducing it (see figure 18.1). The idea has taken particularly strong root in the United Kingdom and in the USA and follows in the footsteps of the 'third way' – a political theory intended to move beyond the relatively rigid ideological prescriptions of left and right (Halpern 1998; Giddens 1998).

There are three broad areas in which social psychology can make contributions to general policy-making. First – and perhaps most importantly – social psychology can help us reflect on what the purpose, or objective, of policy should be. Should policy-making be about making people happy? Second, social psychology can give us insights into the complex causal processes that underlie most social problems. For example, is there a social psychological component to how disadvantage is transmitted across generations? Third, social psychology can help us understand the constraints within which our policy problems arise and which our solutions will have to respect. For example, this includes the ways people think and how people differ from one another.

Objectives: what are we trying to achieve?

Policy-makers must – or should – have some idea of what they are trying to do. We could list a few objectives off the top of our heads: economic growth, lower unemployment, lower inflation and so on. In this list, economic objectives – making us all richer – are likely to loom large.

As a psychologist, you might ask yourself what you think it is policy-makers should try to maximize. Is it gross domestic product (GDP) per capita? Probably not. As a psychologist you might suggest something like psychological well-being, or perhaps just 'happiness'. After all, if money does not make us happy, then why should we be directing our policy at simply making more of it?

This question brings us to the most fundamental way in which social psychology can contribute to policy – by making us think about what is the point of it all. This does not have to be a vague philosophical question. We can ask: what does actually make us happy?

Let us start with the most obvious question: does money make us happy? Well, the answer seems to be that being richer does make us a little happier, but not much (Argyle 1987; Diener et al. 1993). For example, the USA today is much richer than the USA of the 1950s. But the survey data indicates that people do not seem to be much happier (D. G. Myers 1990, p. 381). Another way of looking at it is to compare how happy the rich and poor are. Within countries, the rich are a little happier, but not much (Inglehart 1990). It would seem that, as we get richer, the main thing that happens is that our expectancies increase in line with our new-found wealth. This is known as the relative deprivation effect. It is not how much you have got in an absolute sense that matters, rather it is how much you have got relative to what you used to have and relative to other people. Hence, if you ask people what they consider to be essentials in life, rather than luxuries, they give you a list of all the things they are used to having, be it a washing machine, video, hot water, playstation, or whatever. Similarly, classic studies of work satisfaction showed that people in organizations with rapid promotions were no more satisfied, and often less satisfied, than those in organizations that promoted people slowly (Merton and Kitt 1950). It seems that a corporate culture of rapid promotion raises aspirations faster than it can deliver achievements (Wheeler, Koestren and Driver 1982).

One piece of counterevidence to the relative deprivation hypothesis is that, generally speaking, people living in wealthier nations tend to report being happier (Figure 18.2). These large national differences do not appear to be the result of linguistics. If you compare people living in the same nation but who speak different languages (e.g. in Switzerland), it is the nation they live in rather than the language they speak that determines their satisfaction with life (Inglehart 1990). None the less, this finding does not conclusively demonstrate that it is the nation's wealth that is important. For example, one possibility is that it is the nation's level of 'social capital' that leads to both the economic growth and the happiness (see below). Nations characterized by positive and trusting relationships are likely to have stronger economic growth and happier citizens.

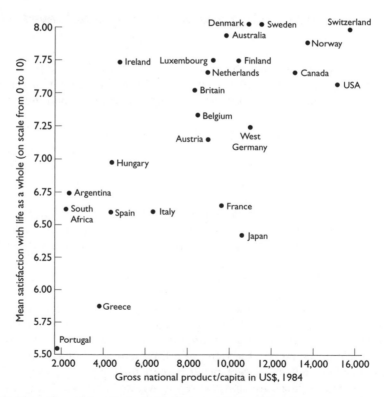

Figure 18.2 Mean life satisfaction by level of economic development

How could economic growth not bring happiness? To economists, it may be a worrying paradox that economic growth could occur but people end up with less happiness or utility. Economic transactions should only happen if both parties feel that they have benefited from them. Unfortunately, developments can occur in an economy – such as the introduction a new piece of machinery – that lead to more efficient yet less satisfying practices for those engaged in them (Scitovsky 1992). For example, it might be that traditional craftsmen greatly enjoy their work and would not trade it in for a better paid but less satisfying job in a factory making the same type of product. But if someone else opens up and staffs such a factory, the craftsmen may be put out of work just the same. Economic growth will have occurred, but the craftmen certainly would not be any happier. The new process may also have side effects, such as pollution, more traffic or worse working conditions, that inadvertently reduce the quality of other people's lives.

So if money does not necessarily bring happiness – or at least not much – then what does? Studies at the individual level show that the best predictors of happiness lie in the quality of our personal relationships. A classic study of 2,000 Americans found that the best predictors of overall life satisfaction were, in descending order, levels of satisfaction with: family life, marriage, financial situation, housing, job, friendship, health and leisure activities (A. Campbell, Converse and Rogers 1976). Interestingly, when these same researchers asked people what they *thought* would be most important, financial situation came at the top of the list, followed by leisure activities, job and housing. So there is an interesting paradox that we might file under the heading 'people don't know themselves as well as they think' (see Nisbett and Wilson 1977). People think that money and material well-being are most important in determining their well-being, yet the evidence shows that it is their satisfaction with personal relationships that counts most.

Of course, what is most important to one person may not be most important to another (see the section below on individual differences). For some people, job satisfaction is the best predictor of their overall satisfaction, while for others it is their family life. Similarly, people living in different countries differ in how satisfied they are with different aspects of their lives. For example, people in Britain seem more satisfied with their jobs than do Americans (Argyle 1987). This latter finding may relate to the fact that, on average, people in Britain work fewer hours than in the USA.

It is likely that what really matters to people's happiness changes according to conditions. The psychologist Abraham Maslow tried to capture this phenomenon by postulating that people have a hierarchy of needs (Maslow 1954). This hierarchy works up through a series of basic needs, such as hunger, affection, security and self-esteem. People prioritize the most basic needs, and only when these are fulfilled do they move on to concentrating on the next in the hierarchy. Hence if you are starving and thirsty, this is what matters to you most. But once you have eaten and drunk your fill, then you start concerning yourself with matters such as having a warm and safe place to live. And when this condition is fulfilled, your focus shifts onto the quality of your relationships, whether people like you or not, and so on.

Maslow argued that once people had satisfied their basic needs, their attention shifted to what he called meta-needs, such as justice, goodness, beauty, order and unity. He argued that unlike the basic needs, meta-needs were not arranged hierarchically and could be substituted one for another. None the less, he believed that once people's basic needs were fulfilled, if they were unable to go on to fulfil their meta-needs, pathology would result. Hence he argued that however wealthy and secure a nation became, if it did not fulfil people's meta-needs, they would feel unhappy, alienated, apathetic and cynical.

Maslow's work has been tested in the more recent research of Ronald Inglehart (Inglehart 1990). Inglehart conducted surveys across the world asking people to rate what is most important to them from a list of alternative items such as:

1 maintain order in the nation;
2 give people more say in the decisions of government;
3 fight rising prices;
4 protect freedom of speech.

If a person rated items (1) and (3) as the most important – items that relate to more basic needs – then Inglehart classed them as materialists. If a person rated items (2) and (4) as most important – items that relate to meta-needs – then he classed them as postmateri- alists. Ingelhart found a remarkable pattern of results. Younger generations, and people brought up in conditions of relative affluence, were far more postmaterialist than older generations and people brought up in conditions of poverty. The results broadly supported Maslow's theory, except that what seemed to matter most were the condi- tions you were brought up in, not your present circumstances, which is a striking illustration of the relevance of developmental issues for social psychology.

The results appear to have huge political and social implications. They indicate that one of the reasons why the economic growth rate of advanced industrialized nations tends to slow down is that young people brought up in conditions of affluence have different priorities to those of their parents brought up in poorer times. Sure enough, Inglehart has shown that the higher the proportion of postmaterialists in a given country and time, the slower the future economic growth. Instead of prioritizing basic needs such as getting a good job and earning a living, the new generation prioritizes meta-needs just as Maslow would have predicted.

Inglehart's work has been criticized, not least because of his use of a forced choice method (Halpern 1995). Other data shows that postmaterialist generations are not really any less materialistic, since they still want to be well paid and have lots of material goods (Halpern 1995; Rahn and Transue 1998). The difference is that people now want to have their cake and eat it – they want to be ever better paid, but now they also want an ever more liberal society and more responsive government. None the less, Inglehart's work is very important in that it has shown that values, and the psychological processes that underpin them, may be of critical importance to the functioning of the economy and society.

Most fundamentally, this line of work is building the foundations for policy based explicitly on quality of life considerations rather than the objectives of conventional economics. It forces policy-makers to think much harder about what it is that we should be trying to maximize, and provides alternative empirical measures. At the same time, this research is enabling us to understand how various aspects of our society and economy may interact to determine our collective and individual well-being.

So next time you watch the news and it tells you how much the Dow Jones index, FT100 or inflation has changed, try to imagine what indices a psychologist might have used. Is it so ridiculous to ask: how much did happiness or well-being change today?

Understanding social processes: the example of social capital

One of the key issues for good policy-making is to understand the processes that underlie a particular problem (see figure 18.1 above). We tend to cast problems in terms of the visible end results. For example, it is easy to see as a problem the physical decay of an urban slum and the poverty and illness of its residents. It is more difficult to see the processes that may have led to this state of affairs. Indeed, we may even end up identifying the victims of the underlying problem as the problem themselves (as we shall see in the next section).

A common problem for policy-makers across the world is that of the disadvantage or 'underperformance' of certain segments of the population, and typically the concentration of these disadvantaged populations in particular urban areas. Often these groups are an ethnic minority population, such as blacks in the USA, certain South Asian groups in the UK, Turks in Germany, and so on. Less visibly, a section of the white working class also may be trapped in a cycle of disadvantage.

Sociologists have had much to say about such cycles of disadvantage. They point to the way in which a background of poverty lends fewer opportunities for education or start-up capital, and thus the disadvantage of one generation is passed to the next. Yet it has become clear, not least as a result of the patchy success of many policy interventions, that cycles of disadvantage have many subtle social psychological aspects to them beyond that of the physical and financial resources available to individuals (Oppenheim 1998).

It has been found that working-class children often underperform not just because of the quality of the schools they have access to, but as a result of their expectations of failure and the nature of their aspirations (Weiner, Russell and Lerman 1979; Kinder 1995; Kinder, Wakefield and Wilkin 1996). Criminal offending has been found to be predicted by patterns of parenting, such as harsh and erratic discipline and a distant father, as well as many other factors (Faulkner, Hough and Halpern 1996). Long-term unemployment has been found to result not just from low skills, but from the nature of the person's social network (Granovetter 1985; White 1991; Wilson 1997). Conflict inside the family has been found to have long-term impacts on children into their adult life, including on their own adult relationships (Hess 1995; and see chapter 6). The list of known social psychological processes contributing to well-known social problems is long and getting longer.

In parallel with this developing understanding, it has become clear that even major economic objectives, such as economic growth, appear to rest significantly on the micro-level character of social interaction in a society (Szreter 1998). In short, there is a growing understanding that quite subtle, humble social psychological processes can and do have big effects at the macro- or societal level.

Perhaps the best example of this growing understanding is the explosion of interest in something called social capital.

Many of these findings, particularly in relation to health, bear a direct relationship to forty years of research in psychology into social networks and social support.

Psychologists have long noted that people with high levels of social support – that is, who have relationships with others on which they can rely for emotional and

---

Box 18.1   Social capital

Social capital has been given a range of definitions, but probably the most frequently cited is that of Robert Putnam. He defined it as: 'features of social life – networks, norms, and trust – that enable participants to act together more effectively to pursue shared objectives…Social capital, in short, refers to social connections and the attendant norms and trust' (Putnam 1995, pp. 664–5). Putnam found, in a path-breaking study, that the roots of very substantial differences in the performance of different regional governments of Italy appeared to lie in the character of everyday associational life in each region. Hence regions with vibrant choral associations and clubs of all kinds were also the regions that had the most efficient governments and the best-performing economies. To the surprise of many, the character of people's everyday social networks in a community, region or nation has been found to have a strong relationship with that community's or region's economic growth, health, crime rate and even the efficiency of its government (Halpern forthcoming).

---

instrumental help – tend to be happier and healthier (Argyle 1987; see also previous chapter). For example, as we saw in chapter 17, people with such supportive relationships are significantly less likely to become depressed in the face of a major life event than those without (G. W. Brown and Harris 1978). One difficulty for psychologists working in this area was that it was often difficult to demonstrate conclusively which way the causality went. Many studies show an association between people's social network and their well-being, but it could be argued that happy, healthy people are more pleasant to be with and therefore have better relationships – a selection effect (Sarason, Sarason and Pierce 1990; Halpern 1995a). None the less, various longitudinal studies and quasi-experimental findings suggest that the link is causal – supportive relationships are indeed good for our health and well-being (Berkman and Glass 2000).

Recent research has shown how the consequences of the quality of a person's social network on his or her health can even be seen at the regional level. People living in states in the USA in which more people respond positively to the question 'Can most people be trusted?' have significantly higher life expectancies (Kawachi et al. 1997). This effect is seen across many different causes of death. It turns out that not only do individuals benefit from having more positive and trusting relationships, but so can whole communities.

Meanwhile, researchers in other areas have been finding parallel effects indicating the importance of relationships. Economists have found that the simple question 'Do you think that most people can be trusted?' is able to predict huge differences between the economic performance of nations (Knack and Keefer 1997; Whiteley 1997). Indeed, social capital appears to be as important to predicting economic growth as a nation's level of human capital (the training and skills of its workforce) and more important than its level of investment in physical capital (machinery, infrastructure etc.). The reason seems to be that where people have relationships such that they can trust one another, information is passed easily and people can trade without the need for expensive and difficult legal arrangements. This is illustrated at the micro-level by the finding that people tend to get out of unemployment by finding jobs through friends and acquaintances rather than through formal channels (White 1991; Wilson 1997; Six 1997). This is one of the major reasons why people living in poor areas find it so difficult to get work, as their friends and peers are also out of work.

Criminologists have similarly come to be very interested in social capital and the quality of relationships between people. A close relationship has been found between the level of violent crime and the level of social trust across areas (Kawachi, Kennedy and Wilkinson 1999; Wilkinson, Kawachi and Kennedy 1998). The evidence suggests that most violent crime has at its root an incident of someone, often with low self-esteem, feeling that she or he is being 'disrespected' (see chapter 9). A community with high status differentials and little trust between people – low social capital – is a ripe breeding ground both for such low self-esteem and for incidents of disrespect to occur. A neighbourhood-level analysis showed that the quality and strength of the relationships at the community level – community efficacy – was predictive of violent crime rates even having controlled for prior levels of violence and neighbourhood characteristics such as racial mix (Sampson, Raudenbush and Earls 1997). The authors suggested that in more cohesive communities, people were more likely to intervene in the precursors to crime and were also more effective at ensuring the statutory services did their job.

Finally, it has been found that there is a close relationship between the performance and lack of corruption in governments and the quality of personal relationships in the society. Confirming Putnam's early work, nations characterized by high personal trust between non-kin have better-performing and less corrupt governments (La Porta et al. 1997).

There is some uncertainty about how these remarkable relationships work (Boix and Posner 1995). For example, is it that nations with more trusting relationships between people have more efficient governments because more people obey the law, or is it because the people running the government are more honest and cooperate together? There are certainly many questions to be answered.

In the USA, there is great concern because lots of the indicators of social capital suggest that it is on the decline. People are becoming less and less likely to join clubs and associations, are less likely to see friends or to sit down as a family together for dinner, and are becoming less trusting of one another (Putnam 2000). Fortunately, this does not appear to be true of the whole world (Hall 1999; Halpern forthcoming). None the less, it could be that developments in the USA are warning us of the shape of things to come, and the long-term knock-on effects in terms of economic growth, crime and health may be very worrying indeed.

In summary, researchers from across a range of disciplines are coming to the conclusion that the quality of personal relationships in a society has a very significant impact on virtually all the major outcomes policy-makers care about, including economic growth, health, crime and the effectiveness of government. Many policy implications follow from this emerging literature. First, policy-makers need to be much more concerned about this supposedly 'soft stuff'. The quality of relationships and the way people treat one another in everyday life have far-reaching consequences. At the very least, policy-makers should be wary of damaging this social fabric. Second, the literature demonstrates dramatic ecological effects. These show that the well-being of any given individual is closely bound up with what is happening in the rest of the society or community. In practical and political terms, this boils down to 'We're all in it together.' Put even more bluntly, it is a mistake for the rich and middle classes, even in terms of their own narrow self-interests, to disregard the interests of the less advantaged.

This literature directs us to consider how policy might actually affect and improve the quality of interpersonal relationships, especially between strangers. Policy options might include: direct pleas ('Please try to be considerate to others'); attempting to bolster existing forms of social capital and create new ones more appropriate to today's world (such as supporting local associations and helping foster new forms, e.g. via electronic media) and attacking the underlying factors that might undermine social capital (e.g. economic inequality). This will be an important and interesting area to follow over the coming years, and one in which social psychology is sure to play an important role alongside its sister disciplines of sociology, economics and politics.

Making judgements: if not rational, then what?

In the introduction to this chapter, it was mentioned that economists and political scientists tend to assume that people are rational. This means that they assume that individuals know what they are trying to maximize and can efficiently and effectively assess the choices before them in order to do this. However, as generations of psychologists have shown, this is often – if not always – not the case (S. T. Fiske and Taylor 1991; see also chapter 4).

We have already seen one important example that illustrates this problem in the section on policy objectives (above). People in the West generally think the most important determinant of their happiness is their financial well-being. Yet the data repeatedly shows that, in reality, factors such as the quality of their relationships are much more important.

Another example of this problem can be seen in selection procedures. There are fairly reliable patterns of individual differences (see chapter 2), and particular employers and institutions will wish to find individuals high or low on some of these characteristics (see the next section). For many selectors, the method of choice is the informal interview. Yet the evidence is that the validity of conventional interviews is extremely low (Hunter and Hunter 1984). This is so for several reasons. Interviewers get distracted by irrelevant information, such as how physically attractive the candidate is, or that they have something in common and so on (Rowe 1994). For example, a person with a minor facial disfigurement is significantly less likely to get a job even when factors such as sex, education and experience are held constant (Stevenage and McKay 1999). Interviewers are often very poor at weighting the various contradictory bits of information that arise, such as grades relative to work experience, and tend to use selection procedures to confirm their initial biases (Dougherty, Turband and Callender 1994). In short, selectors tend to think that they are engaged in some kind of sophisticated weighting of the information, while the evidence is that their judgements tend to be dominated by personal prejudices and unreliable heuristics (see below). In reality, computer-guided and more structured selection procedures lead to better results than informal human judgements (Dawes, Faust and Meehl 1989; S. T. Taylor and Fiske 1991).

Policy-making may also be prone to the same faulty thought processes. A famous example of this is groupthink, whereby a group of people tend to reach a more extreme and unbalanced viewpoint than would have been expected of the individuals making up the group (Janis 1982; see also chapter 8). The desire to achieve consensus leads to a filtering out of contrary information. A lot of work has been done on groupthink in the context of judgements made by juries as well as in the context of certain policy disasters. Groupthink is seen most clearly when examining the behaviour of small groups dealing with a crisis, such as President Kennedy's approval of the disastrous Bay of Pigs invasion in 1961 (Janis 1982). Examples in the UK include the decision to sink the *General Belgrano* during the Falklands War in 1982, and the controversial decision to modernize Britain's nuclear deterrent in the late 1970s (Greenway, Smith and Street 1992, p. 227). The last example is clearly illustrated in subsequent admissions by a senior politician involved, Denis Healey, that he had not wanted to go along with the decisions but had thought that he was the only dissenter and therefore kept quiet. This is the classic pattern of groupthink that Janis describes.

Research has shown that although people are not truly rational in their thinking, they are often predictable and consistent. We tend to use a set of heuristics or short cuts to get to the answer (Tversky and Kahneman 1974; see also chapter 3). For example, we judge the likelihood of an event happening by how readily we can think of an example (the availability heuristic). Hence we tend to think that dying on an aeroplane is much more likely than it really is, because when aeroplanes crash it always makes the news.

Politicians and policy-makers can use their knowledge of the shortcomings in people's rationality to their own advantage. For example, people judge how pleasant or unpleasant an experience was not by a true averaging of the level of pain or pleasure over the period, but by particular reference to the most recent and the most intense peak. Hence if you need to do something unpleasant to someone but want him or her not to notice, then your best bet is to spread it out over a period and decrease it just before you ask him or her if it hurt. This, of course, is exactly what politicians try to do with taxes and spending in relation to elections.

Another example of a distortion in human thought that regularly impacts on policy-making is the way in which we attribute causes (for a discussion of attribution theory, see chapter 11). Our thinking is distorted towards being self-centred and self-interested (S. T. Taylor and Fiske 1991). Hence when things go well for us, we tend to think that this is the result of our own efforts, but when things go badly, we tend to blame others. Interestingly, when this pattern of thought is reversed, we are very likely to end up clinically depressed (see chapter 17). Similarly, when we see someone else struggling in life, we are strongly inclined to blame it on the person themselves, even when there is clear evidence that situational factors are responsible (the fundamental attribution error).

The ramifications of these distortions in thought are widespread. Even the best-intentioned policy-makers tend to find it an uphill struggle to convince the electorate that the underprivileged in society ended up that way through no fault of their own and therefore should be helped by the rest of us. Instead, there is a strong tendency to blame the victim (Lerner 1970). Similarly, while surveys often show that most people are in favour of higher taxes on the affluent, they also tend to show that people think the affluent are those who earn just a little bit more than them, however wealthy they are – so we tend to favour higher taxes for other people (SCPR 1992: F16). Another example is attitudes towards the environment. While the vast majority of people are strongly in favour of policies to protect the environment, that support rapidly evaporates once the policy looks as though it will require some sacrifice from them personally (Stokes and Taylor 1994). Hence while most people think public transport is a great idea, we all want everyone else to use it so that we can drive our cars in freedom.

Policy-makers can use knowledge about the peculiar ways in which we think to positive effect. For example, in the area of health policy, it has been found that quite subtle differences in health promotion campaigns can have dramatic effects on people's behaviour. A campaign to increase breast self-examination (critical in the reduction of breast cancer) was shown to be far more effective when worded in terms of potential loss than when worded in terms of potential gain (Meyerowitz and Chaiken 1987). This finding follows from the work of Tversky and Kahneman (1986) that the threat of a small loss often has more impact than the promise of a small gain. No one likes to lose the benefits she or he already has.

We can expect future policies to be increasingly shaped by the growing psychological knowledge about how people think and make judgements in everyday life. We can expect to see more sophisticated 'selling' of taxation, such as through hypothecation (the linking of specific taxes to specific benefits), and far greater information to taxpayers on how their money is actually being spent. We will see ever more health and crime prevention programmes structured to overcome the biases in our thought that make simple informational campaigns ineffective. In criminal justice policy, we may see a shift away from increasing the average severity of punishments towards increasing the certainty of conviction. Even constitutional arrangements may be altered to make them better rooted in our psychological reality; for example, the decision to introduce directly elected mayors in Britain in order to increase voter interest through personifying politics.

A huge literature now exists exploring how people actually think and how they may be persuaded to change their views or behaviour (S. T. Taylor and Fiske 1991; Zimbardo and Leippe 1991; Cialdini 1993; see also chapter 13). Those in the marketing industry have long followed this literature, but policy-makers are not far behind.

The problem of individual differences in ability

If people were all the same, policy would be a lot easier. Imagine a world in which all people were born with the same resources and abilities. Such a world might seem a little dull, but issues over welfare, education and many other social policy areas would become very much simpler.

Sociologists show us how, in reality, people start with very different financial resources and power in life. For example, a person born to a poor working-class family is much less likely to be able to pay for an enhanced education than one from an affluent middle-class background (Bilton et al. 1996; Adonis and Pollard 1997). The psychology of individual differences suggests a similar story for differences in ability. We are not all born alike – some may have natural endowments that give them advantages over others, at least in some contexts. A well-known, and controversial, example of such psychological differences is in intelligence.

The pattern of individual differences forms a permanent backdrop to policy-making and presents two different types of problem. First, it means that you cannot just assume that a policy that works for one person will work for everyone. Second, more subtly, the policy-maker is forced to consider what causes the pattern of difference. Consider the issue of unemployment. The policy-maker needs to understand why one person but not another ends up unemployed. An understanding of causality will give an indication as to the kind of policies that might reduce the unemployment. If we discover that the reason why the person is unemployed is that he or she lacks skills, then education and training maybe appropriate. But if we decide that the person had such opportunities but is simply lazy, then our approach may be very different. Hence our understanding of root causes of individual differences has a huge effect on the policies we decide to follow.

The study of intelligence, or more specifically of intelligence quotient (*IQ*), shows that people differ widely in their cognitive abilities. In contrast to the spirit of the popular phrase 'Everyone is special in their own way', researchers studying cognitive abilities from Spearman to the present day have come up with a repeated and remarkable finding. People who are good at one cognitive task tend on average to be good in most other cognitive areas (Spearman 1927; N. B. Brody 1992; Mackintosh 1998). This general pattern does not hold for every aspect of our being. For example, musical abilities, social intelligence and bodily-kinaesthetic abilities are not much associated with IQ. None the less, a very large number of measures of ability appear to correlate closely, and the IQ scores derived from these measures appear remarkably stable over time.

None of this would matter much to policy except for the fact that IQ appears to be an exceptionally good general predictor of job performance and therefore of pay (Schmidt, Ones and Hunter 1992). Partly because of this, employers and educational establishments have become steadily more efficient in their ability to select by IQ, though often using indirect measures such as previous educational achievement. A wide range of twin, adoption and family studies have indicated that IQ is very heavily influenced by genes; the population variance explained by genes is estimated to be in the range 50 to 80 per cent. Of course, unless you believe in eugenics or the use of genetic engineering in humans, these genes are beyond the reach of policy-makers.

This pattern of findings has led some prominent researchers to argue that class and pay differences across society are the result of genetic differences over which the state has no control (Hernstein and Murray 1994). Hernstein and Murray, in their book *The Bell Curve*, caused even greater controversy by extending this argument to racial differences in IQ, hinting that the disadvantaged position of black Americans resulted not from prejudice or their poor life chances but from their own genetic make-up. The writers went on to argue that because of the psychological and genetic basis of these social differences, much policy effort and spending was doomed to failure.

Hernstein and Murray's work, like that of Jenson before it, has been very strongly criticized (for example, see the edited volume by Jacoby and Glauberman 1995). University of California psychologist Arthur R. Jensen argued that little could be done to boost IQ, scholastic achievement, and therefore the associated socioeconomic differences, as policy interventions mistook genetic differences as environmental (Jenson 1969). Jenson's article became one of the most cited and controversial of the following decade. Both Hernstein and Murray's original book and many of the responses to it are rather polemical in style. One substantive weakness in the *Bell Curve* argument is that the evidence on heritability (i.e. the relative importance of genes vs. environment) is incorrectly applied to racial differences. Even if heritability estimates for IQ approached 100 per cent inside both populations, it could still be that racial differences were entirely environmentally determined. Second, the few quasi-experimental studies that exist concerning race offer little support for a genetic explanation of the racial differences (e.g. Eyferth 1959; 1961; Tizard 1974; though some cite support in Scarr and Weinberg 1976). Third, we know as a fact that the IQs of many populations have increased by 10–15 points – the same amount as the black–white difference – since the 1950s (Flynn 1987). This shift must have been the result of environmental, not genetic, changes. Though the black–white difference remains in America, such large changes over time suggest that the social environment remains a very plausible causal candidate for explaining similar differences across races.

Picking apart the causes of racial differences in IQ is a difficult task, and cannot be covered adequately here. There are methodological problems associated with even the best studies, not least because it is almost impossible to control for ubiquitous social influences, such as the experience of racism (Mackintosh 1998). What should be clear is that the argument on racial differences in *The Bell Curve* is far from secure.

The weakness with the *Bell Curve* argument over the relationship between class and IQ is more subtle. The basic difficulty is that there is evidence both that class affects IQ – for example, deprivation leads to lower IQ – and that IQ affects class – for example, lower IQ is associated with lower lifetime earnings. Essentially, Hernstein and Murray address this issue by comparing the ability of two different variables to predict earnings. One predictor is the individual's IQ. The second predictor is the person's class background, generally measured by the father's occupation. In this analysis, they find that the individual's IQ is indeed the better predictor. However, subsequent researchers have found that if more sophisticated measures of class are employed, then class becomes the better predictor (Korenman and Winship 1995).

Most importantly, even if one concludes that via IQ, our lifetime earnings result largely from our genes, this does not mean that there is no role for social policy. The former conclusion, if accepted, may imply that there is little we can do about the population distribution of ability. But this does not mean that we have to accept the distribution of earnings that follows from this pattern of ability. For example, we could still collectively agree to tax the more able, higher earners and distribute extra resources to less able, lower earners.

The key, but relatively difficult, point to realize is that understanding what causes the pattern of individual differences has huge political and policy implications. However, these implications are more subtle than the crude nature of the debate around IQ tends to imply. If one believes that differences in earnings – and the psychological attributes these imply – are the result of individual effort and choices, such as how hard people worked at school, then you are likely to conclude that governments should leave the issue alone. You would almost certainly be against any form of redistribution. Note that this argument applies regardless of whether you think the remaining variance is explained by genes or environment. On the other hand, if you believe that the causes of such outcomes are largely the result of brute-luck differences in natural ability or social advantage, you may well conclude that some redistribution is essential for a fair and efficient society. If you think it is the environment that matters, you might focus on schooling. If you think it is genes that matter, you might have to focus on income redistribution (for example, in-work benefits for the less advantaged).

A number of points should be clear from this cursory discussion of IQ. First, it is a highly controversial area. Second, there are some serious weaknesses in the argument presented in the now-infamous *Bell Curve* argument – though also in many of the polemical responses to it. Third, despite those weaknesses, the argument really *does* matter to policy. Furthermore, as societies become more meritocratic, in the sense that people are rewarded according to individual ability rather than the status of their family in society, then an understanding of what leads to differences of ability becomes ever more politically important.

Conclusions

This chapter has shown that social psychology, as well as having a role in more narrowly defined applied social psychology, has the potential to play a major role in policy more generally. The chapter explored four major areas illustrating the contribution that social psychology can make to policy-making.

We saw that a social psychological perspective challenges conventional thinking on the fundamental question of what the objectives of policy should be. It was found that economic well-being is only a relatively poor predictor of subjective well-being, or happiness. A far more important predictor is the quality of people's relationships. The implication is that policies based on maximizing subjective well-being might look significantly different from conventional policies based on maximizing economic objectives such as GDP.

It was shown how social psychology can help illuminate important aspects of the processes that underlie social and economic problems. The emerging literature on social capital was used as an illustration. This literature shows how the structure and quality of people's relationships to one another, including the social norms that characterize the relationships between relative strangers, have significant effects on health, crime, economic growth, and even the performance of governments.

How people think about one another – social cognition – also has many implications for policy. Human thought does not comply with the tidy assumptions of rational-choice theories of economics and political science. None the less, social cognition can be empirically studied, is often predictable, and can therefore be systematically considered by the skilful policy-maker.

Finally, the problem of individual differences in human abilities was considered. These differences throw up many problems for the policy-maker, as well as methodological problems for the psychologist. An understanding of the causes of these differences has many implications for how we, as a society, respond to them.

Despite the range of impressive examples, we should not fall into the trap of thinking that policy can be built on social psychology alone. This would replicate the mistake of thinking that policy can be based on narrow economics or political science alone. Good policy-making must be based on a well-rounded understanding of a wide range of issues, interests and subjects. But social psychology certainly has an important contribution to make.

RECOMMENDED READING

Argyle, M. (1987) *The Psychology of Happiness*. London and New York: Methuen.
On objectives and happiness, Argyle is still a good, and quite easy, overall read.
If you want something a little more challenging than Argyle, you might want to look at
Scitovsky. His book is considered a classic challenge to economics that even lots of
economists read.

Halpern, D. S. (forthcoming) *Social Capital*. Cambridge: Polity
If you want a more international overview of the social capital literature than Putnam's,
try Halpern.

Hernstein, R. J. and Murray, C. (1994) *The Bell Curve: Intelligence and Class Structure
in American Life*. New York: Free Press.
On the psychology of individual differences, and especially IQ, try the book that
everyone loves to hate by Hernstein and Murray.

Mackintosh, N. J. (1998) *IQ and Human Intelligence*. Oxford: Oxford University Press.
For a more balanced point of view than *The Bell Curve* gives, try Mackintosh, a good
scholar trying to get to the truth in a field full of polemics.

Putnam, R. D. (2000) *Bowling Alone: The Collapse and Revival of American Community*.
New York: Simon and Schuster.
On social capital, Bob Putnam's massive analysis of the dramatic decline in social
capital in the USA is comprehensive, influential but still easy to read.

Scitovsky, T. (1992) *The Joyless Economy: The Psychology of Human Satisfaction*.
Revised edn. Oxford and New York: Oxford University Press.

PART V

The Nature of Social Psychology

Research Methods

Introduction

Social Psychology is overwhelmingly an empirical science. By that we mean that social psychologists learn by observing and doing. As we have seen, theory is not unimportant, but in social psychology the main advances in knowledge come not from armchair theorizing but from interacting with the subject matter – people. In this way the social psychologist can be seen to be engaging in the same project as people in their everyday lives – attempting to gain a better understanding of the social world through observation of that world. In fact, it could be argued that good social psychologists learn more about social psychology in their everyday lives than when they are 'in uniform'.

If you have read some or all of chapters 2 to 18 before embarking on this one, you will have noticed a large variety of types of evidence that have been given to support the various arguments in those chapters. Some evidence comes from laboratory experiments, some from observations of individuals, groups, families and even animals in their natural settings, some from observations of 'abnormal' cases such as people with brain injuries or autism, some from analyses of historical records, and so on. But there are very important differences between the ways in which a social psychologist approaches research and the ways a lay person learns about the social world. The gathering of knowledge in social scientific research is more explicitly systematic, such that we can be more certain of the findings, and their interpretation. We hope to avoid some of the errors that are common in the less systematic gathering of knowledge that individuals do in their everyday lives. And, rather than relying on personal hunches, intuitive understandings or emotional attachments, social psychologists attempt to achieve both logical coherence and adequate evidence to support their theories. But, as will become evident as you read this chapter, no one method is perfect in achieving this objective. Indeed, the exact way in which one goes about systematic inquiry in social psychology has caused more controversy than any other single topic. In this chapter several major methods will be discussed in detail, and their strengths and weaknesses contrasted. It will be argued that no one method is considered to be superior to all others. Social psychology has advanced through a multitude of different approaches; and there is every expectation that in the future new methods will be invented or imported from other social sciences.

But to begin this chapter we will consider the method that has been the most dominant, mainstream one in social psychology: the laboratory experiment. We start here, not because we think that it is the best method in social psychology, but because it has undoubtedly been the most widespread in its use over the past century. Indeed, some of the most prestigious journals for the publication of new research in social psychology, as their titles suggest, will only publish research which has been based on experimentation (e.g. the *Journal of Experimental Social Psychology*). But this dominance of experimental methods has its opponents; in chapter 20 it is argued that one of the most important achievements of European social psychology is to have partially broken free of the stranglehold that experimentation has had over so much of social psychology in the USA.

So, what exactly is an experiment?

In psychology we mean something very particular by the term 'experiment', a technique which is uniquely suited to investigating causal relationships between variables by manipulating the variables which are assumed to be causal. Many methods we have can detect correlation; that is, whether two things tend to be related to each other, like alcoholism and unhappiness. But knowing that they go together is of limited use in a scientific investigation; we want to know whether, for instance, people drink because they are unhappy, or are unhappy because they drink. The experiment can unravel such 'chicken and egg' issues, by actually manipulating the variable (or variables) which are assumed to be the most important causes of behaviour, and then carefully measuring the outcome variable or variables. Furthermore, it is essential that the participants in the experiment are randomly allocated to the different levels of the manipulated variable. For instance, let us assume that an investigator is interested in whether watching violent films makes people more aggressive (see chapter 9). She might start with, for instance, three films which pre-testing showed to be high, medium and low in violent content. Participants in the experiment would be allocated at random to watch one of these three films. After they had watched the film they would then be tested to ascertain their level of aggression. For instance, they could be asked to play a game and the frequency with which they use aggressive tactics could be observed and measured. If the participants who watched the high-violence film tended, on average, to behave more aggressively, and the participants who watched the low-violence film to behave least aggressively, then the investigator could conclude that there was a direct, causal link between the level of violence in a film and the level of aggression that people are prone to after watching it. Those are the bare bones of an experiment.

Before we go on to compare it to other methods, let us consider some of the jargon that is used to describe experiments. Typically an experiment starts with a strong and carefully articulated theory about a cause–effect relationship which is hypothesized to exist, whereas other methods sometimes start with a more open-minded approach to the possible ways in which variables might be related to each other. The independent variable (or IV) is the one that the investigator assumes to be the cause (in the above example the level of violence in a film); that is the one that gets manipulated to create different experimental conditions. An experiment can have more than one independent variable; for instance, we could also have compared films where the violence is rewarded with films where the violence is punished to see whether that too has an effect.

It is vital that the only difference between the experimental conditions is that brought about by the manipulation of the IV. If there are other systematic differences between groups, these are called confounding variables, and we cannot be sure whether the results obtained are attributable to the IV or the other variables. For instance, if the participants who saw the violent film were inadvertently kept waiting a long time before the second task (the 'game' to measure their aggression), or if that part of the experiment was conducted on a particularly hot and muggy day, then it would be possible that any differences in aggression could be attributable to the frustration caused by the wait or the climatic conditions rather than the film.

Whether the IV is indeed a cause is judged by its relationship to the dependent variable (DV), the one that is measured at the end of the experiment (in this example, the level of aggression displayed in the game). DVs can take many forms: they could (as in this case) be direct observations of behaviour; or they could be written or verbal reports by the participants of their attitudes or feelings; or they could be physiological measures such as heart rate or pupil dilation as indicators of arousal. Indeed, some experiments would measure several very different DVs.

Typically, statistical procedures are employed to rule out the possibility that the differences between the average levels of the DV in the different conditions might have arisen by chance differences between the groups of participants in, say, their genetic make-up, personality or intelligence. In order to support the link between observed violence and aggression in our example, we need to rule out the possibility that, even though the participants were allocated to the three groups at random, any differences between the groups in their average aggression might have been caused by inadvertently allocating more aggressive individuals to one group or the other. If we can rule out the possibility that our observed differences in the DV between groups have been caused by imperfections in the randomization, then we can be confident that any observed differences really are attributable to differences in the IV. Whether the difference between groups is a spurious, chance occurrence or whether it is indicative of a true relationship between the variables can be tested for statistically, in the same way as a statistician could calculate whether a roulette wheel was probably fair or biased if she or he observed it for long enough, making a careful record of numerous spins. Such statistical calculations have become ubiquitous in the treatment of all numerical research results, and they can get quite complex when, for instance, an experiment involves more than one IV.

'Why go to all this bother?', you might ask. An alternative might be to interview people, or ask them to keep diaries of their television viewing, as a measure of the IV. We could then test for differences between the ones who watch a lot of violent television and the ones who watch few violent television programmes (or if we were ingenious enough we might even be able to think of naturalistic ways of measuring their aggression – perhaps by looking at their school reports or criminal records). If we find a correlation between the measure of television violence observed and our measure of aggression, such that those who watched more violent television also tended to exhibit more aggression, then would this not also support our hypothesis that violence in the media causes aggression?

Unfortunately, the answer is 'No'. You might like to pause for a while and see if you can think what the main weaknesses of this evidence are.

It may be that our hypothesis is true: observing violence causes aggression, displayed diagrammatically in figure 19.1(a). But there are other explanations that could also give us such a correlation. It may be, for instance, that people with higher general levels of aggression typically find violent television more interesting, but that they would be no less aggressive if they did not watch it; in other words there may be a third, confounding,

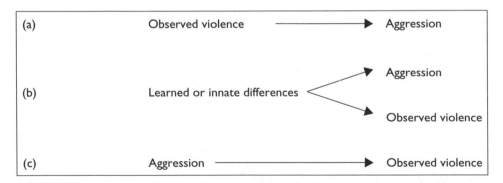

Figure 19.1 Possible cause and effect links between observed violence on television and aggression

variable that affects both our assumed IV and DV, but there is, in fact, no direct link between them (figure 19.1(b)). As a third possibility, the direction of cause may be the exact reverse to that which we had hypothesized. For instance, it may be that individuals who, for whatever reason, were compelled to resort to aggression in their everyday lives find that television programmes with high levels of violence are more relevant to their lives and thus more interesting (figure 19.1(c)).

In this type of survey design, all three causal relationships portrayed in figure 19.1 would give similar results (a correlation between the two variables of interest) that would be indistinguishable to the researcher. Yet the policy implications of the findings are completely different; figure 19.1(a) provides evidence which might be used to support censorship of violence on television, whereas figures 19.1(b) and (c) do not.

In an experiment we can be sure, if our IV and DV are related, that the IV is the cause and the DV the effect. This, a devotee of the experimental method would argue, is the supreme advantage of experiments over all other methods. In all other methods, we can only show that they are associated, but we do not know which one of the two is the cause, or whether they are related only because they both happen, coincidentally, to be related to a third or prior variable such as gender, age or social class. (We can sometimes eliminate these prior or confounding variables statistically, if we have measured them. But we can never be sure that we have measured and eliminated all of them.) And to understand how and why a system works, we always want to know about relationships in terms of causes and effects. There lies the most powerful argument there is for experiments, and that is the reason why psychology has throughout much of its history retained a strong commitment to the experimental method, believing that experiments provided conclusive proof of hypotheses whereas other methods provided little better than suggestive evidence.

To understand the experiment a little better, one needs to understand a little more about its execution, to put some flesh on the bare bones. For a start, social psychology experiments are almost always conducted in a laboratory setting. This provides a very controlled environment, away from any influences (apart from the IV) which might sway the participants. It also allows careful observation of behaviour, such as videotaping, which is more difficult in less controlled environments. There are exceptions to the use of the laboratory: field experiments are considered later in this chapter.

Another common feature of experiments is deception (or, perhaps, being economical with the truth). Think back to our example concerning violence and aggression. If the participants were told that they were being shown the films to see the extent to which it made them more aggressive, and that they were to play games so that their levels of aggression could be measured, then it is highly likely that the participants would have monitored their behaviour very carefully and reacted very atypically. This is often countered by hiding the true purpose of the experiment from them. For instance, in this example the participants could have been told that the experimenters were interested in the physiological responses to films, and measured their heart rate during the film as a decoy to make the deception more plausible. The game to measure aggression could then be presented as a separate exercise which just happened to follow on 'because they finished earlier than expected'. In fact, deceptions of this sort are so clever and pervasive that a perusal of the literature in social psychology might rapidly convince the reader that, if experimentalists were to lose their jobs in academia, they would easily be able to make a good living as confidence tricksters. In the past experimenters did not consider deception to be a problem, as it was being done in the name of science, but more recently the notion of informed consent has become central to debates about the ethics of research, which are considered later in this chapter.

However, as we suggested at the beginning of the chapter, experiments have a number of problems and imperfections which have led some social psychologists to consider that, in fact, they are limited in their usefulness, and others to reject them completely.

Experimenter effects

To start with, there are a number of ways in which experimenters can subtly alter the outcome of experiments in a way that may bias the results of the experiment. One well-known bias is caused by experimenter expectancies. For instance, in the hypothetical experiment described here, experimenters, knowing what results they expected, may inadvertently have introduced the rules of the game to participants who had seen the more violent film in such a way as to encourage them to use more aggressive strategies. Or they may have inadvertently nodded with approval when a participant from the violent-film condition was aggressive in the game, but frowned with disapproval when a participant from the less-aggressive condition was aggressive. Rosenthal (1976) studied such effects at length and concluded that they may be prevalent in many experiments.

Demand characteristics

It is also possible to get people to act in quite bizarre ways under laboratory conditions because of the demands that the situation unwittingly imposes upon them. Orne (1962) used a straightforward laboratory-based study to demonstrate this. Participants were instructed to perform very simple tasks, such as adding up lists of numbers or filling in the noughts in pages of old newspapers. When they had finished a whole page of such dull and pointless activities, they were to take the completed page to the investigator at the front of the room, who would tear up the sheet into tiny pieces, give them another sheet of paper and tell them to start again. One might assume that participants would quickly lose patience with this meaningless task and refuse to continue. To Orne's surprise, participants continued without complaint for hours on end; typically the investigator had to abandon the task well into the evening after a midday start.

Why? It seems as if the participants, finding themselves in such a peculiar situation, tried to make sense of it. Many assumed that it was an experiment to investigate stamina or vigilance in a monotonous task. So, while experimenters may, through deception, manage to conceal the true hypothesis of the experiment, they cannot stop participants trying to guess what the experimenter is trying to prove. And participants' behaviour, as Orne showed, might be more a function of that 'second guessing' than any simple reaction to the experimental manipulation. It should also be remembered that participants may come to an experiment with a clear idea about what they hope to achieve. Often they will be wanting to help the experimenter, seeing taking part as a way in which they can assist the greater goals of science to advance knowledge. Alternatively, some participants will want to show that they are individuals whose reactions do not conform to scientific laws, and may thus attempt to act in unpredictable ways; the technical term for this is the 'screw you' effect.

Experimenter effects and demand characteristics are examples of practical problems which can detract from the validity of psychological experiments. But no method is perfect; they all have their practical weaknesses. (And many non-experimental methods are also prey to demand characteristics or the equivalent of experimenter effects.) All this tells us is that if we are to conduct experiments we need to be very careful in the way that we go about it. We need to take precautions to ensure that the experimenters treat all participants equally, perhaps by designing a 'double-blind' technique whereby even the experimenters do not know which condition the participants are in. This, and the standardization in giving of instructions to participants, can quite easily be achieved with the help of computers to run many parts of an experiment, including the random allocation of participants to conditions, the giving of instructions and the collection of the data (or DV).

But a move to making experiments more 'exact' or 'scientific' may create more problems than it solves. One way of describing the predicament that we find ourselves in is that it is like walking a tightrope between two equally damning downfalls; a lack of internal validity and a lack of external validity. In order for an experiment to contribute usefully to knowledge, we need to avoid both possible undoings.

On the one hand, any investigation must be internally valid (or reliable) to be of any use whatsoever. By this we mean that it must be replicable; if each time an experiment is repeated, either by the same or by a different researcher, a different result is obtained, then little can be learned from the experiment, apart from the fact that something is clearly wrong with the experimental procedure. Like experimenters in the physical sciences, we need to be sure that if the procedure is repeated under similar conditions, and with participants drawn at random from the same populations, then the results will hold. So in order to ensure that experiments are internally valid, researchers will attempt to remove any spurious effects caused by experimenter effects, a failure to standardize procedures, non-random selection and allocation of participants, and so on.

But even if an experiment is internally valid, this does not necessarily mean that it will provide a useful addition to knowledge. As well as being internally valid, it must also have external validity, also known as generalizability. By this we mean that the findings from the experiment hold in the real-world situation which we are interested in. For instance, in the example given here concerning violence and aggression, it could be argued that the experimental situation is so unlike the way in which violence in the media is experienced that it is unlikely that the phenomena observed in the laboratory will resemble the relationship between media violence and aggression in the real world. More specifically, it could be argued that there are many features associated with violence in the media which are completely absent in our experiment, such as the reaction of important others (e.g. parents or peers) to the violence, or extended exposure over many years. And, as social psychology has found on so many occasions, behaviour may be endowed with different meanings in different contexts, and thus create totally different reactions (as has been discussed in chapters 3, 5 and 14).

Another aspect of the same problem of external validity is that some experiments have, from the same data, led researchers to reinterpret the results in a very different way to that conceived of by the original researcher. For instance, some have claimed that the key IV which brought about obedience in Milgram's experiments was not so much authority as trust (Mixon 1972).

Perhaps then the most difficult thing for experiments to achieve is external validity. Without this they are but demonstrations of behaviour in artificial or unusual situations. This can be very important for theory testing, but of no direct relevance to any real situation. But methods other than experiments can also suffer from threats to internal and external validity; when we come to consider them, we can use these two concepts to compare methods one with another.

However, there are other arguments against the use of experiments which do not have simple solutions, and are the reasons why some psychological researchers have become deeply sceptical about the use of experimentation as a method for use in any social science.

The radical critiques of experimentation

The publication of the book *The Explanation of Social Behaviour* by Harré and Secord (1972) was one of the important milestones in the move against experimentation, although there have been many other strands to these arguments originating from a variety of other social sciences and philosophical traditions. Harré and Secord claim that social psychologists have fundamentally misunderstood what it is to be human, and the conceptual differences between the study of inanimate objects (where experimentation has been so successful) and the study of conscious, self-reflexive human beings. (These views are also considered briefly in chapter 20.) Some of these arguments will be presented here, before some of the alternative methods are described and discussed.

Harré and Secord argued that experiments are based on simplistic notions of behaviour, which reflect some of the elementary stimulus–response notions that psychologists have carried over unquestioningly from the physical and biological sciences. But these notions do not adequately describe what it is to be a thinking human being or a social actor. Unlike plants or simpler animals, we do not always react mechanistically or deterministically to a given stimulus. Rather we might think, interpret, attribute meaning or seek further information. In other words we are characteristically active, but Harré and Secord claim that experiments treat participants as if they are passive responders to stimuli.

Another problem with experiments is that they typically investigate participants one at a time, removing people from their normal social worlds. And since, as social psychologists, we fundamentally believe that the social environment affects behaviour, it therefore follows that the typical behaviour of an individual in a laboratory may be very different from typical behaviour in any other situation. It is not quite true to say that individuals are always tested alone in laboratory experiments. For instance, many experiments involve the use of 'stooges' in the experiment – actors employed by the experimenter to pretend that they are other participants. In other cases discussed in chapter 8, to investigate the behaviour of groups, sets of participants might be investigated where they had a task to complete or decision to make. However, in both of these situations the individuals are strangers, and we interact very differently with strangers and with the individuals and groups we normally choose to interact with, such as our friends, parents, enemies, other students, boyfriends, girlfriends and so on (see chapters 6 and 7). For instance, the people with whom we already have relatively permanent relationships know a lot about us, and we know that anything that we do or say may be important to the way in which they perceive us in the future. By contrast, with new acquaintances that we are unlikely to meet again we can present very different sides of ourselves. Similarly, the study of small groups has been a central concern of social psychology (see chapter 8), and for this purpose groups have often been created in a laboratory for careful scrutiny. As was argued in chapter 8, generalizations from these laboratory-concocted groups should be treated with caution.

A further limitation of experiments is the severe restriction of the number of important causal variables that can be manipulated as IVs in experiments. There are a large number of variables which cannot (for practical or ethical reasons) be manipulated in an experiment but which, nevertheless, are among the most important determinants of our social lives; for instance, gender, ethnic group, race, social class, intelligence, personality, unemployment, poverty, style of parenting and political socialization, to name but a few. So, because experiments are limited in the types of social phenomena that they can investigate, any social psychology which relies exclusively on the experiment will necessarily limit itself to a restricted set of social phenomena. Furthermore, laboratory experiments are typically very restricted in the time period they can consider. For instance, watching one violent film may have little impact upon behaviour, whereas watching violent films night after night from a young age may be a very potent cause of aggression.

So, if we are not going to use only experiments, what else can we do? Fortunately there is no shortage of techniques which are also available to social psychologists. Many of them have been developed primarily in other disciplines, such as sociology or social anthropology. Others have been developed within social psychology as an explicit reaction to the criticisms of the experiment which Harré and others have made.

Field experiments and quasi-experiments

It is possible to investigate real or naturally occurring groups experimentally, and there are very good examples of research (particularly in industry and education) that uses natural groups. Excellent examples of this type of research are intervention studies, where participating individuals or families are randomly allocated to conditions, so the rigour of the experimental logic is retained. For instance, in the USA a number of studies called the Head Start experiments have attempted to provide better preschool environments to combat educational underachievement and later juvenile delinquency (Zigler, Taussig and Black 1992). In the UK Murray and Cooper (1997) have followed up their laboratory studies on the effects of maternal deprivation on child development (see chapter 6) by using health visitors to ameliorate these effects. And Grantham-McGregor et al. (1991) have investigated the effects of nutritional supplements on Jamaican children's development. These intervention studies have the dual benefits of experimental rigour and of providing evidence that can be plugged directly into public policy (see chapter 18).

But more often, when we use naturally occurring groups, we are no longer able to retain all of the features of the experimental method – the manipulation of the IV, the random allocation to groups and the exclusion of confounding variables. But, with some ingenuity, as in Sherif and Sherif's (1953) studies of summer camps discussed in chapter 15, many of the desirable features of experiments can still be retained even in these situations – D. T. Campbell and Stanley (1966) called these 'quasi-experimental designs', and discussed their strengths and weaknesses at length.

Surveys and interviewing people

The most common research method in sociology has been the survey, and it is now widely used in many areas within social psychology. It can take many forms, but again we will start by describing the bare bones before considering embellishments and criticisms.

A survey is simply a systematic collection of variables relating to a sample of cases. In social psychology the cases are usually individuals (typically referred to as respondents instead of participants), but could be anything from cities to subcultures or from magazines to psychiatric hospitals. A number (often a very large number) of variables are measured from each respondent, including perhaps measures of their attitudes, experiences, psychological well-being, income, membership of various demographic categories (gender, ethnic group) and so on. The survey relies on naturally occurring variation in the assumed independent variable, and uses statistical procedures to determine whether those variations are correlated to variations in the dependent variable.

For instance, the suggested investigation mentioned earlier in this chapter, correlating the amount of violent television that individuals have watched with their aggression, is a good example of the use of the survey method. As was also mentioned, we can demonstrate that two variables are correlated, but we cannot simply deduce from this that there is a cause–effect relationship in operation. However, we do have some very powerful statistical techniques that can go a long way to settling causal claims. For instance, structural equation modelling is now widely used for the analysis of the interrelationships between variables from survey data. And we can control the influences of other potentially confounding prior variables (such as gender, age, social class etc.) to determine whether the correlation still remains when the influences of those other variables have been removed.

Pettigrew's (1958) investigation into levels of prejudice against blacks in the USA and South Africa provides a good example of the use of the survey (see chapter 15). His findings, that there were marked differences in the levels of prejudice between the two countries, and between different groups of whites within each country, showed the inadequacy of simple individualistic theories of prejudice, and suggested that we need to look for societal influences too.

Survey data can be collected in a variety of ways, with face-to-face interviewing, telephone interviewing and postal questionnaires being the most common. Each is suitable for different sorts of research problem or type of respondent. For instance, postal questionnaires tend to be less expensive to administer but are less suitable for less motivated respondents (who just will not reply) or respondents with poor literacy skills.

Box19.1   Questionnaires

Questionnaires are one of the commonly used methods of collecting data in social psychology research. Here is a short section of a questionnaire which was administered to 1,000 respondents in each of the European Union countries by trained interviewers in 1995, to compare working conditions and investigate their effects on health and attitudes to work. Note how the questionnaire collects a combination of behavioural, attitudinal and situational information

Q.26.   over the past 12 months, have you, or not ... ?

READ OUT	Yes	No	DK
had a frank discussion with your boss about your work performance	73 1	2	3
been consulted about changes in the organisation of work and/or your working conditions	74 1	2	3
discussed work-related problems with your boss	75 1	2	3
discussed work-related problems with your colleagues	76 1	2	3
discussed work-related problems with your employee representatives	77 1	2	3

Q.28.   At your workplace, would you say that men and women have equal opportunities, or not ?

Equal opportunities... 86   1
More opportunities for men...   2
More opportunities for women...   3
Other (SPONTANEOUS)   4
DK...   5

Q.29.   Is your immediate boss a man or woman ?

A man... 87   1
A woman...   2
NOT APPLICABLE (SPONTANEOUS)...   3

Q.32.   Over the past 12 months, how many days, if any, were you absent due to health problems caused by your main paid job ?

Never... 93   1
<5...   2
5–9..   3
10–19..   4
20–29..   5
30–39..   6
40–49   7
50–74..   8
75–99..   9
100+..   10
OTHER ANSWER...   11

Q.36.   On the whole, are you very satisfied, fairly satisfied, not very satisfied or not at all satisfied with your main paid job? would you say you are ... ? (READ OUT)

Very satisfied... 98   1
Fairly satisfied...   2
Not very satisfied...   3
Not at all satisfied...   4
DK...   5

Telephone interviewing had a poor reputation in the past because it missed out those people without telephones in their homes, thus leading to an unrepresentative sample. However, with telephone ownership becoming almost universal among most segments of the population in industrialized societies, and with the added advantage that the responses can be entered directly into the computer by the interviewer, telephone interviewing is again becoming common and respectable. And no doubt with the advent of new technologies, such as the Internet, pocket computers and tiny video cameras, other methods of obtaining survey data will become possible.

But, just as we had to be careful with the 'social psychology of the psychology experiment', we need to be aware of the ways in which the interviewer can influence the respondents. For instance, the gender or ethnic group of the interviewer may influence the respondents; a woman may be more forthcoming about personal issues to another woman than a man; a member of a minority ethnic or religious group may feel that he or she needs to defend that group to an 'outsider'. As with experimenter effects, a knowledge of these potential problems can reduce their effects. Well-worded questions that provide unambiguous answers leave less scope for interviewer bias. Sometimes it may be important to use interviewers of the same sex, age or ethnic origin as the respondents. And well-trained interviewers learn how to ask questions in a consistent manner, showing no emotional reaction, either positive or negative, to the answer.

This may be all well and good for interviews of a very factual nature, but there are many situations where a cold, detached interviewer is going to be completely inappropriate. For instance, if interviewed on such sensitive topics as bereavement or domestic violence, respondents will probably not be very revealing to an interviewer unless they feel that there is a trusting, empathetic and safe environment to do so in. Similarly, if one wants to understand a complex phenomenon, as in Andrews's (1991) study to determine why some individuals remain life-long political activists, then one is unlikely to get anywhere near a complete understanding by asking a set of prepared questions. Rather, Andrews used more detailed, semi-structured interviews and reinterviews to great effect with her respondents. While she had an idea of what sort of questions she wanted to ask, she knew she would also want to follow up on those questions, encouraging the respondent to give more information where she thought it was important or illuminating.

Survey designs

So far we have only considered one type of survey design, where the variables are all measured at the same point in time (commonly called cross-sectional surveys). This is certainly the most frequent way in which surveys are conducted, partly for reasons of simplicity, cost and speed. But there are other types of design that can, in many ways, be superior, particularly in sorting out those knotty cause-and-effect problems. They all involve incorporating change over time into the survey design – that is, they are all longitudinal surveys – but there are several different ways of doing this.

Some surveys, such as ones on which much of the research on children and divorce discussed in chapter 6 is based, take a birth cohort (for instance, all of the children in the United Kingdom born in a particular week) and every few years take detailed measures of their psychological, physical and social development, as well as the circumstances of their families, schools and communities. We can then see how their early experiences affect their later development, and the sequence in which changes take place. If, for instance, children seemed to be thriving before their parents separate, but then start to behave badly afterwards, that would support the view that marital breakdown is directly responsible for children's problems. However, if we noticed that children whose parents separated in their teens were already underperforming at the age of 7, we would need to find some alternative explanation, perhaps based on the quality of the marriage or the pressures that led to the breakdown of that marriage. The British birth cohort studies which were started in 1946, 1958 and 1972 have all produced rich findings that help address these important problems (Scott 1995).

The other common type of longitudinal survey is a panel design. In this case a representative cross-section of the population is interviewed, and then reinterviewed at regular (e.g. annual) intervals. Again, because of the expense of such a design, and the need for a long-term financial commitment to keep it going, such surveys are rare, but one, called the British Household Panel Survey (BHPS), was started in 1991 and will be an enormously fertile source for psychological research for a long time to come. Data from such surveys is made freely available to the research community, so that it can be used widely (see Scott 1995 for a discussion of the advantages of panel and longitudinal designs generally, and the BHPS in particular).

A significant strength of survey methodologies over experimentation is that, for many topics, they are more obviously related to real-world phenomena, and therefore do not so obviously suffer the problems of external validity which can detract from laboratory experiments. There are, however, times when we must treat the results of survey research with some scepticism. For instance, surveys usually rely exclusively on respondents' verbal or written reports, but these can be affected by social desirability biases; people can underestimate the frequency of stigmatized behaviours (e.g. number of cigarettes smoked per day, or frequency of smacking children) and overestimate the frequency of socially desirable ones (e.g. giving to charities). Similarly, respondents may modify the expression of their attitudes to make themselves seem more likeable to the interviewer, for instance by moderating their racism if they think that the interviewer is not racist, or exaggerating it if they think that the interviewer is likely to approve of their racist attitudes. Skilful survey researchers are well aware of these biases that can affect responses, and can sometimes ask questions in such a way as to reduce them, but nevertheless any research which relies exclusively on self-report data has its limitations.

Observation

As an alternative to relying on self-report data from interviews as a way of exploring psychological phenomena, observing behaviour directly is another way of investigating them. Throughout this book there have been numerous and diverse examples of this. For instance, in chapter 9 on altruism and chapter 6 on the development of relationships, much of our understanding comes from observing behaviour, and drawing inferences from those observations.

Sometimes those observations can occur in a laboratory where the investigator can set-up a particular situation and see how children or adults react to it. For instance, in the Ainsworth Strange Situation (see chapters 6 and 7), mothers and their young children were separated, and the behaviour and level of anxiety of the child were observed. Note that, even though this observation might take place in a laboratory, it is not necessarily an experiment. As is often the case, we are interested in naturally occurring variation in the IVs, such as age, gender and relationship between subjects, not manipulated variables.

Alternatively, observations can be made in naturally occurring environments such as nursery schools or school playgrounds. While it may be more difficult to interpret those observations because of the greater diversity of events, and we have less control over our ability to record important details such as facial expressions or eye contact, the greater relevance and external validity or generalizability of observation in a natural situation is very valuable indeed if we want to understand how such processes operate in people's everyday lives. The fact that people are not aware that they are being observed adds greatly to the relevance of the research, although there may be ethical issues if we observe people without their knowledge or consent.

But there are many situations in which it is difficult, impossible or unethical to observe people. For instance, if we are interested in the ways in which gangs of youths or members of a religious cult interact, then we cannot simply observe or video them without causing a major disruption to their activities. As with any research problem, one could think of many ways to proceed. One could interview members, or ex-members, of the gang or cult, but we might be wary of biases in the reinterpretation of evidence; current members may want to portray their own group in a favourable light, whilst ex-members may want to do the exact opposite. And besides, one of the central tenets of social psychology is that we are not always aware of the forces that shape our thoughts and behaviours. There are plenty of examples in social psychology where the things that people say influence them greatly do not, and those things that they claim do not influence them at all can be seen to have an enormous impact on behaviour – some of the experiments on influence in small groups described in chapter 8 are excellent examples of this. For these reasons we could never have a complete picture of a social psychological phenomenon derived entirely from self-report data – for instance from surveys or in-depth interviews.

An alternative possibility may therefore be to ask permission of the group to observe them. Sometimes this will be unproblematic, and the group can get on with their activities regardless. But often this is not the case, particularly if some of the activities of the group are secretive or illegal. In these situations researchers have sometimes joined such groups without revealing their true identity or intentions, and made careful note of all they saw and heard. Festinger, Riecken and Schachter's (1956) observations of the doomsday cult described in chapter 13 is one of the most famous examples of participant observation in social psychology. Such a method has generated considerable controversy too. The advantage is obvious – direct observation in naturally occurring environments, often ones of great policy or theoretical interest. However, the concerns that have been expressed about this technique are wide-ranging, covering both the practical and the ethical.

On a practical level, it is healthy to remain somewhat sceptical of the ability of participant observers to keep an accurate and unbiased record of their observations. They will rarely have the opportunity to take notes while 'in the field', so will have to rely on their memory until they can write their diary or log of events and observations. They may also become emotionally involved with the group they are observing, which will affect the ways in which the researchers interpret the group's actions. And, although participant observers may try not to influence the situation they are observing, this is sometimes easier said than done. As they become group members it may become impossible not to influence the group one way or the other. If, for instance, they are asked to perform an illegal or antisocial act, a refusal may deter others in the group, whilst an acceptance may encourage them. And sometimes researchers may be seen as odd and out-of-place, for instance if they ask too many nosey or naive questions.

Other methods

All of the methods discussed so far are widely used across many fields in social psychology. Many more specialist areas of social psychology have their own particular research methods, sometimes borrowed from other disciplines and modified for use in social psychology. For instance, chapter 5 mentioned conversation analysis as a method for investigating social aspects of language use. And some of the discursive methods mentioned in chapter 14 use discourse analysis, which has been heralded as novel, innovative and developed at least in part within social psychology (although drawing upon many other traditions in the study of language) as part of the reaction against the experimental method (Potter and Wetherell 1987). As a marked break with the bulk of social psychology which treats language as a peripheral or unimportant phenomenon, discourse analysis attempts to deal explicitly with language as the central phenomenon in human interaction. Rather than seeing the imprecise ways in which language is used as an annoyance, and as a source of bias in self-report data, the ways in which meanings are fluid and continually renegotiated by speakers are seen as central to the way in which we make sense of the social world.

Many of the chapters in the book make comparative analyses between different cultures to further understanding of the specificity or universality of certain phenomena, as, for example, in chapter 4's discussion of cultural differences in the expression of emotion, or in chapter 18, where the relationship between the wealth of a country and the happiness of its citizens is considered. And as well as comparisons between human societies, the study of interpersonal relationships makes comparisons between human social relationships and those found in primates in their natural settings. In the past, social psychologists have sometimes experimented on animals in laboratory settings; unfortunately a few of those experiments have caused even greater pain and psychological trauma to animals than many medical experiments.

Other social psychologists have sometimes been lucky enough or perceptive enough to be in the right time and place to study fascinating phenomena such as a riot (Reicher 1984). Others have, in the course of their research, worked with survivors of some of the most brutal social environments, such as the concentration camps in World War II, and have made important advances in our understanding of normal development on the basis of the psychological damage done to the victims of those environments (see chapter 6 for a description of Anna Freud's work with children who survived the Holocaust). The accounts of children raised without any social contact with other humans, or of the deficits in the cognition of autistic children, all share the same logic – that by studying the exceptions to the rule, the rules themselves can be understood in a new light.

Other examples of specialist methods can be found in studies of emotion and health and illness, where sometimes blood or urine samples are used instead of, or as well as, self-report to obtain objective measures of physiological states. And studies of cognition sometimes use individuals with brain injuries (often from war wounds or brain surgery) as evidence for the functioning of normal brains. This innovative methodological eclecticism has often been able to verify or challenge accepted positions, and is one of the great strengths of social psychology.

Quantification

An important decision facing researchers is the extent to which we quantify – or put numbers to – the data which is measured, whether in an experiment, survey or observational study. Some data we routinely deal with in a numerical form. For instance, whenever we talk about our age, how many pints of lager we drank last night, or our blood pressure, we do so in numbers. One of the great achievements of psychology in the twentieth century was to determine techniques to put numbers to many psychological variables. Although we might at times think it a little simplistic, we nevertheless are used to the idea that we can measure attitudes, values and beliefs (chapters 12 and 13), intelligence and personality traits (chapter 2), our psychological health (chapters 16 and 17), and our many other characteristics and behaviours numerically. Such quantification makes the whole process of research much easier – we can apply statistical techniques to compare different conditions in an experiment, the relationship between intelligence, personality and styles of parenting, or lifestyles and stress.

However, there are also disadvantages with the quantification of psychological phenomena. Some researchers have argued that, all too often, such quantification has led to oversimplification, and that concepts such as personality or psychological well-being, once quantified, lose much of their meaning. Instead, these researchers advocate methods that treat data in non-numerical ways. In the past there has been fierce debate between these two positions, and it has often been politicized, with claims that some qualitative methods are more sympathetic to a feminist perspective, while quantitative research is associated with a masculine orthodoxy. Now pragmatism has taken over, as it is increasingly apparent that different types of research are best suited to different types of problem. Very often a particular theoretical or applied problem is best tackled by taking several different approaches. If they all reach the same conclusions, all well and good, but if they do not then that often gives deeper insights into the complexity of the initial problem.

Ethics

All research raises ethical issues. You may well, in the course of reading this book, have raised an eyebrow or two at some of the antics of social psychologists in the course of their research. They have often deceived people; they have caused alarm to young babies (chapter 6); they have deliberately put people into bad moods (chapter 11); and they have injected potent hormones into innocent experimental participants (chapter 4). Other transgressions may be milder; for instance, a participant observer gaining entry to a group by deception. Some of the sensitive topics which social psychologists raise with respondents could leave them feeling upset or disturbed, particularly when using vulnerable participants (e.g. psychiatric patients). These problems are exacerbated in much psychological research because often we cannot ask participants for their consent (for instance, in field experiments or participant observation studies), or because, even if they do consent to take part, they are being kept in the dark about what they have actually consented to (this is particularly a problem in those laboratory experiments which require deception).

Some social psychologists used to be quite cavalier about such things, confident that most things were acceptable if done in the name of science. Such issues would usually now be considered by an ethics committee before such research could proceed. There is not the space here to go into all of the arguments as to what should and should not be permitted and the justifications given, but these issues are now taken much more seriously than was once the case, and some of what has been done in social psychology in the past would send a modern ethics committee apoplectic. The British Psychological Society, the American Psychological Association and their equivalent organizations in other countries now give clear ethical guidelines for research, and make it clear that, as far as possible, participants in research should be fully informed and able to make an informed choice whether to participate in research. Furthermore, the debriefing of subjects is now routine, so that investigators will quickly detect it if their methods are causing any unforeseen stress to the participants.

The research process

Research findings do not stand alone, but build upon each other and form a body of literature. One of the tasks early on in the research process is usually to read any previous research and theorizing on a topic, so that new research can build upon firm foundations without reinventing the wheel each time. Similarly, when a study or series of studies has been completed successfully, it is important to publish that work so that it is available to the rest of the research community and other interested parties.

There are, of course, many ways in which research can be disseminated – for instance, sometimes research produces findings of such importance or topical interest that the researchers issue a press release directly to the popular media. But more generally dissemination takes place through refereed academic journals and books.

Social psychological papers intended for academic journals tend to be written in a very closely defined and formal style. They start with an introduction to the field, a survey of relevant previous research, and a justification for the research to be presented. There then follows a section where the exact method is described in some detail, and then the results of the study, and the results of any statistical work on the data, are presented. The paper ends with a discussion of the interpretation of the results, their relevance to theoretical or applied fields, and perhaps suggestions for further research. Often the whole paper is preceded by a short abstract, giving a brief summary of the most important parts.

Papers submitted to psychological journals are typically read anonymously by at least two referees, experts in that field chosen by the journal editors. The majority of papers submitted (certainly to the more prestigious journals) are rejected as being flawed in their research design or of little relevance to the advancement of knowledge. Referees will often also make suggestions for improving the research paper, perhaps by taking account of other theoretical positions or by improving the statistical analyses of the data. Then, if and when the paper is published, it is open to scrutiny by the rest of the academic community. Its title, authors and abstract are also stored on computer in bibliographic databases, which can be searched by other researchers who are interested in a particular topic. For instance, if one were interested in the effects of unemployment on self-esteem, one could search the database for all of the articles published in, say, the last ten years with those words in the title or abstract. This might suggest ways in which research could further advance knowledge, and so the cycle between the literature and research continues.

With the exponential growth in research and publications in social psychology, it is not unusual to find dozens, or even hundreds, of previous studies in the literature all focusing on one particular issue. And, given all of the difficulties of doing research in social psychology that you have read about in this chapter, it would not surprise you by now if all of those articles seem to be reporting different findings. Even the most patient of scholars might want to throw in the towel.

Fortunately, increasing numbers of social psychologists are taking this problem very seriously by conducting meta-analyses on many of the important questions in social psychology. This involves collecting together all of the research on a particular topic (unpublished as well as published, which causes further headaches). These studies are then very systematically combined, using specialist statistical techniques to arrive at an overall conclusion, and to determine which are the important moderators of the effects in question. For instance, is it important whether the participants are male or female, British or American? Do the types of manipulations used in the experiment matter, or the types of measurements taken, and so on? These meta-analyses, if done with sufficient care, can then provide a more reliable picture, less dependent on any one study or researcher.

Research and theory

The other way in which progress in social psychology can be seen as a cyclical process is in the relationship between theory and empirical research. Traditionally research, particularly experimental research, would be seen as a way of testing a theory; the exact way in which the outcome of the experiment might support or reject the theory could be specified in advance. If the experimental hypotheses were supported, so would be the theory. If, however, the experimental hypotheses were rejected, then the theory could be rejected or, more typically, modified. (It is rarely that simple in practice, as one also has to wonder whether the experiment really was a good test of the theory, or whether it was, after all, testing something quite different, or perhaps subverted by poor internal validity or misinterpretation of the data.)

But others have suggested that instead of a top-down approach, research should start at the bottom with the data and lead from that to theory (Glaser and Strauss 1967). Instead of starting with an abstract theory and a hypothesis derived from that theory, they proposed that it was more useful to start by collecting some data, and being guided by that as to what a useful theory might look like. Thus, they suggest that theory should emerge and be refined as the research progresses; theory should be grounded in observation (thus the term *grounded theory*) rather than from grand theories conjured up in the comfort of an ivory tower. But once a theory has emerged from data, it could be further tested in a more deductive way.

Conclusions

This chapter has permitted only the briefest consideration of an enormous topic, and some issues have received no mention whatsoever – for instance, the special problems associated with researching children, or the value (if any) of using animals in psychology experiments for furthering our understanding of human behaviour. However, the list of suggested further readings at the end of the chapter extends it in both depth and breadth.

There are a number of ways in which to characterize methods within social psychology. For some, the term 'mainstream social psychology' is synonymous with 'experimental social psychology'. This is a position which, many would argue, has done a lot of damage to the discipline; such a narrow methodological basis has limited the scope and relevance of social psychology, and restricted the ways in which it could advance. Topics which were not amenable to experimentation were thus marginalized.

Others see social psychologists as having at their disposal an impressive shopping list of methods, which can be selected and taken off the shelf where appropriate to a particular research problem. Each of these packages comes with a wealth of examples from previous successful and unsuccessful applications, and a literature advising on the most accurate ways of proceeding while successfully avoiding known pitfalls. This can be taken further; because of the inherent complexity of studying human nature, we should be sceptical of the findings of any one method, and can therefore be more confident of any findings or theory if we obtain supportive evidence from more than one method. This 'belt and braces' approach is often termed triangulation. The findings of any one method can be carefully evaluated and interpreted in terms of the pros and cons of the method employed, and different methods can be used to complement each other's deficiencies. For instance, if a researcher investigating the connection between observed violence and aggression could not only establish, under laboratory experimental conditions, that the two are causally related, but could also demonstrate under less artificial conditions that, say, criminals convicted of crimes of violence report in interviews having had a preference for violent television programmes, and if participant observers in violent gangs report that fights are analysed and compared to violent scenes in films, then the weight of evidence is far greater than could be claimed from any one method. And if the findings of such research can be successfully applied in intervention studies, we can be even more confident. It is thus important not to classify some methods as inherently better than others, but rather to be aware of the particular strengths and particular weaknesses of any given technique, so that we can very precisely evaluate what new knowledge a given study contributes, and which questions it leaves unanswered. So whilst we may not find adequate internal validity and external validity and be able to unravel direction of cause in any one study, a carefully designed series of interrelated studies using complementary methods will give a much more complete understanding of a given phenomenon.

But the best research is rarely characterized by mindlessly following the rules. Much research, it could be argued, is simply a demonstration of the obvious (or what is believed to be obvious) because it is thought that an argument with empirical backing will carry more weight than an argument without (Billig 1988; Rogers et al. 1995). Rather, real advances in knowledge occur through careful scholarship, where the methods of research are considered with the same great care as the theoretical coherence of a position.

RECOMMENDED READING

Bannister, P., Burman, E., Parker, I., Taylor, M. and Tindall, C. (1994) *Qualitative Methods in Psychology: A Research Guide*. Buckingham: Open University Press.
This gives a guide to some 'alternative' non-experimental methods.

Breakwell, G. L., Hammond, S. and Fife-Shaw, C. (eds) (2000) *Research Methods in Psychology*. 2nd edn. London: Sage.
This very comprehensive guide to most of the methods you are likely to come across in social psychology also has a section on data analysis.

Dyer, C. (1995) *Beginning Research in Psychology: A Practical Guide to Research Methods and Statistics*. Oxford: Blackwell.
This is a useful book to start you off on a research project.

The Nature of Social Psychology

- Introduction
- A brief history of social psychology
- Alternative conceptions of social psychology
- Conclusions
- Recommended reading

Introduction

So what is social psychology? If, by now, you have not decided that for yourself, let me tell you what it is! This final chapter will attempt to do that in two ways. First, it will offer a short and selective history of social psychology, which should help you understand why the contents and methods you have been reading about have taken the forms that they have. Then, it will discuss briefly some possible alternative conceptions of social psychology, before expanding the definition of social psychology with which we started chapter 1 into the broader view which has provided the distinctive approach of our introduction to social psychology.

A brief history of social psychology

It is possible to claim that the roots of present-day social psychology are just about discernible in the writings of the great Greek philosophers, with the views of Aristotle and Plato, for example, anticipating current disputes about the relative contributions of nature and nurture to social behaviour. And most of the major social and political philosophers since then can be claimed as distant ancestors of our discipline (see G. W. Allport 1985). Although less scholarly, it is much quicker to begin our history more than a couple of millennia later than Allport did, by pointing to the year 1908. In that year there appeared the first two English-language textbooks titled *Social Psychology*. They were by McDougall, a British psychologist of biological leanings, and E. A. Ross, an environmentally oriented American sociologist, which conveniently introduces three contrasts which will reappear in this chapter: psychology vs. sociology; European vs. North American; biological vs. environmental.

Social psychology is often described as having a long past but a short history, in that as a distinct intellectual enterprise it has existed for less than a century. According to Farr (1996), 'modern social psychology' is not much more than half-a-century old. Social psychology's origins are seen as lying in the slightly older 'parent' disciplines of general or experimental psychology and sociology, with the former being the more influential parent – the mother, perhaps. An understanding of the history of social psychology requires a brief excursion into the history of experimental psychology.

An excursion into experimental psychology

Experimental psychology itself broke away from its 'parental' disciplines, philosophy and physiology, from about the middle of the nineteenth century. It is usually claimed, for instance, that the first full-blown, psychological laboratory was established in 1879, in Leipzig, by Wilhelm Wundt. Notice that, from very early in its history, psychology saw itself as not merely an empirical discipline, as opposed to philosophy, but actually a laboratory experimental science (see chapter 19).

Psychology's primary concern, until the early twentieth century, was the study of the higher mental processes or the structure of the mind. Participants in laboratories were asked to report on what they experienced, what images passed through their minds, when carefully controlled stimuli were presented to them. Reporting on one's own mental experiences was dubbed introspection. From around the turn of the century, especially in the USA, objections to this introspective, mentalistic psychology strengthened, and they came from a variety of sources. Some pointed out that such an approach could not be applied to animals or children. Others proposed that psychology should become more functional and applied. Early followers of Freud claimed that the powerful unconscious processes in which they believed – though many academic psychologists did not, and still do not – were not amenable to introspection. The most radical critics, however, were the behaviourists, whose most prominent spokesman was J. B. Watson (1913; 1919). They insisted that introspective, mentalistic psychology was unscientific. There was no way in which claims about the workings of the mind arrived at via introspection could be independently observed and validated. Only overt behaviour was open to direct observation by independent observers. To be accepted as a science, psychology should confine itself to the study of behaviour, and the more extreme behaviourists (e.g. Skinner 1938; J. B. Watson 1919) argued that psychology should avoid all theorizing about unobservable internal processes. The so-called behaviourist revolution came to dominate experimental psychology, especially in North America, for approximately four decades, although as we shall see, it never gained the same domination over the infant social psychology.

In the 1950s, signs of a counter-revolution emerged in experimental psychology (see G. A. Miller 1966), which turned into the so-called cognitive revolution, and the study of cognition has dominated psychology since. From your reading of chapter 3, I hope you will agree that cognition can be roughly defined as 'higher mental processes'. Does that mean that from about 1960 onwards experimental psychology has been, in principle, the same as it had been in 1880? Yes and no. The higher mental processes are the primary concern of contemporary experimental psychology, which has renamed itself 'cognitive psychology'. Cognitive psychologists are usually methodological behaviourists but definitely not conceptual behaviourists. That means they more or less accept the argument that, wherever possible, psychology should work with observable behaviours which can be independently checked, but they reject the claim that there should be no theorizing about unobservable, internal processes. Indeed, cognitive psychology continually constructs theories of how the mind and mental processes work, but it insists that those theories should generate explicit predictions about specific behaviours that should result if the theories are correct. In that way, psychology guards against empty or vacuous 'explanations' based on uncontrolled invention of claimed but unobservable processes.

Much of what has just been asserted of general, experimental psychology also applies to social psychology. Currently, as previous chapters should have made clear, it too is dominated by the study of cognitive processes, though behaviour is also of considerable interest, and as chapter 4 showed, emotions are beginning to receive more attention than hitherto. Social psychologists, in general, also practise methodological behaviourism while strongly rejecting conceptual behaviourism. These similarities are not surprising, because the influence of experimental psychology on social psychology has been considerable, as a brief history of social psychology itself will now demonstrate.

Social psychology's immediate precursors

What preceded the appearance in 1908 of its first two English-language textbooks? Its immediate precursors can be discerned for about half a century beforehand, including the ideas of a number of European thinkers. Gustave Lebon, Gabriel Tarde and the sociologist Emile Durkheim in France; Georg Simmel, Wilhelm Wundt and another major sociologist, Max Weber, in Germany; Sigmund Freud in Austria; and Charles Darwin, Herbert Spencer and William McDougall in Britain can all be seen, in some respects at least, as influences on the emerging discipline. We might speculate that, had their influences prevailed, then social psychology would have emerged as a largely theoretically oriented enterprise with a strong emphasis on biological influences on social functioning. But social psychology did not establish itself readily in Europe. Instead it emerged most obviously in the United States of America. That may have been because a psychologically inclined social analysis was more acceptable there, because of a pervasive individualism in American social and political life. Or perhaps prestigious American universities, such as Harvard, were more ready to institutionalize social psychology and other social sciences than were older, high-status European universities such as Cambridge or Leipzig. It is certainly thought-provoking that early attempts by Wundt (1900–20) in Leipzig, and Bartlett (e.g. 1923) in Cambridge, to develop ambitious social psychologies were ignored, or perhaps suppressed, for decades until their much later 'rediscovery' (see Danziger 1979; Saito 2000b). When social psychology did emerge early in the twentieth century in the United States, it was not the biologically and theoretically oriented discipline speculated about above. Instead it rapidly adopted the environmentalism of early American sociology and the empiricism of American psychology, and those two broad characteristics have continued to be true of social psychology.

Influences from sociology and psychology

The main sociological influence on early social psychology was what has come to be called 'the Chicago school of symbolic interactionism' (Meltzer, Petras and Reynolds 1975; Plummer 1991), derived in turn from American pragmatic philosophy. The gist of symbolic interactionism was presented in chapter 2 on the self, and G. H. Mead's (1934) account of the largely social construction of an individual's sense of self through interaction with others has been substantially absorbed into contemporary social psychology. Other symbolic interactionists who have contributed ideas have included Cooley, Thomas and, more recently, Goffman (e.g. 1959) (see chapter 2). Sociological influences have also been a source of opposition to the uncritical use of laboratory experimenting as the principal methodology of social psychology, which was criticized in the previous chapter. But the influence of sociology has never been as stong as that of experimental psychology and, as judged for example by the frequency of social psychology textbooks emanating from psychology departments or from sociology departments, the disparity may have increased over the years (Jones 1985).

American psychologists who exerted some influence on the beginnings of social psychology included James M. Baldwin, G. S. Hall and William James, but it was less the ideas of particular psychologists and much more the general practices of psychology that proved especially influential. A very early – perhaps the first – line of sustained empirical inquiry in social psychology started with a study in America by Triplett (1898). It is often hailed as social psychology's first laboratory experiment; interestingly, the fact that Triplett also made use of non-laboratory empirical evidence is often overlooked. In order to assess the impact of the presence of others on the efficiency of individual performance, Triplett got children to wind in string on gadgets like large fishing reels either on their own or competitively in pairs. From this study there developed a line of research on the consequences of the presence of others, which has been and is still pursued as *social facilitation* (e.g. Zajonc 1965; Geen 1991). Like numerous other subsequent lines of research in social psychology, this type of research tradition has asked apparently limited questions and has been content to develop limited-scale theories to deal with them. The questions appear to be readily answerable, though frequently they prove to be more complex than originally thought, and they lend themselves to experimental studies in laboratories. When answers start to emerge, investigators are inclined to assume, until evidence to the contrary accumulates, that the answers hold universally. This helps to explain why most empirical evidence in social psychology comes from university undergraduates, for if you assume phenomena and processes are universal, it does not much matter whom you choose to study, and students are conveniently close at hand. Each of these features can be regarded as a legacy from experimental psychology, and the general approach has been and still is typical of most social psychology, especially in North America.

In the first few decades of the twentieth century, research in social psychology, largely in America, slowly increased its scope. The study of 'side-by-side' (i.e. non-interactive) groups extended into the much broader arena of face-to-face interactive groups (e.g. Lewin, Lippitt and White 1939). Terman (1904) commenced the study of leadership, attempting to locate personality traits that characterized leaders. The study of personality itself (see chapter 2) became more common (G. W. Allport 1937). Quite sophisticated scales were devised for measuring attitudes on a wide range of topics (Thurstone 1928; Likert 1932), and Gordon Allport (1935) wrote a very influential chapter on attitudes.

Note that it was Gordon Allport who wrote important pieces about personality and attitudes. His brother, Floyd Allport (1924), had written a textbook which attempted to transform social psychology into a behaviouristic, and rather individualistic, discipline. Some other social psychologists paid forms of lip service to behaviourism by adopting some of its terminology. But, in general, social psychology was never dominated by behaviourism in the way that American experimental psychology was. It was as if dealing with the complexities of social attitudes and actions led social psychologists largely to ignore the self-imposed restrictions of the behaviourists. A good case in point is Gordon Allport. In his chapter on attitudes, which appeared in 1935, in the heyday of behaviourism, he very deliberately asserted the inner reality of attitudes by defining them as 'mental and neural states of readiness' (see chapter 12). Throughout its history, social psychology seems always to have been primarily cognitive in its orientation.

Following the end of World War II, according to Farr (1996), 'modern social psychology' started to flourish in North America, due in part to the influence of Kurt Lewin, who had fled Nazi Germany, and his American students and junior colleagues (see Festinger 1980; Jones 1985). Social psychology became even more cognitive as well as more rigorous and laboratory based. The concern with rigour led to the somewhat self-conscious creation in the 1960s of a view of the future of social psychology as experimental social psychology, whereby prestigious work would virtually be confined to elegant experiments conducted in well-equipped laboratories and interpreted in terms of carefully formulated mini-theories. In this way, it would be demonstrated that social psychology could be as rigorous as experimental psychology itself. A decade of such endeavours was enough to provoke numerous criticisms. Two complementary critiques deserve mention, those of scope and of method.

Critiques of scope and method

Criticisms that social psychology had become too narrow in its interests, by studying cognitive processes of individuals and the minutiae of interaction removed from any broader social concerns or analyses, came primarily from the recently emerged European social psychology (Moscovici 1972; Tajfel 1972). Hitherto, social psychology had not flourished in Europe. By the early 1960s there were only a modest number of research-oriented social psychologists scattered across Europe, and by and large their only contacts with colleagues outside their own country were with American social psychologists. But driven by convictions that an alternative cultural view would be very healthy for social psychology, and that the 'critical mass' of active researchers necessary to generate such a view would not be forthcoming from any single European country, a European organization of social psychology was established in 1966, and it quickly flourished. In 1971 it founded the *European Journal of Social Psychology*, and then came an influential monograph series. New lines of research originated in Europe, including work on social identity and intergroup relations (see chapter 15), social representations (see chapter 14), language (see chapter 5), and group polarization and minority influence (see chapter 8). A recurring theme in these innovations was that social psychology had become too narrow and insufficiently concerned with society at large. What was needed was a broad, fully 'social' social psychology (Tajfel 1984; Himmelweit and Gaskell 1990).

Social psychology in Europe did not wish or try to cut itself entirely free from social psychology in North America. Friendly and constructive rivalry was the goal, not outright rejection. That was symbolized by the title of the new European organization, the 'European Association of Experimental Social Psychology'. The 'experimental' in the title reflected the spirit, the American spirit, of the times. In practice, the association has never attempted to enforce an adherence to experimental methods. Numerous exponents of other methodologies have been elected members. 'Experimental' has seemed to have been taken to mean 'serious', 'high-quality', 'committed' rather than 'laboratory experimenting'. Nevertheless, the title of the Association indicates that although social psychology in Europe was critical of the scope of mainstream American social psychology, it did not launch a critique of its methods.

Almost the reverse is true of an alternative line of criticism. Sociologists interested in social interaction, such as the symbolic interactionists, had always been critical of the use of laboratory experiments, and such criticisms continued in America (Denzin 1978; Garfinkel 1967). In Britain, the philosopher of science Rom Harré mounted a similar attack on the appropriateness of laboratory experiments for the study of human social experience, on the grounds of their artificiality (see chapter 19) and the mechanistic view of the individual which, it was claimed, they imply (Harré and Secord 1972). This line of attack was methodological in a much broader sense than just criticizing a particular research method. It argued that social psychology was unjustifiably positivistic in adopting the approach of the physical sciences in trying to understand human beings. Despite this apparently far-reaching critique, in practice the content of the 'different' social psychology that was envisaged seemed to bear a strong resemblance to that of experimental social psychology, namely the thought processes of individuals and the minutiae of face-to-face interaction, with little concern for a broader social perspective (see Fraser 1981).

Many of the same points can be made about a related, more recent challenge to mainstream social psychology, social constructionism, which you have briefly encountered in chapters 14 and 17. According to its best-known exponent, Gergen (1985; 1999), 'Social constructionist enquiry is principally concerned with explicating the processes by which people come to describe, explain or otherwise account for the world (including themselves) in which they live' (1985, p. 266). Shotter (1993) adds that psychological and sociological 'realities' are socially constructed and sustained within the context of our everyday conversational activities. Social constuctionism appears to see itself as an alternative to the social psychology that has emerged over the past century, being an anti-positivistic enterprise which would reject laboratory methods, and perhaps quantitative methods more generally, in favour of an interpretative approach using qualitative methods (see chapter 19). How far it will succeed remains to be seen. So far it has produced broad statements of intent, some interesting criticisms of certain lines of mainstream ideas and research (e.g. Potter and Wetherall 1987), and analyses of conversation and discourse which usually lack the precision of the work on language in chapter 5. Like much of American social psychology, in practice it uses the term 'social' to mean 'interactional' rather than 'societal'.

Having read the foregoing selective history, you may wonder where this textbook stands with regard to it. This book can be thought of as a broad-ranging work coming from the edge of the mainstream. It is not written from a specific theoretical or methodological stance. Instead it attempts to present major topics in the ways that make most sense to the contributors. It presents a mixture of mainstream and non-mainstream, European and American, ideas and evidence. It accepts the very general assumptions of science that evidence should be reliable and, if possible, replicable, and that theories should be clearly formulated and amenable to empirical testing, while recognizing that there are important differences in how social scientists and physical scientists can proceed. The single most crucial difference is that people, unlike inanimate objects, are conscious, thoughtful beings aware of the context in which they are behaving. We present substantial amounts of American work, including parts of experimental social psychology, without which a textbook of social psychology would be a rather slim volume. However, we sympathize strongly with the critique concerning the scope of social psychology, and that is reflected by the inclusion of a number of chapters on areas not commonly found in standard textbooks, including chapters 2, 6, 10, 14, 16, 17 and 18. Although we do not subscribe to the extreme methodological critiques which advocate the abandonment of much of social psychology, we are sympathetic to the greater use of non-experimental methods. We also accept that social life is largely constructed by social actors and the societies they live in. In short, we believe this book represents a broad view of social psychology.

Alternative conceptions of social psychology

Like any area of academic study, social psychology can be, and has been, conceived of and defined in a number of somewhat different ways. I will present, simply, four possible conceptions of social psychology. The first will be quickly discarded and the remaining three will be collapsed into two current conceptions, namely narrower and broader views of social psychology:

- what social psychologists do;
- the study of individuals;
- the study of social interaction;
- individual, interaction and society.

One very down-to-earth view is that social psychology is simply what social psychologists do. That was the position of as discerning a social psychologist as the late Roger Brown (1965; 1986). In 1965 he wrote that, 'Social psychology . . . is a set of topics that have exceeded the grasp of a non-social psychology but which are being effectively investigated by a psychology which draws upon the social sciences.' And for good measure he added, 'Social psychology is a field of study, an historical development, not a theoretical construct' (1965, pp. xix–xx). In different words, he repeated the argument in 1986. When, at the very beginning of this book, you were invited to start almost immediately reading about the substance of social pschology, that may have seemed to be implying something similar to Brown. But you were told to read chapters 19 and 20 whenever you felt ready to think about the nature of social psychology. The clear implication of that is that social psychology is more than just an arbitrary list of interesting topics. There is an underlying conception that is important. One reason for its importance is that, without such a conception, how would we ever know if we have got the list right? There could be major issues being ignored by social psychologists, and other topics receiving far more attention than their relevance for social psychology merits. So let us proceed on the assumption that we cannot avoid defining social psychology as a discipline by claiming that it is just a changing list or set of topics. What is it then?

One conceivable answer, and our second conception of social psychology, is that it is about individuals. If general, experimental psychology is the scientific study of the experience and behaviour of individual organisms, then social psychology might be the scientific study of the individual as influenced by other individuals. Such a definition might, at first sight, seem to apply quite well to some of the issues in this book, especially part I on personality, for example. But this definition is unsatisfactory. It is overly individualistic and as a result likely to be overly psychological. Surely we want social concepts as well as psychological ones in social psychology. An array of 'other individuals' is not much of a social analysis. An exclusive focus on individuals is likely to lead to reductionism, of two possible types. Psychological reductionism is the attempt to explain social phenomena exclusively in psychological terms, such as trying to account for prejudice and intergroup hostilities in terms of personality characteristics (see chapter 15). Biological reductionism asserts that important aspects of individual functioning are directly the results of genes or instincts or other biological, or quasi-biological, concepts. Individuals are clearly a major part of social psychology's concerns, but conceiving social psychology exclusively in terms of individuals is obviously inadequate.

An alternative, third conception would be to insist that social psychology is really about social interaction processes, including interpersonal relations and small groups. This view might seem to apply well to part II, and there are a few points which can be made in its favour. It avoids an exclusive focus on individuals by implying that, often, the unit of analysis has to be greater than a single person; as we have seen in chapters 6, 7 and 8, for example, it may have to be an interpersonal unit such as a relationship or group. This reveals part of the complexity of the task of the social psychologist; problems of studying and explaining the behaviour and experience of even two people simultaneously can be more than twice as difficult as those involved in dealing with just one individual at a time. An interactional conception of social psychology also makes the point that individuals cannot be understood in isolation. Understanding why individuals do what they do frequently requires an understanding of their relations with family, friends, workmates and others. Emphasizing interaction also helps make social psychology more distinctive. It becomes harder to see it merely as an after-thought of experimental psychology. But do we wish to study interaction processes and groups just to grasp the fine details of interaction processes? Is there not a danger of ending up with a social psychology of nothing but nods and twitches and the obsessive analysis of conversations? Surely social psychology amounts to more than that. There would also be the problem of trying to study interaction in a social vacuum. Just as we have recognized that the individual needs to be understood in terms of relations with others, so interactions between individuals must be put in a broader social context, for that context may well markedly influence the forms that interaction and individual actions take, as we saw in chapters 3 and 4 regarding syllogistic reasoning and the facial expression of emotion, as well as at numerous points in subsequent chapters. Social psychology is not just about possible psychological and interactional universals; it is also about systematic social and cultural variations and differences. Individuals, and their interactions, have to be related to the societies in which they live. Hence our fourth conception of social psychology is the conception summarized in the definition of social psychology offered at the beginning of this book..

Social psychology is the study of the interrelations amongst individuals, their inter-actions and the societies they live in. As explained earlier, the primary focus of social psychology is not the individual or interaction or society, but the interrelations amongst the three. Individuals interact with others and sometimes influence broader aspects of society by doing so. Society and its institutions influence individuals and the ways in which they interact. It is through interaction with others that individuals most com-monly encounter society and its institutions, expectations and influences.

In arriving at the conception of social psychology that underlies this textbook, it may seem as if I have been 'cooking the books' by offering alternatives views of social psychology that are obviously too narrow to be realistic. There may be an element of truth in that, but their brief exposition does permit me to draw one final distinction which I believe is informative regarding contemporary social psychology, and that is a contrast between a broader and a narrower view.

Broader and narrower views of social psychology

A broader view is represented by this book. Where can a narrower view be found? 'In most other textbooks of social psychology, especially North American ones', is my answer. Much of contemporary social psychology seems unduly narrow in a number of respects. Admittedly it is no longer called 'experimental social psychology'. It has been updated, rather thinly disguised and renamed 'cognitive social psychology'. Studies of cognition and interaction still generally seem to take place in psychological laboratories within a social vacuum. In short, the narrower view of social psychology, which is currently the most commonly encountered view, consists of a mixture of two of the simple conceptions outlined above: those focusing on individuals and on social inter-action. In practice, there are a number of differences in emphasis which help to distinguish the broader and narrower views. These are summarized in box 20.2, and help to convey some of the distinctiveness of this textbook.

Box 20.1   Two views of Social Psychology

A broader view	The narrower view
More diffuse	More focused
Individual + Interaction + Society	Individual + Interaction
More European	More American
Independent discipline	Part of general psychology
Developmental	Non-developmental
More interdisciplinary	Less interdisciplinary
Cultural differences	Universals
Multiple research methods	Laboratory experiments
Social = Societal	Social = Interpersonal

In discussing each of these differences in turn, let me emphasize very strongly that I am invoking rough and ready general tendencies that help draw attention to the ways in which a broader conception attempts to move beyond the more standard, narrower conception. There are clear exceptions to every contrast. It would be ridiculous, for example, to claim that all European social psychologists adopt a broader perspective than all their North American counterparts. Indeed, as some European interests become narrower and some American research broader, that difference is probably diminishing.

More diffuse vs. More focused   If I asked you if you favoured the broader or narrower conception of 'phlogiston', you might well claim a preference for the former even if you had not the faintest idea what I was asking you about. After all, on most things it sounds much more enlightened to have a broader than a narrower outlook. So to be fair, I should point out that the price of breadth regarding social psychology can be a relative lack of agreement about boundaries and contents. In the narrower view there is considerable consensus on just what should be included. For example, most American textbooks of social psychology manifest substantial agreement on the chapters, and even the number of chapters, they contain. This textbook has five or six additional chapters, as well as other distinctive emphases, and had pressure on length not prevailed, there could have been even more chapters, on social psychology and economic, environmental, legal and political issues, amongst others.

Individual + Interaction + Society vs. Individual + Interaction   That key contrast has already been discussed, but is included in box 20.2 for completeness sake.

European vs. North American   Much of the impetus for a broader, more social social psychology came with the emergence of social psychology in Europe in the 1960s and 1970s. Criticisms of the then current social psychology were inevitably criticisms of the subject as it existed in America, because that was where most of social psychology had developed. Not all European social psychologists espoused the criticisms. Some accepted the American approach. Some Americans also harbour reservations about the scope of social psychology, and some of the fire has gone out of the European critique. But a broader view is still somewhat more likely to be encountered in European writings in social psychology. It can also be found in the even more recent flourishing of social psychology in Latin America and elsewhere, and in continuing contributions from sociologists.

Independent discipline vs. Part of general psychology   A broader view is more inclined to take it for granted that social psychology is a discipline in its own right. It has been described as an 'interstitial science' which lies between, and attempts to relate, psychology and the biological sciences to sociology and the social sciences. In this view, the ideal training would be to study social psychology in conjunction with both general, experimental psychology and sociology. The narrower view assumes that social psychology is one of a number of subfields of general psychology, and that one should first train in general psychology and subsequently specialize in social psychology, should one wish to do so.

Developmental vs. Non-developmental   Since, in a broader view, social psychology is a discipline in its own right, it makes sense for it to incorporate substantial parts of some subfields of general psychology. It is particularly difficult, within a broader view, to draw a clear distinction between what, in the narrower view, are described as social psychology and developmental psychology. Most of developmental psychology – certainly what is called 'social development' – is social psychology. And social psychology would do well to adopt a life-span developmental approach, instead of confining itself, as in the narrower view, to normal adult functioning between the ages of about 18 and 50 and leaving acquisition and change before and after those ages, as well as changes between them, to developmental psychology. We have not attempted to incorporate most of developmental psychology into this book but we have clearly signalled our convictions on this issue, especially in chapters 6 and 10, and also in parts of other chapters, including 14 and 15.

More interdisciplinary vs. Less interdisciplinary   In a broader view there are at least two other disciplines of major concern for social psychologists, psychology and sociology, and they in turn may be regarded as points of entry into other social and biological sciences, such as social anthropology and genetics. The narrower view tends to be accompanied by a stronger sense of self-sufficiency, in which crossing disciplinary boundaries, particularly between psychology and sociology, is sometimes viewed with suspicion or distaste. This is one respect, and the previous contrast was another, in which the greater diffuseness of the broader view manifests itself.

Cultural differences vs. Universals   It is sometimes said of social psychology, in its narrower version, that most of its evidence comes from sophomores at the University of Michigan. Certainly a preponderance of evidence does come from university students. Whether that is regarded as sensible, because convenient, or problematic, because non-representative, depends, at least in part, on whether you adopt the narrower or broader view. The former, probably because it accepts the approach of a biologically oriented general psychology, tends to follow a strategy of assuming that findings will turn out to have universal applicability unless evidence accrues to the contrary. But searching for contrary evidence often does not seem to have very high priority. A broader view, however, with its close links to the other social sciences, tends to assume that systematic social variations associated with cultural and category differences are a major source of interest for social psychology, rather than unfortunate complications in a search for universal processes.

Multiple research methods vs. Laboratory experiments Despite often paying lip service to the value of using a variety of different research methods, the narrow view still is dominated by the use of laboratory experiments. A broader view is more eclectic. It does not reject rigorous experimenting, but it also values a range of alternatives, including sound observational studies, systematic surveys, ethnographies and qualitative evidence (see chapter 19), arguing that for different purposes in different contexts all have their strengths, just as all have weaknesses. Experiments have been overused and often used prematurely. That, rather than a denial of their potential value if used appropriately, is a broader view's criticism of laboratory experimenting.

Social = Societal vs. Social = Interpersonal The term 'social' can have at least six distinguishable meanings (W. J. McGuire 1986). Two of those meanings are particularly pertinent here. If asked what 'social' in 'social psychology' means, an exponent of a broader view is likely to say it means 'societal', whereas a proponent of the narrower view tends to define it as 'interpersonal' or 'interactional'. When some social psychologists urge the need for a more *social* social psychology, they can leave baffled a number of their colleagues who fail to see how social psychology can be more social when it is already studying interaction processes in great detail. If one of the contrasts just discussed can capture the difference between broader and narrower approaches, it is probably this difference in the implicit meaning of 'social'.

It should be clear from this discussion of broader and narrower views of social psychology that the broader view is a very ambitious conception of social psychology. In practice, it should be capable of accommodating virtually all of the narrower view while moving beyond that in the variety of respects just indicated. It is only honest to admit that the broader view has not yet been fully implemented. What has been outlined is part aspiration, part achievement. The hope of the contributors to this textbook is that we are not just showing you what social psychology is, we are also letting you see what it should be.

Conclusions

Social psychology was defined as the study of the interrelations amongst individuals, their interactions and the societies they live in. That broad and ambitious view of the discipline was elaborated on in two ways. First, a short, selective history of the discipline was offered. This drew attention to the impact on social psychology of general experimental psychology and, to a lesser degree, sociology. It also discussed two lines of critique of mainstream, mainly American, social psychology: critiques of scope and of method. Those issues reappeared in the second part of the chapter, a consideration of alternative conceptions of social psychology. That consideration concluded by elaborating on a contrast between the narrower view and a broader view of social psychology represented by this book.

RECOMMENDED READING

Allport, G. W. (1985) The historical background of social psychology. In G. Lindzey and E. Aronson (eds), *The Handbook of Social Psychology, Vol. 1*. 3rd edn. New York: Random House.
This is the classic, very scholarly account.

Farr, R. M. (1996) *The Roots of Modern Social Psychology 1872–1954*. Oxford: Blackwell.
This is a set of ten, short, related essays.

Jones, E. E. (1985) Major developments in social psychology during the past five decades. In G. Lindzey and E. Aronson (eds), *The Handbook of Social Psychology, Vol. 1*. 3rd edn. New York: Random House.
Jones gives a detailed account of modern, mainly American social psychology. Like Allport's chapter, it is not the easiest of reading for beginners.

Jones, E. E. and Colman, A. M. (1996) Social psychology. In A. and J. Kuper (eds), *The Social Science Encyclopedia*. 2nd edn. London: Routledge.
This is a short, authoritative and by no means extreme account of the narrower conception of social psychology.

Pettigrew, T. F. (1996) *How to Think Like a Social Scientist*. New York: Harper Collins.
This slim but wide-ranging book is written in the spirit of a broader view of social psychology.

Glossary

Terms in *italic* in the definitions refer to other entries in the glossary.

Action   A deliberate and intended behaviour; i.e. actions are a subset of behaviours. See also *theory of reasoned action*.

Actor–observer difference   The tendency for actors to overemphasize *external attributions* in explaining their own behaviour and underemphasize *internal attributions* when explaining the *behaviour* of others.

Aetiology   The study of causes of disease. Also spelled 'etiology'.

Affect   A general term used to refer to *emotions*, feelings, moods etc. Often contrasted with *cognition*.

Agency theory   An approach developed to understand the effects of *unemployment*, in response to Jahoda's analysis of *latent functions* of paid *work*. Agency theory asserts that individuals are active and try to plan for the future – in short, proactive rather than reactive or passive – and it is the frustration of agency that causes poor well-being in unemployment.

Aggression   *Behaviour* intended to harm a victim who is motivated to avoid the infliction of such physical and/or psychological pain. There are different types, such as *hostile aggression* and *instrumental aggression*.

Agreeableness   see *big five*.

Altruism   The motivation to improve someone else's welfare rather than one's own.

Altruistic behaviour   Conduct intended solely to benefit someone else rather than the helper.

Amygdala   An almond-shaped structure in the temporal lobe of the brain which is part of the limbic system. Involved in motivation and *aggression*.

Anchoring   In Moscovici's theory of *social representations*, the process whereby the novel or new is located within existing structures of meaning. In Moscovici's phrase, anchoring refers to the way in which the unfamiliar is made familiar. Contrast with *objectification*.

Anchoring and adjustment heuristic   A *heuristic* which causes ideas generated in the here and now to have biasing effects. When making judgements, the point at which we start our deliberations can have an *anchoring* effect, and subsequent adjustments to that estimate are thereby constrained.

Antisocial personality disorder   A *personality* disorder originating in childhood in which the individual has a chronic history of antisocial *behaviour*. See also *psychopathy* and *sociopathy*.

Artifact   In the context of statistical analysis, an incorrect or misleading inference due to a *bias* in the data collection.

Attachment   In the context of *development*: an emotional bond formed between an infant and one or more adults. In the context of studies of *relationships*: that aspect of a relationship that provides security to the partner.

Attitude   A relatively stable collection of *belief*s, feelings and intentions towards a person, *group* or object, all of which tend to be referred to as attitude objects.

Attitude accessibility   The speed or ease with which an *attitude* can be brought into consciousness.

Attitude change   Any significant alteration in an individual's *attitude*. This may occur through persuasion or following prior *behaviour* change.

Attitude object   See *attitude*.

Attribution   The process of explaining events, usually the actions of other people, by causes. There are different types, such as *internal* or *dispositional* and *external* or *situational attribution*s.

Autism   A condition found in some people in which they are said to display three symptoms: social isolation, poor *communication* skills, and stereotypy or repetitiveness in their *behaviour*.

Autobiographical memory   The memories people have of their own lives.

Autonomous thought   In a literal sense, thought that is not constrained. Although it is not constrained by social relations, it is, in Piaget's *epistemology*, subject to certain rational (or logico-mathematical) constraints. Autonomous thought is only possible from within relations of cooperation and is a feature of more mature moral reasoning. Contrast with *heteronomous thought*, and see also *morality*.

Availability heuristic   The tendency to assume that something which is more easily available in *mind* is more likely to reflect the state of affairs in the world. See also *heuristic*.

Behaviour   Broadly, any measurable response of an organism. Behaviour tends to refer to the observable actions and reactions of individuals and *groups*, in contrast with such *mentalistic* conceptions as thoughts, feelings, *attitudes*, *beliefs* etc.

Behaviourism   The approach to *psychology* which focuses solely on observable, measurable *behaviour*. This argues that mental processes cannot be investigated in a scientific manner. Contrast with *introspection* and *mentalistic*.

Belief   A *cognition* or piece of knowledge believed to be true or false regarding an *attitude* object.

Bias   A tendency towards a particular (often mistaken) position with regard to understanding one's own and other people's *behaviour*. There are different types of bias, such as *confirmation bias*, *self-serving bias*, the *fundamental attribution error* and the *actor–observer difference*.

Big five   The five *personality* dimensions – extroversion, agreeableness, conscientiousness, neuroticism and intellect – which many personality theorists believe underlie differences amongst individuals' *behaviour*.

Bio-psycho-social   Any approach that considers the interaction of biological, psychological and social factors which affect an individual's well-being. Initially developed as a critique of the *medical model*.

Blue-collar worker   Manual worker. Contrast *white-collar worker*.

Bottom-up   That part of perceptual or interpretative processes which is driven by the input to those psychological processes from the external world. Contrast with *top-down*.

Brainwashing   An extreme way of forcibly changing an individual's *attitude*, often using such techniques as sleep deprivation, social isolation and intensive interrogation.

Bystander effect   The tendency of a person to be less likely to help (and slower to respond) when in the presence of others than when alone. The greater the number of bystanders witnessing an emergency the less likely it is that any one of them will help.

Castration anxiety   In *psychoanalytic* theory, the fear of the son that the father as a competitor to the son for the mother's love will emasculate him to eliminate the competition.

Causation   A relationship between two *variables* such that one directly affects the other; changes in the former will cause changes in the latter.

Central route to persuasion   Attempts to persuade via carefully constructed, explicit arguments, according to the *elaboration likelihood model*. Contrast with *peripheral route*.

Child   A human being in the period of childhood. This period can cover birth to maturity, or infancy to adolescence/puberty.

Coercive power   A form of *social influence* involving the use of threats or punishment to gain compliance.

Cognition A term used broadly to refer to mental processes. Often contrasted with *affect*.

Cognitive balance See *cogitive consonance*.

Cognitive congruity See *cognitive consonance*.

Cognitive consistency See *cognitive consonance*.

Cognitive consonance A situation of consistency between the *beliefs* and *attitudes* that an individual holds and external circumstances. Also referred to as cognitive consistency, cognitive balance or cognitive congruity. Contrast with *cognitive dissonance*.

Cognitive dissonance An uneasy feeling claimed by the theory of cognitive dissonance to result from inconsistency between any two *cognitions*, where a cognition can reflect an *attitude*, *belief* or *behaviour*.

Cognitive psychology An approach to *psychology* which focuses on the mental processes and structures which are responsible for activities as diverse as *memory*, reasoning and *perception*.

Cognitive-response model of attitude change Greenwald's explanation of persuasion, emphasizing the receiver's active interpretation and responsiveness.

Cognitive style The typical style in which an individual functions cognitively. See also *cognition*.

Cohesion The tendency of a *group* to stick together and show unity in their *behaviour*s and *beliefs*. Also referred to as cohesiveness.

Cohesiveness See *cohesion*.

Cohort design A research design where a particular *group* of people who share some quality (e.g. all being born in the same week) are followed up over time. Similar to *panel design*.

Commitment The extent to which the participants in a *relationship* direct their *behaviour* towards maintaining the relationship over time or optimizing its properties.

Communication Any *interaction* that involves the transmission of information.

Communication model of attitude change An attempt to understand persuasive *communication* in terms of features of sender, message and receiver.

Compliance Change in overt *behaviour* (although not necessarily in underlying *beliefs*) as a result of *social influence*. Contrast with *conversion*.

Conation An almost archaic term meaning striving or exerting the will. As the third component of *tripartite conception of attitude*, roughly comparable to intention.

Confirmation bias The tendency to seek only information and ideas which support your existing views, and ignore those which reveal their failings.

Conformity The acceptance of *norm*s of a *group* by its members. Used as neutral, non-pejorative term in this book.

Confounding variable An uncontrolled or unintended *variable* which prevents an unambiguous conclusion that variations in the *dependent variable* result from differences in the *independent variable*. See also *prior variable*.

Connectionist See *parallel distributed processing*.

Connotation Associations or implications of a word rather than its literal meaning. To doting owners, the connotations of 'cats' may include company, elegance and homeliness. Contrast with *denotation*.

Conscienciousness See *big five*.

Consensual universe In Moscovici's theory of *social representation*s, a representation of knowledge in which phenomena are described in relation to human interests. The primary example of this form of knowledge is everyday common sense, which is sometimes referred to as taken-for-granted knowledge. Contrast with *reified universe*.

Conservation In Piaget's theory, the understanding that in any transformation something remains unchanged or conserved. For example, when a glass of water is poured into a differently shaped glass, the amount of water is conserved across this transformation. Understanding conservations requires the development of appropriate psychological structures, which for this example are the concrete operations Piaget described as developing in middle *child*hood.

Consistency In the context of *personality* theories, the idea that personality *trait*s will cause a person to behave in a similar way across similar situations (and sometimes across different situations).

Constructionist In *psychology* generally, constructionist (or constructivist) theories suggest that our knowledge and understanding of the world is the primary source for our action or *behaviour*, and that this knowledge is a constructive product of psychological activity. Some recent ideas in *social psychology* have argued that the process of construction is a function of the resources made available through the wider social and cultural environment. Frequently these resources have been considered as linguistic or *discursive* in character, so that construction is seen as emerging from communicative *interaction*.

Constructivist See *constructionist*.

Convention Standard social practice.

Conversation analysis An approach within *sociology* which is concerned with the analysis of *conversational organization*.

Conversational organization The phenomena of structure and regularity in the way that people speak to each other. Examples include regularities in the way conversations are begun and ended, and decisions as to who speaks and when in a multi-party conversation.

Conversion   Change in underlying *belief*s (also leading to change in overt *behaviour*) as a result of *social influence*. Contrast with *compliance*.

Correlation   Two *variables* are said to correlate if variation on one is systematically accompanied by variation on the other. If as one increases the other does, then this is a positive correlation. If, however, as one increases the other decreases, this is a negative correlation.

Cortex   Most usually used to refer to the cerebral cortex, i.e. the outer layer of the brain, in which human higher psychological functions are located.

Cross-sectional study   A type of research design where data collection is carried out, usually with *group*s of different ages, at one particular point in time. Contrast with *longitudinal study*.

Data-driven   See *bottom-up*.

Deduction   A type of reasoning which starts with a set of assumptions and then tries to derive specific conclusions or applications from them. Contrast *induction*.

Defensive mechanism   A *psychoanalytic* term to describe the way in which the *ego* deals with unacceptable unconscious impulses to make them acceptable. Examples include *repression*, *projection*, *reaction-formation* and *displacement*.

Deindividuation   The process of persons losing their sense of individuality. Often claimed to lead to an increase in forms of impulsive and/or deviant *behaviour*.

Demand characteristics   Features of an *experiment* that unintentionally tend to lead participants to behave in a particular way, as they try to be cooperative.

Denotation   The literal meaning of a word. The denotation of the word 'cats' is those four-legged mammals we think of as cats. Contrast with *connotation*.

Dependent variable (DV)   An 'outcome' *variable* which is measured as an indicator of the effects of the *independent variable*(s).

Depression   A condition in which the individual experiences deep levels of sadness and sometimes anxiety, is generally despondent and lethargic, finds it hard to engage in any mental or physical activity and feels inadequate. Depression can be subdivided in a variety of ways, but the simplest division is between 'endogenous', where the condition is driven by factors internal to the person, and 'reactive', where the condition arises in response to events in the external world.

Deprivation   Broadly, the loss of something. Used in developmental *psychology* to describe the lack of affection and contact, and sometimes basic necessities, which some *child*ren experience at the hands of their care-givers.

Development   The sequence of life events and changes over the full life span.

Discourse analysis   In linguistics, the analysis of language in terms of units larger than a sentence.

Discrimination   Distinctive *behaviour* towards a *group* and its members, often based on *prejudice*s held about them. Usually it refers to negative, unfavourable behaviour, although, in a minority of instances, there can be positive discrimination.

Discursive   One line of recent *social psychological* work has suggested that psychological phenomena are constructed in and through the communicative practices of speech acts. Rather than imagining psychological processes as taking place within some inner realm of cognitive organization, discursive *psychology* has focused attention on how such things as thinking, remembering and feeling are achieved through ordinary talk and conversation.

Displacement   A *defensive mechanism* in *psychoanalytic* theory through which the individual handles the anxiety associated with a *belief* or desire. In displacement, a related target is substituted for the true object. For example, an individual might hate his father, but displaces this hate onto his boss rather than face up to his true feeling.

Display rules   In Ekman's theory, the rules on how we are to display our basic *emotion*al expressions. These may vary from culture to culture.

Disposition   A hypothesized internal tendency, such as *attitude*, *trait* etc., to function in a consistent fashion.

Dispositional attribution   See *internal attribution*.

Dissonance   An uncomfortable emotional feeling held to result from recognition that two inconsistent cognitions are being held simultaneously.

Diversity of interaction   The number of different things that individuals do together in an *interaction*.

Domestic work   *Work* pertaining to the home, sometimes also referred to as home-making.

Dyad   Two people in interaction.

Ego   In *psychoanalysis*, the part of the *mind* which is conscious and in touch with external reality, helps to fulfil desires arising from the *id*, and serves to mediate between the *superego* and the id.

Egocentric   Perceiving the world solely from one's own perspective, as Piaget claimed of younger children's reasoning.

Egoism   Exclusive concern with one's own welfare.

Elaboration likelihood model   Petty and Cacioppo's model of *attitude change*. They argue that people process information via one of two different routes (*central* or *peripheral*), and that this processing influences attitude change. Contrast with *heuristic-systematic model*.

Emotion   A subjective, internal experience consisting of *intrapersonal* elements such as how our body seems to feel, our conscious awareness of this and understanding of what it means, as well as *interpersonal* and social elements such as how we express ourselves, the actions and reactions of the other people present, and our understanding of the wider context. This definition is deliberately vague, as more specific definitions tend to reflect particular theoretical underpinnings. Often contrasted with *cognition*.

Emotional contagion   The spread of an *emotion* through a *group* of people, often as a function of them engaging in the same expressive *behaviours*.

Empathic concern   Feelings of warmth, tenderness and compassion caused by taking the perspective of someone in need.

Empathy   The sharing of a feeling with someone by experiencing it at the same time.

Empirical   An approach to research characterized by a focus on measuring and observing phenomena, rather than simply speculating about them.

Employment   Paid *work* of any kind.

Epidemiology   The distribution of illness in the community, and the investigation of reasons for its uneven distribution.

Epistemology   (The study of) theories of knowledge.

Eros   The god of love in classical mythology. Used in classical *psychoanalytic* theory to refer to the individual's instinct for pleasure.

Ethics   A branch of philosophy concerned with what is acceptable in human *behaviour*. Applied to research, ethical debates centre on the treatment of participants.

Ethnic group   A set of people who share a common cultural background. The common culture may be associated with certain common biological characteristics, such as skin colour, but it need not be.

Ethnocentric   An ethnocentric perspective considers (although not always intentionally) the perspective of one culture or ethnic *group* to be primary in evaluating the mores, *beliefs*, *action*s and traditions of other cultures or groups.

Ethology   The study of animal *behaviour*.

Etiology   See *aetiology*.

Evidence-based policy making   The design of policy based on *empirical* evidence about the issues the policy addresses.

Exchange theories   Theories that assume that *behaviour* in *relationships* is in large measure determined by the exchange of rewards and costs, or expectations thereof.

Experiment   A research technique which is uniquely suited to investigating causal relationships between *variables* through the systematic manipulation of postulated *independent variables* and the measurement of their effects on *dependent variables*.

Experimental psychology   A view of *psychology* which places heavy emphasis on the scientific nature of the discipline and the use of *experiments* in gaining understanding of psychological processes.

Expressed emotion A term used to describe the *emotion*al flavour of typical *inter-actions* within a family, particularly where one member is suffering from *mental illness*. The level of expressed emotion is measured by combining ratings of three factors: critical comments, hostility and overinvolvement.

External attribution An explanation of someone's *behaviour* based on the circumstances surrounding it, i.e. the context of the situation. Also called situational attribution.

External validity The extent to which research findings can be generalized beyond the controlled environment in which they were originally found. Contrast with *internal validity*.

Extroversion See *big five*.

Extrinsic rewards Benefits which arise as a consequence of an activity, rather than being part of the activity itself. In *employment*, one of the main extrinsic rewards is pay. Contrast with *intrinsic rewards*.

Factor analysis A statistical technique which is used to identify clusters of *correlations* in large data sets where many individual *variables* may correlate together.

False consensus effect The assumption that our own views of the world are more prevalent in the wider population than they actually are.

Feedback The consequences of an *action* that also affect its causes.

Field experiment A type of *experiment* that is carried out in a natural setting, sometimes without participants' awareness.

Figurative nucleus Moscovici suggests that at the centre of every *social representation* there is a figurative nucleus, i.e. a complex of images that visibly reproduces a complex of ideas. In this way the abstract ideas and values which define a representation are given concrete form.

Forced compliance A *dissonance*-creating technique of encouraging people to behave contrary to their attitudes. Better thought of as induced, or even unforced, *compliance*.

Freudian slip A term commonly applied to those slips of the tongue, the eye and the hand which might reveal an underlying desire or fear. For example, misreading the word 'shopfitting' as 'shoplifting' might reflect a fear of being accused of this crime.

Fundamental attribution error The tendency to overemphasize *internal attributions* and underemphasize *external attributions* when explaining other people's *behaviour*.

Gambler's fallacy The tendency to believe that knowledge of prior events, even if we know them to be random, allows us to predict a chance outcome in the future better.

Gender The social or cultural ideas and values attributed to each *sex*. These may take the form of patterns of thought, feeling and *action* which are held to be appropriate for boys or girls, men or women, in which case they may be referred to as gender *roles*.

The sense of belonging to a gender *group* is referred to as gender identity, which is a specific type of *social identity*.

Generalizability The extent to which research findings from a controlled environment are relevant to the external world.

Generalized other The values, *attitude*s, sentiments etc. which the individual comes to understand and internalize as representing the wider society, according to G. H. Mead's analysis of the *self*. See also I and *me*.

Grammar Loosely, the set of rules which structure a language. Technically, in linguistics grammar equals *morphology* plus *syntax*.

Gross domestic product (GDP) The total value of goods produced and services provided in a country in one year.

Grounded theory A theory which emerges from observations, rather than being postulated in advance of any investigation.

Group A group exists when a set of individuals perceive themselves to be members of the same group. The term is applied to both small face-to-face groups and large social categories.

Group dynamics The study of small *group* processes.

Group polarization The finding that in laboratory settings small *group*s commonly come to more extreme (but not necessarily riskier, as supposed in the *risky shift*) decisions on problems than might have been expected from a knowledge of the initial individual positions of the members of the groups.

Groupthink A mode of thinking that people engage in when they are deeply involved in a cohesive *group*, when the members' strivings for unanimity override their motivation to appraise alternative courses of *action* realistically.

Heteronomous thought In Piaget's theory, a form of reasoning which is a consequence of relations of constraint and corresponds to moral realism. Often a feature of younger children's moral judgements. Questions of truth and falsity are ceded to an authority or authority, figure. Contrast with *autonomous thought*, and see also *morality*.

Heuristic In ordinary language, a rule of thumb. In psychological theories, practices or simple rules followed in an attempt to solve problems or understand states of affairs. They do not guarantee a clear outcome, but might guide us quickly to an acceptable answer.

Heuristic processing Cognitive processing involving the use of rules of thumb, short cuts, *stereotype*s and the like. See also *cognition*.

Heuristic-systematic model Chaiken's model of *attitude change*. People are said to process information in two different ways: systematically (when they attend carefully) or via *heuristic*s (when they do not attend carefully). The type of processing affects how the information influences people's *attitude*s. Contrast with *elaboration likelihood model*.

Hostile aggression   A form of aggressive *behaviour* which occurs when the aggressor's primary intent is to harm the victim. Contrast with *instrumental aggression*.

Human capital   A term used in economics to refer to the training and skills of a nation's *labour force*.

Human relations approach   An employee-centred approach to management. See also *human resource management*.

Human resource management (HRM)   The currently favoured phrase for a *human relations approach*, and meaning rather different things to different exponents.

Hypothecation   A taxation system where specific taxes are linked to specific benefits.

Hypothesis   A theory about a cause–effect relationship between two or more *variables*.

I   In the analysis of the *self* by G. H. Mead, the aspect of the self which is the knower of the self and the source of spontaneous action. See also *me* and *generalized other*.

Id   In Sigmund Freud's account, the instinctual, libidinous, unconscious source of much of our thought and *behaviour*. See also *ego* and *superego*.

Identity   The subjective concept which an individual holds of himself or herself in relation to other people. Also referred to as *self*.

Idiographic   Usually refers to studies of *personality* in which the focus is on the specific characteristics of an individual. Contrast with *nomothetic*.

Impression management theory   A theory which emphasizes individuals' concerns to appear in a favourable and consistent light in the eyes of others.

Incentive-induced change   *Behaviour* change achieved through externally administered incentives rather than via *attitude change* by persuasive *communication*.

Independent variable (IV)   The *variable* that the investigator assumes to be the cause; that is, the one that is manipulated to create different *experiment*al conditions. Its effect is measured by the *dependent variable*.

Induction   A type of reasoning in which general principles are constructed from specific cases or instances. Contrast *deduction*.

Infant   A human being in the period of infancy. This period is variously defined as: up to 1 year (*developmental psychology* definition); up to 2–3 years (lay definition); and up to 18–21 years (legal definitions).

Inferential statistics   Statistical techniques used for making inferences rather than just for pure description.

Informational social influence   *Social influence* which operates through the acceptance of information from another as being evidence of reality. Contrast with *normative social influence*.

Informed consent   Agreement, based on truthful information about a research project from the researcher, to participate in that research.

Instrumental aggression   A form of aggressive *behaviour* which occurs when there is an intent to injure, but the *aggression* is primarily a means towards achieving some other non-injurious goal. Contrast with *hostile aggression*.

Intellect   See *big five*.

Interaction   A process whereby the *behaviour* and ideas of two or more people become mutually influencing and interdependent.

Interdependence theory   A type of *exchange theory* which lays stress on the mutual influence between the participants in a *relationship*.

Intergroup conflict   Hostile *intergroup relations*. These can include *prejudice*, *discrimination* and *racism* as well as the more extreme examples of war and genocide.

Intergroup relations   Patterns of *interactions* between two or more *groups*, where individuals behave in terms of their group membership.

Internal attribution   An explanation of someone's *behaviour* based on his or her supposed personal characteristics. Also called dispositional attribution.

Internal validity   In an *experiment*, the extent to which changes in *dependent variables* can be unambiguously attributed to variations in *independent variables*. High internal validity should result in *replicability*. Contrast with *external validity*.

Interpersonal   Factors and processes operating between persons. Contrast with *intrapersonal*.

Interpersonal perception   How the individuals in a *relationship* perceive each other, including how they perceive the other's view of them.

Intrapersonal   Factors and processes operating within a person. Contrast with *interpersonal*.

Intrinsic rewards   Benefits that are part of an activity, i.e. arise from the very *action* involved. In *employment*, an example would be enjoyment of the work itself. Contrast with *extrinsic rewards*.

Introspection   Focusing on one's inner mental experience in order to gain an understanding of the function of *psychological* processes. This *method* was especially popular with early psychologists in the late nineteenth century. Contrast with *behaviourism*.

Job   A position of *employment*. Contrast with *work*.

Job insecurity   Both the subjective experience and objective circumstances of threat to one's *job*. Situations where job insecurity is likely to be experienced include redundancies in an industry as a whole, the seasonal nature of some jobs (e.g. in the tourist industry), and rapid turnover of jobs, as in temping or contract work.

Job satisfaction   How positive people's *attitudes* are towards their *jobs*. This can be measured in a variety of ways.

Kinship   A general term used to cover any social *relationship* based on family.

Knowledge-driven   See *top-down*.

Labour force   A collective term for everyone in a population who is or wants to be employed. Definitions vary in terms of the inclusiveness of the term. See also *employment*.

Labour market   A hypothetical arena of exchange between demand and supply of workers and *jobs*.

Latent function   A term used by Jahoda to describe benefits of *employment* not directly associated with pay, namely: enforcement of activity; structuring of time; sharing of common goals; insertion in a social network; and provision of status and *identity*. Contrast with *manifest function*.

Learned helplessness   A term coined by Seligman to describe his *empirical* observation of a state of apathy that is induced by an experience of lack of control over unpleasant stimuli.

Libido   In *psychoanalysis*, the sexual energy underlying mental activity as it originates in the *id*.

Life event   Any event, positive or negative, of significance in an individual's life. Examples range from the death of a spouse to more minor events, such as a *child* starting school. Life events are associated with varying levels of psychosocial stress.

Literal meaning   That element of the meaning of a sentence which is associated with its literal truth. See *semantics*.

Longitudinal study   A type of research design where data collection is carried out repeatedly over a period of time. Contrast with *cross-sectional study*.

Macro-level   The level of analysis concerned with society as a whole. Contrast with *micro-level*.

Manifest function   A term used by Jahoda to describe the benefits of *work* directly associated with pay. Contrast with *latent function*.

Me   In the analysis of the *self* by G. H. Mead, the aspect of the self which is known; the reflective, self-conscious self. See also I and *generalized other*.

Medical model   A view of psychological abnormalities and disorders which assumes they can be understood and treated in a similar fashion to physical illness.

Memory   Can refer variously to the information about the world which we store in our *mind*s; the actual storage system; and the process of storing the information.

Mental health   More than the mere absence of *mental illness*; usually denotes a high level of behavioural and emotional adjustment. Also called *psychological well-being*.

Mental illness   A collective term for various *psychological* or behavioural abnormalities which severely affect an individual's ability to function normally. Contrast *mental health*.

Mentalistic   Pertaining to the workings of the *mind*. Contrast with *behaviourism*.

Meta-analysis   A systematic statistical analysis of a large number of related studies which permits the results of different ones to be summed together. A powerful technique for finding the clearest overall patterns where there have been some contradictory findings.

Method   A procedure used to accumulate information.

Methodology   The philosophy behind a *method*.

Micro-level   The level of analysis concerned with individuals. Contrast with *macrolevel*.

Mind   An umbrella term used variously to describe conscious and unconscious mental processes and experiences, or as a synonym for the brain, the soul, the psyche etc.

Modelling   The process of an individual observing another person performing a particular *behaviour* and then imitating it.

Monotropy   The infant's tendency, as postulated by Bowlby, to form only one strong *attachment*.

Morality   In its broadest sense, right and wrong. Morality is concerned with how things *should* be rather than how things *are*. In this sense, morals are fundamentally reasons for *action* and involve prescribing certain rules for *behaviour*.

More exposure effect   The phenomenon where individuals rate something as more pleasant or attractive the more they are exposed to it.

Morphemes   The smallest units of meaning in a language. Many of these may be freestanding, e.g. the word 'walk', but others can only exist in combination with other morphemes, e.g. '-ed' marking the past tense of English verbs.

Morphology   The study of how *morphemes* combine into words. See also *grammar*.

Motivation   The internal state of an organism that drives its *behaviour*.

Motivational bias   See *self-serving bias*.

Multiplex   A term used to describe a *relationship* in which the participants engage in many types of *interaction*. Contrast *uniplex*.

Nature   A term used in *psychology* to refer to all that is innate (genetically programmed) in an individual. Contrast with *nurture*.

Neuroticism   See *big five*.

Nomothetic   Refers to studies of *personality* which seek to discover law-like regularities which apply to large *group*s of people. Contrast with *idiographic*.

Non-linear relationship   A type of *correlation* which is not constant. For example, increases in *variable* A may be associated with increases in variable B, but only up to a certain point, after which further increases in variable A lead to decreases in variable B.

Non-literal meaning All that additional meaning which is communicated above and beyond the *literal meaning*.

Non-vocal communication *Communication* which does not involve verbalizing or vocalizing; e.g. facial expressions, gaze, gestures, proxemics (the distance we maintain between ourselves and others), posture and touch.

Norm A usual way of behaving or of orientation to the social world.

Normative social influence *Social influence* which operates through concern regarding rewards and sanctions from others. Contrast with *informational social influence*.

Nurture The collective impact of the environment on an individual. Contrast with *nature*.

Objectification In Moscovici's theory of *social representations*, the process whereby representations are projected as objective elements of reality. The complementary process to *anchoring*.

Oblique rotation A technique in *factor analysis* which permits factors to be correlated with one another. Contrast with *orthogonal rotation* and see also *correlation*.

Observational learning In *social learning* theory, the process of learning through observing the *behaviour* of others (who are sometimes referred to as models). Also known as vicarious conditioning.

Occupational level The status of an individual's *job*, e.g. manager, sales assistant etc.

Oedipus complex In classical *psychoanalytic* theory, the process through which the male *child* ultimately forgoes his love of his mother in the face of competition for his mother from his father, whom he wishes to kill.

Ordinal position Ranked position in an array or list, e.g. third.

Orthogonal rotation A technique in *factor analysis* which does not permit factors to be correlated with one another. Contrast with *oblique rotation* and see also *correlation*.

Panel design A type of research design where a *group* of people who are representative of the population as a whole are followed up over time. Similar to *cohort design*.

Parallel distributed processing A type of cognitive model in which the individual is held to operate by having a number of *psychological* processes running in parallel to one another. See also *cognition*.

Para-medicine Services supplementing and supporting medicine.

Parenting styles Qualitatively different ways in which parents or guardians discipline (and, for some theorists, educate) their *child*ren.

Participant observation A research *method* that involves the researcher participating in the activities of the people being observed, sometimes covertly.

Peer An individual who can be characterized as an equal in some way (usually age) and who is not a blood relation.

Penis envy In *psychoanalytic* theory, the desire of a woman to gain the penis she believes she has been denied.

Perceived behaviour control Perception by an individual that he or she potentially has control over a type of *behaviour* that might have to be performed. See *theory of planned behaviour*.

Perception The processes which enable us to make sense of sensory input. These can be *top-down* or *bottom-up*, and usually involve a combination of the two.

Peripheral route to persuasion Attempts to persuade via *heuristic* and/or emotional means, according to *elaboration likelihood model*. Contrast with *central route*.

Personality A very broad term, used in many different ways. Generally, different perspectives are united by a focus on those features of a person's *action*s and *behaviour* which reliably distinguish him or her from other people, which are consistent across time and space, and which derive from stable internal factors.

Phonemes The idealized sound components of a language. The initial sound of the word 'cat' is the same at one idealized level for all speakers of English, but may vary quite widely in actual pronunciation.

Phonetics The study of speech sounds which analyses their physical properties as well as the ways in which humans produce and perceive them.

Phonology The study of how the individual sounds in a language combine to make words and other higher-order units.

Physical capital A term used in economics to refer to the machinery and infrastructure available to a nation.

Pleasure–pain principle In *psychoanalytic* theory, the simple principle which all beings follow of avoiding pain and seeking pleasure.

Policy A principle or programme of action, usually proposed by an institution or organization, especially a government.

Power The ability of one participant in a *relationship* to control the other.

Pragmatics The study of those aspects of meaning which derive from the relationship between a speaker and what he or she has said.

Prejudice A set of *attitude*s towards a *group* and its members, often based on premature judgement and sometimes leading to *discrimination*. Usually it refers to negative, unfavourable attitudes, although, in a minority of instances, these can be positive.

Pretend play Play in which childen use one thing to evoke or represent something else, e.g. using a pencil as if it were an aeroplane. Emerges around the end of the child's second year as part of a more general development of *semiotic function*s. Its frequency and complexity increase in subsequent years. Pretend play has frequently been studied for what it reveals about children's understanding of the world around them.

Primary process   The process by which the instincts of the *id* are held to be formed into desires under the influence of the *pleasure–pain principle*. Contrast *secondary process*.

Prior variable   A *variable* that occurs temporally before two variables that we are interested in, and is related to both of them, giving the false impression that the two variables are linked. For instance, it might be observed that taller people are more likely to belch in public, but this is not because height *per se* reduces manners, but because both height and bad manners are related to a prior variable, gender.

Projection   A *defensive mechanism* in *psychoanalytic* theory through which the individual handles the anxiety associated with a *belief* or desire. In projection, individuals impute their own feeling or belief to someone else. For example, if someone hated her father, projection might lead her to believe that the father was the one who did the hating.

Prosocial behaviour   Behaviour that is positively valued by the individual's society as generally beneficial to other people and the on-going social system.

Psychoanalysis   The approach to *psychological* understanding founded by Sigmund Freud. Both a general theory and a specific form of psychotherapy or treatment of mental or emotional difficulties.

Psychological well-being   See *mental health*.

Psychology   Broadly, the scientific study of the *mind* and *behaviour* of individual organisms, including humans and other animals.

Psycho-neuro-immunology   The study of how *psychological* processes affect the immune system via neurophysiological pathways.

Psychopathology   The study of *psychological* pathologies.

Psychopathy   A condition in which the individual pursues his or her own goals in a self-interested way with little understanding for their effect on others or any *emotion*al engagement. See also *antisocial personality disorder*, which has largely replaced this term, and *sociopathy*.

Psychosomatic   The *interaction* of *psychological* and physical processes, and their impact on an individual's health.

Qualitative   An approach to research which is associated with in-depth exploration of an issue. It has also been linked with *induction*, feminism, and a critique of the traditional principles of science.

Quantitative   An approach to research which is associated with a focus on numerical measurement and statistical analysis. It has also been linked with *deduction* and a traditional scientific approach to research.

Quasi-experiment   A 'sort-of' *experiment*. *Field experiments* are often not quite experiments in the strict sense of the term, since the nature of their setting may make random allocation to *groups* or complete control of *variables* impossible.

Racism   Institutionalized prejudice and discrimination based on race or ethnicity.

Randomization   The process by which participants in *experiments* are assigned to experimental *groups* such that there is no systematic difference between the groups other than the manipulation involved in the experiment.

Reaction-formation   A *defensive mechanism* in *psychoanalytic* theory through which the individual handles anxiety associated with a *belief* or desire by reversing the value of the *emotion*. For example, an individual might hate his father but turn the hate into excessive love for him.

Recovered memory   A controversial term referring to *memories* which are believed to have been suppressed or lost, and are subsequently recovered through a therapeutic intervention. Many writers do not accept the existence of recovered memory.

Reciprocal   An *interaction* in which the participants show similar *behaviour*, either simultaneously or alternately, directed towards each other.

Reified universe   In Moscovici's theory, of *social representations*, a representation of knowledge which describes phenomena in terms of impersonal forces and relations. The primary example of this form of knowledge is modern scientific thought. Contrast with *consensual universe*.

Relationship   A series of *interactions* between two individuals who know each other, such that each interaction is affected by preceding ones and usually by the expectation of future ones.

Reliability   See *replicability*. Contrast with *validity*.

Replicability   The extent to which a research procedure or test yields similar results each time it is repeated, i.e. something is being assessed consistently.

Representativeness heuristic   The tendency to assume that something or someone is a member of a category even though we only have partial information about the thing or person.

Repression   A type of *defensive mechanism* which involves preventing unacceptable unconscious material from entering the conscious.

Risky shift   The phenomenon whereby small *groups* were believed to take riskier decisions than might be expected from knowledge of the initial positions of individual members. A somewhat misguided precursor to the notion of *group polarization*.

Role   Expectations about the *behaviour* associated with a particular position in society or in a *group*.

Salary   The monthly pay of a middle-class employee. Contrast *wage*.

Satisfaction   In the context of *relationships*, the extent to which the participant's perception of the relationship overlaps with his or her ideal for the relationship. This can be influenced by the availability of alternatives.

Schema   A structuring of the individual's knowledge which is relevant to how that knowledge is deployed in many *psychological* processes.

Schizophrenia   A serious *mental illness* involving a supposed splitting of the *mind*, in the sense of one mental function, *affect*, being split off from another, *cognition*, so that the coherence of the person's mental functioning is severely impaired. Not to be confused with 'split *personality*', i.e. multiple personality disorder.

Secondary process   The process through which the *ego* is held to relate the desires of the individual to the practical circumstances of the world, and thus how they might be satisfied. Contrast *primary process*.

Security   A sense of confidence, safety and freedom from anxiety, often used in the context of *attachment*.

Selective exposure   The tendency to avoid exposing oneself to information which might lead to *cognitive dissonance*.

Self   The conception which an individual has of himself or herself as a social being. See also *I*, *me* and *social identity*.

Self-categorization theory   A theory, derived by Turner from *social identity theory*, which seeks to explain how categorizing oneself as a member of a *group* alters one's social identity and subsequent *behaviour*.

Self-disclosure   The extent to which the participants in a *relationship* reveal themselves to each other.

Self-esteem   The degree to which one values oneself.

Self-monitoring   A tendency to monitor the immediate social situation before acting. Better thought of as situation monitoring.

Self-perception theory   A model for understanding our own *attitudes*. Just as we infer other people's attitudes from their *behaviour*, Bem argues that we use our own behaviour to infer our underlying attitudes.

Self-presentation   The way an individual presents himself or herself to other people.

Self-serving bias   An attempt to bolster our image to others or to ourselves by portraying positive outcomes as having causes internal to ourselves and negative outcomes as being caused by other people or by the situation. Also known as motivational bias.

Self-system   What a person knows and believes about himself or herself in relation to the social environment.

Semantics   The study of how meaning arises from the relationship between words and the world they are about.

Semiotic function   The capacity for understanding that one thing (a signifier) may represent another (the signified). Developmentally this capacity for representation emerges towards the end of the *child*'s second year, and is most clearly visible in the emergence of imitation, *pretend play* and language. All later thought and *communication* involve some form of semiotic function.

Semi-skilled worker   Manual worker with some training but less than that of a skilled worker.

Sex   The innate, biological distinction between male and female. Contrast with *gender*.

Sibling   A brother or sister, biological or adopted.

Situated cognition   An approach which seeks to understand *cognition* by reference to the circumstances in which it is deployed and the way they support it, rather than by studying it in the laboratory.

Situational attribution   See *external attribution*.

Social   A term with a variety of slightly different meanings at whose heart is probably the notion of a situation involving two or more people, all of whom need not be physically present, as an individual can imagine or represent internally other people.

Social capital   Those features of *social* life that enable people to *work* together more effectively towards common goals, including *norms* and social networks.

Social cognition   The study of the cognitive processes underlying our *social* abilities and *behaviour*. See also *cognition*.

Social comparison   The process of comparing oneself to others in order to evaluate one's opinions and abilities.

Social conditioning   The process whereby certain social *behaviour*s are encouraged (reinforced) and others are discouraged (punished), enabling individuals to learn how to behave in a *social*ly acceptable manner.

Social desirability effect   A *bias* created in the collection of data via self-reports. It arises from the respondent's attempts to present himself or herself in a good light, rather than being completely honest.

Social identity   Tajfel defined social identity as 'that part of an individual's self-concept which derives from his knowledge of his membership of a social *group* (or groups) together with the value and emotional significance attached to that membership' (1981, p. 255). This definition continues to be widely used in *social psychology*, although other perspectives have employed rather different definitions, while agreeing that a social identity expresses a person's *attachment* to a particular social group or social category, an attachment which also serves to locate the person within the social world.

Social identity theory   A theory, originally proposed by Tajfel, that we understand our *social identity* by reference to the social *group*s of which we are part.

Social influence Changes in views and/or *actions* of *group* members as a result of being exposed to the views and/or actions of other group members. A distinction is often drawn between *normative* and *informational social influence*.

Social learning According to Bandura, the process whereby individuals acquire social *behaviour*s through *observational learning* and the process of *modelling*.

Social psychology The study of the interrelations amongst individuals, their *interactions* and the societies they live in

Social representation A theory put forward by Moscovici to explain how people understand the *social* world. Social representations are collective structures of meaning which serve both to give shape and definition to the realities people experience, and to make possible *communication* among members of the *group* sharing the representation.

Social support The support derived from *relationship*s with other people.

Socialization The processes by which a *child* is given the information and skills necessary for successful *social* functioning.

Sociocultural structure The system of *belief*s, values, myths, *convention*s and institutions with their constituent *role*s shared by most or all of the society, *group* or *dyad*.

Socioeconomic status A measure of an individual's status in a stratified society, usually based on some mixture of income, education, family background and the like.

Sociology The systematic study of human societies, especially modern, industrialized ones. It generally operates at a more *macro-level* than does *social psychology*.

Sociometry The study of patterns of personal *relationship*s, with a particular focus on quantifying and formalizing them.

Sociopathy A condition similar to *psychopathy* and *antisocial personality disorder*, in which the individual engages in a variety of unsuccessful and maladaptive *relationship*s because of her or his antisocial and disruptive *behaviour*.

Sound system In linguistics, the structure of the language in relation to the medium in which it is expressed. In this case, it is the vocal-auditory channel which links the speaker's mouth to the listener's ear.

Spurious Not genuine, e.g. of an apparent *correlation* between two *variable*s.

Stereotype A widely shared set of generalizations about a *group*. These can be positive or negative and are used as a mental short cut to understanding the *behaviour* of other people. They may arise in part from an individual's or a group's *prejudice*s.

Subjective norm An individual's perception of what the *norm* is, which may or may not be accurate.

Superego In classical *psychoanalytic* accounts, that part of the psychic structure which represents the demands and standards of the wider world, and is in that sense the basis of the conscience. See also *ego* and *id*.

Survey A systematic collection of data on a range of measures relating to a sample, often a large one, of 'cases'. In *social psychology* the cases are usually individuals but could be anything from cities to subcultures, magazines to psychiatric hospitals. A number of *variable*s are measured from each respondent. The survey relies on naturally occurring variations in assumed *independent variable*s, and examines statistically whether those variations are correlated to variations in assumed *dependent variables*. See also *correlation*.

Syllogism A logical reasoning structure in which there is a major premise, a minor premise, and a conclusion which is drawn from their conjunction.

Symbolic interactionism An approach to *sociology* and *social psychology* following from the work of Mead, and examining the symbolic processes in society through which we construct our *identities* and *social* relations.

Syntax The set of rules for combining words into grammatical sentences. See also *grammar*.

Thanatos The god of death in classical mythology. Used in classical *psychoanalytic* theory to refer to the instinct of all life forms to pursue their ultimate return to a simpler organic state.

Theory of mind The ability to understand that other people have *mind*s (i.e. thoughts, feelings, *belief*s, intentions etc.). A deficit in theory of mind abilities has been put forward as an explanation of the difficulties which people who have *autism* experience in *interacting* with others.

Theory of planned behaviour Ajzen's modification of the *theory of reasoned action*, involving the addition of *perceived behaviour control* as a third predictor of intentions and *behaviour*s.

Theory of reasoned action Fishbein and Ajzen's model of how *attitude*s and *subjective norm*s predict intentions and *action*s.

Time-series analysis The organization of data along a time dimension.

Top-down That part of perceptual or interpretative processes which is driven by the individual's knowledge of the nature and structure of the external world. Contrast with *bottom-up*.

Trait A quality of a person's *behaviour* which is thought to reflect an underlying *personality* disposition.

Triangulation The use of more than one *method* to obtain more reliable results from research.

Tripartite conception of attitude A view that *attitude*s consist of three correlated components, cognitive, affective and intentional.

Two-factor theory of job satisfaction Herzberg's theory of *job satisfaction*, which argues that the aspects of a *job* that lead to satisfaction are different from those that lead to dissatisfaction.

Type A personality A temperament characterized by excessive drive, ambition, competitiveness and a tendency towards stress. Contrast *Type B personality*.

Type B personality A temperament characterized by a relaxed, easy-going approach to life. Contrast *Type A personality*.

Unemployment Definitions vary, but usually refers to those without paid *work* who are able and want to have it. Does not include people not in the *labour force*, e.g. the retired or housewives not wanting paid work.

Uniplex A *relationship* in which the participants engage in only one type of *interaction*. Contrast *multiplex*.

Validity The extent to which a procedure or test measures what it is supposed to measure. Contrast with *reliability*.

Variable Any aspect of a study which varies and is measured. See also *independent variable*, *dependent variable*, *prior variable* and *confounding variable*.

Vicarious conditioning See *observational learning*.

Vitamin model Warr's theory of *mental health* in *employment* and *unemployment*. Different factors contributing to an individual's well-being are compared to vitamins: with some, the relationship between the 'vitamin' and well-being is *linear*; with others, *non-linear*.

Wage The weekly pay of a working-class employee. Contrast *salary*.

White-collar worker Non-manual worker. Contrast *blue-collar worker*.

Work The actual activity of a *job*.

Working model An explicit mini-theory of how a set of processes work.

Picture Credits

Page 21, Mary Evans Picture Library, Sigmund Freud Copyrights.

Page 28, The Granger Collection, New York

Page 59, © Bettmann/Corbis.

Pages 64–5, William Hague © Ian Berry/Magnum. Yasscr Arafat © Peter Marlow/ Magnum. Benazir Bhutto © Abbas/Magnum. Tony Blair © Peter Marlow/Magnum.

Page 69, © Martin Parr/Magnum.

Page 99, © Richard Kalvar/Magnum.

Page 132, © Richard Kalvar/Magnum.

Page 147, William Vandivert.

Page 152, PA Photos.

Page 169, © Abbas/Magnum.

Page 180, © Ian Berry/Magnum.

Page 185, © Guzelian.

Page 188, Copyright 1965 by Stanley Milgram. From the film *Obedience*, distributed by Penn State Media Sales.

Page 200, © Bettman/Corbis.

Page 220, © Richard Kalvar/Magnum.

Page 251, © Peter Marlow/Magnum.

Page 263, PA Photos.

Pages 276–7, Star map © Science Museum/Science and Society Picture Library. Signs of the Zodiac © Mary Evans Picture Library.

Page 293, © Hulton Getty.

Page 307, © Ian Berry/Magnum.

Page 315, © James Nachtwey/Magnum.

Page 320, Photo by Steve McKenna.

Page 345, © Lorne Campbell/Guzelian.

Picture research by Heather Vickers

References

Abelson, R. P. (1981) The psychological status of the script concept. *American Psychologist*, 36, 715–29.

Abelson, R. P. and Rosenberg, M. J. (1958) Symbolic psycho-logic: a model of attitudinal cognition. *Behavioural Science*, 3, 1–13.

Aboud, F. (1988) *Children and Prejudice*. Oxford: Blackwell.

Abraham, S. C. S., Sheeran, P., Spears, R. and Abrams, D. (1992) Health beliefs and the promotion of HIV-preventive intentions among teenagers: a Scottish perspective. *Health Psychology*, 11, 363–70.

Abric, J.-C. (1993) Central system, peripheral system: their functions and roles in the dynamic of social representations. *Papers on Social Representations*, 75–85.

Adams, J. S. (1965) Injustice in social exchange. In L. Berkowitz (ed.), *Advances in Experimental Social Psychology, Vol. 2*. New York: Academic Press.

Adonis, A. and Pollard, S. (1997) *A Class Act: The Myth of Britain's Classless Society*. London: Hamish Hamilton.

Adorno, T. W., Frenkel-Brunswik, E., Levinson, D. J. and Sanford, R. N. (1950) *The Authoritarian Personality*. New York: Harper.

Agassi, J. B. (1982) *Comparing the Work Attitudes of Men and Women*. Aldershot: Gower.

Ahrendt, D. and Young, K. (1994) Authoritarianism updated. In R. Jowell, J. Curtice, L. Brook and D. Ahrendt (eds), *British Social Attitudes: The 11th Report*. Aldershot: Dartmouth.

Ainsworth, M. D. S. (1967) *Infancy in Uganda: Infant Care and the Growth of Attachment*. Baltimore: Johns Hopkins University Press.

Ainsworth, M. D. S., Blehar, M. C., Waters, E. and Wall, S. (1978) *Patterns of Attachment: A Psychological Study of the Strange Situation*. Hillsdale, NJ: Erlbaum.

Ajzen, I. (1988) *Attitudes, Personality and Behaviour*. Milton Keynes: Open University Press.

Ajzen, I. (1991) The theory of planned behaviour. *Organisational Behaviour and Human Decision Processes*, 50, 179–211.

Ajzen, I. and Fishbein, M. (1980) *Understanding Attitudes and Predicting Social Behavior*. Englewood Cliffs, NJ: Prentice-Hall.

Aldag, R. J. and Fuller, S. R. (1993) Beyond fiasco: a re-appraisal of the groupthink phenomenon and a new model of group decision making processes. *Psychological Bulletin*, 113, 533–52.

Alexander, C. N., Jr, Zucker, L. G. and Brady, C. L. (1970) Experimental expectations and autokinetic experiences: consistency theories and judgmental convergence. *Sociometry*, 33, 108–22.

Allen, V. L. (1975) Social support for non-conformity. In L. Berkowitz (ed.), *Advances in Experimental Social Psychology, Vol. 8*. New York: Academic Press.

Allen, V. L. and Wilder, D. A. (1977) Social comparison, self-evaluation and conformity to the group. In J. M. Suls and R. L. Miller (eds), *Social Comparison Processes*. Washington, DC: Hemisphere.

Allport, F. H. (1924) *Social Psychology*. Boston: Houghton Mifflin.

Allport, G. W. (1935) Attitudes. In C. Murchison (ed.), *Handbook of Social Psychology*. Worcester, MA: Clark University Press.

Allport, G. W. (1937) *Personality: A Psychological Interpretation*. New York: Henry Holt.

Allport, G. W. (1954) *The Nature of Prejudice*. Reading, MA: Addison-Wesley.

Allport, G. W. (1985) The historical background of modern social psychology. In G. Lindzey and E. Aronson (eds), *Handbook of Social Psychology, Vol. 1*. 3rd edn. New York: Random House.

Allport, G. W. and Odbert, H. S. (1936). Trait names: a psycho-lexical study. *Psychological Monographs*, 47, 1–171.

Amenson, C. S. and Lewinsohn, P. M. (1981) An investigation of the observed sex difference in prevalence of unipolar depression. *Journal of Abnormal Psychology*, 90, 1–13.

Amir, Y. (1976) The role of intergroup contact in change of prejudice and ethnic relations. In P. A. Katz (ed.), *Towards the Elimination of Racism*. New York: Pergamon.

Andersen, S. M. and Bem, S. L. (1981) Sex typing and androgyny in dyadic interaction: individual differences in responsiveness to physical attractiveness. *Journal of Personality and Social Psychology*, 41, 74–86.

Anderson, C. A. and Anderson, K. B. (1998) Temperature and aggression: paradox, controversy, and a (fairly) clear picture. In R. G. Geen and E. Donnerstein (eds), *Human Aggression: Theories, Research, and Implications for Social Policy*. San Diego: Academic Press.

Anderson, C. A., Anderson, K. B. and Deuser, W. E. (1996) Examining an affective aggression framework: weapon and temperature effects on aggressive thoughts, affect, and attitudes. *Personality and Social Psychology Bulletin*, 22, 366–76.

Anderson, J. R. (2000) *Cognitive Psychology and its Implications*. New York: W. H. Freeman.

Anderson, M. (1992) *Intelligence and Development: A Cognitive Theory*. Oxford: Blackwell.

Anderson, N. H. (1965) Averaging versus adding as a stimulus-combination rule in impression formation. *Journal of Experimental Psychology*, 70, 394–400.

Andrews, M. (1991) *Lifetimes of Commitment: Aging, Politics and Psychology*. Cambridge: Cambridge University Press.

Archer, J. and Lloyd, B. (1985) *Sex and Gender*. Cambridge: Cambridge University Press.

Archibald, W. P. (1978) *Social Psychology as Political Economy*. Toronto: McGraw-Hill Ryerson.

Argyle, M. (1976) Personality and social behaviour. In R. Harré (ed.), *Personality*. Oxford: Blackwell.

Argyle, M. (1987) *The Psychology of Happiness*. London and New York: Methuen.

Argyle, M. and Dean, J. (1965) Eye contact, distance, and affiliation. *Sociometry*, 28, 289–304.

Argyle, M. and Henderson, M. (1985) *The Anatomy of Relationships*. Harmondsworth: Penguin.

Aronfeed, J. (1968) *Conduct and Conscience: The Socialization of Internalized Control over Behaviour*. New York: Academic Press.

Asch, S. E. (1946) Forming impressions of personality. *Journal of Abnormal and Social Psychology*, 41, 258–90.

Asch, S. E. (1951) Effects of group pressure upon the modification and distortion of judgments. In H. Guetzkow (ed.), *Groups, Leadership and Men*. Pittsburg: Carnegie Press.

Asch, S. E. (1952) *Social Psychology*. Englewood Cliffs, NJ: Prentice-Hall.

Asch, S. E. (1956) Studies of independence and conformity: a minority of one against a unanimous majority. *Psychological Monographs: General and Applied*, 70, 1–70 (whole no. 416).

Ashmore, R. D. and Del Boca, F. K. (eds) (1986) *The Social Psychology of Female–Male Relationships*. Orlando: Academic Press.

Auhagen, A.-E. (1991) *Freundschaft in Alltag*. Bern: Hans Huber.

Auhagen, A.-E. and von Salisch, M. (eds) (1992) *Zwischenmenschliche Beziehungen*. Göttingen: Hogrefe.

Auhagen, A.-E. and von Salisch, M. (eds) (1996) *The Diversity of Human Relationships*. Cambridge: Cambridge University Press.

Backman, C. W. (1988) The self: a dialectical approach. *Advances in Experimental Social Psychology*, 21, 229–60.

Baddeley, A. (1990) *Human Memory: Theory and Practice*. Hove: Erlbaum.

Bales, R. F. (1950) *Interaction Process Analysis: A Method for the Study of Small Groups*. Cambridge, MA: Addison-Wesley.

Bandura, A. (1977) *Social Learning Theory*. 2nd edn. Englewood Cliffs, NJ: Prentice-Hall.

Bandura, A. (1986) *Social Foundations of Thought and Action: A Social Cognitive Theory*. Englewood Cliffs, NJ: Prentice-Hall.

Bandura, A. and McDonald, F. J. (1963) Influence of social reinforcement and the behavior of models in shaping children's moral judgments. *Journal of Abnormal and Social Psychology*, 67(3), 274–81.

Bandura, A., Underwood, B. and Fromson, M. E. (1975) Disinhibition of aggression through diffusion of responsibility and dehumanization of victims. *Journal of Research in Personality*, 9, 253–69.

Bannister, P., Burman, E., Parker, I., Taylor, M. and Tindall, C. (1994) *Qualitative Methods in Psychology: A Research Guide*. Buckingham: Open University Press.

Barker, R. G. (1978) *Habitats, environments, and human behavior*. San Francisco: Jossey-Bass.

Baron, R. A. (1989) Personality and organizational conflict: the Type A behavior pattern and self-monitoring. *Organizational Behavior and Human Decision Processes*, 44, 281–97.

Baron, R. A. (1997) The sweet smell of . . . helping: effects of pleasant ambient fragrance on prosocial behavior in shopping malls. *Personality and Social Psychology Bulletin*, 23, 498–503.

Baron, R. A. and Richardson, D. R. (1994). *Human Aggression*. 2nd edn. New York: Plenum Press.

Baron, R. S., Kerr, N. and Miller, N. (1992) *Group Process, Group Decision, Group Action*. Milton Keynes: Open University Press.

Baron-Cohen, S. (1995) *Mindblindness: An Essay on Autism and Theory of Mind*. Cambridge, MA: MIT Press.

Baron-Cohen, S. and Hammer, J. (1997) Parents of children with Asperger Syndrome: what is the cognitive phenotype? *Journal of Cognitive Neuroscience*, 9(4), 548–54.

Baron-Cohen, S., Ring, H. A., Wheelwright, S., Bullmore, E. T., Brammer, M. J., Simmons, A. and Williams, S. C. R. (1999) Social intelligence in the normal and autistic brain: an fMRI study. *European Journal of Neuroscience*, 11(6), 1891–8.

Bar-Tal, D. (1984) American study of helping behavior: what? why? and where? In E. Staub, D. Bar-Tal, J. Karylowski and J. Reykowski (eds), *Development and Maintenance of Prosocial Behaviour*. New York: Plenum.

Bar-Tal, D., Nadler, A. and Blenchman, N. (1980) The relationship between Israeli children's helping behaviour and their perception of parents' socialization practices. *Journal of Social Psychology*, 111, 159–67.

Bartholomew, K. and Horowitz, L. A. (1991) Attachment styles among young adults: a test of a four category model. *Journal of Personality and Social Psychology*, 61, 226–44.

Bartlett, F. C. (1923) *Psychology and Primitive Culture*. Cambridge: Cambridge University Press.

Bartlett, F. C. (1932) *Remembering: A Study in Experimental and Social Psychology*. Cambridge: Cambridge University Press.

Bateson, P. and Martin, P. (1999) *Design for a Life*. London: Vintage Ebury.

Batson, C. D. (1991) The altruism question: toward a social-psychological answer. Hillsdale, NJ: Erlbaum.

Batson, C. D. (1998) Altruism and prosocial behavior. In D. T. Gilbert, S. T. Fiske and G. Lindzey (eds), *The Handbook of Social Psychology*, Vol. 2., 4th edn. New York: McGraw-Hill.

Batson, C. D. and Oleson, K. C. (1991) Current status of the empathy–altruism hypothesis. In M. S. Clark (ed.), *Prosocial Behaviour*. Newbury Park, CA: Sage.

Batson, C. D., Batson, J. G., Griffitt, C. A., Barrientos, S., Brandt, J. R., Sprengelmeyer, P. and Bayly, M. J. (1989) Negative-state relief and the empathy–altruism hypothesis. *Journal of Personality and Social Psychology*, 56, 922–33.

Baumeister, R. F. (1999) *The Self in Social Psychology*. Philadelphia and Hove: Psychology Press/Taylor and Francis.

Baumeister, R. F. and Boden, J. M. (1996) Relation of threatened egotism to violence and aggression: the dark side of high self-esteem. *Psychological Review*, 103, 5–33.

Baumeister, R. F. and Campbell, W. K. (1999) The intrinsic appeal of evil: sadism, sensational thrills, and threatened egoism. In A. G. Miller (guest ed.), *Special Issue:*

Perspectives on Evil and Violence, Personality and Social Psychology Review, 3(3), 210–21.

Baumeister, R. F., Smart, L. and Boden, J. M. (1998) Aggression and the self: high self-esteem, low self-control, and ego threat. In R. G. Geen and E. Donnerstein (eds), *Human Aggression: Theories, Research and Implications for Social Policy*. San Diego: Academic Press.

Baumrind, D. (1971) Current patterns of parental authority. *Developmental Psychology Monographs*, 4 (1 and 2).

Baumrind, D. (1991) The influence of parenting on adolescent competence and substance use. *Journal of Early Adolescence*, 11, 59–95.

Bavelas, J. B., Black, A. and Lemery, C. R. (1986) I show how you feel – motor mimicry as a communicative act. *Journal of Personality and Social Psychology*, 50(2), 322–9.

Bavelas, J. B., Black, A., Chovil, N., Lemery, C. R. and Mullett, J. (1988) Form and function in motor mimicry – topographic evidence that the primary function is communicative. *Human Communication Research*, 14(3), 275–99.

Baxter, L. A. (1990) Dialectical contradictions in relationship development. *Journal of Social and Personal Relationships*, 7, 69–88.

Bebbington, P. and Kuipers, L. (1988) Social influences on schizophrenia. In P. Bebbington and P. McGuffin (eds), *Schizophrenia: The Major Issues*. Oxford: Heinemann/Mental Health Foundation.

Bebbington, P., Hurry, J., Tennant, C., Sturt, E. and Wing, J. (1981) Epidemiology of mental disorders in Camberwell. *Psychological Medicine*, 11, 561–79.

Beck, A. T., Rush, A. J., Shaw, B. F. and Emery, G. (1979) *Cognitive Therapy of Depression*. New York: Guilford Press.

Becker, P. (1999) Beyond the big five. *Personality and Individual Differences*, 26(3), 511–30.

Belansky, E. S. and Boggiano, A. K. (1994) Predicting helping behaviors: the role of gender and instrumental/expressive self-schemata. *Sex Roles*, 30, 647–61.

Bell, R. (1968) A reinterpretation of the direction of effects in studies of socialization. *Psychological Bulletin*, 75, 81–95.

Belsky, J. (1990) Parental and nonparental care and children's socioemotional development: a decade in review. *Journal of Marriage and the Family*, 52, 885–903.

Belsky, J. and Cassidy, J. (1994) Attachment: theory and evidence. In M. Rutter and D. F. Hay (eds), *Development through Life: A Handbook for Clinicians*. Oxford: Blackwell Scientific.

Belsky, J., Woodworth, S. and Crnic, K. (1996) Trouble in the second year: three questions about family interaction. *Child Development*, 67, 556–78.

Belsky, J., Campbell, S. B., Cohn, J. E. and Moore, G. (1996) Instability of infant–parent attachment security. *Developmental Psychology*, 32, 921–4.

Bem, D. J. (1965) An experimental analysis of self-persuasion. *Journal of Experimental Social Psychology*, 1, 199–218.

Bem, D. J. (1972) Self-perception theory. In L. Berkowitz (ed.), *Advances in Experimental Social Psychology, Vol. 6*. New York: Academic Press.

Bem, D. J. and Funder, D. C. (1978) Predicting more of the people more of the time. *Psychological Bulletin*, 85, 485–501.

Bem, S. (1981) Gender schema theory: a cognitive account of sex typing. *Psychological Review*, 88, 354–64.

Bentler, P. M. and Speckart, G. (1979) Models of attitude–behaviour relations. *Psychological Review*, 30, 419–56.

Bentler, P. M. and Speckart, G. (1981) Attitudes 'cause' behaviours: a structural equation analysis. *Journal of Personality and Social Psychology*, 40, 226–38.

Berkman, L. F. and Glass, T. (2000) Social integration, social networks, social support, and health. In L. F. Berkman and I. Kawachi (eds), *Social Epidemiology*. Oxford: Oxford University Press.

Berkowitz, L. (1962) *Aggression: A Social Psychological Analysis*. New York: McGraw-Hill.

Berkowitz, L. (1969) The frustration–aggression hypothesis revisited. In L. Berkowitz (ed.), *Roots of Aggression*. New York: Atherton Press.

Berkowitz, L. (1993) *Aggression: Its Causes, Consequences and Control*. New York: McGraw-Hill.

Berkowitz, L. (1999) Aggression, psychology of. In L. Kurtz (ed.), *Encyclopedia of Violence, Peace and Conflict, Vol. 1*. San Diego: Academic Press.

Berkowitz, L. (2000) *Causes and Consequences of Feelings*. Cambridge: Cambridge University Press.

Berkowitz, L., Fraser, C., Treasure, F. P. and Cochran, S. (1987) Pay, equity, job gratifications and comparisons in pay satisfaction. *Journal of Applied Psychology*, 72, 544–51.

Bethlehem, D. W. (1985) *A Social Psychology of Prejudice*. London: Croom Helm.

Bettencourt, B. A. and Miller, N. (1996) Sex differences in aggression as a function of provocation: a meta-analysis. *Psychological Bulletin*, 119, 422–47.

Beynon, H. (1984) *Working for Ford*. 2nd edn. Harmondsworth: Penguin.

Bhugra, D. (1989) Attitudes towards mental illness: a review of the literature. *Acta Psychiatrica Scandinavia*, 80, 1–12.

Bierhoff, H. W. (1988) Affect, cognition, and prosocial behaviour. In K. Fiedler and J. Forgas (eds), *Affect, Cognition and Social Behaviour*. Toronto: Hogrefe.

Bierhoff, H. W., Klein, R. and Kramp, P. (1991) Evidence for the altruistic personality from data on accident research. *Journal of Personality*, 59, 263–80.

Billig, M. (1987) *Arguing and Thinking: A Rhetorical Approach to Social Psychology*. Cambridge: Cambridge University Press.

Billig, M. (1988) Methodology and scholarship in understanding ideological explanation In C. Antaki (ed.), *Analysing Everyday Explanation: A Casebook of Methods*. London: Sage.

Billig, M. and Tajfel, H. (1973) Social categorisation and similarity in intergroup behaviour. *European Journal of Social Psychology*, 3, 37–52.

Bilton, T., Bonnett, K., Jones, P., Stanworth, M., Sheard, K. and Webster, A. (1996) *Introductory Sociology*. 3rd edn. Basingstoke: Macmillan.

Birchwood, M. J., Hallett, S. E. and Preston, M. C. (1988) *Schizophrenia: An Integrated Approach to Research and Treatment*. London and New York: Longman.

Birdwhistell, R. L. (1970) *Kinesics and Context: Essays on Body Motion Communication*. Philadelphia: University of Pennsylvania Press.

Blackburn, R. (1993) *The Psychology of Criminal Conduct: Theory, Research and Practice*. Chichester: John Wiley.

Blinkhorn, S. and Johnson, C. (1990) The insignificance of personality testing. *Nature*, 348(6303), 671–2.

Block, J. (1995) A contrarian view of the Five Factor approach to personality description. *Psychological Bulletin*, 117, 187–215.

Bohner, G., Moskowitz, G. B. and Chaiken, S. (1995) The interplay of heuristic and systematic processing of social information. In W. Stroebe and M. Hewstone (eds), *European Review of Social Psychology, Vol. 6*. Chichester: John Wiley.

Boix, C. and Posner, D. N. (1995) Making social capital work: a review of Robert Putnam's *Making Democracy Work: Civic Traditions in Modern Italy*. Draft review.

Bolton, W. and Oatley, K. (1987) A longitudinal study of social support and depression in unemployed men. *Psychological Medicine*, 17, 453–60.

Bond, M. and Smith, P. B. (1996) Culture and conformity: a meta-analysis of studies using Asch's (1952b, 1956) line judgment task. *Psychological Bulletin*, 119, 111–37.

Borgida, E., Conner, C. and Manteufel, L. (1992) Understanding living kidney donation: a behavioral decision-making perspective. In S. Spacaman and S. Oskamp (eds), *Helping and Being Helped*. Newbury Park, CA: Sage.

Bothwell, S. and Weissman, M. M. (1977) Social impairments four years after an acute depressive episode. *American Journal of Orthopsychiatry*, 47, 231–7.

Bower, G. H. (1982) Mood and memory. *American Psychologist*, 36, 129–48.

Bowlby, J. (1944) Forty-four juvenile thieves: their characters and home life. *International Journal of Psycho-Analysis*, 25, 19–53. Forty-four juvenile thieves: their character and home life (II). *International Journal of Psycho-Analysis*, 25, 107–28.

Bowlby, J. (1969) *Attachment and Loss, Vol. 1: Attachment*. London: Hogarth Press.

Bowlby, J. (1980) *Attachment and Loss, Vol. 3: Loss, Sadness and Depression*. New York: Basic Books.

Boyanowsky, E. O. and Allen, V. L. (1973) Ingroup norms and self-identity as determinants of discriminatory behaviour. *Journal of Personality and Social Psychology*, 25, 408–18.

Breakwell, G. L., Hammond, S. and Fife-Shaw, C. (eds) (2000) *Research Methods in Psychology*. 2nd edn. London: Sage.

Breckler, S. J. (1984) Empirical validation of affect, behaviour and cognition as distinct components of attitude. *Journal of Personality and Social Psychology*, 47, 1191–1205.

Brenner, M. H. (1973) *Mental Illness and the Economy*. Cambridge, MA: Harvard University Press.

Brenner, M. H. (1979) Mortality and the national economy: a review and the experience of England and Wales 1936–76. *Lancet*, 2(8142), 568–73.

Bretherton, I. (1985) Attachment theory: retrospect and prospect. In I. Bretherton and E. Waters (eds), *Growing Points of Attachment Theory and Research*. Monographs of the Society for Research in Child Development, 50, serial no. 209, 3–35.

Bretherton, I. (1990) Communication patterns, internal working models, and the intergenerational transmission of attachment relationships. *Infant Mental Health Journal*, 11, 237–52.

Brewer, M. B. and Miller, N. (1996) *Intergroup Relations*. Buckingham: Open University Press.

Brewin, C. R. (1985) Depression and causal attributions: what is their relation? *Psychological Bulletin*, 98, 297–309.

Briggs, S. R. and Cheek, J. M. (1986) The role of factor analysis in the development and evaluation of personality scales. *Journal of Personality*, 54, 106–48.

Broberg, A. G., Wessels, H., Lamb, M. E. and Hwang, C. P. (1997) Effects of day care on the development of cognitive abilities in 8-year-olds: a longitudinal study. *Developmental Psychology*, 33, 62–9.

Brody, G. H. and Flor, D. L. (1997) Maternal psychological functioning, family processes, and child adjustment in rural, single-parent, African-American families. *Developmental Psychology*, 33, 1000–11.

Brody, N. B. (1992) *Intelligence*. 2nd edn. San Diego: Academic Press.

Brody, R. (1987) *Stories of Sickness*. New Haven, CT: Yale University Press.

Brown, G. W. and Birley, J. L. T. (1968) Crises and life changes and the onset of schizophrenia. *Journal of Health and Social Behaviour*, 9, 203–14.

Brown, G. W. and Harris, T. (1978) *Social Origins of Depression: A Study of Psychiatric Disorder in Women*. London: Tavistock.

Brown, G. W., Bifulco, A. and Harris, T. (1987) Life events, vulnerability and onset of depression: some refinements. *British Journal of Psychiatry*, 150, 30–42.

Brown, G. W., Birley, J. L. T. and Wing, J. K. (1972) Influence of family life on the course of schizophrenic disorders: a replication. *British Journal of Psychiatry*, 121, 241–58.

Brown, G. W., Harris, T. and Copeland, J. R. (1977) Depression and loss. *British Journal of Psychiatry*, 130, 1–18.

Brown, R. (1965) *Social Psychology*. New York: Free Press.

Brown, R. (1986) *Social Psychology*. 2nd cdn. Ncw York: Free Press/Macmillan.

Brown, R. J. (1978) Divided we fall: an analysis of relations between sections of a factory workforce. In H. Tajfel (ed.), *Differentiation between Social Groups: Studies in the Social Psychology of Intergroup Relations*. London: Academic Press.

Brown, R. J. (1988) *Group Processes: Dynamics Within and Between Groups*. Oxford: Blackwell.

Brown, R. J. (1995) *Prejudice: Its Social Psychology*. Oxford: Blackwell.

Brown, R. J. (2000) *Group Processes*. 2nd edn. Oxford: Blackwell.

Bruner, J. S. (1957) On perceptual readiness. *Psychological Review*, 64, 123–51.

Bruner, J. S. (1990) *Acts of Meaning*. Cambridge, MA: Harvard University Press.

Buck, N., Gershuny, J., Rose, D. and Scott, J. (1994) *Changing Households: The British Household Panel Survey, 1990–1992*. Essex University, ESRC Research Centre on Micro-Social Change.

Buck, R. and Ginsburg, B. (1991) Spontaneous communication and altruism: the communicative gene hypothesis. In M. S. Clark (ed.), *Prosocial Behavior*. Newbury Park, CA: Sage.

Buck-Morss, S. (1975) Socio-economic bias in Piaget's theory and its implications for cross-cultural studies. *Human Development*, 18, 35–49.

Burbank, V. K. (1987) Female aggression in cross-cultural perspective. *Behavior Science Research*, 21, 70–100.

Burchell, B. J. (1992a) Changes in the labour market and the psychological health of the nation. In J. Michie (ed.), *The Economic Legacy, 1979–1992*. London: Academic Press.

Burchell, B. J. (1992b) Towards a social psychology of the labour market: or why we need to understand the labour market before we can understand unemployment. *Journal of Occupational and Organisational Psychology*, 65, 345–54.

Burchell, B. J. (1994) Who is affected by unemployment? Job insecurity and labour market influences on psychological health. In D. Gallie, C. Marsh and C. Vogler (eds), *Social Change and the Experience of Unemployment*. Oxford: Oxford University Press.

Burchell, B. J. and Rubery, J. (1990) An empirical investigation into the segmentation of the labour supply. *Work, Employment and Society*, 4(4), 551–75.

Burchell, B. J., Day, D., Hudson, M., Ladipo, D., Mankelow, R., Nolan, J., Reed, H., Wichert, I. and Wilkinson, F. (1999) *Job Insecurity and Work Intensification: Flexibility and the Changing Boundaries of Work*. Joseph Rowntree Foundation Report.

Burgoon, J. K., Parrott, R., Le Poire, B. A., Kelley, D. L., Walther, J. B. and Perry, D. (1989) Maintaining and restoring privacy through communication in different types of relationships. *Journal of Social and Personal Relationships*, 6, 131–58.

Burnstein, E., Crandall, C. and Kitayama, S. (1994) Some neo-Darwinian rules for altruism: weighing cues for inclusive fitness as a function of the biological importance of the decision. *Journal of Personality and Social Psychology*, 67, 773–89.

Busfield, J. (1996) *Men, Women and Madness: Understanding Gender and Mental Disorder*. Basingstoke: Macmillan.

Bushman, B. J. (1996) Individual differences in the extent and development of aggressive cognitive-associative networks. *Personality and Social Psychology Bulletin*, 22, 811–19.

Bushman, B. J. and Anderson, C. A. (1998) Methodology in the study of aggression: integrating experimental and non-experimental findings. In R. G. Geen and E. Donnerstein (eds), *Human Aggression: Theories, Research and Implications for Social Policy*. San Diego: Academic Press.

Buss, A. H. (1989) Personality as traits. *American Psychologist*, 44, 1378–88.

Buss, D. M. (1999) *Evolutionary Psychology*. Boston: Allyn and Bacon.

Buss, D. M. and Kenrick, D. T. (1998) Evolutionary social psychology. In D. T. Gilbert, S. T. Fiske and G. Lindzey (eds), *The Handbook of Social Psychology, Vol. 2*. 4th edn. New York: Mc Graw-Hill.

Buunk, B. and Bringle, R. G. (1987) Jealousy in love relationships. In D. Perlman and S. Duck (eds), *Intimate Relationships*. Beverley Hills, CA: Sage.

Byrne, R. W. (1995) The thinking ape: evolutionary origins of intelligence. Oxford: Oxford University Press.

Byrne, R. W. and Whiten, A. (1988) *Machiavellian Intelligence: Social Expertise and the Evolution of Intellect in Monkeys, Apes and Humans*. Oxford: Clarendon Press.

Cairns, R. B. and Cairns, B. D. (1994) *Lifelines and Risks: Pathways of Youth in Our Time*. Cambridge: Cambridge University Press.

Callaway, M. R. and Esser, J. K. (1984) Groupthink: effects of cohesiveness and problem-solving procedures on group decision making. *Social Behaviour and Personality*, 12, 157–64.

Calnan, M. (1987) *Health and Illness: The Lay Perspective*. London: Tavistock.

Cameron, D. (1995) *Verbal Hygiene*. London: Routledge.

Campbell, A. (1986) *The Girls in the Gang*. Oxford: Blackwell.

Campbell, A. (1993) *Out of Control: Men, Women and Aggression*. New York: Basic Books.

Campbell, A. and Muncer, S. (1998) *The Social Child*. Hove: Psychology Press.

Campbell, A., Converse, P. E. and Rogers, W. L. (1976) *The Quality of American Life*. New York: Sage.

Campbell, C. (1997) Migrancy, masculine identities and AIDS: the psychosocial context of HIV transmission in the South African gold mines. *Social Science and Medicine*, 45 (2), 273–81.

Campbell, D. T. (1963) Social attitudes and other acquired behavioural dispositions. In S. Koch (ed.), *Psychology: A Study of a Science, Vol. 6*. New York: McGraw-Hill.

Campbell, D. T. (1965) Ethnocentric and other altruistic motives. In D. Levine (ed.), *Nebraska Symposium on Motivation*. Lincoln, NE: University of Nebraska Press.

Campbell, D. T. and Stanley, J. (1966) *Experimental and Quasi-experimental Designs for Research*. Chicago: Rand McNally.

Cannon, W. B. (1927) The James–Lange theory of emotions: a critical examination and an alternative theory. *American Journal of Psychology*, 39, 106–24.

Caplan, M. Z., Vespo, J. E., Pedersen, J. and Hay, D. F. (1991) Conflict and its resolution in small groups of one-and two-year-olds. *Child Development*, 62, 1513–24.

Caprara, G. V., Barbaranelli, C., Pastorelli, C. and Perugini, M. (1994) Individual differences in the study of aggression. *Aggressive Behaviour*, 20, 291–303.

Carmelli, D., Dame, A., Swan, G. and Rosenman, R. (1991) Long-term changes in Type A behaviour: a 27 year follow-up of the Western Collaborative Group Study. *Journal of Behavioural Medicine*, 14, 593–606.

Carraher, T. N., Carraher D. W. and Schliemann, A. D. (1985) Mathematics in the streets and in schools. *British Journal of Developmental Psychology*, 3, 21–9.

Carraher, T. N., Carraher, D. W. and Schliemann, A. D. (1987) Written and oral mathematics. *Journal for Research in Mathematics Education*, 18(2), 83–97.

Carugati, F. (1990) Everyday ideas, theoretical models and social representations: the case of intelligence. In G. Semin and K. Gergen (eds), *Everyday Understanding*. London: Sage.

Carver, C. S. and Glass, D. C. (1978) Coronary-prone behavior pattern and interpersonal aggression. *Journal of Personality and Social Psychology*, 36, 361–6.

Catalano, R. A. and Dooley, D. (1983) Health effects of economic instability: a test of economic stress hypothesis. *Journal of Health and Social Behaviour*, 24, 46–60.

Chaiken, S. (1980) Heuristic versus systematic information processing and the use of source versus message cues in persuasion. *Journal of Personality and Social Psychology*, 39, 752–66.

Chaiken, S. (1987) The heuristic model of persuasion. In M. P. Zanna, J. M. Olson and C. P. Herman (eds), *Social Influence: The Ontario Symposium, Vol. 5*. Hillsdale, NJ: Erlbaum.

Charman, T., Swettenham, J., Baron-Cohen, S., Cox, A., Baird, G. and Drew, A. (1997) Infants with autism: an investigation of empathy, pretend play, joint attention, and imitation. *Developmental Psychology*, 33(5), 781–9.

Christensen, A. and Heavey, C. L. (1993) Gender differences in marital conflict. In S. Oskamp and M. Costanzo (eds), *Gender Issues in Contemporary Society*. Newbury Park, CA: Sage.

Cialdini, R. B. (1993) *Influence: The Psychology of Persuasion*. New York: Quill.

Cialdini, R. B. and Fultz, J. (1990) Interpreting the negative mood/helping literature via mega-analysis: a contrary view. *Psychological Bulletin*, 107, 210–14.

Cialdini, R. B., Darby, B. L. and Vincent, J. E. (1973) Transgression and altruism: a case for hedonism. *Journal of Experimental Social Psychology*, 9, 502–16.

Clary, E. G. and Snyder, M. (1991) A functional analysis of altruism and prosocial behaviour: the case of volunteerism. In M. S. Clark (ed.), *Review of Personality and Social Psychology*, 12, 119–48. Newbury Park, CA: Sage.

Clary, E. G., Snyder, M., Ridge, R. D., Copeland, J., Stukas, A. A., Haugen, J. and Miene, P. (1998) Understanding and assessing the motivations of volunteers: a functional approach. *Journal of Personality and Social Psychology*, 74, 1516–30.

Cleckley, H. (1988) *The Mask of Sanity: An Attempt to Clarify Some Issues about the So-called Psychopathic Personality*. Augusta, GA: Emily S. Cleckley.

Clegg, C. W. (1983) Psychology of employee lateness, absence, and turnover: a methodological critique and an empirical study. *Journal of Applied Psychology*, 68, 88–101.

Coates, J. (1993) *Women, Men, and Language: A Sociolinguistic Account of Gender Differences in Language*. 2nd edn. London and New York: Longman.

Coates, J. (1998) *Language and Gender: A Reader*. Oxford and Malden, MA: Blackwell.

Cochrane, R. (1983) *The Social Creation of Mental Illness*. London and New York: Longman.

Cohen, C. (1987) Nuclear language. *Bulletin of the Atomic Scientist*, June, 17–24.

Cohen, D. (1995) *Psychologists on Psychology*. London and New York: Routledge.

Cohen, S. and Wills, T. A. (1985) Stress, social support and the buffering hypothesis. *Psychological Bulletin*, 98, 310–57.

Cohn, J. F. and Tronick, E. Z. (1983) Three-month-old infants' reaction to simulated maternal depression. *Child Development*, 54, 185–93.

Coie, J. D., Dodge, K. A. and Coppotelli, H. (1982) Dimensions and types of social status: a cross-age perspective. *Developmental Psychology*, 18, 557–70.

Colby, A. and Kohlberg, L. (1987) *The Measurement of Moral Judgment*. Cambridge: Cambridge University Press.

Colby, A., Kohlberg, L., Gibbs, J. and Liebermann, M. (1983) A longitudinal study of moral development. *Monographs for the Society for Research in Child Development*, 48 (1 and 2).

Cole, M. and Scribner, S. (1974) *Culture and Thought: A Psychological Introduction*. New York: John Wiley.

Collins, J., Krietman, N., Nelson, B. and Troop, J. (1971) Neurosis and marital inter-action. III: Family roles and functions. *British Journal of Psychiatry*, 119, 233–42.

Constanzo, P. R., Coie, J. D., Grumet, J. and Farnill, D. (1973) A reexamination of the effects of intent and consequences on children's moral judgments. *Child Development*, 45, 799–802.

Cook, S. W. (1978) Interpersonal and attitudinal outcomes in cooperating interracial groups. *Journal of Research and Development in Education*, 12, 97–113.

Cooper, J. and Fazio, R. H. (1984) A new look at dissonance theory. In L. Berkowitz (ed.), *Advances in Experimental Social Psychology, Vol. 17*. New York: Academic Press.

Corsaro, W. A. (1990) The underlife of the nursery school: young children's social representations of adult rules. In G. Duveen and B. Lloyd (eds), *Social Representations and the Development of Knowledge*. Cambridge: Cambridge University Press.

Costa, P. T., Jr, and McCrae, R. R. (1994) The Revised NEO Personality Inventory. In R. Briggs and J. M. Cheek (eds), *Personality Measures: Development and Evaluation*. Greenwich, CT: JAI Press.

Cotton, J. L. and Baron, R. S. (1980) Anonymity, persuasive arguments and choice shifts. *Social Psychology Quarterly*, 43, 391–404.

Cowan, P. A. and Cowan, C. P. (1978) Changes in marriage during the transition to parenthood: must we blame the baby? In G. Y. Michaels and W. A. Goldberg (eds), *The Transition to Parenthood: Current Theory and Research*. New York: Cambridge University Press.

Cox, M. J. and Paley, B. (1997) Families as systems. *Annual Review of Psychology*, 48, 243–67.

Coyne, J. C., Kessler, R. C., Tal, M., Turnbull, J., Wortman, C. B. and Greden, J. F. (1987) Living with a depressed person. *Journal of Consulting and Clinical Psychology*, 9, 148–58.

Cramer, R. E., McMaster, M. R., Barrell, P. A. and Dragna, M. (1988) Subject competence and minimization of the bystander effect. *Journal of Applied Social Psychology*, 18, 1133–48.

Crick, N. R. and Dodge, K. A. (1994) A review and reformulation of social information processing mechanisms in children's adjustment. *Psychological Bulletin*, 115, 74–101.

Crick, N. R. and Dodge, K. A. (1996) Social information-processing mechanisms in reactive and proactive aggression. *Child Development*, 67, 993–1002.

Cronbach, L. J. (1975) Beyond the two disciplines of scientific psychology. *American Psychologist*, 30, 116–27.

Crook, T. and Eliot, J. (1980). Parental death during childhood and adult depression: a critical review of the literature. *Psychological Bulletin*, 87, 252–9.

Crystal, D. (1997) *A Dictionary of Linguistics and Phonetics*. 4th edn. Oxford and Cambridge, MA: Blackwell.

Csikszentmihalyi, M. (1991) *Flow: The Psychology of Optimal Experience*. New York: Harper Perennial.

Curtice, J. (1993) Satisfying work – if you can get it. In R. Jowell, L. Brooks and L. Dowds (eds), *British Social Attitudes: The 10th Report*. Aldershot: Dartmouth.

Curtiss, S. (1977) *Genie: A Psycholinguistic Study of a Modern Day 'Wild Child'*. London: Academic Press.

D'Alessio, M. (1990) Social representations of childhood: an implicit theory of development. In G. Duveen and B. Lloyd (eds), *Social Representations and Development of Knowledge*. Cambridge: Cambridge University Press.

Dalgleish, T., Joseph, S., Thrasher, S., Tranah, T. and Yule, W. (1996) Crisis support following the *Herald of Free Enterprise* disaster: a longitudinal perspective. *Journal of Traumatic Stress*, 9, 833–46.

Damasio, A. R. (1994) *Descartes' Error*. New York: Putnam.

Damon, W. (1977) *The Social World of the Child*. San Francisco: Jossey-Bass.

Damon, W. (ed.) (1998) *Handbook of Social Psychology, Vol. 4*. Chichester: John Wiley.

Danziger, K. (1979) The positivistic repudiation of Wundt. *Journal of the History of the Behavioural Sciences*, 15, 205–30.

Danziger, K. (1997) The varieties of social construction. *Theory and Psychology*, 7, 399–416.

Darley, J. M. (1999) Methods for the study of evil – doing actions. In A. G. Miller (guest ed.), *Special Issue: Perspectives on evil and violence, Personality and Social Psychology Review*, 3(3), 269–75.

Darwin, C. (1872) *The Expression of Emotion in Man and Animals*. London: John Murray.

Davey, A. G. (1983) *Learning to be Prejudiced*. London: Edward Arnold.

Davidson, P., Turiel, E. and Black, A. (1983) The effect of stimulus familiarity on the use of criteria and justifications in children's social reasoning. *British Journal of Development Psychology*, 1, 49–65.

Dawes, R., Faust, D. and Meehl, P. E. (1989) Clinical versus actuarial judgement. *Science*, 243, 1668–74.

Deaux, K. and Lafrance, M. (1998) Gender. In D. T. Gilbert, S. T. Fiske and G. Lindzey (eds), *The Handbook of Social Psychology, Vol. 1*. 4th edn. New York: McGraw-Hill.

Deaux, K. and Philogene, G. (eds) (2000) *Social Representations: Introductions and Explorations*. Oxford: Blackwell.

DeCasper, A. J. and Fifer, W. P. (1980) Of Human bonding: newborns prefer their mothers' voices. *Science*, 208, 1174–6.

De Jonge, J. and Schaufeli, W. B. (1998) Job characteristics and employee well-being: a test of Warr's Vitamin Model in health care workers using structural equation modelling. *Journal of Organisational Behaviour*, 19, 387–407.

Dell, G. S., Chang, F. and Griffin, Z. M. (1999) Connectionist models of language production: lexical access and grammatical encoding. *Cognitive Science*, 23(4), 517–42.

Denham, S., McKinley, M., Couchoud, E. A. and Holt, R. (1990) Emotional and behavioral predictors of preschool peer ratings. *Child Development*, 61, 1145–52.

Denzin, N. K. (1978) *The Research Act*. 2nd edn. Chicago: Aldine.

De Paolis, P. (1990) Prototypes of the psychologist and professionalisation: diverging social representations of a developmental process. In G. Duveen and B. Lloyd (eds), *Social Representations and Development of Knowledge*. Cambridge: Cambridge University Press.

Depaulo, B. M. (1992) Nonverbal behavior and self-presentation. *Psychological Bulletin*, 111(2), 203–43.

De Rosa, A. M. (1987) The social representations of mental illness in children and adults. In W. Doise and S. Moscovici (eds), *Current Issues In European Social Psychology, Vol. 2*. Cambridge: Cambridge University Press.

Deschamps, J.-C. and Doise, W. (1978) Crossed category memberships in intergroup relations. In H. Tajfel (ed.), *Differentiation between Social Groups: Studies in the Social Psychology of Intergroup Behaviour*. London: Academic Press.

Deutsch, M. and Gerard, H. B. (1955) A study of normative and informational influence upon individual judgement. *Journal of Abnormal and Social Psychology*, 51, 629–36.

Deutscher, I. (1984) Choosing ancestors: some consequences of the selection from intellectual traditions. In R. M. Farr and S. Moscovici (eds), *Social Representations*. Cambridge: Cambridge University Press.

Devlin, K. (1997) *Goodbye Descartes: The End of Logic and the Search for a New Cosmology of the Mind*. New York: John Wiley.

De Wolff, M. S. and van Ijzendoorn, M. H. (1997) Sensitivity and attachment. a meta-analysis on parental antecedents of infant attachment. *Child Development*, 68, 571–91.

Dickson, K. L., Walker, H. and Fogel, A. (1997) The relationship between smile type and play type during parent–infant play. *Developmental Psychology*, 33, 925–33.

Diener, E., Sandvik, E., Seidlitz, L., and Diener, M. (1993) The relationship between income and subjective well-being: relative or absolute? *Social Indicators Research*, 28, 195–223.

Digman, J. M. (1990) Personality structure: emergence of the five-factor model. *Annual Review of Psychology*, 41, 417–40.

DiLalla, L. F. and Gottesman, I. J. (1991) Biological and genetic contributors to violence – Widom's untold tale. *Psychological Bulletin*, 109, 125–9.

Dodge, K. A. (1986) A social-information processing model of social competence in children. In M. Permutter (ed.) *Minnesota Symposium on Child Psychology*, 18. Hillsdale, NJ. Erlbaum.

Dodge, K. A. (1997) *How Early Peer Rejection and Acquired Autonomic Sensitivity to Peer Conflicts Influence Each Other to Produce Conduct Problems in Adolescence.* Washington, DC: Society for Research in Child Development.

Dohrenwend, B. S. and Dohrenwend, B. P. (1969) *Social Status and Psychological Disorder: A Causal Enquiry.* New York: John Wiley.

Doise, W. (1969) Intergroup relations and polarisation of individual and collective judgments. *Journal of Personality and Social Psychology*, 12, 136–43.

Doise, W. (1978) *Groups and Individuals: Explanations in Social Psychology.* Cambridge: Cambridge University Press.

Doise, W. and Mackie, D. (1981) On the social nature of social cognition. In J. P. Forgas (ed.), *Social Cognition: Perspectives on Everyday Understanding.* London: Academic Press.

Doise, W., Clémence, A. and Lorenzi-Cioldi, F. (1993) *The Quantitative Analysis of Social Representations.* London: Harvester Wheatsheaf.

Doise, W., Clémence, A. and Lorenzi-Cioldi, F. (1994) Le charme discret des attitudes. *Papers on Social Representations*, 3, 26–8.

Dollard, J., Doob, L. W., Miller, N. E., Mowrer, O. H. and Sears, R. R. (1939) *Frustration and Aggression.* New Haven, CT: Yale University Press.

Doms, M. and van Avermaet, E. (1980) Majority influence, minority influence and conversion behaviour: a replication. *Journal of Experimental Social Psychology*, 16, 283–92.

Dooley, D. and Catalano, R. A. (1986) Do economic variables generate psychological problems? Different methods, different answers. In: A. J. MacFadyen and H. W. MacFadyen (eds), *Economic Psychology: Intersections in Theory and Application.* Amsterdam: North-Holland.

Dooley, D., Catalano, R. and Rook, K. S. (1988) Personal and aggregate unemployment and psychological symptoms. *Journal of Social Issues*, 44, 107–23.

Dooley, D., Rook, K. and Catalano, R. (1987) Job and non-job stressors and their moderators. *Journal of Occupational Psychology*, 60, 115–32.

Dougherty, T. W., Turban, D. B. and Callender, J. C. (1994) Confirming first impressions in the employment interview: a field study of interviewer behaviour. *Journal of Applied Psychology*, 79(5), 659–65.

Dovidio, J. F. and Fazio, R. H. (1992) New technologies for the direct and indirect assessment of attitudes. In J. M. Tanur (ed.), *Questions about Questions: Inquiries into the Cognitive Bases of Surveys.* New York: Russell Sage Foundation.

Dovidio, J. F., Allen, J. and Schroeder, D. A. (1990) The specificity of empathy-induced helping: evidence for altruism. *Journal of Personality and Social Psychology*, 59, 249–60.

Dovidio, J. F., Piliavin, J. A., Gaertner, S. L., Schroeder, D. A. and Clark, R. D. III. (1991) The arousal: cost–reward model and the process of intervention: a review of the evidence. In M. S. Clark (ed.), *Prosocial Behaviour*. Newbury Park, CA: Sage.

Dowds, L. (1994) Victim surveys: exploring the nature of violent crime. *Psychology, Crime and the Law: Special Issue on British Research*, 1, 125–32.

Drewery, J. and Rae, J. B. (1969) A group comparison of alcoholic and non-alcoholic marriages using the interpersonal perception technique. *British Journal of Psychiatry*, 11, 287–300.

Duck, S. W. and Craig, G. (1978) Personality similarity and the development of friendship: a longitudinal study. *British Journal of Social and Clinical Psychology*, 17, 237–42.

Duckitt, J. (1992) *The Social Psychology of Prejudice*. Westport, CT: Praeger.

Duclos, D. (1998) *The Werewolf Complex: America's Fascination with Violence*. Oxford: Berg.

Dunn, J. (1988) *The Beginnings of Social Understanding*. Cambridge, MA: Harvard University Press.

Dunn, J. (1993) *Young Children's Close Relationships: Beyond Attachment*. London: Sage.

Dunn, J. and Kendrick, C. (1982) *Siblings*. Cambridge, MA: Harvard University Press.

Dunn, J. and Plomin, R. (1990) *Separate Lives: Why Siblings are So Different*. New York: Basic Books.

Dunn, J., Stocker, C. and Plomin, R. (1990) Nonshared experiences within the family: correlates of behavioral problems in middle childhood. *Development and Psychopathology*, 25, 835–45.

Durkheim, E. (1925/1961) *L'Education Morale*. Glencoe, IL: Free Press.

Durkheim, E. (1906/1974) *Sociology and Philosophy*. New York: Free Press.

Durkin, K. (1995) *Developmental Social Psychology: From Infancy to Old Age*. Oxford: Blackwell.

Duveen, G. (1998) The psychosocial production of knowledge: social representations and psychologic. *Culture and Psychology*, 4, 455–72.

Duveen, G. (2000) Representations, identities, resistance. In K. Deaux and G. Philogene (eds), *Social Representations: Introductions and Explorations*. Oxford: Blackwell.

Duveen, G. and Lloyd, B. (1986) The significance of social identities. *British Journal of Social Psychology*, 25, 219–30.

Duveen, G. and Lloyd, B. (eds) (1990) *Social Representations and Development of Knowledge*. Cambridge: Cambridge University Press.

Dyer, C. (1995) *Beginning Research in Psychology: A Practical Guide to Research Methods and Statistics*. Oxford: Blackwell.

Eagly, A. H. (1995) The science and politics of comparing women and men. *American Psychologist*, 50, 145–58.

Eagly, A. H. and Chaiken, S. (1984) Cognitive theories of persuasion. In L. Berkowitz (ed.), *Advances in Experimental Social Psychology, Vol. 17*. New York: Academic Press.

Eagly, A. H. and Chaiken, S. (1993) *The Psychology of Attitudes*. San Diego: Harcourt Brace Jovanovich.

Eagly, A. H. and Crowley, M. (1986) Gender and helping behaviour: a meta-analytic review of the social psychological literature. *Psychological Bulletin*, 100, 283–308.

Eagly, A. H. and Steffen, V. J. (1986) Gender and aggressive behavior: a meta-analytic review of the social psychological literature. *Psychological Bulletin*, 100, 309–30.

Ebbinghaus, H. (1885) *Uber das Gedachtnis: Untersuchungen zur experimentellen Psychologie.* Leipzig: Duncker & Humblot.

Ebbinghaus, H. (1913) *Memory: A Contribution to Experimental Psychology.* New York: Teachers College, Columbia University.

Egeland, B., Jacobvitz, D. and Sroufe, L. A. (1988) Breaking the cycle of abuse: factors related to its development and changes over time. *Child Development*, 59, 1080–8.

Egeland, J. A. and Hostetter, A. M. (1983) Amish study: 1. Affective disorders among the Amish, 1976–1980. *American Journal of Psychiatry*, 140, 56–61.

Eisenberg, N. (1992) *The Caring Child.* Cambridge, MA: Harvard University Press.

Eisenberg, N. and Fabes, R. A. (1990) Empathy: conceptualization, assessment, and relation to prosocial behaviour. *Motivation and Emotions*, 14, 131–49.

Eisenberg, N., Fabes, R. A., Carlo, G. and Karbon, M. (1992) Emotional responsibility to others: behavioural correlates and socialization antecedents. *New Directions in Child Development*, 55, 57–73.

Eisenberg, N., Fabes, R. A., Schaller, M. and Miller, P. A. (1989) Sympathy and personal distress: development, gender differences, and interrelations of indexes. *New Directions in Child Development*, 44, 107–26.

Eisenman, R. (1993) Belief that drug usage in the United States is increasing when it is really decreasing – an example of the availability heuristic. *Bulletin of the Psychonomic Society*, 31(4), 249–52.

Ekman, P. (1994) Strong evidence for universals in facial expressions – a reply to Russell's mistaken critique. *Psychological Bulletin*, 115(2), 268–87.

Ekman, P. and Friesen, W. V., (1971) Constants across cultures in the face and emotion. *Journal of Personality and Social Psychology* 17(2), 124–9.

Ekman, P., Friesen, W. V. O'Sullivan, M., Chan, A., Diacoyannitarlatzis, I., Heider, K., Krause, R., Lecompte, W. A., Pitcairn, T., Riccibitti, P. E., Scherer, K., Tomita, M. and Tzavaras, A. (1987) Universals and cultural differences in the judgments of facial expressions of emotion. *Journal of Personality and Social Psychology*, 53(4), 712–17.

Elder, G. H., Jr, and Caspi, A. (1988) Economic stress in lives: developmental perspectives. *Journal of Social Issues*, 4, 25–45.

Elder, G. H., Jr, Modell, J. and Parke, R. D. (eds) (1993) *Children in Time and Place: Developmental and Historical Insights.* Cambridge: Cambridge University Press.

Emler, N. (1987) Socio-moral development from the perspective of social representations. *Journal for the Theory of Social Behaviour*, 17, 371–88.

Epstein, S. (1979) The stability of behaviour I: on predicting most of the people much of the time. *Journal of Personality and Social Psychology*, 37, 1097–1126.

Epstein, S. and O'Brien, E. J. (1985) The person-situation debate in historical and current perspective. *Psychological Bulletin*, 98, 513–37.

Eron, L. D., Huesmann, L. R., Dubow, E., Romanoff, R. and Yarmel, P. (1987) Aggression and its correlates over 22 years. In D. Crowell, I. Evans and C. O'Donnell (eds), *Childhood Aggression and Violence.* New York: Plenum Press.

Esterling, B. A., Kiecolt-Glaser, J. K. and Glaser, R. (1996) Psychosocial modulation of cytokine-induced natural killer cell activity in older adults. *Psychosomatic Medicine*, 58, 264–72.

Eyferth, K. (1959) Eine untersuchung der Neger-Mischlingskinder in West-deutschland. *Vita Humana*, 2, 102–13.

Eyferth, K. (1961) Leistungen verschiedener Gruppen von Besatzungskindern in Hamburg-Weschler Intelligenztest fur kinder (HAWIK). *Archiv fur die Gesamte Psychologie*, 113, 222–41.

Eysenck, H. J. (1954) *The Psychology of Politics*. London: Routledge and Kegan Paul.

Eysenck, H. J. (1977) *Crime and Personality*. (3rd edn.) London: Routledge and Kegan Paul.

Eysenck, H. J. (1978) *Sex and Personality*. London: Abacus.

Eysenck, H. J. (1980) *The Causes and Effects of Smoking*. London: Temple Smith.

Eysenck, H. J. (1982) *The Scientific Study of Personality*. Westport, CI: Greenwood Press.

Eysenck, H. J. (1991) *Smoking, Personality, and Stress: Psychosocial Factors in the Prevention of Cancer and Coronary Heart Disease*. New York: Springer-Verlag.

Eysenck, H. J. (1997) *Rebel with a Cause: The Autobiography of Hans Eysenck*. Rev. and expanded edn. New Brunswick, NJ: Transaction.

Eysenck, H. J. (1998) *Dimensions of Personality*. New Brunswick, NJ: Transaction.

Eysenck, H. J. (1999) *The Psychology of Politics*. Rev. edn. New Brunswick, NJ: Transaction.

Eysenck, H. J. and Nias, D. K. B. (1978) *Sex, Violence, and the Media*. New York: St Martin's Press.

Eysenck, H. J. and Wilson, G. D. (1973) *The Experimental Study of Freudian Theories*. London: Methuen.

Fagin, L. and Little, M. (1984) *The Forsaken Families*. Harmondsworth: Penguin.

Fagot, B. (1997) Attachment, parenting, and peer interactions of toddler children. *Developmental Psychology*, 33, 489–99.

Farr, R. M. (1994) Attitudes, social representations and social attitudes. *Papers on Social Representations*, 3, 33–6.

Farr, R. M. (1996) *The Roots of Modern Social Psychology 1872–1954*. Oxford: Blackwell.

Farr, R. M. (1998) From collective to social representations: aller et retour. *Culture and Psychology*, 4, 275–96.

Farrington, D. P. (1993) Understanding and preventing bullying. In M. Tonry and N. Morris (eds), *Crime and Justice: An Annual Review of Research*, 17. Chicago: University of Chicago Press.

Farrington, D. P. (1994) Childhood, adolescent and adult features of violent males. In L. R. Huesmann (ed.), *Aggressive Behaviour: Current Perspectives*. New York: Plenum Press.

Farrington, D. P. and West, D. J. (1990) The Cambridge Study in Delinquent Development: a long-term follow-up of 411 London males. In H. J. Kerner and G. Kaiser (eds), *Criminality: Personality, Behaviour and Life History*. Berlin: Springer-Verlag.

Fasold, R. W. (1984) *The Sociolinguistics of Society*. New York: Blackwell.

Faulkner, D., Hough, M. and Halpern, D. S. (1996) Crime and criminal justice. In D. S. Halpern, S. Wood, S. White and G. Cameron (eds), *Options for Britain: A Strategic Policy Review*. Aldershot: Dartmouth.

Fazio, R. H. (1986) How do attitudes guide behaviour? In R. M. Sorrentino and E. T. Higgins (eds), *Handbook of Motivation and Cognition: Foundations of Social Behaviour*. New York: Guilford Press.

Fazio, R. H. (1989) On the power and functionality of attitudes: the role of attitude accessibility. In A. R. Pratkanis, S. J. Breckler and A. G. Greenwald (eds), *Attitude Structure and Function*. Hillsdale, NJ: Erlbaum.

Fazio, R. H. and Zanna, M. P. (1978) Attitudinal qualities relating to the strength of the attitude–behaviour relationship. *Journal of Experimental Social Psychology*, 14, 398–408.

Fazio, R. H., Zanna, M. P. and Cooper, J. (1977) Dissonance and self-perception: an integrative view of each theory's proper domain of application. *Journal of Experimental Social Psychology*, 13, 464–79.

Feather, N. T. (1990) *The Psychological Impact of Unemployment*. New York: Springer-Verlag.

Felson, R. B. (1978) Aggression as impression management. *Social Psychology*, 41, 205–13.

Felstead, A., Burchell, B. and Green, F. (1998) Insecurity at work. *New Economy*, 5(3), 180–4.

Feshbach, N. D. (1989) Empathy training and prosocial behaviour. In J. Groebel and R. A. Hinde (eds), *Aggression and War: Their Biological and Social Bases*. Cambridge: Cambridge University Press.

Festinger, L. (1950) Informal social communication. *Psychological Review*, 57, 271–82.

Festinger, L. (1954) A theory of social comparison processes. *Human Relations*, 7, 117–40.

Festinger, L. (1957) *A Theory of Cognitive Dissonance*. Evanston, IL: Row, Peterson.

Festinger, L. (1964) *Conflict, Decision and Dissonance*. Stanford, CA: Stanford University Press.

Festinger, L. (ed.) (1980) *Retrospection on Social Psychology*. New York: Oxford University Press.

Festinger, L. and Carlsmith, J. M. (1959) Cognitive consequences of forced compliance. *Journal of Abnormal and Social Psychology*, 58, 203–10.

Festinger, L., Riecken, H. W. and Schachter, S. (1956) *When Prophecy Fails*. Minneapolis: University of Minnesota Press.

Fhaner, G. and Hane, M. (1979) Seat belts: opinion effects of law-induced use. *Journal of Applied Psychology*, 64, 205–12.

Field, T. M., Healy, B. and Goldstein, S. (1988) Infants of depressed mothers show 'depressed' behaviour even with nondepressed adults. *Child Development*, 59, 1569–79.

Field, T. M., Woodson, R., Greenberg, R. and Cohen, D. (1982) Discrimination and imitation of facial expressions by neonates. *Science*, 146, 668–70.

Fincham, F. D. and Bradbury, T. N. (1992) Assessing attributions in marriage: the relationship attribution measure. *Journal of Personality and Social Psychology*, 62, 457–68.

Fincham, F. D. and Jaspers, J. M. (1980) Attribution of responsibility: from man the scientist to man the lawyer. In L. Berkowitz (ed.), *Advances in Experimental Social Psychology, Vol 13*. New York: Academic Press.

Fineman, S. (1983) *White Collar Unemployment: Impact and Stress*. Chichester: John Wiley.

Fineman, S. (1987) Back to employment: wounds and wisdoms. In D. Fryer and P. Ullah (eds), *Unemployed People: Social and Psychological Perspectives*. Milton Keynes: Open University Press

Finkelhor, D., Gelles, R. J., Hotaling, G. T. and Straus, M. A. (1990) *Physical Violence in American Families: Risk Factors and Adaptations to Violence in 8,145 Families*. New Brunswick, NJ: Transaction.

Fishbein, M. and Ajzen, I. (1975) *Belief, Attitude, Intention and Behaviour: An Introduction to Theory and Research*. Reading, MA: Addison-Wesley.

Fisher, W. A. (1984) Predicting contraceptive behaviour among university men: the role of emotions and behavioural intentions. *Journal of Applied Social Psychology*, 14, 104–23.

Fishman, P. (1978) Interaction: the work women do. *Social Problems*, 25(4), 397–406.

Fiske, A. P. (1991) The cultural relativity of selfish individualism: anthropological evidence that humans are inherently sociable. In M. S. Clark (ed.), *Prosocial Behaviour*. Newbury Park, CA: Sage.

Fiske, D. W. (1949) Consistency of the factorial structures of personality ratings from different sources. *Journal of Abnormal and Social Psychology*, 44, 329–44.

Fiske, S. T. (1992) Thinking is doing: portraits of social cognition from Daguerreotype to Laserphoto. *Journal of Personality and Social Psychology*, 63, 877–89.

Fiske, S. T. and Neuberg, S. T. (1990) A continuum of impression formation, from category-based to individuating processes: influences of information and motivation on attention, and interpretation. In M. P. Zanna (ed.), *Advances in Experimental Social Psychology, Vol. 23*. New York: Academic Press.

Fiske, S. T. and Taylor, S. E. (1991) *Social Cognition*. 2nd edn. New York: McGraw-Hill.

Flick, U. (ed.) (1998) *The Psychology of the Social*. Cambridge: Cambridge University Press.

Flowers, M. L. (1977) A laboratory test of some implications of Janis's groupthink hypothesis. *Journal of Personality and Social Psychology*, 35, 888–96.

Flynn, J. R. (1987) Massive IQ gains in 14 nations: what IQ tests really measure. *Psychological Bulletin*, 95, 29–51.

Foa, U. G. and Foa, E. B. (1974) *Social Structures of the Mind*. Springfield: Thomas.

Foa, U. G., Converse, J., Törnblom, K. Y. and Foa, E. B. (eds) (1993) *Resource Theory: Explorations and Applications*. San Diego: Academic Press.

Fogel, A. (1979) Peer-vs. mother-directed behaviour in 1- to 3-month-old infants. *Infant Behavior and Development*, 2, 47–54.

Foley, W. A. (1997) *Anthropological Linguistics: An Introduction*. Cambridge, MA: Blackwell.

Ford, M. R. and Lowery, C. R. (1986) Gender differences in moral reasoning: a comparison of the use of justice and care orientations. *Journal of Personality and Social Psychology*, 50, 777–83.

Ford, W. S. (1986) Favourable intergroup contact may not reduce prejudice: inconclusive journal evidence. *Sociological Social Research*, 70, 256–8.

Forgas, J. P. (1983) What is social about social cognition? *British Journal of Social Psychology*, 22, 129–44.

Forgas, J. P. (1985) Person prototypes and cultural salience: the role of cognitive and cultural factors in impression formation. *British Journal of Social Psychology*, 24, 3–17.

Forgas, J. P. (1992) Affect in social judgements and decisions: a multiprocess model. In M. P. Zanna (ed.), *Advances in Experimental Social Psychology, Vol. 25*. New York: Academic Press.

Forgas, J. P. (1998a) Asking nicely? The effects of mood on responding to more or less polite requests. *Personality and Social Psychology Bulletin*, 24, 173–85.

Forgas, J. P. (1998b) On being happy and mistaken: mood effects on the fundamental attribution error. *Journal of Personality and Social Psychology*, 75, 318–31.

Forgas, J. P. and Moylan, S. (1987) After the movies: the effect of mood on social judgements. *Personality and Social Psychology Bulletin*, 13 465–77.

Foster, D. and Louw-Potgieter, J. (eds) (1991) *Social Psychology in South Africa*. Johannesburg: Lexicon.

Foucault, M. (1967) *Madness and Civilization: A History of Insanity in the Age of Reason*. London: Tavistock.

Foucault, M. (1973) *The Birth of the Clinic*. London: Tavistock.

Fox, N. A., Kimmerly, N. L. and Schafer, W. D. (1991) Attachment to mother/attachment to father: a meta-analysis. *Child Development*, 62, 210–25.

Frank, R. (1988) *Passions within Reasons: The Strategic Role of Emotions*. New York: Norton.

Fraser, C. (1971) Group risk-taking and group polarisation. *European Journal of Social Psychology*, 1, 493–510.

Fraser, C. (1973) *Determinants of Individual and Group Decisions Involving Risk*. Final report on SSRC project HR 542, available from British Library Lending Division.

Fraser, C. (1981) Review of R. Harré's *Social Being*. *European Journal of Social Psychology*, 11, 445–50.

Fraser, C. (1994) Attitudes, social representations and widespread beliefs. *Papers on Social Representations*, 3, 13–25.

Fraser, C. and Foster, D. (1984) Social groups, nonsense groups and group polarisation. In H. Tajfel (ed.), *The Social Dimension: European Developments in Social Psychology, Vol. 2*. Cambridge: Cambridge University Press.

Fraser, C. and Gaskell, G. (eds) (1990) *The Social Psychological Study of Widespread Beliefs*. Oxford: Clarendon Press.

Fraser, C., Gouge, C. and Billig, M. (1971) Risky shifts, cautious shifts and group polarisation. *European Journal of Social Psychology*, 1, 7–30.

Freud, A and Dann, S. (1951) An experiment in group upbringing. *Psychoanalytic Study of the Child*, 6, 127–68.

Freud, S. (1900/1976) *The Interpretation of Dreams*. Penguin Freud Library Vol. 4. Harmondsworth: Penguin.

Freud, S. (1905/1953–74) Three essays on the theory of sexuality. In J. Strachey (ed.), *The Standard Edition of the Complete Works of Sigmund Freud, Vol. 7*. London: Hogarth Press.

Freud, S. (1907/1953–74) The psychotherapy of everyday life. In J. Strachey (ed.), *The Standard Edition of the Complete Works of Sigmund Freud, Vol. 6*. London: Hogarth Press.

Freud, S. (1919) *Totem and Taboo: Resemblances between the Psychic Lives of Savages and Neurotics*. London: Kegan Paul Trench Trubner.

Freud, S. (1921/1960) *Group Psychology and the Analysis of the Ego*. New York: Bantam Books.

Freud, S. (1927) *The Ego and the Id*. London: Hogarth Press.

Freud, S. (1930) *Civilization and its Discontents*. London: Hogarth Press.

Freud, S. (1938) *An Outline of Psychoanalysis*. London: Hogarth Press.

Frey, D. (1986) Recent research on selective exposure to information. In L. Berkowitz (ed.), *Advances in Experimental Social Psychology, Vol. 19*. New York: Academic Press.

Fried, I., Wilson, C. L. MacDonald, K. A. and Behnke, E. J. (1998) Electric current stimulates laughter. *Nature*, 391(6668), 650.

Frith, U. (1989) *Autism: Explaining the Enigma*. Oxford: Blackwell.

Frodi, A., Macaulay, J. and Thome, P. R. (1977) Are women always less aggressive than men? A review of the experimental literature. *Psychological Bulletin*, 84, 634–60.

Fromkin, V. and Rodman, R. (1998) *An Introduction to Language*. 6th edn. Fort Worth, TX: Harcourt Brace.

Fry, D. P. (1999) Aggression and altruism. In L. Kurtz (ed.), *Encyclopedia of Violence, Peace and Conflict, Vol. 1*. San Diego: Academic Press.

Fryer, D. M. (1986) Employment deprivation and personal agency during unemployment: a critical discussion of Jahoda's explanation of the psychological effects of unemployment. *Social Behaviour*, 1, 3–24.

Fryer, D. M. (1987) Monmouthshire and Marienthal: sociographies of two unemployed communities. In D. Fryer and P. Ullah, *Unemployed People: Social and Psychological Perspectives*. Milton Keynes: Open University Press.

Fryer, D. M. (1992) Psychological or material deprivation: why does unemployment have mental health consequences? In E. McLauglin (ed.), *Understanding Unemployment: New Perspectives On Active Labour Market Policies*. London: Routledge.

Fryer, D. M. (1995) Agency theory. In Nigel Nicholson (ed.), *The Blackwell Dictionary of Organisational Behaviour*. Oxford: Blackwell.

Fryer, D. M. (1999) Marie Jahoda: a social psychologist for and in the real world. In K. Isaksson, C. Hogstedt, C. Eriksson and T. Theorell (eds), *Health Effects of the New Labour Market*. New York: Kluwer Academic/Plenum. Press.

Fryer, D. M. and Fagan, R. (1993) Coping with unemployment. *International Journal of Political Economy*, 23, 95–120.

Fryer, D. M. and Payne, R. L. (1984) Proactivity in unemployment: findings and implications. *Leisure Studies*, 3, 273–95.

Fryer, D. M. and Payne, R. (1986) Being unemployed: a review of the literature on the psychological experience of unemployment. In C. L. Cooper and I. T. Robertson (eds), *International Review of Industrial and Organisational Psychology*, Vol 1. Chichester: John Wiley.

Funder, D. C. (1987) Errors and mistakes: evaluating the accuracy of social judgement. *Psychological Bulletin*, 101, 75–90.

Furnham, A. (1997) *The Psychology of Behaviour at Work*. Chichester: Taylor and Francis.

Furnham, A. and Lewis, A. (1986) *The Economic Mind: The Social Psychology of Economic Behaviour*. New York: St Martin's Press.

Furth, H. G. (1996) *Desire for Society: Children's Knowledge as Social Imagination*. New York: Plenum Press.

Gaertner, S., Dovidio, J. F., Anastasio, P. A., Bachevan, B. A. and Rust, M. C. (1993) The common ingroup identity model: recategorisation and the reduction of intergroup bias. In W. Stroebe and M. Hewstone (eds), *European Review of Social Psychology, Vol. 4*. Chichester: John Wiley.

Garfinkel, H. (1967) *Studies in Ethnomethodology*. Englewood Cliffs, NJ: Prentice-Hall.

Gaskell, G. (1994) Survey research and consensuality: statistical and natural groups. *Papers on Social Representations*, 3, 29–32.

Gay, P. (ed.) (1995) *The Freud Reader*. London: Vintage.

Geen, R. G. (1991) Social motivation. *Annual Review of Psychology*, 42, 377–99.

Geen, R. G. (1998a) Aggression and antisocial behaviour. In D. T. Gilbert, S. T. Fiske and G. Lindsey (eds), *The Handbook of Social Psychology Vol. 2*. 4th edn. New York: McGraw-Hill.

Geen, R. G. (1998b) Processes and personal variables in affective aggression. In R. G. Geen and E. Donnerstein (eds), *Human Aggression: Theories, Research and Implications for Social Policy*. San Diego: Academic Press.

Geen, R. G. and Donnerstein, E. (eds) (1998) *Human Aggression: Theories, Research and Implications for Social Policy*. San Diego: Academic Press.

Gelder, M. G., Mayou, R. and J. Geddes (1999) *Psychiatry*. 2nd edn. Oxford: Oxford University Press.

Gergen, K. J. (1985) The social constructionist movement in modern psychology. *American Psychologist*, 40, 266–75.

Gergen, K. (1999) *An Invitation to Social Construction*. London: Sage.

Gershuny, J. (1994) The psychological consequences of unemployment: an assessment of the Jahoda thesis. In D. Gallie, C. Marsh and C. Vogler (eds), *Social Change and the Experience of Unemployment*. Oxford: Oxford University Press.

Gervais, M. C. and Jovchelovitch, S. (1998) *The Health Beliefs of the Chinese Community in England: A Qualitative Study*. London: Health Education Authority.

Giddens, A. (1998) *The Third Way*. Cambridge: Polity.

Gilbert, G. M. (1951) Stereotype change and persistence among college students. *Journal of Abnormal and Social Psychology*, 46, 245–54.

Giles, H. and Coupland, N. (1991) *Language: Contexts and Consequences*. Pacific Grove, Ca: Brooks/Cole.

Gilligan, C. (1982) *In a Different Voice: Psychological Theory and Women's Development*. Cambridge, MA: Harvard University Press.

Gilligan, C. (1993) *In a Different Voice: Psychological Theory and Women's Development*. Repr. Cambridge, MA: Harvard University Press.

Gilligan, C. and Attanucci, J. (1988) Two moral orientations: gender differences and similarities. *Merrill-Palmer Quarterly*, 34, 223–37.

Glaser, B. G. and Strauss, A. L. (1967) *The Discovery of Grounded Theory*. Chicago: Aldine.

Goffman, E. (1959) *The Presentation of Self in Everyday Life*. Harmondsworth: Penguin.

Goffman, E. (1961) *Asylums: Essays on the Social Situation of Mental Patients and Other Inmates*. New York: Anchor Books

Goffman, E., Lemert, C. C. and Branaman, A. (1997) *The Goffman Reader*. Cambridge, MA: Blackwell.

Goldberg, D. and Huxley, P. (1980) *Mental Illness in the Community: The Pathway to Psychiatric Care*. London: Tavistock.

Goldberg, E. M. and Morrison, F. S. (1963) Schizophrenia and social class. *British Journal of Psychiatry*, 109, 785–802.

Goldberg, L. R. (1990) An alternative description of personality – the big-5 factor structure. *Journal of Personality and Social Psychology*, 59(6), 1216–29.

Goldberg, L. R. and Shmelov, A. G. (1993) Intercultural study of personality-traits vocabulary – the big 5 factors in English and in Russian. *Psikhologicheskii Zhurnal*, 14(4), 32–9.

Goldman, W. and Lewis, P. (1977) Beautiful is good: evidence that the physically attractive are more socially skilled. *Journal of Experimental Social Psychology*, 13, 125–30.

Goldstein, A. P. (1989) Aggression reduction: some vital steps. In J. Groebel and R. A. Hinde (eds), *Aggression and War: Their Biological and Social Bases*. Cambridge: Cambridge University Press.

Golombok, S. and Fivush, R. (1994). *Gender Development*. Cambridge: Cambridge University Press.

Golombok, S., Tasker, F. and Murray, C. (1997) Children raised in fatherless families from infancy: family relationships and the socioemotional development of children of lesbian and single heterosexual mothers. *Journal of Child Psychology and Psychiatry*, 28, 783–91.

Goodman, S. H. and Gotlib, I. H. (1999) Risk for psychopathology in the children of depressed mothers: a developmental, model for understanding mechanisms of transmission. *Psychological Review*, 106, 458–90.

Goody, E. (1991) The learning of prosocial behaviour in small-scale egalitarian societies: an anthropological view. In R. A. Hinde and J. Groebel (eds), *Cooperation and Prosocial Behaviour*. Cambridge: Cambridge University Press.

Goody, E. N. (1995) *Social Intelligence and Interaction: Expressions and Implications of the Social Bias in Human Intelligence*. Cambridge and New York: Cambridge University Press.

Goody, J. (1968) *Literacy in Traditional Societies*. Cambridge: Cambridge University Press.

Gotlib, I. H. and Hammen, C. L. (1992) *Psychological Aspects of Depression: Toward a Cognitive-Interpersonal Integration*. Chichester: John Wiley.

Gotlib, I. H. and McCabe, S. B. (1990) Marriage and psychopathology: a critical examination. In F. Fincham and T. Bradbury (eds), *The Psychology of Marriage: Conceptual, Empirical and Applied Perspectives*. New York: Guilford Press.

Gottesman, I. I. (1991) *Schizophrenia Genesis: The Origins of Madness*. New York: Freeman.

Gould, L. (1992) *The Mismeasure of Man*. Harmondsworth: Penguin.

Gove, W. R. and Tudor, J. F. (1973) Adult sex roles and mental illness. *American Journal of Sociology*, 78, 812–35.

Graddol, D. and Swann, J. (1989) *Gender Voices*. Oxford and New York: Blackwell.

Granovetter, M. S. (1985) Economic action and social structure: the problem of embeddedness. *American Journal of Sociology*, 91, 481–510.

Grantham-McGregor, S. M., Powell, C. A., Walker, S. P. and Himes, J. H. (1991) Nutritional supplementation, psychosocial stimulation, and mental development of stunted children: the Jamaican Study. *Lancet*, 338, 1–5.

Graumann, C. (1988) Introduction to a history of social psychology. In M. Hewstone, W. Stroebe, J. P. Codol and G. Stephenson (eds), *Introduction to Social Psychology*. Oxford: Blackwell.

Green, L. R., Richardson, D. R. and Lago, T. (1996). How do friendship, indirect and direct aggression relate? *Aggressive Behaviour*, 22, 81–6.

Greenaway, J., Smith, S. and Street, J. (1992) *Deciding Factors in British Politics: A Case-studies Approach*. London: Routledge.

Greenberg, R. P. and Fisher, S. (1977) *The Scientific Credibility of Freud's Theories and Therapy*. Hassocks: Harvester Press.

Greenberg, R. P. and Fisher, S. (1996) *Freud Scientifically Reappraised: Testing the Theories and Therapy*. New York and Chichester: John Wiley.

Greenwald, A. G. (1968) Cognitive learning, cognitive response to persuasion, and attitude change. In A. G. Greenwald, T. C. Brock and T. M. Ostrom (eds), *Psychological Foundations of Attitudes*. New York: Academic Press.

Greenwald, A. G. (1981) Cognitive response analysis: an appraisal. In R. E. Petty, T. M. Ostrom and T. C. Brock (eds), *Cognitive Responses in Persuasion*. Hillsdale, NJ: Erlbaum.

Greer, S. (1983) Cancer and the mind. *British Journal of Psychiatry*, 143, 535–43.

Gross, R. and McIlveen, R. (1998) *Psychology: A New Introduction*. London: Hodder and Stoughton.

Grote, N. K. and Frieze, I. H. (1994) The measurement of friendship-based love in intimate relationships. *Personal Relationships*, 1, 275–300.

Guest, D. and Conway, N. (1997) *Employee Motivation and the Psychological Contract*. London: Institute of Personnel and Development

Guest, D. and Conway, N. (1999) *How Dissatisfied and Insecure are British Workers? A Survey of Surveys*. London: Institute of Personal Development.

Guimelli, C. (1993) Locating the central core of social representations: towards a method. *European Journal of Social Psychology*, 23, 555–9.

Haddon, A. C. (1901) *Physiology and Psychology*. Cambridge: Cambridge University Press.

Hagan, J. (1994) Crime, inequality and inefficiency. In A. Glyn and D. Miliband (eds), *Paying for Inequality: The Economic Costs of Social Injustice*. London: IPPR/Rivers Oram Press.

Hakim, C. (1996) *Key Issues in Women's Work: Female Heterogeneity and the Polarisation of Women's Employment*. London: Athlone.

Hall, C. S., Lindzey, G. and Campbell, J. B. (1998) *Theories of Personality*. 4th edn. New York: John Wiley.

Hall, P., Brockington, I., Levings, J. and Murphy, C. (1993) A comparison of responses to the mentally ill in two communities. *British Journal of Psychiatry*, 162, 99–108.

Hall, P. A. (1999) Social capital in Britain. *British Journal of Political Science*, 29(3), 417–61.

Halpern, D. S. (1995a) *Mental Health and the Built Environment: More than Bricks and Mortar?*. London: Taylor and Francis.

Halpern, D. S. (1995b) Values, morals and modernity: the values, constraints and norms of European youth. In M. Rutter and D. J. Smith (eds), *Psychosocial Disorders in Young People: Time Trends and their Causes*. Chichester: John Wiley.

Halpern, D. S. (1998) *The Third Way: Summary of the Nexus Debate*. London: Nexus.

Halpern, D. S. (forthcoming) *Social Capital*. Cambridge: Polity.

Hamilton, D. L. and Gifford, R. K. (1976) Illusory correlation in interpersonal perception: a cognitive basis of stereotypic judgements. *Journal of Experimental Social Psychology*, 12, 392–407.

Hamilton, D. L. and Sherman, S. J. (1989) Illusory correlations: implications for stereotype theory and research. In D. Bar-Tal, C. F. Grauman, A. W. Kruglanski and W. Stroebe (eds), *Stereotypes and Prejudice: Changing Conceptions*. New York: Springer-Verlag.

Hammen, C. (1991) *Depression Runs in Families: The Social Context of Risk and Resilience in Children of Depressed Mothers*. New York: Springer-Verlag.

Hampson, S. E. (1984) Personality traits: in the eye of the beholder or the personality of the perceived? In M. Cook (ed.), *Issues in Person Perception*. London: Methuen.

Handy, C. (1984) *The Future of Work*. Harmondsworth: Penguin.

Haney, C., Banks, C. and Zimbardo, P. B. (1973) Interpersonal dynamics in a simulated prison. *International Journal of Criminology and Penology*, 1(1), 69–97.

Haraszti, M. (1977) *A Worker in a Worker's State: Piece-rates in Hungary*. Tr. M. Wright. Harmondsworth: Penguin/New Left.

Harold, G. T., Fincham, F. D., Osborne, L. N. and Conger, R. D. (1997) Mom and dad are at it again: adolescent perceptions of marital conflict and adolescent psychological distress. *Developmental Psychology*, 33, 333–50.

Harré, R. and Gillett, G. (1994) *The Discursive Mind*. London: Sage.

Harré, R. and Secord, P. F. (1972) *The Explanation of Social Behaviour*. Oxford: Blackwell.

Harris, J. A., Rushton, J. P., Hampson, E. and Jackson, D. N. (1996) Salivary testosterone and self-report aggressive and pro-social personality characteristics in men and women. *Aggressive Behavior*, 22, 321–31.

Harris, T., Brown, G. W. and Bifulco, A. (1986) Loss of parent in childhood and adult psychiatric disorder: the role of lack of adequate parental care. *Psychological Medicine*, 16, 641–59.

Harrower, J. (1998). *Applying Psychology to Crime*. London: Hodder and Stoughton.

Hart, P. T. (1990) *Groupthink in Government: A Study of Small Groups and Policy Failure*. Amsterdam: Swets and Zeitlinger.

Hastie, R. and Kumar, P. A. (1979) Person memory: personality traits as organising principles in memory for behaviours. *Journal of Personality and Social Psychology*, 37, 25–38.

Hatfield, E., Cacioppo, J. T. and Rapson, R. L. (1994) *Emotional Contagion*. Cambridge, New York and Paris: Cambridge University Press/Editions de la Maison des sciences de l'homme.

Hay, D. F. (1977) Following their companions as a form of exploration for human infants. *Child Development*, 48, 1624–32.

Hay, D. F., Castle, J. and Davies, L. (2000) Toddlers' use of force against familiar peers: a precursor of serious aggression? *Child Development*, 71, 457–67.

Hay, D. F., Nash, A. and Pedersen, J. (1981) Responses of six-month-olds to the distress of their peers. *Child Development*, 52, 1071–5.

Hay, D. F., Nash, A. and Pedersen, J. (1983) Interaction between six-month-old peers. *Child Development*, 54, 557–62.

Hay, D. F., Vespo, J. E. and Zahn-Waxler, C. (1998) Young children's quarrels with their siblings and mothers: links with maternal depression and bipolar illness. *British Journal of Developmental Psychology*, 16, 519–38.

Hays, R. B. (1985) A longitudinal study of friendship development. *Journal of Personality and Social Psychology*, 48, 909–24.

Hays, R. B. (1988) Friendship. In S. Duck (ed.), *Handbook of Personal Relationships*. Chichester: John Wiley.

Hazan, C. and Shaver, P. (1994) Attachment as an organizational framework for research on close relationships. *Psychological Inquiry*, 5, 1–22.

Heal, J. (1991) Altruism. In R. A. Hinde and J. Groebel (eds), *Cooperation and Prosocial Behaviour*. Cambridge: Cambridge University Press.

Hearold, S. (1986) A synthesis of 1043 effects of television on social behavior. In G. Comstock (ed.), *Public Communications and Behavior, 1*. New York: Academic Press.

Heider, F. (1958) *The Psychology of Interpersonal Relations*. New York: John Wiley.

Helman C. G. (1990) *Culture, Health and Illness: An Introduction for Health Professionals*. London: Wright.

Helwig, C. C., Tisak, M. S. and Turiel, E. (1990) Children's social reasoning in context: a reply to Gabennesch. *Child Development*, 61, 2068–78.

Henderson, S., Byrne, D. G., Duncan-Jones, P., Scott, R. and Adcock, S. (1980) Social relationships, adversity and neurosis: a study of associations in a general population sample. *British Journal of Psychiatry*, 136, 574–83.

Hendrick, C. and Hendrick, S. S. (1986) A theory and method of love. *Journal of Personality and Social Psychology*, 50, 392–402.

Hendrick, C., Hendrick, S., Foote, F. H. and Slapion-Foote, M. J. (1984) Do men and women love differently? *Journal of Social and Personal Relationships*, 1, 177–96.

Hendriks, A. A. J., Hofstee, W. K. B. and De Raad, B. (1999). The Five-Factor Personality Inventory (FFPI). *Personality and Individual Differences*, 27(2), 307–25.

Hensley, T. R. and Griffin, G. W. (1986) Victims of groupthink: the Kent State University Board of Trustees and the 1977 gymnasium controversy. *Journal of Conflict Resolution*, 30, 497–531.

Herek, G. M. and Glunt, E. K. (1988). An epidemic of stigma: public reaction to AIDS. *American Psychologist*, 43, 886–91.

Heritage, J. (1984). *Garfinkel and Ethnomethodology*. Cambridge: Polity.

Herle, A. and Rouse, S. (1998) *Cambridge and the Torres Strait: Centenary Essays on the 1898 Anthropological Expedition*. Cambridge: Cambridge University Press.

Hernstein, R. J. and Murray, C. (1994) *The Bell Curve: Intelligence and Class Structure in American Life*. New York: Free Press.

Herrera, C. and Dunn, J. (1997) Early experiences with family conflict: implications for arguments with a close friend. *Developmental Psychology*, 33, 869–81.

Herzberg, F. (1966) *Work and the Nature of Man*. Cleveland, OH: World Books.

Herzberg, F., Mausner, B. and Synderman, B. (1959). *The Motivation to Work*. New York: John Wiley.

Herzlich, C. (1973). *Health and Illness: A Social Psychological Analysis*. London: Academic Press.

Hess, L. E. (1995) Changing family patterns in Western Europe: opportunity and risk factors for adolescent development. In M. Rutter and D. J. Smith (eds), *Psychosocial Disorders in Young People: Time Trends and their Causes*. Chichester: John Wiley.

Hetherington, E. M. and Stanley-Hagan, M. (1999) The adjustment of children with divorced parents: a risk and resiliency perspective. *Journal of Child Psychology and Psychiatry*, 40, 129–40.

Hewitt, J. K., Silberg, J. L., Rutter, M., Simonoff, E., Meyer, J. M., Maes, H., Pickles, A., Neale, M. C., Loeber, R., Erickson, M. T., Kendler, K. S., Heath, A. C., Truett,

K. R., Reynolds, C. A. and Eaves, L. J. (1998) Genetics and developmental psychopathology: I. Phenotypic assessment in the Virginia Twin Study of Adolescent Behavioral Development. *Journal of Child Psychology and Psychiatry*, 38, 943–63.

Hewstone, M. (1989) *Causal Attribution: From Cognitive Processes to Collective Beliefs*. Oxford: Blackwell.

Hewstone, M. and Brown, R. J. (eds) (1986) *Contact and Conflict in Intergroup Encounters*. Oxford: Blackwell.

Hewstone, M., Islam, M. R. and Judd, C. M. (1993) Models of crossed categorisation and intergroup relations. *Journal of Personality and Social Psychology*, 64, 779–93.

Hilton, J. L. and Darley, J. M. (1991) The effects of interaction goals on person perception. In M. P. Zanna (ed.), *Advances in Experimental Social Psychology, Vol. 24*. New York: Academic Press.

Himmelweit, H. T. and Gaskell, G. (eds) (1990) *Societal Psychology*. Newbury Park, CA: Sage.

Hinde, R. A. (1974) *The Biological Bases of Human Social Behaviour*. New York: McGraw-Hill.

Hinde, R. A. (1984) Why do the sexes behave differently in close relationships? *Journal of Social and Personal Relationships*, 1, 471–501.

Hinde, R. A. (1997) *Relationships: A Dialectical Perspective*. Hove: Psychology Press.

Hinde, R. A. and Stevenson-Hinde, J. (1988) *Relationships within Families: Mutual Influences*. Oxford: Clarendon Press.

Hinde, R. A., Tamplin, A. and Barrett, J. (1993a) Home correlates of aggression in preschool. *Aggressive Behaviour*, 19, 85–105.

Hinde, R. A., Tamplin, A. and Barrett, J. (1993b) A comparative study of relationship structure. *British Journal of Developmental Psychology*, 32, 191–207.

Hinkle, S. and Brown, R. J. (1990) Intergroup comparisons and social identity: some links and Lacunae. In D. Abrams and M. A. Hogg (eds), *Social Identity Theory: Constructive and Critical Advances*. Hemel Hempstead: Harvester Wheatsheaf.

Hinton, P. R. (1993) *The Psychology of Interpersonal Perception*. London: Routledge.

Hodges, J. and Tizard, B. (1989) Social and family relationships of ex-institutional adolescents. *Journal of Child Psychology and Psychiatry*, 30, 77–97.

Hoffman, E. (1989) *Lost in Translation: A Life in a New Language*. London: Heinemann.

Hoffman, M. L. (1989) Moral development. In M. H. Bornstein and M. E. Lamb (eds), *Developmental Psychology: An Advanced Textbook*. 2nd edn. Hillsdale, NJ: Erlbaum.

Hoffman, M. L. (1990) Empathy and justice motivation. *Motivation and Emotion*, 14, 151–72.

Hoffman, M. L. and Saltzstein, H. D. (1967) Parent discipline and the child's moral development. *Journal of Personality and Social Psychology*, 5, 45–7.

Hofstee, W. K. B., Kiers, H. A. L., De Raad, B., Goldberg, L. R. and Ostendorf, F. (1997). A comparison of big-five structures of personality traits in Dutch, English, and German. *European Journal of Personality*, 11(1), 15–31.

Hogarty, G. E., Anderson, C. M., Reiss, D. J., Kornblith, S. J., Greenwald, D. P., Ulrich, R. F. and Carter, M. (1991) Family psychoeducation, social skills training and maintenance chemotherapy in the aftercare treatment of schizophrenia II: Two-year effects of a controlled study on relapse and adjustment. *Archives of General Psychiatry*, 48, 340–7.

Hogg, M. A. (1992) *The Social Psychology of Group Cohesiveness: From Attraction to Social Identity*. Hemel Hempstead: Harvester Wheatsheaf.

Hogg, M. A. and Abrams, D. (1990) Social motivation, self-esteem and social identity. In D. Abrams and M. A. Hogg (eds), *Social Identity Theory: Constructive and Critical Advances*. Hemel Hempstead: Harvester Wheatsheaf.

Hokanson, J. E., Rubert, M. P., Welker, R. A., Hollander, G. R. and Hedeen, C. (1989) Interpersonal concomitants and antecedents of depression among college students. *Journal of Abnormal Psychology*, 98, 209–17.

Hollin, C. and Howells, K. (1997) Controlling violent behaviour. *Psychology Review*, 3, 10–14.

Homans, G. C. (1974) *Social Behaviour: Its Elementary Forms*. New York: Harcourt Brace Jovanovich.

Hooley, J. M. and Teasdale, J. D. (1989) Predictors of relapse in unipolar depressives: expressed emotion, marital distress, and perceived criticism. *Journal of Abnormal Psychology*, 98, 229–37.

Hoppock, R. (1935) *Job Satisfaction*. New York: Harper.

Hovland, C. I., Janis, I. L. and Kelley, H. H. (1953) *Communication and Persuasion: Psychological Studies of Opinion Change*. New Haven, CT: Yale University Press.

Howes, C. (1983) Patterns of friendship. *Child Development*, 54, 1041–53.

Howitt, D., Billig, M., Cramer, D., Edwards, D., Kniveton, B., Potter, J. and Radley, A. (1989) *Social Psychology: Conflicts and Continuities*. Milton Keynes: Open University Press.

Hudson, R. A. (1996) *Sociolinguistics*. 2nd edn. Cambridge: Cambridge University Press.

Huesmann, R. L. (1998) The role of social information processing and cognitive schema in the acquisition and maintenance of habitual aggressive behaviour. In R. G. Geen and E. Donnerstein (eds), *Human Aggression: Theories, Research and Implications for Social Policy*. San Diego: Academic Press.

Hunt, M. (1997) *How Science Takes Stock: The Story of Meta-analysis*. New York: Russell Sage Foundation.

Hunter, J. E. and Hunter, R. F. (1984) Validity and utility of alternate predicators of job performance. *Psychological Bulletin*, 83, 1053–71.

Huston, T. L. (ed.) (1974) *Foundations of Interpersonal Attraction*. New York: Academic Press.

Hutchins, E. (1995) *Cognition in the Wild*. Cambridge, MA, and London: MIT Press.

Iaffaldano, M. T. and Muchinsky, P. M. (1985) Job satisfaction and job performance: a meta-analysis. *Psychological Bulletin*, 97, 251–73.

Ibanez, T. (1997) *Critical Social Psychology*. London: Sage.

Imamoglu, E. M. (1975) Children's awareness and usage of intention cues. *Child Development*, 46, 39–45.

Inglehart, R. (1990) *Culture Shift in Advanced Industrialised Nations*. Princeton, NJ: Princeton University Press.

Isen, A. M. (1984) Toward understanding the role of affect in cognition. In S. R. Wyer and T. K. Srull (eds), *Handbook of Social Cognition, Vol. 3*, Hillsdale, NJ: Erlbaum.

Isen, A. M., Shalker, T. E., Clark, M. and Karp, L. (1978) Affect, accessibility of material in memory, and behavior. *Journal of Personality and Social Psychology*, 36, 1–12.

Isenberg, D. J. (1986) Group polarisation: a critical review and meta-analysis. *Journal of Personality and Social Psychology*, 50, 1141–51.

Ispa, J. (1981) Peer support among Soviet day care toddlers. *International Journal of Behavioural Development*, 4, 255–69.

Israel, J. and Tajfel, H. (1972) *The Social Context of Social Psychology*. London: Academic Press.

Itard, J. M. G. (1801/1962) *The Wild Boy of Aveyron*. Tr. G. and M. Humphrey. East Norwalk, CT: Appleton-Century-Crafts.

Jack, D. C. (1999) *Behind the Mask: Destruction and Creativity in Women's Aggression*. Cambridge, MA: Harvard University Press.

Jacobs, R. and Campbell, D. T. (1961) The perpetuation of an arbitrary tradition through several generations of a laboratory microculture. *Journal of Abnormal and Social Psychology*, 62, 649–58.

Jacoby, R. and Glauberman, N. (eds) (1995) *The Bell Curve Debate: History, Documents, Opinions*. New York: Random House.

Jahoda, G. (1988) Critical notes and reflections on 'social representations'. *European Journal of Social Psychology*, 18, 195–209.

Jahoda, M. (1982) *Employment and Unemployment: A Social Psychological Analysis*. Cambridge: Cambridge University Press.

Jahoda, M. (1988) Economic recession and mental health: some conceptual issues. *Journal of Social Issues*, 44, 13–23.

Jahoda, M. (1995) Manifest and latent functions. In Nigel Nicholson (ed.), *The Blackwell Dictionary of Organisational Behaviour*. Oxford: Blackwell.

Jahoda, M., Lazarsfeld, P. F. and Zeisel, H. (1972) *Marienthal: The Sociography of an Unemployed Community*. London: Tavistock.

James, W. (1884) What is an emotion? *Mind*, 9, 188–205.

James, W. (1890) *The Principles of Psychology*. London: Macmillan.

Janis, I. (1972) *Victims of Groupthink*. Boston: Houghton Mifflin.

Janis, I. (1982) *Groupthink: Psychological Studies of Policy Decisions and Fiascoes*. 2nd edn. Boston: Houghton Mifflin.

Jaspars, J. M. F. (1978) Determinants of attitudes and attitude change. In H. Tajfel and C. Fraser (eds), *Introducing Social Psychology*. Harmondsworth: Penguin.

Jaspars, J. and Fraser, C. (1984) Attitudes and social representations. In R. M. Farr and S. Moscovici (eds), *Social Representations*. Cambridge: Cambridge University Press.

Jenkins, J. M., Oatley, K. and Stein, N. (eds) (1998) *Human Emotions: A Reader*. Oxford: Blackwell.

Jenson, A. R. (1969) How much can we boost IQ and scholastic achievement? *Harvard Educational Review*, 39, 1–123.

Jo, E. and Berkowitz, L. (1994) A priming effect analysis of media influences: an update. In J. Bryant and D. Zillmann (eds), *Media Effects*. Hillsdale, NJ: Erlbaum.

Jodelet, D. (1989/1991) *Madness and Social Representations*. Hemel Hempstead: Harvester Wheatsheaf.

Joffe, H. (1996) AIDS research and prevention: a social representational approach. *British Journal of Medical Psychology*, 69, 169–90.

Johnson, T. J., Fiegenbaum, R. and Weiby, M. (1964) Some determinants and consequences of teacher's perception of causality. *Journal of Educational Psychology*, 55, 237–46.

Johnson-Laird, P. N. (1988) *The Computer and the Mind: An Introduction to Cognitive Science*. Cambridge, MA, and London: Harvard University Press.

Jones, B., Gray, A., Kavanagh, D., Moran, M., Norton, P. and Seldon, A. (1994) *Politics UK*. 2nd edn. Hemel Hempstead: Harvester Wheatsheaf.

Jones, E. E. (1985) Major developments in social psychology during the past five decades. In G. Lindzey and E. Aronson (eds), *The Handbook of Social Psychology, Vol. 1*. New York: Random House.

Jones, E. E. (1998) Major developments in five decades of social psychology. In D. T. Gilbert, S. T. Fiske and G. Lindzey (eds), *The Handbook of Social Psychology, Vol. 1*. 4th edn. New York: McGraw-Hill.

Jones, E. E. and Colman, A. M. (1996) Social psychology. In A. Kuper and J. Kuper (eds), *The Social Science Encyclopedia*. 2nd edn. London: Routledge.

Jones, E. E. and Davis, K. E. (1965) From acts to dispositions: the attribution process in person perception. In L. Berkowitz (ed.), *Advances in Experimental Social Psychology, Vol. 2*. New York: Academic Press.

Jones, E. E. and Gerard, H. B. (1967) *Foundations of Social Psychology*. New York: John Wiley.

Judge, T. A. and Church, A. H. (2000) Job satisfaction: research and practice. In C. L. Cooper and E. A. Locke (eds), *Industrial and Organisational Psychology: Linking Theory with Practice*. Oxford: Blackwell.

Kahneman, D., Slovic, P. and Tversky, A. (1982). *Judgment under Uncertainty: Heuristics and Biases*. Cambridge and New York: Cambridge University Press.

Kanner, L. (1943) Autistic disturbances of affective contact. *Nervous Child*, 2, 217–50.

Kardes, F. R., Sanbonmatsu, D. M., Voss, R. T. and Fazio, R. H. (1986) Self-monitoring and attitude accessibility. *Personality and Social Psychology Bulletin*, 12, 468–74.

Kasl, S. V. and Cobb, S. (1982) Variability of stress effects among men experiencing job loss. In L. Goldberger and S. Breznitz (eds), *Handbook of Stress: Theoretical and Clinical Aspects*. New York: Free Press.

Katz, D. and Braly, K. (1933) Racial stereotypes of one hundred college students. *Journal of Abnormal and Social Psychology*, 28, 280–90.

Kavanagh, D. J. (1992) Recent developments in expressed emotion and schizophrenia. *British Journal of Psychiatry*, 160, 601–20.

Kawachi, I., Kennedy, B. P. and Wilkinson, R. G. (1999) Crime: social disorganisation and relative deprivation. *Social Science and Medicine*, 48(6), 719–31.

Kawachi, I., Kennedy, B. P., Lochner, K. and Prothrow-Stith, D. (1997) Social capital, income inequality and mortality. *American Journal of Public Health*, 89(9), 1491–8.

Keenan, K. and Shaw, D. (1997) Developmental and social influences on young girls' early problem behavior. *Psychological Bulletin*, 121, 95–113.

Kelley, H. H. (1972) Causal schemata and the attributional process. In E. E. Jones, D. E. Kanouse, H. H. Kelley, R. E. Nisbett, S. Valins and B. Weiner, *Attribution: Perceiving the Causes of Behaviour*. Morristown, NJ: General Learning Press.

Kelley, H. H. (1973) The processes of causal attribution. *American Psychologist*, 28, 107–28.

Kelley, H. H. (1979) *Personal Relationships*. Hillsdale, NJ: Erlbaum.

Kelley, H. H. and Thibaut, J. W. (1978) *Interpersonal Relations*. New York: John Wiley.

Kelley, H. H., Berscheid, E., Christensen, A., Harvey, J. H., Huston, T. L., Levinger, G., McClintock, E., Peplau, L. A. and Peterson, D. R. (eds) (1983) *Close Relationships*. New York: W. H. Freeman.

Kelvin, P. (1977) Predictability, power and vulnerability in interpersonal attraction. In S. Duck (ed.), *Theory and Practice in Interpersonal Attraction*. London: Academic Press.

Kelvin, P. and Jarrett, J. E. (1985) *Unemployment: Its Social and Psychological Effects*. Cambridge: Cambridge University Press.

Kennepohl, S. (1999) Toward a cultural neuropsychology: an alternative view and a preliminary model. *Brain and Cognition*, 41(3), 365–80.

Kenny, D. A. and Kashy, D. A. (1994) Enhanced co-orientation in the perception of friends: a social relations analysis. *Journal of Personality and Social Psychology*, 67, 1024–33.

Kinder, K. (1995) *Three to remember: Strategies for Disaffected Pupils*. Slough: National Foundation for Educational Research.

Kinder, K., Wakefield, A. and Wilkin, A. (1996) *Talking Back: Pupils' Views on Disaffection*. Slough: National Foundation for Educational Research.

Knack, S. and Keefer, P. (1997) Does social capital have an economic payoff? A cross-country investigation. *Quarterly Journal of Economics*, 112(4), 1251–88.

Koch, H. (1960) The relation of certain formal attributes of siblings to attitudes held toward each other and toward their parents. *Monographs of the Society for Research in Child Development*, 25, serial no. 78.

Kochanska, G. (1993) Toward a synthesis of parental socialization and child temperament in the early development of a conscience. *Child Development*, 64, 325–47.

Kogan, N. and Wallach, M. A. (1967) Risk-taking as a function of the situation, the person and the group. In G. Mandler, P. Mussen and N. Kogan (eds), *New Directions in Psychology II*. New York: Holt, Rinehart & Winston.

Kohlberg, L. (1963) The development of children's orientation towards a moral order: I. Sequence in the development of moral thought. *Vita Humana*, 6, 11–33.

Kohlberg, L. (1969) Stage and sequence: the cognitive-developmental approach to socialization. In D. A. Goslin (ed.), *Handbook of Socialization Theory and Research*. Chicago: Rand McNally.

Kohlberg, L. (1971) From is to ought: how to commit the naturalistic fallacy and get away with it in the study of moral development. In T. Miscel (ed.), *Psychology and Genetic Epistemology*. New York: Academic Press.

Kohlberg, L. (1976) Moral stages and moralization: the cognitive-developmental approach. In T. Lickona (ed.), *Moral Development and Behavior: Theory Research and Social Issues*. New York: Holt.

Kohlberg, L. (1981) *Essays on Moral Development, Vol. 1: The Philosophy of Moral Development*. New York: Harper & Row.

Kohlberg, L. (1984) *Essays on Moral Development, Vol. 2: The Psychology of Moral Development*. New York: Harper & Row.

Kohlberg, L. and Kramer, R. B. (1969) Continuities and discontinuities in childhood and adult moral development. *Human Development*, 12, 93–120.

Korenman, S. and Winship, C. (1995) *A Reanalysis of the Bell Curve*. National Bureau of Economic Research, Working Paper 5230. Cambridge, MA: NBER.

Kruger, A. C. (1992) The effect of peer and adult–child transactive discussions on moral reasoning. *Merrill-Palmer Quarterly*, 38, 191–211.

Kruglanski, A. W. (1980) Lay epistemo-logic – process and content: another look at attribution theory. *Psychological Review*, 89, 70–89.

Kruglanski, A. W. and Ajzen, I. (1983) Bias and error in lay attribution. *European Journal of Social Psychology*, 13, 1–44.

Kruglanski, A. W. and Mackie, D. M. (1990) Majority and minority influence: a judgemental process analysis. In W. Stroebe and M. Hewstone (eds), *European Review of Social Psychology, Vol. 1*. Chichester: John Wiley.

Kuipers, L. and Bebbington, P. (1988) Expressed emotion research in schizophrenia: theoretical and clinical implications. *Psychological Medicine*, 18, 893–909.

Kunda, Ziva (1999) *Social Cognition: Making Sense of People*. Cambridge, MA: MIT Press.

Kunda, Z. and Oleson, K. C. (1997) When exceptions prove the rule: how extremity of deviance determines the impact of deviant examples on stereotypes. *Journal of Personality and Social Psychology*, 72, 965–79.

Lakoff, R. T. (1975) *Language and a Woman's Place*. New York: Harper & Row.

Lamb, M. E. (1977) Father–infant and mother–infant interaction in the first year of life. *Child Development*, 48, 167–81.

Lamb, M. E., Frodi, A. M., Hwang, C. P., Frodi, M. and Steinberg, J. (1982) Mother- and father–infant interaction involving play and holding in traditional and nontraditional Swedish families. *Developmental Psychology*, 18, 215–21.

Lampard, R. (1994) An examination of the relationship between marital dissolution and unemployment. In D. Gallie, C. Marsh and C. Vogler (eds), *Social Change and the Experience of Unemployment*. Oxford: Oxford University Press.

Landy, F. J. (1989) *The Psychology of Work Behaviour*. 4th edn. Pacific Grove, CA: Brooks/Cole.

Lange, C. G. and James, W. (1922) *The Emotions*. Baltimore: Williams & Wilkins.

Langer, E. J. (1978) Rethinking the role of thought in social interaction. In J. H. Harvey, W. J. Ickes and R. F. Kidd (eds), *New Directions in Attribution Research, Vol. 2*. Hillsdale, NJ: Erlbaum.

Langer, E. J. (1989a) Minding matters: the consequences of mindlessness-mindfulness. In L. Berkowitz (ed.), *Advances in Experimental Social Psychology, Vol. 22*. New York: Academic Press.

Langer, E. J. (1989b) *Mindfulness*. Reading, MA: Addison-Wesley.

Langer, E. J., Blank, A. and Chanowitz, B. (1978) The mindlessness of ostensibly thoughtful action. *Journal of Personality and Social Psychology*, 36, 635–42.

La Porta, R., Lopez-de-Silanes, F., Shleifer, A. and Vishny, R. W. (1997) Trust in large organisations. *American Economic Review*, 87 (Papers and Proceedings), 333–8.

LaPiere, R. T. (1934) Attitudes versus actions. *Social Forces*, 13, 230–7.

Lasker, B. (1929) *Race Attitudes in Children*. New York: Holt, Rinehart & Winston.

Latané, B. (1981) The psychology of social impact. *American Psychologist*, 36, 343–56.

Latané, B. and Darley, J. M. (1970) *The Unresponsive Bystander: Why Doesn't He Help?*. New York: Appleton-Century-Crofts.

Latané, B. and Darley, J. M. (1976) *Help in a Crisis: Bystander Response to an Emergency*. Morristown, NJ: General Learning Press.

Latané, B. and Wolf, S. (1981) The social impact of majorities and minorities. *Psychological Review*, 88, 438–53.

Laupa, M. (1991) Children's reasoning about three authority attributes: adult status, knowledge and social position. *Developmental Psychology*, 27(2), 321–9.

Laupa, M. and Turiel, E. (1986) Children's conceptions of adult and peer authority. *Child Development*, 57, 405–12.

Lave, J. (1988) *Cognition in Practice: Mind, Mathematics and Culture in Everyday Life*. Cambridge: Cambridge University Press.

Lave, J., Murtaugh, M. and de la Rocha, O. (1984) The dialectic of arithmetic in grocery shopping. In B. Rogoff and J. Lave (eds), *Everyday Cognition: Its Development in Social Context*. Cambridge, MA: Harvard University Press.

Lawler, E. E. (1971) *Pay and Organisational Effectiveness: A Psychological View*. New York: McGraw-Hill.

LeDoux, J. E. (1993) Emotional networks in the brain. In M. Lewis and J. M. Haviland (eds), *Handbook of emotions*. New York: Guilford Press.

Leff, J. and Vaughn, C. (1985) *Expressed Emotion in Families: Its Significant for Mental Illness*. New York: Guilford Press.

Leman, P. J. and Duveen, G. (1999) Representations of authority and children's moral reasoning. *European Journal of Social Psychology*, 29, 557–75.

Lepore, L. and Brown, R. (1997) Category and stereotype activation: is prejudice inevitable? *Journal of Personality and Social Psychology*, 72, 275–87.

Lerner, M. J. (1970) The desire for justice and reactions to victims. In J. Macaulay and L. Berkowitz (eds), *Altruism and Helping Behaviour*. New York: Academic Press.

Lessing, D. M. (1972) *The Golden Notebook*. London: Granada.

Le Unes, A. D., Nation, J. R. and Turley, N. M. (1980) Male–female performance in learned helplessness. *Journal of Psychology*, 104, 255–58.

Levin, J. and Fox, J. A. (1985) *Mass Murder: America's Growing Menace*. New York: Plenum Press.

Levine, J. M. and Moreland, R. (1994) Group socialisation: theory and research. In W. Stroebe and M. Hewstone (eds), *European Review of Social Psychology, Vol. 5*. London: John Wiley.

Levy, D. (1939) Sibling rivalry studies in children of primitive groups. *American Journal of Orthopsychiatry*, 9, 205–14.

Lévy-Bruhl, L. (1910/1926) *How Natives Think*. London: George Allen & Unwin.

Lewin, K., Lippitt, R. and White, R. K. (1939) Patterns of aggressive behaviour in experimentally created 'social climates'. *Journal of Social Psychology*, 10, 271–99.

Lichtenstein, S., Slovic, P., Fischhoff, B. and Combs, B. (1978) Judged frequency of lethal events. *Journal of Experimental Psychology: Human Learning and Memory*, 4, 551–78.

Likert, R. (1932) A technique for the measurement of attitudes. *Archives of Psychology*, 140, 5–53.

Lloyd, B. and Duveen, G. (1989) The reconstruction of social knowledge in the transition from sensorimotor to conceptual activity: the gender system. In A. Gellatly, J. Sloboda and D. Rogers (eds), *Cognition and Social Worlds*. Oxford: Oxford University Press.

Lloyd, B. and Duveen, G. (1990) A semiotic analysis of the development of social representations of gender. In G. Duveen and B. Lloyd (eds), *Social Representations and the Development of Knowledge*. Cambridge: Cambridge University Press.

Lloyd, B. and Duveen, G. (1992) *Gender Identities and Education: The Impact of Starting School*. Hemel Hempstead: Harvester Wheatsheaf.

Locke, E. A. (1984) Job satisfaction. In M. Gruneberg and T. Wall (eds), *Social Psychology and Organisational Behaviour*. Chichester: John Wiley.

Locke, E. A. and Henne, D. I. (1986) Work motivation theories. In C. L. Cooper and I. T. Robertson (eds), *International Review of Industrial and Organisational Psychology 1986*. Chichester: John Wiley.

Locke, J. L. (1998) *The De-voicing of Society: Why We Don't Talk to Each Other Anymore*. New York: Simon & Schuster.

Loeber, R. and Hay, D. (1997) Key issues in the development of aggression and violence from childhood to early adulthood. *Annual Review of Psychology*, 48, 371–410.

Loftus, E. F. (1979) *Eyewitness Testimony*. Cambridge: Cambridge University Press.

Loftus, E. F. and Ketcham, K. (1991) *Witness for the Defense: The Accused, the Eyewitness, and the Expert Who Puts Memory on Trial*. New York: St Martin's Press.

Loftus, E. F. and Ketcham, K. (1996) *The Myth of Repressed Memory: False Memories and Allegations of Sexual Abuse*. New York: St Martin's Press.

Lollis, S., Ross, H. and Leroux, L. (1996) An observational study of parents' socialization of moral orientation during sibling conflicts. *Merrill-Palmer Quarterly*, 42, 475–94.

London, P. (1970) The rescuers: motivational hypotheses about Christians who saved Jews from the Nazis. In J. Macaulay and L. Berkowitz (eds), *Altruism and Helping Behaviour: Social Psychological Studies of Some Antecedents and Consequences*. New York: Academic Press.

Lorenz, K. (1966) *On Aggression*. New York: Harcourt Brace and World.

Luckenbill, D. F. (1977) Criminal homicide as a situated transaction. *Social Problems*, 25, 176–86.

Lund, M. (1985) The development of investment and commitment scales for predicting continuity of personal relationships. *Journal of Personal and Social Relationships*, 2, 3–24.

Luria, A. R. (1969) *The Mind of a Mnemonist*. London: Cape.

Luria, A. R. (1977) Tr. M. Lopez-Morillas and L. Solotaroff. *Cognitive Development: Its Cultural and Social Foundations*. Cambridge, MA, and London: Harvard University Press.

Maass, A. and Clark, R. D., III (1984) Hidden impact of minorities: fifteen years of minority influence research. *Psychological Bulletin*, 95, 428–50.

Maccoby, E. E. (1988) Gender as a social category. *Developmental Psychology*, 24, 735–65.

Maccoby, E. E. (1998) *The Two Sexes*. Cambridge, MA: Harvard University Press.

Maccoby, E. E. and Jacklin, C. N. (1974) *The Psychology of Sex Differences*. Stanford, CA: Stanford University Press.

MacKinnon-Lewis, C., Starnes, R., Volling, B. and Johnson, S. (1997) Perceptions of parenting as predictors of boys' sibling and peer relations. *Developmental Psychology*, 33, 1024–31.

Mackintosh, N. J. (1998) *IQ and Human Intelligence*. Oxford: Oxford University Press.

MacMillan, J. F., Gold, A., Crow, T. J., Johnson, A. L. and Johnstone, E. C. (1986) Expressed emotion and relapse in schizophrenia. *British Journal of Psychiatry*, 148, 741–4.

Madden, T. J., Ellen, P. S. and Ajzen, I. (1992) A comparison of the theory of planned behaviour and the theory of reasoned action. *Personality and Social Psychology Bulletin*, 18, 3–9.

Main, M. and Cassidy, J. (1988) Categories of response with the parent at age six: predicted from infant attachment classifications and stable over a one month period. *Developmental Psychology*, 24, 415–26.

Main, M. and Solomon, J. (1990) Procedures for identifying infants as disorganised/disoriented during the Ainsworth Strange Situation. In M. Greenberg, D. Cicchetti and E. M. Cummings (eds), *Attachment in the Pre-school Years*. Chicago: Chicago University Press.

Mann, L. (1981) The baiting crowd in episodes of threatened suicide. *Journal of Personality and Social Psychology*, 41, 703–9.

Manstead, A. S. R. and Parker, D. (1995) Evaluating and extending the theory of planned behaviour. In W. Stroebe and M. Hewstone (eds), *European Review of Social Psychology, Vol. 6*. Chichester: John Wiley.

Marañon, G. (1924) Contribution a l'étude de l'action émotive de l'andrenoline. *Revue Française d'Endocronologie*, 21, 301–25.

Markovà, I. and Farr, R. (eds) (1995) *Representations of Health, Illness and Handicap*. Chur: Harwood Academic.

Marshall, G. D. and Zimbardo, P. G. (1979) Affective consequences of inadequately explained emotional arousal. *Journal of Personality and Social Psychology*, 37, 970–85.

Martin, R. (1994) Majority and minority influence using the afterimage paradigm: a series of replications. Unpublished ms. University College, Swansea.

Martin, R. (1995) Majority and minority influence using the afterimage paradigm: a replication with an unambiguous blue slide. *European Journal of Social Psychology*, 25, 373–81.

Maslach, C. (1979) Negative emotional biasing of unexplained arousal. *Journal of Personality and Social Psychology*, 37, 953–69.

Maslow, A. K. (1954) *Motivation and Personality*. New York: Harper & Row.

Masters, J. C. and Wellman, H. M. (1974) The study of human infant attachment: a procedural critique. *Psychological Bulletin*, 81, 218–37.

May, M. A. and Hartshorne, H. (1928) *Studies in the nature of character I & II*. New York: Macmillan.

McCauley, C. and Stitt, C. L. (1978) An individual and quantitative measure of stereotypes. *Journal of Personality and Social Psychology*, 36, 929–40.

McCauley, C., Stitt, C. L. and Segal, M. (1980) Stereotyping: from prejudice to prediction. *Psychological Bulletin*, 87, 195–208.

McDougall, W. (1908) *An Introduction to Social Psychology*. London: Methuen.

McDougall, W. (1913) *An Introduction to Social Psychology*. 5th edn. Boston: Luce.

McFadyan, R. (1992) Conflicts and consistencies in stereotypes and identities of unemployed people. Doctoral dissertation, University of Cambridge.

McGhee, J. and Fryer, D. (1989) Unemployment, income and the family: an action research approach. *Social Behaviour*, 4, 237–52.

McGuire, A. M. (1994) Helping behaviors in the national environment: dimensions and correlates of helping. *Personality and Social Psychology Bulletin*, 20, 45–56.

McGuire, W. J. (1968) Personality and attitude change: an information-processing theory. In A. G. Greenwald, T. C. Brock and T. M. Ostrom (eds), *Psychological Foundations of Attitudes*. New York: Academic Press.

McGuire, W. J. (1969) The nature of attitudes and attitude change. In G. Lindzey and E. Aronson (eds), *Handbook of Social Psychology, Vol. 3*. 2nd edn. Reading, MA: Addison-Wesley.

McGuire, W. J. (1985) Attitudes and attitude change. In G. Lindzey and E. Aronson (eds), *Handbook of Social Psychology, Vol. 2*. 3rd edn. New York: Random House.

McGuire, W. J. (1986) The vicissitudes of attitudes and similar representations in twentieth century psychology. *European Journal of Social Psychology*, 16, 89–130.

McKenna, S. P. and Fryer, D. M. (1984) Perceived health during lay-off and early unemployment. *Occupational Health*, 36, 201–6.

McKenzie, J. (1998) Fundamental flaws in the five factor model: a re-analysis of the seminal correlation matrix from which the 'openness-to-experience' factor was extracted. *Personality and Individual Differences*, 24(4), 475–80.

McNulty, S. C. and Swann, W. B. (1994) Identity negotiation in room-mate relationships: the self as architect and consequence of social reality. *Journal of Personality and Social Psychology*, 67, 1012–23.

Mead, G. H. (1934) *Mind, Self and Society*. Chicago: University of Chicago Press.

Mead, G. H. and Strauss, A. L. (1964) *On Social Psychology: Selected Papers*. Chicago and London: University of Chicago Press.

Mealey, L. (1995) The sociobiology of sociopathy – an integrated evolutionary model. *Behavioral and Brain Sciences*, 18(3), 523–41.

Mealey, L. (1999) Human evolution, reproduction, and morality. *Archives of Sexual Behavior*, 28(5), 423–5.

Medcof, J. W. (1990) An integrative model of attribution processes. In M. P. Zanna (ed.), *Advances in Experimental Social Psychology, Vol. 23*. New York: Academic Press.

Meloy, J. R. (1998) The psychology of stalking. In J. R. Meloy (ed.), *The Psychology of Stalking: Clinical and Forensic Perspectives*. San Diego: Academic Press.

Meltzer, B. N., Petras, J. W. and Reynolds, L. T. (1975) *Symbolic Interactionism: Genesis, Varieties and Criticism*. London: Routledge and Kegan Paul.

Meltzoff, A. N. (1988) Infant imitation after a 1-week delay – long-term memory for novel acts and multiple stimuli. *Developmental Psychology*, 24(4), 470–6.

Meltzoff, A. N. and Moore, M. K. (1992) Early imitation within a functional framework: the importance of personal identity, movement, and development. *Infant Behavior and Development*, 15, 479–505.

Meltzoff, A. N. and Moore, M. K. (1997) Explaining facial imitation: a theoretical model. *Early Development and Parenting*, 6(3–4), 179–92.

Merton, R. K. (1949) Manifest and latent functions In R. K. Merton (ed.), *Social Theory and Social Structure*. Glencoe, IL: Free Press.

Merton, R. K. (1957) *Social Theory and Social Structure*. New York: Free Press.

Merton, R. K. and Kitt, A. S. (1950) Contributions to the theory of reference group behaviour. In R. K. Merton and P. F. Lazarfeld (eds), *Continuities in Social Research: Studies in the Scope and Method of the American Soldier*. Glencoe, IL: Free Press.

Meyerowitz, B. E. and Chaiken, S. (1987) The effect of message framing on breast self examination attitudes, intentions, and behaviour. *Journal of Personality and Social Psychology*, 52, 500–10.

Midlarsky, E. (1991) Helping as coping. In M. S. Clark (ed.), *Prosocial Behaviour*. Newbury Park, CA: Sage.

Miles, A. (1987) *The Mentally Ill in Contemporary Society*. 2nd edn. Oxford: Blackwell.

Milgram, S. (1965) Liberating effects of group pressure. *Journal of Personality and Social Psychology*, 1, 127–34.

Milgram, S. (1974) *Obedience to Authority*. New York: Harper & Row.

Milgram, S. (1984) Cities as social representations. In R. M. Farr and S. Moscovici (eds), *Social Representations*. Cambridge: Cambridge University Press.

Miller, A. G. (guest ed.) (1999) *Special issue: Perspectives on Evil and Violence. Personality and Social Psychology Review*, 3(3), 176–275.

Miller, D. T. and Ross, M. (1975) Self-serving biases in the attribution of causality: fact or fiction? *Psychological Bulletin*, 82, 213–25.

Miller, G. A. (1966) *Psychology: The Science of Mental Life*. Harmondsworth: Penguin.

Miller, G. A. (1968) The magical number seven plus or minus two. In G. A. Miller, *The Psychology of Communication*. Harmondsworth: Penguin.

Miller, J. G. and Bersoff, D. M. (1992) Culture and moral judgment: how are conflicts between justice and interpersonal responsibilities resolved? *Journal of Personality and Social Psychology*, 62, 541–54.

Miller, L. C. (1990) Intimacy and liking: mutual influence and the role of unique relationships. *Journal of Personality and Social Psychology*, 59, 50–60.

Miller, N. and Brewer, M. B. (eds) (1984) *Groups in Contact: The Psychology of Desegregation*. New York: Academic Press.

Milner, D. (1975) *Children and Race*. Harmondsworth: Penguin.

Milner, D. (1996) Children and racism. In W. P. Robinson (ed.), *Social Groups and Identities*. London: Butterworth Heinemann.

Milroy, L. (1980) *Language and Social Networks*. Oxford: Blackwell.

Mischel, W. (1968) *Personality and Assessment*. New York: John Wiley.

Mischel, W. (1996) *Personality and Assessment*. Rev. edn. Mahwah, NJ: Erlbaum.

Mixon, D. (1972) Instead of deception. *Journal for the Theory of Social Behaviour*, 2, 142–78.

Molinari, L. and Emiliani, F. (1990) What is an image? The structure of mothers' images of the child and their influence on conversational styles. In G. Duveen and B. Lloyd (eds), *Social Representations and Development of Knowledge*. Cambridge: Cambridge University Press.

Moliner, P. (1994) A two-dimensional model of social representations. *European Journal of Social Psychology*, 25, 27–40.

Morant, N. (1998) The social representation of mental ill-health in communities of mental health practitioners in the UK and France. *Social Science Information*, 37 (4), 663–85.

Moreno, J. L. (1943) *Who Shall Survive? A New Approach to the Problems of Human Interrelations*. Washington, DC: Nervous and Mental Disease Publishing.

Moriarty, T. (1975) Crime, commitment, and the responsive bystander: two field experiments. *Journal of Personality and Social Psychology*, 31, 370–6.

Moscovici, S. (1961/1976). *La Psychanalyse, son image et son public*. Paris: Presses Universitaires de France.

Moscovici, S. (1972) Society and theory in social psychology. In J. Israel and H. Tajfel (eds), *The Context of Social Psychology: A Critical Assessment*. London: Academic Press.

Moscovici, S. (1973) Foreword. In C. Herzlich, *Health and Illness*. London: Academic Press.

Moscovici, S. (1976) *Social Influence and Social Change*. London: Academic Press.

Moscovici, S. (1980) Towards a theory of conversion behaviour. In L. Berkowitz (ed.), *Advances in Experimental Social Psychology, Vol. 13*. New York: Academic Press.

Moscovici, S. (1981) On social representations. In J. P. Forgas (ed.), *Social Cognition: Perspectives on Everyday Understanding*. London: Academic Press.

Moscovici, S. (1982) Perspectives d'avenir en psychologie sociale. In P. Fraisse (ed.), *Psychologie de demain*. Paris: Presses Universitaires de France.

Moscovici, S. (1984) The phenomena of social representations. In R. M. Farr and S. Moscovici (eds), *Social Representations*. Cambridge: Cambridge University Press.

Moscovici, S. (1985) *The Age of the Crowd*. Cambridge: Cambridge University Press.

Moscovici, S. (1996) *The Invention of Society*. Cambridge: Polity.

Moscovici, S. (1997) *Chronique des années égarées* (*Chronicle of Stray Years*). Paris: Editions Stock.

Moscovici, S. (1998) The history and actuality of social representations. In U. Flick (ed.), *The Psychology of the Social*. Cambridge: Cambridge University Press.

Moscovici, S. (2000) *Social Representations: Explorations in Social Psychology*. Ed. Gerard Duveen. Cambridge: Polity.

Moscovici, S. and Doise, W. (1994) *Conflict and Consensus: A General Theory of Collective Decisions*. London: Sage

Moscovici, S. and Personnaz, B. (1980) Studies in social influence. V: Minority influence and conversion behaviour in a perceptual task. *Journal of Experimental Social Psychology*, 16, 270–82.

Moscovici, S. and Personnaz, B. (1991) Studies in social influence VI: Is Lenin orange or red? Imagery and social influence. *European Journal of Social Psychology*, 21, 101–8.

Moscovici, S. and Zavalloni, M. (1969) The group as a polariser of attitudes. *Journal of Personality and Social Psychology*, 12, 125–35.

Moscovici, S., Lage, E. and Naffrechoux, M. (1969) Influence of a consistent minority on the responses of a majority in a colour perception task. *Sociometry*, 32, 365–80.

Moser, K. A., Fox, A. J. and Jones, D. R. (1984) Unemployment and mortality in the OPCS longitudinal survey. *Lancet*, 2, 1324–9.

Moshman, D. (1994) Reason, reasons and reasoning: a constructivist account of human rationality. *Theory and Psychology*, 4, 245–60.

Moshman, D. (1995) The construction of moral rationality. *Human Development*, 38, 265–81.

Motowidlo, S. J. (1982) Relationship between self-rated performance and pay satisfaction among sales representatives. *Journal of Applied Psychology*, 67, 209–13.

Mugny, G. (1982) *The Power of Minorities*. London: Academic Press.

Mullen, B. (1986) Atrocity as a function of lynch mob composition: a self-attention perspective. *Personality and Social Psychology Bulletin*, 12, 187–97.

Mullen, P. E., Path, M. and Purcell, R. (2000) *Stalkers and their Victims*. Cambridge: Cambridge University Press.

Murphy, E. (1991) *After the Asylum*. London: Faber.

Murphy, H. B. M. (1983) Sociocultural variations in symptomatology, incidence and course of illness. In M. Shepard and O. L. Sangwill (eds), *Handbook of Psychiatry, Vol. I: General Psychopathology*. Cambridge: Cambridge University Press.

Murray, L. (1992) The impact of postnatal depression on infant development. *Journal of Child Psychology and Psychiatry*, 33, 543–61.

Murray, L., and Cooper, P. (eds) (1997) *Postpartum Depression and Child Development*. New York: Guilford Press.

Murstein, B. I. (1972) Person perception and courtship progress among premarital couples. *Journal of Marriage and the Family*, 34, 621–6.

Myers, D. G. (1990) *Social Psychology*. 3rd edn. New York: McGraw-Hill.

Myers, D. G., Bach, P. J. and Schreiber, F. B. (1974) Normative and informational effects of group interaction. *Sociometry*, 37, 275–86.

Myers, S. K., Wiseman, M. M., Tichsler, G. L., Holzer, C. E., Leaf, P. J., Orvasihel, H., Anthony, J. C., Boyd, J. H., Burke, J. D., Kramer, M. and Stoltzman, R. (1984) Six month prevalence of psychiatric disorders in three communities, 1980–1982. *Archives of General Psychiatry*, 41, 959–67.

Nadler, A. (1987) Determinants of help-seeking behaviour: the effects of helper similarity, task centrality, and recipient self-esteem. *European Journal of Social Psychology*, 17, 57–67.

Nadler, A. (1991) Help-seeking behavior: psychological costs and instrumental benefits. In M. S. Clark (ed.), *Review of Personality and Social Psychology, Vol. 12*. Newbury Park, CA: Sage.

Neisser, U. (1981) John Dean's memory: a case study. *Cognition*, 9, 1–22.

Neisser, U. (1988) What is ordinary memory the memory of? In U. Neisser and E. Winograd, *Remembering Reconsidered: Ecological and Traditional Approaches to the Study of Memory*. Cambridge and New York: Cambridge University Press.

Nemeth, C., Swedland, M. and Kanki, B. (1974) Patterning of the minority's response and their influence on the majority. *European Journal of Social Psychology*, 4, 53–64.

Neuman, J. H. and Baron, R. A. (1997) Aggression in the workplace. In R. A. Giacalone and J. Greenberg (eds), *Antisocial Behaviour in Organizations*. Thousand Oaks, CA: Sage.

Newcomb, T. N. (1937) Attitudes. In G. Murphy, L. B. Murphy and T. N. Newcomb (eds), *Experimental Social Psychology*. (Rev. edn.) New York: Harper.

Newcomb, T. M. (1953) An approach to the study of communicative acts. *Psychological Review*, 60, 393–404.

Newcomb, T. M. (1961) *The Acquaintance Process*. New York: Holt, Rinehart & Winston.

NICHD Early Child Care Research Network (1997) The effects of infant child care on infant–mother attachment security: results of the NICHD Study of Early Child Care. *Child Development*, 68, 860–79.

Nisbett, R. E. and Ross, L. (1980) *Human Inference: Strategies and Shortcomings of Social Judgement*. Englewood cliffs, NJ: Prentice-Hall.

Nisbett, R. E. and Wilson, T. D. (1977) Telling more than we can know: verbal reports on mental processes. *Psychology Review*, 84, 231–59.

Nisbett, R. E., Caputo, C., Legant, P. and Maracek, J. (1973) Behaviour as seen by the actor and as seen by the observer. *Journal of Personality and Social Psychology*, 27, 154–64.

Nolan, J., Wichert, I. and Burchell, B. J. (1999) Job insecurity, psychological well-being, work orientation and family life. In E. Heery (ed.), *The Insecure Workforce*. London: Routledge.

Nolen-Hoeksema, S. (1987) Sex differences in unipolar depression: evidence and theory. *Psychological Bulletin*, 101, 259–82.

Nolen-Hoeksema, S. (1990) *Sex Differences in Depression*. Stanford, CA: Stanford University Press.

Noller, P. (1987) Non-verbal communication in marriage. In D. Perlman and S. Duck (eds), *Intimate Relationships*. Beverley Hills, CA: Sage.

Norman, D. A. (1980) Twelve issues for cognitive science. *Cognitive Science*, 4, 1–33.

Norman, W. T. (1963) Toward a taxonomy of personality attributes: replicated factor structure in peer nomination personality ratings. *Journal of Abnormal and Social Psychology*, 66, 574–83.

Nuckolls, K. B., Cassel, J. and Kaplan, B. J. (1972) Psychosocial assets, life crisis and the prognosis of pregnancy. *American Journal of Epidemiology*, 95, 431–41.

Oakes, P. J., Haslam, A. and Turner, J. C. (1994) *Stereotyping and Social Reality*. Oxford: Blackwell.

Oatley, K. (1992) *Best Laid Schemes: The Psychology of Emotions*. Cambridge: Cambridge University Press.

Oatley, K. and Jenkins, J. M. (1995) *Understanding Emotions*. Oxford: Blackwell.

O'Leary, K. D. and Beach, S. R. H. (1990) Marital therapy: a viable treatment for depression. *American Journal of Psychiatry*, 147, 183–6.

Oliner, S. P. and Oliner, P. M. (1988) *The Altruistic Personality: Rescuers of Jews in Nazi Europe*. New York: Free Press.

Olson, D. (1995) Writing and the mind. In J. V. Wertsch, P. D. Río and A. Alvarez (eds), *Sociocultural Studies of Mind*. Cambridge: Cambridge University Press.

Omoto, A. M. and Snyder, M. (1995) Sustained helping without obligation: motivation, longevity of service and perceived attitude change among AIDS volunteers. *Journal of Personality and Social Psychology*, 68, 671–86.

Oppenheim, C. (ed.) (1998) *An Inclusive Society: Strategies for Tackling Poverty*. London: IPPR.

O'Reilly, J. and Fagan, C. (eds) (1998) *Part-time Prospects: An International Comparison of Part-time Work in Europe, North America and the Pacific Rim*. London: Routledge.

Orne, M. T. (1962) On the social psychology of the psychology experiment: with particular references to demand characteristics and their implications. *American Psychologist*, 17, 776–88.

Orwell, G. (1949) *Nineteen Eighty-four*. London: Secker & Warburg.

Osgood, C. E. and Tannenbaum, P. H. (1955) The principle of congruity in the prediction of attitude change. *Psychological Review*, 62, 42–55.

Osterman, K., Bjorkqvist, K., Lagerspetz, K. M. J., Kaukiainen, A., Landua, S. F., Fraczek, A. and Caprara, G. V. (1998) Cross-cultural evidence of female indirect aggression. *Aggressive Behavior*, 24, 1–8.

Ostrom, T. M. (1969) The relationship between the affective, behavioural and cognitive components of attitudes. *Journal of Experimental Social Psychology*, 5, 12–30.

Paicheler, G. (1988) *The Psychology of Social Influence*. Cambridge: Cambridge University Press.

Palkowitz, R. (1985) Fathers' birth attendance, early contact, and extended contact with their newborns: a critical review. *Child Development*, 56, 392–406.

Palnalp, Sally (1999) *Communicating Emotion: Social, Moral and Cultural Processes*. Cambridge: Cambridge University Press.

Parker, D., Manstead, A. S. R. and Stradling, S. G. (1995) Extending the theory of planned behaviour: the role of personal norm. *British Journal of Social Psychology*, 34, 127–37.

Parkin Alan, J. (2000) *Essentials of Cognitive Psychology*. Hove: Psychology Press.

Parry, G. (1988) Mobilising social support. In F. N. Watts (ed.), *New Developments in Clinical Psychology, Vol. II*. Leicester: BPS Books.

Patterson, G. R. (1979) A performance theory for coercive family interactions. In R. Cairns (ed.), *Social Interaction: Methods, Analysis, and Illustration*. Hillsdale, NJ: Erlbaum.

Patterson, G. R. (1982) *Coercive Family Process, 3*. Eugene, OR: Castalia.

Patterson, G. R. (1986) The contribution of siblings to training for fighting: a micro-social analysis. In D. Olweus, J. Block and M. Radke-Yarrow (eds), *The Development of Antisocial and Prosocial Behavior: Research, Theories, and Issues*. New York: Academic Press.

Patterson, G. R., DeBaryshe, B. D. and Ramsey, E. (1989) A developmental perspective on antisocial behavior. *American Psychologist*, 44, 329–35.

Payne, R. L. and Jones, J. G. (1987) Social class and re-employment: changes in health and perceived financial circumstances. *Journal of Occupational Behaviour*, 8, 175–84.

Penner, L. A. and Finkelstein, M. A. (1998) Dispositional and structural determinants of volunteerism. *Journal of Personality and Social Psychology*, 74, 525–37.

Pennington, D. (2000) *Social Cognition*. London: Routledge.

Peplau, L. A. and Perlman, D. (1982) Perspectives on loneliness. In L. A. Peplau and D. Perlman (eds), *Loneliness*. New York: John Wiley.

Pepler, D. and Craig, W. M. (1995) A peek behind the fence: naturalistic observations of aggressive children with remote audiovisual recording. *Developmental Psychology*, 31, 548–53.

Perlman, M. and Ross, H. S. (1997) The benefits of parent intervention in children's disputes: an examination of concurrent changes in children's fighting styles. *Child Development*, 68, 690–700.

Perry, D. G., Kusel, S. J. and Perry, L. C. (1988) Victims of peer aggression. *Developmental Psychology*, 24, 807–14.

Perry, S., Difede, J., Musgni, G., Frances, A. J. and Jacobsberg, L. (1992) Predictors of posttraumatic stress disorder after burn injury. *American Journal of Psychiatry*, 149(7), 931–5.

Pervin, L. A. (1990) *Handbook of Personality: Theory and Research*. New York: Guilford Press.

Pervin, L. A. (1999) *Handbook of Personality: Theory and Research*. 2nd edn. New York: Guilford Press.

Pervin, L. A. and John, O. P. (1997) *Personality: Theory and Research*. 7th edn. New York: John Wiley.

Pettigrew, T. F. (1958) Personality and socio-cultural factors in intergroup attitudes: a cross-national comparison. *Journal of Conflict Resolution*, 2, 29–42.

Pettigrew, T. F. (1996) *How to Think Like a Social Scientist*. New York: HarperCollins.

Pettigrew, T. F. (1998) Intergroup contact theory. *Annual Review of Psychology*, 49, 65–85.

Pettigrew, T. F. and Meertens, R. W. (1995) Subtle and blatant prejudice in Western Europe. *European Journal of Social Psychology*, 25, 57–75.

Pettigrew, T. F. and Tropp, L. (2000) Does intergroup contact reduce prejudice? Recent meta-analytic findings. In S. Oskamp (ed.), *Reducing Prejudice and Discrimination: Social Psychological Perspectives*. Mahwah, NJ: Erlbaum.

Petty, M. M., McGee, G. W. and Cavender, J. W. (1984) A meta-analysis of the relationship between individual job satisfaction and individual job performance. *Academy of Management Review*, 9, 712–21.

Petty, R. E. and Cacioppo, J. T. (1981) *Attitudes and Persuasion: Classic and Contemporary Approaches*. Dubuque, IA: Brown.

Petty, R. E. and Cacioppo, J. T. (1986) *Communication and Persuasion: Central and Peripheral Routes to Attitude Change*. New York: Springer-Verlag.

Petty, R. E., Priester, J. R. and Wegener, D. T. (1994) Cognitive processes in attitude change. In R. S. Wyer Jr and T. K. Srull (eds), *Handbook of Social Cognition, Vol. 2*. Hillsdale, NJ: Erlbaum.

Petty, R. E., Wells, G. L. and Brock, T. C. (1976) Distraction can enhance or reduce yielding to propaganda: thought disruption versus effort justification. *Journal of Personality and Social Psychology*, 34, 874–84.

Philo, G. (ed.) (1996) *Media and Mental Distress*. London: Longman.

Piaget, J. (1926) *The Child's Conception of the World*. London: Granada.

Piaget, J. (1932) *The Moral Judgment of the Child*. London: Routledge.

Piaget, J. (1970) Piaget's theory. In P. H. Mussen (ed.), *Carmichael's Manual of Child Psychology*. London: John Wiley.

Piaget, J. and Inhelder, B. (1969) *The Psychology of the Child*. London: Routledge and Kegan Paul.

Piliavin, J. A. and Charng, H. W. (1990) Altruism: a review of recent theory and research. *American Sociological Review*, 16, 27–65.

Piliavin, J. A., Dovidio, J. F., Gaertner, S. L. and Clark, R. D., III (1981) *Emergency Intervention*. New York: Academic Press.

Pipp, S., Easterbrooks, M. A. and Harmon, R. J. (1992) The relation between attachment and knowledge of self and mother in one- to three-year-old infants. *Child Development*, 63, 738–50.

Planalp, S. and Rivers, M. (1996) Changes in knowledge of personal relationships. In G. J. O. Fletcher and J. Fitness (eds), *Knowledge Structures in Close Relationships*. Hillsdale, NJ: Erlbaum.

Plomin, R. (1989) *Nature and Nurture: An Introduction to Human Behavioural Genetics*. New York: Brooks / Cole.

Plous, S. (1993) *The Psychology of Judgement and Decision Making*. New York: McGraw-Hill.

Plummer, K. (ed.) (1991) *Symbolic Interactionism*. 2 vols. London: Edward Elgar.

Podsakoff, P. M. and Williams, L. J. (1986) The relationship between job performance and job satisfaction. In E. A. Locke (ed.), *Generalising from Laboratory to Field Settings*. Brookfield, VT: Gower.

Potter, J. (1996) *Representing Reality: Discourse, Rhetoric and Social Construction*. London and Thousand Oaks, CA: Sage.

Potter, J. and Edwards, D. (1999) Social representations and discursive psychology: from cognition to action. *Culture and Psychology*, 5, 447–58.

Potter, J. and Wetherell, M. (1987) *Discourse and Social Psychology: Beyond Attitudes and Behaviour*. London and Newbury Park, CA: Sage.

Power, M. J. and Dalgleish, T. (1997) *Cognition and Emotion: From Order to Disorder*. Hove: Psychology Press.

Power, T. G. and Parke, R. D. (1986) Patterns of early socialization: mother– and father–infant interaction in the home. *International Journal of Behavioural Development*, 9, 331–41.

Pratt, M. W., Golding, G. and Hunter, W. J. (1983) Ageing as ripening: character and consistency of moral judgment in young, mature and older adults. *Human Development*, 26, 277–88.

Prentice-Dunn, S. and Spivey, C. B. (1986) Extreme deindividuation in the laboratory: its magnitude and subjective components. *Personality and Social Psychology Bulletin*, 12, 206–15.

Prior, L. (1993) *The Social Organisation of Mental Illness*. London: Sage.

Protopapas, A. (1999) Connectionist modeling of speech perception. *Psychological Bulletin*, 125(4), 410–36.

Putnam, R. D. (1993) *Making Democracy Work: Civic Traditions in Modern Italy*. Princeton, NJ: Princeton University Press.

Putnam, R. D. (1995) Tuning in, tuning out: the strange disappearance of social capital in America. *Political Science and Politics*, 28(4), 664–83.

Putnam, R. D. (2000) *Bowling Alone: The Collapse and Revival of American Community*. New York: Simon and Schuster.

Pylyshyn, Z. W. (1973) What the mind's eye tells the mind's brain: a critique of mental imagery. *Psychological Bulletin*, 80, 1–24.

Quatrone, G. A. (1986) On the perception of a group's variability. In S. Worchel and W. Austin (eds), *Social Psychology of Intergroup Relations*. Chicago: Nelson.

Quatrone, G. A. and Jones, E. E. (1980) The perception of variability within ingroups and outgroups: implications for the law of small numbers. *Journal of Personality and Social Psychology*, 38, 141–52.

Quinton, D., Rutter, M. and Liddle, C. (1984) Institutional rearing, parenting difficulties and marital support. *Psychological Medicine*, 14, 107–24.

Quinton, D., Pickles, A., Maughan, B. and Rutter, M. (1993) Partners, peers, and pathways: assortative pairing and continuities in conduct disorder. *Development and Psychopathology*, 5, 763–83.

Rabbie, J. M., Schot, J. C. and Visser, L. (1989) Social identity theory: a conceptual and empirical critique from the perspective of a behavioural interaction model. *European Journal of Social Psychology*, 19, 171–202.

Radley, A. (1994) *Making Sense of Illness: The Social Psychology of Health and Disease*. London: Sage.

Rahn, W. E. and Transue, J. E. (1998) Social trust and value change: the decline of social capital in American youth. *Political Psychology*, 19(3), 545–65.

Rajecki, D. W. (1990) *Attitudes*. 2nd edn. Sunderland, MA: Sinauer.

Ramon, S. (1996) *Mental Health in Europe: Ends, Beginnings and Rediscoveries*. London: Macmillan.

Randall, P. (1997) *Adult Bullying: Perpetrators and Victims*. London: Routledge.

Read, S. J. and Miller, L. C. (eds) (1998) *Connectionist Models of Social Reasoning and Social Behaviour*. Mahwah, NJ: Erlbaum.

Reber, A. S. (1985) *The Penguin Dictionary of Psychology*. Harmondsworth: Penguin.

Reddy, V., Hay, D. F., Murray, L. and Trevarthen, C. (1997) Communication in infancy: mutual regulation of affect and attention. In G. Bremner, A. Slater and G. Butterworth (eds), *Infant Development: Recent Advances*. Hove: Psychology Press.

Reicher, S. D. (1984) St Paul's: a study in the limits of crowd behaviour. In J. Murphy, M. John and H. Brown (eds), *Dialogues and Debates in Social Psychology*. London and Milton Keynes: Erlbaum Open University Press.

Reis, T. H., Nezlek, J. and Wheeler, L. (1980) Physical attractiveness in social interaction. *Journal of Personality and Social Psychology*, 38, 604–17.

Rentsch, J. R. and Heffner, T. S. (1994) Assessing self-concept – analysis of Gordon Coding Scheme using who am I responses. *Journal of Social Behavior and Personality*, 9(2), 283–300.

Renzetti, C. M. (1992) *Violent Betrayal: Partner Abuse in Lesbian Relationships*. Newbury Park, CA: Sage.

Resnick, L. B. and North Atlantic Treaty Organization. Scientific Affairs Division (1997) *Discourse, Tools, and Reasoning: Essays on Situated Cognition*. Berlin and New York: Springer-Verlag.

Rest, J. R. (1983) Morality. In J. H. Flavell and E. M. Markman (eds), *Handbook of Child Psychology, Vol. 3*. New York: John Wiley.

Rheingold, H. L. (1969a) The effect of a strange environment on the behaviour of infants. In B. M. Foss (ed.), *Determinants of Infant Behaviour, Vol. 4*. London: Methuen.

Rheingold, H. L. (1969b) The social and socializing infant. In D. A. Goslin (ed.), *Handbook of Socialization Research*. Chicago: Rand McNally.

Rheingold, H. L. and Eckerman, C. O. (1973) Fear of the stranger: a critical re-examination. *Advances in Child Development and Behavior*, 8, 186–222.

Ribble, M. A. (1944) Infantile experiences in relation to personality development. In J. McV. Hunt (ed.), *Personality and the Behavior Disorders*. New York: Ronald.

Robarchek, C. A. and Robarchek, C. J. (1996) Waging peace: the psychological and sociocultural dynamics of positive peace. In A. W. Wolfe and H. Yang (eds), *Anthropological Contributions to Conflict Resolution*. Athens, GA: University of Georgia Press.

Rodgers, G., with J. B. de Figueiredo, C. Gore, F. Lapeyre and H. Silver (1994) *Overcoming Exclusion: Livelihood and Rights in Economic and Social Development*. International Institute for Labour Studies Discussion Paper, Geneva.

Rogers, R. S., Stenner, P., Gleeson, K. and Rogers, W. S. (1995) *Social Psychology: A Critical Agenda*. Cambridge: Polity.

Rojahn, K. and Pettigrew, T. F. (1992) Memory for schema-relevant information – a metaanalytic resolution. *British Journal of Social Psychology*, 31, 81–109.

Romaine, S. (1994) *Language in Society: An Introduction to Sociolinguistics*. Oxford and New York: Oxford University Press.

Romaine, S. (1999) *Communicating Gender*. Mahwah, NJ: Erlbaum.

Rosch, E. (1977) Linguistic relativity. In P. N. Johnson-Laird and P. C. Wason (eds), *Thinking*. Cambridge: Cambridge University Press.

Rose, D. (1996) *Living in the Community*. London: Sainsbury Centre for Mental Health.

Rose, D. (1998) Television, madness and community care. *Journal of Community and Applied Social Psychology*, 8, 213–28.

Rosen, B., Klein, D. F. and Gittleman-Klein, R. (1971) The prediction of rehospitalisation: the relationship between age of first psychiatric treatment contact, marital status and pre-morbid social adjustment. *Journal of Nervous and Mental Diseases*, 152, 17–22.

Rosenberg, M. I. and Hovland, C. I. (1960) Cognitive, affective and behavioural components of attitudes. In C. I. Hovland and M. I. Rosenberg (eds), *Attitude Organisation and Change: An Analysis of Consistency among Attitude Components*. New Haven, CT: Yale University Press.

Rosenman, R. H., Brand, R. J., Sholtz, R. I. and Friedman, M. (1976) Multivariate prediction of coronary heart disease during 8.5 year follow-up in the Western Collaborative Group Study. *American Journal of Cardiology*, 37, 903–10.

Rosenman, R., Brand, R. J., Jenkins, C. D., Friedman, M., Straus, R. and Wurm, M. (1975) Coronary heart disease in the Western Collaborative Group study: final follow-up experience at 8.5 years. *Journal of the American Medical Association*, 233, 872–7.

Rosenthal, R. (1976) *Experimenter Effects in Behavioral Research*. New York: Irvington.

Ross, E. A. (1908) *Social Psychology: An Outline and Source Book*. New York: Macmillan.

Ross, H. S. and Goldman, B. D. (1977) Infants' sociability toward strangers. *Child Development*, 48, 638–42.

Ross, H. S. and Kay, D. A. (1980) The origins of social games. *New Directions for Child Development*, 9, 17–31.

Ross, H. S., Martin, J., Perlman, M., Smith, M., Blackmore, E. and Hunter, J. (1996) Autonomy and authority in the resolution of sibling disputes. *New Directions for Child Development*, 13, 71–90.

Ross, L., Bierbrauer, G. and Polly, S. (1974) Attribution of educational outcomes by professional and non-professional instructors. *Journal of Personality and Social Psychology*, 29, 609–18.

Rothbart, M., Evans, M. and Fulero, S. (1979) Recall for confirming events: memory processes and the maintenance of social stereotypes. *Journal of Experimental Social Psychology*, 15, 343–55.

Rowe, C. (1994) Picking the winners: the thorny issue of assessing leadership potential. *Leadership and Organisation Development Journal*, 15(6), 1–4.

Rowland, K. F. (1977) Environmental events predicting death for the elderly. *Psychological Bulletin*, 84, 349–72.

Rozin, P., Lowery, L., Imada, S. and Haidt, J. (1999) The CAD triad hypothesis: a mapping between three moral emotions (contempt, anger, disgust) and three moral codes (community, autonomy, divinity). *Journal of Personality and Social Psychology*, 76(4), 574–86.

Rubin, J. Z., Provenzano, F. J. and Luria, Z. (1974) The eye of the beholder: parents' views on the sex of new borns. *American Journal of Orthopsychiatry*, 44, 512–19.

Ruble, D. and Martin, C. (1997) Gender development. In W. Damon (ed.), *Handbook of Child Psychology, Vol. 3*. New York: John Wiley.

Ruffman, T., Perner, J., Naito, M., Parkin, L. and Clements, W. A. (1998) Older (but not younger) siblings facilitate false belief understanding. *Developmental Psychology*, 34, 161–74.

Rumelhart, D., McClelland, J. and the PDP Research Group (1986) *Vol. 1. Foundations. Parallel distributed processing: explorations in the microstructure of cognition. Vol. 2. Psychological and Biological Models.* Cambridge, MA: MIT Press.

Rusbult, C. E. and Zembrodt, I. M. (1983) Responses to dissatisfaction in romantic involvements: a multidimensional scaling analysis. *Journal of Experimental Social Psychology*, 19, 274–93.

Rusbult, C. E., Verette, J., Whitney, G. A., Slovik, L. P. and Lipkus, I. (1991) Accommodation processes in close relationships: theory and preliminary empirical evidence. *Journal of Personality and Social Psychology*, 60, 53–78.

Rush, A. J., Shaw, B. F. and Khatami, M. (1980) Cognitive therapy for depression: utilising the couples system. *Cognitive Therapy and Research*, 4, 103–13.

Rutter, D. R. (1984) *Looking and Seeing: The Role of Visual Communication in Social Interaction.* Chichester and New York: John Wiley.

Rutter, D. R. (1987) *Communicating by Telephone.* Oxford and New York: Pergamon Press.

Rutter, M. and Redshaw, J. (1991) Growing up as a twin: twin–singleton differences in psychological development. *Journal of Child Psychology and Psychiatry*, 32, 885–95.

Rutter, M., Quinton, D. and Hill, J. (1990) Adult outcome of institution-reared children. In L. Robins and M. Rutter (eds), *Straight and Devious Pathways from Childhood to Adulthood.* Cambridge: Cambridge University Press.

Saito, A. (2000a) Multilevel analyses of social bases of cognition. In A. Saito (ed.), *Bartlett, Culture and Cognition.* Hove: Psychology Press.

Saito, A. (ed.) (2000b) *Bartlett, Culture and Cognition.* Hove: Psychology Press.

Salovey, P., Mayer, J. D. and Rosenhan, D. L. (1991) Mood and helping: mood as a motivator of helping and helping as a regulator of mood. In M. S. Clark (ed.), *Prosocial Behaviour.* Newbury Park, CA: Sage.

Sampson, R. J., Raudenbush, S. W. and Earls, F. (1997) Neighbourhoods and violent crime: a multilevel study of collective efficacy. *Science*, 277(5328), 918–24.

Sanders, G. S. and Baron, R. S. (1977) Is social comparison irrelevant for producing choice shifts? *Journal of Experimental Social Psychology*, 13, 303–14.

Spier, L. A., Hallowell, I. and Newman, S. S. (eds) (1983) *Language, culture, and personality: essays in memory of Edward Sapir.* Westport, CT: Greenwood Press.

Sarason, B. R., Sarason, I. G. and Pierce, G. R. (1990) *Social Support: An Interactional View.* Chichester: John Wiley.

Savin-Williams, R. C. (1987) *Adolescence: An Ethological Perspective.* New York: Springer-Verlag.

Savitz, L. D., Kumar, K. S. and Zahn, M. A. (1991) Quantifying Luckenbill. *Deviant Behavior*, 12, 19–29.

Sayers, J. (1986) *Sexual Contradictions: Psychology, Psychoanalysis and Feminism.* London: Tavistock.

Sayers, S. (1988) The meaning of work. In R. E. Pahl (ed.), *On Work: Historical, Comparative and Theoretical Approaches.* Oxford: Blackwell.

Scarr, S. and McCartney, K. (1983) How people make their own environments: a theory of genotype–environment effects. *Child Development*, 54, 424–35.

Scarr, S. and Weinberg, R. A. (1976) IQ test performance of black children adopted by white families, *American Psychologist*, 31, 726–39.

Schachter, S. (1951) Deviation, rejection and communication. *Journal of Abnormal and Social Psychology*, 46, 190–207.

Schachter, S. and Singer, J. E. (1962) Cognitive, social and physiological determinants of emotional state. *Psychological Review*, 69, 379–99.

Schaffer, H. R. (1995) *Social Development*. Oxford: Blackwell.

Schaffer, H. R. and Emerson, P. E. (1964) The development of social attachments in infancy. *Monographs of the Society for Research in Child Development*, 29, serial no. 94.

Schegloff, E. A. (1992) Repair after next turn – the last structurally provided defense of intersubjectivity in conversation. *American Journal of Sociology*, 97(5), 1295–345.

Schegloff, E. A., Jefferson, G. and Sacks, H. (1977) The preference for self-correction in the organization of repair in conversation. *Language*, 53, 361–82.

Schlenker, B. R. (1982) Translating actions into attitudes: an identity-analytic approach to the explanation of social conduct. In L. Berkowitz (ed.), *Advances in Experimental Social Psychology, Vol. 15*. New York: Academic Press.

Schmidt, F. L., Ones, D. S. and Hunter, J. E. (1992) Personnel selection. *Annual Review of Psychology*, 43, 627–70.

Schneider, D. J. (1973) Implicit personality theory: a review. *Psychological Bulletin*, 79, 294–309.

Schneider, D. J., Harstorf, A. H. and Ellsworth, P. C. (1979) *Person Perception*. 2nd edn. Reading, MA: Addison-Wesley.

Schneider, M. E., Major, B., Luhtanen, R. and Crocker, J. (1996) Social stigma and the potential costs of assumptive help. *Personality and Social Psychology Bulletin*, 22, 201–9.

Schroeder, D. A., Penner, L. A., Dovidio, J. F. and Piliavin, J. A. (1995) *The Social Psychology of Helping and Altruism: Problems and Puzzles*. New York: McGraw-Hill.

Schroeder, D. A., Dovidio, J. F., Sibicky, M. E., Matthews, L. L. and Allen, J. L. (1988) Empathy and helping behavior: egoism or altruism. *Journal of Experimental Social Psychology*, 24, 333–53.

Schwartz, N., Bless, H., Strack, F., Klump, G., Rittenaver-Schatra, H. and Simons, A. (1991) Ease of retrieval as information: another look at the availability heuristic. *Journal of Personality and Social Psychology*, 61, 195–202.

Scitovsky, T. (1992) *The Joyless Economy: The Psychology of Human Satisfaction*. Rev. edn. Oxford: Oxford University Press.

Scott, J. (1995) Using household panels to study micro-social change. *Innovation*, 8, 61–73.

SCPR (1992) *British Social Attitudes: Cumulative Sourcebook*. Aldershot: Gower.

Scribner, S. and Tobach, E. (1996) *Mind and Social Practice: Selected Writings of Sylvia Scribner*. Cambridge: Cambridge University Press.

Searcy, E. and Eisenberg, N. (1992) Defensiveness in response to aid from a sibling. *Journal of Personality and Social Psychology*, 62, 422–33.

Seidenberg, M. S. and MacDonald, M. C. (1999) A probabilistic constraints approach to language acquisition and processing. *Cognitive Science*, 23(4), 569–88.

Seligman, M. E. P. (1975) *Helplessness: On Depression, Development, and Death*. San Francisco: W. H. Freeman.

Selman, R. L. (1971) The relation of role taking to the development of moral judgment in children. *Child Development*, 42, 79–91.

Semin, G. (1990) Everyday assumptions, language and personality. In G. Semin and K. Gergen (eds), *Everyday Understanding*. London: Sage.

Semin, G. R. and Fiedler, K. (1989) Cited in M. Hewstone (1989). Relocating attributional phenomena within a language-cognition interface: the case of actors' and observers' perspectives. Unpublished ms, University of Sussex.

Semin, G. R. and Glendon, A. I. (1972) Polarisation and the established group. *British Journal of Social and Clinical Psychology*, 11, 213–21.

Sherbourne, C. D., Hayes, R. D. and Wells, K. B. (1995) Personal and psychosocial risk factors for physical and mental health outcomes and course of depression amongst depressed patients. *Journal of Consulting and Clinical Psychology*, 63(3), 345–55.

Sherif, M. (1935) A study of some social factors in perception. *Archives of Psychology*, 27(187), 1–60.

Sherif, M. (1936) *The Psychology of Social Norms*. New York: Harper & Row.

Sherif, M. (1966) *In Common Predicament: Social Psychology of Intergroup Conflict and Cooperation*. Boston: Houghton Mifflin.

Sherif, M. and Sherif, C. W. (1953) *Groups in Harmony and Tension: An Integration of Studies on Intergroup Relations*. New York: Octagon.

Sherif, M., Harvey, O. J., White, B. J., Hood, W. R. and Sherif, C. W. (1961) *Intergroup Conflict and Cooperation: The Robbers Cave Experiment*. Norman, OK: University of Oklahoma Book Exchange.

Sherwood, R. (1980) *The Psychodynamics of Race*. London: Harvester.

Shotland, R. L. and Stebbins, C. A. (1980) Bystander response to rape: can a victim attract help? *Journal of Applied Social Psychology*, 10, 510–27.

Shotland, R. L. and Straw, M. K. (1976) Bystander response to an assault: when a man attacks a woman. *Journal of Personality and Social Psychology*, 34, 990–9.

Shotter, J. (1993) *Conversational Realities*. Newbury Park, CA: Sage.

Shweder, R. A. (1990) In defense of moral realism: reply to Gabennesch. *Child Development*, 61, 2060–7.

Shweder, R. A. (1991) *Thinking through Cultures: Expeditions in Cultural Psychology*. Cambridge, MA: Harvard University Press.

Shweder, R. A. and Much, N. (1987) Determinations of meaning: discourse and moral socialization. In W. Kurtines and J. Gewirtz (eds), *Moral Development through Social Interaction*. New York: John Wiley.

Shweder, R. A., Mahapatra, M. and Miller, J. G. (1987) Culture and moral development. In J. Kagan and S. Lamb (eds), *The Emergence of Morality in Young Children*. Chicago: University of Chicago Press.

Siegal, M. (1982) *Fairness in Children: A Social-cognitive Approach in the Study of Moral Development*. London: Academic Press.

Sigall, H. and Aronson, E. (1967) Opinion-change and the gain–loss model of interpersonal attraction. *Journal of Experimental Social Psychology*, 3, 128–88.

Simmel, G. (1950) *The Sociology of Georg Simmel*. Tr. and ed. K. H. Wolff. Glencoe, IL: Free Press.

Simpson, G. E. and Yinger, J. M. (1985) *Racial and Cultural Minorities: An Analysis of Prejudice and Discrimination*. 5th edn. New York: Harper & Row.

Six, P. (1997) *Escaping Poverty: From Safety Nets to Networks of Opportunity*. London: Demos.

Skinner, B. H. (1938) *The Behaviour of Organisms*. New York: Appleton-Century-Crofts.

Slaby, R. G. and Guerra, N. G. (1988) Cognitive mediators of aggression in adolescent offenders: 1. Assessment. *Developmental Psychology*, 24, 580–8.

Slater, A. and Butterworth, G. (1997) Perception of social stimuli: face perception and imitation. In G. Bremner, A. Slater and G. Butterworth (eds), *Infant Development: Recent Advances*. Hove: Psychology Press.

Smedslund, J. (1998) Social representations and psychologic. *Culture and Psychology*, 4, 435–54.

Smetana, J. (1981) Preschool children's conceptions of moral and social rules. *Child Development*, 52, 1333–6.

Smetana, J. G. (1995) Parenting styles and conceptions of parental authority during adolescence. *Child Development*, 66, 299–316.

Smith, C. (1982) Mothers' attitudes and behaviour with babies and the development of sex-typed play. Unpublished DPhil thesis, University of Sussex.

Smith, C. and Lloyd, B. (1978) Maternal behaviour and perceived sex of infant: revisited. *Child Development*, 49, 1263–5.

Smith, E. R. and DeCoster, J. (1998) Knowledge acquisition, accessibility, and use in person perception and stereotyping: simulation with a recurrent connectionist network. *Journal of Personality and Social Psychology*, 74, 21–35.

Smith, E. R., Coats, S. and D. Walling (1999) Overlapping mental representations of self, in-group, and partner: further response time evidence and a connectionist model. *Personality and Social Psychology Bulletin*, 25(7), 873–82.

Smolensky, P. (1988) On the proper treatment of connectionism. *Behavioural and Brain Sciences*, 11(1), 1–74.

Snarey, J. R. (1985) Cross-cultural universality of social-moral development: a critical review of Kohlbergian research. *Psychological Bulletin*, 97, 202–32.

Snyder, M. (1979) Self-monitoring processes. In L. Berkowitz (ed.), *Advances in Experimental Social Psychology, Vol. 12*. New York: Academic Press.

Snyder, M. and Cantor, N. (1998) Understanding personality and social behavior: a functionalist strategy. In D. T. Gilbert, S. T. Fiske and G. Lindzey (eds), *The Handbook of Social Psychology, Vol. 1*. New York: McGraw-Hill.

Snyder, M. and Monson, T. C. (1975) Persons, situations, and the control of social behaviour. *Journal of Personality and Social Psychology*, 32, 637–44.

Snyder, M. and Omoto, A. M. (1992a) Volunteerism and society's response to the HIV epidemic. *Current Directions in Psychological Science*, I, 113–16.

Snyder, M. and Omoto, A. M. (1992b) Who helps and why? The psychology of AIDS volunteerism. In S. Spacaman and S. Oskamp (eds), *Helping and Being Helped*. Newbury Park, CA: Sage.

Snyder, M. and Omoto, A. M. (1995) Sustained helping without obligation: motivation, longevity of service, and perceived attitude change among AIDS volunteers. *Journal of Personality and Social Psychology*, 68, 671–86.

Snyder, M. and Tanke, E. D. (1976) Behaviour and attitude: some people are more consistent than others. *Journal of Personality*, 44, 501–17.

Sochting, I., Skoe, E. E. and Marcia, J. E. (1994) Care-oriented moral reasoning and prosocial behaviour – a question of gender or sex-role orientation. *Sex Roles*, 31(3–4), 131–47.

Somer, O. and Goldberg, L. R. (1999) The structure of Turkish trait-descriptive adjectives. *Journal of Personality and Social Psychology*, 76(3), 431–50.

Spearman, C. (1927) *The Abilities of Man*. London: Macmillan.

Spence, J. T., Helmreich, R. and Stapp, J. (1975) Ratings of self and peers on sex role attributes and their relation to self-esteem and conceptions of masculinity and feminity. *Journal of Personality and Social Psychology*, 32, 29–39.

Spender, D. (1980) *Man Made Language*. London and Boston: Routledge & Kegan Paul.

Spitz, R. (1946) Anaclitic depression. *Psychoanalytic Study of the Child*, 2, 313–42.

Sroufe, L. A. (1983) Infant–caregiver attachment and patterns of adaptation in pre-school. In M. Perlmutter (ed.), *Minnesota Symposia on Child Psychology*, 16, 41–83. Hillsdale, NJ: Erlbaum.

Sroufe, L. A. (1985) Attachment classification from the perspective of infant–caregiver relationships and infant temperament. *Child Development*, 56, 1–14.

Stafford-Clark, D. (1965) *What Freud Really Said*. London: Macdonald.

Stainton-Rogers, W. (1991) *Explaining Health and Illness: An Exploration of Diversity*. Hemel Hempstead: Harvester Wheatsheaf.

Stattin, H. and Magnusson, D. (1989) The role of early aggressive behavior in the frequency, seriousness and type of later crime. *Journal of Consulting and Clinical Psychology*, 57, 710–18.

Staub, E. (1989) *The Roots of Evil: The Psychological and Cultural Origins of Genocide and Other Forms of Group Violence*. Cambridge: Cambridge University Press.

Staub, E. (1996) Cultural-societal roots of violence: the examples of genocidal violence and of contemporary youth violence in the United States. *American Psychologist*, 51(2), 117–32.

Staub, E. (1999) The roots of evil: social conditions, culture, personality, and basic human needs. In A. G. Miller (guest ed.), *Special Issue: Perspectives on Evil and Violence, Personality and Social Psychology Review*, 3(3), 179–92.

Staw, B. M. Organizational behavior: a review and reformulation of the field outcome variables. *Annual Review of Psychology*, 35, 627–66.

Stefanek, M. E., Ollendick, T. H., Baldock, W. P., Francis, G. and Yaeger, N. J. (1987) Self-statements in aggressive, withdrawn, and popular children. *Cognitive Research and Therapy*, 11, 229–39.

Stevenage, S. V. and McKay, Y. (1999) Model applicants: the effect of facial appearance on recruitment decisions. *British Journal of Psychology*, 90, 221–34.

Stevenson, H. W. (1991) The development of prosocial behaviour in large scale collective societies: China and Japan. In R. A. Hinde and J. Groebel (eds), *Cooperation and Prosocial Behaviour*. Cambridge: Cambridge University Press.

Stevenson-Hinde, J. (1991) Temperament and attachment: an eclectic approach. In P. Bateson (ed.), *The Development and Integration of Behaviour*. Cambridge: Cambridge University Press.

Stevenson-Hinde, J. and Glover, A. (1996) Shy girls and boys: a new look. *Journal of Child Psychology and Psychiatry*, 37, 181–7.

Stokes, G. and Taylor, B. (1994) Where next for transport policy? In R. Jowell, J. Curtice, L. Brook and D. Ahrendt (eds), *British Social Attitudes: The 11th Report*. Aldershot: Dartmouth.

Stoner, J. A. F. (1961) A comparison of individual and group decisions involving risk. Unpublished Master's thesis, School of Industrial Management, MIT.

Stoner, J. A. F. (1968) Risky and cautious shifts in group decisions: the influence of widely held values. *Journal of Experimental Social Psychology*, 4, 442–59.

Storms, M. D. (1973) Videotape and the attribution process: reversing actor's and observer's points of view. *Journal of Personality and Social Psychology*, 27, 165–75.

Stouffer, S. A. et al. (1949) *The American Soldier. Studies in Social Psychology in World War II*. 4 vols. Princeton, NJ: Princeton University Press.

Strack, F., Stepper, L. L. and Martin, S. (1988) Inhibiting and facilitating conditions of the human smile – a nonobtrusive test of the facial feedback hypothesis. *Journal of Personality and Social Psychology*, 54(5), 768–77.

Stroebe, W. and Jonas, K. (1996) Principles of attitude formation and strategies of change. In M. Hewstone, W. Stroebe and G. M. Stephenson (eds), *Introduction to Social Psychology: A European Perspective*. Oxford: Blackwell.

Stroebe, W. and Stroebe, M. (1995) *Social Psychology and Health*. Buckingham: Open University Press.

Strongman, K. T. (1996) *The Psychology of Emotion*. 4th edn. Chichester: John Wiley.

Strube, M. J. (1989) Evidence for the type in Type A behavior: a taxonometric analysis. *Journal of Personality and Social Psychology*, 56, 972–87.

Strube, M., Turner, C. W., Cerro, D., Stevens, J. and Hinchey, F. (1984) Interpersonal aggression and the Type A coronary-prone behavior pattern: a theoretical distinction and practical implications. *Journal of Personality and Social Psychology*, 47, 839–47.

Struch, N. and Schwartz, S. H. (1989) Intergroup aggression: its predictors and distinctness from in-group bias. *Journal of Personality and Social Psychology*, 56, 364–73.

Stuart-Hamilton, I. (1996) *Dictionary of Cognitive Psychology*. London: Jessica Kingsley.

Sulloway, F. J. (1996) *Born to Rebel: Birth Order, Family Dynamics, and Creative Lives*. London: Little, Brown.

Suls, J. and Wan, C. K. (1989) The relation between Type-A behavior and chronic emotional distress – a meta-analysis. *Journal of Personality and Social Psychology*, 57(3), 503–12.

Swann, W. B. (1987) Identity negotiation: where two roads meet. *Journal of Personality and Social Psychology*, 53, 1038–51.

Swann, W. B., de la Ronde, C. and Hixon, J. G. (1994) Authenticity and positivity showings in marriage and courtship. *Journal of Personality and Social Psychology*, 66, 857–69.

Szreter, S. (1998) A new political economy for New Labour: the importance of social capital. University of Sheffield, Political Economy Research Centre, Political Paper no. 13.

Tajfel, H. (1959) Quantitative judgement in social perception. *British Journal of Psychology*, 50, 16–29.

Tajfel, H. (1969) Cognitive aspects of prejudice. *Journal of Social Issues*, 25, 79–97.

Tajfel, H. (1972) Experiments in a vacuum. In J. Israel and H. Tajfel (eds), *The Context of Social Psychology: A Critical Assessment*. London: Academic Press.

Tajfel, H. (1974) Social identity and intergroup behaviour. *Social Science Information*, 13, 65–93.

Tajfel, H. (ed.) (1978a) *Differentiation between Social Groups: Studies in the Social Psychology of Intergroup Relations*. London: Academic Press.

Tajfel, H. (1978b) Intergroup behaviour: I. Individualistic perspectives and Intergroup behaviour: II. Group perspectives. In H. Tajfel and C. Fraser (eds), *Introducing Social Psychology*. Harmondsworth: Penguin.

Tajfel, H. (1981) *Human Groups and Social Categories: Studies in Social Psychology.* Cambridge and New York: Cambridge University Press.

Tajfel, H. (1982) *Social Identity and Intergroup Relations.* Cambridge, New York and Paris: Cambridge University Press/Editions de la Maison des sciences de l'homme.

Tajfel, H. (ed.) (1984) *The Social Dimension: European Developments in Social Psychology.* 2 vols. Cambridge: Cambridge University Press.

Tajfel, H. and Forgas, J. P. (1981) Social categorisation: cognitions, values and groups. In J. P. Forgas (ed.), *Social Cognition: Perspectives on Everyday Understanding.* London: Academic Press.

Tajfel, H. and Turner, J. C. (1979) An integrative theory of intergroup conflict. In W. G. Austin and S. Worchel (eds), *The Social Psychology of Intergroup Relations.* Monterey, CA: Brooks/Cole.

Tajfel, H. and Wilkes, A. L. (1963) Classification and quantitative judgement. *British Journal of Psychology*, 54, 101–14.

Tajfel, H., Flament, C., Billig, M. and Bundy, R. (1971) Social categorisation and intergroup behaviour. *European Journal of Social Psychology*, 1, 149–78.

Tangney, J. P. (1991) Moral affect: the good, the bad, and the ugly. *Journal of Personality and Social Psychology*, 61, 598–607.

Tannen, D. (1990) *You Just Don't Understand: Women and Men in Conversation.* New York: Morrow.

Taylor, D. M. and Moghaddam, F. M. (1994) *Theories of Intergroup Relations.* 2nd edn. Westport, CT: Praeger.

Taylor, S. E., Crocker, J., Fiske, S. T., Sprinzen, M. and Winkler, J. D. (1979) The generalisability of salience effects. *Journal of Personality and Social Psychology*, 37, 357–68.

Taylor, S. T. and Fiske, S. E. (1991) *Social Cognition.* 2nd edn. New York: McGraw-Hill.

Teasdale, J. D. (1988) Cognitive vulnerability to persistent depression. *Cognition and Emotion*, 2, 247–74.

Tedeschi, J. T. (1983) Social influence theory and aggression. In R. G. Geen and E. I. Donnerstein (eds), *Aggression: Theoretical and Empirical Reviews, 1.* New York: Academic Press.

Tedeschi, J. T. and Felson, B. R. (1994) *Violence, Aggression, and Coercive Actions.* Washington, DC: American Psychological Association.

Teichman, Y. and Teichman, M. (1990) Interpersonal view of depression: review and integration. *Journal of Family Psychology*, 3, 349–67.

Terman, L. M. (1904) A preliminary study of the psychology and pedagogy of leadership. *Pedagogical Seminary*, 11, 413–51.

Teti, D. and Ablard, K. E. (1989) Security of attachment and infant–sibling relationships: a laboratory study. *Child Development*, 60, 1519–28.

Tetlock, P. E. and Manstead, A. S. R. (1985) Impression management versus intrapsychic explanations in social psychology: a useful dichotomy? *Psychological Review*, 92, 59–77.

Thagard, P. and Kunda, Z. (1998) Making sense of people: coherence mechanisms. In S. V. Read and L. C. Miller (eds), *Connectionist Models of Social Reasoning and Social Behaviour.* Mahwah, NJ: Erlbaum.

Thayer, S. (1969) The effect of interpersonal looking on dominance judgements. *Journal of Social Psychology*, 79, 285–6.

Thibaut, J. W. and Kelley, H. H. (1959) *The Social Psychology of Groups*. New York: John Wiley.

Thomas, W. I. and Znaniecki, F. (1918–20) *The Polish Peasant in Europe and America*. 5 vols. Boston: Badger.

Thurstone, L. L. (1928) Attitudes can be measured. *American Journal of Sociology*, 33, 529–54.

Tienari, P. (1991) Interaction between genetic vulnerability and family environment: the Finnish adoptive family study of schizophrenia. *Acta Psychiatrica Scandinavica*, 84, 460–5.

Tiger, L. (1995) Men, women and aggression. *Transaction Social Science and Modern Society*, 32, 79–83.

Tisak, M. S. and Turiel, E. (1988). Variation in seriousness of transgressions and children's moral and conventional concepts. *Developmental Psychology*, 24, 352–7.

Tizard, B. (1974) IQ and race. *Nature*, 247, 316.

Tizard, B. and Hodges, J. (1978) The effect of early institutional rearing on the development of eight-year-old children. *Journal of Child Psychology and Psychiatry*, 19, 99–118.

Tjaden, P. and Thoennes, N. (1997) *Stalking in America: Findings from the National Violence against Women Survey*. Denver, CO: Center for Policy Research.

Tobias, B. A., Kihlstrom, J. F. and Schacter, D. L. (1992). Emotion and implicit memory. In S. A. Christianson (ed.) *The Handbook of Emotion and Memory: Research and Theory*. Hillsdale, NJ: Erlbaum.

Toch, H. (1969). *Violent Men*. Chicago: Aldine.

Toch, H. and Adams, K. (1989) *The Disturbed Violent Offender*. New Haven, CT: Yale University Press.

Tomasello, M., Kruger, A. C. and Ratner, H. H. (1993) Cultural learning. *Behavioural and Brain Sciences*, 16(3), 495–552.

Townsend, P. (1979) *Poverty in the UK*. Harmondsworth: Penguin.

Trehub, S., Unyk, A. M., Kamenetsky, S. B., Hill, D. S., Trainor, L. J., Henderson, J. L. and Sanoza, M. (1997) Mothers' and fathers' singing to infants. *Developmental Psychology*, 33, 500–7.

Triandis, H. C. (1991) Cross-cultural differences in assertiveness/competition vs group loyalty/cooperation. In R. A. Hinde and J. Groebel (eds), *Cooperation and Prosocial Behaviour*. Cambridge: Cambridge University Press.

Triplett, N. D. (1898) The dynamogenic factor in pacemaking and competition. *American Journal of Psychology*, 9, 507–33.

Trudgill, P. (1972) Sex, covert prestige and linguistic change in the urban British English of Norwich. *Language in Society*, 1, 179–95.

Tuckman, B. W. (1965) Developmental sequence in small groups. *Psychological Bulletin*, 63, 384–99.

Turiel, E. (1978) Social regulations and domains of social concepts. In W. Damon (ed.), *New Directions for Child Development, Vol. 1. Social Cognition*. San Francisco: Jossey-Bass.

Turiel, E. (1983) *The Development of Social Knowledge*. Cambridge: Cambridge University Press.

Turiel, E. and Wainryb, C. (1994) Social reasoning and the varieties of social experiences in cultural contexts. *Advances in Child Development and Behaviour*, 25, 289–326.

Turner, J. C. (1991) *Social Influence*. Milton Keynes: Open University Press.

Turner, J. C., Hogg, M. A., Oakes, P. J., Reicher, S. D. and Wetherell, M. S. (1987) *Rediscovering the Social Group: A Self-categorisation Theory*. Oxford: Blackwell.

Tversky, A. and Kahneman, D. (1974) Judgement under uncertainty: heuristics and biases. *Science*, 185, 1124–31.

Tversky, A. and Kahneman, D. (1981) The framing of decisions and the psychology of choice. *Science*, 211, 453–8.

Tversky, A. and Kahneman, D. (1983) Extensional versus intuitive reasoning: the conjunction fallacy in probability judgements. *Psychological Review*, 90, 293–315.

Tversky, A. and Kahneman, D. (1986) Rational choice and the framing of decisions. *Journal of Business*, 59, S251–S278.

Tweedie, J. (1979) *In the Name of Love*. London: Cape.

Urberg, K. A., Değirmencioğlu, S. M. and Pilgrim, C. (1997) Close friend and group influence on adolescent cigarette smoking and alcohol use. *Developmental Psychology*, 33, 834–44.

Ussher, J. (1991) *Women's Madness: Misogyny or Mental Illness?* Hemel Hempstead: Harvester Wheatsheaf.

Vanbeselaere, N. (1983) Mere exposure: a search for an explanation. In W. Doise and S. Moscovici (eds), *Current Issues in European Social Psychology, Vol. 1*. Cambridge: Cambridge University Press.

Vanbeselaere, N. (1991) The different effects of simple and crossed categorisations. In W. Stroebe and M. Hewstone (eds), *European Review of Social Psychology, Vol. 2*. Chichester: John Wiley.

van Ijzendoorn, M. J. H. (1995) Adult attachment representations, parental responsiveness and infant attachment. *Psychological Bulletin*, 117, 387–403.

van Ijzendoorn, M. H. and De Wolff, M. S. (1997) In search of the absent father – meta-analyses of infant–father attachment: a rejoinder to our discussants. *Child Development*, 68, 604–9.

Van Overwalle, F. (1998) Causal explanation as constraint satisfaction: a critique and a feedforward connectionist alternative. *Journal of Personality and Social Psychology*, 74, 312–28.

Vaughn, C. and Leff, J. (1976) The influence of family and social factors in the course of psychiatric patients. *British Journal of Psychiatry*, 129, 125–37.

Vinokur, A. and Burnstein, E. (1974) Effects of partially shared persuasive arguments on group-induced shifts: a group-problem-solving approach. *Journal of Personality and Social Psychology*, 29, 305–15.

Vroom, V. H. (1964) *Work and Motivation*. New York: John Wiley.

Wagner, W. (1994) The fallacy of misplaced intentionality in social representations research. *Journal for the Theory of Social Behaviour*, 24, 243–66.

Wagner, W., Duveen, G., Themel, M. and Verma, J. (1999) The modernization of tradition: thinking about madness in Patna, India. *Culture and Psychology*, 5, 413–45.

Walker, L. E. and Meloy, J. R. (1998) Stalking and domestic violence. In J. R. Meloy (ed.), *The Psychology of Stalking: Clinical and Forensic Perspectives*. San Diego: Academic Press.

Walker, L. J. (1984) Sex differences in the development of moral reasoning: a critical review. *Child Development*, 55, 677–91.

Walker, L. J. (1986) Experiential and cognitive sources of moral development in adulthood. *Human Development*, 29, 113–24.

Walker, L. J. and Taylor, J. H. (1991) Family interaction and the development of moral reasoning. *Child Development*, 62, 264–83.

Walker, T. G. and Main, E. C. (1973) Choice-shifts in political decision-making: federal judges and civil liberties cases. *Journal of Applied Social Psychology*, 3, 39–48.

Walsh, D. (1986) *Heavy Business*. London: Routledge and Kegan Paul.

Walster, E., Walster, G. W. and Berscheid, E. (1978) *Equity Theory and Research*. Boston: Allyn & Bacon.

Walters, G. C. and Grusec, J. E. (1977) *Punishment*. San Francisco: W. H. Freeman.

Warr, P. (1982) A national study of non-financial employment commitment. *Journal of Occupational Psychology*, 55, 297–312.

Warr, P. (1987) *Work, Unemployment and Mental Health*. Oxford: Clarendon Press.

Warr, P. (1999) Wellbeing and the workplace. In D. Kahnemann, E. Diener and N. Schwartz (eds), *Wellbeing: The Foundations of Hedonic Psychology*. New York: Sage.

Warr, P. and Jackson, P. R. (1985) Factors affecting the psychological impact of prolonged unemployment and re-employment. *Psychological Medicine*, 15, 795–807.

Warr, P. and Payne, R. L. (1982) Experiences of strain and pleasure amongst British adults. *Social Science and Medicine*, 16, 1691–7.

Warr, P., Jackson, P. R. and Banks, M. (1985) Unemployment and mental health: some British studies. *Journal of Social Issues*, 44, 47–68.

Wason, P. C. (1960) On the failure to eliminate hypotheses in a conceptual task. *Quarterly Journal of Experimental Psychology*, 12, 129–40.

Wason, P. C. (1968) Reasoning about a rule. *Quarterly Journal of Experimental Psychology*, 20, 273–81.

Waters, E. and Sroufe, L. A. (1983) Social competence as a developmental construct: perceiving the coherence of individual differences across age, across situations, and across behavioral domains. *Developmental Review*, 3, 79–97.

Watson, D. (1982) The actor and the observer: how are their perceptions of causality different? *Psychological Bulletin*, 92, 682–700.

Watson, J. B. (1913) Psychology as a behaviourist views it. *Psychological Review*, 20, 158–77.

Watson, J. B. (1919) *Psychology from the Standpoint of a Behaviourist*. Philadelphia: Lippincott.

Watts, F. N. (1983) Socialisation and social integration. In F. N. Watts and D. H. Bennett (eds), *Theory and Practice of Psychiatric Rehabilitation*. Chichester: John Wiley.

Watts, F. N. (1991) Socialisation and social integration. In F. N. Watts and D. H. Bennett (eds), *Theory and Practice of Psychiatric Rehabilitation*. Chichester: John Wiley.

Weaver, C. N. (1977) Relationships among pay, race, sex, occupational prestige, supervision, work autonomy, and job satisfaction in a national sample. *Personnel Psychology*, 30, 437–45.

Weaver, C. N. (1980) Job satisfaction in the United States in the 1970s. *Journal of Applied Psychology*, 65, 364–7.

Weiner, B. (1979) A theory of motivation for some classroom experiments. *Journal of Educational Psychology*, 71, 3–25.

Weiner, B. (1985) 'Spontaneous' causal thinking. *Psychological Bulletin*, 97, 74–84.

Weiner, B., Russell, D. and Lerman, D. (1979) The cognition–emotion process in achievement-related contexts. *Journal of Personality and Social Psychology*, 37, 1211–20.

Weinreich-Haste, H. (1982) Piaget on morality: a critical perspective. In S. Modgil and C. Modgil (eds), *Jean Piaget: Consensus and Controversy*. London: Holt, Rinehart & Winston.

Weissman, M. M. and Klerman, G. L. (1977) Sex differences and the epidemiology of depression. *Archives of General Psychiatry*, 34, 98–111.

Weissman, M. M. and Olfson, M. (1995) Depression in women: implications for health care research. *Science*, 269 (5225), 799–801.

Weissman, M. M. and Paykel, E. S. (1974) *The Depressed Woman: A Study of Social Relationships*. Chicago: University of Chicago Press.

Wheeler, L., Koestner, R. and Driver, R. E. (1982) Related attributes in the choice of comparison others: it's there, but it isn't all there is. *Journal of Experimental Social Psychology*, 18, 489–500.

White, M. (1991) *Against Unemployment*. London: Policy Studies Institute.

Whiteley, P. (1997) *Economic Growth and Social Capital*. Sheffield: Political Economy Research Centre.

Whiten, A. and Byrne, R. W. (1997) *Machiavellian Intelligence II: Extensions and Evaluations*. New York: Cambridge University Press.

Whiting, B. (1983) The genesis of prosocial behavior. In D. Bridgeman (ed.), *The Nature of Prosocial Development: Interdisciplinary Theories and Strategies*. New York: Academic Press.

Whorf, B. L. (1956) *Language, Thought, and Reality: Selected Writings*. [Cambridge, MA]: Technology Press of MIT.

Wichert, I. C., Nolan, J. P. and Burchell, B. J. (2000) *Workers on the Edge: Job Insecurity, Psychological Well-being and Family Life*. Washington, DC: Economic Policy Institute.

Wicker, A. W. (1969) Attitudes vs. actions: the relationship of verbal and overt behavioural responses to attitude objects. *Journal of Social Issues*, 25, 41–78.

Wicklund, R. A. and Frey, D. (1981) Cognitive consistency: motivational vs. non-motivational perspectives. In J. P. Forgas (ed.), *Social Cognition: Perspectives on Everyday Understanding*. London: Academic Press.

Widom, C. S. (1989) Does violence beget violence? A critical examination of the literature. *Psychological Bulletin*, 106, 3–28.

Wigboldus, D. H. J., Semin, G. R. and Spears, R. (2000) How do we communicate stereotypes? Linguistic bases and inferential consequences. *Journal of Personality and Social Psychology*, 78, 5–18.

Wiggins, J. S. (1996) *The Five-factor Model of Personality: Theoretical Perspectives*. New York: Guilford Press.

Wilder, D. A. (1981) Perceiving persons as a group: categorisation and intergroup relations. In D. L. Hamilton (ed.), *Cognitive Processes in Stereotyping and Intergroup Behaviour*. Hillsdale, NJ: Earlbaum.

Wilkinson, R. (1996) *Unhealthy Societies: The Afflictions of Inequality*. London: Routledge.

Wilkinson, R. G., Kawachi, I. and Kennedy, B. (1998) Mortality, the social environment, crime and violence. *Sociology of Health and Illness*, 20(5): 578–97.

Williams, A. W., Ware, J. E., Jr, and Donald, C. A. (1981) A model of mental health, life events, and social supports applicable to general populations. *Journal of Health and Social Behaviour*, 22, 324–36.

Williamson, G. M. and Schulz, R. (1995) Caring for a family member with cancer: past communal behavior and affective reactions. *Journal of Applied Social Psychology*, 25, 93–116.

Wilson, M. and Daly, M. (1985) Competitiveness, risk taking and violence: the young male syndrome. *Ethology and Sociology*, 6, 59–73.

Wilson Robert, A. and Keil Frank, C. (1999) *The MIT Encyclopedia of the Cognitive Sciences*. Cambridge, MA, and London: MIT Press.

Wilson, W. J. (1997) *When Work Disappears: The World of the New Urban Poor*. New York: Alfred Knopf.

Wimmer, H. and Perner, J. (1983) Beliefs about beliefs: representation and constraining function of wrong beliefs in young children's understanding of deception. *Cognition*, 13(1), 103–28.

Woehrle, L. (1999) Gender studies. In L. Kurtz (ed.), *Encyclopedia of Violence, Peace, and Conflict, Vol. 2*. San Diego: Academic Press.

Wolfe, J. L. and Russianoff, P. (1997) Overcoming self-negation in women. *Journal of Rational-Emotive and Cognitive-Behavioural Therapy*, 15(1), 81–92.

Wollheim, R. (1991) *Freud*. London: Fontana Press.

Woo, S. M., Goldstein, M. J. and Nuechterlein, K. H. (1997) Relatives' expressed emotion and non-verbal signals of subclinical psychopathology in schizophrenic patients. *British Journal of Psychiatry*, 170, 58–61.

Word, C. O., Zanna, M. P. and Cooper, J. (1974) The non-verbal mediation of self-fulfilling prophecies in interracial interaction. *Journal of Experimental Social Psychology*, 10, 109–20.

Wu, X. and DeMaris, A. (1996) Gender and marital status differences in depression: the effects of chronic strains. *Sex Roles*, 34(5–6), 299–319.

Wundt, W. (1900–20) *Volkerpsychologie*. 10 vols. Leipzig: Englemann.

Yang, B., Ollendick, T. H., Dong, Q., Xia, Y. and Lin, L. (1995) Only children and children with siblings in the People's Republic of China: levels of fear, anxiety, and depression. *Child Development*, 66, 1301–11.

Youniss, J. (1980) *Parents and Peers in Social Development*. Chicago: University of Chicago Press.

Youniss, J. and Damon, W. A. (1992) Social construction in Piaget's theory. In H. Beilin and P. B. Pufall (eds), *Piaget's Theory: Prospects and Possibilities*. Hillsdale, NJ: Erlbaum.

Youniss, J. and Volpe, J. (1978) A relational analysis of children's friendships. In W. Damon (ed.), *New Directions for Child Development, Vol. 1*. San Francisco: Jossey-Bass.

Zajonc, R. B. (1965) Social facilitation. *Science*, 149, 269–74.

Zajonc, R. B. (1968) Attitudinal effects of mere exposure. *Journal of Personality and Social Psychology*, 9, 1–27.

Zajonc, R. B. (1980) Feeling and thinking: preferences need no inferences. *American Psychologist*, 35, 151–75.

Zanna, M. P., Olson, J. M. and Fazio, R. H. (1980) Attitude–behavior consistency: an individual difference perspective. *Journal of Personality and Social Psychology*, 38, 432–40.

Zigler, E., Taussig, C. and Black, K. (1992) Early childhood intervention: a promising preventative for juvenile delinquency. *American Psychologist*, 47, 997–1006.

Zimbardo, P. G. (1969) The human choice: individuation, reason and order versus deindividuation, impulse and chaos. In W. J. Arnold and D. Levine (eds), *Nebraska Symposium on Motivation*, 17. Lincoln, NE: University of Nebraska Press.

Zimbardo, P. G. (1980) Philip Zimbardo. In R. Evans (ed.), *The Making of Social Psychology: Discussions with Creative Contributors*. New York: Gardner Press.

Zimbardo, P. G. and Leippe, M. R. (1991) *The Psychology of Attitude Change and Social Influence*. New York: McGraw-Hill.

Zola, I. (1972) Medicine as an institution of social control. *Sociological Review*, 20, 487–504.

Zuckerman, M. (1991) *Psychobiology of Personality*. Cambridge: Cambridge University Press.

Name Index

Subject Index

Note: Main references to subjects are signified by **bold** print.